# Issues in the Psychology
of Women

# Issues in the Psychology of Women

Edited by

**Maryka Biaggio**

and

**Michel Hersen**

*Pacific University*
*Forest Grove, Oregon*

**Kluwer Academic / Plenum Publishers**
New York • Boston • Dordrecht • London • Moscow

ISBN 0-306-46321-0

©2000 Kluwer Academic / Plenum Publishers
233 Spring Street, New York, N.Y. 10013

http://www.wkap.nl/

10   9   8   7   6   5   4   3   2   1

A C.I.P. record for this book is available from the Library of Congress.

To my parents,
who taught me the value
of determination and integrity.
—M.B.

To Vicki.
—M.H.

# Contributors

**Kristine M. Baber,** Department of Family Studies, University of New Hampshire, Durham, New Hampshire 03824

**Mary Ballou,** Northeastern University, Boston, Massachusetts 02478

**Tammy A. R. Bartoszek,** Department of Psychology, Indiana University of Pennsylvania, Indiana, Pennsylvania 15705

**Maryka Biaggio,** School of Professional Psychology, Pacific University, Forest Grove, Oregon 97116

**Joan C. Chrisler,** Department of Psychology, Connecticut College, New London, Connecticut 06320

**Shiata Forcet,** Cora Neumann Job Training Center, Philadelphia, Pennsylvania 19124

**Linda B. Gallahan,** College of Arts and Sciences, Pacific University, Forest Grove, Oregon 97116

**Angela R. Gillem,** Beaver College, Glenside, Pennsylvania 19038-3295

**Rhonda Felece Jeter,** Department of Education, Bowie State University, Bowie, Maryland 20715

**Ingrid Johnston-Robledo,** Department of Psychology, Connecticut College, New London, Connecticut 06320

**Maureen C. McHugh,** Department of Psychology, Indiana University of Pennsylvania, Indiana, Pennsylvania 15705

**Susan L. Morrow,** Faculty of Educational Psychology, University of Utah, Salt Lake City, Utah 84112-9255

**Linda Krug Porzelius,** School of Professional Psychology, Pacific University, Forest Grove, Oregon 97116

**Laurie A. Roades,** Department of Behavioral Sciences, California State Polytechnic University, Pomona, California 91768

**Patricia D. Rozee,** Women's Studies Program, California State University, Long Beach, California 90840

**Radhika Sehgal,** Beaver College, Glenside, Pennsylvania 19038-3295

**Carolyn West,** Western New England College, Springfield, Massachusetts, 01119

**Janice D. Yoder,** Department of Psychology, University of Akron, Akron, Ohio 44325-4301

# Preface

Over the past 15 years, I (MB) have taught a graduate-level course in Psychology of Women to students in two different professional psychology programs. Because my students were at the doctoral level and often had some familiarity with the psychology of women, these courses focused on bringing a feminist analysis of psychology and integrating a feminist analysis into one's scholarly work and professional activities. Although I used several fine psychology of women textbooks during this time, I found none that was specifically designed for graduate students. Thus, I always augmented the textbook with journal articles on specific aspects of the topic, and these focused articles have typically been well received by the students. The students whom I have encountered in these courses have often expressed a wish for a textbook that is designed for their needs; I think what they are asking for is one that could serve as a foundation for their scholarly analysis of psychology as well as a springboard for thoughtful application of a feminist perspective to the profession of psychology. Therefore, *Issues in the Psychology of Women* has been designed to serve as a textbook for advanced undergraduate or graduate courses including Psychology of Women or Feminist Analysis of Psychology.

This book is the collective work of authors with special expertise in their chapter topic. The authors were directed to write on focused aspects of their topic, ground the material in current research and theory, and bring a social constructionist perspective to bear. The text is divided into four parts: (1) Historical and Scientific Foundations; (2) Social Issues and Problems; (3) Relationships and Sexuality; and (4) Psychological and Health Issues. Diversity and developmental issues are integrated into each chapter. Thus, the organization and coverage are somewhat different from that found in a text designed to survey the psychology of women. But the format should lend itself to a progression of topics, starting with foundations and theoretical/conceptual frameworks, moving to more specific and practical issues, and concluding with a chapter on feminist therapy.

We believe that the focus on specific topics or issues in psychology of women will facilitate in-depth exploration of such issues by our students. It may be especially fitting for graduate courses in clinical and counseling psychology. Chapters on historical and scientific foundations are intended to allow for a scholarly focus on research in psychology. Also, the issues approach is designed to lend itself to an examination of specific concerns of women, including clinical the implications of these concerns.

We have found, and believe students would agree as well, that the academic experience for a course such as Psychology of Women or Feminist Analysis of Psychology is unlike that of most other courses. That is, the learning experience encompasses far more than a body of knowledge, the discussion quickly moves beyond a mere exchange of abstract ideas, and the exploration of one's perspective and attitudes often touches unexamined parts of the developing student. It is our hope that this textbook will serve to facilitate the special learning experience that can occur when an instructor and students come together to examine the discipline and perspective that is feminist psychology.

Many individuals have contributed to the fruition of the textbook. First we thank our eminent authors for taking time out to write the chapters. Second, we are most appreciative of the technical help of Carole Londoreé, Erika Qualls, Eleanor Gil, and Megan Schmidt. Third, we are grateful to Eliot Werner, our editor, for understanding the need for this text.

Maryka Biaggio
Michel Hersen

# Contents

## IV. PSYCHOLOGICAL AND HEALTH ISSUES

# I

# Historical and Scientific Foundations

---

This section provides an overview of the historical and scientific foundations of the psychology of women, first by reviewing the history of the contemporary women's movement, then by examining feminist perspectives on the discipline of psychology and feminist approaches to understanding gender.

Maryka Biaggio's chapter illustrates the impact of the women's movement on contemporary society and demonstrates how the cultural zeitgeist fostered this movement. Notice the changes that were wrought by the movement. It is interesting to speculate what women's lives would be like today if this movement had not swept our society. As you read this chapter, consider the ways that the movement has opened doors for today's women. And think about how this history sets the scene for the chapters that follow: Do you believe it would have been possible for the feminist perspective to take hold in the discipline of psychology, or any other discipline, had a grassroots women's movement not paved the way?

The next chapter, by Sue Morrow, holds up a feminist lens to the discipline of psychology, showing how early musings led to feminist critiques of psychology and the scientific enterprise. Morrow, an expert in qualitative research approaches, explains how feminist paradigms for inquiry emerged. She describes social constructionism, the perspective utilized in this textbook. Notice as you read this chapter how the analysis of the discipline emerged and evolved. Do you see parallels between developments in the culture at large and the discipline of psychology? Morrow mentions many early pioneers of the feminist perspective. How do you think these women were received when they first criticized the androcentrism of the discipline? Do you believe that there have been changes in the discipline as a result of the critiques articulated by these women? What have we learned about our discipline as a result of bringing a feminist lens to our analysis?

Linda Gallahan's chapter on approaches to understanding gender specifically focuses on how traditional psychological theory and contemporary feminist perspectives conceptualize gender. Obviously, an understanding of gender and how it affects individual development and experiences is central to feminist theory. As Gallahan points out, theories may be either essentialist (presuming that sex differences are fixed) or constructionist (assuming that gender is a "constructed" way of understanding men and women). As you will see here, the view that is adopted by a particular theory of development has ramifications for what is considered normative and possible behavior for men and women. This, then, gives rise to an important question—can scientific theory be a vehicle for oppression? You may wish to reflect on the real-life implications of the essentialist versus constructionist perspectives on gender, ethnicity, sexual orientation, and other important categories for understanding human differences.

As you will note from Chapter 1, an important tenet of the women's movement is that "the personal is political." As you will see from Chapters 2 and 3, the scholarly and scientific are also political! As you complete this section, ask yourself about the tangible ways in which this is true.

# 1

# History of the Contemporary Women's Movement

## Maryka Biaggio

## INTRODUCTION

The purpose of this chapter is to provide an overview of the contemporary women's movement in the United States as well as a context for understanding its impact on modern women and the discipline of psychology. The women's movement has had a significant impact on U.S. society and women's roles and opportunities, and a review of its history demonstrates its influence on current circumstances. Further, an articulation of the values espoused by the movement illustrates how contemporary beliefs have evolved from our culture and history. Also, an explanation of the feminist critique of psychology shows how feminism has been instrumental in shaping views within the discipline and profession.

This chapter is, by necessity, not a detailed treatment of the history of the movement, since the purpose is simply to provide an overview of the movement's history. Also, the explanations of feminist ideologies and feminist perspectives in the mental health field and discipline of psychology are intended to present basic concepts rather than a detailed explication of these views.

## THE WOMEN'S MOVEMENT AND ITS SOCIAL CONTEXT

The contemporary women's movement in the United States, also known as the second wave of feminism, emerged during the 1960s, driven by a wide variety of women's concerns, including sex discrimination; limited opportunities in employment; restraints on reproductive freedom; and concerns about domestic violence, sexual victimization, and women's unpaid labor. Like similar movements of the time, this was a grassroots endeavor, and it gave rise to a number of organizations that focused on women's rights and concerns, most notably the National Organization for Women (which was founded in 1966 and is still in existence). The women who identified with the contemporary women's movement came to be known as feminists, while those who had identified with the first wave of feminism, which emerged in the

Maryka Biaggio ● School of Professional Psychology, Pacific University, Forest Grove, Oregon 97116

*Issues in the Psychology of Women,* edited by Biaggio and Hersen. Kluwer Academic/Plenum Publishers, New York, 2000.

late nineteenth century, were known as women suffragists, since their primary focus was on gaining the vote for women.

The women's movement cannot be considered a discrete organizational movement, but rather a political force that has broad ideological variety and a range of organizational expressions (Katzenstein, 1987). As Katzenstein has explained:

> One reason for the diversity of feminism is the fact that the women's movement is a potentially *transformational* social movement and thus draws supports with a range of different agendas. The movement is transformational in the sense that it engages both a *broad* range of issues and a set of issues that can *deeply* affect the daily experiences of an individual's life. Thus, feminism addresses economic concerns (the existence of job discrimination; the valuation of women's work); sexual issues (the existence of sexual pleasure; the problem of rape, harassment, battering, and homophobia); family issues (the provision of child care; the division of labor in the household; maternity/paternity leave; reproductive rights); and a range of matters less easily catalogued (the demilitarization of society, the deconstruction and critical analysis of language, the rewriting of women's history). What this "agenda" entails is nothing less than the reformulation of public life, the educational sphere, the workplace, and the home—that is, a total transformation of society. (p. 5)

The contemporary women's movement was part of the cultural zeitgeist that characterized the 1960s and 1970s—the questioning of the political status quo, a focus on the rights of the disenfranchised, and a strong anti-Vietnam War sentiment. A number of leftist groups emerged, and there were some overlaps in ideology and membership across these New Left groups, as well as some differences in philosophy and strategy. Many women had been treated as second class citizens within some of these leftist groups, and this experience became part of the impetus for their own political awakening. As Whalen (1996) has pointed out, "Despite the purported equality within these leftist groups, women found themselves denied leadership, their voices silenced by males. . . . New Left women began talking among themselves, giving voice to their concerns as women and, more important, organizing for change" (pp. 144–145).

Federal actions and legislation played a key role in spurring women's awareness of inequity and demands for equality. In 1961, at the request of the Labor Department Women's Bureau Director Esther Peterson, President John Kennedy appointed a commission to study the status of women; the resulting report named and described sex discrimination in employment (Freeman, 1973; Tiefer, 1991). This report called for policies to improve women's opportunities in employment and the political arena. Investigations by state commissions subsequent to the report revealed evidence of pervasive legal and economic inequities, and "created a climate of expectations that something would be done" (Freeman, 1973, p. 798).

Two government initiatives on behalf of employed women—the Equal Pay Act of 1963, which required equal pay for equal work, and Title VII of the Civil Rights Act of 1964, which applied to wages as well as to all aspects of employment including hiring and promotion— played important roles in fueling the women's movement (Hartmann, 1989), and provided a foundation for complaints and lawsuits in cases of discrimination. Interestingly, the original version of Title VII barred discrimination only on the basis of race, religion, or national origin. Some conservative legislators opposed this bill, and decided to try to kill it by also barring discrimination on the basis of sex, thinking that this would be sufficiently outrageous to undermine the whole bill. Their miscalculation allowed for inclusion of women as a protected group under this bill. In 1972, Congress passed the Equal Rights Amendment (ERA), and the campaign to ratify this amendment mobilized many women into feminism and brought liberal feminists into the political mainstream (Rollins, 1996). By 1982, the ERA had failed to garner the requisite number of state ratifications and subsequently was defeated. It is somewhat astounding that this amendment, which simply intended to affirm equality on the basis of sex, was so controversial that it failed to gain sufficient support for ratification.

During the early years of the women's movement several writings presented feminist analyses that influenced large numbers of women; these writings have come to be considered classics of the movement. Simone de Beauvoir, a French philosopher, published *Le Deuxieme Sexe* in France in 1949; it was published as *The Second Sex* in the United States in 1953. This book "was one of the earliest inquiries into the social construction of 'femininity' and sparked a great deal of debate" (Ruth, 1990, p. 115). The translator's preface by Parshley presents the unifying theme as:

> Since patriarchal times women have in general been forced to occupy a secondary place in the world in relation to men . . . and further that this secondary standing is not imposed of necessity by natural "feminine" characteristics but rather by strong environmental forces of educational and social tradition under the purposeful control of men. This, the author maintains, has resulted in the general failure of women to take a place of human dignity as free and independent existents, associated with men on the plane of intellectual and professional equality, a condition that not only has limited their achievement in many fields but also has given rise to pervasive social evils and has had a particularly vitiating effect on the sexual relations between man and women. (p. vii)

Simone de Beauvoir's book was very provocative when it was released, and spurred analyses of men's and women's views of women as well as relationships between men and women.

In 1963 Betty Friedan published *The Feminine Mystique*, an influential book that exposed the myth of the happy housewife and sparked an examination of a woman's role in the traditional middle-class family. This book struck a chord with middle-class women, and 300,000 copies of Friedan's book were sold in the first six months of publication. It became a bestseller and prompted growing numbers of women to question the status quo (Tiefer, 1991). According to Ruth (1990, p. 252), Friedan's book

> describes the inchoate sense of something wrong lodged in the minds and feelings of countless American housewives, a sense that puts the lie to the "feminine mystique," the cultural image of wifely and domestic bliss. Friedan's work is powerful not only because it so accurately delineates the nature of the mystique, but because it also captures the flaws in the image as well, the fall from grace of happily-ever-after-land and the dangers for those who believe in or seek it. (p. 252)

Friedan referred to the "problem that had no name" as the stifling of women's potential; by naming this problem she hoped to foster greater awareness of its costs to women and society.

Kate Millett's 1970 book *Sexual Politics* unabashedly examined the nature of power in sexual relationships, claiming that domination of men over women is perhaps the most pervasive ideology of our culture and provides its most fundamental understanding of power. "Using literary and historical models to support her thesis, she argues that social and sexual relations between women and men are not-so-nice power arrangements, grounded in misogyny, expressing themselves as a life view (patriarchy), and resulting in the worldwide oppression of women on both an institutional and a personal level" (Ruth, 1990, p. 496).

In 1970, Robin Morgan published her famous anthology *Sisterhood Is Powerful*, and in 1984 she extended her work in a second anthology, *Sisterhood Is Global*. These books gave voice to the many who were concerned about women and their place in society. Through *Sis-

*terhood Is Global,* "we see that women all over the world experience many of the same feelings, beliefs, and reactions. What is more, there is a universal spark, a sensitivity that raises humor and pride and affection among us. This is what 'sisterhood' means" (Ruth, 1990, p. 149). Both of these books resonated widely with women's voices and fostered a sense of sisterhood among feminists around the world.

An important vehicle of the early period of the women's movement was the consciousness-raising group. These "CR" groups focused on facilitating personal awareness of a central tenet of the movement: the personal is political. All across the country, as if by spontaneous combustion, women were meeting to discuss their personal plights and arriving at the same conclusion: that their problems were not unique or isolated phenomena, but rather reflections of a political environment that devalued and subjugated women. One of the most exciting aspects of these early days was the sudden and widespread understanding that so many women achieved through these CR discussions—they felt empowered and took on the ideology of the movement with great enthusiasm. This is how the movement caught fire; women bonded around the new insight that they were being treated as second-class citizens. They realized that they had grown so accustomed to this status that they had been blind to its very existence. This awareness and the fervent sense of sisterhood it gave rise to fueled the movement.

As more and more women embraced feminism and the women's movement, questions arose about what strategies to employ to counter sexism and discriminatory practices. Divergent voices emerged, and one group of women advocated for changes in policy and law. These women, generally referred to as "liberal feminists," believed that it was possible and feasible to work "within the system" to achieve equality for women. On the other hand, radical feminists called for more extreme actions, contending that it was not fruitful to work within a system that was structurally biased against women; they promulgated confrontational and revolutionary tactics. Other strains of feminism developed as the women's movement evolved, including radical lesbian feminism and socialist feminism. Radical lesbian feminists contended that lesbianism was a political choice and they focused their energy on building separatist societies that could develop their own social and economic orders. Jill Johnston's book *Lesbian Nation* (1973) was highly influential among lesbian feminists, many of whom felt silenced by the homophobia within the early women's movement. Johnston contended that lesbianism offered the true political solution to a feminist revolution, and this idea provided an impetus for those choosing a separatist solution.

As the women's movement gained visibility complaints and attacks from outside the movement appeared. Some journalists trivialized the movement by referring to feminists as "bra burners," after the symbolic burning of the item that some women considered an implement of repression. Further, Lesbian-baiting by reactionaries put the movement on the defensive, since referring to feminists as a "pack of lesbians" was at that time a very effective means of denigrating and discounting the entire movement.

There was also criticism and splintering within the movement. Liberal and radical feminists differed sharply in terms of activist strategies. African-American feminists criticized the feminist movement as being too unidimensional, dominated by a white middle-class view of the world, and ignoring the role of class and race hierarchies in the oppression of women (hooks, 1993; Rollins, 1996). African-American women in the civil rights movement pointed out that the predominantly white women's movement neither understood nor addressed their issues and concerns.

These critical voices did not silence the movement, but rather facilitated examination and growth within it, although this process was sometimes painful. In its beginnings the women's movement was largely dominated by white women and white women's concerns; there was limited awareness of racism or the impact of racism and sexism on women of color. Criticism by African-American women forced white feminists to examine their own racism and find ways to embrace women of various ethnic groups. And an understanding of the tactics used by reactionaries to discount the movement led to a more sophisticated understanding of how to counter negative press attacks and how to effect positive change.

The early years of the contemporary women's movement saw internal struggles and questions about the meaning of feminism, although the movement gave expression to many women and won many victories for them over the next several decades. Although the movement continues to this day it is not characterized by the widespread groundswell, public demonstration, and heady excitement of its early days. It has evolved into a more mature movement, although questions about the nature of feminism still persist, some of which are raised by those outside the movement, and some debated by those who identify with feminism.

The women's and civil rights movements led to many tangible changes and improvements in the status of women and racial/ethnic minority groups. The Equal Pay Act of 1963 specifically countered employment discrimination. The Civil Rights Act of 1964 gave the courts the authority to enforce nondiscriminatory policies not only in employment, but also in housing and education. Barriers to educational access were challenged, and affirmative action programs opened the door to many who had previously been denied access to certain educational and employment opportunities. The women's movement has fostered examination of numerous issues: women's status in the family, domestic violence, restraints on reproductive freedom, sexual victimization, and many others. There have been some very specific and positive outcomes of these somewhat public discussions and debates: we now have better laws and programs to address domestic violence; there are rape shield laws protecting such victims from being questioned about their sexual histories; some company policies now provide day-care for the children of working parents; more women have been elected and appointed to important government positions; and police are more sensitive when dealing with rape victims, to name just a few. So significant have been many of these gains that some who lived through the early period of the women's movement now claim that young women take for granted the struggles that brought about these gains.

## FEMINIST IDEOLOGIES

The women's movement gave rise to various explanations for sexism as well as to different strategies for ameliorating its effects. Over time these perspectives developed into somewhat distinct, albeit overlapping, feminist ideologies. The ideologies gaining the most prominence in the United States included liberal feminism, radical feminism, cultural feminism, and socialist feminism. Table 1.1 provides an overview of these ideologies, showing how they differ on key dimensions.

Liberal feminism is the offspring of the women's suffrage movement, and has its roots in the rationalist tradition. Liberal feminists contend that because women "do not differ in this essential human capacity to reason, men and women ought to participate as equals in society" (Whalen, 1996, p. 14). Liberal feminists generally embrace the democratic political system and believe that women can achieve equality through systematic legal and social change. "Liberal feminism is what sociologists would consider a reform social movement that seeks to bring about change within the existing social framework by reforming rather than overturning the basic institutions of society" (Rollins, 1996, p. 3).

Radical feminists contend that subjugation of women is the primary form of oppression, and that it has spawned patriarchal societal structures that have institutionalized sexism. Un-

**Table 1.1.** Views and Characteristics of Selected Feminist Ideologies

| Feminist ideologies | Explanation for women's oppression | Remedies for inequity | View of the genders |
|---|---|---|---|
| Liberal feminism | Irrational prejudice, inequity in legal and social policies, institutionalized discrimination | Enactment of new laws, changes in social policies | Men and women are imbued with same capacity for reasoning and rationality, and thus should be treated equally in the eyes of the law and society. |
| Radical feminism | Institutionalized sexism due to entrenched patriarchy. (Sexism is the most fundamental form of oppression.) | Significant and revolutionary social and political changes to eliminate sexism, the patriarchal system, and other forms of oppression | Men and women are basically the same and ought to have same access to power. |
| Cultural feminism | Cultural devaluation of women's traits | Focus on the individual woman, revealing women's unique traits and contributions to society, cultural transformation via feminization of culture | There are essential differences between men and women; there is a female nature (essentialist). |
| Socialist feminism | Oppression is rooted in the economic system. (Sexism, racism and classism are inseparable forms of oppression.) | Economic revolution from capitalistic to socialistic economies that do not exploit workers | Individuals are marginalized and exploited by and because of gender, race, ethnicity, and class status. |

like liberal feminists, radical feminists believe that there must be significant political and social upheaval in order to root out and restructure patriarchal institutions. Radical feminists argue that "men and women are, or have the potential to be, essentially the same—biologically, psychologically, socially, and politically. . . . The political project of radical feminists, therefore, is to work actively at subverting the existing political system and developing radically new societal forms" (Whalen, 1996, p. 15).

Socialist feminism developed out of socialist political and economic analysis, and is concerned with the interlocking nature of sexual, racial, and economic forms of oppression. Socialist feminists believe that capitalism promulgates oppressive economic practices by subordinating people on the basis of gender, race, and class. Capitalistic systems exploit the labor of many powerless persons for the benefit of a few powerful ones. Like radical feminists, socialist feminists contend that radical social, political, and economic changes are necessary to subvert oppressive systems and build a society in which persons can be treated equally. This form of feminism has "aided the cause of women's liberation by focusing attention on multiple systems of oppression and dominance and their interactive effect on women in varying circumstances and historical periods. The political project of social feminists is to subvert not only the patriarchal structures of oppression but also its racist, classist, heterosexist, ageist, and ableist structures" (Whalen, 1996, p. 16).

Cultural feminists focus less on political structures than any of the other feminist ideologies, instead attending to attitudes and values. They generally contend that sexism is the result of a devaluing of what they believe are inherent female traits. Thus, they also differ from liberal and radical feminists in their contention that there are clear differences between men and women. According to Whalen (1996):

> Cultural feminists, however, have tended to embrace the biological and psychological understandings of the differences between men and women. From their perspective, the social problem women encounter is not the differences per se but rather the differential value placed on those differences. In our culture, men's capacities are valued while women's are devalued. The goal of cultural feminists is the revaluing of women's capacities and women's nature and the effort to reverse (or for some, to equalize) the current differential valuing of men and women. (p. 23)

Cultural feminists have an affinity with spiritualist perspectives, since there is much emphasis on the individual woman valuing herself and the inherently positive aspects of woman's nature. Many cultural feminists contend that women are morally superior to men, since women are more nurturant and value peacekeeping over competition and aggression. They thus believe that the revaluing of feminine traits can foster a cultural transformation to a more peaceful society.

## THE WOMEN'S MOVEMENT AND MENTAL HEALTH ISSUES

Phyllis Chesler's 1972 book *Women and Madness* was influential in shaping a feminist analysis of women's psychiatric treatment. Chesler contended that a double standard of mental health—one for women and another for men—dominated clinical theory and practices, leading to the pathologizing of the very traits that were expected of women in their prescribed social roles. She also held that the types of behavior for which people are hospitalized are related to sex, race, age, class, and marital status. Her detailed analysis prompted research and reflection about how women were treated by clinicians and about the relationship among women's roles, experiences of oppression and exploitation, and psychological distress.

Such analysis led to concerns about the plight of victims of domestic violence, childhood sexual abuse, sexual exploitation, and rape, as well as of women who sought treatment for the aftereffects of these traumas or for other distress. In keeping with the credo that the personal is political, there were attempts to bring to light the injustices of the system that silenced rape and childhood sexual abuse victims, that minimized domestic violence, and that discounted women's distress as "hysterical female problems." Attitudes and policies that promulgated these injustices were challenged, and victim-blaming reactions to them were excoriated. The shamefully high rates of domestic violence, rape, and childhood sexual abuse were publicized. Empowerment of victims became the byword of the movement; as victims came to understand that they were not at fault for their victimization, they became empowered by the understanding that an injustice had been done *to* them.

Professional as well as nonprofessional women took up these causes. The battered women's movement was their answer to the specific but widespread problem of domestic violence. Around the country women banded together to obtain funding and community support for the development of safe havens for battered women. As the various programs began to network among themselves, most eventually established formalized connections in state coalitions and with the National Coalition Against Domestic Violence (Whalen, 1996). Today the shelters developed by these groups continue in many communities, and they have gained sufficient visibility that most battered women now know they have a place to go to escape their immediate situation. The battered women's movement has also branched out into other areas, training police officers to effectively intervene in domestic disputes, advocating for changes in laws to facilitate arrest and prosecution of batterers, and developing treatment programs for batterers.

Feminist mental health workers were concerned about an array of barriers to naming and treating women's problems—overprescription of pharmacological treatments for women, stigmatization of victims of violence and sexual assault, and paternalistic treatment of women by many medical and mental health workers. Such concerns led to the birth of feminist therapy, which was specifically intended to validate women's experiences, to provide appropriate and respectful treatment for women, and to provide a foundation for political activism on behalf of women. Feminist mental health professionals who began to discuss these concerns found much in common with each other and, out of a desire to work together on their concerns, formed professional associations or treatment collectives. One such highly influential association was the Feminist Therapy Institute, founded in 1982, an organization of feminist therapists that continues to the present day. The Feminist Therapy Institute provided an opportunity for feminist therapists to come together and discuss their ideas about the practice of feminist therapy. These experienced therapists went on to formulate positions relevant to a feminist philosophy of treatment, to articulate feminist therapeutic techniques, and to discuss violence against women, power and advocacy, ethics, and training in an early book on feminist therapy, the *Handbook of Feminist Therapy: Women's Issues in Psychotherapy* (Rosewater & Walker, 1985). They have been in the forefront in elucidating a set of feminist ethical principles, and in 1995 published a book specifically on ethics: *Ethical Decision Making in Therapy: Feminist Perspectives* (Rave & Larsen, 1995).

Feminist mental health professionals have had a significant impact on the profession of psychology through the actions of small groups of feminists as well as through a variety of organizations, including the Association for Women in Psychology (founded in 1969) and the American Psychological Association's Division 35 (Psychology of Women division; founded in 1973). The Association for Women in Psychology (AWP) was founded when a group of women psychologists met at the 1969 American Psychological Conference over concerns about sexist practices at the conference, discrimination in the academic and professional worlds of psychology, and the contribution of psychological theory to women's oppression (Tiefer, 1991). AWP developed a feminist governance structure and went on to offer an annual conference that is still very popular among its members. In 1973 the American Psychological Association approved the Psychology of Women Division, and this division has grown considerably since its birth, bringing a feminist perspective to governance meetings and association policies. These groups and the women and men in them have offered critiques of sexist therapy and research practices, newly proposed diagnostic categories, and ethical guidelines.

## EMERGING CHALLENGES FOR MODERN FEMINISM

One of the challenges for modern feminism in general, and for a feminist psychology in particular, has been how to truly understand and incorporate women's diversities into its models and actions. The women's movement has at times ignored differences among women, and mainstream feminist psychology has had a white, middle-class focus. In the United States modern feminists are more and more examining diversities among women and how they impact individuals' identities, circumstances, values, and opportunities.

For instance, in recent years there has been increased attention to differences among women from different ethnic/racial heritages and to the diversity of concerns among these different groups. Although the U.S. feminist movement has been predominantly a white women's movement, women of color are, more and more, voicing their criticisms about the failure of white feminists to understand their perspectives and address their concerns. Green and Sanchez-Hucles (1997) have pointed out that feminist psychology has been characterized by an overrepresentation of white, middle-class women, and that it does not well represent the effects of race, culture, ethnicity, socioeconomic class, age, sexual orientation, and able-bodied status on women's lives. Feminist psychologists are in the beginning stages of incorporating a cultural analysis into feminist psychological theory, research, and practice. For example, a recent publication edited by Landrine (1995) focused on bringing cultural diversity to feminist psychology. Landrine explains that "to bring cultural diversity to feminist psychology requires not only a focus on the cultures of others but a focus on European American cultures" (1995, p. 16). That is, Euro-American culture should not be taken as a "standard" against which other cultures are judged, but rather it should also be subjected to scrutiny. Also, as Unger (1995) has pointed out in her discussion of conceptual issues in the study of cultural diversity, culture is a rich variable, requiring analysis along many dimensions and levels.

Similarly, there has been a recognition among contemporary feminists that as a culture we have generally neglected and even denied the impact that class has on the individual. In the introduction to a special journal issue on classism and feminist therapy, Hill (1996) notes, "Class and classism is [sic] in the position that gender and sexism was [sic] thirty years ago; denied, surrounded with myth, and silenced. Class is complicated and difficult, but the first problem with class is that we don't talk about it." In recent years, however, there has been increased dialogue about how class affects values, interpersonal perceptions, and opportunities. There are those who have not shrunk from bringing these issues to public attention. For instance, Angela Davis' important 1981 work *Women, Race, and Class* criticizes the women's movement for its racist and classist biases. However, feminist psychologists have only recently entered into the dialogue about class and its impact.

With development of worldwide communication systems and increased travel across countries there has been increased attention to the plight of women around the world. The United Nations declared 1975–1985 the United Nations Decade for Women, and they have sponsored several conferences over the intervening decades addressing women's circumstances internationally. These actions helped focus attention on women's circumstances around the world. There is now greater awareness of oppressive conditions for many girls and women in some areas around the world. For instance, a recent report examining gender differences in access to education in 132 countries found that 51 of these countries still have serious gender gaps (Briscoe, 1998). Further, women continue to be overrepresented among the world's poor: most of the world's women are poor, and most of the poor are women. Feminists in the United States have been challenged by this greater awareness of the problems of women around the world to better understand the intersection of cultural values and political views and how these forces impact women in diverse societies. However, the United States is not viewed positively among women of all nations and the liberal feminist perspective of many United States feminists is considered culture-bound and especially irrelevant to the concerns of women from developing countries.

## FEMINIST SCHOLARSHIP AND PSYCHOLOGY

Not surprisingly, feminist thinking has had a great influence on the scholarly disciplines, psychology included. Two feminist ideologies in particular have held much sway in the discipline: liberal feminism and cultural feminism, although the radical and socialist perspectives have found expression in some circles.

Early feminist analyses challenged the androcentric biases of psychological theory and knowledge. Debates at this time focused on questions about the extent and ramifications of any gender differences in abilities or traits, the origins of any gender differences, the problem of considering men as the standard against which women were measured, and the lack of attention to women's experiences.

These early feminist analyses and research approaches were characterized by the logical empiricist paradigm that had prevailed in the social sciences for several decades. This paradigm assumed the possibility of an objective researcher. "Feminist-empiricist psychologists initially located sexist practices not in epistemology (i.e., in the theories of knowledge) but in methodology, and they believed that the construction of nonsexist science required simply that bias be eliminated from empirical methods" (Morawski & Bayer, 1995, p. 122). These feminist empiricists generally utilized the same methods as the traditional scientific endeavor, while also recommending strategies for eliminating bias (cf. Denmark, Russo, Frieze, & Sechzer, 1988; McHugh, Koeske, & Frieze, 1986). According to Enns (1992) this perspective is consistent with the liberal feminist orientation. Riger (1992) has pointed out, however, that continuing identification of numerous instances of androcentic bias in research casts doubts on the feminist empiricist's contention that there can be a value-free science.

But a different perspective, that of standpoint feminism, broke with the feminist empiricist approach, questioning "the very methods and nature of science, such as assumptions that truth is objective, rational, and ahistorical, and that the inquirer must maintain distance from the subject matter being studied" (Enns, 1992, p. 461). This perspective differed sharply from the feminist empiricist view that operated on the assumption that there could be an objective scientist and science. The feminist standpoint approach gave rise to research which placed women at the center of inquiry and tried to erase the boundaries between researchers and the persons studied (Fee, 1986), thus utilizing the qualitative, in-depth approach to studying women's lives (Enns, 1992). Carol Gilligan's work on moral development (1982) is perhaps the best known example of feminist standpoint research. Enns (1992) has noted that standpoint feminism is consistent with the emphases of many cultural, radical, and socialist feminists. Riger (1992) identifies a number of problems with this perspective: assuming a commonality among all women ignores differences among racial/ethnic and social classes (Spelman, 1988); carried to an extreme, this approach seems to dissolve science into autobiography; and, since we all have multiple status identities, it is difficult to generalize about women's experiences (Harding, 1987).

Yet a third major feminist perspective, that of feminist postmodernism, grew out of the contemporary revolution in scientific thinking that fomented a critique of traditional epistemological models and precipitated the development of postmodernism or social constructionism. Feminists were "frontrunners" in exploring the possibilities of a postmodern or social constructionist analysis (Gergen, 1985). According to Enns (1992),

> Feminist postmodernism rejects the search for a distinctive, universal female standpoint because the identities of women are influenced by many other potential standpoints, such as race, ethnicity, sexual orientation, class, and disability. A postmodern view proposes that reality is embedded within social relationships and historical contexts and is socially constructed or invented. Rather than searching for 'a' truth, the inquirer focuses on how meaning is negotiated, and how persons in authority maintain control over these meanings" (p. 461)

At its most basic, social constructionism is concerned with explaining the processes by which people come to describe, explain, or otherwise account for the world in which they live (Gergen, 1985). Enns (1992) contends that this epistemological position can be integrated with many aspects of socialist feminist philosophy.

The social constructionist framework is now very much a part of contemporary feminist psychology. This framework has facilitated critiques of traditional theories, analyses of the scientific enterprise, and an appreciation of the ways in which science affects our worldview. According to Morawski and Bayer (1995), in their presentation on feminist critiques of the social sciences:

> (P)sychologists' tools of knowledge production can never be assumed to be politically neutral. Rather, they must be scrutinized for ways in which they function to reproduce hierarchical social relations among women of differing races, ethnicities, and sexual orientation. We must also see how our traditional approaches direct us toward individual-centered psychological theories instead of toward the historical, social, and cultural contingencies of psychological phenomena, as well as ways of seeing and thinking about our everyday lives. Similarly, psychologists' routine investigative practices need be examined for how our theorizing, research designs, questions, and writing style impose limitations on a multicultural psychology. We must consider how these "tools of the trade" can arrange the inclusion of forgotten and ignored "others," of voices silenced by assumptions of a universal psychological subject and subjectivity. We also need to move back several steps to ask ourselves about the very categories of race, class, ethnicity, and sexual orientation that we take to be "natural" givens rather than cultural constructions. (p. 119)

The framework used by the authors of this book is social constructionist, and there are a number of specific assumptions that underlie this perspective. Davis and Gergen (1997) have articulated these key features:

1. Facts are dependent on the language used to create and sustain them; all forms of naming are socially constructed, including such seemingly basic biological categories as the female–male sex distinction.
2. People generate their truths from the language available to them.
3. Any description of the nature of reality is dependent on the historical and cultural location of that description; thus, it is possible to acknowledge a multiplicity of worldviews.
4. There are no universal ethical principles but one cannot ignore value considerations in scientific inquiry.
5. We must recognize that we ourselves are embedded in cultural communities.

## SUMMARY

This chapter has provided an overview of the women's liberation movement of the 1960s and 1970s, from its emergence out of the New Left, to its maturation as a force influencing legislation, judicial rulings, attitudes about women and men, and public and private treatment of women. A liberal feminist ideology permeated the early years of the women's movement, but various other ideologies, including radical feminism, socialist feminism, and cultural feminism, emerged and led to splintering and challenging within the movement, and subsequently to further elucidation of the meanings of feminism. These various ideologies spurred the development of feminist scholarship. The women's movement and feminist psychologists challenged the discipline and profession of psychology to examine its views and practices with respect to women and other disenfranchised persons, and individuals as well as feminist organizations provided rallying points for those interested in advancing feminist views. Without a doubt, the women's movement in the United States has had far-reaching impact, and has played a key role in shaping attitudes and policies toward contemporary women.

# REFERENCES

Beauvoir, S. de (1953). *The second sex* (H. M. Parshley, Ed. and Trans.). New York: Knopf.

Briscoe, D. (1998, October 19). More girls in school worldwide, study says. *The Oregonian*, p. A4.

Chesler, P. (1972). *Women and madness*. New York: Avon Books.

Davis, A. Y. (1981). *Women, race, and class*. New York: Random House.

Davis, S. N., & Gergen, M. (1997). Toward a new psychology of gender: Opening conversations. In S. N. Davis & M. Gergen (Eds.), *Toward a new psychology of gender* (pp. 1–27). New York: Routledge.

Denmark, F., Russo, N. F., Frieze, I. H., & Sechzer, J. A. (1988). Guidelines for avoiding sexism in psychological research. *American Psychologist, 43,* 582–585.

Enns, C. Z. (1992). Toward integrating feminist psychotherapy and feminist philosophy. *Professional Psychology: Research and Practice, 23,* 453–466.

Fee, E. (1986). Critiques of modern science: The relationship of feminism to other radical epistemologies. In R. Bleier (Ed.), *Feminist approaches to science* (pp. 42–56). New York: Pergamon Press.

Freeman, J. (1973). The origins of the women's liberation movement. *American Journal of Sociology, 78,* 792–811.

Gergen, K. J. (1985). The social constructionist movement in modern psychology. *American Psychologist, 40,* 266–275.

Gilligan, C. (1982). *In a different voice*. Cambridge, MA: Harvard University Press.

Green, B., & Sanchez-Hucles, J. (1997). Diversity: Advancing an inclusive feminist psychology. In J. Worrell & N. G. Johnson (Eds.), *Shaping the future of feminist psychology: Education, research, and practice*. Washington, DC: American Psychological Association.

Harding, S. (1987). Introduction: Is there a feminist method? In S. Harding (Ed.), *Feminism and methodology: Social science issues* (pp. 1–14). Bloomington, IN: Indiana University Press.

Hartmann, S. M. (1989). *From margin to mainstream: American women and politics since 1960*. Philadelphia, PA: Temple University Press.

Hill, M. (1996). We can't afford it: Confusions and silences on the topic of class. *Women & Therapy, 18,* 1–5.

hooks, b. (1993). Black women and feminism. In L. Richardson & V. Taylor (Eds.), *Feminist frontiers III* (pp. 499–507). New York: McGraw-Hill. (Reprinted from *Ain't I a women: Black women and feminism*, 1981. Boston: South End Press.)

Johnston, J. (1973). *Lesbian nation*. New York: Simon & Schuster.

Katzenstein, M. F. (1987) Comparing the feminist movements of United States and Western Europe: An overview. In M. F. Katzenstein & C. M. Mueller (Eds.), *The women's movement of the United States and Western Europe* (pp. 3–20). Philadelphia, PA: Temple University Press.

Landrine, H. (Ed.). (1995). *Bringing cultural diversity to feminist psychology: Theory, research, and practice*. Washington, DC: American Psychological Association.

McHugh, M., Koeske, R., & Frieze, I. (1986). Issues to consider in conducting nonsexist psychological research: A guide for researchers. *American Psychologist, 41,* 879–890.

Millett, K. (1970). *Sexual politics*. New York: Doubleday.

Morawski, J. G., & Bayer, B. M. (1995). Stirring trouble and making theory. In H. Landrine (Ed.), *Bringing cultural diversity to feminist psychology: Theory, research, and practice* (pp. 113–137). Washington, DC: American Psychological Association.

Morgan, R. (1970). *Sisterhood is powerful*. New York: Doubleday.

Morgan, R. (1984). *Sisterhood is global*. New York: Doubleday.

Rave, E. J., & Larsen, C. C. (Eds.)(1995). *Ethical decision making in therapy: Feminist perspectives*. New York: Guilford.

Riger, S. (1992). Epistemological debates, feminist voices: Science, social values, and the study of women. *American Psychologist, 47,* 730–740.

Rollins, J. H. (1996). *Women's minds women's bodies: The psychology of women in a biosocial context*. Upper Saddle River, NJ: Prentice Hall.

Rosewater, L. B., & Walker, L. E. A. (Eds.)(1985). *Handbook of feminist therapy: Women's issues in psychotherapy*. New York: Springer.

Ruth, S. (1990) *Issues in feminism: An introduction to women's studies* (2nd ed.). Mountain View, CA: Mayfield.

Spelman, E. V. (1988). *Inessential women: Problems of exclusion in feminist thought*. Boston: Beacon Press.

Tiefer, L. (1991). *A brief history of the Association for Women in Psychology (AWP): 1969–1991*. Indiana, PA: Association for Women in Psychology.

Whalen, M. (1996). *Counseling to end violence against women: A subversive model*. Thousand Oaks, CA: Sage Publications.

Unger, R. (1995). Conclusion: Cultural diversity and the future of feminist psychology. In H. Landrine (Ed.), *Bringing cultural diversity to feminist psychology: Theory, research, and practice* (pp. 413–431). Washington, DC: American Psychological Association.

# 2

# Feminist Reconstructions
of Psychology

## Susan L. Morrow

## INTRODUCTION

The women's liberation movement of the 1960s and 1970s provided the groundwork and consciousness for the development of a psychology of women. In the early 1960s, feminist author Betty Friedan (1963) proposed a sociopolitical analysis of the source of women's depression or "the problem that has no name" (p. 11; that is, women's confinement in roles for which they find themselves unsuitable) and critiqued psychoanalytic and anthropological perspectives on women. Later, Phyllis Chesler (1972) addressed issues related to women's mental health that were subsequently incorporated in the early literature on psychology of women. These early works were foreshadowed by some women novelists, for instance, Charlotte Perkins Gilman (1973, orig. 1899) in *The Yellow Wallpaper.* These works contributed to a growing consciousness among feminist psychologists regarding the treatment of women by the field of psychology as a whole, resulting in a groundswell of critiques of the field.

This chapter begins with a focus on androcentric views of women's psychology, followed by an overview of early attempts by women scholars to respond to those views in a way that centralized women's experiences and began to touch on sociopolitical components of women's psychology. Next, I address early feminist critiques of psychology's treatment of women and historical perspectives on the psychology of women. Finally, I examine feminist critiques of science and emerging feminist paradigms for inquiry, with a particular focus on a feminist social constructionist view of psychology of women.

## WHAT DO WOMEN WANT?
## ANDROCENTRIC VIEWS OF WOMEN'S PSYCHOLOGY

"What do women want?" (Freud, communique to Marie Bonaparte, in Young-Bruehl, 1990, p. xi)

Despite Freud's apparent naiveté concerning women, he had a great deal to say about women and their psychology. In fact, as Gallahan notes in Chapter 3, Freud and those who fol-

Susan L. Morrow ● Faculty of Educational Pyschology, University of Utah, Salt Lake City, Utah 84112–9255

*Issues in the Psychology of Women,* edited by Biaggio and Hersen. Kluwer Academic/Plenum Publishers, New York, 2000.

lowed him dedicated a considerable amount of time theorizing about women, usually without consulting them. However, lest Freud himself be singled out as the psychonemesis of women, it is important to understand the social and historical context from which women's place in psychology emerged. Bohan (1992) argued that "psychology has not *treated* women well" (p. 9, emphasis mine) in terms of its treatment of the subject of women, its treatment of women as psychologists, and its treatment of women as clients or patients.

After psychology began to separate itself from philosophy as a discipline at the end of the nineteenth century, its focus shifted from an interest in understanding the human psyche to that of controlling human behavior. As Furumoto (1998) pointed out, psychology at the beginning of the twentieth century "mirrored many aspects of the new ideal of manliness" (p. 72) of the time—including masculine action and objective measurement—and repudiated feminine reflection (introspection). Cattell, in his 1904 address to the International Congress of Arts and Sciences, embellished these perspectives with metaphors of territorial conquest, exploitation, hierarchy, competition, and domination, which Grossberg (1990) labeled "the institutionalizing of masculinity"(p. 134). This androcentric bias of psychology has affected the psychology of women by emphasizing values of objectivity and value-neutrality at the cost of understanding contextual bases for women's experience (Bohan, 1992).

With technology as the new deity of the turn of the twentieth century—and science (and consequently academe) its mentor—scientists and intellectuals such as Einstein and Darwin used their newfound authority to reinforce the positioning of women as baby makers and as less civilized than men. The study of psychology of women focused primarily on sex differences, with women "discussed only in relation to the male" and "the function of the female . . . thought to be distinctly different from and complementary to the function of the male" (Shields, 1975, p. 739). Evolutionary theory emphasized the biological bases of temperament, resulting in an emphasis on maternal instinct. In addition, because white men were viewed as the pinnacle of evolution, women were necessarily defined as deficient in "sensory, motor, and intellectual abilities" (Shields, 1975, p. 740). These deficiencies were focused on (1) differences between men and women in brain structure and therefore intelligence, (2) the variability hypothesis (that men, by virtue of the greater variability evidenced by their greater activity and achievements, were superior to women); and (3) the place of maternal instinct in women's "nature" (Shields, 1975). Education was thought to defeminize women and to endanger their reproductive and mothering capabilities (Bohan, 1992; Shields, 1975). These underpinnings of the new discipline of psychology set the stage for psychology to define women's "true" nature as if it were a biologically, not culturally, determined phenomenon. Science was called upon to reinforce roles formerly enforced by the church and society. Scientific sexism both supported and gave additional credence to societally determined subservient and domesticated roles for women (Bohan, 1992).

In addition to sexism, scientific racism predominated, particularly following Darwin's *The Origin of Species* in 1859. From 1860 through 1910, psychology ignored the powerful influences of white imperialism on its endeavors while defining European "man" as the pinnacle of creation. Like sex, race was viewed as independent of culture, and investigations of racial differences—in hair type, lip form, skin color and hue—became associated with characteristics believed to be "true" of people of various ancestries without attention to context. Races were even placed on a hierarchy of superiority and inferiority with—you guessed it—those most similar to Euro-Americans in appearance and values closest to the top. Race differences between "Caucasians" and "Negroes" gained the most attention. Galton, Spencer, and Hall contributed immensely to scientific racism, with African men gaining most salience (although negative), while African women remained largely invisible (Guthrie, 1998; Richards, 1997).

Research on women at the turn of the twentieth century focused primarily on sex and race differences in brain structures and functions (note that "sex and race," not "gender" or "culture" are the key words here). Helen Thompson Wooley (1910), in a scathing review of "this motley mass of material" (p. 340), asserted, "There is perhaps no field aspiring to be scientific where flagrant personal bias, logic martyred in the cause of supporting a prejudice, unfounded assertions, and even sentimental rot and drivel, have run riot to such an extent as here [in psychology]" (p. 340). She argued that despite research demonstrating that there were few, if any, biologically based psychological sex differences, proponents of sex differences ignored research that did not support their biased views of women. In addition, she noted that most sex differences were sociological, not psychological, thus foreshadowing a more explicit incorporation of the social construction of gender in the future. She pointed out that the trend away from a psychological focus and toward a sociological one had resulted in a shift away from the view that woman would injure herself mentally and physically by using her intellect, and toward the view that women would harm society itself by emphasizing intellectual activity at the expense of reproducing children and "thus lessen[ing] the chances of the best element to perpetuate itself" (p. 342).

It is important to understand the historical context in which early women psychologists such as Wooley entered the field. The sphere of North American middle-class white women's activity was to be the home, whereas women of color and working-class women were basically ignored by psychology in the United States as well as Europe. Women were exhorted to adhere to prescribed feminine behaviors and roles that "exalted the virtues of 'piety, purity, submissiveness, and domesticity' (Welter 1966, p. 152)" (Scarborough & Furumoto, 1987, p. 2). Several societal changes served to disturb this perspective, including "westward migration, industrialization, . . . urbanization" (Scarborough & Furumoto, 1987, p. 3), and the Civil War. Women began to demand—often in the face of tremendous resistance—to be allowed into the formerly all-male halls of academe.

Psychology in the United States began as a formal discipline in the 1880s, and the American Psychological Association was founded in 1892. Women were readily accepted into the new organization and comprised 13 percent of the organization by 1917. Yet these women— and indeed women in general—were rendered invisible in psychology until the women's movement of the 1960s and 1970s acted as a catalyst for historians to unearth these lost pioneers in psychology and other disciplines. The 25 "first generation" women in psychology, according to Scarborough and Furumoto (1987), were those who entered academic psychology around the turn of the century. They confronted a broad spectrum of challenges while pursuing doctoral degrees and careers in psychology, including emphasis on "the family claim" on daughters, pressure to choose between marriage and career, roadblocks to obtaining faculty positions in universities, and uncollegial treatment by male peers in the academic setting.

It is notable that women of color entered psychology later than white women and typically were not in positions to address issues related to their treatment by psychology until later than white women—indicative of their dual oppression as women and people of color. Ines Beverly Prosser, likely the first woman of color to enter psychology in 1933, wrote her dissertation on Negro children in mixed and segregated schools, but the majority of early women of color, like their white counterparts in the field, conducted research on traditional topics.

Prior to the most recent North American women's liberation movement, psychology could best be described as "womanless" (Crawford & Marecek, 1989), because women and women's experiences were omitted from investigation; men were used disproportionately as research subjects, with results generalized to women; and gender was not considered a legitimate variable in studies that included both women and men. Men's activities were seen as central to human experience, and women rarely had access to the means of knowledge production.

Bohan (1992) has noted that the marginalization of women in psychology is twofold: first, women as scholars in the discipline of psychology have been silenced and ignored; second, the concerns of women have been neglected throughout psychology's history, including the present. She noted the circularity of women psychologists' position in the field, whereby, due to the construction of gender, women's place has typically been one of ministering to suffering, not producing scientific knowledge; that is, women have been urged toward and even forced into applied rather than academic psychology. It is also frequently the case that when women take their places in professional arenas those arenas quickly become devalued economically and in terms of prestige (Touhey, 1974). Even those women who have made it to the halls of academe have traditionally been subordinated for various reasons.

The double entendre of "treatment" of women in psychology relates both to the academic "treatment" of the subject of woman or femininity *and* to how women clients/patients have been "treated" in psychotherapy. In both cases, psychology failed women miserably. Freud was, of course, a key proponent of an androcentric psychology of women, on the one hand admitting the limitations of his understanding of women by acknowledging that women's sexuality "is still veiled in an impenetrable obscurity" (Freud, 1905, p. 551) and that "the sexual life of adult women is a 'dark continent' for psychology" (Freud, 1926, p. 212). On the other hand, however, Freud devoted much of his speaking and writing to theorizing about women, drawing his theories from both his personal life experiences and his clinical work with his Viennese female patients. Freud viewed biology as destiny; however, as Lerman (1986) pointed out, a look at Freud's own sexual development reveals that, in the case of his theories, his personal history became a destiny that had far-reaching consequences for women.

Initially, Freud's interpretation of hysteria in women was based on his belief that the stories of his female patients (indicating that an overwhelming number of fathers were incestuously abusing their daughters) were in fact true and that this incest was the source of their hysterical symptomatology. Although he attempted to disguise the prevalence of abuse by the father by attributing much of it to wet nurses and nannies, he exhibited horror over its prevalence. However, a number of influences in his personal life converged to cause him to give up this viewpoint. He reported to his colleague Fleiss that he had had a dream in which he had "overly affectionate" feelings for his own 10-year-old daughter. In addition, through his own psychoanalysis, he began to have a growing awareness that his own father had abused, if not Freud himself, at least his siblings. These highly personal experiences were accompanied by growing controversy and lack of acceptance by professional peers of his "seduction theory" (note here that "seduction" refers to the activity of the perpetrator, not the child; and that Freud often used such words as "rape" and "sexual attack" as well as seduction to describe this abuse). In the midst of feeling intellectually and emotionally shunned and isolated as a result of his seduction theory, Freud found some of his closest friends drifting away. The influence of these factors may have been exacerbated by Freud's status as a Jew in anti-Semitic Vienna, driving him, consciously or unconsciously, to gradually come to see "scenes of seduction" reported by his patients as fantasies (Lerman, 1986; Masson, 1985). It should be noted, in relation to Freud's experiences of anti-Semitism, that he was a proponent of a nonracist psychology, although he remained oblivious to class privilege.

Ultimately, Freud's theories became almost exclusively intrapsychic: biology was destiny; and male power, female subordination, and the formation of subsequent personality structures (e.g., women's passivity, masochism, and narcissism; Gallahan, Chapter 3, *this vol-*

*ume*) were believed to have originated in the presence or absence of the penis and in complexes that sexualized the girl's attachments to her mother and father. As Horney would later argue, his perceptions were limited by his own cultural context; however, he generalized from his personal and historical milieu to women in general, with a resulting influence that is still felt today.

Early misogyny and misunderstandings in psychology have left their legacy as male psychologists over the years have perpetuated themes of "biology as destiny," women as inferior or incomplete men, and woman as nurturer/mother. According to Weisstein (1971), Bettelheim allowed for women to choose enterprises such as science and engineering, but he insisted that they wanted "first and foremost to be womanly companions of men and to be mothers" (Weisstein, 1971, p. 363). Erikson proposed that a woman's definition of her identity must be postponed as she waits to discover who she will marry (Weisstein, 1971)—presumably, then, she will define herself as the doctor's or grocer's *wife*. In addition, Erikson defined woman's psyche as a reflection of her biology, that is, as the receptive, passive, "inner space" that nurtures men and children. These sentiments were echoed throughout psychology's early and recent history; indeed, remnants of these ideas are still found in psychology today.

In addition to the pervasive gender stereotyping in psychology, women of color and poor women were marginalized into invisibility. Lesbian women have been the subject of considerable pathologizing by psychology, while bisexual women have been relegated to invisibility along with women of color, poor women, women with disabilities, and others.

## USING THE MASTER'S TOOLS:
## EARLY ATTEMPTS TO ADDRESS ANDROCENTRISM

It may be virtually impossible, given the hegemony of Freudian psychoanalytic thinking, for us to conceptualize a psychology of women not grounded in or reactive to psychodynamic theories. Building on and sometimes reacting against Freud were his dutiful and not-so-dutiful daughters, who used psychoanalytic theory to expand upon and, in some instances, oppose Freud's original formulations.

Helene Deutsch, born in 1884, published her two-volume work, *Psychology of Women* in 1944 and 1945. She was truly a "dutiful daughter" (Chesler, 1972) of Freud, having spent a year in analysis with him and working entirely within a Freudian theoretical framework. Gallahan (Chapter 3, *this volume*) describes the key points of Deutsch's work, which expanded on classical Freudian concepts. Penis envy took a secondary role to the concept of envy itself, which is experienced by both boys and girls over anything that someone else has that they do not, particularly if that "something" takes parental attention away from them. In addition, Deutsch argued that the girl's bond with her mother is never completely broken, and the mother remains a more central figure in the girl's development than the father.

Karen Horney, born a year after Deutsch and thirty years after Freud, broke with classical psychoanalytic tradition by proposing what she termed a "holistic" view of the person in which individual constitution and the environment interacted reciprocally. She critically examined Freud's theories on women, expressing the view that because civilization is dominated by men, the psychology of women had evolved from a masculine point of view and that women were unfairly and inaccurately being evaluated according to male standards and points of view. Horney (1967, originally published in 1935) insisted on rigorous examination of behavioral data across cultures as a standard for generating theory about women's psychology. She pointed to cultural factors as contributors to such concepts as female masochism and noted that "these ideologies [which attribute the cultural experiences of women to biology] function not only to reconcile women to their subordinate role" (Horney, 1967, p. 237), but also to define that role as their "hope of fulfillment, and to define it as desirable" (Williams, 1987, p. 76). Horney had completely disengaged herself from Freudian psychoanalysis by 1950, preferring a more optimistic view of human nature in which humans strive toward knowledge, spirituality, moral courage, achievement, intellect, and imagination.

It is interesting to wonder about the personal experiences of these women who were so immersed in androcentric analytic theories. Did they, like later feminists, experience a vague undefined unease when they learned about women from the influential men in their profession? Did a voice inside protest, "That is not my experience"?

Clara Thompson, born in 1893 in Rhode Island, was strongly influenced by Horney. Thompson criticized Freud for viewing female development through a masculine lens and from a masculine perspective. In addition, she argued, he generalized from women in his own culture to women as a whole. She did not object to Freud's observations of his women patients; rather, she challenged his interpretations of those observations. She addressed issues such as penis envy, as well as women's ability to grow and mature emotionally and intellectually, by arguing that the differential privilege and power attached to the roles of men and women in society explained these constructs. Like Horney, Thompson believed psychological views that evolve from a masculinist ideology serve to limit women's potential for growth and freedom. Thompson (1971, originally written in 1943) also identified women in terms of minority-group status, likening discrimination against women to that against people of color and noting that white skin and the penis both symbolize power and engender feelings of inferiority and even envy in people who are less powerful.

## DISMANTLING THE MASTER'S HOUSE: FEMINIST CRITIQUES OF TRADITIONAL PSYCHOLOGY

The women's liberation movement of the late 1960s and early 1970s brought a new critique to psychology of women. In concert with concerns raised by the fledgling feminist professional organizations, Association for Women in Psychology (AWP) in 1969 and Division 35 (Psychology of Women) of the American Psychological Association in 1973 (Biaggio, Chapter 3, *this volume;* Tiefer, 1991), individual feminist psychologists began identifying the androcentric biases in psychology that had for so long kept women in their place and pathologized those who could not or refused to stay there. There were many spokeswomen for a growing critique of traditional psychology. Stephanie Shields, cited earlier in this chapter, framed this critique historically. Rhoda Kessler Unger, cited later in the chapter, framed it epistemologically. In the following paragraphs, I address critiques by Naomi Weisstein, Carolyn Woods Sherif, Martha Mednick, and Carolyn Payton.

*Naomi Weisstein.* In 1968 Naomi Weisstein "fired a feminist shot that ricocheted down the halls between psychology's laboratories and clinics, hitting its target dead center" (Sherif, 1979, p. 93). Her original manuscript, titled *Kinder, Kuche, Kirche as Scientific Law: Psychology Constructs the Female,* was later expanded and published in 1971 with the title, *Psychology Constructs the Female, or, The Fantasy Life of the Male Psychologist (with Some Attention to the Fantasies of His Friends the Male Biologist and the Male Anthropologist).* She argued that psychological views depicting women as first and foremost suited to and concerned with marriage and motherhood were not, as the experts of the day promulgated, the "true" intrapsychic natures of women, but were constructed in the absence of data and based on societal stereotypes. She challenged the field to consider social context to understand female psychology. Like Helen Thompson Wooley 58 years before her, Weisstein (1971) blew the whistle on psychology for its biased views: "Psychology has functioned as a pseudo-scientific buttress for our cultural sex-role notions, that is, as a buttress for patriarchal ideology and patriarchal social organization: women's liberation and gay liberation fight against a common victimization" (p. 366).

*Carolyn Wood Sherif.* Laying the groundwork for her critique of psychology in her 1979 chapter entitled "Bias in Psychology," Carolyn Wood Sherif described psychology's heirarchy at the time of World War II, in which experimentalists occupied the topmost rung of the ladder of prestige and power, followed by "testers," those psychologists engaged in mental measurement. The lower rungs consisted of developmentalists, social psychologists, and clinicians. The highest levels of the hierarchy were occupied predominantly by men, with the lower, more applied levels consisting of more women. Sherif noted that these hierarchies had persisted into the late 1970s when she wrote her chapter, with each subdiscipline attempting to prove its worth by appearing as scientific (i.e., experimental) as possible.

Sherif identified psychological scientific perspectives as social myth, or the ideology of psychology's elite. The dominant beliefs in psychology at the time served to enforce sexism and racism—a focus on the physical world and physical processes, the reduction of human behavior to biological structures, an ahistorical perspective, the use of "objective language," and the glorification of the experiment. Sherif argued that this love affair with the physical and natural sciences was at the heart of sex bias in psychology. The "hard" (masculine) sciences were given precedence over the "soft" (feminine), human sciences; and male psychologists strove mightily to demonstrate that psychology was "hard"—a sort of "my science is harder than your science" argument. Psychology's pursuit of credibility as a "hard" science dominates the field to this day.

Sherif warned against experimental comparative psychology's tendency to place humans alongside the "other" animals in an attempt to explain human behavior. She also criticized the study of sex differences and trait theory, arguing that "the entire literature on sex differences reflects certain assumptions of its founding father, Sir Fancis Galton," who "found that women are inferior, just as he found the British superior to those of their subject peoples" (p. 115). Galton had founded a Eugenics Society "for the purpose of improving and purifying British blood, even if it had to be contaminated by that of women" (p. 115). Sherif pointed out that a particular bias in sex differences research was the press to find differences in order to get published. She also noted that focusing on traits necessarily led to ignoring human interaction as a powerful source of behaviors often labeled "traits."

In her critique of behavioral theorizing, Sherif argued that behavioral psychology, by ignoring human consciousness and self-awareness, has failed to deal with human experience. Further, by ignoring environmental influences—or by categorizing those influences as mere rewards and punishments—the behaviorist effectively dismisses issues of social values that influence women and men and fails to acknowledge differences in power and powerlessness that come to bear on human behavior. Noting that it has typically been privileged white men who have promulgated behavior theories and conducted behavioral experiments, she argued that projecting their conceptualizations of reward and punishment "into another sex, another group, or another culture produce[s] a bizarre psychology, replete with androcentric, ethnocentric, or nationalistic biases" (p. 118).

Sherif reserved her most scathing criticism for "psychodynamic visions of women's place" (p. 119). She argued, "If one were to design a theory to keep women in an inferior position and at lowered worth, none is more suitable than one locating the causes of women's behavior and problems inside the woman" (p. 119). She viewed the "equitable pursuit of knowledge [as] totally impossible within a Freudian framework" (p. 199), and she expressed the fervent "hope that the movement toward equality of men and women [would] deliver the final blow to any attempt to explain behavior in terms of inner psychodynamics alone" (p. 120). Sherif advocated a coordination of psychological and sociocultural explanations of human behavior, seeking new ways of producing knowledge and drawing on multiple disciplines to understand the impact of culture on individual psychology.

*Martha Schuch Mednick.* Martha Mednick (1978), addressing the "new" psychology of women, described the field as young, interdisciplinary, and in some disarray, which she found desirable as it could stimulate new ideas. She warned that an overemphasis on sex-differences research would continue to influence discriminatory policy decisions that negatively affect women, and she distinguished sex differences research from the new, feminist psychology of women. The new psychology of women, she argued, included a critique of the status quo, including biological explanations that placed woman in a victim position and rendered her invisible. In addition, she noted that feminist critiques of psychology include a focus on methodology that frequently biases research against women and ignores the historico–socio–political context. Mednick recommended that psychology of women address four neglected areas: (1) issues of power in women's lives, (2) the study of women's life cycle, (3) interpersonal issues in women's lives, and (4) research on women of color. She also proposed that psychology of women examine sex roles and sex-role change, particularly from a cross-cultural perspective, and that male psychologists begin studying their own misogyny and sexism.

*Carolyn R. Payton.* Carolyn Payton, in her 1984 American Psychological Association (APA) Award for Public Service address, castigated the APA for its reluctance to take a stand on social issues affecting women and people of color. She argued that psychologists were proposing deficit models for black people without taking into account the context of poverty, inadequate educational systems, and racism. She contended that "to view psychology as a science devoid of social implications or responsibilities will not advance our profession but will rather lead to its demise" (p. 394). Payton (1984) questioned the validity of a psychological science devoid of context, and she told the following story from her experience as director of the Peace Corps:

> More than a decade ago, a private voluntary agency working in a small community in what is now Bangladesh decided that installing flush toilets would help separate the sewage from the drinking water and cut down on waterborne diseases. The organization's workers did everything right—they thought. They consulted with community leaders about placement of the toilets, ran education programs, and handed out leaflets explaining the importance of the toilets. Agency staff met with the men working on the project to talk to them about what they were doing and why, with the result that their efforts were so successful that it became a status symbol among community leaders to be among the first to have the new toilets.
>
> When the agency went back 10 years later for a field check, it found the toilets in disrepair because no one had used them for such a long time. Staff members investigated and came back to the agency very embarrassed. Despite all its efforts to involve people, the agency had failed to note that the five gallons of water it took for each flush had to be hauled by hand, and the village women were the water bearers. Since nobody had bothered to convince the women of the importance of flush toilets, they had refused to carry the extra water. (p. 396)

In closing, she advocated adequate representation of women and people of color in all areas of APA governance and concluded with these words: "Who must do the impossible things? Those who care" (p. 397).

A common theme among feminist psychological writers building on grassroots feminist analyses was the need to examine the psychology of women in social context. In addition, they criticized mainstream psychology for its androcentric, misogynist, and racist perspectives and its treatment of women in the field of psychology. Throughout these critiques, parallels were often drawn between gender and race, the two most salient forms of marginalization in the field. In addition, a narrow "science" dominated by positivism came under heavy criticism, with feminists and feminist psychologists in the forefront of the argument.

## FEMINIST CONTRIBUTIONS TO EPISTEMOLOGY AND METHODOLOGY

Feminist contributions to epistemology and methodology are twofold. First, feminist and womanist scholars have criticized what they have termed the "scientific myths" that pervade masculinist science (Hubbard, 1988). Second, feminists and multiculturalists have contributed to an ongoing dialogue that not only investigates issues of importance to women, people of color, and other marginalized groups, but also contributes to a new worldview and methods of inquiry that make the honest study of those issues more possible.

### Feminist Critiques of Science

Feminists have criticized conventional (i.e., white, male, middle-to upper-middle-class) science for a number of shortcomings: (1) that those who are allowed to "do" science are members of a privileged and elite group, (2) that the basic underpinnings of accepted scientific inquiry are at core masculinist and racist, and (3) that the treatment of women, people of color, and other such groups marginalizes those groups, who are then viewed through a biased lens.

Hubbard (1988) pointed out that those who have been permitted to make scientific facts are typically highly educated Western European and American white men of the upper-middle and upper classes. Although some white women and a few people of color have gained access to academe, by and large the socioeconomic class makeup of the scientific community remains one of privilege. Hubbard noted that science is not only conducted by the elite, but it is also defined by the elite. The rules of what constitutes science are made by those with privilege and power, and those rules are highly resistant to change. When women, people of color, and others who have been marginalized point out the emperor's nakedness, it is a small matter for the emperor and those who serve him to discount his detractors as emotional, crazy, or nonobjective (thus using the rules to reinforce the rules).

Masculinity has powerfully influenced science, according to Benjamin (1993), Furumoto (1998), Keller (1992), and others. Psychology as a science emerged during "a crisis of masculinity" (Furumoto, p. 72) in which social roles were shifting and a new idea of masculinity was emerging. Feminist theorists (Gergen, 1988; Hubbard, 1988) have implicated science as essentially masculine, including its basic ontological structure, its emphasis on objectivity, the invisibility of the researcher and her or his social context, its tendency toward context-stripping, and its apolitical stance.

The basic ontological structure or orienting assumptions of science represent those historical masculine perspectives described earlier that are psychology's heritage from the turn of the twentieth century. These assumptions "frame the categories of subsequent understanding, the kinds of questions toward which research can be directed, and the kinds of answers that can be derived" (Gergen, 1988). Ontology dictates what counts as data and how those data may be interpreted, thus limiting the potential for findings outside the boundaries of its structure. In addition, the hegemony of the Euro-American white middle- and upper-class male perspective dictates who may study and generate knowledge, whose ontology will predominate, what kinds of questions may be asked, and what methods may be used. Questions that would be asked by marginalized peoples remain unasked or, if asked, are simply ignored.

Noting that "The scientific method rests on a particular definition of objectivity" (p. 9), Hubbard (1988) argued that this definition of objectivity functions to exclude those who are not part of the privilege/power structure. Objectivity as defined by androcentric science is nonrelational in regard to the "subjects" or objects of study. This nonrelationality means that the object of investigation is separate from the investigator, other objects, and the context or environment in which it resides. Fine (1992) noted that all research psychologists make choices about epistemologies and political stances; however, most "deny these choices within veils of 'objectivity,' describing behaviors, attitudes, and preferences as if these descriptions were static and immutable, 'out there,' and unconnected to political contexts" (p. 211). She identified these researchers as "ventriloquists" who are "vehicles for transmission, with no voices of their own" (p. 211).

In addition to context-stripping in relation to subjects/objects of research, conventional androcentric, "objective" science renders the person and social context of the researcher invisible (Hubbard, 1988). Myths of objectivity and separateness between researcher and researched have perpetuated the practice of nondisclosure by the researcher. Although the orienting assumptions and worldviews of investigators have potent effects on the paradigms and methodologies used to "discover" information, objectivity remains a mask behind which the investigator can avoid being known. Thus, the person of the researcher remains safely outside the realm of criticism.

Stripped of context, human experience must be viewed intrapsychically. History is replete with examples of ways women have been silenced, marginalized, misunderstood, misrepresented, and, indeed, abused at the hands of science. Context-stripping results in blaming women for problems imposed by a misogynist society (Bohan, 1997). This context-stripping violates basic feminist principles viewing humans as embedded in a social context that reciprocally influences and is influenced by the individual. Thus, "awareness of subjectivity and context must be part of doing science because our subjectivity and our context are part of being human" (Hubbard, 1998, p. 12).

Objective science is, by definition, apolitical (Tieffer, 1988). In its claims of being neutral or value-free, psychological science has managed to perpetuate a particular worldview without acknowledging the existence of that worldview. Collins (1990) argued that "Knowledge claims are evaluated by a community of experts whose members represent the standpoints of the groups from which they originate" (p. 203). Thus, by dismissing competing knowledge claims (such as those from feminists and people of color) because those claims fall outside the dominant paradigm, the hegemony of the "Eurocentric masculinist knowledge validation process" (p. 203) is ensured.

All research, the feminist researcher would argue, is political. To maintain the stance that research is value-free is to actively uphold the status quo of misogyny, racism, and all the other "isms" that characterize North American culture and science. The researcher has a choice to support that status quo or to conduct research that furthers liberation, social empowerment, and social change.

## Feminist Contributions to Science

Feminist psychological scientists and theorists embrace the challenge of change. Feminist research empowers women as well as other marginalized and disempowered peoples.

Feminist contributions to science attempt to address the problems of masculinist traditional science, including its basic ontological structure, its emphasis on objectivity, the invisibility of the researcher and her or his social context, its tendency toward context-stripping, and its apolitical stance.

Feminist science centralizes the female experience. Although gender tends to be used as a template for understanding oppressions, feminist science attempts to step into the experiences and worlds of those whose lives we study and to centralize the salient aspects of their experience as the lens through which those experiences are viewed. Feminist theorists attempt to centralize and validate instead of marginalizing the experiences of those who have traditionally been silenced. As opposed to having its roots in the masculinity crisis of the late nineteenth and early twentieth centuries, the roots of feminist psychology have emerged largely from the women's liberation movement of the 1960s and 1970s.

Feminists and liberation psychologists have called for "the indispensable unity between subjectivity and objectivity in the act of knowing" (Freire, 1985, p. 51; Hubbard, 1988). This unity restores relationship between researcher and researched, among those who are the participants of research, and between participant and context or environment. Feminist research recognizes this unity by being nonexploitative and by treating participants with respect and care (Reinharz, 1992). Research participants are viewed in positive, nonpathologizing ways. In addition, feminist research invites multiple viewpoints and attends to the political realities of participants' lives. Feminist research offers the possibility of social change as part of its very process, using participatory and action-oriented methods to engage participants in their own empowerment and in changing social structures that oppress them.

One aspect of context addressed by feminists has been the social context of the researcher, including the social structure of the laboratory as well as the community and interpersonal relationships in which research is conducted (Hubbard, 1988). Feminist researchers have often identified themselves somewhere in the text of their research in order that the reader may understand more fully the "lens" through which the research was conceived and conducted. Fine (1992) suggested that, in contrast to the "ventriloquist" stance adopted in conventional research, researchers might adopt other stances, those of "voice" and of participatory activist. Fine referred to the "voice" stance as one of "dis-stance, importing to their work the voices of Discarded Others, . . . [while] typically claim[ing] little position for self" (p. 211). This perspective can be seen in early works of Gilligan (1982) and Belenky, Clinchy, Goldberger, and Tarule (1986), in which the authors "gave" voice to participants but in which their own personhood remained relatively invisible. In contrast, Fine advocated a position of "participatory activism, . . . which seeks to unearth, disrupt, and transform existing institutional arrangements" (p. 211). In this approach, the investigator is an integral part of the inquiry process and is explicit about her or his involvement, politics, and perspectives. Hubbard (1988) proposed that feminist scientists acknowledge our values and subjectivities, enabling us to "understand the world . . . from inside instead of pretending to be objective outsiders looking in" (p. 13).

This understanding of "the world from inside" has been powerfully illustrated in the work of Patricia Hill Collins (1990), who articulated an Afrocentric feminist epistemology in which the subjective experiences of Black women undergird and pervade scholarship. In her synthesis of Afrocentric and feminist perspectives, she noted that "Afrocentric feminist epistemology is rooted in the everyday experiences of African-American women" (p. 208). Thus, the subjectivities of African-American women become infused in Afrocentric feminist scholarship in the form of personal experiences of the author, voices of these women, folk wisdom, concrete practical images, stories, Biblical principles, and political analysis. Similarly, Theresa Martínez (1996) defined a Chicana feminist epistemological standpoint as one of "resistance, resilience, humor and wit" (p. 114) grounded in the struggles of family and people "against discrimination in a racist, classist, and sexist society" (p. 114). She argued for the integration of theorizing and storytelling, for the inclusion of the author's personal and historical realities within the context of theory and scholarship. Bringing to light such concepts as colonization, resilience, resistance, and oppositional consciousness (Sandoval, 1991), women scholars of color have effectively illustrated that epistemology cannot be separated from the human and political realities of women's lives.

Thus, feminist psychological science is, one hopes, incurably political. Its perspective is not so much female as feminist, with the underpinnings of a social movement for change and the credo, "The personal is political." Although feminist researchers are diverse in their epistemological and methodological approaches, most would agree that feminist science goes beyond a focus on women and includes a commitment to some kind of change. Comas-Díaz (1994) argued that an integrative, pluralistic perspective examines and combats the psychological colonization experienced by women of color. A key element in combatting this colonization is *conscientizaçáo,* or an awakening of consciousness. This process involves both personal and social transformation. Thus, feminist psychology is viewed as a tool for political change, regardless of the specific methods employed.

Because conventional research methods remain the most well-understood and credible approaches in psychology at the present time, quantitatively and statistically oriented feminist researchers have argued for the importance of conducting generalizable research that will contradict misogynistic, biased research on women. By bringing scientific and public attention to findings that put women in a positive light and that view women of color from a model of resilience instead of deficiency, researchers may contribute to positive social change. Feminist quantitative researchers can provide important information to change policy and speak to power structures accustomed to the concise results that characterize these methods. Feminist survey researchers and experimentalists increasingly attend to context in their work.

Feminists have also been strong proponents of qualitative research methods, attractive primarily because the genre facilitates an opportunity for those who have been traditionally silenced to give "voice" to their experiences and oppressions and to tell their "stories." Qualitative methods encourage relational values embraced by many feminists and make participatory and action-oriented research more possible.

Feminist researchers of all persuasions are interested in issues of power and representation in research relationships. That is, who holds the power in researcher–participant relationships, and how is that power used? Whose realities are represented? Who gains from the research endeavor? Who owns the products of research (Fine, 1992; Lather, 1991)? These questions, initiated by feminist, critical, and poststructuralist theorists and qualitative researchers, are important regardless of method. In voicing these concerns, the feminist researcher recognizes that knowledge is generated in a sociopolitical context.

## SOCIAL CONSTRUCTIONIST PERSPECTIVES ON PSYCHOLOGY OF WOMEN

Building on feminist critiques that psychology has ignored the social realities of women's lives, a social constructionist perspective of psychology of women is rooted in an understanding of "reality" as constructed within a social context. Instead of a reality "out there," noted Hare-Mustin and Marecek (1990), this perspective contends that reality is invented. "Rather than passively observing reality, we actively construct the meanings that frame and organize our perceptions and experience" (p. 455). All knowledge is contextual and embedded in social interaction (Bohan, 1992), and what we humans conceive of as reality are "shared meanings that derive from language, history, and culture" (Hare-Mustin & Marecek, 1988, p. 456). Social constructionism rests on an understanding of critical history, in which values in psychology are examined and value judgments are made about psychology's history (Crawford & Marecek, 1989).

## Essentialism

To fully understand feminist constructionism, it is important to look at essentialism—the view that gender and other traits lie within the individual. A feminist essentialist perspective would argue for the existence of a unique way of knowing (Belenky et al., 1986) or of making moral decisions (Gilligan, 1982). This position views gender differences as essential to femaleness and maleness, as exemplified by the popular book *Men are from Mars, Women are from Venus* (Gray, 1992). Essentialist perspectives often resonate powerfully with women, in part because those perspectives give women validation for previously undervalued qualities such as nurturance, emotionality, and relationality. Now, instead of being "wrong" (codependent, histrionic, or some other "feminine" disorder), we are valued for the same female virtues that male scientists of yore said made us unfit for higher education, nontraditional work, or the professions.

Despite its appeal, an essentialist perspective has some inherent problems. Bohan (1992) pointed out that "these understandings, though laudable for their affirmation of women's experience, also raise important theoretical, empirical, and political difficulties for feminist psychology" (p. 34). Bohan identified five criticisms of essentialism: (1) its claim to universality, (2) the political dilemma created by glorifying characteristics that may be products of oppression, (3) its limiting implications for collective feminist action, (4) limitations of alternate modes of being and acting, and (5) essentialist implications for understanding gender differences. Essentialism, at its core, views qualities attributed to women as universal and timeless, not as socio–historico–political constructs. Thus, the diversity of women's experience is ignored, and this has resulted in the justifiable conclusion on the part of women of color and others marginalized within feminism that such conclusions are biased and exclusionary.

Bohan (1997) asks a disturbing question: "If women's relationality is a product of oppression . . . , then when we cherish our relationality, are we legitimizing the oppression that created it . . . ?" (p. 35). She painted a picture of how women might be coerced to collaborate in their own oppression; her suggestion might be ludicrous were it not already an integral part of the philosophy and actions of the radical right. She argued:

> Although we may cherish these qualities associated with women, wish them for ourselves, and also encourage them in men, both political experience and systematic research demonstrate that these traits are not those most respected by the culture. Collaboration with essentialist interpretations of gender might, if inadvertently, contribute to a recreation of earlier understandings of gender, with women deemed not different and equal but, once again, deficient. (p. 36)

Bohan (1997) also argued that considering qualities associated with women to be essential encourages individual responsibility and change, indeed promotes victim-blaming in that the very qualities that are supposed to "belong" to women may be viewed as contributing to their oppression. Thus, women strive for personal change (e.g., assertiveness training or self-defense classes) and neglect collective political action. She argued that "if we succumb to the temptation of compelling person-blame explanations, feminism is at risk of becoming a mental health rather than a social change movement" (p. 37).

Essentializing women's ways of knowing and being limits both women and men to their prescribed roles. In part, this limits the possibilities for nurturing behavior by men. In addition, it marginalizes women who do not "possess" the stereotypic female characteristics.

Finally, Bohan (1997) argued that there is weak empirical support for essential gender characteristics. The research that does exist either lacks methodological rigor, has not been replicated, or is qualitative and therefore not intended to be generalized. She raises the question, "If behavior is not differentiated by sex as portrayed by essentialist models, why have these depictions of gender enjoyed such widespread support, and why, as we have discussed them among ourselves, have they seemed to resonate so with women's personal experience?" (p. 38). Bohan responds by identifying the paradox: "Women are different; it is not because women are different" (p. 38).

## Social Constructionism

A social constructionist view of women and gender has the potential to resolve the foregoing dilemma. The basic underpinnings of social constructionism include the beliefs that: (1) there is no way to know the nature of reality or truth; (2) reality is constructed, not discovered; (3) reality is inextricably intertwined with social context; (4) knowledge is constructed by discourse (language) in social interchange; and (5) what we agree to call reality is mutually constructed and agreed upon (Bohan, 1997).

Reality, then, is constructed by mutual agreement that takes place in social interactions. Gender is one of those agreements. As Bohan (1997) argued, "one does not *have* gender; one *does* gender" (p. 39, emphasis added; West & Zimmerman, 1987). Further, gender is done in specific contexts despite biological sex. In other words, "gendered actions are shaped not by the sex but by the social location of the individual" (Bohan, 1997, p. 39). Unger and Crawford (1996) described "gender as a process rather than as something that people possess . . . more a verb than a noun" (p. 146). The traits and characteristics that we typically have considered as qualities of a person are seen by social constructionists as constructed by interactions between people in the context of social expectations and demands (Unger & Crawford, 1996). In particular, gender is constructed in the context of power and status; consequently "gender and status may be hopelessly confused in the way people organize social reality" (Unger & Crawford, 1996, p. 147).

Social constructionism promises to remedy the problems of essentialism (Bohan, 1997). First, constructionism embraces the diversity of women's experience and centralizes context as an integral component of that diversity. It recognizes the mutidimensionality of women's lives and indicates that gender may be more or less salient to any given woman in the context of multiple oppressions. Responsibility for women's oppression and victimization is placed in a socio–politico–historical context, with a clear examination of how privilege and power function to keep women "in their place." By understanding gender in context, women are no longer blamed for their victimization or for traits and characteristics deemed "feminine" (Bohan, 1997; Unger, 1989).

An important contribution of social constructionism is that it frees women (and men) from the defining boxes of appropriate femaleness (and maleness). Simplistic essentialist perspectives on sex differences give way to more sophisticated and interesting dialogues about context. As Bohan (1997) argued, "There are no 'women's ways'; there are modes of being that we have agreed to understand as gendered" (p. 42). We are able, then, to more clearly understand the role of status, dominance and submission, and power in relation to gender, particularly as we examine the research on gendered behavior. It has been found, for example, that women's and men's gendered behavior changes based on context, such as when women in leadership positions exercise more typically "masculine" forms of power, or when a single fathers exhibit "mothering" behaviors. From a social constructionist perspective, we are also able to examine the complexities of status, stigma, and the power of social forces to control women who deviate from their expected roles and behaviors (Bohan, 1997; Unger & Crawford, 1996).

## SUMMARY AND CONCLUSIONS

The history of feminist reconstructions of psychology can be traced back to the late nineteenth and early twentieth centuries, when women scholars first confronted psychology's insistence on treating characteristics and traits of women as purely psychological. The women's liberation movement of the 1960s and 1970s fueled renewed critiques of psychology by feminist psychologists, placing issues of gender squarely on psychology's agenda amidst considerable resistance that continues to the present day. Psychology's "treatment" of women—as subject matter, as research subjects, and as professional colleagues—has come under fire throughout this evolution.

Freudian psychodynamic theory had a tremendous impact on the psychology of women; those women analysts who followed Freud became known as his "dutiful daughters" and attempted to make adjustments to his theory that would more accurately describe the female experience. The next wave of feminist scholars critiqued Freud and introduced issues of privilege and power in their analyses. Weisstein, Sherif, Mednick, Payton, and others confronted androcentric theories of psychology of women, exposed misogynist biases, opened the doors to the study of gynocentric issues, and insisted that psychology must take a stand on social issues affecting women and people of color.

Feminist scholars have criticized conventional, white, male, middle- and upper-class science for its masculinist bias; its exclusion and marginalization of women, people of color, and other disenfranchised groups; its notions of objectivity and resultant context-stripping; and its claims to being value-neutral and apolitical. Feminists centralized the female experience; insisted on an essential unity of subjectivity and objectivity, as well as an understanding of the relationships among reasearcher, participant, and context; made the investigator visible in the research process; and advocated a political stance in which a purpose of research is social change. Feminist science promotes methods that reflect feminist values of empowerment, social action, and voice.

A social constructionist perspective, in contrast to essentialism, views reality as mutually constructed in social interaction between and among people in the contexts of their lives. Gender, then, is not a characteristic or trait of women or men, but is something one *does*. Gendered behaviors are context-dependent and related to status and power. A feminist constructionist view of the psychology of women, consequently, places our understanding of women within a political framework in which power is centralized, multidimensionality embraced, and complexity celebrated. The "hard issues" such as racism, classism, heterosexism, antisemitism, ageism, able-bodiedism, looksism, and others are integral to our understanding of women's psychology, and a social constructionist perspective engages feminist psychologists in the challenges of continually centralizing what we would otherwise marginalize and of exploring the complexities of—and our complicities in—processes of privilege and power.

# REFERENCES

Belenky, M. F., Clinchy, B. M., Goldberger, N. R., & Tarule, J. M. (1986). *Women's ways of knowing: The development of self, voice, and mind.* New York: Basic Books.

Benjamin, M. (1993). A question of identity. In M. Benjamin (Ed.), *A question of identity: Women, science, and literature* (pp. 1–21). New Brunswick, NJ: Rutgers University Press.

Bohan, J. S. (1992). *Seldom seen, rarely heard: Women's place in psychology.* Boulder, CO: Westview.

Bohan, J. S. (1997). Regarding gender: Essentialism, constructionism, and feminist psychology. In M. M. Gergen & S. N. Davis (Eds.), *Toward a new psychology of gender* (pp. 31–47). New York: Routledge.

Chesler, P. (1972). *Women and madness.* New York: Avon.

Collins, P. H. (1990). *Black feminist thought: Knowledge, consciousness, and the politics of empowerment.* New York: Routledge.

Comas-Díaz, L. (1994). An integrative approach. In L. Comas-Díaz & B. Greene, *Women of color: Integrating ethnic and gender identities in psychotherapy* (pp. 287–318). New York: Guilford.

Crawford, M., & Marecek, J. (1989). Psychology reconstructs the female: 1968–1988. *Psychology of Women Quarterly, 13,* 147–165.

Fine, M. (1992). *Disruptive voices: The possibilities of feminist research.* Ann Arbor: University of Michigan Press.

Friedan, B. (1963). *The Feminine Mystique.* New York: Norton.

Friere, P. (1985). *The politics of education.* South Hadley, MA: Bergin and Garvey.

Freud, S. (1905). Three essays on the theory of sexuality. In Strachey, J. (Tr. and Ed., 1976). *The complete psychological works* (Vol. VII, pp. 135–243). New York: Norton.

Freud, S. (1926). The question of lay analysis. In Strachey, J. (Tr. and Ed., 1976). *The complete psychological works* (Vol. XX, pp. 183–258). New York: Norton.

Furumoto, L. (1998). Gender and the history of psychology. In B. M. Clinchy & J. K. Norem (Eds.), *The gender and psychology reader* (pp. 69–77). New York: New York University Press.

Gergen, K. J. (1988). Feminist critique of science and the challenge of social epistemology. In M. M. Gergen (Ed.), *Feminist thought and the structure of knowledge* (pp. 27–48). New York: New York University Press.

Gilligan, C. (1982). *In a different voice: Psychological theory and women's development.* Cambridge, MA: Harvard University Press.

Gilman, C. P. (1973). *The yellow wallpaper* (Reprint of the 1899 ed. published by Small, Maynard, Boston). Old Westbury, NY: The Feminist Press.

Gray, J. (1992). *Men are from Mars, women are from Venus: A practical guide for improving communication and getting what you want in your relationships.* New York: HarperCollins.

Grossberg, M. (1990). Institutionalizing masculinity: The law as a masculine profession. In M. C. Carnes & C. Griffen (Eds.), *Meanings for manhood: Constructions of masculinity in Victorian America* (pp. 133–151). Chicago: University of Chicago Press.

Guthrie, R. V. (1998). *Even the rat was white: A historical view of psychology.* Boston: Allyn and Bacon.

Hare-Mustin, R. T., & Marecek, J. (1988). The meaning of difference: Gender theory, postmodernism, and psychology. *American Psychologist, 43,* 455–464.

Horney, K. (1967). The problem of feminine masochism. In K. Horney, *Feminine psychology* (pp. 214–233). New York: W. W. Norton.

Hubbard, R. (1988). Some thoughts about the masculinity of the natural sciences. In M. M. Gergen (Ed.), *Feminist thought and the structure of knowledge* (pp. 1–15). New York: New York University Press.

Keller, E. F. (1992). *Secrets of life, secrets of death: Essays on language, gender, and science.* New York: Routledge.

Lather, P. (1991). *Getting smart: Feminist research and pedagogy with/in the postmodern.* New York: Routledge.

Lerman, H. (1986). *A mote in Freud's eye: From psychoanalysis to the psychology of women.* New York: Springer.

Martínez, T. A. (1996). Toward a Chicana feminist epistemological standpoint: Theory at the intersection of race, class, and gender. *Race, Gender, & Class, 3,* 107–128.

Masson, J. M. (1985). *The assault on truth: Freud's suppression of the seduction theory.* New York: Viking Penguin.

Mednick, M. T. S. (1978). Psychology of women: Research issues and trends. *New York Academy of Sciences Annals, 309,* 77–92. Reprinted in S. Cox (Ed.), *Female Psychology: The Emerging Self* (2nd ed.) (pp. 91–107). New York: St. Martin's.

Payton, C. R. (1984). Who must do the hard things? *American Psychologist, 39,* 391–397.

Reinharz, S. (1992). *Feminist methods in social research.* New York: Oxford University Press.

Richards, G.(1997). *"Race," racism and psychology: Towards a reflexive history.* London and New York: Routledge.

Sandoval, C. (1991). U. S. third world feminism: The theory and method of oppositional consciousness in the postmodern world. *Genders, 10,* 1–24.

Scarborough, E., & Furumoto, L. (1987). *Untold lives: The first generation of American women psychologists.* New York: Columbia University Press.

Sherif, C. W. (1979). Bias in psychology. In J. Sherman & E. T. Beck (Eds.), *The prism of sex: Essays in the sociology of knowledge* (pp. 93–133). University of Wisconsin Press.

Shields, S. A. (1975). Functionalism, Darwinism, and the psychology of women: A study in social myth. *American Psychologist, 30,* 739–754.

Thompson, C. M. (1971). *On women.* New York: New American Library.

Tiefer, L. (1988). A feminist perspective on sexology and sexuality. In M. M. Gergen (Ed.), *Feminist thought and the structure of knowledge* (pp. 16–26). New York: New York University Press.

Tiefer, L. (1991). A brief history of the Association for Women in Psychology (AWP) 1969–1991. *Psychology of Women Quarterly, 15,* 635–649.

Touhey, J. C. (1974). Effects of additional women professionals on ratings of occupational prestige and desirability. *Journal of Personality and Social Psychology, 29,* 86–89.

Unger, R. (1989). Sex, gender, and epistemology. In M. Crawford & M. Gentry (Eds.), *Gender and thought: Psychological perspectives* (pp. 17–35). New York: Springer-Verlag.

Unger, R., & Crawford, M. (1996). *Women and gender: A feminist psychology.* New York: McGraw-Hill.

Weisstein, N. (1971). Psychology constructs the female, or the fantasy life of the male psychologist (with some attention to the fantasies of his friends the male biologist and the male anthropologist). *Social Education, 35,* 362–373.

West, C., & Zimmerman, D. H. (1987). Doing gender. *Gender & Society, 1,* 125–151.

Williams, J. H. (1987). *Psychology of women: Behavior in a biosocial context* (3rd ed.). New York: W. W. Norton.

Wooley, H. T. (1910). Psychological literature: A review of the recent literature on the psychology of sex. *Psychological Bulletin, 7,* 335–342.

Young-Bruehl, E. (1990). *Freud on women: A reader.* New York: W. W. Norton.

# 3

# Research and Conceptual Approaches to the Understanding of Gender

## Linda B. Gallahan

## INTRODUCTION

This chapter presents and critiques the concept of gender from the psychoanalytic, social learning, cognitive developmental, and social constructionist perspectives. Each of these theoretical perspectives views the development and conceptualization of gender differently. Psychoanalytic theories regard gender as a component, and a distinctly salient one, of a person's identity and personality, such that a person's desires, motives, and interests derive from and enforce such an identity, thereby leading the person to behave in ways consistent with that identity. The Social Learning theory purports that while individuals may learn the roles of females and males through their interaction with the environment, it is only when they are reinforced for and subsequently imitate role-related behaviors that they acquire a sex-role identity. Cognitive Developmental theories focus on the processes of gender categorization and discrimination, and suggest that knowledge of gender is a function of the individual's active construction of stimuli in the environment, and that behavior related to that knowledge is purposefully directed by it in attempts to adopt socioculturally accepted standards. Finally, social constructionists explore the meanings of gender through sociocultural frameworks and attempt to show how such meaning-making by the dominant social group sustains sex-based inequality.

Historically, an androcentric, male-centered or single-sexed view has permeated research on gender. This traditional view is rooted in a belief in sex differences in which female identity is distinct from, or in opposition to, normative male identity. This biological essentialist view, in which sex and gender are separable constructs, has its roots in Freudian psychoanalysis and explanations of male and female gender identity development.

Linda B. Gallahan ● College of Arts and Sciences, Pacific University, Forest Grove, Oregon 97116

*Issues in the Psychology of Women,* edited by Biaggio and Hersen. Kluwer Academic/Plenum Publishers, New York, 2000.

# THEORIES OF GENDER IDENTITY DEVELOPMENT

## Psychoanalytic Perspectives

Psychoanalytic theory describes the development of gender identity from two perspectives—the phallocentric Freudian view of Oedipal-based psychosexual development, and the gynocentric view of mother-centered affiliation and differentiation. Both views embrace the basic psychoanalytic premises that the unconscious houses repressed thoughts and desires that are the sources of all motivations and behaviors; that psychosexual development begins at birth; and that early experiences determine adult personality development. Each view differs with respect to the emphasis it places on male and female gender identity development and the respective roles of the father and the mother in that development; the phallocentric view places greater emphasis on the former and the gynocentric view on the latter.

### *The Phallocentric View*

The phallocentric view is best represented by Freud's account of the Oedipus Complex. According to Freud (1933/1964), in early childhood both boys and girls recognize their mother as their primary caregiver and, because she fulfills their basic needs, they love and feel attached to her. As children move from the anal to the phallic stage of psychosexual development, their erogenous zone shifts to their genitalia. Their primary source of need satisfaction, the mother, then becomes an object of sexual desire.

Freud believed that small children enter the phallic stage with a potential for bisexual identity development—the desire to both possess and to be possessed. Only with recognition of anatomical differences do boys' and girls' psychic energies shift. For boys, this shift comes when they realize that they share anatomical similarities with their fathers and are anatomically different from their mothers. Concomitantly, the boy recognizes the social superiority of the father who wields power over the submissive, inferior mother. He comes to associate having a penis, the phallus, with power, and comes to believe that such power is an inherent characteristic of the male sex to which he belongs. He also comes to desire the mother in the same active, masculine way the father does. As his desire for the mother increases, his fear of the more powerful father also increases. His realization that the powerful father stands between him and his desired love object, the mother, and that the father is capable of punishment, potentially in the form of castration (the mother's own castration and lack of phallus, or power, is evidence of this capability) causes the boy to abandon his active masculine desire for the mother and to value and identify with the father. As he identifies with the more powerful father, he learns the rules of society and his place in the social structure. Freud believed that it was this process that caused males to have a well-developed sense of morality and understanding of social order, or what he termed a strong superego psychic structure.

For girls, the shift of psychic energy from one erogenous zone to another occurs in the same way that it does for boys. Young girls discover that they too possess the phallus in the form of the smaller, less well developed clitoris. They also express a desire to possess their mothers but soon realize that, relative to the penis, the clitoris is an inferior, less powerful organ:

> The discovery of her castration is a turning-point in the life of the girl. [The] little girl, who has hitherto lived a masculine life, and has been able to obtain pleasure through excitation of her clitoris, and has connected this behavior with the sexual wishes (often of an active character) which she has directed towards her mother, finds her enjoyment of phallic sexuality spoilt by the influence of penis envy.

> She is wounded in her self-love by the unfavorable comparison with the boy who is so much better equipped, and therefore gives up the masturbatory satisfaction which she obtained from her clitoris, repudiates her love towards her mother, and at the same time often represses a good deal of her sexual impulses in general. (p. 172)

The girl then believes that, like her mother, she has already been punished for her desires by being castrated. Nonetheless, she hopes to regain the phallus by turning her attention to the father. Freud hypothesized that young girls believed they could regain the phallus—and the concomitant superiority that it represented—through impregnation and birth (particularly of a male child). When the girl child realizes that the father will not accede to this desire and that the mother is a barrier to this outcome and most likely responsible for the girl's castration, she abandons her desires for her father.

Freud believed that the girl's abandonment of the desire for the phallus and her subsequent ambivalent relationship with the mother causes her to have a less well developed sense of morality, or superego. This lack of complete Oedipal resolution on the part of girls led to what Freud called the "feminine" personality, which consisted of the key elements of *passivity*—marked by the resignation of active sexual desire and inferior status; *masochism*—the desire/willingness to endure suffering through intercourse and childbirth; and *narcissism*—the motivation to present herself as an object of desire for males in order to possess the phallus. He also believed that, in place of a feminine identity, girls may develop a masculine identity typified by their refusal to abandon an active masculine sexual desire for the mother and for their own phallus—the clitoris. This identity development would then lead to hypermasculinity or homosexuality in adulthood.

Although he acknowledged that his theory of female gender identity development was "incomplete and fragmentary" (1933/1964; p. 184), Freud's account of how girls come to identify themselves as feminine, and as women, has been subjected to much scrutiny. That both boys and girls come to devalue the female—boys through their fear of castration and girls through their anger toward their mothers for it—has also provoked considerable debate. Some of Freud's earliest students attempted to extend and modify his views, while others attempted to discredit them.

## Extensions and Modifications of Freud's Views

Some of the best known contributions to the field of psychology came from the many students Freud trained in psychoanalytic therapeutic techniques. Several went on to become well-known psychologists in their own right, although not all continued to share his views. Responding to Freud's androcentrism and biological essentialism, neo-Freudians such as Clara Thompson, Carl Jung, and Erik Erikson pointed to the symbolic importance of anatomical sex, which was derived from social relationships between women and men. These relationships were particularly pronounced in patriarchal societies.

Clara Thompson (1893–1958) posited that a girl's desire to be male, rooted in her desire to possess the phallus, was a product of sociocultural rather than biological factors. Thompson (1943) believed that the penis represented a symbol of male status and, as a consequence, female inferiority. Thompson observed that this sex-based hierarchy was played out in cultures in the form of male aggression, through active participation in the public realm of social and work relationships and in the private realm of active sexuality. Thompson noted that child bearing and rearing were of value apart from their relation to the phallus; women achieved status in both domestic and public arenas through such activities. These activities, however, were in opposition to activities of self-actualization that women suspended while engaging in them. Thompson believed that the greater the social value placed on procreative activity for females in a given society, the more male-dominant and oppressive the society and the less likely females were to hold other socially valued positions. Thus, according to Thompson, a female's feminine identity lay not in penis envy, but in her desire to be a valued member of her society. She also noted that as females aspired to more socially valued positions, the emphasis a society placed on procreative activities increased, as did the oppression of females, publicly through discrimination and privately through demands for sexual passivity.

Carl Jung (1875–1961), another of Freud's students, worked with Freud until 1913, when they parted following heated debates over the basic nature of humans. Contrary to Freud, Jung did not believe that all motives were sexual in nature; individuals could be motivated by a sense of purpose and creativity. Jung's contribution to the study of the development of gender includes his concepts of archetypes—collective memories that contribute to an individual's personality development. The two most important of these archetypes to the study of gender are the anima and the animus. The anima represents a male's feminine archetype and the animus a female's masculine archetype. Both the individual's biological sex and these unconscious archetypes help to form an individual's gender identity. Jung believed that these archetypes could represent both positive and negative forces: the best and worst of women and men throughout history and within societies. He also believed that a well-developed, functioning personality depended on a balance between these forces within the individual and within society.

Another psychoanalyst, Erik Erikson (1902–1994), was trained at the Psychoanalytic Institute in Vienna and accepted most of Freud's basic premises. Erikson, however, focused on psychosocial rather than psychosexual development and was the first identity theorist to offer a life span perspective of development. Like Freud, Erikson believed that biological differences were foundational to sex differences and individual personality development. However, unlike Freud, he believed such differences were shaped by culture. Erikson believed that children did not focus on what they lacked (the phallus), but rather on what they possessed; for boys this is the penis and comes through identification with the father to represent the phallus; for girls this is the clitoris and other reproductive organs, and comes, as does the phallus for boys, to represent a form of social power.

Erikson posited that the anatomical placement of boys' and girls' genitalia—externally and internally, respectively—influenced their self-image as well as their view of others. He believed that boys external genitalia produced in them an "externalized" view of the world, which he referred to as "outer space." This external view is demonstrated by boys through their greater and more overt activity, their more adventuresome strivings, and their louder and more boisterous play. Conversely, girls' internal genitalia contributed to their internalized, or "inner space" view. Such a view is characterized by more subdued and covert activity, more circumspect and thoughtful strivings, and quieter, less physical play.

Erikson (1968) tested these premises among prepubescent children. In his studies, he gave children blocks of various shapes and sizes and asked them to construct a scene. Girls built lower level scenes marked by open entries and paths with static characters:

> The girl's scene is a house *interior* scene, represented either as a configuration of furniture without any surrounding walls or by a *simple enclosure* built with blocks. In the girl's scene, people and animals are mostly *within* such an interior or enclosure, and they are primarily people or animals in a *static* [position]. (pp. 270–271)

Boys' scenes included towering walls and buttresses, with gated or barred entries, and mobile characters:

Boys' scenes are either houses with elaborate walls or facades with *protrusions* such as cones or cylinders representing ornaments or cannons. There are *high towers*; and there are *exterior scenes*. In boys' constructions more people and animals are *outside* enclosures or buildings, and there are more *automotive objects* and *animals moving* along streets and intersections. (p. 271).

While the scenes of both sexes represented both inner and outer spaces, one or the other type dominated. Erikson believed these scenes represented how girls and boys, and then women and men, conceived of themselves in their social world; he considered the spaces as complementary rather than oppositional, with both representing necessary forces in society.

Erikson rejected the Freudian notion that feminine identity development was ultimately inferior and rather held that females, especially in the role of mothers, were a powerful, positive social force. He also noted that the belief that a female experiences a sense of "lack" over her "missing" organ is less sound than is the claim that she experiences a sense of interiority.

Erikson's account of gender identity development explores the cultural foundations of the mother–child relationship and recognizes that such foundations are shaped by societal norms and change with history. The influence of such forces has also been explored by those psychoanalytic theorists who adopt the gynocentric view of identity development.

## The Gynocentric Perspective

The gynocentric view of gender identity development posits that a feminine, rather than a bisexual or masculine orientation, predominates a child's perspective throughout development and that this perspective is evident prior to the phallic stage. Gynocentric theorists, like phallocentric theorists, posit that a child's primary interest from birth is the mother. The mother satisfies the child's needs and desires and thus becomes an object of affection. Unlike phallocentric theorists, however, gynocentric theorists consider female identity development as the standard for normative development rather than merely a derivative of masculine identity development. Also, the role of the mother rather than that of the father is emphasized in development.

Early psychoanalytic theorists, such as Karen Horney and Melanie Klein, and later theorists, such as Nancy Chodorow, have articulated this view. While initially considered a contributor to the phallocentric psychoanalytic view, Helene Deutsch's later writings on women's developmental stages critique and support a gynocentric view.

Karen Horney (1885–1952), born at the beginning of the European feminist movement, was one of a handful of females to attend medical school at the beginning of the twentieth century. She attended the Psychoanalytic Institute in Vienna and began working closely with Freud in 1910. Her disagreements with her mentor began early and became legendary; Horney was the first of Freud's students to take a professional and public stand against his theory of female psychology. The main differences between their theories can be found in their relative accounts of gender identity development. Unlike Freud, Horney believed the foundations of that development were sociocultural, that its processes differed by sex, and that females came to possess active, rather than passive, sexual drives.

Horney (1939) believed that males held beliefs about females that were similar to those posited by Freud regarding female identity development: males initially believed that all people have penises and that girls, upon realization that they *lack* a penis, must experience a sense of loss. Horney believed that males were much more interested in development that centered on genitalia than were females, though she did believe that females experienced penis envy. This envy, however, was note a result of a girl's desire to possess the mother or to replace her lost organ, but rather her realization that the penis represented greater social power.

Horney also believed that a female's desire for a child was not the necessary outcome of penis envy, but a primary, instinctual, biological need. She also held that males attribute penis envy to women because of a fear of women that originated in their early fear of the mother and their own desire to reproduce as women do; Horney also suggested that men experience "womb envy" derived from their *lack of* ability to bear offspring.

Horney postulated that the exploration of female neurosis through psychic development, or what was known as "egopsychology," detracted from its causal factors: the cultural conditions established by and sustained through patriarchy. Following her break from Freudian psychoanalysis and egopsychology, Horney went on to contribute to the literature that examined the sociocultural foundations of female oppression. Her work has been a catalyst for subsequent critiques of the psychoanalytic perspective of gender.

Melanie Klein (1882–1960) is often credited with providing one of the first detailed accounts of object relations between mothers and infants. Klein contended that the Oedipal conflict began at the intersection of the oral and anal stages of infant development and was centered on the frustrations experienced by the infant in its attempts to breast feed during weaning and to toilet train. Accordingly, the infant feels simultaneously deprived of the mother's breast—literally in terms of nourishment and figuratively in terms of affection, nurturance, and withholding of the love object—and concomitantly pressured to conform to social standards of cleanliness and responsibility. Such frustrations toward the mother create in the child anxieties that are then exacerbated during the phallic stage when the child notes anatomical distinctions between the sexes. The boy child believes that the mother, not the father, may again deny him need or pleasure through castration, as she has done previously through withholding the breast and enforcing toilet training. The girl child believes such needs and pleasures have already been denied—first through denial of the breast, then denial of anal stimulation, and then removal of the phallus.

Helene Deutsch (1884–1946) embraced Freud's basic tenets of gender identity development and extended his work on female frigidity and masochism. While Freud believed these two pathologies developed as a consequence of unresolved Oedipal conflict, Deutsch postulated that their origins were in earlier development.

In her later writings, Deutsch (1944/45) posited that, because of her close attachment and identification with the primary caregiver mother, the girl child must go through a process of affiliation to and differentiation from the mother during the phallic stage. This process produces greater tension between the girl and her mother than is found in the boy's relationship with either parent. She postulated that the Oedipal conflict was stimulated not so much by a girl's desire to be masculine, but by her desires to break her dependent ties on her mother. Her eventual development of feminine passivity, which Deutsch described as the female psyche turned inward, contributes to her greater intuition, subjectivity, and emotionality. Deutsch noted that this developmental process also led to a woman's self-loathing—through acceptance of her own inferiority—and to hatred of all females—through her recognition of their collective inferiority.

Deutsch believed that both boys and girls observe the dual roles of women: as the sexual, base lover of men (father) and as the nurturant, chaste mother. Deutsch believed that males come to accept and value the sexualized image of females during the process of their identity development. Disregarding or rejecting the nurturant, chaste mother image allows a boy to separate from his mother and to form a separate distinct identity. Conversely, girls accept the mother image and reject the sexualized lover image. However, a girl's knowledge that females are comprised of both images makes her separation process more difficult. Her desire to be like the chaste, nurturant mother and unlike the base, whorelike lover of men creates a dilemma. Deutsch observed that during this crisis of identity girls experimented with the mother image through their play with dolls by engaging in "motherlike" behaviors associated with affection and punishment. She further noted that during this time girls often rejected their mothers' attention.

Deutsch's social–psychological perspective provided an alternative to Horney's explanation of the development of female gender identity and was later used, as was the work of Melanie Klein, as a foundation to Nancy Chodorow's explanation of mother–daughter relationships in her Object Relations theory.

Chodorow (1978), like other students of psychoanalytic theory, accepted Freud's basic premises. She believed, however, that identity development began earlier, during the pre-Oedipal stage. Like Erikson, Chodorow believed that children begin the process of individuation and separation from the primary caregiver when they experience autonomy for the first time during late infancy. All children go through a process of separating from the caregiver to achieve greater autonomy, but the task is more difficult for girls who physically identify with the mother. According to Chodorow, girls, unlike boys, never fully separate from the mother. While striving to be independent from the primary caregiver, they recognize and, if encouraged by the mother, come to value their similarity with the powerful kind mother. Chodorow believed this process produces a sense of similarity, continuity, and connectedness among females and helps to explain why it is more difficult for females to achieve a sense of independence and autonomy. On the other hand, boys develop a greater sense of distinction by coming to value what is dissimilar.

Both male and female children, as a consequence of being cared for by women, know more about being female than being male. This makes the identity process easier for girls and more difficult for boys, who must "learn" to be male. In their efforts to separate from the mother, a process the mother both supports and encourages, boys must come to value what is different. Given the paucity of males in their daily lives, difference for boys is represented by what is "not-female." Chodorow believed that males come to conceive of themselves as unique and dissimilar to others, even to other males. The process of differentiation causes boys to perceive females as not only distinct, but also as inferior, for they come to believe that what is unique is, essentially, superior. The emphasis on learning about being male through focusing on what is "not-female" affects the value males ascribe to each sex. To value their own identity, males must reject female interests and objects. That they learn to reject all that is female leads to fear and mistrust and, ultimately, to the denigration of all women.

How boys and girls separate from or affiliate with the mother begins with their understanding of the roles of other family members as well. Chodorow's (1989) observations of mother–infant dyads showed that mothers encourage and support affiliation/separation through their behaviors toward their children. For example, mothers encourage independence in their sons by holding them facing outward, allowing them to move farther away during play, and not looking at them while directing or instructing them. Also, they encourage dependency in their daughters by holding them facing the breast, monitoring their movements and keeping them nearby, and making eye contact during verbalization. The mother's behaviors are supported and exaggerated by other male family members who witness them.

While Chodorow accepted many of the premises of psychoanalytic theory, including Deutsch's explanation of female identity development, she rejected the emphasis on biological causal factors, believing instead, as did other gynocentric theorists, that gender development is grounded in cultural norms, particularly since females are responsible for child rearing in most cultures. Chodorow also believed that male identity development need not proceed from the rejection of all that is female. But she did acknowledge that this rejection was usually the only option given to boys in most cultures; boys are admonished for engaging in stereotypically feminine activities and behaviors. In turn, girls never learn to reject what is "not-male" because they have a standard, the mother, for their behavior.

> At the same time, core gender identity for a girl is not problematic in the sense that it is for boys. It is built upon, and does not contradict, her primary sense of oneness and identification with her mother and is assumed easily along with her developing sense of self. Girls grow up with a sense of continuity and similarity to their mother, a relational connection to the world. For them, difference is not originally problematic nor fundamental to their psychological being or identity. They do not define themselves as not-men, or not-male, but as "I, who is female." (p. 59)

Drawing on Horney's premise that because she has full power over need satisfaction the mother becomes an object to be feared, Chodorow (1989) posited that the fear of the mother was extended to the fear of women in general. Chodorow believed that this fear, which Horney referred to as dread, was illustrated and perpetuated through folk legends and beliefs and through men's repeated attempts to gain and hold power within the family and society at large. She believed that through time males developed "masculine" attributes such as aggression to sustain their power. Ultimately, then, boy's gender identity development follows narrowly defined social parameters that include the rejection of all that is feminine:

> Boys conform closely to the masculine goals and behavior required of them. They learn early not to exhibit feminine personality traits—to hide emotions and pretend even to themselves that they do not have them, to be independent participants on activities rather than personally involved with friends. (p. 37)

and,

> It is apparent [that] in our society male roles and activities are more prestigious and privileged than female roles and activities. [The] extreme unwillingness of boys to make cross-sex choices indicates that they have been taught very early, [that] it is right for them to prefer masculine things. Therefore they are extremely reluctant to make feminine choices. More important, it would seem that these boys, in contrast to the girls, believe that making such choices helps to ensure their masculinity, and alternatively, that different choices would not be different choices among a number of possible alternatives, but rather threatening in the deepest sense. (pp. 37–38)

Chodorow purports that the elevated status of males and the devaluation of all that is associated with being female is pervasive and found most distinctly in highly patriarchal cultures. Further, she attributes the devaluation of women to the boy child's need to differentiate from his mother and individuate as a male while at the same time recognizing that he has been raised and loved by women.

In terms of female identity development, Chodorow recognizes that girls too are affected by the greater social status accorded males. While girls note that females possess power and prestige as mothers, they also note that the female role is far less valued than the male role in the greater social context. A girl's initial ambivalence about adopting a feminine identity, according to Chodorow, does not stem from her "uncertainty about feminine identity"—for she has been raised by a woman and, thus, her primary identification is female—"but from [her] knowledge *about it*" (p. 43). It is only in early adolescence, however, that a girl's desire to possess or demonstrate the more socially valued masculine behaviors and interests is considered inappropriate. Prior to that time, her role, unlike that of boys, is more flexible.

Chodorow concludes that social systems that perpetuate the devaluation of women produce distinctly different gender identities, built and sustained on that devaluation, for women and men alike:

> [As] long as women must live through their children, and men do not genuinely contribute to socialization and provide easily accessible role models, women will continue to bring up sons whose sexual identity depends on devaluing femininity inside and outside themselves, and daughters who must accept this devalued position and resign themselves to producing more men who will perpetuate the system that devalues them. (p. 44)

## FEMINIST RESPONSES TO PSYCHOANALYTIC THEORIES OF GENDER

The relationship between Freudian psychoanalysis and contemporary psychoanalytic writings has appeared tenuous and strained by its ambivalent relations with patriarchy and feminism (see Morrow, Chapter 2, *this volume*). While early feminist theorists railed against psychoanalysis as the embodiment of patriarchy, because of its focus on female psychopathology as the root of social angst, others were rediscovering and reinterpreting the work of Freud, Horney, Deutsch, and Klein in ways that illustrated their value to the understanding of female identity and its relation to social structures.

In their critique of the psychoanalytic perspective of gender identity development, some feminist theorists question whether investigating the origins of gender identity is productive for feminist inquiry and, more importantly, whether such investigation may actually lead to practices aimed at remediation of "deviant" or "abnormal" identities. Such questions have often been explored in the context of gender equity/equality, the relationship of sexual orientation to identity, and patriarchal power systems.

Challenges to the phallocentric psychoanalytic perspectives of gender identity development most often focus on the relative importance of biological sex. Feminist theorists from a broad range of academic disciplines and political agendas criticized Freudian psychoanalytic accounts of gender identity development for focusing on anatomy and unconscious motives and ignoring the sociocultural conditions that better accounted for the relatively inferior status of women.

In *The Feminine Mystique,* Betty Friedan (1974) argued that the widespread acceptance of Freud's account of "normal" female identity development led women to accept their passive, nurturing wife and mothering roles. She called for women to reject this *mystique* and instead to focus on the true mechanisms of their relatively lower social status: socioeconomic conditions that supported patriarchy.

Like Friedan, Shulamith Firestone (1970) noted that the ideal nuclear family, in which women were responsible for the care of husbands and children, supported sexual inequality and sustained patriarchy. She advocated the abandonment of the nuclear family as a way to disentangle the mythical relationship between biology and gender roles, and claimed that doing so would allow us to examine how patriarchy constructs the meaning of gender.

In response to these early criticisms of Freud, psychoanalytic revisionist and feminist theorist Juliette Mitchell (1971, 1974) recommended a less literal and more symbolic interpretation of Freud's writing. She argued that such an interpretation renders it of value to a feminist understanding of gender identity development. Mitchell posited that the outcome of the

Oedipal situation depends on several sociocultural factors, the most important being the degree to which a society embraces patriarchal values. In her analysis of Freud's premise that social beings develop from biological ones, Mitchell concluded that these social beings reflect relationships between family members and the larger social patriarchal structure. She argued that appropriate feminist analyses of Freud's work should focus on how women come to mentally represent their social position. Only then might women be able to create new and different representations that would eventually eliminate oppression and elevate their status.

Each of these theorists addressed womens' perceptions of their status as a part of their unconscious motives and the ways in which these motives, in turn, direct and guide behavior. Friedan argued that psychoanalysis set the condition for female subordination by showing how women accept the myth of these unconscious motives; Firestone argued that Freud failed to examine the social context of unconscious motives; and Mitchell argued that womens' mental representations will lead to changes in cultural practices that promote equality.

Other theorists, such as Hannah Lerman (1986), argue that the construct of gender identity is not a primary part of the unconscious and that to attribute gender-related behavior to unconscious motives is inappropriate. Lerman explains that while psychoanalysis has permeated our culture and our consciousness, it has done so in ways not unlike those of a religion or cult. It attempts to explain a broad range of human identity and behaviors, offering singular causal mechanisms and narrow parameters for analysis. Its lack of falsifiability and replicability through experimental methods lends to its obscure complexity. That it disregards or at the very least diminishes the sociocultural contexts of patriarchy renders it useless to a feminist critique of power relations.

Lerman also evaluates other psychoanalytic contributions, such as that offered by Chodorow. Although Lerman acknowledges that Chodorow's analysis of sociocultural forces moves beyond traditional phallocentric psychoanalysis, she also points to a lack of empirical support for Chodorow's premises and conclusions. She further argues that, while an implied shift from biological essentialism to social construction in Chodorow's conclusions is appealing, her extensive use of psychoanalytic tenets and language makes its acceptance all the more likely—a dangerous side effect of her writing.

Lerman calls for consideration of the specific contexts of womens' lives when theorizing about gender; these include, for example, child bearing and rearing; homecare; relationships to men and to the patriarchal power structure; and individual characteristics such as class, race, and sexual preference. She also calls for a woman-based theory of personality development that encompasses the "diversity and complexity of women and their lives" that views "women positively and centrally" that "[arises] from women's experience," and that recognizes "that the internal world is inextricably intertwined with the external [one]" (pp. 8–9).

## THE LEARNING THEORIES OF DEVELOPMENT

While the psychoanalytic or "identity" theories of gender development describe how a child develops a gender *identity* by taking on the characteristics and behaviors of the same-sex parent, learning theories describe how a child acquires all types of *behaviors,* with sex-role-related behaviors being only one set.

There exist several important differences between psychoanalytic gender identification and learning theories. Learning theorists, unlike identity theorists, believe that: behaviors are neither stable nor necessarily permanent, but that they are shaped, modified, or eliminated through various processes; while early experience is important in shaping early behavior patterns, it does not result in fixed patterns in that new behaviors can replace old ones; the parent–child relationship is only one of and not necessarily the most influential relationship in the shaping of a child's sex-role identity; and, finally, behaviors, attitudes, and interests are not internally motivated by desires or needs, but are externally reinforced.

## The Social Learning Perspective

Social Learning theories emerged largely from the work of behaviorist B. F. Skinner in the 1940s and 1950s. Skinner (1938) extended the previously developed classical conditioning model and demonstrated that reinforcement could be used to modify and strengthen conditioned behaviors. Social learning theorists extended Skinner's behaviorist theory, noting that the processes of observation, imitation, and modeling are additional means by which individuals acquire behaviors. While behaviorists regarded the environment and external stimuli as tantamount to the learning process, social learning theorists claimed that cognitive processes, primarily those of attention and memory, were equally, if not more, important.

Social learning theory holds that individuals learn by observing the behaviors of others and the consequences of those behaviors. Others serve as models and, while individuals may learn all sorts of behaviors, they adopt only those with favorable outcomes for the model (Bandura, Ross, & Ross, 1963). Early social learning theory research (Bandura & Walters, 1963) suggested that the effect of reinforcement was direct and immediate, while later work (Bandura, 1977a; Rosenthal & Zimmerman, 1978) emphasized the indirect effects of reinforcement on subsequent behavioral changes. Finally, social learning theorists assert that learning and performance are distinct from one another, such that while individuals may acquire specific behaviors they do not necessarily perform those behaviors or may do so only under certain circumstances (Bandura, 1977b). That learning can occur *in the absence* of behavioral change further suggests that mental processes are distinct from the individual's overt behavioral repertoire.

Children learn about their sex and the sex of others, according to social learning theorists, in the same way that they learn about other aspects of their lives. Social learning theorists acknowledge, however, that the salience of sex and gender in our culture, as in most cultures, makes these aspects of identity fundamental to a person's identity or role identification. Because the concepts of sex and gender permeate all venues in our culture, children are exposed early and frequently to stimulus–response patterns that they may observe, imitate, and generalize.

According to social learning theorist Mischel (1966), children attend to and imitate those models with favorable characteristics and acquire sex-role characteristics based on that imitation. Mischel describes sex-typed behaviors as those behaviors that "typically elicit different rewards for one sex [more] than the other" (p. 56). He asserts that the acquisition of sex-typed behaviors occurs in the same way as any other cluster of behaviors—through processes of stimuli discrimination, generalization, observational learning, and reinforcement—and that sex-typing includes both behavioral acquisition *and performance.* Mischel notes that while both boys and girls acquire the behaviors of both sexes, they do not necessarily perform those behaviors.

Parents, family members, and society in general support distinctions by sex through clothing, toy, and activity choices. Boys are often clothed in loose fitting durable clothes, given toys designed for large motor manipulation, and allowed and encouraged to play in open, outdoor spaces. Conversely, girls are often clothed in more restrictive and delicate garments, given toys designed for fine motor manipulation, and allowed and encouraged to play in more closed, indoor spaces.

Social learning theorists also note that while parents actively engage in sex-typing behavior with their children, other social forces are as, if not more, important in the sex-role learning process. The manufacturing and media industries, for example, actively engage in sex stereotyping. In sum, children are exposed to various stimuli in their environment, and come to imitate those people and adopt those activities that they see are reinforced.

The social learning theory of sex-role identity development, however, fails to explain several phenomena: how or why a particular behavior or set of behaviors may be maintained in the absence of reinforcement; the existence of wide individual, within-sex variations in behavior; and why children continue to engage in cross-sex behaviors even when being negatively reinforced or punished for doing so. Some explanations have been offered in response to these criticisms. For example, stimuli in the environment may elicit certain behaviors without directly reinforcing them (i.e., a mother elicits nurturance behavior); not all behaviors that are learned are necessarily performed; and same-sex modeling occurs only when models exhibit sex appropriate behaviors.

If the processes of observing, imitating and modeling sufficiently explain how children learn sex appropriate behaviors, then we should expect that girls, by virtue of being exposed to a same sex model, would be more likely to learn behaviors associated with the female role, and that boys, without similar same sex model exposure, would have greater difficulty learning behaviors associated with the male role. This, however, is not the case. Bem (1983) has shown that girls of feminine mothers, for example, exhibit no more feminine characteristics than those of less feminine mothers. Because both boys and girls learn their relative roles and possess knowledge of the roles of the other sex, cognitive processes must be involved at more than the attentional and memory levels. Cognitive developmental theories of gender role acquisition attempt to identify and explain these processes.

## The Cognitive Developmental Perspective

Cognitive developmental theorists describe how individuals come to *understand and evaluate their environment*, rather than to simply adopt and engage in behaviors. In cognitive developmental explanations of learning, cognitive processes are primary whereas behaviors are secondary manifestations of those cognitive processes. Cognitive developmental theorists argue that children are not simply passive observers, but rather that they actively structure their own experiences and make sense of their own environment based on their current cognitive ability. This constructivist premise underlies a crucial factor in the process of a child's *gender identification*, that of the child's developing *cognitive ability to categorize* herself as female or himself as male.

Drawing on Jean Piaget's stage theory of cognitive development, Lawrence Kohlberg (1966) developed a theory of cognitive sex-typing. Retaining Piaget's basic premises about cognitive structures and processes, Kohlberg demonstrated that children were active processors of the gender-related information in their environment. According to Kohlberg, children seek information from the environment in order to master that environment. In their attempt to understand the environment, children first organize information in simple, meaningful ways. They do this by mentally categorizing stimuli based first on their physical and then conceptual properties. As mental categories or schema develop and are modified with new, alternative, and conflicting information, children learn to actively select from the environment information that closely fits the modified schema.

In terms of gender development, girls and boys categorize stimuli into what they have come to label as male and female objects and activities. They note the appearance and behaviors of males and females and cluster this information accordingly. They also self-categorize their own behavior based on their observations of sex differences and similarities in appearance. These are the first processes in the child's development of gender identity. Once the child self-identifies as male or female, stimuli identification and categorization processes become more selective.

According to Kohlberg, children self-identify before they acquire what is known as "gender constancy," the knowledge that one's biological sex is immutable or unchangeable. This understanding begins to emerge around age three. Prior to and during this time, children acquire and categorize physical information from the environment that pertains to either sex. A person's clothing, facial hair, or size are judged as "gender appropriate" for the child because he or she has not yet learned that one's sex is not changeable based on one's appearance. Once a child achieves gender constancy, other environmental cues, such as activities and behaviors that are associated with sex, become more salient in the process of identifying and selecting gender-related information. At that point, children begin to actively seek information pertaining only to their own sex. They come to value this information and engage in behaviors consistent with what they perceive to be appropriate for their own sex.

There are several limitations to cognitive developmental explanations of gender-role identity development. For example, if a child recognizes and then chooses stimuli, including behaviors and expressed attitudes and interests consistent with his or her sex, and is simultaneously aware of the social mores that define sex-roles, why would girls purposefully select the less socially valued female role? Further, this theory does not explain why sex, rather than class or race, for example, is a highly salient category in the process of self-identification. Finally, research demonstrating that children engage in sex-typing prior to achieving gender constancy and before they have a fully developed understanding of gender, suggests that some cognitive processes may be less purposefully directed and active than claimed (Bussey & Bandura, 1992; Fagot & Lienbach, 1989).

## Gender Schema Theory

Drawing on both social learning and cognitive developmental accounts of sex role acquisition, gender schema theorists describe how children's conceptual categories are shaped by sociocultural standards and practices. Cognitive developmental theorists describe a schema as a cognitive structure, a set of associations that organize and guide an individual's perceptions of environmental stimuli. Gender schema theorists believe that gender schema guide an individual's gender-role identity development. While cognitive developmental theorists also discuss the formation and use of gender schema, they believe such schema are developed as a consequence rather than as a determinant of gender-related information categorization.

Gender schema theorist Sandra Bem (1981) notes that culture determines which schema are salient and contends that we pay greater attention to and have more memory for information related to important schema. In highly patriarchal cultures, gender is an important schema. Children raised in such cultures are more likely to attend to and remember gender-related than nongender-related information. Bem asserts that, based on the amount and type of information available in the environment, individuals develop a wide range of gender schema. The more gender-related or sex-typed information in a child's environment, the more likely she or he is to develop strongly sex-typed gender schema.

In her research, Bem has shown that individuals with weak or nonsex-typed gender schema are more likely to rely on a broader range of schema to process new information than highly sex-typed individuals, who rely on gender schema initially and more frequently. Sex-typed individuals are particularly sensitive to gender-related information in the environment, even to the extent that they may categorize neutral information by gender because of the limited development of other, non-gender-related schema.

Bem has also shown that children whose environments include a wide variety of gender-related and gender-neutral stimuli are more likely to be considered "aschematic." Such individuals may also develop schema based on individual differences in which they recognize there is wide individual within-sex variation, or culturally relative schema in which they recognize that definitions of gender are socially or culturally bound rather than attributable to biological sex.

Other gender schema theorists believe that rudimentary schema consist of two types: "in group/out group" schema and "own self" schema. Martin and Halvorson (1981) describe *group-based gender schema* as those that children use to categorize environmental stimuli for either members of their own sex or the other sex and *individualized own self schema* as those that children use to categorize stimuli for themselves. Martin and Halvorson have shown that young children use both types of schema to select toys, clothing, and activities for themselves and to modify their own behavior in their interactions with members of the same and the other sex. Through these processes of selection and modification, children first learn information about their own sex, then information about the other. Consequently, a person's "own sex" schema are broader, more detailed, and more diverse than her or his "other sex" schema.

Other gender schema theorists, such as Fagot and Leinbach (1989), have pointed to the importance of labeling in the schema formation process. Children are able to distinguish females and males from a very early age, long before they develop gender constancy. Fagot and Leinbach have shown that gender-related behavior is related to labeling objects and activities by sex. For example, once boys begin to label playing with dolls as "girl's play" they decrease their own doll play and engage in more same-sex play. Children who use gender relative labels are more likely to have parents who are highly sex-typed and who encourage sex-specific play while discouraging cross-gender play, and are also more likely to self-segregate and self-label than later labelers. Thus, the confluence of cognitive process and environmental factors perpetuates greater distinction and division by sex for these children.

In their longitudinal study of gender labeling and sex-role behaviors, Fagot and Leinbach have shown that labeling objects, people, and activities by sex occurs after perceptual discrimination of males and females, but before the development of gender constancy. The acquisition and use of labels, then, contributes to the formation of gender schema that are used to adopt sex-role behaviors. Fagot and Leinbach also found that parents of early and later labelers failed to differ in their sex-role related instructional behaviors toward their children during play. From this, they concluded that an *affective*, rather than *cognitive*, component in parents' behaviors may be more salient to children's labeling acquisition processes.

Other researchers, such as Martin and Little (1990), have shown that a child's gender-labeling ability is related to gender discrimination (the ability to distinguish between the sexes based on appearance), gender group membership (the ability to self-identify with either one sex or the other), and gender stability (the belief that one's sex will not change with time). They believe that these constructs, taken together as a global measure of gender concept understanding, are believed to be related to children's sex-typed clothing and toy knowledge and to their same-sex toy and peer preferences. These researchers concluded that only a "rudimentary understanding of gender is acquired by children before the sex-typing process begins. Once children can accurately label the sexes, they begin to form gender stereotypes and their behavior is influenced by these gender associated expectations." (p. 1438). Thus, through labeling, children's gender schema are defined and modified and used to gauge their own behavior.

Cognitive developmental accounts of sex-role development emphasize the importance of cognitive processes in the acquisition of gender knowledge, and the influence that knowledge has on the acquisition and performance of sex-typed behaviors. While children may acquire knowledge of both sexes, gender schema accounts point to the importance of labeling, social and cultural standards for behavior, and children's understanding of power relations between the sexes.

Both identification (i.e., psychoanalytic) and learning (i.e., social learning, cognitive developmental, gender schema) theories describe how boys and girls identify with or take on the characteristics of maleness (or masculinity) and femaleness (femininity). Both perspectives articulate differences between females and males, although such differences are attributed to different causal mechanisms. While the former holds that these differences are distinct and enduring, thus essential, the latter shows that sex-related behaviors can be shaped, modified, and extinguished.

With the understanding that sex-related behaviors could be attributed to exogenous factors, the social learning, then cognitive developmental and gender schema theories became more widely accepted. This acceptance coincided with various sociopolitical movements in the United States, such as the Civil Rights and women's movements (see Biaggio, Chapter 1, *this volume*) that further demonstrated human diversity. As researchers began to explore various aspects of human diversity, they also began to call into question the meanings of gender that had been articulated by traditional theories. As a result, psychological research began to move away from exploring the mechanisms that contributed to the development of sex-related behaviors and characteristics, to an examination of the meaning of gender.

## THE MEANING OF GENDER

The essentialist view that behavioral differences are rooted in biological differences presumes that an individual's core personality, which determines such behaviors, is separable from the individual's social and cultural contexts. Gender researchers adopting this perspective focus on biological sex, and ignore other salient characteristics such as race or ethnicity, class, and age in their analyses and point to within-sex and between-culture "universals" to support their view that women and men are inherently distinct. Conversely, gender researchers adopting a gender socialization view examine those social conditions that influence behaviors and attitudes and their relation to a person's biological sex. Thus, within-sex and between-culture variations support their view.

Regardless of perspective, researchers in both arenas consider gender a salient category for analysis. Research on sex differences prior to the 1960s was aimed at describing inherent differences between women and men and was largely influenced by the essentialist view. Research from the 1970s onward was aimed at debunking the stereotypes associated with each sex, particularly those of women, and considered the social and cultural locations of gender.

One goal of early gender socialization researchers was to show that males and females were more similar than different (Maccoby & Jacklin, 1974) and that such similarities could be measured within individuals by using the construct of psychological androgyny (Bem, 1974).

### Androgyny

Historically, masculinity and femininity had been considered mutually exclusive, bipolar constructs that represented attitudes, behaviors, and personality dimensions of individuals. Early research attempted to identify specific characteristics, or attributes, of masculinity and femininity that could be measured. Early measures of these characteristics conceptualized masculinity and femininity as polar, stable, and enduring traits that could be inferred through self-identification of sex-stereotyped adjectives (Spence, Helmreich, & Stapp, 1975). These measures focused on the traits of instrumentality and expressiveness as indicators of masculinity and femininity, respectively.

Masculinity and femininity have also been conceived of as complementary traits, behaviors, and attitudes (Bem, 1974). How an individual self-describes him- or herself according to these traits indicates his or her degree of sex-typing, that is, how strictly the individual has internalized social standards for behavior proscribed for one or the other sex. According to this conceptualization, those individuals who self-describe using many adjectives associated with both masculine and feminine characteristics are considered "androgynous." Such individuals are believed to possess those socially defined positive traits associated with both sexes and to have greater sex-role flexibility.

Androgynous individuals are believed to have moved beyond the sex-typed categories of masculinity and femininity, are considered capable of functioning in both socially defined roles, and, as a result, are thought to be more well adjusted (Bem, 1977; Spence & Helmreich, 1978). Further, that androgynous individuals possess *both* masculine and feminine traits shows that the constructs of masculinity and femininity are neither mutually exclusive nor polar, as early trait dimension researchers hypothesized. However, analysis of those characteristics identified as socially desirable for men and women show that those characteristics ascribed to males, which define "masculine" attributes, are more socially valued than those ascribed to females. Furthermore, masculine attributes are more closely associated with power and resourcefulness than are feminine attributes. Finally, individuals who are aschematic—those who rely on attributes other than those associated with gender for self-description—are found to have greater social role flexibility than those individuals who self-identify as masculine, feminine, *or* androgynous (Bem, 1983).

While such definitions of masculinity, femininity, and androgyny locate these constructs within socio-cultural, rather than personality domains, they are, nonetheless, narrow definitions of a person's potential self-conceptualization. Nevertheless, the concept of androgyny provided feminist theorists and researchers with alternate ways to define and locate gender. Further, it has provoked serious debate over the relative value of the component constructs masculinity and femininity and forced examination of the social, cultural, and historical constructions of gender and irregularities based on sex.

In her response to the feminist critique that early conceptions of androgyny detracted from the political analysis of gender inequality by rendering such inequality at the personal rather than institutional level, Bem (1993) argued for the import of shifting conceptual frameworks. She asserted that even though the concept of androgyny may provide no political forum or may even reinforce the gender dichotomy it seeks to ameliorate, it does provoke discourse. Such discourse underlies a shift in gender research from examination of the origins and outcomes of identity development to exploration of the meaning of gender itself.

For example, Unger (1979) distinguishes between the essentialist view of sex as a *subject* variable—with sex differences located *within* individuals—and the socialization view of sex as a *stimulus* variable—with sex differences located *within* others or within social systems in which the individual operates. She further notes that the essentialist and individual differences biases of psychology have led researchers to interpret sex differences found in the latter as derived from sex differences in the former.

According to Unger, conceptualizing sex as a stimulus variable influences our perceptions of and explanations for our own behavior. Moreover, the power of sex as a stimulus varies from public to private settings—with the former more powerful than the latter—and this illustrates that the social desirability of acting in accordance with social standards for behavior outweighs any physical, or physiological causal factors related to one's sex.

Unger notes that, because biological sex is a stimulus variable that alters or shapes our views of a person, to identify someone simply by his or her biological sex obscures other features of that person. She recommends the more appropriate use of the term "gender" when identifying someone since it more adequately refers to those "traits and behaviors characteristic of and appropriate to members of each sexual category" (p. 1092). She warns, however, that a substitution of terms will not solve the problems researchers have had in conflating sex as a subject variable with sex as a stimulus variable or in emphasizing sex differences while ignoring sex similarities. Further, simply making a language-based distinction between biological sex and socioculturally constructed gender fails to address the frameworks that researchers and consumers of research bring to their conceptions of women and men. Unger and Crawford (1993) argue that specific terminology will not clear the confusion over sex and gender in that doing so obscures the interrelatedness of the terms and presumes rigid distinctions between categories within each term (male/female; masculine/feminine) when such presumptions cannot, even for biological sex, be made. Further, one's "identity" is shaped by and composed of not only sex or gender, but also of race and class, and each of these interacts with and is determined by the individual's position within cultural systems of power and privilege.

An understanding of how cultural systems shape our perceptions of individuals as a function of their biological sex, and how we attach meaning to those sex-linked conceptualizations, underlies the social constructionist perspective of gender.

## The Social Construction of Gender

The construct of androgyny showed that females and males, because they could share characteristics, were more similar than different. However, the finding that masculine characteristics were more socially valued than feminine characteristics prompted some theorists to return to an essentialist view with the aim of showing that female characteristics should be equal in value to male characteristics. Feminist scholarship derived from this perspective stipulated that the unique characteristics of women, such as nurturance and connectivity, gave women a social advantage in areas such as mothering (i.e., Nancy Chodorow), morality (i.e., Carol Gilligan), subjectivity (i.e., Evelyn Fox Keller), and relationships (i.e., Jean Baker Miller).

A feminist, or woman-centered, discourse began to replace the discourse of gender similarity. By the late 1970s researchers had begun to focus on those social, cultural, political, and economic forces that contributed to the devaluation of women. Scholars walked a fine line between acceptance of enduring, essential female qualities and examination of sociocultural conditions that "created" those qualities or the perception of those qualities. This shift in research and theorizing marked the movement to the social constructionist perspective. Social constructionists show how social contexts create the meaning of gender. How that meaning-making occurs is determined by those in power, by those with control over the resources that allow the dissemination of meaning.

Social constructionists Hare-Mustin and Marecek (1990) argue that the meaning of gender is created by males and disseminated through language. They note that males have historically had control over those institutions that support the production and dissemination of knowledge: academia and the media. They also note that the meaning of gender is incomplete in that it is created and sustained only by the dominant group and excludes all other social groups. In our culture these other groups include women, persons of both sexes from racial and ethnic minorities and lower socioeconomic classes, and nonheterosexuals. Given the paucity of power holders in these groups, the meaning of gender is narrowly represented by a select special interest. To maintain power in our culture, then, it serves those who hold such power to create meanings that favor men and diminish women.

Some social constructionists argue that role distinctions by sex are determined through a given society's division of labor by sex, which is further determined by that society's modes of production and reproduction. Further, the value that a given society places on women is reflected in women's access to that society's modes of production (or resources) and control over her own reproduction. In strongly patriarchal societies, women's access and control is limited, and conceptions of gender are very distinct.

Examination of the theories of gender identity development and sex-role acquisition show how the meaning of "woman" has been constructed in negative, less valued, or "different" terms relative to the meaning of "man"; Freud asserted that women *lack* the phallus and develop an *inferior* ego identity; learning theorists assert that girls adopt *receptive* and *responsive* behaviors that are directed by others; cognitive developmental and schema theorists assert that children recognize and choose distinctly different characteristics associated with gender and that characteristics chosen by girls are of *lesser* social value than those chosen by boys.

Further, social constructionists argue that gender cannot be conceived of consistently across time, situations, or persons, in that it is not a static construct:

> Gender is an invention of human societies, a feat of imagination and industry. This feat is multifaceted. One facet involves laborious efforts to transform male and female children into masculine and feminine adults . . . ,[another] involves creating and maintaining the social arrangements that sustain differences in men's and women's consciousness and behavior . . . , [and a third] involves meaning: creating the linguistic and conceptual structures that shape and discipline our imagination of male and female, as well as creating the meaning of gender itself. Thus, gender is a way of organizing everyday life. (p. 4).

Thus, gender as a construct is one way that we sustain unequal distributions of power. Social constructionists call for the analysis of meanings of race, class, and sexual preference in ways similar to the analysis of gender. Such analyses will help illustrate the many ways that power holders have conflated these constructs to maintain the status quo.

In conclusion, conceiving of gender as something that we "do" rather than what we "are," an aim of the social constructionist perspective, allows us to identify those cultural standards that contribute to our definitions of "maleness" and "femaleness" or "masculinity" and "femininity."

## SUMMARY AND CONCLUSIONS

From psychoanalytic to gender schema theories, psychologists have attempted to show how boys and girls develop identities or adopt behaviors attributable to men and women in their given societies. While identity, learning, and cognitive theories aim to describe the process and outcomes of gender identification or behavior acquisition, they often fail to address the import of how gender is conceived or constructed or how such concepts and constructions are instituted and maintained by dominant groups. The aim of social constructionist theories of gender is to describe these processes and, moreover, to dispel falsely constructed notions of gender that sustain unequal power relations between the sexes.

If we are asked to identify someone's sex, we typically rely on dichotomous categories related to the individual's chromosomal or anatomical composition. When asked to identify the individual's gender, we may rely, erroneously, on the same dichotomy. Yet, gender is neither dichotomous nor mutually exclusive but instead, a socially constructed continuum of characteristics related to personality, appearance, and attitudes. It is a stimulus variable that invokes specific responses from others which, in turn, shape and modify our behaviors. Moreover, how behaviors, interactions, and attitudes are shaped and modified is a function of the meaning attached to gender within a given society or culture and such meanings vary by age, race, ethnicity, and social class. Thus, gender is neither static nor enduring, but malleable, transient, and, ultimately, a tool we use to organize our lives.

In sum, the question of how gender develops or is adopted is no longer salient. Rather, the question of how gender is constructed and why such constructions persist and have such profound implications for our behavior is of greater import. Only by disentangling biological sex from systems of power and privilege, by deconstructing the meaning of gender itself, can we begin to recognize and value the broad spectrum of characteristics that comprise individuals of all ages, ethnicities, sexualities, and socioeconomic groups.

ACKNOWLEDGMENTS  I would like to thank Maryka Biaggio for her generous and unconditional assistance in editing; Julie Wilkins for her marvelous ability to read my sloppy handwriting; and Ray and Lindsay for their patience and encouragement.

## REFERENCES

Bandura, A. (1977a). Self-efficacy mechanism in human agency. *American Psychologist, 37*, 122–147.

Bandura, A. (1977b). *Social learning theory*. Englewood Cliffs, NJ: Prentice-Hall.

Bandura, A., Ross, D., & Ross, S. A. (1963). Imitation of film-mediated aggressive models. *Journal of Abnormal and Social Psychology, 66*, 3–11.

Bandura, A., & Walters, R. H. (1963). *Social learning and personality development*. New York: Holt, Rinehart & Winston.

Bem, S. L. (1974). The measurement of psychological androgyny. *Journal of Consulting and Clinical Psychology, 42*, 155–162.

Bem, S. L. (1977). On the utility of alternative procedures for assessing psychological androgyny. *Journal of Consulting and Clinical Psychology, 45*, 196–205.

Bem, S. L. (1981) Gender schema theory: A cognitive account of sex-typing. *Psychological Review, 88*, 354–364.

Bem, S. L. (1983). Gender schema theory and its implications for child development: Raising gender aschematic children in gender-schematic society. *Signs: Journal of Women in Culture and Society, 10*, 598–616.

Bem S. L. (1993). *The lenses of gender: Transforming the debate on sexual inequality*. New Haven, CT: Yale University Press.

Bussey, K., & Bandura, A. (1992). Self-regulatory mechanisms governing gender development. *Child Development, 63*, 1236–1250.

Chodorow, N. (1978). *The reproduction of mothering: Psychoanalysis and the psychology of gender*. Berkeley, CA: University of California Press.

Chodorow, N. (1989). *Feminism and psychoanalytic theory*. New Haven, CT: Yale University Press.

Deutsch, H. (1944/1945). *The psychology of women* (Vols. I and II). New York: Grune & Stratton.

Erikson, E. (1968). *Womanhood and the inner space*. In E. Erikson, *Identity, youth, & crisis* (pp. 261–294). New York: W.W. Norton & Co.

Fagot, B. I., & Leinbach, M. D. (1989). The young child's gender schema: Environmental input, internal organization. *Child Development, 60*, 663–672.

Firestone, S. (1970). *The dialectic of sex*. New York: W. Morrow & Co.

Freud, S. (1905/1953). Three essays on the theory of sexuality. In J. Strachey (Ed. and Trans.), *The standard edition of the complete psychological works of Sigmund Freud* (pp. 125–222). London: The Hogarth Press.

Freud, S. (1933/1964). The psychology of women. In J. Strachey (Ed. and Trans.), *New introductory lectures on psychoanalysis* (pp. 112–135). New York: W. W. Norton & Co.

Friedan, B. (1974). *The feminine mystique*. New York: Norton.

Hare-Mustin, R. T., & Marecek, J. (1990). On making a difference. In R. T. Hare-Mustin & J. Marecek (Eds.), *Making a difference: Psychology and the construction of gender* (pp. 1–21). New Haven: Yale University Press.

Horney, K. (1939). *New ways in psychoanalysis.* New York: W. W. Norton & Co.

Kohlberg, L. (1966) A cognitive-developmental analysis of children's sex-role concepts and attitudes. In E. E. Maccoby (Ed.), *The development of sex differences* (pp. 82–173). Stanford, CA: Stanford University Press.

Lerman, H. (1986). From Freud to feminist personality theory: Getting here from there. *Psychology of Women Quarterly, 10,* 1–18.

Maccoby, E. E., & Jacklin, C. N. (1974). *The psychology of sex differences.* Stanford: Stanford University Press.

Martin, C., & Halverson, C. F. (1981). A schematic processing model of sex-typing and stereotyping in children. *Child Development, 52,* 119–1134.

Martin, C. L., & Little, J. K. (1990). The relation of gender understanding to children's sex-typed preferences and gender stereotypes. *Child Development, 61,* 1427–1439.

Mischel, W. (1966). A social-learning view of sex differences in behavior. In E. E. Maccoby (Ed.), *The development of sex differences* (pp. 56–81). Stanford, CA: Stanford University Press.

Mitchell, J. (1971). *Woman's estate.* New York: Pantheon Books.

Mitchell, J. (1974). *Psychoanalysis and feminism.* New York: Vintage Press.

Rosenthal, T. L., & Zimmerman, B. J. (1978). *Social learning and cognition.* New York: Academic Press.

Skinner, B. F. (1938). *The behavior of organisms: An experimental analysis.* Englewood Cliffs, NJ: Prentice Hall.

Spence, L. T., & Helmrich, R. (1978). *Masculinity and femininity: The psychological dimensions, correlates, and antecedents.* Austin, TX: University of Texas Press.

Spence, L. T., Helmreich, R., & Stapp, L. (1975). Ratings on self and peers on sex role attributes and their relation to self-esteem and conceptions of masculinity and femininity. *Journal of Personality and Social Psychology, 32,* 29–39.

Thompson, C. (1943). 'Penis Envy' in Women. *Psychiatry , 6,* 123–125.

Unger, R. K. (1979). Toward a redefinition of sex and gender. *American Psychologist, 34,* 1085–1094.

Unger, R. K. & Crawford, M. (1993). Commentary: Sex and gender-the troubled relationship between terms and concepts. *Psychological Science, 4,* 122–124.

# II

# Social Issues and Problems

This section is concerned with women's experiences in the social context, specifically in the world of work, and with some of the social problems that confront women in the larger cultural context—discrimination, sexual harassment and rape, and intimate violence. The authors in this section bring their expertise in the discipline of social psychology to bear on these topics.

Chapter 4, on understanding prejudice and discrimination, explains the mechanisms underlying sexism and the parallels between sexism and racism. Sexism and racism can take overt or subtle, old-fashioned or modern, forms. Have you observed or experienced these forms? Do you respond differently to overt versus subtle forms of sexism or racism? The authors of this chapter present a thought-provoking discussion of privilege, power, and reverse discrimination. Do you believe that reverse discrimination is a real form of discrimination or is it more accurately characterized as a threat to privilege and power? This question has been much debated in recent years in both scholarly and public arenas. Chapter authors Gillem, Sehgal, and Forcet also address some forms of prejudice that are discussed less often—classism and heterosexism. You may want to consider parallels and differences between these latter forms of prejudice and sexism and racism.

Jan Yoder's chapter on women and work details the realities of women's employment, including the persistent wage gap. Yoder points out that the workplace is different for women and men: You may find it interesting to ask yourself how your experience or views of work would differ if you were of the opposite sex. Is it possible that sexism plays some role in defining occupational "choice" or opportunity for women? The author of this chapter also provides overviews of the controversial topics comparable worth and affirmative action, topics which have far-reaching political and policy implications. If you were to find yourself in the midst of a discussion about these topics, what position would you take? How would you support your position?

The chapters on violence against women are by Patricia Rozee, an expert on the topic of rape, Maureen McHugh, a well-known authority on intimate violence; and her coauthor Tammy Redhead Bartoszek. Violence in American society is a problem of significant proportions and violence against women is an especially insidious problem, affecting large numbers of women. It is easy to feel discouraged and disheartened after reading about the prevalence and pernicious impacts of violence against women. You may want to reflect on how sexist attitudes contribute to this violence and think about how attitudes and policies can be changed so as to decrease the occurrence and minimize the negative effects of rape, sexual harassment, and domestic violence. How can you use your knowledge to challenge attitudes that may contribute to or desensitize us to the harassment and violence that plague women?

# 4

# Understanding Prejudice and Discrimination

## Angela R. Gillem, Radhika Sehgal, and Shiata Forcet

---

### INTRODUCTION

In this chapter, we discuss theories and research on sexism, which can be defined as prejudiced attitudes and discriminatory behaviors toward women. These prejudiced attitudes toward women generally involve stereotypical gender constructions and a belief in traditional gender roles for men and women (Campbell, Schellenberg, & Senn, 1997). Sex discrimination involves unequal and harmful behavior toward women only because they are women (Benokraitis, 1997).

Research clearly indicates the existence of widely held sex-role stereotypes in the United States. Women are characterized as more interpersonally sensitive, warm, and expressive than men; men are characterized as more competent, independent, objective, and logical than women. Stereotypically masculine traits are viewed in our society as more desirable and "adult" than stereotypically feminine characteristics (Broverman, Vogel, Broverman, Clarkson, & Rosenkrantz, 1972). Since stereotypes about women both describe how they behave and prescribe how they should behave (Haslett & Lipman, 1997), these constructions force women into a double bind. They are not feminine (as constructed by societal norms) if their behaviors are congruent with those specified for adults; however, if they adopt prescribed behaviors that are defined as feminine, they are inadequate in comparison to the standards for adult behaviors (Broverman et al., 1972). These societal constructions of women as being less competent or capable lead women to have lower self-esteem and less confidence in their abilities than men (Bartholomew & Schnorr, 1994) and, consequently, may lead to reduced productivity in a number of spheres (Haslett & Lipman, 1997).

Much of the theory on sexism is rooted in theory and research on racism. In fact, Dovidio and Gaertner (1983, cited in Campbell et al., 1997) suggest that sexism and racism are parallel belief systems such that historical trends in sexist attitudes tend to parallel trends in racist attitudes. For example, some of the models that we will discuss in this chapter—individual, institutional, and structural sexism; modern versus old-fashioned sexism; and subtle, covert, and

---

Angela R. Gillem and Radhika Sehgal ● Beaver College, Glenside, Pennsylvania 19038-3295
Shiata Forcet ● Cora Neumann Job Training Center, Philadelphia, Pennsylvania 19124

*Issues in the Psychology of Women,* edited by Biaggio and Hersen. Kluwer Academic/Plenum Publishers, New York, 2000.

overt sexism—are all direct derivatives of theories on racism. Other theories, for example, the ambivalent sexism model, have emerged as the result of exploration of these various manifestations of sexism and efforts to understand the complexities of prejudice against women. All of these models have been found to have some validity in describing and explaining sexism, which is a multidimensional and multiply caused phenomenon.

Given its roots in theory and research on racism, it is ironic that theory and research on sexism has, for a long time, excluded consideration of the impact of sexism on women of color. Much of the research that will be reported here involved predominantly white samples. We take this up in a later section as we discuss the ways that racism, classism, and heterosexism (among other isms) complicate the impact of sexism on women of color in ways that have been, until recently, ignored.

We turn now to a discussion of theories and research on sex discrimination and later we will discuss sexual attitudes.

## SEX DISCRIMINATION

One way of viewing sexism is that it is a system of beliefs, policies, and practices designed to maintain male privilege and status which is manifested individually, institutionally, and structurally. Individual or interpersonal discrimination involves the behavior of individual persons that intentionally (or unintentionally) has a differential and/or harmful effect on women (Pincus, 1996). It occurs between two individuals and is embedded in a context of institutional discrimination (Lott & Maluso, 1995). Institutional discrimination involves the policies of male-dominant institutions, and the behavior of those who control those institutions and implement policies, that are *intended* to have a differential, harmful, and/or exclusionary effect on women (Lott & Maluso, 1995; Pincus, 1996). Structural discrimination, which is related to institutional discrimination, refers to those policies of male-dominant institutions that are *neutral in intent* but that still have a differential, harmful, or exclusionary effect on women (Pincus, 1996).

Empirical research provides strong evidence that discrimination against women is widespread and that sexist events range from subtle to blatant. Blatant or overt sex discrimination has been characterized as unequal and harmful behavior toward women that is intentional, visible, documentable, and unambiguous (Benokraitis, 1997; Swim & Cohen, 1997). It includes a range of behaviors from salary differentials and job discrimination to sexual harassment and physical violence (Benokraitis, 1997; Klonoff & Landrine, 1995). For example, overt sexism is blatantly manifested in differences in salary earnings and job positions. In today's workforce, women are more likely to be in low-paid and part-time positions and earn approximately 75 cents to a man's dollar (Benokraitis, 1997). Jobs are categorized according to gender and based upon society's stereotypes of men and women. Women's roles are characterized as passive, nurturing, emotional, nonaggressive, and nonassertive and thus positions such as nurse, secretary, and teacher are defined as women's jobs. On the other hand, traditional male positions are described as requiring logical thinking, manual dexterity, aggressiveness, or some type of hard labor, and thus doctor, police officer, and garbage collector are defined as men's jobs. Many times, occupational salary is contingent upon job positions. If the position is gender sensitive, then there will be a difference in pay based on position/gender, with the "male" positions earning more than the "female" positions. Glick, Zion, and Nelson (1988) found that male and female job applicants were relegated to stereotypic positions, suggesting that gender discrimination was mediated by occupational stereotypes. Glick (1991) concluded from his study of sex-based occupational discrimination that, while men and women do pursue jobs that are dominated by the other sex, gender inequalities continue to be prevalent in the U.S. job market.

Sexual harassment is another form of overt sexism. While sexual harassment happens to both men and women, it is a more common experience for women. Sexual harassment can be exhibited either physically or verbally. For example, one women described how male co-workers gathered around her, grabbing her breast and crotch; they drew obscene pictures of her with her name attached and placed them on cars; and one exposed himself to her. This type of behavior is frequently institutionalized, accepted as the norm, and ignored by many companies. It may lead to demoralization and decreased self-esteem in women (Benokraitis, 1997). Also, women are likely to avoid situations that are oppressive or in which there is a likelihood of sexual harassment (Swim, Cohen, & Hyers, 1998). Thus, workplace environments that place women in compromising situations may lead to reduced productivity, feelings of incompetence and inferiority, and low job satisfaction.

In contrast to overt discrimination, subtle sex discrimination involves unequal and harmful behavior toward women that is less visible and often goes unnoticed because it is so common and perceived as normal in the culture and society (Benokraitis, 1997). The perpetrators of subtle sexism may not know they are doing it. In fact, they may espouse egalitarian attitudes about women and not realize that their behaviors are indicative of prejudice (Swim & Cohen, 1997). Subtle sexism includes such behaviors as sexist jokes that put women down and reinforce male dominance over women (Benokraitis, 1997). People often interpret jokes as being harmless and a safe way to express otherwise demeaning remarks. What is not apparent is the discriminatory effect of these statements. A study conducted by LaFrance and Woodzicka (1998) revealed that women are negatively affected by sexist jokes and that sexist humor creates a hostile work environment for them. Sexist jokes place women in the difficult position of having to choose whether to laugh in order to not offend colleagues and superiors, or to not laugh and be seen as humorless and uncollegial (Benokraitis, 1997). Another example of subtle sexism is gender discrimination in classrooms. In a review of the literature, Myers and Dugan (1996) noted that sexist images of male and female roles were reinforced in classrooms, and sexist humor that demeaned women's abilities was used. They also found that the effects could not only be emotionally damaging to a woman's educational endeavors, but could also interfere with the student–teacher relationship. Other forms of subtle sexism include "condescending chivalry," which places men in a one-up position while at the same time appearing to be simply protective or kind (Benokraitis, 1997, p. 14) and "collegial exclusion," in which women are subtly excluded or ignored in professional discussions (p. 22).

Covert sex discrimination involves unequal and harmful behavior toward women that is hidden, but, unlike subtle discrimination, it is often deliberate and has malicious intent. It includes sabotage or intimidation of women. Covert sexism is often manifested only in circumstances in which the behavior is not likely to be challenged as sexism (Benokraitis, 1997). Using drugs to render a woman incapacitated in order to rape her is an example of this kind of manipulation. For example, the drug Rohypnol, also known as "the date rape drug," is a sedative drug that is ten times more powerful than valium, sedates for up to eight hours, and produces amnesia for the period of sedation. The drug leaves a woman defenseless and unable to fight off a rapist as well as unable to remember the events that occurred while she was under its influence, making her an unreliable witness to the crime. The outcome of this type of control can be deadly if the drug is slipped into a woman's alcoholic beverage, leading to a potential overdose (Benokraitis, 1997).

To document the frequency with which women experience sexist discrimination, Klonoff and Landrine (1995) developed the Schedule of Sexist Events (SSE). They defined sexist events as "negative events (stressors) that happen *to women, because they are women* . . . [that are] inherently demeaning, degrading, and highly personal" [their italics] (pp. 441–442). Their administration of the SSE to 631 women was quite revealing of the experiences of white women and women of color in the United States. They found that, at least once in their lives, 94.1 percent of the women experienced being forced to listen to sexist or degrading jokes; about 82 percent had been sexually harassed, called sexist names, or had been treated disrespectfully because they were women; 56.4 percent experienced being "picked on, hit, shoved, or threatened with harm because of being a woman" (p. 445); and 40.4 percent were denied a raise or promotion because they were female. They found no difference among women across education and social class in their experiences of sexist discrimination. However, among white women, younger women reported more sexist degradation than older women; also, Latina women and Asian-American women reported more sexism in their close relationships than did white women.

Experiences of sexist discrimination can cause a woman to be less confident in future endeavors, jobs, or other activities. This is supported by Elmslie and Sedo's (1996) findings that discrimination leads to helplessness, which further leads to decreased motivation, reduced ability to perform, and impairment of ability to seek future employment. Thus, when a woman experiences this form of discrimination, she may internalize the negative messages and develop a sense of helplessness. Also, according to Ancis and Phillips (1996), who conducted a study of undergraduate students, the more gender bias a woman experiences, the more her sense of self-efficacy may be diminished.

Sexism can act as an environmental stressor that can also play a role in a woman's physical and/or psychological well-being. Gender-specific stressors can contribute to depressive and anxiety symptoms in women, and Landrine, Klonoff, Gibbs, Manning, and Lund (1995) found that sex discrimination correlates with premenstrual symptoms, obsessive–compulsive symptoms, and depressive symptoms more than other life stressors do.

## Distancing from Women

Allport (1954, cited in Lott & Maluso, 1995) described discriminatory behavior as existing on a continuum ranging from avoidance to active exclusion to violent attack. Lott (1995, 1996) conceptualizes sexism as having as its purpose the distancing from, avoidance of, or exclusion of women. In fact, the definition of manhood in sexist societies seems, by implication, to include the requirement that they distance from and exclude women (Lott, 1995). In our exploration of the phenomenon of sexism, we will now turn to the ways in which men distance from and exclude women.

Sexism involves constructing man as norm and woman as the "other" (Lott, 1995, p. 12) by exaggerating the differences and distance between men and women and privileging the characteristics of men. This places men in a position of power and higher status compared to women. Since sexism leads to such positive status outcomes for men, distancing attitudes and behaviors that contribute to those outcomes are strengthened. Based on the research on distancing behaviors dating as far back as 1925, it appears that interpersonal distancing represents an important indicator of interpersonal discrimination, and that women are more often on the receiving end of distancing behaviors than are men (Lott, 1995).

Much of the research on sexism has focussed on sexist attitudes and very little attention has been paid to men's sexist behaviors when they interact with women (Lott, 1995). However, there are several empirically documented ways in which men distance from women. For example, men dream less frequently about women than about men, while women dream equally about both men and women (Hall, 1984, cited in Lott, 1996). Men in the United States continue to strongly believe in the existence of major differences between men and women

(Lott, 1995) despite research evidence that men and women are more alike than they are different (Tavris, 1996). Men tend to give negative evaluations of women's competence and lower evaluations of women's leadership abilities compared to their evaluations for men (Lott, 1995). Women's space is more likely to be intruded upon than men's when men are attempting to achieve some objective. For example, men are more likely to reach over a woman than over another man to push an elevator button (Buchanan, Juhnke, & Goldman, 1976, cited by Lott, 1995). This suggests a "distancing" from women by ignoring the importance of their personal space.

Lott (1995, 1996) examined whether in neutral situations the dominant response of men toward women would be to distance, exclude, or separate themselves from women even when there is no reinforcing consequence for doing so. She conducted a study in which naïve observers observed predominately white mixed-sex and same-sex pairs building a domino structure. None of the participants had admitted to other-gender bias on any of the attitude scales administered earlier. However, the observers noted that the men "more frequently made negative statements and turned away from their partners when the partners were women than when they were men, and that men also less frequently followed the advice of women partners than that of men partners" (p. 34). The women showed no similar tendencies toward either male or female partners. Thus, she found that despite the fact that there were no self-reports of biased attitudes toward women, the men did demonstrate discriminatory behavior that they may not have been consciously aware of in the form of distancing toward women. She later studied the behavior of television characters and observed a similar pattern of distancing behavior of men toward women that was not engaged in by the women toward either men or women (Lott, 1995, 1996).

## SEXIST ATTITUDES TOWARD WOMEN

Despite the fact that sexist events are still so prevalent in women's lives, several studies indicate that, between 1970 and 1995, there has been an increasing trend toward both women and men developing more egalitarian attitudes toward women (Spence & Hahn, 1997; Twenge, 1997). Research also indicates that, consistent with this change over time, older men and women espouse more conservative attitudes toward women than younger ones, and southerners have more conservative attitudes toward women's roles than are found in other regions of the United States. In fact, during every time period examined, the attitudes of both women and men in the South have lagged behind those of the other regions by 5 to 10 years (Twenge, 1997).

Twenge (1997) performed a meta-analysis of data on attitudes toward women from 71 studies of college undergraduates done between 1970 and 1995 and found the same pattern of change. Interestingly, she found that women's attitudes were consistently and significantly more egalitarian than men's. In fact, it was not until 1986–1990 that men's attitudes caught up with attitudes that women held in the early 1970s! Perhaps it is more difficult or threatening for men to liberalize their attitudes because it involves giving up privilege. It is noteworthy that evidence from a study by Spence and Hahn (1997) suggests that women might also be reluctant to give up some of the privileges gained from a sexist environment. In 1992, they found that women's attitudes about sharing expenses on a date (they preferred not to) had not changed since 1972; and women's attitudes toward women being able to propose marriage, which involves a certain amount of interpersonal risk, were *less* egalitarian than men's in their 1976, 1980, and 1992 samples. Privilege may be appealing and hard to give up for both men and women!

How do we account for these changes in attitudes toward women? They may be due to changing family environments over time, with more working mothers influencing their children's attitudes. Research suggests that children of mothers who work outside the home have more liberal attitudes toward women than children of nonworking mothers. The changes may also be due to differences in the social climates of the times during which the various cohorts grew up (Twenge, 1997). Related to this is the issue of social desirability: the participants may have been giving the answers that were socially desirable during the particular cultural climate of their lifetimes (Campbell et al., 1997; Twenge, 1997). Regardless of why the changes have occurred, it is important to remember that change in attitudes does not necessarily predict change in behavior, as we have seen in the previous discussion of Lott's research on distancing from women.

A final word on the evolution of attitudes toward women: Spence and Hahn (1997) found the beginning of a "ceiling effect" by 1992 in which both men's and women's scores on the Attitudes Toward Women Scale (AWS) approached the maximum score possible on the scale (high scores reflect more egalitarian attitudes). The AWS was designed by Spence and her colleagues in the early 1970s "to assess people's beliefs about the responsibilities, privileges, and behaviors in a variety of spheres that have traditionally been divided along gender lines but could, in principle, be shared equally by men and women" (Spence & Hahn, 1997, p. 17). The ceiling effect that has been found when using this scale in contemporary times may be explained by the apparent trend in more recent years toward covert or subtle forms of sexism that may not be adequately measured by the AWS (Swim & Cohen, 1997). The following section will explain why caution is warranted when using scales developed in the 1970s to assess the attitudes of the 1990s (and of the new millenium!).

## Modern and Old-Fashioned Sexism

Although recent research suggests that attitudes toward women have been liberalizing over the past 20 to 30 years, there is evidence that blatantly negative attitudes toward women have not diminished. They have merely gone underground and become subtle or covert as a result of the second wave of the feminist movement (Haslett & Lipman, 1997). In the current cultural climate in which it is considered politically incorrect to express blatantly prejudiced attitudes toward any oppressed group, it is not surprising that those attitudes might begin to be expressed more subtly or covertly.

Old-fashioned sexism was characterized by overt or blatant discrimination, negative stereotypes about women, and blatant belief in unequal rights and roles based on gender. Modern sexism is characterized by unsympathetic responses toward women's issues, including denial of sex discrimination, resistance to women's demands for equity which are seen as excessive, and opposition to progressive social policies, such as affirmative action, which are perceived as giving women unfair advantage (Swim, Aikin, Hall, & Hunter, 1995; Swim & Cohen, 1997). These more subtle forms of sexism allow men to express sexist attitudes without admitting to belief in the inferiority of women, which makes measuring modern sexist attitudes much more difficult than measuring old-fashioned ones (Campbell et al., 1997). In fact, research has demonstrated that measures developed in the 1970s to measure more blatantly negative attitudes toward women cannot adequately measure these types of subtle modern attitudes (Swim & Cohen, 1997).

Haslett and Lipman (1997) refer to subtle sexist behaviors as "micro inequities" and found that the women in their study of female attorneys commonly responded to these with frustration, stress, and anger. Their respondents saw micro inequities as major sources of stress on their jobs because they contributed to a hostile work environment. However, because micro inequities are so often difficult to respond to, these women internalized the subtle sexism and began to wonder if they were to blame. They began to question their own competence and to feel guilty for not being able to adequately respond. Thus, taken separately, each micro inequity seems minor, especially to the perpetrator of the discrimination; however, taken cumulatively, the subtle sexism of modern times constitutes a significant burden to those on the receiving end.

## Ambivalent Sexism

Glick and his colleagues (Glick, Diebold Bailey-Werner, & Zhu, 1997; Glick & Fiske, 1997) have observed that most definitions of sexism found in the literature involve two components: hostile feelings toward and negative stereotypes about women, and benevolent endorsement of traditional gender roles that restrict women's behavior and confine women to lower status and less powerful roles than men. They believe that this "ambivalent sexism" is due to the dual nature of men's relationships to women. On one hand, men possess dominance, power, and privilege and a need to maintain their position by subordinating women; on the other hand, men depend on women to meet their sexual, familial, and intimate needs. Thus, "*Hostile sexism* seeks to justify male power, traditional gender roles, and men's exploitation of women as sexual objects through derogatory characterizations of women. *Benevolent sexism* . . . relies on kinder and gentler justifications of male dominance and prescribed gender roles . . . [expressed as] feelings of protectiveness and affection toward women" [their italics] (Glick & Fiske, 1997, p. 121).

The research of Glick and his colleagues (Glick et al., 1997; Glick & Fiske, 1997) supports this characterization of men who are ambivalently sexist. They found that, compared to nonsexists, ambivalent sexist men tended to spontaneously divide women into subgroups about which they had polarized opinions, that is, into liked and disliked subtypes (Glick et al., 1997). Specifically, they found that hostile sexism was related to negative attitudes toward career (nontraditional) women, and benevolent sexism was related to positive attitudes toward homemakers (traditional women).

They explain these findings by suggesting that ambivalently sexist men tend to categorize women into two mutually exclusive groups in order to avoid experiencing ambivalence toward any particular woman, and to avoid the dissonance produced by hostility toward women on whom they depend to fulfill important needs. Thus, men may feel benevolently toward women in traditional roles of wife, mother, and homemaker, but may feel hostility toward more independent, modern women who have careers and feminist/egalitarian attitudes that preclude meeting the needs of men (Glick et al., 1997; Glick & Fiske, 1997). This may be a good point at which to turn to a discussion of male privilege, an area of research that has begun to intrigue contemporary feminist psychologists.

## PRIVILEGE, POWER, AND REVERSE DISCRIMINATION

White men are still in a better social and economic position than all other racial/ethnic and gender groups in our society, with women still earning only about 75 cents for every dollar that white men make (Benokraitis, 1997). However, white men have begun to experience an erosion of their privileged position and have consequently raised cries of reverse discrimination in response to their perception that women are now receiving special privileges and unfair advantages (Swim et al., 1995). However, there is evidence that men may tend to exaggerate the severity of the sexist discrimination that they experience, particularly those with low self-esteem, in order to make an external, self-protective attribution that explains why they are not continuing to receive their expected amount of privilege (Swim et al., 1995).

Research by Heilman, McCullough, and Gilbert (1996) supports this interpretation. They used an affirmative action analog to determine under what circumstances preferential selection can lead to negative reactions and the experience of "reverse discrimination" on the part of nonbeneficiaries. Male research participants were given a bogus test that they were told would help determine whether they or a female (confederate) participant would be awarded the leadership position on a task in which the leader would verbally instruct the subordinate. The male participants were told that the female confederate would be given preferential treatment because she was a woman. They found that when the men were given *no information* regarding their performance on the test as compared to the woman (analogous to real life in which scores of the selected competitor are rarely given), they responded in the same way they did when given the information that their scores were *superior to* the preferentially selected woman's. The men in the no information condition saw themselves as more deserving of the leadership position awarded to the female; they rated the female leader's competence more negatively than did the men who were told that their scores were equal to or lower than the preferentially selected female leader's scores; and they believed the selection process was less fair than did participants in the equal and inferior conditions. Thus, "without information to the contrary, [the] male participants acted as if they were in fact superior, and . . . more deserving of the position than the female beneficiary" (p. 354). This finding makes sense of white men's claims that they are victims of "reverse discrimination" when they lose out on positions that go to women. Apparently, white male socialization includes being taught, either explicitly or implicitly, that white males are superior and should expect special privileges (Smith, 1998) whether they earned them or not.

Another explanation for this finding comes from research that demonstrates that acknowledging their male privilege negatively affects men's self-esteem, life satisfaction, and self-confidence. Thus, to avoid these damaging consequences, men must disavow the unearned privilege that appears so obvious to many women, making it more likely that they will feel discriminated against when any of that privilege is tampered with (Branscombe, 1996, cited in Swim et al., 1995).

Conversely, recognizing *disadvantage* can be psychologically harmful to women. Research has demonstrated that the more women perceive that they are being discriminated against because of their sex, the more depressed they feel (Kobrynowicz & Branscombe, 1997). Kobrynowicz and Branscombe (1997) found that, for women, high need for approval was related to lower admissions of personal discrimination but not to perceptions of group discrimination. This suggests that those women with high need for social approval may not be willing to risk social disapproval from men by admitting to experiencing personal discrimination, although they may recognize that women as a group are discriminated against. Gaining men's disapproval apparently is a realistic concern: it has been found that dominant group members do become annoyed by reports of discrimination from disadvantaged group members (Dijker et al., 1996, cited in Kobrynowicz & Branscombe, 1997). It has also been demonstrated that the beneficiaries of preferential selection develop unfavorable self-views and are stigmatized as incompetent by others (Heilman et al., 1996). Thus, women may deny discrimination and disadvantage in order to avoid the damaging effects of preferential programs developed to compensate for their lack of privilege.

Thus, denying or exaggerating discrimination serves self-protective purposes for women and men respectively (Kobrynowicz & Branscombe, 1997). Women minimize or deny discrimination in order to avoid depression and loss of social approval, while men exaggerate discrimination in order to avoid loss of power, privilege, and self-esteem.

## COMPLICATED SEXISM

The manifestations and consequences of sexism are complicated by its interaction with other "isms" such as racism, classism, and heterosexism. Historically, mainstream feminist psychology has ignored these complications and treated sexism as if it occurs in a social vacuum. Consequently, the experiences of women of color, poor women, and lesbians, who have had to deal with the effects of multiple membership in disadvantaged groups, have remained unexplored until fairly recently (Bristor & Fischer, 1995; Weber, 1998). When these issues have been addressed, they have been simply added on to the experience of white, middle-class, heterosexual women. The use of the adding-on approach to the race, class, and sexual orientation of women of color, poor women, or lesbian women also ignores the race, class, and sexual orientation of white, middle-class, heterosexual women (Harding, 1991; Palmer, 1983 as cited in Bristor & Fischer, 1995) and overlooks their privilege (Bristor & Fischer, 1995).

Admittedly, sex is a salient characteristic in identifying and distinguishing individuals, and it is used by almost every society to construct roles for males and females. In most societies, men hold positions of public importance, they dominate and control family resources, and they are assigned status and power as their birthright. In contrast, women typically play private personal roles, they have little control of their lives, and they frequently have difficulty earning and keeping power and status (Reid & Comas-Diaz, 1990). However, the existing literature indicates that ethnic or racial characteristics surpass sex as social cues to family background and social status. Characteristics such as skin color, facial features, and use of nonstandard English are assumed to reveal personality, mental abilities, and behavioral traits of minority individuals. Based on these characteristics, white men and women are typically assigned superior status in professional and social settings, and members of other ethnic/ racial groups are assumed to be inferior and to possess negative characteristics (Reid & Comas-Diaz, 1990). Social class also influences our perceptions of individuals and our expectations regarding their behaviors. Individuals with high social status are perceived and accepted as leaders and role models while low status individuals are devalued and ignored (Wentworth & Anderson, 1984, as cited in Reid & Comas-Diaz, 1990). Thus, all forms of discrimination limit and control the lives of women and result from status and power inequity in our society (Lott & Maluso, 1995).

Race, class, gender, and sexuality are contextual for each other. These contexts are used to construct different meanings of masculinity and femininity throughout history for different social groups through social processes that produce and help maintain racialized, class-bound, heterosexist environments (Weber, 1998). The dominant culture defines the categories within race, gender, and sexuality as polar opposites (for instance, white and black [or nonwhite], men and women, heterosexual and homosexual) to create social rankings: good and bad, worthy and unworthy, right and wrong (Lorber, 1994, as cited in Weber, 1998). It also links these concepts to biology to imply that the rankings are fixed, permanent, and embedded in nature. Thus, race, gender, and sexuality are defined as ranked dichotomies with whites, men, and heterosexuals assumed to be superior. Since race, gender, and sexuality are social constructs that create contexts for each other, their interaction in an individual's life cannot be fully understood when they are treated as discrete variables, as this implies individuals can belong to one and only one category (Weber, 1998).

Several authors have begun to examine the effects of multiple "isms" and have referred to those effects as double, triple, or multiple jeopardy (e.g., see Gillem, 1996; Greene, 1994; King, 1988). They suggest that when these "isms" are combined, they have more than just an additive effect. They often have a potentiating or multiplicative impact, producing psychological damage that is more than just the sum of the effects of each form of discrimination. We refer to this multiplicative interaction with sexism as "complicated sexism."

## Sexism and Racism

Ethnic minority women's multiple identities may increase their risk of encountering prejudice. Discrimination based on gender may come from both within and outside of their communities, while that based on race/ethnicity may come from other women as well as from men (Reid & Comas-Diaz, 1990). In addition, race becomes more salient than gender for women of color, as their oppression tends to be more on the basis of race than of gender. Thus, many women of color tend to give more importance to the oppression from whites (of both sexes) while viewing their oppression by men (of all races) secondary (Kliman, 1994).

A review of the literature shows that white women as a group are more likely to finish high school and graduate from college, resulting in higher incomes and a brighter future than many women of color can attain (with the exception of certain groups of Asian women). More and more women are becoming responsible for supporting their families; however, in comparison to white women, women of color are more likely to maintain families, more likely to be heads of households living in poverty, more likely to be divorced, and more likely to have larger families. Thus, women of color have lower incomes and bear more economic burdens than any other group in this country. Although white women also suffer economically, their relationship to white men (the highest earners in society) as daughters, wives, or sisters often gives them an "economic cushion" (Hurtado, 1994).

While the definition of women is differently constructed for white women and women of color, gender is nonetheless the salient mechanism through which each group is subordinated (West & Zimmerman, 1987, as cited in Hurtado, 1994). White men need white women in ways that they do not need women of color because women of color cannot fulfill white men's need for racially pure offspring. White middle-class women are groomed from birth to be the lovers, mothers, and partners (however unequal) of white men because of the economic and social benefits attached to these roles. Upper and middle-class white women are supposed to be the biological bearers of those members of the next generation who will inherit positions of power in society. They are thus seduced into accepting subservient roles that meet the material needs of white men.

Women of color, in contrast, are groomed from birth to be primarily the lovers, mothers, and partners (however unequal) of men of color, who are also oppressed by white men. They are also perceived by white men as workers and as objects of sexual power and aggression. This objectification allows white men to express power and aggression in sexual terms that are not complicated by the emotional entanglements that are present in their relationships with white women. Women have been conceptualized in terms of dual dichotomies: "white goddess/black she-devil, chaste virgin/nigger whore; the blond blue-eyed doll/the exotic 'mulatto' object of sexual craving" (Rich, 1979). This distance from and access to the source of white male privilege creates differences in the relational power of women of color and white women. The avenues of advancement that are open to white women who conform to prescribed standards of middle-class femininity are not even a theoretical possibility for women of color. This is not to say that women of color are more oppressed than white women but, rather, that white men use different forms of oppression on white women than on women of color. White women, as a group, are subordinated through seduction, and women of color, as a group, are subordinated through rejection and objectification (Hurtado, 1994).

## Sexism, Classism, and Racism

Class position also affects the probability of obtaining the rewards of seduction and the sanctions of rejection. Working-class and poor white women are socialized to believe in the advantages of marrying somebody economically successful, but the probability of obtaining that goal is lower for them than for middle- or upper-class white women. Class position affects women of color as well. Although rejected by white men as candidates to reproduce offspring, middle-class women of color may be accepted into some white middle-class social circles in the role of the token if they conform to white middle-class standards (Apfelbaum, 1979, as cited in Hurtado, 1994).

Internalizing society's stereotypes can result in women modifying their behaviors in order to avoid social class stereotypes. For example, Gordon (1997) found that to avoid the negative stereotypes (e.g., sexual promiscuity and loose morals) that are associated with the lower class, middle-class women tend to use prestige speech patterns. By doing this, listeners will focus less on stereotyping her social status as a woman and be less likely to place moral judgment on her.

Gender roles and expectations, as well as the dynamics of patriarchy, differ for oppressed and dominant cultural groups and play out in different ways for each group. For instance, women can be hired at lower wages as a result of sexism. This makes black and Latina women more employable than their husbands and brothers. Thus, men of color are less likely to find work and are then blamed for it and labeled "shiftless," while women of color can generally find work, but are also exploited. Thus, as a result of job discrimination against black men, black women are required to work outside the home and not depend financially on black men. This is in contrast to white women, who have been socialized to depend on white men financially by marrying them. This mechanism of adaptation to the combined impact of racism, sexism, and classism has been referred to pejoratively as the "black matriarchy," which is in itself sexist, implying that it is pathological for women to be primary breadwinners and hold power in the family (Kliman, 1994).

In talking about the experiences of women of color on college campuses, DeFour (1996) explains that sex, race, and socioeconomic status interact to increase the vulnerability of women of color to harassment in academic settings and combine to undermine their self-concept. Financial vulnerability increases women's risk of being harassed. As undergraduate students, they are often dependent upon financial aid to fund their education because their families may not be able to finance their education from family funds. As graduate students they are more likely to have loans and fellowships than research assistantships (Blackwell, 1981, as cited in DeFour, 1996). In addition, female faculty members are often concentrated in adjunct positions with one-year or even one-semester/quarter contracts. A large number of women of color in academic settings are outside of the classroom in positions as administrative staff, secretaries, cooks, and housekeepers, positions in which they are most often supervised by men (DeFour, 1996).

The stereotypes of minority women may also influence their credibility and likelihood of being taken seriously at work by male colleagues (Comas-Diaz & Greene, 1994). The stereotypes and perceptions of women, which portray them either as weak or as very sexual, also increase their vulnerability to harassment. Thus, women are perceived as either unlikely to fight back if harassed or as actually desiring the sexual attention. For instance, Latinas have been described as hot-blooded, ill-tempered, religious, overweight, lazy, always pregnant, loud-mouthed, and deferent to men. Native American women have been perceived as poor, sad, un-educated, isolated, and devoted to male elders, as the American Indian princess or the Poca-hontas figure (Comas-Diaz & Greene, 1994). Asian women are described either as small, docile, and submissive, like China dolls, or as the exotic "sexpots" who will cater to any man's whims (Kumagai, 1978/1988, as cited in DeFour, 1996). Black women are perceived as domi-neering heads of households, having low morals, being highly sexed, and "loose" (DeFour, 1996). These stereotypes are a far cry from the socially constructed norms and stereotypes es-tablished for white middle-class women which, if conformed to as prescribed, place them in a better position to command respect from white men.

## Sexism, Heterosexism, and Racism

Heterosexism and homophobia serve to perpetuate misogyny and sexism (Pharr, 1988). Male dominance and female dependence are preserved through heterosexist attitudes and in-stitutions that keep women subordinate to men. This is done through the belief that women need men to be secure, fulfilled, and functioning properly, thereby rejecting the possibility that women can do things on their own or even with other women. The label "lesbian" affects all women as it is used as a threat against and a put-down of all women who reject male domina-tion and control. Misogyny, sexism, heterosexism, and homophobia interact to influence every sphere of a lesbian's life: identity, self-esteem, sexuality and sexual identity, relationships with family and intimate partners, attitudes and feelings about men, and sense of safety. These ef-fects vary according to the personal history, race, class, age, disability, and sexual orientation of women. However, even with individual variations, what is common to each story is the sub-ordination, separation, and devaluation of women on the basis of their gender and the fact that they face resistance and retaliation for challenging patriarchal rules and heterosexual systems (Ellis & Murphy, 1994).

Having examined how the various "isms" interact to complicate sexism as it is experi-enced by women in America, let us focus briefly on the impact of these "isms" on lesbians of color. The development of a lesbian sexual identity and the coming out process for lesbians of color, as compared to that for white lesbians, becomes even more complicated by the addition of issues realted to race/ethnicity. To understand the impact of gender, ethnicity, sexual orien-tation, and the interaction of these factors upon a lesbian of color, Greene (1994) suggests that one has to take into account the fluidity or rigidity of gender role stereotypes in her specific culture, as well as the cultural importance of family, community, and religion/spirituality. Ad-ditional factors influencing a lesbian of color's experience include racial and ethnic stereo-types of minority women in the dominant culture, and both heterosexism and sexism experi-enced from the dominant culture as well as from within the minority culture. These factors place the lesbian of color in what Greene (1994) calls triple jeopardy, increasing the risk of greater isolation, estrangement, and mental health vulnerability.

For women of color, the family is very often the primary social unit, providing not only emotional and material support, but also positive cultural mirroring which helps to counteract distorted and stereotyped messages about minority individuals from the dominant culture. The family, along with the ethnic community, also functions as a buffer against racism (Greene, 1994). Thus, the coming out process for lesbians of color may bring up fears of rejection and alienation by their family and culture of origin, leaving them without refuge in the face of ra-cial discrimination.

Greene (1994) has articulated additional factors that influence the experiences of lesbians of color, including the views in many minority communities that only heterosexual orientation is normal, that homosexuality is a Western or white man's disease, and that being homosexual is a choice. All of these force the lesbian of color into the quandary of choosing either her family and community of origin or the larger lesbian community. Choosing the lesbian community is also fraught with many difficulties; the racism and negative stereotyping that a woman of color encounters in the dominant culture is equally prevalent in the lesbian community, which is predominantly white. Thus, lesbians of color often are left feeling conflicted about both communities because they have to hide or minimize an integral part of their identities. At times, they end up feeling isolated and estranged from both.

## SUMMARY

In this chapter we have examined theories and research on several current models of sexism and have found that sexism is a multidimensional, multiply caused phenomenon that is complicated by other forms of discrimination. We have found that, although expressed attitudes toward women have liberalized over the years, men continue to discriminate against women just because they are women. The way in which a woman handles the discrimination depends on how she perceives the maltreatment, whether she sees herself as having choices in dealing with it, and whether experience with other oppressions renders her more or less capable of coping. Whether a woman is aware of the effects of oppression or not, there are studies that demonstrate that both sexism and complicated sexism act as stressors, resulting in increased risks of physical and psychological impairment. Although oppression has the potential to cause debilitating effects, a woman does not have to remain powerless when she is faced with discriminatory attitudes and behavior. However, women who demand to be heard and dare to speak against male dominance are faced with the consequences of their actions, often in the form of institutionalized sanctions against women. Finally, we have learned that if we want to understand and eliminate sexism, then we must take all of the oppressions that impact women into account. We must not arrange them hierarchically or examine them singly; we must understand their commonalities as well as their differential effects and how they complicate women's lives by their interaction. Only when the complexities of all women's lives are taken into account can we really understand the impact and complications of sexism.

## REFERENCES

Ancis, J. R., & Phillips, S. D. (1996). Academic gender bias and women's behavioral agency self-efficacy. *Journal of Counseling and Development, 75*, 131–137.

Bartholomew, C. G., & Schnorr, D. L. (1994). Gender equity: Suggestions for broadening career options of female students. *The School Counselor, 41*, 245–255.

Benokraitis, N. V. (1997). *Subtle sexism: Current practice and prospects for change.* Thousand Oaks, CA: Sage.

Bristor, J., & Fischer, E. (1995). Exploring simultaneous oppressions: Toward the development of consumer research in the interest of diverse women. *American Behavioral Scientist, 38*, 526–536.

Broverman, I. K., Vogel, S. R., Broverman, D. M., Clarkson, F. E., & Rosenkrantz, P. S. (1972). Sex-role stereotypes: A current appraisal. In B. Puka (Ed.), *Caring voices and women's moral frames: Vol. 6. Gilligan's view* (pp. 191–210). New York: Garland.

Campbell, B., Schellenberg, E. G., & Senn, C. Y. (1997). Evaluating measures of contemporary sexism. *Psychology of Women Quarterly, 21*, 89–102.

Comas-Diaz, L., & Greene, B. (1994). Women of color with professional status. In L. Comas-Diaz & B. Greene (Eds.), *Women of color: Integrating Ethnic and Gender Identities in Psychotherapy* (pp. 347–388). New York: Guilford Press.

DeFour, D. D. (1996). The interface of racism and sexism on college campuses. In M. A. Paludi (Ed.), *Sexual harassment on college campuses: Abusing the ivory power* (Rev. ed.) (pp. 49–56). New York: State University of New York Press.

Ellis, P., & Murphy, B. C. (1994). The impact of misogyny and homophobia on therapy with women. In M. P. Mirkin (Ed.), *Women in context: Toward a feminist reconstruction of psychotherapy* (pp. 25–47). New York: Guilford Press.

Elmslie, B., & Sedo, S. (1996). Discrimination, social, psychology, and hysteresis in labor markets. *Journal of Economic Psychology, 17*, 465–478.

Gillem, A. R. (1996). Beyond double jeopardy: Female, biracial and perceived to be black. In J. C. Chrisler, C. Golden, & P. D. Rozee (Eds.), *Lectures on the psychology of women* (pp. 199–209). New York: McGraw-Hill.

Glick, P. (1991). Trait-based and sex-based discrimination in occupational prestige, occupational salary, and hiring. *Sex Roles, 25*, 351–378.

Glick, P., Diebold, J., Bailey-Werner, B., & Zhu, L. (1997). The two faces of Adam: Ambivalent sexism and polarized attitudes toward women. *Personality and Social Psychology Bulletin, 23*, 1323–1334.

Glick, P., & Fiske, S. T. (1997). Hostile and benevolent sexism: Measuring ambivalent sexist attitudes toward women. *Psychology of Women Quarterly, 21*, 119–135.

Glick, P., Zion, C., & Nelson, C. (1988). What mediates sex discrimination in hiring decisions? *Journal of Personality and Social Psychology, 55*, 178–186.

Gordon, E. (1997). Sex, speech and stereotypes: Why women use prestige speech forms more than men. *Language in Society, 26*, 47–63.

Greene, B. (1994). Lesbian women of color: Triple jeopardy. In L. Comas-Diaz & B. Greene (Eds.), *Women of color: Integrating ethnic and gender identities in psychotherapy* (pp. 389–427). New York: Guilford Press.

Haslett, B. B., & Lipman, S. (1997). Micro inequities: Up close and personal. In N. V. Benokraitis (Ed.), *Subtle sexism: Current practice and prospects for change* (pp. 34–53). Thousand Oaks, CA: Sage.

Heilman, M. E., McCullough, W. F., & Gilbert, D. (1996). The other side of affirmative action: Reactions of nonbeneficiaries to sex-based preferential selection. *Journal of Applied Psychology, 81*, 346–357.

Hertzberg, J. F. (1996). Internalizing power dynamics: The wounds and the healing. *Women and Therapy, 18*, 129–148.

Hurtado, A. (1994). Relating to privilege: Seduction and rejection in the subordination of white women and women of color. In A. C. Herrmann & A. J. Stewart (Eds.), *Theorizing feminism: Parallel trends in the humanities and social sciences* (pp. 136–154). Boulder, CO: Westview Press.

King, D. K. (1988). Multiple jeopardy, multiple consciousness: The context of a Black feminist ideology. *Signs, 14*(1), 42–72.

Kliman, J. (1994). The interweaving of gender, class, and race in family therapy. In M. P. Mirkin (Ed.), *Women in context: Toward a feminist reconstruction of psychotherapy* (pp. 25–47). New York: Guilford Press.

Klonoff, E. A., & Landrine, H. (1995). The schedule of sexist events: A measure of lifetime and recent sexist discrimination in women's lives. *Psychology of Women Quarterly, 19*, 439–472.

Kobrynowicz, D., & Branscombe, N. R. (1997). Who considers themselves victims of discrimination? Individual difference predictors of perceived gender discrimination in women and men. *Psychology of Women Quarterly, 21*, 347–363.

LaFrance, M., & Woodzicka, J. A. (1998). No laughing matter: Women's verbal reactions to sexist humor. In J. K. Swim & C. Stangor (Eds.), *Prejudice: The targets perspective* (pp. 61–80). San Diego, CA: Academic Press.

Landrine, H., Klonoff, E. A., Gibbs, J., Manning, V., & Lund, M. (1995). Physical and psychiatric correlates of gender discrimination: An application of the schedule of sexist events. *Psychology of Women Quarterly, 19*, 473–492.

Lott, B. (1995). Distancing from women: Interpersonal sexist discrimination. In B. Lott & D. Maluso (Eds.), *The social psychology of interpersonal discrimination* (pp. 12–49). New York: Guilford Press.

Lott, B. (1996). The perils and promise of studying sexist discrimination in face-to-face situations. In M. A. Paludi (Ed.), *Sexual harassment on college campuses: Abusing the ivory power* (pp. 57–71). Albany, NY: State University of New York Press.

Lott, B., & Maluso, D. (1995). Introduction: Framing the questions. In B. Lott & D. Maluso (Eds.), *The social psychology of interpersonal discrimination* (pp. 1–11). New York: Guilford Press.

Myers, D., & Dugan, K. (1996). Sexism in graduate school classrooms: Consequences for students and faculty. *Gender and Society, 10*, 330–350.

Pharr, S. (1988). *Homophobia: A weapon of sexism.* Chardon Press.

Pincus, F. L. (1996). Discrimination comes in many forms. *American Behavioral Scientist, 40*, 186–194.

Reid, P. T., & Comas-Diaz, L. (1990). Gender and ethnicity: Perspectives on dual status. *Sex Roles, 22*, 397–408.

Rich, A. (1979). *On lies, secrets and silence: Selected prose (1966-1973).* New York: Norton.

Smith, R. (1998). Challenging privelege: White male middle-class opposition in the multicultural education terrain. In R. C. Chavez & J. O'Donnell (Eds.), *Speaking the unpleasant: The politics of (non)engagement in the multicultural education terrain* (pp. 197–210). Albany, NY: State University of New York Press.

Spence, J. T., & Hahn, E. D. (1997). The attitudes toward women scale and attitude change in college students. *Psychology of Women Quarterly, 21*, 17–34.

Swim, J. K., Aikin, K. J., Hall, W. S., & Hunter, B. A. (1995). Sexism and racism: Old-fashioned and modern prejudices. *Journal of Personality and Social Psychology, 68*, 199–214.

Swim, J. K., & Cohen, L. L. (1997). Overt, covert, and subtle sexism: A comparison between the attitudes toward women and modern sexism scales. *Psychology of Women Quarterly, 21,* 103–118.

Swim, J. K., Cohen, L. L., & Hyers, L. L. (1998). Experiencing everyday prejudice and discrimination. In J. K. Swim & C. Stangor (Eds.), *Prejudice: The target's perspective* (pp. 37–60). San Diego, CA: Academic Press.

Tavris, C. (1996). The mismeasure of woman. In K. E. Rosenblum & T-M. C. Travis (Eds.), *The meaning of difference* (pp. 336–353). New York: McGraw-Hill.

Twenge, J. M. (1997). Attitudes toward women, 1970-1995: A meta-analysis. *Psychology of Women Quarterly, 21,* 35–51.

Weber, L. (1998). A conceptual framework for understanding race, class, gender, and sexuality. *Psychology of Women Quarterly, 22*, 13–32.

# 5

# Women and Work

## Janice D. Yoder

## INTRODUCTION

Before reading this chapter, if you are a college student, pause for a moment to consider what your plans are for after graduation. Do you project that you will work full-time, get married, have a child or children, etc.? Also think about the sequence of these plans. If some of these decisions have already been made in your life, consider someone younger such as a daughter or friend or remember what you planned in your early twenties. It also makes a difference if these projections are for women or men, so think about a woman (if not yourself, then a potential or real wife, daughter, etc.).

Karen Schroeder and her colleagues (1992) asked these questions of 292 traditional aged undergraduate women and their parents at the University of Rhode Island. The most popular sequence, endorsed by 56 percent of the students and a majority of parents for their daughters, projected graduation, full-time employment, then marriage, children, stopping work at least until the youngest child is in school, then returning to full-time employment. An additional 18 percent selected the same scenario but planned to return to work earlier. Not one student described a full-time career with no marriage.

Only 12 percent of these undergraduate women expected to graduate, work full-time, get married, have children, and continue work with only minor interruptions for childbirth. Indeed, other research finds that continuously employed mothers are regarded less favorably by college students than mothers who interrupt their careers (Bridges & Etaugh, 1995). Employed mothers are regarded by student raters as less well adjusted (Etaugh & Poertner, 1991) and as less dedicated to their families (Etaugh & Nekolny, 1990) than nonemployed mothers. These projections stand in stark contrast to the demographic facts that in 1998 a majority of women with a child age one or under (61.8 percent) and with preschoolers (65.7 percent) were employed (U.S. Bureau of the Census, 1999).

In this chapter, we grapple with some basic issues about women and work. We begin by exploring the meaning of work in women's lives, then go on to describe the reality of women's employment in the United States. We note that the workplace is different for women and men, then continue on to explore two areas that may contribute to this difference: women's occupa-

Janice D. Yoder • Department of Psychology, University of Akron, Akron, Ohio 44325–4301

*Issues in the Psychology of Women,* edited by Biaggio and Hersen. Kluwer Academic/Plenum Publishers, New York, 2000.

tional "choices" and family-to-work "conflict." We conclude by describing some changes designed to create a women-friendly workplace.

## THE MEANING OF WORK

Social scientists generally define work as the production of goods and services that are of value to others (Fox & Hesse-Biber, 1984). Using this definition, women's "work" monopolizes much of their waking lives. Globally, unpaid work includes family-related services (e.g., childcare and housework), subsistence and nonmarket activities (e.g., agricultural production for household consumption), and household enterprises (e.g., keeping the books for a family business) (United Nations, 1995). A disproportionate share of this unpaid and undervalued work is done by women. In developed countries, we typically think of what we "do" as our employment status, and it is this admittedly narrow definition of work that is used in this chapter.

Women accounted for fully 46 percent of the labor force in the United States in 1994 (U.S. Department of Labor, 1995). Nearly 6 of every 10 women over 16 years old (58.8 percent) were employed, with participation rates of more than 70 percent for women in their prime employment years (ages 20 to 54). Overall participation rates vary little by race and ethnicity: 60 percent of Asian and Pacific Islander women, 58.9 percent of white women, 58.7 percent of African-American women, 55 percent of American Indian women, and 52.9 percent of Latinas worked for pay in 1994 (Herz & Wootton, 1996). This translates into 57 million employed U.S. women, 41 million of whom worked more than 35 hours each week. Of the 16 million women employed part-time, 3.3 million held multiple jobs.

Surveys of why women work conclude that they are employed for the same reasons as men: for financial reasons, to fulfill identity needs (James, 1990), and to function as competent and productive members of society (Chester & Grossman, 1990). Financial reasons are often more pressing than stereotypes about women working for discretionary "pin money" suggest. Fully 43 percent of employed U.S. women support themselves, with workforce participation rates of 65.1 percent for never married, 17.3 percent for widowed, and 73.9 percent for divorced women (Herz & Wootton, 1996). Families maintained solely by a woman in 1994 accounted for one-quarter of those with children (8 million families compared to 1.4 million supported by single men). Fully 23 percent of mothers in the workforce are single parents (compared to only 4 percent of fathers) (Galinsky & Bond, 1996). And, single-parenting is associated with poverty, but more so for women (in 1993, half of female-headed families with children lived in poverty compared to 25 percent for parallel male-headed families).

## THE REALITY OF WOMEN'S EMPLOYMENT

Stop for a moment and think about women and men workers. Whom do you picture? Think across a wide range of jobs: college professors, maintenance workers, firefighters, senators, physicians and nurses, telephone operators, and so on. Who comes to mind? How does this relate to the pay and prestige associated with these occupations? Two fundamental features distinguish women's experiences in the U.S. workplace from those of men: the wage gap and the occupations in which women and men cluster (occupational segregation).

### The Wage Gap

The wage gap is the simple ratio of women's to men's earnings subtracted from 1.0. If women's and men's earnings were identical, this earnings ratio would be 1.0 and the wage gap would be nonexistent. In real life, there is a gap (of 28.6 percent) (Institute for Women's Policy Research, 1997), and it disadvantages women:

$$\text{1995 Earnings Ratio} = \frac{\text{median annual earnings of full–time employed women}}{\text{median annual earnings of full–time employed men}} = \frac{\$22,497}{\$31,496} = 0.714$$

Different sources may use different measures of earnings (e.g., weekly wages) to calculate the earnings ratio, but the definition above is the one recommended by the U.S. Census Bureau as best representative of actual incomes. Whatever definitions are used, no one has managed to close the gap simply by using different measures.

## Facts about the Gap

The wage gap tends to widen as women and men spend more time working, but even at career entry, the earnings ratio is estimated to be 84 percent, yielding a gap in starting salaries of 16 percent (Marini & Fan, 1997). Earnings ratios vary across race and ethnicity. Using white men as the denominator (base), the earnings ratio for white women is 71.2 percent; 64.2 percent for African-American women; and 53.4 percent for Latinas (Institute for Women's Policy Research, 1997). Lesbians earn less than heterosexual women (Institute for Gay and Lesbian Strategic Studies, 1996), and disabled women earn 69 percent of what women in general earn (Russo & Jansen, 1988).

The gap has narrowed somewhat recently. From 1955 through 1987, the earnings ratio in the United States fluctuated between 58.8 percent and 65.2 percent. The earnings ratio crept into the low 70 percents in the early 1990s, but stalled in the mid-1990s (Lewin, 1997). If the earnings ratio is calculated in dollars adjusted for inflation, fully 75 percent of the narrowing in the gap between 1979 and 1995 is accounted for by losses in men's wages (Roos & Reskin, 1992). Although reducing men's wages indeed would narrow the gap, this certainly is not what labor activists are advocating.

The United States lags behind other countries in closing the wage gap. During the 1970s and 1980s, when the earnings ratio was relatively stable in the United States, substantial gains were being made in European countries to narrow the gap (Hewlett, 1986). Looking globally in the 1990s, the earnings ratio was highest (around 90 percent) in Tanzania, Iceland, France, and Australia; only Japan (50 percent), Korea, Cyprus, and Egypt reported lower earnings ratios than the United States (United Nations, 1991).

## Closing the Gap

A complex and highly controversial debate has raged over what causes the gap between earnings of women and men. Some potential causes can be discarded when we compare women and men with parallel characteristics.

For example, one argument contends that the wage gap will narrow when women achieve the same educational credentials as men. The education gap between women and men has narrowed and even closed at some levels: in 1993–94, women earned 59 percent of all associate's degrees, 54 percent of all bachelor's degrees, 55 percent of all master's degrees, 39 percent of all doctorates, and 41 percent of all professional degrees (U.S. Department of Education, 1996, Table 239, p. 253). For differences in education to explain the wage gap, however, we would expect women and men with similar educational backgrounds to earn comparable incomes. This is not the case. In 1995, women college graduates earned wages (mean = $26,841) close to those of male high-school graduates ($26,333), not male college graduates ($46,111) (Institute for Women's Policy Research, 1997). Although higher levels of education indeed are associated with higher earnings, education is not a plausible explanation for the wage gap.

Similar reasoning debunks other proposed explanations for the wage gap. When continuously employed women were compared to noninterrupting men, the gap in their earnings remained (Rix, 1988). When women who relocated for the purpose of career advancement were compared to relocated men, the gap persisted (Stroh, Brett, & Reilly, 1992). Although women do differ from men in general on these dimensions, even when women have "all the right stuff," that is, when women do not interrupt and relocate just like men, the wage gap is unaffected.

There are other proposed explanations for the wage gap that can be discarded because they predict differences between women and men that are not supported by gender comparisons. For example, psychologists have suggested that women lack the achievement motivation of men (Horner, 1970; Piedmont, 1995; Thorne, 1995). There is no solid research evidence to suggest that women are any more or less driven to succeed than men given comparable circumstances for advancement (Jacobs & McClelland, 1994). Similarly, when circumstances are parallel, women and men are just as likely to view their successes as products of their own ability (Mednick & Thomas, 1993). Thus, a key to finding similarities between women and men may be to situate them in the same occupational context.

## Occupational Segregation

The obvious next question then becomes: What occupational contexts are parallel for women and men? The simple answer is "whenever they do the same work," but let us not be too quick to accept this. A good starting point is to ask how often women and men indeed do the same work.

### Facts about Occupational Segregation

The second basic fact about the reality of the contemporary American work force is that women and men tend to work in different occupations. The top ten occupations for women in 1990 were secretary, elementary school teacher, cashier, registered nurse, bookkeeper and accounting clerk, nurse's aide, salaried manager and administrator, sales representative for minor commodities, waitress, and salaried sales supervisor and proprietor (Reskin & Padavic, 1994). When you think of these occupations, do you picture men? Only two of these occupations make men's top-ten list (salaried manager and administrator; salaried sales supervisor and proprietor). Furthermore, women's top-ten list has been remarkably stable: since 1940, the only change has been the addition of salaried managers (also see Biblarz, Bengston, & Bucur, 1996).

The extent to which the labor force is gender segregated is captured in the index of segregation, a figure that represents the proportion of all female and male workers who would need to exchange occupations in order to achieve genuine integration with 50:50 representation across the board. With zero indicating a completely integrated work force and 100 a completely segregated one, the 1990 index of segregation was 53, meaning that 53 percent of working women and men would need to switch occupations. Although this figure is an improvement over the 65 to 69 rate that characterized 1900–1970 (Jacobs, 1989; Reskin, 1993), for every woman lawyer in 1990, there were 101 women doing clerical work, 33 women operating factory machines, 30 sales clerks, 9 nurses' aides, and 8 waitresses (Reskin & Padavic, 1994).

Adjusting for the influx of women into the labor force between 1960 and 1980, over-representation of white men in prestigious male-dominated occupations actually increased across this 20-year span (Sokoloff, 1988). This pattern of gendered occupations extends within women to racial and ethnic groupings (Anderson & Shapiro, 1996). For example, the occupation of cook is unique to the top-ten list for African-American women; janitor/cleaner and maid/"houseman" appear only in the lists for African-American and Latina women; and accountant/auditor emerges only for Asian-American women (Reskin & Padavic, 1994). The critical factor that links occupational segregation to the wage gap is the truism that "women's work" is typically low paying, even for men employed in these occupations (England & Herbert, 1993).

In sum, although there is some overlap between the occupations pursued by women and men, many American workers share occupations mostly with members of their own sex. According to the 1990 census, fully one-third of the 56 million employed U.S. women were concentrated in those top-ten occupations we discussed, and remember that only two of these attracted large numbers of men (Reskin & Padavic, 1994). One of every ten employed women worked in the clerical occupations of secretary, typist, stenographer, and office clerk. Looked at another way, only 11 percent of employed women worked in occupations that were at least 75 percent male. This division of the workplace into "women's" and "men's" work perpetuates the wage gap by making it difficult to directly compare the contributions of women and men. In fact, demographers estimate that fully one-third of the earnings gap is accounted for by gender segregation (Cotter, DeFiore, & Hermsen, 1995).

## Same Occupation, Different Context

What happens when women and men do the same work? Is being a firefighter, for example, the same for women and men? Given the extent of occupational segregation in the American workforce, it makes sense that when women and men are in the same occupation, they are not necessarily in similar contexts. For example, women who do "men's work" break occupational norms about what jobs are appropriate for women, and they typically are employed in work groups of mostly men. Researchers find that costs accrue to both of these "deviations."

Undergraduate students regard women doing "men's" work (such as engineers and electricians) as less positively feminine, less likeable, and less attractive, and they socially distance themselves from these workers (Yoder & Schleicher, 1996). Women in nontraditional occupations are least preferred as heterosexual romantic partners (Pfost & Fiore, 1990). In sum, these women are regarded as occupational deviates (Laws, 1975).

Other researchers have explored what it is like for women to work in skewed groups composed of 85 percent or more men where they operate as "tokens" (Kanter, 1977). Looking across a wide range of diverse occupations from military cadets to transit operatives and firefighters, a consistent pattern emerges (see Zimmer, 1988; Yoder, 1991, for reviews). Because of their difference and heightened visibility, these women report high levels of stress, social isolation, role conflicts, sexual harassment, wage inequities, and blocked upward mobility. These negative outcomes are intensified and expanded to other costs for women who differ from the dominant group of workers along multiple dimensions, such as African-American women firefighters (Yoder & Aniakudo, 1997) and police officers (Martin, 1994). These women describe continual attempts to subordinate and exclude them, oftentimes coming from multiple sources including African American male and white female co-workers.

# UNDERSTANDING WOMEN'S WORK

The argument that I am making here is that employment is different for women and men: different in terms of wages and different in terms of occupations, at times even when women and men perform the same work. I believe these differences undermine the possibility of developing a single approach to understanding employment that works for both women and men (Osipow & Fitzgerald, 1996). Instead, girls and boys grow up in different environments, and as adults, work in different environments (Betz, 1989).

Although there is a wide array of areas through which we might explore this thesis, I have elected to concentrate on two here: (1) occupational "choice" (how women come to pursue one occupation over a vast array of possibilities) and (2) family–work involvement, a combination that affects many women and in ways that vary for women and men. Both merit a discussion that is specific to women and women's lives independent from normative expectations we typically hold about men and men's employment.

## Occupational "Choice"

When I ask my 14-year-old daughter, Kate, what she wants to be when she grows up, I like to think that the possibilities are boundless, that only her interests and abilities will limit her free choices. To explain how workers select their occupations, most theories of career development incorporate concepts of expectancies and values (Astin, 1984; Eccles, 1994; Farmer, 1985; Hackett & Betz, 1981). To pursue an occupation, Kate needs to feel that she can succeed at it (expectancies) and value that type of work. Researchers find that girls as young as kindergartners aspire to traditional female careers (Stroeher, 1994). Even their made-up stories reflect these limitations: male characters are portrayed in a wide range of exciting and attainable occupations (e.g., doctor, astronaut, and police officer) in contrast to female characters who are consigned to "women's" work (e.g., princess, cook, nurse, babysitter, and teacher) (Trepanier & Romatowski, 1985).

Obviously, girls' and boys' expectations and values do not develop in a vacuum; rather, they are influenced significantly by socialization experiences in childhood and throughout their lives by the culture's structure of opportunity including the gender-typing of occupations, hiring biases, discrimination, and so on (Astin, 1984). It is these external pressures that may limit the pool of occupations Kate may even consider and that may promise costs for making "wrong" choices. Thus we need to ask how much choice is truly involved in vocational "choice."

Two strands of research are consistent with this speculation. The first looks at "unsocialized" women, that is, exceptional women who break away from prevailing socialization practices that channel girls and women into traditional pursuits. Women who pursue male-dominated occupations tend to exhibit high levels of instrumentality combined with positive aspects of expressiveness (Lemkau, 1979), to express egalitarian attitudes toward women's roles in society, to feel self-confident, to report a high achievement orientation and feminist identification, and to describe a high quality relationship with their mother (Betz, 1993; Fassinger, 1985; O'Brien & Fassinger, 1993). This research explores the factors that *pull* girls and women in unlikely directions.

The second strand of research explores barriers to women's full participation across occupations, examining the factors that *push* girls and women away from nontraditional pursuits. The range of these barriers is extensive, and the following list is far from exhaustive, although each item is firmly rooted in empirical findings. For example, researchers find that there is a tendency to devalue work attributed to women working in groups of mostly men

(Sackett, DuBois, & Noe, 1991). This promises that women doing "men's" work will have to work harder and be more capable than their male co-workers (Pugh & Wahrman, 1983). Stereotypes of leadership encourage men to emerge as the leaders of leaderless groups, suggesting that women who aspire to leader roles must overcome much bias (Eagly & Karau, 1991). In fact, this preference for male leaders translates into a view of "think manager, think male" (Schein, Mueller, Lituchy, & Lui, 1996). Hiring biases are documented such that business professionals prefer women for feminine jobs and men for masculine ones (Branscombe & Smith, 1990; Glick, Zion, & Nelson, 1988) and evaluate gender-congruent candidates as stronger applicants (Towson, Zanna, & MacDonald, 1989). These patterns predict problems for women seeking to access male-dominated occupations. Finally, evidence of "glass ceilings" and "concrete walls" suggests that promotion opportunities open to women and men of color will be blocked (Federal Glass Ceiling Commission, 1995). Given the reality of all these barriers, is it so surprising that many girls dream about being princesses and nurses, not astronauts and police*men*?

## Family–Work Involvement

Whether a woman's employment is traditional or not, a commonly cited barrier to women's full participation in the workforce is the distraction of familial obligations. We saw at the beginning of this chapter that many college women believe that combining employment with mothering (at least of young children) is personally undesirable and fraught with negative expectations about working mothers. Interestingly, Kathleen Gerson (1985) reports that attitudes of seemingly different childless careerists and full-time homemakers converge around a shared belief that employment and childrearing are incompatible (the two groups just made opposite choices). Even intellectually gifted high-school girls report that they would be willing to make occupational sacrifices for family, reflecting an assumption that work and family are incompatible (Jozefowicz, Barber, & Eccles, 1993). Management students and executives believe that women's career success unfavorably impacts family life (Westman & Etzion, 1990) and that women should relinquish employment in response to familial demands (Janman, 1989). In sum, popular attitudes across a wide range of respondents indicate that people believe that employment affects family life and that women shoulder the responsibility for remedying this.

Jacquelynne Eccles (1994) argues that women are expected to assume this responsibility because women and men have different work/family mandates. Because men are expected to be breadwinners, they fulfill their family role through successful employment. In contrast, work and family are expected to be separate, and sometimes conflicting, spheres for women. Indeed, interviews with 40 employed and married mothers and fathers of children under 18 revealed that men's definition of "good fathers" as economic supporters contrasted with women's description of "good mothers" for whom employment was an added responsibility separate from their primary obligations to family (Simon, 1995). Women's family obligations are expected to encompass household chores and caregiving, activities totally separate from work-related success.

### Women's Domestic Workload

Moving from expectations about women's roles to what women actually do, family–work conflict is predominantly a women's problem only if women are doing more of this unpaid and undervalued work. Looking at household tasks, an extensive body of research evidence leads to the same conclusion: women perform a disproportionate share of household labor (Baxter, 1992; Beckwith, 1992; Biernat & Wortman, 1991; Moore, 1995; Starrels, 1994). This pattern holds regardless of socioeconomic class (Wright, Shire, Hwang, Dolan, & Baxter, 1992) and regardless of race and ethnicity (John & Shelton, 1997).

How much time are we describing? The household tasks with the greatest time demands (because they must be done repeatedly and within a limited timeframe) include meal preparation, clean-up, grocery shopping, housecleaning, and laundry—that is, chores typically designated as "women's" work (Beckwith, 1992). On average, women do about 80 percent of these tasks, contributing about 30 hours per week (Blair & Lichter, 1991). This pattern is constant across Anglo, African-American, and Latina/Latino couples (John, Shelton, & Luschen, 1995) and across many developed countries (United Nations, 1995). If this runs counter to your sense that men are doing more around the house, contrast their current 20 percent with their contributions in 1965: 8 percent (Robinson, 1988).

If such division has something to do with who has more time to expend on these tasks, we might predict that dual-earner families will have a more egalitarian split. Research findings are not consistent with this reasoning: there are no increases in men's participation when comparing dual-earning to male-earning families (Baxter, 1992; Bittman & Lovejoy, 1993; Douthitt, 1989; Shelton, 1990) or women's full-time to part-time employment (Hossain & Roopnarine, 1993). What does seem to change with women's employment is not the proportion of their contributions but the absolute time involved. Employed women's time contributions often shrink so that household chores are done more efficiently, less elaborately, or not at all (Baxter, 1992; Douthitt, 1989; Robinson, 1988).

Turning to caregiving, a parallel pattern emerges. If we define caregiving in a broad sense as informal caregiving to parents, adult children, and friends and formal caregiving in volunteer and local groups, then married women contribute about twice as many hours per month (over 60 hours) as their husbands (Gerstel & Gallagher, 1994). When caretaking is confined to the care of children, fathers contribute fewer hours (about 26 percent) and tend to do the less nitty-gritty tasks (e.g., playing with children) (Tiedje & Darling-Fisher, 1993). Although these figures reveal disparate time contributions, they do little to elucidate our understanding of who does the caring-about, as opposed to the caring-for (caretaking), aspect of "mothering" (Traustadottir, 1991).

The relative contributions of women and men to family life fit with speculation that family–work conflict is more pressing for more women than men. However, even this statement makes a questionable assumption focused on the word "conflict." We assume that multiple roles lead to overload and conflict, affecting both the well-being of the "juggler" and her ability to contribute fully to her career.

## Multiple Roles and Well-being

There is some evidence to support the notion that multiple roles negatively affect women. For example, employed mothers report more role overload than employed fathers (Cooke & Rousseau, 1984; Crosby, 1991; Pleck, 1985). Multiple role demands have even been linked to psychophysiological arousal both on and off work (Lundberg, 1996). However, a competing theory, the enhancement hypothesis, posits that multiple roles serve as buffers against undesirable consequences in any subset of roles. For example, if difficulties arise at work, the enhancement hypothesis predicts that people who can go home and find solace in strong family ties will be less seriously affected (Baruch & Barnett, 1986).

Faye Crosby (1991) concludes that at least three benefits may accrue from holding multiple roles such as spouse, parent, and worker. When multiple roles create true variety, not just interruptions, they enrich women's psychological well-being. Multiple roles provide multiple audiences—a variety of people to talk to and get feedback from. In addition, multiple roles can provide refuge when difficulties arise in one role. However, the likelihood of realizing any of these benefits is reduced if one does not control her or his own time.

Crosby's observations fit with other research evidence. For example, multiple roles have been associated with longevity (Moen, Dempster-McClain, & Williams, 1989) and, re-latedly, physical health (Adelmann, 1994a; Hibbard & Pope, 1991) for both African-American and white women (Waldron & Jacobs, 1989). This relationship extends to psychological well-being (Vandewater, Ostrove, & Stewart, 1997) and a sense of self-efficacy (Adelmann, 1994b), as well as mental health outcomes (Barnett, 1997). Women returning to school at a community college were found to be happier if they occupied the three roles of partner, mother, and paid employee than if they filled none or only one of these (Kopp & Ruzicka, 1993). Finally, employment has been shown to buffer against family strain (Barnett & Marshall, 1992); single and childless women experienced more distress as their job-role quality declined than did similarly job-disillusioned partnered women and mothers (Barnett, Marshall, & Singer, 1992). This last relationship is moderated by how challenging employment is—parental distress is lowered only for women employed in challenging jobs (Barnett, Marshall, & Sayer, 1992).

This combination of perspectives and findings merges in a single study of 118 employed mothers of preschoolers aged 23 to 43 months (Rankin, 1993). Of the 100 mothers who described their lives as stressful, fully 62 percent reported high levels of stress. The major sources of their stress were lack of time, child-related problems, and maternal guilt. At the same time, these women reported rewards including personal benefits, financial rewards, and improved family lives.

A key to understanding how holding many roles may affect an individual may rest not in the simple number of roles assumed, but in the quality of those roles. When the balance of pluses and minuses associated with a role is favorable, then this role is related to positive psychological well-being (Baruch & Barnett, 1986). Also, individuals differ in what they want from the roles they enact. For example, 118 women college seniors who were autonomous in defining their roles across the next 14 years of their lives, and thus felt less restricted by conventional dictates, sought excellence in multiple roles with low levels of role conflict (Jenkins, 1996). Finally, doing what one believes in is important. Employed single mothers of preschool children reported strong psychological well-being when they believed that maternal employment does not harm children and regarded their childcare arrangements as of high quality (Goldberg et al., 1992). In sum, multiple roles appear positive for some women and under some supportive circumstances.

## Family–Work Effects

We have seen that women shoulder a disproportionate share of domestic responsibilities in terms of household chores and caregiving contributions. Although assuming many roles may lead to overload and role conflict at times, it also is possible for multiple role holders to derive benefits from their many and varied responsibilities. The critical role that family–work involvement plays in understanding women's work focuses on the assumption that women's family commitments interfere with their full participation in the workplace. We already have seen that people expect that workers, mostly women, with heavy family obligations will be less productive employees (Janman, 1989). Indeed, one justification for the wage gap is that women voluntarily pursue lower paying occupations that are more compatible with children's schedules. However, an analysis of the occupations in which women dominate finds these to be no more compatible with family responsibilities than other occupations (Glass, 1990).

The bottom line question is: Are family-committed employees less effective workers? The research findings to date are inconsistent. Nancy Betz and Louise Fitzgerald (1987) reviewed this literature and concluded that being married and having children negatively affect career involvement and achievement. This conclusion is supported by recent studies finding lower earnings among women with children (Waldfogel, 1997) and with disproportionate responsibility for domestic chores (Cannings, 1991). On the other hand, a study of women scientists found no difference in the number of research papers published by married women with children and single women without children (Cole & Zuckerman, 1987). Another study with women personnel professionals uncovered no relationship between family-work conflict and career progress (Nelson, Quick, Hitt, & Moesel, 1990).

The most direct test of whether family obligations affect wages comes from a survey of 925 women and men who earned their MBA degrees between 1975 and 1980 (Schneer & Reitman, 1993). Controlling for age, hours worked, experience, employment discontinuities, and field of responsibility, single women without children earned about 12 percent *less* than married women with children and an employed spouse (the circumstances under which we'd expect the most family-to-work disruption). Furthermore, the family-involved women were at least as satisfied with their careers as women with other familial configurations. Speculating about their findings, Joy Schneer and Freida Reitman suggest that although single, childless women have been considered the least encumbered employees, they also are the most mobile and thus less attached to an organization. This may translate into greater acceptance of employed mothers as valuable resources (Vanderkolk & Young, 1991).

General employment trends make it clear that employed mothers are not an anomaly, and there is nothing to suggest that mothers' participation in the workforce will decline in the near future.[1] Rather than questioning if mothers are effective workers, both women and employers might be better served if we strive to make the workplace work for women. We have seen that many people expect family demands to interfere with work responsibilities, and we know that expectancies can become self-fulfilling. Might expectations that women will be encumbered by families limit the opportunities some women are given? If so, workplace effectiveness is not being restricted by family itself, but rather by stereotyped expectations. Following this reasoning, we might want to compare family-friendly with family-incompatible workplaces. If we find family-to-work costs in nonsupportive contexts but not in supportive ones, this may help account for some of the inconsistencies in this literature. Certainly more research looking for possible contextual variation is warranted. Recent data suggest that although families add significantly to the workloads of women (and some men), they do not interfere significantly with workplace participation.

## CREATING A WOMEN-FRIENDLY WORKPLACE

Across all the topics explored in this chapter, we have seen that employment is not the same for women and men. In general, women are paid less, are likely to work in a restricted number of female-dominated occupations, are subtly pulled into traditional choices and pushed away from nontraditional pursuits, and are expected to be less productive because of the competing demands of family life (although the reality of these expectations is debatable). Two undeniable truisms of the contemporary American work force are that women are a sizable part of it and that their numbers are unlikely to shrink (Outtz, 1996). This understanding

---

[1] It is easy to find stories in the media about "dropout moms" who leave the workforce to raise children. Although dropout rates among women of childbearing age were substantial through the 1970s, since then women's labor force participation rates have been stable among these age groups (Outtz, 1996).

leads us to explore what supports can be provided for women to increase their productivity and satisfaction as employees. The possibilities presented here include individual, organizational, and societal strategies. Although far from exhaustive, each suggestion is grounded in supportive research findings.

## Individual Possibilities

A recurring theme in this chapter is that there is little, if any, solid evidence from which to argue that deficiencies in women as a group are responsible for their devalued status in the workplace. Women with "all the right stuff," such as education, high levels of career commitment and aspirations, willingness to relocate, assertiveness, and so on, still face barriers. Although this approach does not blame women for their status, neither does it reduce them to helpless pawns in an immutable system. In this section, we discuss some ideas about what individual women can do to both expand their "choices" and work to remove barriers. We explore socialization practices, language, domestic sharing, individuation strategies, mentoring, and working in unity with other women as ways to contribute at an individual level to creating a women-friendly workplace.

### Socializing Nontraditional Workers

We have seen that "unsocialized" women, that is women who reject gender-limited stereotypes about occupations, are more likely to pursue nontraditional options. As socializing agents for the next generation of workers, we each can strive to expand the occupational choices considered realistic by girls.

Sandra Bem (1983) offers one suggestion for doing this. Bem recognizes that there are strong and persistent societal pressures, such as media representations, peers' and teachers' attitudes and sanctions, language, and even the people children encounter doing different jobs. These pressures converge to teach children that there are separate spheres for women and men workers. One way for parents and others to challenge these trends is to help children develop a "sexism schema": that is, a cognitive framework for thinking about the gendered nature of occupations. For example, when girls hear discussions about firemen and see mostly, if not all, portrayals of firefighters as men, their sexism schema will help them not internalize the notion that firefighting excludes women, but rather regard this outcome as a product of sexism. In this way, "unsocialized" girls can grow up in a context they indeed understand, but reject its message.

### Watch Your Language!

The language we use to describe people and things, including workers and occupations, can influence how we think about them (Whorf, 1956). For example, Janet Hyde (1984) described the fictional job of "wudgemaking" to elementary school children. One-quarter of the children heard wudgemakers described using masculine pronouns (he, his); others heard feminine pronouns (she, her); and the remaining children heard gender-inclusive (he or she) or gender-neutral (they) language. Children thought men would make good wudgemakers regardless of the pronoun used. In contrast, the pronoun affected their projections for women. Both girls and boys who heard wudgemakers described with "he" evaluated women as "just OK" potential wudgemakers. Children's ratings of women wudgemakers became more positive in response to both gender-neutral (they) and gender-inclusive (he or she) versions. Women were considered the best at wudgemaking when the description used the female-specific pronoun "she." These data lead me to speculate that when we hear terms such as fire*men* and phrases such as "the nurse, she . . . ," our language contributes to our views about the gender-appropriateness of firefighting and nursing and thus helps channel our "choices."

## Domestic Sharing

Although we have seen that there is little empirical support for our expectations that family demands will interfere with work productivity and satisfaction, it seems intuitively reasonable to argue that more egalitarian sharing of domestic responsibilities would benefit employed women. There is ample evidence to conclude that egalitarian attitudes are not sufficient to produce egalitarian behaviors (Bittman & Lovejoy, 1993; Hochschild, 1989). Rather, equal sharing results from continual vigliance and commitment to achieving equity (Blaisure & Allen, 1995; Gerson, 1993). These sentiments are captured in the words of a husband whom both partners regard as equal-sharing:

> I think it is really possible to have equality or a nonoppressive marriage but it is not something that sort of happens and you say "Zap, now we got it," and you go on. You have to constantly communicate and sometimes it swings a little bit more toward the other . . . You have to ensure that equality maintains itself. (Blaisure & Allen, 1995, p. 13)

## Individuating Job Applicants

We have seen that women's access to nontraditional occupations may be compromised by hiring biases that disadvantage gender-incongruent candidates. To directly counter the tendency to prefer men for masculine and women for feminine jobs, individuating information is helpful (but not fully compensatory).

For example, Peter Glick and his colleagues (1988) "masculinized" the fictitious resumes of female and male applicants by giving them summer jobs in a sports store (as opposed to a feminine jewelry store), a work-study job in grounds maintenance (vs. aerobics instructor), and captain of the varsity basketball team (vs. pep squad). They found that masculinizing information about female candidates for a position in sales management in a heavy machinery company enhanced their likelihood of being interviewed, although being male was an even stronger predictor (also see Branscombe & Smith, 1990). In general, candidates who seem to mesh with the gender orientation of a job are considered stronger applicants (Towson, Zanna, & MacDonald, 1989). Sometimes giving the impression of a good fit simply requires some semantic reframing. For example, my husband advised a woman graduate student to list her hobby truthfully as a "marathoner," not a "jogger," when she applied for a masculine-typed position.

## Mentoring

Individual women can help promote other women on the job by mentoring them. Although a stereotype about women "queen bees" portrays women as refusing to mentor junior women (Staines, Tauris, & Jayaratne, 1974), researchers find high levels of interest in being a mentor among women (Ragins & Cotton, 1993), especially when the work climate encourages it (Yoder, Adams, Grove, & Priest, 1985). Mentoring works. Business school graduates, both women and men, who experienced extensive mentoring reported more promotions, higher incomes, and greater satisfaction with their pay and benefits than those for whom mentoring was superficial or nonexistent (Dreher & Ash, 1990). These benefits extend to global job satisfaction (Mobley, Jaret, Marsh, & Lim, 1994) and to a diversity of women, such as African-American university administrators (Ramey, 1995).

## *Unity with Diversity*

Finally, individual action for change can be very effective when it is conducted in unison with others. For example, Ann Bookman and Sandra Morgen (1988) present case studies of working-class women in a variety of occupations from domestic service to electronics factory workers and street vendors that illustrate how women can work together to empower themselves and promote community activism.

Somewhat paradoxically, central to bringing women together is understanding diversity (Collins, 1986; Dill, 1983; hooks, 1984; MacPherson & Fine, 1995). Throughout this section on creating a women-friendly workplace, the emphasis is on "women" (plural). A women-friendly workplace must include all women as well as recognize and respond to their differences (Sanchez-Hucles, 1997).

For example, when the U.S. Department of Labor formed a Federal Glass Ceiling Commission to examine blocked promotion opportunities for women, it used as its central metaphor, the "glass ceiling." A key feature of the glass ceiling is its transparency: promotions are cloaked in a guise of fairness so that women cannot readily see the barriers that are holding them back. This is not the case for many women of color who realize, quite clearly, that their upward progress is blocked by an intertwining of sexism and racism. In recognition of this key difference, the Federal Glass Ceiling Commission captured the perceptions of African-Americans with the imagery of a "concrete wall."

## Organizational Possibilities

Here we explore some actions organizations, such as businesses, colleges and universities, the military, and so on, can take to reduce barriers to women's full and equitable participation. Some possibilities grow from and support what we have covered under individual possibilities. For example, educational institutions could include gender-sensitivity as part of the curriculum for teacher training. Although far from comprehensive, two areas studied by researchers involve hiring practices and on-the-job supports.

### *Hiring Practices*

For women to access male-dominated occupations (and men to enter female-dominated ones), employers need to scrutinize and monitor their hiring practices. Bernice Lott (1985) concluded that women's competence is most likely to be devalued when little is know about the candidate by the evaluator, when the evaluation is real (as opposed to a laboratory simulation), and when the evaluator's decision has consequences for her or him. Such a combination of factors frequently describes job hiring. This trend can be countered by providing more individuating information about candidates, especially if it "masculinizes" women applying for masculine jobs (Glick, Zion, & Nelson, 1988). The inclusion of evaluators not directly affected by the hiring decision would work to offset the final tendency noted by Lott.

### *On-the-Job Supports*

Our understanding of how women's competence is evaluated carries over from hiring to working on the job and being promoted (or not). For example, psychological testimony in a Supreme Court case, *Price Waterhouse v. Hopkins*, highlighted the role negative stereotyping played in the accounting firm's decision to deny promotion to Ann Hopkins (Fiske, Borgida, Deaux, & Heilman, 1991). Ms. Hopkins logged more billable hours than any of the other 87 all-male candidates being considered with her, but she was described as a "lady partner candidate" who was "macho," "overcompensated for being a woman," and needed a "course at charm school." Indeed, a U.S. Department of Labor report (1991) on top women executives found that women were more likely to be evaluated according to their ability to get along with people, in contrast to men, whose work-related productivity was assessed. In sum, despite similar education, ability, and experience, researchers find that women working in groups of mostly men challenge male-congenial stereotypes (Sackett, DuBois, & Noe, 1991).

Organizations can take positive steps to offset these biases. Researchers find that reliance on sexist stereotypes is reduced when evaluators are freed from competing demands and thus can spend sufficient time on constructing their evaluations (Martell, 1991). Gender bias in performance appraisals and salary allocation increases as tasks become more unpredictable, variable, complex, and interdependent (Auster, 1989). Thus, biases are minimized when evaluation criteria are linked to well-defined, observable behaviors (Fiske & Taylor, 1991) and evaluators are publicly accountable for their decisions (Tetlock, 1992). Finally, the more individuating information a rater has about an employee, the less she or he will rely on stereotypes (Fiske & Von Hendy, 1992).

Organizations can work to empower individuals. For example, followers' evaluations of a leader's effectiveness were influenced more by their perceptions of the leader's power than by the leader's gender (Ragins, 1991). One way that organizations can empower women is to legitimate their expertise. In a laboratory simulation conducted with my students, we appointed a woman to lead an all-male group on a masculine task, giving her position power (Yoder, Schleicher, & McDonald, 1998). In the control condition, this is all we did. In a second condition, we trained the woman leader by giving her task-relevant information. In a third condition, we trained the woman and legitimated her expertise to the group by telling followers of her specialized knowledge. We found that groups led by our trained-only leader did no better than the controls, ignoring the information offered by the woman leader. In contrast, the legitimated, trained leaders' groups outscored the controls. This suggests that businesses must do more than train women. They must empower women so that they can overcome discriminatory expectations.

Finally, organizations can institute policies and procedures designed to address problems more frequently encountered by women. These include development of sexual harassment remedies (Fiske & Glick, 1995) and family-friendly policies. For example, flexible schedules can reduce role strain for women (Matsui, Ohsawa, & Onglatco, 1995). A critical part of flexibility may be the autonomy to be absent (Moen & Forest, 1990) and to work at home. Wage-earning and salaried parents with less stress and better coping were found to have jobs with greater autonomy, more schedule control in their own hands, fewer demands, greater security, and more support, including supportive supervisors, workplace cultures, and opportunities for advancement (Galinsky, Bond, & Friedman, 1996). The provision by employers of on-site childcare has been linked to improved attitudes about managing work and family (Kossek & Nichol, 1992). It is clear that there are ample contributions organizations can make toward creating a women-friendly workplace, yet these family-friendly benefits rarely extend to most women (and men) (Galinsky & Bond, 1996).

## Societal Possibilities

At the broadest level, there are societal-wide changes that could promote women's participation in the workplace, many of which parallel and support what we have already discussed. For example, nonsexist socialization practices could extend beyond parents to the media, and language conventions could describe occupations in gender-inclusive terms. Research specific to this level of analysis has focused on three large-scale policy recommendations: equal pay for equal work, comparable worth, and affirmative action. Equal pay for equal work defines "equal" as "identical," and these forms of readily identifiable discrimination have been challenged most favorably for women through legal action (Pinzler & Ellis, 1989).

## Comparable Worth

Comparable worth is designed to use job content, including skill, effort, responsibility, and working conditions, as the critical determinant of compensation (Aaronson, 1995; Steinberg, 1987; Wittig & Lowe, 1989). This means that workers in different occupations might be compensated equally because their jobs are deemed to be comparable in job content. It is offered as a way to deal with gendered occupational segregation and the devaluing of "women's" work. It does not change the structure of the workforce, but rather seeks to equitably compensate workers in different occupations.

Attempts to implement comparable worth raise serious questions about how we think about skills and the values we give to these (Steinberg, 1990). For example, dog pound attendant, parking lot attendant, and zookeeper were rated as more complex jobs than nursery school teacher and childcare worker in 1974 (cited in Steinberg, 1990). Researchers repeatedly find that the content of a job is inextricably connected with the gender of the jobholder (McArthur & Obrant, 1986) and that the prerequisites, tasks, and work context associated with "women's" work are valued less (Steinberg, 1990). Thus, "women's" work is devalued in part because it is done by women. Furthermore, job evaluation systems are often designed to evaluate "men's" work so that their direct application to "women's" work is questionable. For example, job responsibility often is framed in terms of how many people are supervised rather than served. Although these limitations raise serious questions about how to best implement comparable worth pay policies, they do not undermine the value of job evaluation reform (Taylor, 1989).

## Affirmative Action

The fairness and effectiveness of affirmative action programs are being painstakingly questioned by politicians and the American public. Much of this debate is muddied by our failure to clearly define affirmative action. The original definition of affirmative action, outlined in President Johnson's 1965 Executive Order 11246, called for people to take positive action to increase the likelihood of genuine equality for individuals of differing categories (Crosby & Cordova, 1996). These actions might include special recruitment efforts, giving preference points to applicants from select groups, use of temporary set-asides, or simply paying closer attention to treatment that has disparate impact (see Edwards, 1995; Konrad & Linnehan, 1995, for specific examples). The effectiveness of this approach is gauged by monitoring the extent to which diverse groups of people are represented in an organization.

In recent years, affirmative action has taken on new meanings that include unjustified set-asides ("quotas") and preferential treatment. Interestingly, these new meanings are expressly forbidden under the classical definition of affirmative action; organizations rarely implement affirmative action in these ways (Crosby & Cordova, 1996); and there is strong public sentiment against these operationalizations (Plous, 1996).

Putting aside these myths and concentrating on the original formulation and actual implementation of affirmative action, there is substantial evidence that affirmative action programs, along with other antidiscriminatory efforts, have had a significant impact on women's and minority men's access to employment, education, and business opportunities (Murrell &

Jones, 1996). Still, the evidence presented in this chapter argues that the goal of equitable access sought by affirmative action advocates has not been reached. Toward this end, social psychologists are helping to identify those actions that are most effective and most acceptable for implementing affirmative action (Pratkanis & Turner, 1996). Effective programs target discriminatory barriers, for example, by focusing helping efforts away from promoting individuals and toward removing social barriers. Such an approach is consistent with the focus on contextual inequities in this chapter.

## SUMMARY

A central theme of this chapter is that women and men typically work in different environments, frequently in segregated occupations, and they achieve different outcomes such as unequal pay, even though what they want from their employment is similar. There is ample evidence to suggest that these differences have more to do with the structure of the workplace than with any characteristics that are deficient in women or exemplary in men. If this indeed is the case, we would expect women to be as productive and satisfied with work as men when they share similar contexts. Individuals, organizations, and society as a whole can work together to create supportive workplaces for women (and not incidentally, for men as well). By taking this enriched contextual perspective, we can make work work for women.

ACKNOWLEDGMENTS   I wish to thank Rosalie Hall, Mary Hogue, Paul Levy, Jennifer Ludwig, Andrea Snell, and Linda Subich for their helpful comments and support.

## REFERENCES

Aaronson, S. (1995, January). *Pay equity and the wage gap: Success in the states.* Washington, DC: Institute for Women's Policy Research.

Adelmann, P. K. (1994a). Multiple roles and physical health among older adults: Gender and ethnic comparisons. *Research on Aging, 16,* 142–166.

Adelmann, P. K. (1994b). Multiple roles and psychological well-being in a national sample of older adults. *Journals of Gerontology, 49,* S277–S285.

Anderson, D., & Shapiro, D. (1996). Racial differences in access to high-paying jobs and the wage gap between black and white women. *Industrial and Labor Relations Review, 49,* 273–286.

Astin, H. S. (1984). The meaning of work in women's lives: A sociopsychological model of career choice and work behavior. *The Counseling Psychologist, 12,* 117–126.

Auster, E. R. (1989). Task characteristics as a bridge between macro- and microlevel research on salary inequities between men and women. *Academy of Management Review, 14*(2), 173–193.

Barnett, R. C. (1997). How paradigms shape the stories we tell: Paradigm shifts in gender and health. *Journal of Social Issues, 53*(2), 351–368.

Barnett, R. C., & Marshall, N. L. (1992). Worker and mother roles, spillover effects, and psychological distress. *Women and Health, 18,* 9–40.

Barnett, R. C., Marshall, N. L., & Sayer, A. (1992). Positive-spillover effects from job to home: A closer look. *Women and Health, 19,* 13–41.

Barnett, R. C., Marshall, N. L., & Singer, J. D. (1992). Job experiences over time, multiple roles, and women's mental health: A longitudinal study. *Journal of Personality and Social Psychology, 62,* 634–644.

Baruch, G. K., & Barnett, R. (1986). Role quality, multiple role involvement, and psychological well-being in midlife women. *Journal of Personality and Social Psychology, 51,* 578–585.

Baxter, J. (1992). Power attitudes and time: The domestic division of labour. *Journal of Comparative Family Studies, 23,* 165–182.

Beckwith, J. B. (1992). Stereotypes and reality in the division of household labor. *Social Behavior and Personality, 20,* 283–288.

Bem, S. L. (1983). Gender schema theory and its implications for child development: Raising gender-aschematic children in a gender-schematic society. *Signs, 8,* 598–616.

Betz, N. E. (1989). Implications of the null environment hypothesis for women's career development and for Counseling Psychology. *The Counseling Psychologist, 17*, 136–144.

Betz, N. E. (1993). Women's career development. In F. L. Denmark & M. A. Paludi (Eds.), *Psychology of women: A handbook of issues and theories*. Westport, CT: Greenwood Press.

Betz, N. E., & Fitzgerald, L. F. (1987). *The career psychology of women*. Orlando, FL: Academic Press.

Biblarz, T. J., Bengtson, V. L., & Bucur, A. (1996). Social mobility across three generations. *Journal of Marriage and the Family, 58*, 188–200.

Biernat, M., & Wortman, C. B. (1991). Sharing of home responsibilities between professionally employed women and their husbands. *Journal of Personality and Social Psychology, 60*, 844–860.

Bittman, M., & Lovejoy, F. (1993). Domestic power: Negotiating an unequal division of labor within a framework of equality. *Australian and New Zealand Journal of Sociology, 29*, 302–321.

Blair, S. L., & Lichter, D. T. (1991). Measuring the division of household labor: Gender segregation of housework among American couples. *Journal of Family Issues, 12*, 91–113.

Blaisure, K. R., & Allen, K. R. (1995). Feminists and the ideology and practice of marital equality. *Journal of Marriage and the Family, 57*, 5–19.

Bookman, A., & Morgen, S. (Eds.). (1988). *Women and the politics of empowerment*. Philadelphia, PA: Temple.

Branscombe, N. R., & Smith, E. R. (1990). Gender and racial stereotypes in impression formation and social decision-making processes. *Sex Roles, 22*, 627–647.

Bridges, J. S., & Etaugh, C. (1995). College students' perceptions of mothers: Effects of maternal employment-childrearing pattern and motive for employment. *Sex Roles, 32*, 735–751.

Cannings, K. (1991). An interdisciplinary approach to analyzing the managerial gender gap. *Human Relations, 44*, 679–695.

Chester, N. L., & Grossman, H. Y. (1990). Introduction: Learning about women and their work through their own accounts. In H. Y. Grossman & M. L. Chester (Eds.), *The experience and meaning of work in women's lives* (pp. 1–9). Hillsdale, NJ: Lawrence Erlbaum.

Cole, J. R., & Zuckerman, H. (1987). Marriage, motherhood and research performance in science. *Scientific American, 256*, 119–125.

Collins, P. H. (1986). Learning from the outsider within: The sociological significance of Black feminist thought. *Social Problems, 33*, S14-S32.

Cooke, R. A., & Rousseau, D. M. (1984). Stress and strain from family roles and work-role expectations. *Journal of Applied Psychology, 69*, 252–260.

Cotter, D. A., DeFiore, J. M., & Hermsen, J. M. (1995). Occupational gender desegregation in the 1980s. *Work and Occupations, 22*, 3–21.

Crosby, F. J. (1991). *Juggling: The unexpected advantages of balancing career and home for women and their families*. New York: Free Press.

Crosby, F. J., & Cordova, D. I. (1996). Words worth of wisdom: Toward an understanding of affirmative action. *Journal of Social Issues, 52*(4), 33–49.

Dill, B. T. (1983). Race, class and gender: Prospects for an all-inclusive sisterhood. *Feminist Studies, 9*, 131–150.

Douthitt, R. A. (1989). The division of labor within the home: Have gender roles changed? *Sex Roles, 20*, 693–704.

Dreher, G. F., & Ash, R. A. (1990). A comparative study of mentoring among men and women in managerial, professional, and technical positions. *Journal of Applied Psychology, 75*, 539–546.

Eagly, A. H., & Karau, S. J. (1991). Gender and the emergence of leaders: A meta-analysis. *Journal of Personality and Social Psychology, 60*, 685–710.

Eccles, J. S. (1994). Understanding women's educational and occupational choices: Applying the Eccles et al. model of achievement-related choices. *Psychology of Women Quarterly, 18*, 585–609.

Edwards, J. (1995). *When race counts*. London: Routledge.

England, P., & Herbert, M.S. (1993). The pay of men in "female" occupations: Is comparable worth only for women? In C. L. Williams (Ed.), *Doing "women's" work: Men in nontraditional occupations* (pp. 28–48). Newbury Park, CA: Sage.

Etaugh, C., & Nekolny, K. (1990). Effects of employment status and marital status on perceptions of mothers. *Sex Roles, 23*, 273–280.

Etaugh, C., & Poertner, P. (1991). Effects of occupational prestige, employment status, and marital status on perceptions of mothers. *Sex Roles, 24*, 345–353.

Farmer, H. S. (1985). Model of career and achievement motivation for women and men. *Journal of Counseling Psychology, 32*, 363–390.

Fassinger, R. E. (1985). A causal model of career choice in college women. *Journal of Vocational Behavior, 36*, 225–240.

Federal Glass Ceiling Commission. (1995, March). *Good for business: Making full use of the nation's human capital.* Washington, DC: U.S. Department of Labor.

Fiske, S. T., Bersoff, D. N., Borgida, E., Deaux, K., & Heilman, M. E. (1991). Social science research on trial: Use of the sex stereotyping research in *Price Waterhouse v. Hopkins. American Psychologist, 46,* 1049–1060.

Fiske, S. T., & Glick, P. (1995). Ambivalence and stereotypes cause sexual harassment: A theory with implications for organizational change. *Journal of Social Issues, 51*(1), 97–115.

Fiske, S. T., & Taylor, S. E. (1991). *Social cognition* (2nd ed.). New York: McGraw-Hill.

Fiske, S. T., & Von Hendy, H. M. (1992). Personality feedback and situational norms can control stereotyping processes. *Journal of Personality and Social Psychology, 62,* 577–596.

Fox, M., & Hesse-Biber, S. (1984). *Women at work.* Palo Alto, CA: Mayfield.

Galinsky, E., & Bond, J. T. (1996). Work and family: The experiences of mothers and fathers in the U.S. labor force. In C. Costello & B. K. Krimgold (Eds.), *The American woman, 1996–97* (pp. 79–103). New York: Norton.

Galinsky, E., Bond, J. T., & Friedman, D. E. (1996). The role of employers in addressing the needs of employed parents. *Journal of Social Issues, 52*(3), 111–136.

Gerson, K. (1985). *Hard choices: How women decide about work, career and motherhood.* Berkeley, CA: University of California Press.

Gerson, K. (1993). *No man's land: Men's changing commitments to family and work.* New York: Basic.

Gerstel, N., & Gallagher, S. (1994). Caring for kith and kin: Gender, employment, and the privatization of care. *Social Problems, 41,* 519–539.

Glass, J. (1990). The impact of occupational segregation on working conditions. *Social Forces, 68,* 779–796.

Glick, P., Zion, C., & Nelson, C. (1988). What mediates sex discrimination in hiring decisions? *Journal of Personality and Social Psychology, 55,* 178–186.

Goldberg, W. A., Greenberger, E., Hamill, S., & O'Neil, R. (1992). Role demands in the lives of employed single mothers with preschoolers. *Journal of Family Issues, 13,* 312–333.

Hackett, G., & Betz, N. E. (1981). A self-efficacy approach to the career development of women. *Journal of Vocational Behavior, 18,* 326–339.

Herz, D. E., & Wootton, B. H. (1996). Women in the workforce: An overview. In C. Costello & B. K. Krimgold (Eds.), *The American Woman: 1996–97* (pp. 44–78). New York: Norton.

Hewlett, S. A. (1986). *A lesser life: The myth of women's liberation in America.* New York: Morrow.

Hibbard, J. H., & Pope, C. R. (1991). Effect of domestic and occupational roles on morbidity and mortality. *Social Science and Medicine, 32,* 805–811.

Hochschild, A. R. (1989). *The second shift: Working parents and the revolution at home.* New York: Viking.

hooks, b. (1984). *Feminist theory: From margin to center.* Boston, MA: South End Press.

Horner, M. S. (1970). Femininity and successful achievement: A basic inconsistency. In J. M. Bardwick, E. Douvan, M. S. Horner, & D. Gutman (Eds.), *Feminine personality and conflict* (pp. 45–74). Belmont, CA: Brooks/Cole.

Hossain, Z., & Roopnarine, J. L. (1993). Division of household labor and child care in dual-earner African-American families with infants. *Sex Roles, 29,* 571–583.

Hyde, J. S. (1984). Children's understanding of sexist language. *Developmental Psychology, 20,* 697–706.

Institute for Gay and Lesbian Strategic Studies. (1996, July). *Economic issues for lesbian and bisexual women.* Washington, DC.

Institute for Women's Policy Research. (1997, February). *Research in brief: The wage gap: Women's and men's earnings.* Washington, DC.

Jacobs, J. A. (1989). Long-term trends in occupational segregation by sex. *American Journal of Sociology, 95,* 160–173.

Jacobs, R. L., & McClelland, D. C. (1994). Moving up the corporate ladder: A longitudinal study of the leadership motive pattern and managerial success in women and men. *Consulting Psychology Journal: Practice and Research, 46,* 32–41.

James, J. B. (1990). Women's employment patterns and midlife well-being. In H. Y. Grossman & M. L. Chester (Eds.), *The experience and meaning of work in women's lives* (pp. 103–120). Hillsdale, NJ: Lawrence Erlbaum.

Janman, K. (1989). One step behind: Current stereotypes of women, achievement, and work. *Sex Roles, 21,* 209–230.

Jenkins, S. R. (1996). Self-definition in thought, action, and life path choices. *Personality and Social Psychology Bulletin, 22,* 99–111.

John, D., & Shelton, B. A. (1997). The production of gender among black and white women and men: The case of household labor. *Sex Roles, 36,* 171–193.

John, D., Shelton, B. A., & Luschen, K. (1995). Race, ethnicity, gender, and perceptions of fairness. *Journal of Family Issues, 16,* 357–379.

Jozefowicz, D. M., Barber, B. L., & Eccles, J. S. (1993, March). *Adolescent work-related values and beliefs: Gender differences and relation to occupational aspirations*. Paper presented at biennial meeting of the Society for Research on Child Development, New Orleans, LA.

Kanter, R. M. (1977). *Men and women of the corporation*. New York: Basic.

Konrad, A. M., & Linnehan, F. (1995). Formalized HRM structures: Coordinating equal employment opportunity or concealing organizational practices? *Academy of Management Journal, 38*, 787–820.

Kopp, R. G., & Ruzicka, M. F. (1993). Women's multiple roles and psychological well-being. *Psychological Reports, 72*, 1351–1354.

Kossek, E. E., & Nichol, V. (1992). The effects of on-site child care on employee attitudes and performance. *Personnel Psychology, 45*, 485–509.

Laws, J. L. (1975). The psychology of tokenism: An analysis. *Sex Roles, 1*, 51–77.

Lemkau, J. P. (1979). Personality and background characteristics of women in male-dominated occupations: A review. *Psychology of Women Quarterly, 4*, 221–240.

Lewin, T. (1997, Sept. 15). Wage difference between women and men widens. *The New York Times*, p. A1.

Lott, B. (1985). The devaluation of women's competence. *Journal of Social Issues, 41*(4), 43–60.

Lundberg, U. (1996). Influence of paid and unpaid work on psychophysiological stress responses of men and women. *Journal of Occupational Health Psychology, 1*, 117–130.

MacPherson, P., & Fine, M. (1995). Hungry for an us: Adolescent girls and adult women negotiating territories of race, gender, class and difference. *Feminism & Psychology, 5*, 181–200.

Marini, M. M., & Fan, P. (1997). The gender gap in earnings at career entry. *American Sociological Review, 62*, 588–604.

Martell, R. F. (1991). Sex bias at work: The effects of attentional and memory demands on performance ratings of men and women. *Journal of Applied Social Psychology, 21*(23), 1939–1960.

Martin, S. E. (1994). "Outsider within" the station house: The impact of race and gender on Black women police. *Social Problems, 41*, 383–400.

Matsui, T., Ohsawa, T., & Onglatco, M. (1995). Work-family conflict and the stress-buffering effects of husband support and coping behavior among Japanese married working women. *Journal of Vocational Behavior, 47*, 178–192.

McArthur, L. Z., & Obrant, S. W. (1986). Sex biases in comparable worth analyses. *Journal of Applied Social Psychology, 16*, 757–770.

Mednick, M. T., & Thomas, V. G. (1993). Women and the psychology of achievement: A view from the eighties. In F. L. Denmark & M. A. Paludi (Eds.), *Psychology of women: A handbook of issues and theories*. Westport, CT: Greenwood Press.

Mobley, G. M., Jaret, C., Marsh, K., & Lim, Y. (1994). Mentoring, job satisfaction, gender, and the legal profession. *Sex Roles, 31*, 79–98.

Moen, P., Dempster-McClain, D., & Williams, R. M. (1989). Social integration and longevity: An event history analysis of women's roles and resilience. *American Sociological Review, 54*, 635–647.

Moen, P., & Forest, K. B. (1990). Working parents, workplace supports, and well-being: The Swedish experience. *Social Psychology Quarterly, 53*, 117–131.

Moore, D. (1995). Gender role attitudes and division of labor: Sex or occupation-type differences? An Isreali example. *Journal of Social Behavior and Personality, 10*, 215–234.

Murrell, A. J., & Jones, R. (1996). Assessing affirmative action: Past, present, and future. *Journal of Social Issues, 52*(4), 77–92.

Nelson, D. L., Quick, J. C., Hitt, M. A., & Moesel, D. (1990). Politics, lack of career progress, and work-home conflict: Stress and strain for working women. *Sex Roles, 23*, 169–185.

O'Brien, K. M., & Fassinger, R. E. (1993). A causal model of the career orientation and career choice of adolescent women. *Journal of Counseling Psychology, 40*, 1–14.

Osipow, S. H., & Fitzgerald, L. F. (1996). *Theories of career development*. Boston, MA: Allyn and Bacon.

Outtz, J. H. (1996). *Are Mommies dropping out of the labor force?* Washington, DC: Institute for Women's Policy Research.

Pfost, K. S., & Fiore, M. (1990). Pursuit of nontraditional occupations: Fear of success or fear of not being chosen? *Sex Roles, 23*, 15–24.

Piedmont, R. L. (1995). Another look at fear of success, fear of failure, and test anxiety: A motivational analysis using the five-factor model. *Sex Roles, 32*, 139–158.

Pinzler, I. K., & Ellis, D. (1989). Wage discrimination and comparable worth: A legal perspective. *Journal of Issues, 45*(4), 51–65.

Pleck, J. H. (1985). *Working wives/working husbands*. Beverly Hills: Sage.

Plous, S. (1996). Ten myths about affirmative action. *Journal of Social Issues, 52*(4), 25–31.

Pratkanis, A. R., & Turner, M. E. (1996). The proactive removal of discriminatory barriers: Affirmative action as effective help. *Journal of Social Issues, 52*(4), 111–132.

Pugh, M. D., & Wahrman, R. (1983). Neutralizing sexism in mixed-sex groups: Do women have to be better than men? *American Journal of Sociology, 88*, 746–762.

Ragins, B. R. (1991). Gender effects in subordinate evaluations of leaders: Real or artifact? *Journal of Organizational Behavior, 12*, 259–268.

Ragins, B. R., & Cotton, J. L. (1993). Gender and willingness to mentor in organizations. *Journal of Management, 19*, 97–111.

Ramey, F. H. (1995). Obstacles faced by African American women administrators in higher education: How they cope. *Western Journal of Black Studies, 19*, 113–119.

Rankin, E. D. (1993). Stresses and rewards experienced by employed mothers. *Health Care for Women International, 14*, 527–537.

Reskin, B. F. (1993). Sex segregation in the workplace. *Annual Review of Sociology, 19*, 241–270.

Reskin, B. F., & Padavic, I. (1994). *Women and men at work.* Thousand Oaks, CA: Pine Forge Press.

Rix, S. E. (Ed.). (1988). *The American Woman 1988–89.* New York: Norton.

Robinson, J. P. (1988). Who's doing the housework? *American Demographics, 10*, 24–28, 63.

Roos, P. A., & Reskin, B. F. (1992). Occupational desegregation in the 1970s: Integration and economic equity? *Sociological Perspectives, 35*, 69–91.

Russo, N. F., & Jansen, M. A. (1988). Women, work, and disability: Opportunities and challenges. In M. Fine & A. Asch (Eds.), *Women with disabilities: Essays in psychology, culture, and politics* (pp. 229–244). Philadelphia, PA: Temple.

Sackett, P. R., DuBois, C. L. Z., & Noe, A. W. (1991). Tokenism in performance evaluation: The effects of work group representation on male-female and white-black differences in performance ratings. *Journal of Applied Psychology, 76*, 263–267.

Sanchez-Hucles, J. V. (1997). Jeopardy not bonus status for African American women in the work force: Why does the myth of advantage persist? *American Journal of Community Psychology, 25*, 565–580.

Schein, V. E., Mueller, R., Lituchy, T., & Lui, J. (1996). Think manager—think male: A global phenomenon? *Journal of Organizational Behavior, 17*, 33–41.

Schneer, J. A., & Reitman, F. (1993). Effects of alternate family structures on managerial career paths. *Academy of Management Journal, 36*, 830–843.

Schroeder, K. A., Blood, L. L., & Maluso, D. (1992). An intergenerational analysis of expectations for women's career and family roles. *Sex Roles, 26*, 273–291.

Shelton, B. A. (1990). The distribution of household tasks: Does wife's employment status make a difference? *Journal of Family Issues, 11*, 115–135.

Simon, R. W. (1995). Gender, multiple roles, role meaning, and mental health. *Journal of Health and Social Behavior, 36*, 182–194.

Sokoloff, N. J. (1988). Evaluating gains and losses by black and white women and men in the professions, 1960–1980. *Social Problems, 35*, 36–53.

Staines, G., Tavris, C., & Jayaratne, T. E. (1974, January). The queen bee syndrome. *Psychology Today*, pp. 55–58, 60.

Starrels, M. E. (1994). Husbands' involvement in female gender-typed household chores. *Sex Roles, 31*, 473–491.

Steinberg, R. (1987). Radical challenges in a liberal world: The mixed success of comparable worth. *Gender & Society, 1*, 466–475.

Steinberg, R. (1990). Social construction of skill: Gender, power, and comparable worth. *Work and Occupations, 17*(4), 449–482.

Stroeher, S. K. (1994). Sixteen kindergartners' gender-related views of careers. *Elementary School Journal, 95*, 95–103.

Stroh, L. K., Brett, J. M., & Reilly, A. H. (1992). All the right stuff: A comparison of female and male managers' career progression. *Journal of Applied Psychology, 77*, 251–260.

Taylor, S. H. (1989). The case for comparable worth. *Journal of Social Issues, 45*(4), 23–37.

Tetlock, P. (1992). The impact of accountability on judgment and choice: Toward a social contingency model. In M. P. Zanna (Ed.), *Advances in Experimental Social Psychology* (Vol. 25, pp. 331–376). New York: Academic Press.

Thorne, Y. M. (1995). Achievement motivation in high achieving Latina women. *Roeper Review, 18*, 44–49.

Tiedje, L. B., & Darling-Fisher, C. S. (1993). Factors that influence fathers' participation in child care. *Health Care for Women International, 14*, 99–107.

Towson, S. M. J., Zanna, M. P., & MacDonald, G. (1989). Self-fulfilling prophecies: Sex role stereotypes as expectations for behavior. In R. K. Unger (Ed.), *Representations: Social constructions of gender* (pp. 97–107). Amityville, NY: Baywood.

Traustadottir, R. (1991). Mothers who care: Gender, disability, and family life. *Journal of Family Issues, 12*, 211–228.

Trepanier, M. L., & Romatowski, J. A. (1985). Attributes and roles assigned to characters in children's writing: Sex differences and sex-role perceptions. *Sex Roles, 13*, 263–272.

United Nations. (1991). *The world's women: Trends and statistics, 1970–1990*. New York: United Nations Publications.

United Nations. (1995). *The world's women 1995: Trends and statistics*. New York: United Nations Publications.

U.S. Bureau of the Census. (1999). *Statistical abstract of the United States: 1999* (119th ed.). Washington, DC: Government Printing Office.

U.S. Department of Education, National Center for Education Statistics. (1996). *Digest of Educational Statistics 1996*, NCES 96–133. Washington, DC: U.S. Government Printing Office.

U.S. Department of Labor. (1991). *A report on the glass ceiling initiative* (#91–656-P). Washington, DC: Government Printing Office.

U.S. Department of Labor. (1995, May). *Twenty facts on women workers*. Washington, DC: Women's Bureau of the Department of Labor.

Vanderkolk, B. S., & Young, A. A. (1991). *The work and family revolution: How companies can keep employees happy and business profitable*. New York: Facts on File.

Vandewater, E. A., Ostrove, J. M., & Stewart, A. J. (1997). Predicting women's well-being in midlife: The importance of personality development and social role involvements. *Journal of Personality and Social Psychology, 72*, 1147–1160.

Waldfogel, J. (1997). The effect of children on women's wages. *American Sociological Review, 62*, 209–217.

Waldron, I., & Jacobs, J. A. (1989). Effects of multiple roles on women's health: Evidence from a national longitudinal study. *Women and Health, 15*, 3–19.

Westman, M., & Etzion, D. (1990). The career success/personal failure phenomenon as perceived in others: Comparing vignettes of male and female managers. *Journal of Vocational Behavior, 37*, 209–224.

Whorf, B. L. (1956). *Language, thought, and reality*. Cambridge, MA: MIT Press.

Wittig, M. A., & Lowe, R. H. (1989). Comparable worth theory and policy. *Journal of Social Issues, 45*(4), 1–21.

Wright, E. O., Shire, K., Hwang, S., Dolan, M., & Baxter, J. (1992). The non-effects of class on the gender division of labor in the home: A comparative study of Sweden and the United States. *Gender & Society, 6*, 252–282.

Yoder, J. D. (1991). Rethinking tokenism: Looking beyond numbers. *Gender & Society, 5*, 178–192.

Yoder, J. D., Adams, J., Grove, S., & Priest, R. F. (1985). To teach is to learn: Overcoming tokenism with mentors. *Psychology of Women Quarterly, 9*, 119–131.

Yoder, J. D., & Aniakudo, P. (1997). "Outsider within" the firehouse: Subordination and difference in the social interactions of African American women firefighters. *Gender & Society, 11*, 324–341.

Yoder, J. D., & Schleicher, T. L. (1996). Undergraduates regard deviation from occupational gender stereotypes as costly for women. *Sex Roles, 34*, 171–188.

Yoder, J. D., Schleicher, T. L., & McDonald, T. W. (1998). Empowering token women leaders: The importance of organizationally legitimated credibility. *Psychology of Women Quarterly, 22*, 209–222.

Zimmer, L. (1988). Tokenism and women in the workplace: The limits of gender-neutral theory. *Social Problems, 35*, 64–77.

# 6

# Sexual Victimization
## *Harassment and Rape*

### Patricia D. Rozee

## INTRODUCTION

Violence against women is socially constructed (Edwards, 1987). Just as gender identity is constructed by teaching girls to be feminine and compliant and boys to be tough and aggressive, so an understanding of violence is constructed by teaching what is and is not acceptable with regard to interpersonal aggression. This is true not only in the United States but also around the world. All cultures have differing understandings of what is considered normative, condoned, or approved behavior for members of that culture (Rozee, 1993). Normative behavior for violence against women varies by culture and historical period. Within every culture and at all time periods, however, there have been forms of violence against women considered legitimate, condoned by social norms and enforced by the institutions of the society. In the early nineteenth century in the United States the sexual assault of children and the battering of wives were considered the private business of individual families and carried no legal sanctions. Early twentieth century feminists questioned this laissez-faire attitude and fought for enactment and enforcement of laws against such acts. It is only recently, however, that domestic violence has become an issue of concern to lawmakers and to the general public. The Centers for Disease Control and Prevention cite violence between intimates as the leading cause of injury for women between the ages of 15 and 44, a problem that continues due in part to the lack of support for domestic violence victims. One study found that citizens were less likely to help a woman being assaulted by a man on the street if they thought the two were married (Shotland & Straw, 1976). Domestic violence is a felony offense, yet even today only the most brutal domestic violence cases are actually tried as felonies and not as misdemeanors.

Violence against women is universal (Heise, Ellsberg, & Gottemoeller, 1999). It is pervasive and persistent worldwide precisely because the social institutions of every society implicitly or explicitly condone it (Rozee, 1993). Legal, judicial, medical, religious, educational, and familial institutions often support the social acceptability of violence against women. In male-dominated, patriarchal cultures, such institutions serve to enforce gender inequality, one outcome of which is violence against women. Until recently in the United States, it was perfectly

Patricia D. Rozee ● Women's Studies Program, California State University, Long Beach, California 90840.

*Issues in the Psychology of Women,* edited by Biaggio and Hersen. Kluwer Academic/Plenum Publishers, New York, 2000.

legal to rape one's wife. The first law against spousal assault was enacted in the state of Oregon in 1977 when the marital rape exemption clause was deleted from its rape statute. Women rarely report sexual assaults by dates and intimates because, even though date rape is illegal, it is still socially condoned to such an extent that it is difficult to get police and juries to believe the victim. Rape survivors are often further victimized by a medical system that treats sexual assault the same as any other medical emergency, with little regard for the social and psychological context of the crime. Marie Fortune (1983, 1987) has documented the callous disregard of some religious institutions for the problem of violence against women. She reports that many ministers have counseled abused women to go back to their husbands and "strive to be better wives." Educational institutions perpetuate gender inequality by differential treatment of girls and boys and enforcement of traditional gender roles that promote violence against women. Many authors have pointed to the socialization practices of U. S. society that teach young girls to be submissive, deferential, weak, and passive and boys to be strong, aggressive, tough, and unemotional. Women are still to some extent raised to defer to men, to support men in their goals, and to expect men to take care of and protect them (Rozee, 2000). Girls are expected to be timid and dependent and never to embarrass anyone or make a scene. Many of these socialized traits leave women vulnerable to aggressive men, insecure about their strength and ability to physically defend themselves, and psychologically ill-prepared to do so.

There are many forms of violence against women: sexual assault, sexual harassment, stalking, child sexual assault and molestation, battering, slavery, trafficking in women and forced prostitution, violent pornography, genital mutilations, and so on. This chapter focuses on two of the most pervasive forms: sexual assault and sexual harassment. These two crimes are similar in etiology. Both are crimes of violence resulting from the perpetrator's need to control, dominate, and intimidate another. It is important to note that both sexual harassment and sexual assault can be perpetrated *by* both males and females *on* either males or females. However, these are termed gendered crimes because the vast majority of perpetrators are males and nearly all the victims are female. Thus, we know that gender is an important factor in both crimes—women are raped *because* they are women (Heise, 1989). Women are raped and sexually harassed because gender inequality and its supporting institutions make it possible. Sexual assault and sexual harassment are behaviors that are chosen by perpetrators who have reason to believe they are unlikely to suffer any negative consequences for their crimes. Rozee (1993) defines rape without punishment as normative rape. Since scholars agree that 80 to 98 percent of rapes go unpunished in the United States, rape is normative to the culture. Yet, gender does not explain the whole story. It does not explain, for example, homosexual rape or same-sex sexual harassment. Thus, we must look beyond gender alone for explanations.

Most scholars and activists agree that rape and sexual harassment are crimes of power and domination. While most power relations in our society are gendered (that is, men as a class have power over women as a class) powerful people do come in both genders. In the case of sexual harassment particularly, same-sex harassment occurs when one person (male or female) exercises power over another (male or female) in the workplace or educational setting. The power dynamics and consequences are similar regardless of the victim's gender, race, ethnicity, social class, sexual orientation, age, or ability/disability.

## SEXUAL ASSAULT

The United States has been referred to by many writers as a rape culture. The rate of rape in the United States is higher than in any other industrialized nation in the world (Lott, 1994). According to the Bureau of Justice Statistics (1997), in 1995 there were 355,300 reported attempted and completed sexual assaults in the United States—a woman reports a forcible rape every five minutes. Based on estimates generated from random sample studies, one in four women will experience rape or attempted rape at some point in her lifetime (Russell, 1990; Koss, 1993). The U. S. Department of Justice calls rape the fastest growing crime in the United States. Official statistics on rape are always suspect because what constitutes rape varies according to the agency doing the recording. For example, FBI statistics on rape do not include child sexual assault, statutory rape, marital rape, or attempted rape. What is defined as sexual assault also varies from state to state. In some states there must be penile penetration of the vagina for an assault to be considered a rape. Many states include penetration by objects and fingers, as well as anal penetration, in their definition of sexual assault.

## The Cultural Context of Rape

Race, class, culture, age, and sexual orientation affect every aspect of the rape experience. According to Holzman (1994), "The dynamics of rape involve the ways in which power and violence are structured by a particular culture, not just the psychodynamics of the individual perpetrators or victims. Rape is both a tool and a consequence of an interlocking system of oppressions based on these factors. Those who have the least power in a society are the most vulnerable to rape" (p. 83). Thus rape must be understood in the context of the survivor's own culture.

Women of color are underrepresented in prevalence studies of violence against women. However, Goodman, Koss, Fitzgerald, Russo, and Keita (1993) suggest that street crimes such as rape by strangers are more prevalent among ethnic and poor women. This may explain Wyatt's (1992) finding that Black women are more likely than white women to be raped by strangers and to give as explanations the riskiness of their living situation, such as use of public transportation, walking in unlit neighborhoods, and living in high crime areas (Wyatt, 1992). Yet Koss and Dinero (1989) found lower victimization rates for black than for white women when all types of rape were assessed. There may be two reasons for this finding. First, black women are more likely than white women to possess a strong sense of self, profess principles of self-reliance, self-protection, and avoidance of interpersonal exploitation (Holland & Eisenhart, 1990). Thus, they are more likely to physically resist rape, using multiple methods of self-defense (Bart & O'Brien, 1985). Second, black women may be less likely to report rape. Black women live with the knowledge that they are even less likely than white women to have the benefit of society's protections against rape. In our society there is still the perception that the rape of a black woman is somehow less serious than that of a white woman (Foley, Evancic, Karnik, King, & Parks, 1995), and that black women cannot be raped (Fonow, Richardsen, & Wemmerus, 1992). According to Wyatt (1992), "If African American women perceive that society does not consider that they can be raped, and that they would not be believed if they disclosed their assault, the chances are minimal that they will disclose or seek help from authorities that represent societal views regarding 'real rape'" (p. 78). According to Wyatt, African-American women's beliefs about rape are couched in their own cultural experience of being black and female—rape may be seen as something that happens to you because you are black and female (Wyatt, 1992). In addition, black women may not find support in their own community, especially if their rape did not meet the perceptions of "real rape." In general, African-American women are less accepting of rape myths and gender role stereotypes than white women (Kalof & Wade, 1995). However, if a black woman does not fight back others may think that she is now someone's "sexual property" and the consequent perception of being "ruined" may be part of the victim's own belief system (Wyatt, 1992).

African-American women may feel an obligation to maintain a "code of silence" about sexual victimization when the victimizer is an African-American man (Bell, 1992). According to Ella Louise Bell (1992), black women know the devastating effects of racism on black men and their silence is intended to protect the black man from jeopardy by the white power structure. The racist portrayal by the media of rapists as disproportionately black men, as well as the greater frequency of arrests of black men due to inequities in the criminal justice system, support this position. There is still a strong societal myth that most rapes are committed by black men despite the fact that the majority of rapes are committed by white men (Fonow, Richardsen, & Wemmerus, 1992). Indeed, most rapes are intraracial, occurring primarily between people of the same race and socioeconomic class (O'Brien, 1987; Fonow, Richardsen & Wemmerus, 1992). Bell (1992) claims that when a black woman speaks out about sexual exploitation by black men she is verbally attacked and disbelieved and seen as a co-conspirator with the white power structure. This leaves African-American women with limited options for legal redress of their victimization.

Community-based surveys have found that the lifetime prevalence rate for rape is two and one half times higher for white women than for Latinas (20 percent vs. 8 percent). Latina rape victims have more traditional attitudes and are more likely to subscribe to rape myths than either blacks or whites (Lefley, Scott, Llabre, & Hicks, 1993). They are also likely to attribute victim blaming views to most women and men in their own ethnic community, a fact that Lefley links with a higher prevalence of psychological symptomology and lower use of health services among Latina rape survivors (Sorenson & Siegel, 1992).

Mills and Granoff (1992), in their study of Asian-American women, found that while 28 percent of the women were victims of rape or attempted rape by legal definition, only one third of these so labeled themselves. Mori et al. (1995) suggest that Asian women will thus be less likely to report the rape because of failure to recognize it, fear of negative repercussions, and self-blame. Mori et al. (1995) report that Asians are more likely to endorse negative attitudes toward rape victims and greater belief in rape myths than whites. They also report that Asians who were more acculturated to U. S. culture were more positive toward victims and less likely to believe rape myths (Mori et al., 1995).

Immigrant women, especially the undocumented and refugee women, are at risk for rape owing to their general unfamiliarity with local customs and resources and the barrier of language differences. Many of these women cannot turn to social institutions because of fear of discovery and deportation or fear of authority figures in general. In their work with Cambodian refugees, Rozee and Van Boemel (1995) witnessed these women's fear of authorities and institutions as a result of being tormented, tortured, or seeing people killed by those in positions of authority among the Khmer Rouge communist guerrillas. Rape was not spoken of, even though most had been processed through Thai refugee camps where rape was "as common as the night." The refugee experience for women coming from war-torn countries is one of forced labor, torture, starvation, beatings, and rape (Rosee & Van Boemel, 1989; Van Boemel & Rozee, 1992). One of the so-called "spoils of war" is the raping of enemy women. It is estimated that 95 percent of Cambodian refugees to the United States had been sexually assaulted (Mollica, 1986). In traditional cultures a woman who loses her virginity, even by rape, is considered soiled; thus it is always a matter of shame (Rosee & Van Boemel, 1989; Van Boemel & Rozee, 1992). Holtzman (1994) points out that in Southeast Asia women are often sexually exploited and victimized by sexual tourism and by so-called "R & R" for male U. S. military personnel and the female sex slave trade is flourishing in that region (Funk, 1993).

While some older studies showed that some women, particularly Asian-American women and Latinas, had more difficult recoveries from rape, recent comparisons find no ethnic differences in the impact of rape (Koss, 1993; Wyatt, 1992).

Older women are especially vulnerable to rape, and the outcomes can be especially severe. Often the rape results in profound and debilitating physical and psychological effects on older victims, effects that can be permanent (Tyra, 1993). The psychological effects of rape for older survivors can be particularly severe due to the loss of power and control, both issues that may already have been of concern (Tyra, 1993). Disabled women are three times more likely to be raped than able-bodied women, and often the perpetrator is their caregiver on whom they may be physically and financially dependent (Holzman, 1994). Self-defense classes are currently in high demand among older and disabled women who wish to empower themselves by learning self-protection.

People who challenge the system of power are often targeted by rapists as a form of punishment for presumed transgressions (Holzman, 1994). Thus, the rape of lesbians (and gay men) is often part of the enactment of a hate crime (Garnets, Herek, & Levy, 1993). Lesbians may be subjected to "punitive rape," defined as any rape that is used as a discipline or punishment (Rozee, 1993). Some rapists perceive lesbians as "open targets" who deserve punishment because they are not under the protection of a man (Garnets et al., 1993). Lesbians have been sexually harassed and raped for being "out" (Funk, 1993). Lesbians must also confront the impact of victimization on their identity as lesbians and may experience the rape as an attempt to undermine the worth of lesbian sexuality. Relationship problems may develop because, like male partners of heterosexual victims, her partner may be uncomfortable with the fact that she has been with a man, however involuntarily. A lesbian may be particularly impacted by the effect the rape has on undermining her feelings of independence from the actions of men. According to Garnets et al. (1993): "Because many lesbians are not accustomed to feeling dependent on or vulnerable around men, a sexual attack motivated by male rage at their life-style constitutes a major assault on their general sense of safety, independence, and well-being" (p. 584).

## Normative Rape

Rape is normative in the United States and in many other cultures throughout the world (Rozee, 2000). The lack of reporting, arrests, convictions, and prison time served by rapists are all evidence of the social tolerance for rape in the United States. Rape has the lowest conviction rate of any violent crime; rape cases do not reach the courtroom because of underreporting; police considering the claims unfounded; and cases dropped by prosecutors, dismissed by judges, or plea-bargained (Sinclair & Bourne, 1998).

Other evidence of the normative nature of rape is discussed below. This includes prevalence of rape myths and victim-blaming, researchers' inability to distinguish rapists from normal men, the inability of many normal men to distinguish rape from nonrape behaviors, and the conditional support for rape among young people.

### Rape Myths

Rape myths have been described and discussed by virtually all scholars and activists as a factor in the persistence of rape in the United States (Lonsway & Fitzgerald, 1994; Rozee, 2000). Burt (1991) defines rape myths as prejudicial, stereotypical, or false beliefs about rape, rape victims, or rapists. Rape myths serve as a mechanism of social control and oppression of women in a patriarchal society (Brownmiller, 1975; Lonsway & Fitzgerald, 1994; Rozee, 1993). All women are controlled by the threat of rape, resulting in the practice of myriad preventive behaviors, especially those behaviors that result in restrictions on their own freedom, such as avoiding going out alone at night, taking night classes, night jobs, or travel to unfamiliar places (Rozee, 1993, 2000). Rape myths serve to justify and excuse rape and deny victims appropriate support (Burt, 1980; 1991). Even though rape is illegal in all states, rape myths influence the enforcement of rape laws by influencing the public perception of what is or is not "real rape" (Estrich, 1987). The more rape myths people endorse the more restrictive the definition of rape and the less likely they are to consider a rape to be "real rape." Rape myths generally have one of three primary themes: "She asked for it," "She liked it," or "She lied about it."

"She asked for it" myths generally revolve around beliefs that the victim in some way deserved or caused the rape by something in her manner, behavior, attitude, or appearance. The evidence is clear that rapists plan their crimes in advance with no consideration of the characteristics or behavior of the victim (Burt, 1991). The rapist's choice of a victim is an opportunistic event, a random choice, based on availability rather than on any known characteristic of the victim. Victim-blaming is a common phenomenon in all kinds of crimes, but nowhere is the bias against women so evident as in rape. The fact that men are more likely to blame the victim than are women speaks to the differential meaning of the crime to each gender. Rape myth beliefs among jurors are a strong contributor to the persistently low conviction rate for rape (Sinclair & Bourne, 1998).

"She liked it" myths generally involve a general belief that women are supersexualized, always want it, and that "no" never really means "no." This is a very common theme portrayed in violent pornography: the woman initially gives a token resistance only to find out during the rape that she likes it. This belief among men may explain why some rapists subsequently phone their victims to ask for another "date." Warshaw (1994) cites evidence that 70 percent of date rape victims fought back physically, yet their dates still interpreted no to mean yes. In this myth, the burden of proof is on the victim to show evidence that she did not consent or that she resisted, such as bruises or other injuries.

The "She lied about it" myth denies that a rape ever happened. This belief revolves around the common belief that women use the charge of rape to "get even" with errant boyfriends, to cover up a sexual relationship about which they now have second thoughts, or that resulted in an unwanted pregnancy. Researchers have found that rape has about the same "unfounded" rate as any other felony crime. And often, when police do find the rape charge unfounded, it is based on their own belief in rape myths (Rozee-Koker & Polk, 1986). "She lied about it" myths may also involve the belief that women have so-called "rape fantasies." Both men and women have fantasies of being "taken," having an attractive person find them irresistible, sweep them off their feet, and take over control of sex (with no performance anxieties, pregnancy, or disease risks). In these fantasies, the woman (or man) chooses the partner, the acts, and can end it at will. Few people have "rape fantasies" that include forced sex with a partner not of their choosing, physical injury, degradation, and/or threat of death that are always a part of actual rape.

Martha Burt (1991) succinctly expresses the effects of rape myths on the perpetuation of rape: "Rape myths allow rapists to rape with near-impunity. They teach women to blame themselves for their own victimization. They transform rape by acquaintances, friends, and intimates to no rape at all. They support the use of violence, coupled with sexuality, as a mechanism for keeping women powerless" (p. 37). In short, rape myths form the foundation for the structural acceptance of rape in our society—they allow rape to become normative.

## Characteristics of Rapists

Other evidence of the normative nature of rape in our culture concerns the inability of researchers to discern a difference between rapists and normal American males. Most studies with college students have failed to show reliable differences between known rapists and non-rapists on a variety of measures. Neil Malamuth and his colleagues have conducted a series of studies to discover the rape proclivity of college males (see Malamuth & Donnerstein, 1984 for an overview). Across his studies he found that an average of 35 percent of male college students stated that there was some likelihood of raping of woman if they could be assured of not being caught and punished. Men who report some proclivity to rape were similar to convicted rapists in their belief in rape myths and their arousal to rape depictions. An additional 30 percent said there was some likelihood of using force but no likelihood of raping. This finding demonstrates the difficulty that many men have in defining rape from nonrape behaviors. Mary Koss and her associates in their research on date rape found that while 12 percent of men in her study reported behavior that met the legal definition of rape, nearly all of them said that the behavior was definitely not rape (Koss, Leonard, Beezley, & Oros,1985).

Young men already espouse these rape supportive values by the time they are in junior high and high school. A recent incident in Lakewood, California, is indicative of the way in which boys are socialized to think about girls. The community was stunned when seven young women filed charges against members of the Spur Posse, a group of 25 to 30 popular middle-class teenage boys. The Spur Posse had a competition to "score" on as many girls as possible by whatever means. The boys kept count of the young girls with whom they had sex, many of them scoring 60 or more conquests (Gelman, 1993). One 16-year-old girl reported that during a sexual encounter a Posse member took her clothes and refused to return them unless she had sex with other Posse members. Eight of the boys were arrested on charges ranging from rape to unlawful intercourse with underage girls. Only two of the Spur Posse members were charged, one with having sex with a 10-year-old girl (Smolowe, 1993). The rest of the Spur Posse were released after the district attorney concluded that the sexual contact was consensual. While the parents of the girls were outraged, many of the parents of the boys took a "Boys will be boys" attitude and made disparaging comments about the girls' reputations. Some fathers even bragged about the sexual virility of their sons (Gelman, 1993). This case is indicative of the general tolerance for the sexually aggressive behavior of young men and the sense of sexual entitlement with which they are raised.

Studies of the attitudes of young people toward forced and coerced sexual contact give a frightening view of future heterosexual relationships. Numerous researchers have documented that both boys and girls agree that under certain circumstances it is okay for a man to hold a woman down and force her to have sex. They thought it was okay for a man to force a woman if any of the following occurred: she asked him out, he spent a lot of money on her, she "led him on" by allowing kissing and petting, he got aroused, or she had been sexually intimate with him or with other men previously (cf. Goodchilds, Zellman, Johnson, & Giarusso, 1988). Lott (1994) found that a majority of young men thought it was okay to force sex on a woman if they had been dating a long time (65 percent); if they were planning to get married (75 percent); or if they are married (87 percent). Rape by intimates is the most prevalent form of sexual assault. The closer the relationship of the victim to the aggressor, the less likely she is to report the sexual assault. Young people learn very early that forced sex among intimates is not "real rape."

## RAPE PREVENTION

Sexual assault has multiple overlapping causes and any effective intervention strategy must provide multiple approaches to the problem. The solutions must relate to the needs of a society in which rape has become epidemic as well as to the needs of a woman faced with an assailant or a woman trying to avoid sexual assault. Sole emphasis in rape prevention on what women can do to prevent rape supports the attitude that they are responsible for its occurrence.

Appropriate interventions will require multilevel approaches to prevention: societal or perhaps global responsibility, group and individual awareness and education, and self-protection and resistance (Rozee, Bateman, & Gilmore, 1991).

As Charlotte Bunch (1997) so succinctly expresses it, "There is nothing immutable about the violent oppression of women and girls. It is a construct of power, as was apartheid, and one that can be changed" (p. 44). Violence against women is so embedded in cultural tradition that it is almost invisible (Bunch, 1997) and is seen as normative, a normal part of life, the "way things are" (Rozee, 2000). Changing these constructs will require action at all levels of society, beginning with social policy decisions, legal structures and policies, economic access, and political representation.

Violence against women has finally been recognized by the United Nations as a fundamental human rights issue. This has led to widespread grassroots movements against violence by hundreds of women's organizations on every continent around the world. As a result of such efforts many countries have revised or enacted rape laws. Louise Heise and her colleagues report that in Bolivia women organized a massive campaign to reform rape laws, collecting 40,000 signatures in one month; hundreds of Zambian women took to the streets to show support for rape law reform; and Malaysia launched a five-year educational campaign (Heise, Raikes, Watts, & Zwi, 1994). In the United States hundreds of women and men every year show support for rape victims and rape law reform by organizing Take Back the Night marches all over the country.

Effectiveness of legal reform is dependent on public access to legal redress, implementation of laws, and enforcement priorities. Changes are required in the processing of rape through criminal justice systems and other institutions. Rapists are deterred by formal sanctions such as arrests (Bachman, 1998). In the United States there is still considerable state-to-state variability in the implementation of legal reforms to the treatment of rape victims (Bachman, 1993). Recent discussions of releasing names of rape victims to the news media has resulted in overwhelming opposition by rape crisis groups. One survey found that 86 percent of respondents felt that fewer rape victims would report rape if they thought their names would be disclosed to the media (Bachman, 1993). To increase the apprehension, conviction, and incarceration rates for rape, conditions must be changed that discourage victim reporting (Bachman, 1998).

Heise et al. (1994) note that policy reform requires a great deal of political pressure from grassroots organizations, coalitions, allies from different sectors of society and the state, and increasing the political "cost" of not working to end gender violence. Other activists argue that to make progress in this area, women must work to change the status quo: changing the ways in which societies differentially value women and men; establishing women as full and active participants in the legal, economic, and political processes, insuring the education of girls as a route to economic and political empowerment; and promoting women to positions of power and authority so they can work on behalf of women from the inside (cf. Bunch, 1997).

Many writers have pointed to the role violent pornography plays in encouraging callous attitudes toward women. Researchers in this field generally do not define all sexually explicit material as pornography. Instead, researchers have found that it is not sexually explicit material per se but rather sexually explicit scenes containing violence against women that has the most dramatic effects on attitudes and behavior. Linz, Donnerstein, and Penrod (1984) found that experimental groups exposed to violent images embedded in sexually explicit scenes, or even violent images alone, compared to control groups and those exposed to X-rated films, were more likely to discount the experience of rape victims. The victim's injuries were seen as less severe and the experimental groups judged her more worthless as a person. Other experimental research confirms these findings and suggests that exposure to violent pornography results in increased callousness toward women, acceptance of rape myths, and increased aggression toward women in the laboratory (Donnerstein & Berkowitz, 1981; Malamuth & Check, 1981). In addition, studies of domestic violence have found that battered women are more likely than other women to report sexual aggression from their partners. Such sexual aggression often occurs in the context of the batterer trying to force the woman to perform acts seen in pornographic books, films, or photographs (Cramer & McFarlane, 1994). Pornography also depicts women of color in stereotypical and uniquely demeaning ways (Collins, 1997).

Given the weight of research evidence linking violent depictions and violent pornography, however indirectly, with violence against women, it seems reasonable to consider these facts in any prevention efforts. Interestingly, most people are more vocal in their protests against nudity and depictions of consensual sex in film, music video, or printed materials, than against violent depictions. Until we come to terms with our own ambivalence around these issues, violence against women will continue to be associated with the coupling of sex and violence in pornographic images.

## Self-Protection and Resistance

Many of the global efforts by women's organizations are focused on political resistance to gender violence. Yet, individual women in all societies make personal decisions every day about the nature and vigor of their resistance to male violence. In the United States, as in other societies throughout the world, women are still socialized to be "ladylike": silent, acquiescent, compliant, and nonassertive. It is unacceptable for women to be hostile toward men, while men's hostility toward women is not only acceptable, but also expected. As Martha Burt (1991) points out, if a man has hostile feelings toward women "the culture will provide ample support for the 'truth' of these feelings . . . and he will not therefore have to confront them as feelings. . . . However, if a woman feels hostile to men, she will experience a lot of baiting and rejection. The culture does not support women's hostility toward men, however justified" (p. 33). If a woman comments negatively about men's behavior she is labeled a "bitch, a man-hater, or a ball-buster." After I had presented the FBI and U. S. Department of Justice incidence and prevalence rates for crimes against women, a student in my Women and Violence course told me that her boyfriend's response was that I must be a man-hater or why would I say such things. Even the presentation of factual information is taboo. A "good woman" is supposed to be silent about male violence.

Closely aligned with women's silence is women's enforced inaction. Women are raised to take up less space than men, to yield to men, to avoid contact sports, and when accosted by a rapist, not to resist for fear of making him angry and thus "being hurt" more, or even killed. In the early part of the twentieth century in the United States it was believed that women's inherently weak physical and emotional constitution made sports participation a health risk; if women engaged in sports (especially basketball) they could damage their reproductive organs and perhaps cause infertility (Griffin, 1998). Such social myths were eventually debunked by science. In the United States today there are certain myths about rape resistance and self-defense that are largely believed by a majority of people and these myths persist despite widespread evidence to the contrary. These myths feed on women's fears of rape and their physical insecurity and create a psychology of helplessness. Many women have told me they fear that their first reaction if confronted by a rapist would be to totally freeze. In a recent pilot study that I conducted with 79 first-year college women, 48 percent of the women said they were afraid they would freeze if accosted by a rapist. Most women believe that they are physically inferior to most men and thus could not effectively defend themselves. Women are socialized to focus on beauty first, and more recently, on physical fitness (i.e., aerobic endurance), but not on physical strength. Like the women of the early twentieth century, modern women believe in their "natural" physical weakness and do little to change it. These beliefs persist in spite of evidence that shows women are four times more likely to escape a would-be rapist than they are to be raped by him (Riger & Gordon, 1989).

Again, we must turn to the scientific evidence to put these myths to rest. The most comprehensive information on rape resistance to date is found in a recent review article by Sarah Ullman (1997). After reviewing all published studies on rape resistance she concludes that forceful physical resistance by the victim is consistently related to rape avoidance. Furby and Fischhoff (1986), who conducted an earlier review of the literature, found the same results. In fact, they found that forceful resistance strategies were related to rape avoidance even for acquaintance rapes and attacks with weapons. Ullman and Knight (1993) found that women who fought back were more likely to avoid rape than women who did not fight back, regardless of whether or not a weapon was present. One study did find that physical resistance may be less effective in avoiding acquaintance rape (Levine-MacCombie & Koss, 1986), but this may be an artifact of the *manner* of physical resistance. Physically "struggling" as a method of self-defense described by Levine-MacCombie and Koss is less effective than the physical kicks and punches typically taught in self-defense courses. Such powerful techniques are less likely to be used on dates than on strangers, and this may contribute to the finding of less effectiveness (Rozee, Bateman, & Gilmore, 1991). Most researchers conclude that traditional advice from authorities telling women to refrain from resisting is unsupported by virtually every research study on the topic. It also has the unintended effect of increasing the percentage of completed rapes.

A related self-defense myth is that if you try to resist your attacker you are more likely to get hurt. First, only three percent of rapes involve some additional injury that is serious; usually the rape itself is the most serious injury suffered (Kleck & Sayles, 1990). Second, a woman who fights back is *no* more likely to be hurt than one who does not fight back. Virtually all women who do not resist are raped, but the research evidence also shows that those who fight back are far less likely to be raped and no more likely to be hurt (Bart & O'Brien, 1985; Furby & Fischhoff, 1986; Kleck & Sayles, 1990; Ullman, 1997). Brown (1995) points out that many police officers and even some rape investigators share the common belief that if women fight back they will be hurt more. She points out that these myths persist despite a 1989 FBI study that found no correlation between victim resistance and physical injury.

Some early studies on rape resistance did find a *noncausal* relationship between fighting back and physical injury. These studies may have fueled rape myths because they failed to study the sequence of offender attack, victim resistance, and injury. Most of these studies correctly pointed out that the relationship they found was *not* causal because they had not looked at which came first: the injury or the fighting back. Was she being physically injured which then prompted her to fight back, or was she injured because she fought back? The answer can be found in several recent studies that did analyze the sequence of events. A large-scale study using a representative sample from the National Crime Surveys from 1979–1985 found that resistance was not significantly related to higher rates of injury since the attack against the victim provoked the victim resistance rather than the reverse (Kleck & Sayles, 1990). Quincey and Upfold (1985) found that physical resistance was related to less injury. Ullman and Knight (1991, 1992) found that women who fought back forcefully experienced less severe sexual abuse and no more injury than those who did not. In a study of police files, Zoucha-Jensen and Coyne (1993) found that women who used forceful resistance were no more likely to be injured than women who did not resist. All of these studies also found that rape resistance was associated with rape avoidance and no resistance was associated with being raped. Yet, as a culture we dissuade women from defending themselves by persuading them that they are likely to be hurt by fighting back.

A related myth is that physical resistance provokes increased violence in particular types of rapists, such as sadists (see Groth, 1990). Recently, Ullman and Knight (1995) conducted a study to examine this myth. Based on a random sample of incarcerated rapists, they found that women who fought in response to sadistic rapists were no more likely to experience physical injury than women who did not. These researchers caution against issuing warnings against the supposed dangers of physical resistance to sadistic rapists in the absence of empirical data to support such claims. They also note the absurdity of advising women to assess the "type" of rapist before determining whether or not to resist. Rus Funk (1993) questions the usefulness of classifying rapists as power, anger, or sadistic rapists. He asserts that rape is a consciously chosen behavior. It follows that claims that men who rape are driven by power, anger, or sadism take rape out of the realm of personal choice by men who rape and carry it into the arena of psychotherapy, which tends to depoliticize sexual violence. According to this argument, with occasional exceptions, rape is not a pathological behavior; rather it is chosen by the men who do it and condoned by the social and cultural institutions of our society.

As summarized elsewhere (Rozee, 2000; Rozee, 1999), resistance studies (Bart & O'Brien, 1985; Brown, 1995; Furby & Fischhoff, 1986; Kleck & Sayles, 1990; Ullman, 1997; Ullman & Knight, 1991, 1992, 1993, 1995; Ullman & Siegel, 1993; Koss & Mukai, 1993; Zoucha-Jensen & Coyne, 1993) show a consistent pattern of results:

1. Women who fight back and fight back immediately are less likely to be raped than women who do not.
2. Women who fight back are no more likely to be injured than women who do not fight back (victim resistance often occurred in response to physical attack).
3. Pleading, begging, crying, and reasoning are ineffective in preventing rape or physical injury (Bart & O'Brien, 1985; Ullman & Knight, 1995; Zoucha-Jensen & Coyne, 1993).
4. Women who fight back experience less post-assault symptomatology (both physical and psychological) due to avoidance of being raped (Ullman & Knight, 1995; Ullman & Siegel, 1993).
5. Women who fight back have faster psychological recoveries whether or not they are raped.
6. Fighting back strengthens the physical evidence should the survivor decide to prosecute for rape or attempted rape (Bachman, 1993).

Ellen Snortland's (1998) book, *Beauty Bites Beast: Awakening the Warrior within Women and Girls*, attacks the social promotion of passive womanhood and encourages rape resistance. Victim resistance makes rape completion more difficult, increases the effort required by the rapist, and prolongs the attack, thereby increasing the risk of discovery and capture. It also increases the probability of injury to the rapist, and may leave marks that could contribute to later discovery. Warning women not to fight back because they might get hurt is based in myth, not scientific evidence, and contributes to a destructive pattern of silence and inaction among women.

Rape prevention will require more than efforts by women to learn and practice self-defense and rape resistance or other prevention strategies. It will require more than the exemplary efforts by some cities to form Sexual Assault Response Teams (SARTs) to facilitate the victim being required to tell her story only once to a SART team composed of district attorney, police, forensic nurse, and rape crisis advocates. While all these efforts help ameliorate the trauma of rape and, in the case of self-defense, may even prevent individual victimization, seldom does effort *by* the victim or *for* the victim result in significant changes in a social problem (Levine & Perkins, 1987). Rather, it will require a paradigmatic shift for psychologists and activists to view this problem from another angle. Instead of focusing on "repairing" the damage to the victims of rape, we must focus on rape as a social problem requiring interventions with perpetrators, with "normal" men, and with the social institutions that serve to perpetuate rape by blaming the victim, shifting blame away from the perpetrators, and ignoring the social conditions that condone rape.

## SEXUAL HARASSMENT

Thirty to fifty percent of women students (Fitzgerald, 1993) and as many as 75 percent of women workers have been sexually harassed (Wood, 1997). Female workers or students have a 40 percent chance of encountering some form of sexual harassment in their work or school lives (Barak, Fisher, & Houston, 1992). Sexual harassment is characterized as a hidden crime because it is rarely reported. Many women respond to sexual harassment by transferring from, or quitting, schools or jobs; thus the statistics we have may be suspect (Gutek, 1985).

The nation became aware of the nature of sexual harassment in 1991 when a renowned law professor, Dr. Anita Hill, came forward to charge a Supreme Court nominee, Dr. Clarence Thomas, with sexual harassment. Anita Hill was ridiculed and humiliated by the senators who questioned her. Despite the fact that several other women also came forward to claim he harassed them at work, Clarence Thomas was appointed as a Supreme Court Justice. Nowhere has the gendered nature of this form of violence against women been so clearly delineated. For women across America, the Hill–Thomas hearings drew the battle lines of the "gender war." As Margaret Randall (1992) points out in her introduction to the book, *Sexual Harassment: Women Speak Out*, the people listening to Anita Hill's testimony heard two different stories. Those with an awareness of the sexual oppression of women (mostly women) heard a different story than those with a vested interest in patriarchal values (mostly men). A *Los Angeles Times* staff writer, Marlene Cimons, called it the *Click!* heard around the nation. Suddenly the silent majority of women "got it." Hill's testimony helped to break the silence of many women who had suffered sexual harassment but had never spoken of it. Feminist attorney Gloria Allred's office was logging 300 calls a day instead of the usual 400 calls per month from women seeking legal advice about sexual harassment. The Equal Employment Opportunity Commission (EEOC) received 6883 sexual harassment complaints in 1991. This number skyrocketed to 10,522 complaints in 1992 following the Hill–Thomas hearings. Never again would the silence and shame of sexual harassment isolate its victims. Women began to speak out.

## Legal Definitions

Sexual harassment is a relatively recent addition to legal discourse. It was only in the mid-1960s that women first petitioned the U. S. legal system to create a separate statute against sexual harassment in the workplace. In the landmark case of *Meritor vs. Vinson,* the U. S. Supreme Court defined sexual harassment precisely (Ford & Donis, 1996) as a form of sex discrimination. It was defined as unwanted and unwelcome verbal or nonverbal behavior of a sexual nature that links academic or professional status to sexual favors or that hinders work or learning (Wood, 1997).

There are two types of sexual harassment: quid pro quo and hostile environment. *Quid pro quo* harassment is actual or threatened use of rewards or punishments to obtain sexual submission. Some examples are the promise of raises or promotions for sexual favors, or the denial of a scholarship for refusal of sexual advances. *Hostile environment* was recognized in 1986 as a common type of sexual harassment involving a pattern of hostile or intimidating conditions in the work or learning environment that hinders one's ability to function effectively. This may include the display of pornographic depictions in a faculty office, lewd remarks by a supervisor, or sexual language that is demeaning. Till (1980) gives the most comprehensive definition of the five most common types of sexual harassment, ranging from generalized sexist remarks or behaviors; inappropriate and offensive sexual advances; coercion by threat of punishment; gross sexual imposition (fondling, touching, grabbing); to sexual assault.

## Gender Differences

Many studies have confirmed that males tend to see female behavior as having more sexual meaning than women do. While men may interpret a conversation to be flirtatious, women interpret the same conversation as merely friendly. Women perceive a greater variety of sexual behaviors as sexual harassment compared with men. Men believe that social–sexual behavior in the workplace is appropriate and have broader definitions as to what is acceptable (Thacker & Gohmann, 1996). Women are less tolerant of sexually harassing behaviors (Ford & Donis, 1996). This differing perspective of women was recently used as psychological evidence to justify a shift from a "reasonable person" standard to a "reasonable woman" standard in determining if a particular behavior was sexual harassment. The difference was codified into law in the landmark case of Ellison vs. Brady. In this case, jurors were instructed to take the woman's perspective (e.g., feeling vulnerable to sexual violence) and consider the effects of this perspective on her perceptions of sexual harassment.

## Characteristics of Offenders

In a comprehensive examination of correlates of a proclivity to sexually harass, Bartling and Eisenman (1993) looked at many of the same beliefs that we have previously examined when discussing perpetrators of rape. They found that there is a significant relationship between the self-professed likelihood to rape and the likelihood to sexually harass. Men who said they were likely to sexually harass a woman also scored higher in adversarial sexual beliefs, rape myth acceptance, and acceptance of interpersonal violence than men who reported no likelihood of harassing (Bartling & Eisenman, 1993). Research by Reilly, Lott, Caldwell and DeLuca (1992) confirms these findings and extends them by finding that these variables were also significantly related to actual confessed experience as a sexual victimizer as measured by the Koss Sexual Experiences Survey. A vivid example of the demonstration of this constellation of traits is the recent Navy Tailhook incident. During this incident, 83 women and 7 men were sexually assaulted and harassed by naval officers at a La Vegas convention in 1991 (Lott, 1994). These men created a violent ritual of forcing women to "run the gauntlet" while men grabbed and groped them sexually. The ritual allowed the kind of exclusionary fraternal bonding typical of group rapists (Rozee-Koker & Polk, 1986). The behaviors and attitudes of these soldiers are correlated with the likelihood of rape and sexual harassment described by the research mentioned earlier. Women in such rituals are seen as sexual objects solely for men's pleasure (adversarial sexual beliefs); women are thought to like rough treatment and deserve it (belief in rape myths); and the ritual itself is violent (acceptance of interpersonal violence) in an occupational setting that is founded on male values of dominance and control through war and fighting—the U. S. Military.

## Characteristics of Victims

Anyone can be sexually harassed, but the vast majority of victims are female. All woman can be sexually harassed, although younger, unmarried (single, divorced, or lesbian) women are most vulnerable (Fitzgerald & Ormerod, 1993; Riger, 1991). Women students and professionals in all fields have been harassed, but those in nontraditional fields are especially likely to experience sexual harassment. Women in nontraditional fields face more severe sexual harassment with greater risk of physical harm such as physical hazing, receiving faulty or dangerous equipment, or not receiving backup on emergency calls (Fitzgerald, 1993). In a unique study of African-American women firefighters, Janice Yoder and Patricia Aniakudo (1996) reported that 77 percent of the women perceived that they had been sexually harassed since they became firefighters. Most of the women reported being the target of behaviors indicative of a hostile work environment, such as negative verbal insults, being called names such as bitch, dyke, whore, load (dead weight), or militant. These women were also subjected to flashing, lack of privacy in bathrooms, pornographic images left in lockers, and ill-fitting gear that jeopardized physical safety. Women of color face a double jeopardy situation in such jobs, making it impossible to distinguish the effects of race and gender in creation of a hostile climate. In fact Yoder and Aniakudo (1996) report a .68 correlation between perceptions of racial climate and gender climate; women who reported an unfavorable gender climate also perceived the environment to be unfriendly to racial minorities.

Despite the risks women in nontraditional careers face, Burgess and Borgida (1997) report that people are less likely to see incidents as sexual harassment when a woman is in a nontraditional career, especially blue collar work. They were also less likely to endorse disciplinary actions by supervisors against perpetrators (Burgess & Borgida, 1997). Participants in this study were also less likely to recommend the victim file a formal complaint or initiate legal action against the harassor if she was in a nontraditional career.

Women in professional fields can also be vulnerable to sexual harassment. In a review of the literature on sexual harassment in medical education, Lois Margaret Nora (1996) reports that 34 percent to 73 percent of women and 15 percent to 22 percent of men reported experiencing sexual harassment during their medical education. Women tended to perceive sexual harassment as happening more often than did men. Neither was likely to report such experiences despite negative outcomes such as interference with ability to work and participate in the learning environment, avoidance of training opportunities, and drops in performance (Nora, 1996). In another study of medical school students, it was found that 46 percent of female medical students (and 15% of males) had experienced sexual harassment from a professor and 70 percent of students reported having observed such sexual harassment (Bergen, Guarino, & Jacobs, 1996). These experiences were associated with a decrease in feelings of a positive campus climate and an increase in negative ratings of the campus. This was true whether the student merely observed or actually experienced sexual harassment. Completing medical school does not seem to stop the harassment. Phillips and Schneider (1993) found that 77 percent of female physicians reported being sexually harassed on the job.

Research with female psychologists found that 53 percent were sexually harassed in clinical practice by patients (deMayo, 1997). These therapists drew the distinction between normal transference and sexual harassment or countertherapeutic behavior. Although Robert deMayo (1997) estimates incidence of sexual harassment of women physicians and psychologists at only about one in 5000 therapeutic contacts, he advocates graduate and postgraduate training so that women are prepared to handle it if it happens.

Nora (1996) contends that the problem of sexual harassment is even more severe for minority women who are even more likely to be subjected to it, although this has been inadequately studied. In a stratified community sample of African-American and white American women, Gail Wyatt and Monika Riederle (1995) found a 44 percent incidence of sexual harassment of women at work. Single African-American women who were currently working were at a greater risk of being sexually harassed than their white cohort. Overall, however, Wyatt and Riederle (1995) found more white than African-American women reporting an incident of harassment. Wyatt points out that black women tend to underreport sexually abusive incidents compared to white women. Ella Louise Bell (1992) concurs with Gail Wyatt's view regarding the underreporting by black women. As mentioned earlier, there may be a "code of silence" surrounding sexual harassment, especially if the harassor is a black man. Bell (1992) points out the complexity inherent in sexual harassment when sex and race are intertwined. In the case of Clarence Thomas, Bell states that if he was the victim of a "high tech lynching" then Anita Hill was the victim of a "high tech raping" (p. 365) by an all white male committee of the U. S. Senate. The Hill–Thomas hearings perpetuated a number of myths about black women, especially professional women (Bell, 1992), that served to undermine the faith of all women in our system of justice.

## Power and Sexual Harassment

It is widely acknowledged that power is at the root of sexual harassment. It is easy to identify power difference due to role status: professor/student; supervisor/worker; rich/poor. This is called *achieved power*—that which someone earns—money, formal role, position, or information, and the like. The cases of sexual harassment that have been discussed thus far in this chapter fall primarily into this category. However, there are other categories of power that are equally potent and have recently become the focus of research. Stringer, Remick, Salisbury, and Ginorio (1990) describe the following power categories as important to the consideration of sexual harassment.

### Ascribed Power

Ascribed power is that which is given to someone and cannot be taken away, such as gender, race, age, and so on. Even though a woman may have role power, such as a professor, she does not have access to the societal value placed on the male gender, that is, *ascribed*, to maleness. When a woman with achieved power is sexually harassed by a male student with ascribed power, it is called *contrapower* harassment (McKinney, 1992). Female professors are "powerless" in terms of gender (assuming a male student), and this may be the essential power difference in the case of sexual harassment (Grauerholz, 1989). The male student carries the whole weight of the patriarchal social structure with him as protection from the female professor whom he is harassing. While students may not be much of a professional threat, men do represent a physical threat to women despite the woman's formal power. Prevalence of contrapower harassment among female faculty is estimated at 6 percent to 50 percent (McKinney, 1992). Grauerholz (1989) reports that 82 percent of women faculty stated that male students were exclusively the perpetrators. Harassment ranges from sexist comments and obscene phone calls to sexual assault. It is common for contrapower harassment to be anonymous because of the threat of retaliation. Most faculty feel they should handle this form of sexual harassment rather than report it (Grauerholz, 1989; McKinney, 1992). It is also possible that the professor's complaint may be disregarded because others feel that she had the formal power to stop the harassment if she really wanted to (Stringer et al., 1990). Although it may be easier for women professors to deal effectively with such sexual harassment simply because they do have access to the trappings of authority, it is important to note that all forms of harassment undermine one's confidence, quality of work, and professional growth. Male professors are not likely to feel harassed by students, nor can they be harassed in the gendered way that female professors can, thus it may be difficult for them to understand contrapower harassment (Grauerholz, 1989).

### Ethnic Power

Ethnic power can also affect sexual harassment because whites are more powerful and valued in U. S. culture than people of color (Stringer et al., 1990). Often, complaints by ethnic victims are not taken as seriously, investigated as thoroughly, or punished as strongly. On the contrary, ethnic harassors of white women are often more severely disciplined (Stringer et al., 1990).

## Peer Harassment

The power that the harassor has over the victim is a key contextual variable in sexual harassment (Bursik, 1992). However, harassment by peers is very common; in fact, co-workers may constitute the majority of harassors (Ivy & Hamlet, 1996). Women are most often the targets of peer harassment. Ivy and Hamlet (1996) report that among women college students, 68 percent to 92 percent perceived sexual harassment by peers, including unwanted and repeated touching or lewd or sexist comments. The classroom was one of the most common locales for sexual harassment. Both women and men thought peer harassment was a problem on college campuses. Faculty women are more likely to be harassed by peers than by students, while the opposite is true for male faculty members (McKinney, 1990).

## Outcomes of Sexual Harassment

The negative outcomes of sexual harassment include physical, emotional, and job-related factors. In general, severity of sexual harassment determines strength of the reaction (Baker, Terpstra, & Larntz, 1990). Michelle Paludi describes the psychological effects of sexual harassment in her formulation of the Sexual Harassment Trauma Syndrome (Paludi & Barickman, 1991). The syndrome contains a constellation of reactions: emotional (anxiety, denial, anger, fear, shame); physical (headaches; sleep disturbances; stomach, respiratory, and urinary problems; substance abuse); self-perception (negative self-concept, hopelessness, powerlessness, isolation); social (withdrawal, lack of trust, fear of others, sexual problems, changes in dress or physical appearance); and career (drop in performance, loss of job or promotion, absenteeism, changes in career goals). It is important to note that both male and female sexual harassment victims are equally traumatized by the experience; the psychological outcomes are very similar regardless of victim gender (Thacker & Gohmann, 1996). Such personal trauma and changes in behavior will have effects on co-workers and the workplace in general. Many authors have addressed the consequences to employers of unchecked sexual harassment: high turnover, sick leaves, reduced productivity, poor attitudes toward work, and loss of quality employees (Goodman, Koss, Fitzgerald, Russo, & Keita, 1993; Thacker & Gohmann, 1996). A recent survey of Fortune 500 companies found that sexual harassment costs a typical company

$6.7 million per year in absenteeism, turnover, and loss of productivity (Stanko & Miller, 1996). The financial burden of sexual harassment on the entire country in terms of costs to the health care, educational, and criminal justice systems is obvious (Goodman et al., 1993).

It is crucial that the institutional response to sexual harassment be immediate and direct. The only effective response is corrective action, from verbal reprimand to termination, depending on the frequency and intensity of the sexual harassment (Stringer et al., 1990). Preventive programs such as educational workshops and informal reporting mechanisms are basic. Research has shown that educational interventions are effective in increasing sensitivity to sexual harassment and, in fact, may even bring men up to the level of sensitivity of women (Bonate & Jessell, 1996). In a comprehensive review of the current state of sexual harassment in the United States, Fitzgerald (1993) outlines three categories of needed initiatives, including research, legal reform, and prevention. Federal funding for harassment research has been practically nonexistent, thus research has been severely limited. More research is needed to understand the dynamics and outcomes of sexual harassment, especially with respect to women of color and other high-risk groups. Fitzgerald suggests that legislation be introduced to require all employers to develop clear sexual harassment policies, to remove caps on damages, extend the statute of limitations (currently only 180 days for the EEOC), and ensure that the legal system does not represent a second victimization. There is currently no shield law for sexual harassment that would prevent a woman's sexual history from being introduced as evidence against her. Finally, Fitzgerald (1993) points out, primary prevention is the only real solution.

## SUMMARY

Rape, sexual harassment, and other forms of violence against women are normative in U. S. and other cultures. To change such social mores, efforts must be made to bring such assumptions to light. Women's organizations all over the world are now working to change such horrific practices as dowry death, the killing of 5000 women a year in India because in-laws are disappointed in the size of the dowry; and the forced genital mutilation (removal of the clitoris) that is suffered by 6000 girls every day in parts Africa and the Sudan; and rape as the "spoils" of war in male battles all over the world (Bunch, 1997). In the United States the fight against domestic violence, sexual assault, and sexual harassment has made some progress in the last 10 to 20 years. Wife beating and rape are illegal in all states, marital rape is illegal in almost all states, and sexual harassment policies are in place in most major universities and corporations. The progress that has been made in changing the way we think about such violent acts is notable because it has been made solely through the efforts of grassroots groups of women. As Charlotte Bunch (1997) points out: "Few social movements have registered as great an impact in as short a time—and with such remarkably peaceful methods. And yet, these small, determined groups continue to work largely alone. How many government officials have staked their careers on resolving the problem of gender-based violence?"(p. 45). Women learned how to use politics to persuade policy makers and legislators to make change. We learned to say "NO" at the same time as we learned not take no for an answer.

## REFERENCES

Bachman, R. (1993). Predicting the reporting of rape victimizations: Have reforms made a difference? *Criminal Justice and Behavior, 20,* 254–270.

Bachman, R. (1998). The factors related to rape reporting behavior and arrest. *Criminal Justice and Behavior, 25,* 8–29.

Baker, D. D., Terpstra, D. E., & Larntz, K. (1990). The influence of individual characteristics and severity of harassing behavior on reactions to sexual harassment. *Sex Roles, 22,* 305–323.

Barak, A., Fisher, W. A., & Houston, S. (1992). Individual difference correlates of the experience of sexual harassment among female university students. *Journal of Applied Social Psychology, 22,* 17–37.

Bart, P. B., & O'Brien, P. (1985). *Stopping rape: Successful survival strategies.* New York: Pergamon Press.

Bartling, C. A., & Eisenman, R. (1993). Sexual harassment proclivities in men and women. *Bulletin of the Psychonomic Society, 31,* 189–192.

Bell, E. L. (1992). Myths, stereotypes, and realities of Black women: A personal reflection. *Journal of Applied Behavioral Science, 28,* 363–376.

Bergen, M. R., Guarino, C. M, & Jacobs, C. D. (1996). A climate survey for medical students: A means to assess change. *Evaluation and the Health Professions, 19*(1), 30–47.

Bonate, D. L., & Jessell, J. C. (1996). The effects of educational intervention on perceptions of sexual harassment. *Sex Roles, 35,* 751–764.

Brown, M. (1995, July 23). Should you fight? No easy answers. *The Sacramento Bee,* p. A10.

Brownmiller, S. (1975). *Against our will: Men, women and rape.* New York: Simon & Schuster.

Bunch, C. (1997). The intolerable status quo: Violence against women and girls. *The Progress of Nations* (pp. 41–49). New York: UNICEF.

Bureau of Justice Statistics. (1997). *Sex offenses and offenders* (DOJ Publication No. NCJ-163931). Washington, DC: U.S. Government Printing Office.

Burgess, D., & Borgida E. (1997). Sexual harassment: An experimental test of sex-role spillover theory. *Personality and Social Psychology Bulletin, 23,* 63–75.

Bursik, K. (1992). Perceptions of sexual harassment in an academic context. *Sex Roles, 27,* 401–412.

Burt, M. R. (1991). Rape myths and acquaintance rape. In A. Parrot & L. Bechhofer (Eds.), *Acquaintance rape: The hidden crime* (pp. 26–40). New York: John Wiley & Sons, Inc.

Collins, P. H. (1997). Pornography and Black women's bodies. In L. L. O'Toole & J. R. Schiffman (Eds.), *Gender violence: Interdisciplinary perspectives* (pp. 395–399). New York: New York University Press.

Cramer, E. & MacFarlane, J. (1994). Pornography and abuse of women. *Public Health Nursing, 11,* 268–272.

deMayo, R. A. (1997). Patient sexual behavior and sexual harassment: A national survey of female psychologists. *Professional Psychology: Research and Practice, 28,* 58–62.

Donnerstein, E. & Berkowitz, L. (1981). Victim reactions in aggressive-erotic films as a factor in violence against women. *Journal of Personality and Social Psychology, 41,* 710–724.

Edwards, C. (1987). Public opinion on domestic violence: A review of the New Jersey survey. *Response to the Victimization of Women and Children, 10*(1), 6–9.

Estrich, S. (1987). *Real rape: How the legal system victimizes women who say no.* Cambridge, MA: Harvard University Press.

Fitzgerald, L. F. (1993). Sexual harassment: Violence against women in the workplace. *American Psychologist, 48,* 1070–1076.

Fitzgerald, L. F., & Ormerod, A. J. (1993). Breaking silence: The sexual harassment of women in academia and the workplace. In F. L. Denmark & M. A. Paludi (Eds.), *Psychology of women: A handbook of issues and theories* (pp. 553–581). Westport, CT: Greenwood Press/Greenwood Publishing Group.

Foley, L. A., Evancic, C., Karnik, K., King, J., & Parks, A. (1995). Date rape: Effects of race of assailant and victim and gender of subjects on perceptions. *Journal of Black Psychology, 21,* 6–18.

Fonow, M. M., Richardson, L., & Wemmerus, V. A. (1992). Feminist rape education: Does it work? *Gender and Society, 6,* 108–121.

Ford, C. A., & Donis, F. J. (1996). The relationship between age and gender in workers' attitudes toward sexual harassment. *Journal of Psychology, 130,* 627–633.

Fortune, M. M. (1983). *Sexual violence: The unmentionable sin.* Cleveland: Pilgrim Press.

Fortune, M. M. (1987). *Keeping the faith.* San Francisco: Harper & Row.

Funk, R. E. (1993). *Stopping rape: A challenge for men.* Philadelphia: New Society Publishers.

Furby, L., & Fischhoff, B. (1986). *Rape self-defense strategies: A review of their effectiveness.* Eugene, OR: Eugene Research Institute.

Garnets, L., Herek, G. M., & Levy, B. (1993). Violence and victimization of lesbians and gay men: Mental health consequences. In L. Garnets & D. Kimmel (Eds.), *Psychological perspectives on lesbian and gay male experiences* (pp. 579–597). New York: Columbia University Press.

Gelman, D. (1993, April 12). Mixed messages. *Newsweek,* pp. 28–29.

Goodchilds, J. D., Zellman, G. L., Johnson, P. B., Giarusso, R. (1988). Adolescents and their perception of sexual interactions. In A. W. Burgess (Ed), *Rape and sexual assault* (Vol. 2, pp. 245–270). New York: Garland.

Goodman, L. A., Koss, M. P., Fitzgerald, L. F., Russo, N. F., & Keita, G. P. (1993). Male violence against women: Current research and future directions. *American Psychologist, 48*, 1054–1058.

Grauerholz, E. (1989). Sexual harassment of women professors by students: Exploring the dynamics of power, authority, and gender in a university setting. *Sex Roles, 21*, 789–801.

Griffin, P. (1998). *Strong women, deep closets: Lesbians and homophobia in sport*. Champaign, IL: Human Kinetics.

Groth, A. N. (1990). *Men who rape: The psychology of the offender*. New York: Plenum Press.

Gutek, B. A. (1985). *Sex and the workplace*. San Francisco: Jossey-Bass.

Heise, L. L. (1989). International dimensions of violence against women. *Response to the Victimization of Women and Children, 12*(1), 3–11.

Heise, L. L., Ellsberg, M., & Gottemoeller, M. (1999). Ending violence against women. *Population Reports, 27*(4), 1–43.

Heise, L. L., Raikes, A., Watts, C. H., & Zwi, A. B. (1994). Violence against women: A neglected public health issue in less developed countries. *Social Science Medicine, 39*(9), 1165–1179.

Holland, D. C., & Eisenhart, M. A. (1990). *Educated in romance: Women, achievement, and college culture*. Chicago: University of Chicago Press.

Holzman, C. G. (1994). Multicultural perspectives on counseling survivors of rape. *Journal of Social Distress and the Homeless, 3*(1), 87–97.

Ivy, D. K., & Hamlet, S. (1996). College students and sexual dynamics: Two studies of peer sexual harassment. *Communication Education, 45*, 149–166.

Kalof, L., & Wade, B. H. (1995). Sexual attitudes and experiences with sexual coercion: Exploring the influence of race and gender. *Journal of Black Psychology, 21*, 224–238.

Kleck, G., & Sayles, S. (1990). Rape and resistance. *Social Problems, 37*(2), 149–162.

Koss, M. P. (1993). Rape: Scope, impact, interventions, and public policy responses. *American Psychologist, 48*, 1062–1069.

Koss, M. P., & Dinero, T. E. (1989). Discriminant analysis of risk factors for sexual victimization among a national sample of college women. *Journal of Consulting and Clinical Psychology, 57*, 242–250.

Koss, M. P., Leonard, K. E., Beezley, D. A., & Oros, C. J. (1985). Nonstranger sexual aggression: A discriminant analysis of the psychological characteristics of undetected offenders. *Sex Roles, 12*, 981–992.

Koss, M. P., & Mukai, T. (1993). Recovering ourselves: Frequency, effects and resolution of rape. In F. L. Denmark & M. A. Paludi (Eds.), *Psychology of women: A handbook of issues and theories* (pp. 477–512). Westport, CT: Greenwood Press.

Lefley, H. P., Scott, C. S., Llabre, M., & Hicks, D. (1993). Cultural beliefs about rape and victims' response in three ethnic groups. *American Journal of Orthopsychiatry, 63*, 623–632.

Levine, M., & Perkins, D. V. (1987). *Principles of community psychology: Perspectives and applications*. New York: Oxford University Press.

Levine-MacCombie, J., & Koss, M. P. (1986). Acquaintance rape: Effective avoidance strategies. *Psychology of Women Quarterly, 10*, 311–319.

Linz, D., Donnerstein, E., & Penrod, S. (1984). The effects of long-term exposure to filmed violence against women. *Journal of Communication, 34*, 130–147.

Lonsway, K. A., & Fitzgerald, L. F. (1994). Rape myths: In review. *Psychology of Women Quarterly, 18*, 133–164.

Lott, B. (1994). *Women's lives: Themes and variations in gender learning*. Pacific Grove, CA: Brooks-Cole.

Malamuth, N. M., & Donnerstein, E. (Eds.). (1984). *Pornography and sexual aggression*. Orlando: Academic Press.

Malamuth, S. E., & Check, J. V. P. (1981). The effects of mass media exposure on acceptance of violence against women: A field experiment. *Journal of Research in Personality, 15*, 436–446.

McKinney, K. (1990). Sexual harassment of university faculty by colleagues and students. *Sex Roles, 23*, 421–438.

McKinney, K. (1992). Contrapower sexual harassment: The effects of student sex and type of behavior on faculty perceptions. *Sex Roles, 27*, 627–643.

Mills, C. S., & Granoff, B. J. (1992). Date and acquaintance rape among a sample of college students. *Social Work, 37*, 504–509.

Mollica, R. (1986, August). *Cambodian refugee women at risk*. Paper presented at the American Psychological Association Annual Meeting, Washington, DC.

Mori, L., Bernat, J. A., Glenn, P. A., Selle, L. L., & Zarate, M. G. (1995). Attitudes towards rape: Gender and ethnic differences across Asian and Caucasian college students. *Sex Roles, 32*, 457–467.

Nora, L. M. (1996). Sexual harassment in medical education: A review of the literature with comments from the law. *Academic Medicine, 71*(1), S113-S118.

O'Brien, R. M. (1987). The interracial nature of violent crimes: A reexamination. *American Journal of Sociology, 92*, 817–835.

Paludi, M. A., & Barickman, R. (Eds). (1991). *In their own voices: Responses from individuals who have experienced sexual harassment and supportive techniques for dealing with victims of sexual harassment. Academic and workplace sexual harassment: A resource manual.* Albany: State University of New York: Bantam Books.

Phillips, S., & Schneider, M. (1993). Sexual harassment of female doctors by patients. *New England Journal of Medicine, 329*(6), 1936–1939.

Quincey, V. L., & Upfold, D. (1985). Rape completion and victim injury as a function of female resistance strategy. *Canadian Journal of Behavioral Science, 17,* 40–50.

Randall, M. (1992). Introduction. In A. C. Sumrall & D. Taylor (Eds.*),. Sexual harassment: Women speak out* (pp. 18–22). Freedom, CA: The Crossing Press.

Reilly, M. E., Lott, B., Caldwell, D., & DeLuca, L. (1992). Tolerance for sexual harassment related to self-reported sexual victimization. *Gender and Society, 6,* 122–138.

Riger, S. (1991). Gender dilemmas in sexual harassment policies and procedures. *American Psychologist, 46,* 497–505.

Riger, S., & Gordon, M. (1989). *The female fear.* New York: Free Press.

Rozee, P. (1993). Forbidden or forgiven: Rape in cross-cultural perspective. *Psychology of Women Quarterly, 17,* 499–514.

Rozee, P. D. (1999). Stranger rape. In M. Paludi (Ed.), *The psychology of sexual victimization: A handbook.* New York: Greenwood Press.

Rozee, P. (2000). Freedom from fear of rape: The missing link in women's freedom. In J. Chrisler, C. Golden, & P. Rozee (Eds.), *Lectures in the psychology of women* (2nd edition) (pp. 255–260). New York: McGraw-Hill.

Rozee, P., Bateman, P., & Gilmore, T. (1991). The personal perspective of acquaintance rape prevention: A three-tier approach. In A. Parrot & L. Bechhofer (Eds.), *Acquaintance rape: The hidden crime* (pp. 337–354). New York: John Wiley & Sons.

Rozee, P., & Van Boemel, G. (1989). The psychological effects of war trauma and abuse among older refugee women. *Women and Therapy, 8,* 23–50.

Rozee, P. & Van Boemel, G. (1995). Seeing Cambodia: A new view of the research process. *Reflections: Narratives of Professional Helping, 1,* 19–25.

Rozee-Koker, P., & Polk, G. A. (1986). The social psychology of group rape. *Sexual Coercion and Assault: Issues and Perspectives, 1*(2), 57–65.

Russell, D. E. H. (1990). *Rape in marriage* (Rev. ed.). Bloomington: Indiana University Press.

Shotland, R.L., & Straw, M. K. (1976). Bystander response to an assault: When a man attacks a woman. *Journal of Personality and Social Psychology, 34,* 990–999.

Sinclair, H. C., & Bourne, L. E., Jr. (1998). Cycle of blame or just world: Effects of legal verdicts on gender patterns in rape-myth acceptance and victim empathy. *Psychology of Women Quarterly, 22,* 575–588.

Smolowe, J. (1993, April 5). Sex with a scorecard. *Time,* p. 41.

Snortland, E. (1998). *Beauty bites beast: Awakening the warrior within women and girls.* Pasadena, CA: Trilogy Press.

Sorenson, S. B., & Siegel, J. M. (1992). Gender, ethnicity, and sexual assault: Findings from the Los Angeles epidemiological catchment area study. *Journal of Social Issues, 48,* 93–104.

Stanko, B., & Miller, G. J. (1996). Sexual harassment and government accountants: Anecdotal evidence from the profession. *Public Personnel Management, 25*(2), 219–235.

Stringer, D. M., Remick, H., Salisbury, J., & Ginorio, A. B. (1990). The power and reasons behind sexual harassment: An employer's guide to solutions. *Public Personnel Management, 19*(1), 43–52.

Thacker, R. A., & Gohmann, S. F. (1996). Emotional and psychological consequences of sexual harassment: A descriptive study. *Journal of Psychology, 130,* 429–446.

Till, F. J. (1980). *Sexual harassment: A report on the sexual harassment of students.* Washington, DC: National Advisory Council on Women's Educational Programs.

Tyra, P. A. (1993, May). Older women: Victims of rape. *Journal of Gerontological Nursing,* 7–12.

Ullman, S. E. (1997). Review and critique of empirical studies of rape avoidance. *Criminal Justice and Behavior, 24*(2), 177–204.

Ullman, S. E., & Knight, R. A. (1991). A multivariate model for predicting rape and physical injury outcomes duing sexual assaults. *Journal of Consulting and Clinical Psychology, 59,* 724–731.

Ullman, S. E., & Knight, R. A. (1992). Fighting back: Women's resistance to rape. *Journal of Interpersonal Violence, 7,* 31–43.

Ullman, S. E., & Knight, R. A. (1993). The efficacy of women's resistance strategies in rape situations. *Psychology of Women Quarterly, 17,* 23–38.

Ullman, S. E., & Knight, R. A. (1995). Women's resistance strategies to different rapist types. *Criminal Justice and Behavior, 22*(3), 263–283.

Ullman, S. E., & Siegel, J. M. (1993). Victim–offender relationship and sexual assault. *Violence and Victims, 8*(2), 121–134.

Van Boemel, G. & Rozee, P. (1992). Treatment efficacy for psychosomatic blindness among Cambodian refugee women. *Women and Therapy: A Feminist Quarterly, 13*, 239–266.

Warshaw, R. (1988, 1994). *I never called it rape.* New York: Harper Perennial.

Wood, J. (1997). *Gendered lives: Communication, gender and culture.* Belmont, CA: Wadsworth.

Wyatt, G. E. (1992). The sociocultural context of African American and White American women's rape. *Journal of Social Issues, 48*, 77–91.

Wyatt, G. E., & Riederle, M. (1995). The prevalence and context of sexual harassment among African American and White American women. *Journal of Interpersonal Violence, 10*, 309–321.

Yoder, J. D., & Aniakudo, P. (1996). When pranks become harassment: The case of African American women firefighters. *Sex Roles, 35*, 253–270.

Zoucha-Jensen, J. M., & Coyne, A. (1993). The effects of resistance strategies on rape. *American Journal of Public Health, 83*(11), 1633–1634.

# 7

# Intimate Violence

## Maureen C. McHugh
## and Tammy A. R. Bartoszek

## INTRODUCTION

Since the 1970s when feminists called attention to the problem of men beating their wives, widespread changes have occurred in our consciousness concerning this phenomenon. Over the past three decades, approaches to domestic violence have "evolved from male prerogative, to female pathology, to pervasive social problem" (Lipchik, Sirles, & Kubicki, 1997, p. 131). Within the proliferation of research on partner violence, some topics, such as the prevalence of domestic violence and the characteristics and reactions of the victim, have received extensive attention. Other topics such as the reason(s) why men beat women are less frequently and only more recently the focus of study. This chapter critiques the existing research in terms of focus, examines the appropriateness and efficacy of clinical interventions, and argues for viewing intimate violence in a sociocultural context.

## NAMING THE VIOLENCE

What we name a phenomenon both reflects and determines how we conceptualize it. Without a name, we have difficulty discussing our experience. As our conception of the problem develops or changes, so does our vocabulary. Early researchers used terms such as *wife abuse* and *domestic violence*; this reflected the initial focus on the physical violence experienced by married, heterosexual women. Once the silence about battering was broken, additional victims were identified (including lesbians and gay men, unmarried cohabiting couples, dating couples, and women in the process of separation and divorce). Terms such as *wife abuse* and *wife battering* are not inclusive enough to cover all these experiences. Many women are battered by intimates in nonmarital relationships.

Maureen C. McHugh and Tammy A. R. Bartoszek ● Department of Psychology, Indiana University of Pennsylvania, Indiana, Pennsylvania 15705

*Issues in the Psychology of Women,* edited by Biaggio and Hersen. Kluwer Academic/Plenum Publishers, New York, 2000.

Debates about definitions and labels are struggles about conceptualization and ideology (Kelly & Radford, 1998), and may not be resolvable. For example, feminist critics have objected to the use of the terms *domestic violence, family violence,* and *spouse abuse.* In addition to limiting our conception to marital and family relationships, these terms obscure the dimensions of gender and power that are fundamental to understanding the abuse of women (Breines & Gorden, 1983; Schecter, 1982). Generic terms such as *domestic violence* do not distinguish between battering and mutually combative relationships; such terms ignore the context of the violence, its nature and consequences, the role obligations of family members, and the processes that lead to abuse. Such terms can lead to biases as to how the causes and solutions of wife abuse are conceptualized and treated (Bograd, 1988).

Typically, researchers have employed social, legal, conceptual, or methodological perspectives in deciding what constitutes wife abuse. Women's definitions and conceptualizations, (i.e., how a woman labels or defines the "problem") are not considered. Kelly (1988) examined battered women's own conceptualization of their experiences. She reports that the terms typically used to label partner violence caused problems for some of the women in her study. The term *wife beating* was seen as applying only in marital situations, and *battering* tended to be understood in terms of severe frequent physical violence. Kelly (1988) also reported that women changed their labels of their experiences over time. As the episodes increased and escalated, women were likely to relabel earlier incidents as abusive.

The emergence of new terminology, such as *dating violence* and *lesbian battering,* allows more women to speak about their experiences with violence in intimate relationships. Having a label for our experiences helps us to organize and understand the patterns of our daily lives. Yet, giving each form of violence experienced by women in their intimate relationships a different name or term may obscure the persistent and pervasive nature of such violence and may prevent us from examining such violence for underlying causes. Assigning different women different labels for their experienced violence may divide and isolate them.

## INTIMATE VIOLENCE

Today, researchers and clinicians do not agree on the terms, labels, or measures to be used to discuss the coercion, intimidation, or physical assault perpetrated on women in the context of their intimate relationships (Geffner, 1997; Pagelow, 1997). The interchangeable use of terms, such as assaultive, abusive, aggressive, and violent has led to conceptual ambiguity and confusion (Browne, 1989; Brush, 1990). Geffner (1997) suggests the term *partner maltreatment* to refer to the psychological and physical coercion used by one partner against the other to gain control in a relationship. The following review uses the term *intimate violence* to refer to physical injury to women in the context of intimate (romantic/sexual) relationships; *intimate abuse* refers to physical, psychological, and/or sexual coercion exerted on a woman in the context of an intimate relationship. *Intimate violence* has been defined elsewhere as violence between individuals who are known to each other, including: female infanticide; incest and other physical and sexual child abuse; elder abuse; date, acquaintance, and marital rape; bride and gender-related murder; as well as courtship/dating/marital violence (Goodman, Koss, & Russo, 1993; Koss et al., 1994; Russo, Koss, & Goodman, 1995). It is used here in the more circumscribed or limited meaning—to refer to physical, sexual, and psychological coercion; intimidation; and injury to an intimate adult partner—in recognition of the connections between such partner abuse and the other manifestations included in the broad definition. At times the terms *partner abuse* and *partner maltreatment* are used as alternative labels for *intimate abuse.*

## ASSESSING THE VIOLENCE

### Estimated Prevalence

Estimates are that more than one fourth of intimate relationships involve at least one incident of physical assault. Koss (1990) reports that 25 percent to 33 percent of married individuals engage in some form of domestic violence at some point in their relationship. Straus, Gelles, and Steinmetz (1980) report 28 percent in their national survey of more than 2,000 homes. Russell (1982) reports 21 percent for her San Francisco sample of current or previously married women. Frieze and her colleagues found that 34 percent of a general community group of ever married women reported being attacked at least once by a male partner (Frieze, Knoble, Washburn, & Zomnir, 1980). Others indicate lifetime prevalence rates of being a victim of domestic violence at between 18 percent and 30 percent of women, with yearly rates of husband to wife violence at 10 percent to 12 percent (Hotaling & Sugarman, 1986; Schulman, 1979; Smith, 1987). A Canadian national population survey of 12,300 women conducted in 1993 indicated that 29 percent of ever married women have been assaulted by a spouse, and 16 percent of women had been assaulted by a date or boyfriend (Johnson, 1998). The reported experience of wife assault (201,000) was four times higher than the number of cases reported to/by the police. Rates of assault were higher for past unions (48 percent) than for current relationships (15 percent), suggesting that some violent relationships end (Johnson, 1998).

In the past decade we have come to realize that violence is as prevalent among cohabitating and dating couples as it is among married couples. Prevalence rates for violence among nonmarried heterosexual couples are consistently about 25 percent (Cate, Henton, Koval, Christopher, & Lloyd, 1982; Makepeace, 1983), but some research suggests an even higher rate. For example, Deal and Wampler (1986) report that 47 percent of their college sample has some experience with violence in dating relationships. Possibly because the participants are likely to be young (Henton, Cate, Koval, Lloyd, & Christopher, 1983), only about on half of the victims involved will terminate the relationship (Makepeace, 1986).

Rates of intimate abuse have been found to differ among various cultural and ethnic groups. African American women experience intimate violence at a higher rate than European Americans (Cazenave & Straus, 1979) and are more likely to be killed by a partner or former partner (O'Carroll & Mercy, 1986). Latina women also have a greater risk of partner abuse than Anglo women, but less risk than African-American women (Neff, Holamon, & Schluter, 1995). Latina women are likely to experience violence for a longer duration and may feel cultural pressure to remain in a violent relationship (Gondolf, Fisher, & McFerron, 1991). Native Americans in urban areas have been found to have histories of family violence as high as 80 percent (Chester, Robin, Koss, Lopez, & Goldman, 1994). While Asian women may have lower rates of intimate abuse than other ethnic groups (Koss et al., 1994), some Asian women such as military wives and "mail order brides" may be particularly vulnerable to abuse (Jang, 1994).

Violence is also prevalent in gay male and lesbian relationships. In a study of 90 lesbian couples, Coleman (1991) found that 46 percent used repeated acts of physical abuse. Research has indicated that violence occurs in lesbian relationships at the rate of 25 percent (Brand & Kidd, 1986) to 48 percent (Gardner, 1989), which are comparable to the rates established for heterosexual relationships. Gardner (1989) explicitly compared rates of violence reported by individuals in heterosexual (28 percent), gay male (38 percent), and lesbian couples (48 percent). Like the violence in heterosexual couples, violence in lesbian couples increases in frequency and severity over time (Renzetti, 1988).

## Studying the Prevalence of Intimate Violence

A substantial amount of research effort has been focused on prevalence of woman battering, and this question continues to be a central and controversial issue. Early estimates of both incidence and prevalence were based on reports from intact couples, and were applied only to abuse occurring within current marital relationships. Later, community (urban) samples yielded higher estimates when women respondents were asked if they had ever been assaulted. Incidence rates are further increased if we include women who are battered in the context of nonmarital relationships.

By providing statistical evidence of the extent of wife abuse, researchers have played a critical role in making this a social issue (Caplan, 1985). McHugh (1993) examines the relevance of prevalence research. Estimates of intimate abuse are necessary for obtaining resources to address the issue on a local or societal level. Funding for police training, shelters, and additional research is dependent on our ability to demonstrate the extent and severity of the problem. Incidence and prevalence rates can be used to document increases and decreases in the phenomena over time. Incidence rates also have important etiological and intervention implications. The perspective that abuse of women by their partners is the result of individual pathology is less convincing as an explanation for a phenomenon that occurs in approximately one fourth of relationships. High incidence rates are typically interpreted as indicating existence of structural or societal causes, such as societal support of male aggression, relationship scripts that include woman battering, institutional support for battering, and others. McHugh (1993) questions whether documented prevalence rates have impacted on our theoretical or clinical perspectives on partner maltreatment. Researchers continue to investigate primarily individual or dyadic level variables, and clinicians continue to attempt to intervene at the individual behavioral or intrapsychic level or at the dyadic or family process level.

## Assessing Intimate Abuse

More than 10 validated and standardized scales to measure partner mistreatment have been published (Gondolf, 1998). For example, the Index of Spouse Abuse (ISA) developed by Hudson and McIntosh (1981) is recommended by Gondolf (1998). The 30 items of the ISA addresses psychological as well as physical abuse. Instruments such as the ISA may be administered as a follow-up to screening questions about violence. Questions about violence should be included in intake interviews but typically are not (von Erden & Goodwin, 1992). Von Erden and Goodwin (1992) caution that initial responses to direct questions about violence may not be revealing; battered women may hesitate to reveal the source of their distress to strangers who may or may not report back to the abusive partner. For example, 6 percent of women seeking couples' therapy voluntarily presented the issue of relationship violence; 44 percent of this sample reported violence when specifically and directly asked, and 53 percent reported violence using a standardized measure. Goldberg and Tomlanovich (1984) report that more than three fourths of known battered women failed to identify themselves on a confidential questionnaire in a medical setting. Other research suggests that only a small proportion of women inform their doctors of their experience of abuse (Drossman et al., 1990).

When corroborating evidence is available, it has suggested that battered women, especially those who have been battered over a long period of time, tend to underestimate both the frequency and the severity of the violence they experience. Kelly (1988) suggests that forgetting and minimizing are two coping strategies used by battered women. Experts working with battered men note that they greatly underreport their violent actions, and will exaggerate the involvement of their female partner in the commission of the violence (Browne & Dutton,

1990; Sonkin & Durphy, 1985). In interviewing or treating male perpetrators and women victims one should seek third party corroboration and/or seriously question the accuracy of the reports of both partners.

Ethnic and cultural differences and issues are important to consider when conducting an assessment for intimate violence. Cultural norms about relationship behaviors, help-seeking, and differences in interpersonal behaviors and communication can influence the way that a battered woman communicates her experience. A clinician who fails to consider differences in cultural background is in danger of misinterpreting her and her difficulties. For example, African-American women who have been victims of intimate abuse may appear on the surface to be more assertive and confident; this may be misinterpreted as lower distress and greater resiliency (Coley & Beckett, 1988). Also, for Latina women, level of acculturation needs to be assessed and carefully considered in any intervention attempted as acculturation has been found to increase the likelihood of being battered (Kantor, Jasinski, & Aldarondo, 1994). The value placed on family loyalty in many cultures may deter many women from disclosing instances of abuse. Immigrant women may face additional concerns about their immigrant status and possibility of deportation that leave them reluctant to share detailed information about their abuse experiences (Gondolf, 1998). While no formula exists for the proper way to address or consider all of the complex cultural issues that may influence the assessment of intimate abuse, clinicians should be mindful of differences in cultural norms regarding disclosure of information, communication patterns, and that women from diverse cultural backgrounds face many pressures and challenges that may make assessment difficult.

## Assessing Lethality

Partner violence often escalates in severity and frequency over time (Pagelow, 1981, 1997). Intimate violence may end in death. Approximately 4000 women are killed by their spouses or lovers each year (U.S. Department of Justice, Bureau of Statistics, 1994, as cited in Stahly, 1996). The rates of spouse and partner homicides have remained consistently high over time. In 1992, 41 percent of the homicides of women (when the offender was identified) were committed by a husband or boyfriend (Bachman & Saltzman, 1996). Walker (1995) and Stahly (1996) state that women are at especially high risk for severe violence and homicide when they are leaving or have just left their abusive partner.

It is important to recognize the potential lethality of partner maltreatment for both legal and clinical reasons. Browne (1987) compared battered women who killed their partners with others who did not. She identified some patterns present prior to partner homicide: the men abused alcohol and/or drugs; the men made threats to kill their partners; the physical attacks increased in frequency and the women sustained severe injuries; and the women were likely to have been raped or forced into other sexual acts by the male partner. Similarly, Gelles, Lackner, and Wolfner (1994) used the literature to identify 10 risk factors that are associated with severe violence. Risk factors associated with the male are: age between 18 and 30 years; unemployment; use of illicit drugs; having a high school education or less, and/or a blue collar job; and being raised in a home with domestic violence. Relationship characteristics related to severe violence include: the male and female have different religious backgrounds; the male and female cohabitate; the male or female uses severe violence toward children in the home; and the total family income is below the poverty line.

Hart (1992) suggests a checklist to assess the lethality of the abuser or situation. Based on a literature review her checklist includes: threats or fantasies of homicide or suicide; weapon possession and use; escalation of personal risk; stalking; extreme depression and alcohol binges; separation violence and threats; and ideas about ownership and centrality of the partner. Other instruments have been developed to assess for lethality. The Danger Assessment Instrument (Campbell, 1986; 1995) is administered by nurses to assess battered women's risk of killing or being killed. A second instrument has been developed by Sonkin, Martin, and Walker (1985). Assessment for lethality, however, may be misleading; we may not have the knowledge base to accurately assess for lethality (Gondolf, 1988; Gondolf & Hart, 1994; Hart & Gondolf, 1994).

## Measuring Intimate Violence

In the literature on battered women, most of the research has relied on use of the Conflicts Tactics Scale (CTS) designed by Straus (1979) and used extensively by Straus, Gelles, and their colleagues (e.g., Straus, 1979; Straus & Gelles, 1986; Straus, Gelles, & Steinmetz, 1980). Continued use of this scale allows for comparability of results, but also perpetuates inadequacies in the literature. The Conflict Tactics Scale has been seriously criticized; many of these criticisms are reviewed briefly here (for an extensive critique of this scale, see Yllo & Bograd, 1988; Johnson, 1998).

On the CTS, respondents indicate how often, in the context of a disagreement, they perpetrated various acts (e.g., threw something, used a gun or knife) and how often they were the recipients of such actions. The scale does not differentiate initiated violence from acts of self-defense nor does the CTS assess the seriousness of the injuries inflicted. The CTS does not allow for consideration of the victims' ability to repel or restrain offenders, or to retaliate against them. As a direct result of these inadequacies, use of the scale has led to confusion over the mutuality of domestic violence. Strauss (1979) and Steinmetz (1978) have interpreted symmetry in incidences reported by males and females as indicative of mutual violence. Others (Browne, 1989; Browne & Dutton, 1990; Dobash, Dobash, Cavanagh, & Lewis, 1998) have challenged this conclusion. (Mutual and woman-initiated violence are discussed in more depth in the final section.) The interpretation that men and women are mutually combative ignores the physical and economic power disparities between men and women, and fails to consider the motive for or consequences of aggressive acts (Johnson, 1998).

Questions on the Conflict Tactics Scale are set in the context of settling disputes in a conflict situation. Respondents may not include violence that does not occur in the context of a disagreement, that is, violence not precipitated by a disagreement (Browne, 1987). Moreover, the CTS does not include questions about psychological abuse, verbal assaults, or sexual abuse. Others have devised measurement instruments to assess sexual coercion (Koss, 1990) and psychological abuse (Tolman, 1989). A revised Conflict Tactics Scale (CTS2) has been developed to include sexual coercion and emotional abuse and to measure injuries (Straus, Hamby, Boney-McCoy, & Sugarman, 1996). The CTS2, however, still fails to place intimate abuse in the context of gender relations and male dominance (Johnson, 1996). For these reasons, the recent Canadian survey developed a new measure, the Violence Against Women Survey (Johnson, 1998).

## Psychological Abuse

Partly as a result of reliance on the CTS, little research has been conducted on the effects of psychological and sexual abuse within intimate relationships. Psychological abuse has been studied primarily as an aspect of a physically abusive relationship (e.g., Tolman, 1989; Walker, 1979). There is increasingly an understanding of both the prevalence and the seriousness of psychological abuse (Chang, 1996; Tolman, 1992). More than one half of women reported emotional abuse as the reason for divorce (Cleek & Pearson, 1985), and 27 percent of college women characterized at least one of their dating relationships as abusive (Raymond & Brushi, 1989).

Stets (1991) defined psychological abuse as offensive and degrading verbal behavior that results in feelings of guilt, upset, or worthlessness. Tolman (1989) constructed the Psychological Maltreatment of Women Scale to explore psychological abuse. The 58 items relate to six themes of abuse: defining her reality; controlling her contacts; withholding positive rewards; demanding subservience; attacking her personhood; and threatening punishment. Chang (1996) describes the process of psychological abuse; the abused partner, in an attempt to please the abuser and avoid criticism, censors herself until all sense of the unique self is lost. With development of new scales and inclusion of questions about psychological/emotional abuse on other instruments, we anticipate greater attention to psychological abuse and its relation to other aspects of intimate abuse in the future.

## FOCUS ON THE VICTIM

### Who Is the Victim?

Early research focused on characteristics of women who were battered. Initially battered women were seen as causing their own suffering. Subsequently feminist research challenged misconceptions about the identity of battered women. Research documented that abuse can occur across regional, occupational, ethnic, racial, and class groups. A review of the first 15 years of research indicated that characteristics of the battered woman did not predict violence (Hotaling & Sugarman, 1986; Sugarman & Hotaling, 1989).

However, the process of challenging our conceptions of the identity of victims of intimate battering continues; "new" victim groups have recently been identified. An expanding literature on dating violence confirms Makepeace's (1986) contention that dating violence is as extensive as marital violence. Makepeace (1983) and others have suggested that "discovery" of dating violence calls into question many of our interpretations and explanations for partner mistreatment.

Research has suggested that we have ignored at least one other group of victims of relationship violence: battered lesbians. Documentation that lesbian women are often abused by other women (Bologna, Waterman, & Dawson, 1987; Kelly & Warshafsky, 1987; Myers, 1989; Renzetti, 1993) raises new questions for researchers. For example, theories that tie wife battering to legal and social codes of marital conduct may not be helpful in explaining either dating violence or lesbian battering, and theories that tie woman battering to male aggression cannot easily explain lesbian battering.

Very little research has been conducted on lesbian or gay male couples even though such couples seem to be a good comparison for heterosexual couples given theoretical models of battering that are based on male sex roles or marital roles. Such oversight reflects the operation of heterosexism in our selection of research questions and populations. Lesbians have remained invisible in the psychological literature even when we have attempted to study women's experiences. Problems and experiences of lesbians are not seen as informing us about the nature of human relationships.

### Why Does She Stay?

This is probably the most often asked question about woman abuse. In class discussions, in public forums, and in the research literature, people continue to voice this question first and foremost. This question may reveal our basic premises about woman battering—if the woman would leave, she would not get beaten. The primary and most popular intervention strategy is focused on the victim; the solution is to physically and psychologically relocate the woman. This perspective is increasingly seen as both victim-blaming and counterproductive.

Early research focused on the logistical reasons why some women did not leave an abusive husband. Not having the money, transportation, or a safe place to go were initially emphasized (Bowker, 1983; Browne & Williams, 1989). Other social factors affecting the woman's decision to stay were also explored. Loss of social status, disapproval of family and friends, and feelings of failure or guilt for abandoning the relationship have been suggested as factors (Dobash & Dobash, 1979; Frieze, 1979; Walker, 1979). Abused women's perceptions of alternatives may be influenced by societal expectations related to gender and role relationships that encourage women to be self-sacrificing and adaptive, and to care for and protect those close to them regardless of the cost (Browne, 1987; Walker & Browne, 1985).

Subsequently, researchers and clinicians began to emphasize psychological factors underlying women's decisions not to leave. Walker's work suggested that battered women have learned helplessness (Walker, 1977, 1979, 1983, 1984). They allegedly have developed motivational, cognitive, and behavioral deficits as a result of the battering. Woman battering has been compared to being a prisoner of war (Romero, 1985) or a torture victim (Chandler, 1986). Chandler's phenomenological analysis of battered women's experiences suggests that overriding fear and a loss of a sense of self characterize the severely battered woman. Other research perspectives emphasize the emotional bonds that battered women form with their abusers (Browne, 1987; Dutton & Painter, 1981; Walker, 1983). Browne (1987) and Walker (1984) note that abused women report that their partners were extremely attentive and affectionate early in the relationship. They showed great interest in the woman's whereabouts, a desire to be with her all the time, intense expressions of affection and jealousy, and wanted an early commitment to a long-term relationship. Over time these behaviors that were initially seen as evidence of love became intrusive, controlling, and triggers to assault. The woman has become emotionally and geographically isolated, making her vulnerable to abuse. The abuser's concern for the wife's whereabouts becomes a form of surveillance, and the batterers are often described as evidencing severe and delusional jealousy (Frieze et al., 1980; Hotaling & Sugarman, 1986).

The fact that women stay in relationships because they fear retaliation from the violent partners has been obscured by our attention to economic, social, and psychological factors. The battered woman fears that her husband will retaliate against her, her children, or her family if she tries to leave (Ridington, 1978). Threats of kidnapping and custody battles are common tactics used by abusive partners to keep women in violent relationships (Stahly, 1996). This fear of her abuser finding her or others he has threatened is a realistic one. Women who have left an abusive partner have been followed and harassed for months or even years, and some have been killed (Browne, 1987; Jones, 1981; Pagelow, 1981). Evidence suggests that in many cases the man's violence escalates in response to a separation (Fields, 1978; Fiora-Gormally, 1978; Pagelow, 1981). Stahly (1996) reports the National Crime Survey of the Department of Justice documenting that 70 percent of domestic violence crime doesn't occur until after the relationship has ended. Walker (1995) reports that women are at increased risk for severe violence and homicide after leaving the batterer. Goodwin and McHugh (1990) have labeled the stalking, coercive harassment, and threats of violence that occur in the context of the attempted breakup of a romantic relationship "termination terrorism."

## Victims or Survivors?

Thus, even a woman's decision to stay may actually reflect her survival instinct, rather than either masochism or helplessness as had been repeatedly suggested. An important feminist criticism of the woman battering research is that it has focused attention on her as victim while ignoring her strengths and efforts to leave. Use of both of these labels, *victim* and *survivor*, has been challenged by Kelly, Burton, and Regan (1994), who argue that neither victim nor survivor is likely to be helpful as a core identity.

Researchers have begun to emphasize the help-seeking, coping mechanisms, and survival skills of battered women. For example, Gondolf and Fisher (1988) critique the learned helplessness model of wife abuse, and examine the ways in which battered women in their Texas sample acted assertively and logically in response to the abuse. The women in their sample, like the women studied by Bowker (1983), persistently sought help from a wide range of sources. The more intensified and prolonged the abuse, the greater the variety and the extent of their help seeking. These studies suggest that there are cognitive, motivational, and behavioral deficits, not within the battered woman, but within the individuals and agencies that fail to adequately respond to her request for help. Many women return to or remain with their abusers because they lack access to community resources (Gondolf, 1988; Sullivan, Basta, Tan, & Davidson, 1992). "I was one of those women. One of the horrible aspects of being battered as a woman is that when you try to escape, people will refuse to help you. They justify this refusal to help by saying that you wanted to be hit, or that you provoked it and/or deserved it" (Dworkin & Brooks, 1995, p. 174).

## Implications of a Victim Focus

Most of the research on wife abuse has focused on the supposed inadequacies of the battered woman. Original formulations of the battered woman as masochistic or pathological have been repeatedly challenged (e.g., Caplan, 1985; Gondolf & Fisher, 1988; Yllo & Bograd, 1988). Yet, this perspective and other newer victim-blaming perspectives continue to influence both the research and treatment of wife abuse. For example the "theory" that some women who have experienced abuse seek out abusive situations and partners is a new variation on a worn masochism hypothesis. Further, the formulation that battered women are suffering from helplessness is widely held even though newer evidence indicates that abused female partners actively seek help and demonstrate cognitive and behavioral coping strategies (Bowker, 1983, 1984; Gondolf & Fisher, 1988).

Why has the research focused so heavily on the inadequacies of the battered women? McHugh (1987, 1990, 1993) outlines some of the explanations for victim-blaming. Victim blame is viewed by social psychologists as resulting from the individual's need to believe in a just world (Lerner, 1980) and in her/his own invulnerability. Caplan (1985) has argued that the focus on the female victim as responsible for the violence is the legacy of Freud. Alternatively, it can be argued that the focus on battered women, both in the research and in clinical practice, stems from the fact that the victimized women are the ones who have most typically sought professional help (McHugh, 1990; 1993). Thus, women's help seeking, a positive coping response, might ironically have led to them being labeled as inadequate and pathological. Not only does their entry into shelters and therapy make them more assessable to researchers, but the woman's presentation as client makes them available for intervention by professionals. Since it is the woman's behavior and personality that we can measure, and possibly change, it must therefore be her behavior and personality that are viewed as problematic. Rosewater

(1987) argues that "Many of the behaviors used to describe a personality disorder are traits that are reactive responses to victimization and tend to disappear or lower in frequency when the abuse is eliminated" (p. 193). A feminist analysis suggests that we challenge both the view of women as passive victims and our tendency to focus our research and intervention efforts on them.

## Shelters as Interventions

Originally, shelter was provided by a network of women to prevent the maiming or murder of an abused wife. Shelters were established as a last resort in terms of resolving violence in the lives of women. Early shelter workers resisted the professional tendency to pathologize the battered woman. Eventually, however, the shelter movement was taken over by professionals and, in the United States, was funded by the government. Today a network of funded shelters provides refuge along with individual counseling, support groups, legal advice, advocacy, and educational workshops. The battered women's movement raised public consciousness, developed the shelters, and obtained government funding. This aspect of the women's movement has made a difference in the lives of hundreds of thousands of women.

Shelters were designed, however, as a last resort, and can never be the solution to partner violence. Shelters provide only *temporary* refuge for a small portion of battered women. Shelters are not an option for all women. Shelters turn away more women than they can accommodate, and every county does not have a shelter. Women with sons who are more than 10 years of age are typically not welcome in the shelter. So some women are never accepted into a shelter, and others eventually have to leave the shelter and find housing elsewhere. An alarming proportion of homeless women and children are refugees from abusive homes. Most women exiting a shelter reported that they lacked the resources (e.g., housing, a job, transportation, child care, education and legal assistance) necessary to permanently leave the abuser (Sullivan, Basta, Tan, & Davidson, 1992).

In some ways existence of shelters has provided the public with the illusion of a solution. Shelters unwittingly have reinforced the public perception that the solution to battery is for the abused partner to leave. Krenek (1998) addresses the inadequacy of shelters as THE solution to partner violence. She points out that now police and prosecutors may expect the battered woman to go to the shelter, and to leave the abuser and the domicile. She suggests that in some localities police punish women who do not leave by arresting them. Krenek (1998) and Stahly (1996) both ask the same question: *Why should a woman and her children have to leave home to feel safe?*

Even if a woman were able to leave an abusive relationship and physically relocate, she remains at risk for violence and homicide as discussed previously. Research has also demonstrated that a man who is violent in a relationship is likely to be violent in subsequent relationships (Kalmuss & Seltzer, 1986). Thus, the solution to intimate violence is not to have women go to temporary shelters, or to live in the streets with their children, but to intervene with the batterer.

## REFOCUSING ON THE BATTERER

The shelter movement has brought attention to occurrence of battering and helped to define it as a social problem. Shelter and other services have become available to women and children to provide them with more options than have been available in the past. Resources and research have been devoted to the question of "How can we help battered women and their children?" While provision of services to women and children certainly has been the greatest priority of the shelter movement, and rightly so, other questions have often been left unasked. The perpetrator and what to do about his behavior is notably absent from many discussions about the problem of battering, particularly given that the perpetrator would seem to be at the heart of the issue. "Who are these men who batter?" "Why do men batter?" "How do we stop a man from battering?" These are vital questions if we are to have an impact on the problem of battering.

A sole focus on the victims of battering has previously led to theories that blame the woman for the abuse. A focus on the batterer is necessary to hold him responsible for his behavior. To develop theories that consider the batterer as central to the occurrence of domestic violence, we must look at batterers for clues that may tell us who he is, why he batters, and how he may be able to change. Research conducted over the last two decades has begun to address these questions.

## Who Is He? Batterer Characteristics

Who are these men that batter their intimate female partners? Batterers have been compared with other violent and nonviolent men to get a sense of what makes them different. While these descriptive characteristics cannot be said to cause a man to batter his partner, they can aid in theory development and indicate who may be at risk for battering.

One of the most consistent findings with regard to batterers is that they are more likely to have a history of violence in their family of origin (Hotaling & Sugarman, 1986). Men who have witnessed parental violence and men who have been abused as children or adolescents are more likely to become batterers than those who have not (Caesar, 1988; Coleman, Weinman, & Hsi, 1980; Fitch & Papantonio, 1983; Hastings & Hamberger, 1988; MacEwen & Barling, 1988; Rosenbaum & O'Leary, 1981; Sugarman & Hotaling, 1989; Telch & Lindquist, 1984). Witnessing parental violence has been found to be more predictive than experiencing abuse as a child (Tolman & Bennett, 1990). As many as three quarters of men seeking counseling for battering witnessed abuse between their parents, whereas half were abused as children (Fitch & Papantonio, 1983).

Early studies concluded that battering was more prevalent among lower socioeconomic families, but that it existed at all levels of SES (Gelles, 1980; Sugarman & Hotaling, 1989). Higher rates of battering have been found among the unemployed (Fitch & Papantonio, 1983; Roberts, 1987), blue collar workers (Gelles et al., 1994), and those with lower levels of education (Hamberger & Hastings, 1988). Some of the largest, most representative studies, however, have failed to find this relationship (e.g., Hornung, McCullough, & Sugimoto, 1981; Hotaling & Sugarman, 1986; Schulman, 1979; Straus et al., 1980). Batterers who are poor or working class may be more likely to be reported to the police, or called to "official" attention. The exact relationship between battering and SES remains unclear.

While researchers have been unable to identify a unitary batterer personality profile (Hamberger & Hastings, 1988), higher rates of certain psychiatric conditions have been found among batterers (Rosenbaum, Geffner, & Benjamin, 1997). Personality disorders and characteristics, such as antisocial, borderline, and narcissistic, occur at higher rates among batterers (Hamberger & Hastings, 1991; Hart, Dutton, & Newlove, 1993; Hastings & Hamberger, 1988), particularly among those who have been identified by community agencies. Based on MCMI tests administered to men in four batterer programs, Gondolf (1998) reported levels of narcissism (1/4), passive-aggressiveness (1/4), depression (1/5), and antisocial tendencies (1/5). A study of men who voluntarily entered a batterer treatment found that they had significant psychiatric symptoms as measured by the Minnesota Multiphasic Personality Inventory (MMPI); these included elevated anxiety, schizophrenia-like symptoms, inability to appreciate social customs and conform to social rules, and significant physical concerns (Bernard & Bernard, 1984). Depression is also more common among batterers, occurring in as many as two thirds of men referred to batterer intervention programs (Maiuro, Cahn, Vitaliano, Wagner, & Zegree, 1988).

Drug and alcohol use has been found to be a consistent risk marker for use of violence toward a female partner (Coleman et al., 1980; Hotaling & Sugarman, 1986; Telch & Lindquist, 1984). There is, however, no direct relationship between the amount of alcohol consumed and battering (Leonard, Bromet, Parkinson, Day, & Ryan, 1985; Van Hasselt, Morrison, & Bellack, 1985), and the violence/battering occurs independently of alcohol and drug abuse. Chronic alcohol abuse is more predictive of battering than acute intoxication, although both are predictive (Tolman & Bennett, 1990). Binge drinkers have the highest rates of battering (Gelles et al., 1994).

Various skill deficits and belief systems have been proposed to contribute to the incidence of battering. Batterers have been found to be lower in assertiveness than nonabusive, nonmaritally distressed men, but similar to nonabusive, maritally distressed men (Dutton & Strachan, 1987; Maiuro, Cahn, & Vitaliano, 1986; O'Leary & Curley, 1986; Rosenbaum & O'Leary, 1981). Men who are abusive are also lower in self-esteem (Neidig, Freidman, & Collins, 1986), attribute more negative intent to others (Holtzworth-Munroe & Hutchinson, 1993; Neidig et al., 1986), and have a higher need for power (Dutton & Strachan, 1987).

## Types of Batterers

The clearest conclusion one can draw from the available literature is that batterers are a heterogeneous group, and there is a great deal of inconsistency in the literature (Hamberger & Hastings, 1991; Rosenbaum et al., 1997). It makes sense that not all batterers are alike. There may be various types of batterers, with different etiological and abuse patterns, and with implications for diverse interventions (Dutton, 1988; Gondolf, 1988; Saunders, 1992). Further, results of a particular study may depend on how the sample was recruited. Batterers who have been reprimanded by the courts to batterer groups may differ significantly from men in a community survey who admit to use of violence toward their partners.

One approach to reconciling inconsistencies in the literature is the development of typologies of batterers. Distinctions have been made between men who have used severe versus minor forms of violence and between batterers who abuse drugs and/or alcohol and those who do not. Caesar (1986) suggests a four-category system based on personality (tyrant, exposed rescuer, nonexposed altruist, and psychotic). Gondolf (1988) presents an empirically derived, behavior-based typology; he labeled the three groups: sociopathic, antisocial, and typical batterers. Others have found differences between generally violent and family-only batterers (Saunders, 1992; Shields, McCall, & Hanneke, 1988), and clusters of batterers that differ in emotional volatility (Saunders, 1992). Based on an extensive review of the literature, Holtzworth-Munroe and Stuart (1994) proposed three subtypes of batterers: family only; dysphoric/borderline; and generally violent/antisocial. Some support has been provided for this model (Hamberger, Lohr, Bonge, & Tolin, 1995).

Saunders (1996) provides some validation for the typology approach. He reports an interaction between personality characteristics as measured by the Millon Clinical Multiaxial Inventory and treatment approach on reports of recidivism. Saunders (1996) found that men scoring higher on dependent personality characteristics had a better outcome when treated using a process psychodynamic model, while those scoring higher on antisocial characteristics had a better outcome after completing a feminist cognitive-behavioral approach. Findings such as this can lead the way to developing interventions that are most likely to be effective for particular types of batterers.

## Interventions with Batterers

### Mandatory Arrest

The response of police to violence in the family in the 1970s and early 1980s centered on "family crisis intervention," in which attempts were made to mediate the dispute or separate the involved parties. Pressures from women's groups and advocates for victim's rights encouraged police departments to treat battering and domestic crimes as equal to street crimes (Eisikovits & Edleson, 1989). A highly influential study, the Minneapolis Spouse Abuse Experiment, found that arrest significantly reduced recidivism over mediation or separation (Sherman & Berk, 1984). Largely as a result of this finding, many states enacted mandatory arrest laws in efforts to increase the likelihood that a batterer would be arrested following a domestic disturbance call.

Currently, many states have mandatory or pro-arrest laws (Mignon & Holmes, 1995). While some may see this as a positive step toward changing the cultural norms that have supported the use of violence against women, mandatory arrest laws have their difficulties. Most mandatory arrest laws indicate that a person should be arrested if there is evidence of an assault; however, they provide no guidance for situations in which there is evidence that both parties have engaged in violence. As a result, there has been an increase in the number of women being arrested for domestic assault and instances of dual arrest are frequent (Hamberger & Potente, 1994; Martin, 1997). Also, attempts to replicate the findings of a positive outcome for arrest have had mixed results (Davis & Smith, 1995). It seems as if arrest may be an effective deterrent of future battering for men who are married and employed, but that arrest may be associated with an increase in the likelihood of violence for the unemployed (Pate & Hamilton, 1992; Sherman, Smith, Schmidt, & Rogan, 1992). Arrest alone will clearly not provide the solution to the problem of intimate abuse.

### Groups for Batterers

In part based on the characteristics that have been discovered to be more prevalent in batterers, psychological and educational treatments have been proposed, often in groups where isolation can be broken and cultural norms can be challenged. Same-sex groups for men who abuse their intimate partners are generally of two types. The psychoeducational/cognitive-behavioral skill building approach addresses behavioral skill deficits, whereas the resocialization approach addresses the cultural norms that support abuse of women including traditional sex roles. The groups vary in other ways: in the number of sessions, in the recruitment of participants (court-mandated vs. voluntary participants), and in their relationship to the criminal justice system. Many batterer groups offer a combination of skills training and resocialization; groups sessions address definitions of abuse, anger management, assertiveness training, challenging negative sex-role stereotypes, and communication skills.

Outcomes have been mixed in studies of the effects of group treatment for male batterers. Reviews indicate that between 53 percent and 85 percent of men who complete such programs are deemed nonviolent at follow-up (Russell, 1988; Tolman & Bennett, 1990). Lower success rates are reported by programs in which women report on recurrence of violence, and there is a longer follow-up period (Tolman & Bennett, 1990). Preliminary results from a large multi-site study indicate that 72 percent of program completers were reported as nonviolent at 15 months follow-up (Gondolf, 1997) in contrast with 60 percent of program dropouts who were reported as nonviolent.

The men who are likely to repeat violence even after treatment are: those with higher levels of substance abuse before and after treatment (DeMaris & Jackson, 1987; Hamberger & Hastings, 1990), those with high scores on narcissism (Hamberger & Hastings, 1990), those who had witnessed violence between their parents (DeMaris & Jackson, 1987), and men who were living with their partners upon termination of counseling (DeMaris & Jackson, 1987).

### Intervention Innovation

Armed with the knowledge that narrowly focused, single-target interventions are limited in their efficacy, communities are making efforts to develop coordinated responses to the problem of intimate abuse. In some communities, police actions and other criminal justice system sanctions, victim services, and batterer treatment are coming together toward the same end: cessation of abuse among intimate partners. Steinman (1988) found that police actions that were not coordinated with other criminal justice sanctions led to increased violence, while actions, particularly arrest, that were coordinated with other sanctions served as significant deterrents for violence. In certain communities, like the Domestic Abuse Project in Minneapolis, a central clearinghouse exists for all intimate abuse cases so that the victim and the perpetrator will receive direct referral to many services (Brygger & Edleson, 1987, as cited in Gondolf & Fisher, 1988). Others have found that coordinated responses decreased the subsequent use of violence (Tolman & Weisz, 1995), and that women were generally satisfied with the police response (Jaffe, Hastings, Reitzel, & Austin, 1993). Women increased their use of social services because they became more aware of coordinated services (Jaffe et al., 1993).

## FOCUS ON THE FAMILY

### The Family Systems Approach

Interventions with men and women separately as described earlier have not been the only methods attempting to address intimate abuse. Along with development of organized group interventions for the batterer, work with couples has sought to have both partners participate in the work. Those working with couples often cite systems theory as guiding their approach to treatment. Systems theory is often used in the context of family therapy as a way of understanding difficulties, not as caused by the dysfunction of a single individual, but as the product of dysfunctional interactions among members. These difficulties may then be maintained by members attempting to maintain homeostasis in the family. Systems theories indicated that there are a complexity of factors that contribute to violence among intimates. These theories suggest that both partners participate in abusive behavior and the escalation of conflict, although not necessarily equally (Neidig, Friedman, & Collins, 1985). Circular rather than linear explanations are sought to understand the interactional sequence that maintains the violence behavior (Margolin & Burman, 1993). From this perspective, it is important to intervene with the couple, either individually or in a group with other couples, to help them understand their own contributions to the interaction and to teach skills to change the pattern.

Information on the occurrence of mutual violence supports this perspective. Neidig (1986) notes in his article on the development of a spouse abuse treatment program for a military setting that many of the couples interviewed acknowledged mutual and reciprocal violence. Data from a national survey assessing domestic violence confirmed that both men and women frequently report engaging in violence (Straus & Gelles, 1986). As has been found elsewhere, Neidig (1986) also noted that violence was related to significant conflict and stress in the relationship. Couples programs have emphasized development of relationship skills, such as communication and conflict containment, stress management and anger control, and problem solving. This has been stated to be an appropriate intervention when the couple expresses a desire to remain together and the violence is at "mild to moderate" levels such that safety is not jeopardized (Eisikovits & Edleson, 1989).

## Feminist Critique

Many feminist writers have taken issue with the family systems approach to intervening in cases of intimate abuse (e.g., Bograd, 1984). They indicate that implicit within the perspective of violence as the result of an interactional pattern is the assumption that the victim is responsible for the abuse as well as the batterer. This form of victim-blaming, they state, relieves the batterer of responsibility for his behavior (Adams, 1986; Harris, Savage, Jones, & Brooke, 1988; Yllo & Bograd, 1988). In addition, this perspective has been criticized for ignoring the criminal aspects of intimate violence, the effect of the trauma on the victim, and the cultural aspects of gender socialization and use of violence to perpetuate the power differential between men and women (Pressman, 1989).

As a result of this position, and the lobbying efforts of domestic violence advocates, some states have prescribed group programs for batterers as the primary (mandatory) treatment and forbade couples treatment except under special circumstances (Lipchik et al., 1997). Lipchik and her colleagues (1997) argue that some couples want couple counseling, and that the multifaceted reality of domestic violence suggests that it should be an option in some cases. As previously discussed, not all batterers are alike. There is evidence that some couples engage in mutual and/or less serious violence for extended periods of time (Frieze & McHugh, 1992). Perhaps work in the area of batterer typologies will provide a scientific basis for decisions about the safety and appropriateness of couple's treatment (Lipchik et al., 1997). When we can distinguish mutual violence from woman battering (discussed later), couple treatment can be evaluated as a possible option.

## Newer Models of Couples Therapy

Several programs have been described that seek to intervene at the level of the couple or family while remaining mindful of the criticisms put forth by feminist writers (Harris, 1986; Harris et al., 1988; Lipchik et al., 1997; Shaw, Bouris, & Pye, 1996; Weidman, 1986). These programs show promise for integrating the wishes of the couple, formulations that place each person responsible for their own behavior, while not sacrificing concerns for safety.

Harris (1986) describes a model for couples treatment originally proposed by Walker. The goals of this model include stopping the violence and for each partner to accept appropriate responsibility for behavior surrounding the violence; therefore, the treatment can be viewed as successful even if the relationship dissolves. For these goals to occur the batterer needs to accept responsibility for his behavior and the victim is helped to stop feeling responsible for his. Initial individual sessions are held to gather information, to engage in safety planning, and to educate clients about the cycle of violence and appropriate responsibility. Conjoint sessions are held later to address problems in the relationship and facilitate problem solving. Male and female cotherapists are used and Walker believed that the couple should be separated and living apart when starting counseling to increase motivation. Lipchik et al. (1997) also work with couples in individual and conjoint sessions from a solution-focused approach, in which attention is directed to their strengths as individuals and as a couple and to exceptions to their complaints. Safety is a primary concern, and both partners must agree that they want no further violence and be willing to make changes in their own behavior.

Groups have also been used for working with batterers and their families when the couple wishes to remain together (Shaw et al., 1996; Weidman, 1986). Both of the approaches describe a combination of the use of same-sex groups, groups for children, and conjoint couples sessions or family therapy. In the family safety model, groups for women, men, and children are conducted to provide information about violence, to educate about appropriate responsibility for the violence, and encourage appropriate behavioral change that is focused on the safety of all members of the family (Shaw et al., 1996). Couples must complete an "assessment" phase in which the violence is specifically addressed. If this phase is completed without further violence from the man, the couple may then progress to "treatment" in which relationship issues may be addressed. Throughout the program, cessation of violence and safety for all members is of utmost concern, as is the coordination of services and acceptance of appropriate responsibility.

## Efficacy of Couples/Family Interventions

Outcome studies of couples interventions have reported some success, but often lack control groups to make comparisons. Neidig (1986) found that a majority of military couples completing a 10-week program were nonviolent at follow-up, as did Harris (1986) with 73 percent of his civilian couples. Others, however, have reported that of couples completing a group approach, 50 percent had again experienced violence after only 6 weeks (Lindquist, Telch, & Taylor, 1985). Harris et al. (1988) found that couples treated in a couples group had a lower dropout rate than couples treated conjointly. More evaluative research is needed to assess couples/family approaches to intimate abuse, particularly for the programs that specifically address a family systems perspective.

## Rethinking Explanatory Models

We have traced progression of beliefs about causes and appropriate interventions for intimate abuse—from a focus on the characteristics of the victim/survivor and attempts to shelter her from the violence, to a concern with the attributes of the batterer and intervention efforts directed toward him, and then to an analysis of the violent relationship and family therapy. These approaches may be considered inadequate, both theoretically and pragmatically, for a number of reasons. Theoretical explanations that focus on the characteristics or psychopathology of individuals or on the interaction patterns of couples are not sufficient to explain the documented prevalence of intimate violence. Further, we cannot provide shelter and other resources for all the women and children affected by domestic violence, cannot effectively "heal" all the scars of the violence, cannot arrest and rehabilitate all the perpetrators, and cannot counsel all the violent couples. Critics charge that such theories and interventions do not challenge or change the cultural attitudes and societal structures that underlie the violence (Pence, 1989; Tifft, 1993). "As long as therapists confine themselves to treating the relative handful of casualties of the patriarchal system who can afford therapy, they will contribute little or nothing to changing the male-dominated family structure and other social institutions that place so many females and children at risk. . . . " (Russell, 1995, p. 432).

## NEW DIRECTIONS IN THEORY AND RESEARCH

Feminists contend that gender and unequal distribution of power between men and women are important explanatory factors in intimate violence (e.g., Dobash & Dobash, 1979). Others have consistently argued that intimate violence is a human issue, and that women are as likely as men, or even more prone than men, to use physical violence in intimate relationships (McNeely & Mann, 1990). Bograd (1990) argues that the importance of gender in understanding violence is not contingent on data establishing men as the (only) batterers. Yet, recent research that challenges our conceptions of who is a victim and who is a perpetrator also argues for new conceptualizations of intimate violence.

### Mutual and Woman-Initiated Violence

Recent evidence suggests that women's participation in and even initiation of violence is higher than we originally thought. Using the CTS in a nationally representative sample, Straus and his colleagues (Straus & Gelles, 1986; Straus, Gelles, & Steinmetz, 1980) report that women initiate both minor and severe forms of physical violence with the same frequency as men. Saunders (1986) indicates that as many of 75 percent of battered women report using minor forms of violence as measured by the CTS.

The CTS does not distinguish between use of violence and initiation of violence. Women defending themselves against hostile or even deadly attacks would be classified as engaging in mutual domestic violence in this research. Further, Hamberger (1997) argues that asking who initiated the violence is too simplistic. He argues that it is necessary to understand partner violence as having occurred in a context. The history of the violence, the development and patterns of the violence, and the personal definitions of the individuals involved are part of this context (Hamberger, 1997). For example, a woman pushing or slapping her partner may be viewed as a case of primary aggression. However, our label and interpretation may be different when we know that she has been battered on a regular basis for 16 years, and has just recently begun to retaliate or to defend herself.

In a study of women arrested for domestic violence, Hamberger (1997) found that about two thirds of the women were battered and used violence to protect themselves or to retaliate. Although many of the women acknowledged initiating violence, they generally did so in the context of a relationship in which the male partner initiated violence more often, and was likely to have initiated the overall pattern of violence. Studies have found that women are more likely to use violence in self-defense or retaliation and are significantly more likely to sustain injuries (Makepeace, 1986). Men, however, are more likely to use violence for intimidation and forced sex and use more severe forms of violence (Bookwala, Frieze, Smith, & Ryan, 1992; Makepeace, 1986). Frieze and McHugh (1992) document the impact that male violence has on the power dynamics within marriage. Abusive husbands, by their own admission, use force to get what they want (Bograd, 1988) whereas women report using violence in self-defense (Saunders, 1986). Under current research practices (i.e., use of the CTS) and current legal approaches (i.e., mandatory arrest of anyone who hits), however, these women are likely to be labeled *mutual combatants* or *husband beater,* and are likely to be arrested and prosecuted.

Given these perspectives, we must still acknowledge the existence of female-initiated violence. In his study of women arrested for domestic violence, Hamberger (1997) found that 25 percent of the women reported starting the violence 100 percent of the time and that one third of the sample could not be classified as battered women. Similarly, Pagelow (1985) acknowledges existence of violent women who "create an atmosphere of fear for their husbands" (p.

274). Until researchers, clinicians, and police can distinguish battered women who act to defend themselves from women who initiate violence in their relationships, battered women will be arrested and prosecuted under the laws originally designed to protect them.

Many individuals have reviewed differences in perspective taken by feminist and domestic violence researchers. In addition, we have examined here how the research questions and measures may impact on our conclusions about the mutuality of violence versus battering. There are additional explanations for differences in conclusions reached by different authors. Much of the research has been conducted on women who have sought shelter after years of battering. Probably very few of these women, if any, are intimate abusers or mutual combatants. However, in samples of women from the community, or in samples drawn from college populations we may be more likely to see a range of intimate abuse situations that include women who abuse their partners and mutually violent couples. Even within a small clinic sample, Vivian and Langhinrichsen-Rohling (1994) identified three subgroups of spouses: a large number of couples who reported mutual but low level violence, a small subgroup of battered men (by female partners), and a substantial number of couples identified as battered wives and male batterers. Further, age or cohort effects might account for some of the differences in findings. Female-initiated and mutual violence may be more common among younger women. One interpretation is that post-feminist young women see violence as a gender neutral behavior, or as much their prerogative as men's. Unfortunately, the results are often the same as in the past, with the woman sustaining serious injuries.

Acknowledging that women are (increasingly) violent has profound implications for both individuals and social movements (Hamberger, 1997). Even while rejecting the conclusion that women's violence is equivalent to men's, we may need to rethink our conceptions of gender issues in partner violence (Frieze, 1999).

## Gay Male and Lesbian Battering

Analyses of intimate abuse have tended to be heterosexist; they exclude violence that occurs between same-sex partners. The feminist focus on men who batter and women as victim/survivor contributed to the invisibility of gay male and lesbian intimate abuse (Letellier, 1994). The gender categorization of perpetrators (as male) and victims (as female) is challenged by the existence of gay and lesbian intimate violence (Hamberger, 1994). Gender and other theories of violence developed in reference to heterosexual intimate abuse may impede our understanding of gay and lesbian violence. Battered gay men differ from battered heterosexual women in their conceptualizations and responses to the violence (Letellier, 1994). Letellier claims that many battered gay and bisexual men lack both the language and the awareness to declare themselves "battered." Individuals may assume that when violence occurs in gay male or lesbian relationships that it tends to be mutual. This assumption is also accepted and reported by battered gay men (Letellier, 1994). Distinctions between initiation of violence and defensive violence are unlikely to be made. Renzetti (1992) calls for an analysis of the motives, patterns, and uses of violence in lesbian relationships to challenge the myth of mutual combat. Most importantly we have structured the services around our heterosexist conceptions of intimate violence. A battered gay man or lesbian will most likely have difficulty finding assistance, and he may be reluctant to report to the police (Letellier, 1994). The lesbian community would probably not endorse widespread arrest and incarceration as the solution to the high levels of lesbian battering indicated. Thus, the recognition of gay male and lesbian partner mistreatment challenges both our explanatory models of intimate violence and our current intervention efforts.

## Cross-Cultural Research

The United Nations recognizes physical violence against women in marriage as a human rights issue. This issue, violence against women, was addressed at the 1995 United Nations Conference on Women in Beijing as a result of women organizing around violence in various parts of the world. At international meetings discussion among women attests to the universal nature of male violence directed toward women. The fact that male violence against women is universal has also been systematically documented (Counts, Brown, & Campbell, 1992; Levinson, 1989; Smuts, 1992).

Cross-cultural research emphasizes the need to consider the cultural context in both theory and practice, in explanations of intimate abuse, and in how we "treat" it. For example, Gondolf (1998) and Sev'er (1997) acknowledge the complexities in understanding and treating violence in the lives of immigrant women, whose values and expectations are cultivated in one culture, but whose experience of violence occurs in another.

Despite the universality of male violence against women, cross-cultural comparisons can be used to understand how culture can contribute to variations in the patterns and prevalence of intimate violence. Although such cross-cultural explorations of wife abuse have recently been published (e.g., Counts et al., 1992; Gelles & Cornell, 1983; Sev'er, 1997), researchers are critical of the previous invisibility of wife abuse in the ethnographic record (Brown, 1997). Cultural factors can be identified that help or hinder wife abuse (Brown, 1997; Counts et al., 1992; Levinson, 1989). For example, McWilliams (1998) describes violence against women in societies under stress (e.g., involved in ethnic violence, civil disorder, terrorism, war, or political oppression) as a special problem. Women's groups may protect women from violence (Counts, Brown, & Campbell, 1992) and mothers-in-law may play a cultural role that either protects younger women or contributes to wife beating (Brown, 1997). Dutton and van Ginkel (1997) offer an etiological explanation that combines personality and cultural context. Using data from five ethnic groups within Canada, Dutton and van Ginkel (1997) provide support for their contention that certain men with an "abusive personality" are more likely to batter their partners in a cultural context where negative and blaming attitudes toward women are supported by cultural belief systems. In an analysis of 90 societies, Levinson (1989) links wife beating with cultural factors: male control of the wealth, use of violence to resolve conflict, the domestic authority of men, and women's limited access to divorce. According to Tifft (1993), an analysis of the cross-cultural research indicates that intrafamily violence is associated with: societal violence, specific family organizational patterns, and cultural supports or limits on male dominance.

A cross-cultural perspective urges us to view intimate battering in a cultural context as well as realizing it is a universal phenomena. What about OUR culture contributes to the prevalence of intimate violence? Do our cultural conceptions of love or intimate relationships contribute to intimate violence (Martin, 1981; Tifft, 1993)? Do our family organizational patterns [i.e., isolated nuclear families with an individual (woman) providing all the child care], contribute to patterns of violence? Is there a connection between other forms of violence and partner abuse?

## Battering in Relation to Violence

Thus, our explanations for intimate violence may involve relating it to other cultural patterns of aggression. Surprisingly, research and theory on violent behavior has treated aggression between intimates and aggression between strangers as separate phenomena (Fagan &

Wexler, 1987; Shields et al., 1988). Researchers and theorists have generally adopted a "family violence perspective" in which domestic violence is viewed as different from violence between nonfamilial individuals (Hotaling & Straus, 1980; Shields et al., 1988). An emphasis on family specific factors makes family violence seem distinct from general violence.

Yet, as a group, men who batter are more likely than nonviolent partners to be violent or aggressive in other ways and with other people. They are more likely to have a criminal history (Roberts, 1987; Bland & Orn, 1986; White & Straus, 1981) and to have used violence outside of the home (Graff, 1979; Hotaling & Sugarman, 1986; Rouse, 1984; Shields et al., 1988). White and Straus (1981) report that batterers are twice as likely as nonviolent husbands to have an arrest record for a serious crime, and Gayford (1975) reports that 50 percent of his sample of male batterers had spent time in prison. Somewhere between one third (Flynn, 1977) and 46 percent of batterers (Fagan, Stewart, & Hansen, 1983) have been arrested for other violence. Batterers have consistently higher rates of committing child abuse than men who are not violent with their partners (Hotaling & Sugarman, 1986). Thus, the violence and aggression used by at least some batterers is not confined to their partners.

Batterers have been found to have higher levels of anger and hostility than nonviolent controls, but they do not differ significantly from other violent men in this regard (Maiuro et al., 1986, 1988). Batterers did differ from generally violent men in reporting higher levels of guilt and self-criticism. The most violent spouse abusers are those who are also violent toward strangers (Fagan et al., 1983; Frieze et al., 1980). Use of psychological forms of aggression (Murphy & O'Leary, 1989) and sexual aggression toward their partners (Hotaling & Sugarman, 1986) is more common for men who become physically violent in general. In a study by Shields and Hanneke (1981) men who were violent at home *and* with strangers were indistinguishable from men violent only outside the home in terms of background characteristics. Batterers who limited their violence to family members differed from generally violent men in terms of education, socioeconomic status, and attitudes. These findings support the perspective that there are different types of batterers. However, the findings also suggest that at least a portion of battering may be related to (male) aggression in general.

## Intergenerational Transmission of Violence

Exposure to violence as a child is an important precursor for both stranger and family violence of adult males (Fagan & Wexler, 1987). Childhood exposure to violence as the strongest predictor for both intra- and extrafamilial violence (Fagan et al., 1983). Pagelow (1982) examines the processes that underlie this intergenerational transmission of violence, including: modeling, reinforcement, internalization, practice opportunities, and teaching the functional value of violence. Intergenerational theory suggests that parents serve as role models for children. The children learn that violent or aggressive behavior is an acceptable way to deal with anger and conflict, and learn that a benefit of violence is control and dominance (Straus, 1979). Fagan and Wexler (1987) argue that it is necessary to explain how or why some individuals raised in violent homes grow up nonviolent. Pagelow (1984) argues that this theory of intergenerational transmission of violence is more appropriate for sons of violent fathers than for other combinations. Fagan and Wexler (1987) present a theoretical framework in which violent behaviors learned during childhood are either strengthened or inhibited during later developmental stages by sociocultural factors (e.g., peer group attitudes, sex-role norms) or by perceived deterrence or sanctions (e.g., societal disapproval or illegality). Several theorists have encouraged primary prevention efforts directed at breaking the cycle of intergenerational transmission (Gelles, 1979; Tifft, 1993; Walker, 1979).

## Intimate Abuse in a Violent Culture

The political rhetoric and media coverage of increasing and endemic violence in our society rarely addresses or includes reference to family forms of violence. Although partner battering is illegal and a violent crime, rates of domestic violence are not reported as violent crimes in the Uniform Crime Statistics, except for partner homicides. Similarly, individuals working with batterers or victims may not view spouse or intimate abuse as an aspect of escalating violence in our culture.

Some theorists, however, have argued that spouse abuse, like gang violence and stranger crime, is the result of a culture of violence (e.g., Straus, 1973; Tifft, 1993). In such a culture, physical force is an acceptable method of conflict resolution, and social controls are weak or inadequate. Tifft (1993) argues for a connection between the deployment of violence by nation-states and ethnic groups to address regional, national, and international conflicts, and the use of violence at the dyadic level. Further, he contends that hierarchical, competitive, and dehumanizing workplaces contribute to intrafamily violence. Tifft (1993) argues that prevalent intimate abuse can be linked to "decision-making and economic arrangements that foster hierarchical nonparticipation, severely restrict access to collective resources, and de-emphasize collective accomplishment and responsibility" (p. 13). He suggests that a primary preventative approach to intimate violence would involve the reducing power inequalities and eliminating the use of violence to solve conflicts in all contexts and at all levels of society.

## SUMMARY

Implicitly or explicitly the research we conduct on intimate violence and our intervention efforts reflect underlying ideological perspectives. The focus of our research, the terms and measures we use, and the intervention strategies we employ both inform and are directed by our theories of intimate violence. An initial focus on wife beating led to theories of marital dynamics and deficiencies in the wives who were beaten, and intervention efforts entailed sheltering and counseling the abused wife. Research that employs the terms and measures of the domestic violence perspective emphasizes the mutuality and interactive aspects of intimate violence and supports interventions directed toward dyadic or family conflict resolution. Feminist research has directed our attention toward the (male) batterer, and has coined terms that embody the gendered aspects of intimate violence. Feminist theories focus on the unequal distribution of power in intimate relationships as supported by cultural beliefs and institutions. Feminists support interventions directed at rehabilitating the batterer, and work for the transformation of male–female relationships and societal structures. Cross-cultural research directs our attention to cultural factors that contribute to intimate violence and also calls for explanations of the universality of male violence against women. Previously, heterosexist biases rendered violence in gay and lesbian relationships invisible. The research documenting the prevalence of violence across all forms of intimate relationships, and research increasingly indicating that women can be perpetrators calls for new theoretical perspectives. The authors endorse a culture of violence perspective that encourages intensive primary prevention efforts. The incidence of intimate violence indicates the futility of intervening at the individual level. We must find ways to reduce the levels of violence experienced in our lives and in our intimate relationships.

## REFERENCES

Adams, D. (1986). *Counseling men who batter: A profeminist analysis of five treatment modes.* Paper presented at the Annual Meeting of the American Psychiatric Association.

Bachman, R., & Saltzman, L. E. (1996). *Violence against women: Estimates from the redesigned survey.* [Bureau of Justice Statistics special report]. Rockville, MD: U. S. Department of Justice.

Bernard, J. L., & Bernard, M. L. (1984). The abusive male seeking treatment: Jekyll and Hyde. *Family Relations, 33,* 543–547.

Bland, R., & Orn, H. (1986). Family violence and psychiatric disorder. *Canadian Journal of Psychiatry, 31,* 129–137.

Bograd, M. (1984). Family systems approaches to wife battery: A feminist critique. *American Journal of Orthopsychiatry, 54,* 558–565.

Bograd, M. (1988). Feminist perspectives on wife abuse: An introduction. In K. Yllo & M. Bograd (Eds.), *Feminist perspectives on wife abuse.* Beverly Hills, CA: Sage.

Bograd, M. (1990). Why we need gender to understand human violence. *Journal of Interpersonal Violence, 5(1),* 132–135.

Bologna, M. J., Waterman, C. K., & Dawson, L. J. (1987, July). *Violence in gay male and lesbian relationships.* Paper presented at the Third National Conference for Family Violence Researchers, Durham, NH.

Bookwala, J., Frieze, I. H., Smith, C., & Ryan, K. (1992). Predictors of dating violence: A multivariate analysis. *Violence and Victims, 7,* 297–311.

Bowker, L. H. (1983). *Beating wife beating.* Lexington, MA: Lexington Books.

Bowker, L. H. (1984). Coping with wife abuse: Personal and social networks. In A. R. Roberts (Ed.), *Battered women and their families.* New York: Springer.

Brand, P. A., & Kidd, A. H. (1986). Frequency of physical aggression in heterosexual and female homosexual dyads. *Psychological Reports, 59,* 1307–1313.

Breines, W., & Gorden, L. (1983). The new scholarship on family violence. *Signs: A Journal of Women in Culture and Society, 8 (3),* 490–531.

Brown, J. K. (1997). Agitators and peace-makers: Cross cultural perspectives on older women and the abuse of young wives. In A. Sev'er (Ed.), *A cross-cultural exploration of wife abuse: Problems and prospects* (pp. 79–100). Lewiston, NY: The Edwin Mellen Press.

Browne, A. (1987). *When battered women kill.* New York: Macmillan Free Press.

Browne, A. (1989). *Are women as violent as men?* Commentary at the meeting of the American Society of Criminology, Reno, NV.

Browne, A., & Dutton, D. G. (1990). Escape from violence: Risks and alternatives for abused women. In R. Roesch, D. G. Dutton, & V. F. Sacco (Eds.), *Family violence: Perspectives in research and practice.* Burnaby, BC: Simon Fraser University Press.

Browne, A., & Williams, K.R. (1989). Exploring the effect of resource availability and the likelihood of female-perpetrated homicides. *Law and Society Review, 23(1),* 75–94.

Brush, L. (1990). Violent acts and injurious outcomes in married couples: Methodological issues in the national survey of families and households. *Gender & Society, 4,* 56–67.

Caesar, P. L. (1986, August). Men who batter: A heterogeneous group. In L. K. Hamberger (Chair), *The male batterer: Characteristics of a heterogeneous population.* Symposium conducted at the Annual Meeting of the American Psychological Association, Washington, DC.

Caesar, P. L. (1988). Exposure to violence in the families of origin among wife-abusers and maritally nonviolent men. *Violence and Victims, 3,* 49–63.

Campbell, J. C. (1986). Nursing assessment for risk of homicide with battered women. *Advances in Nursing Science, 8,* 36–51.

Campbell, J. C. (1995, July). *Depression in battered women.* Paper presented at the Fourth International Family Violence Research Conference, Durham, NH.

Caplan, P. (1985) *The myth of women's masochism.* New York: E. P. Dutton.

Cate, R. M., Henton, J. M., Koval , J., Christopher, F. S., & Lloyd, S. (1982). Premarital abuse: A social psychological perspective. *Journal of Family Issues, 3,* 79–91.

Cazenave, N., & Straus, M. (1979). Race, class network embeddedness and family violence: A search for potent support systems. *Journal of Comparative Family Studies, 10,* 281–299.

Chandler, S. (1986). *The psychology of the battered woman.* Unpublished doctoral dissertation. Department of Education, University of California, Berkeley.

Chang, V. N. (1996). *I just lost myself: Psychological abuse of women in marriage.* Westport, CT: Praeger.

Chester, B., Robin, R., Koss, M., Lopez, J., & Goldman, D. (1994). Grandmother dishonored: Violence against women by male partners in American Indian communities. *Violence and Victims, 9,* 259–274.

Cleek, M. G., & Pearson, T. A. (1985). Perceived causes of divorce: An analysis of interrelationships. *Journal of Marriage and the Family, 47 (1),* 179–183.

Coleman, K. H., Weinman, M. L., & Hsi, B. P. (1980). Factors affecting conjugal violence. *The Journal of Psychology, 105,* 197–202.

Coleman, V. E. (1991). Violence in lesbian couples: A between groups comparison. (Doctoral dissertation, California School of Professional Psychology—Los Angeles, 1990). *Dissertation Abstracts International, 51*, 5634B.

Coley, S., & Becket, J. (1988). Black battered women: Practice issues. *Social Casework, 69*, 483–490.

Counts, P. A., Brown, J. K., & Campbell, J. C. (1992). *Sanctions and sanctuary: Cultural perspectives on the beating of wives.* Boulder, CO: Westview Press.

Davis, R. C., & Smith, B. (1995). Domestic violence reforms: Empty promises or fulfilled expectations? *Crime and Delinquency, 41*, 541–552.

Deal, J. E., & Wampler, K. S. (1986). Dating violence: The primacy of previous experience. *Journal of Social and Personal Relationships, 3*, 457–471.

DeMaris, A., & Jackson, J. (1987). Batterers' reports of recidivism after counseling. *Social Casework, 68*, 142–154.

Dobash, R. E., & Dobash, R. P. (1979). *Violence against wives.* New York: The Free Press.

Dobash, R. P., Dobash, R. E., Cavanagh, K., & Lewis, R. (1998). Separate and intersecting reality: A comparison of men's and women's accounts of violence against women. *Journal of Violence Against Women, 4(4)*, 382–414.

Drossman, D. A., Leserman, J., Nachman, G., Zhiming, L., Gluck, H., Toomey, T. C., & Mitchell, C. M. (1990). Sexual and physical abuse in women with functional or gastrointestinal disorders. *Annals of Internal Medicine, 113*, 828–833.

Dutton, D. G. (1988). Profiling of wife assaulters: Preliminary evidence for a trimodal analysis. *Violence and Victims, 3*, 5–29.

Dutton, D. G., & Painter S. L. (1981). Traumatic bonding: The development of emotional attachments in battered women and other relationships of intermittent abuse. *Victimology, 6*, 139–155.

Dutton, D. G., & Strachan, C. E. (1987). Motivational needs for power and spouse-specific assertiveness in assaultive and non-assaultive men. *Violence and Victims, 2*, 145–156.

Dutton, D. G., & van Ginkel, C. (1997). The interaction of cultural and personality factors in the etiology of wife assault. In A. Sev'er (Ed.), *A cross-cultural exploration of wife abuse: Problems and prospects* (pp.101–122). Lewiston, NY: The Edwin Mellen Press.

Dworkin, A., & Brooks, T. (1995). Fighting sexual abuse. In P. Chesler, E. D. Rothblum, & E. Cole (Eds.), *Feminist foremothers women's studies, psychology, and mental health.* Binghamton, NY: Haworth Press.

Eisikovits, Z. C., & Edleson, J. L. (1989). Intervening with men who batter: A critical review of the literature. *Social Science Review, 37*, 385–414.

Fagan, J. A., Stewart, D. K., & Hansen, K. V. (1983). Violent men or violent husbands? Background factors and situational correlates. In D. Finkelhor, R. Gelles, G. Hotaling, & M. A. Straus (Eds.), *The dark side of families: Current family violence research.* Beverly Hills, CA: Sage.

Fagan, J., & Wexler, S. (1987). Crime at home and in the streets: The relationship between family and stranger violence. *Violence and Victims, 2, 1*, 5–23.

Fields, M. D. (1978). Does this vow include wife beating? *Human Rights, 7*, 40–45.

Fiora-Gormally, N. (1978). Battered women who kill: Double standard out of court, single standard in? *Law and Human Behavior. 2*,133- 165.

Fitch, F. J., & Papantonio, A. (1983). Men who batter: Some pertinent characteristics. *The Journal of Nervous and Mental Disease, 171*, 190–192.

Flynn, J. P. (1977). Recent findings related to wife abuse. *Social Casework, 58*, 13–20.

Frieze, I. H. (1979). Perceptions of battered wives. In I. H. Frieze, D. Bar-Tal, & J. S. Carroll (Eds.), *New approaches to social problems: Applications of attribution theory.* San Francisco: Jossey Bass.

Frieze, I. H. (March, 1999). *Violence in female-male relationships: Women as victims and perpetrators.* Paper presented to The Association for Women in Psychology, Providence, RI.

Frieze, I. H., Knoble, J., Washburn, C., & Zomnir, G. (1980). *Types of battered women.* Paper presented at Association for Women in Psychology. Santa Monica, CA.

Frieze, I. H., & McHugh, M. C. (1992). Power and influence strategies in violent and nonviolent marriages. *Psychology of Women Quarterly, 16*, 449–465.

Gardner, R. A. (1989). *The parental alienation syndrome and the differention between fabricated and genuine child sex abuse.* Cresskill, NJ: Creative Therapeutics.

Gayford, J. J. (1975). Wife battering: A preliminary study of 100 cases. *British Medical Journal, 1* (January), 194–197.

Geffner, R. (1997). Family violence: Current issues, interventions, and research. In R. Geffner, S. B. Sorenson, & P. K. Lundberg-Love (Eds.), *Violence and sexual abuse at home: Current issues in spousal battering and child maltreatment* (pp. 1–26). New York: Haworth Maltreatment & Trauma Press.

Gelles, R. J. (1979). *Family violence.* Beverly Hills, CA: Sage.

Gelles, R. J. (1980). Violence in the family: A review of research in the seventies. *Journal of Marriage and the Family, 42*, 873–885.

Gelles, R. J., & Cornell, C. P. (1983). *International perspectives on family violence.* Toronto: Lexington.

Gelles, R. J., Lackner, R., & Wolfner, G. D. (1994). Men who batter: The risk markers. *Violence Up Date, 4(12),* 1, 2, 4, 10.

Goldberg, W. G., & Tomlanovich, M. C. (1984). Domestic violence victims in the emergency departments: New findings. *Journal of the American Medical Association, 251,* 3259–3264.

Gondolf, E. W. (1988). Who are those guys? Toward a behavioral typology of batterers. *Violence and Victims, 3,* 187–203.

Gondolf, E. W. (1997). *Multi-site evaluation of batterer intervention systems.* Unpublished manuscript.

Gondolf, E. W. (1998). *Assessing woman battering in mental health services.* Thousand Oaks, CA: Sage.

Gondolf, E., & Fisher, E. R. (1988). *Battered women as survivors: An alternative to treating learned helplessness.* Lexington MA: Lexington Books.

Gondolf, E. W., Fisher, E. R., & McFerron, R. (1991). Racial differences among shelter residents: A comparison of anglo, black, and hispanic battered women. In R. Hampton (Ed.), *Black family violence: Current research and theory.* Newbury Park, CA: Sage.

Gondolf, E. W., & Hart, B. (1994). Lethality and dangerous assessments. *Violence Update, 4,* 7–10.

Goodman, L., Koss, M.P., & Russo, N.F. (1993). Violence against women: Physical and mental health effects. Part I: Research findings. *Applied & Preventive Psychology: Current Scientific Perspectives, 2,* 79–89.

Goodwin, B. E., & McHugh, M. C. (1990). *Termination terrorism.* Panel presented at the Association for Women in Psychology, Tempe, AZ.

Graff, T. T. (1979). *Personality characteristics of battered women.* Unpublished doctoral dissertation, Brigham Young University.

Hamberger, L. K. (1994). Domestic partner abuse: Expanding paradigms for understanding and intervention. *Violence and Victims, 9, 2,* 91–94.

Hamberger, L. K. (1997). Female offenders in domestic violence: A look at actions in their context. In R. Geffner, S. B. Sorenson, & P. K. Lundberg-Love (Eds.) *Violence and sexual abuse at home: Current issues in spousal battering and child maltreatment* (pp. 117–130). New York: Haworth Press.

Hamberger, L. K., & Hastings, J. E. (1988). Skills training for treatment of spouse abusers: An outcome study. *Journal of Family Violence, 3,* 121–130.

Hamberger, L. K., & Hastings, J. E. (1990). Recidivism following spouse abuse abatement counseling: Treatment program implications. *Violence and Victims, 5,* 157–170.

Hamberger, L. K., & Hastings, J. E. (1991). Personality correlates of men who batter and nonviolent men: Some continuities and discontinuities. *Journal of Family Violence, 6,* 131–147.

Hamberger, L. K., Lohr, J. M., Bonge, D., & Tolin, D. (1995, July). *A typology of men who batter: Relationship to violence severity.* Paper presented at the 4th International Family Violence Research Conference, Durham, N. H.

Hamberger, L. K., & Potente, T. (1994). Counseling heterosexual women arrested for domestic violence: Implications for theory and practice. *Violence and Victims, 9,* 125–137.

Harris, J. (1986). Counseling violent couples using Walker's model. *Psychotherapy, 23,* 613–621.

Harris, R., Savage, S., Jones, T., & Brooke, W. (1988). A comparison of treatments for abusive men and their partners within a family service agency. *Canadian Journal of Community and Mental Health, 7,* 147–155.

Hart, B. (1992). Assessing whether batterers will kill. *Ending Men's Violence Network Newsletter, 8,* 16.

Hart, B. J., & Gondolf, E. W. (1994, June). Lethality and dangerousness assessments. *Violence Up Date,* 7–8, 10.

Hart, S. D., Dutton, D. G., & Newlove, T. (1993). The prevalence of personality disorders among wife assaulters. *Journal of Personality Disorders, 7,* 329–341.

Hastings, J. E., & Hamberger, L. K. (1988). Personality characteristics of spouse abusers: A controlled comparison. *Violence and Victims, 3,* 31–47.

Henton, J., Cate, R., Koval, J., Lloyd, S., & Christopher, S. (1983). Romance and violence in dating relationships. *Journal of Family Issues, 4,* 467–482.

Holtzworth-Munroe, A., & Hutchinson, G. (1993). Attributing negative intent to wife behavior: The attributions of maritally violent versus nonviolent men. *Journal of Abnormal Psychology, 102,* 206–211.

Holtzworth-Munroe, A. & Stuart, G. (1994). Typologies of male batterers: Three subtypes and the differences among them. *Psychological Bulletin, 116,* 476–497.

Hornung, C. A., McCullough, B. C., & Sugimoto, T. (1981). Status relationships in marriage: Risk factors in spouse abuse. *Journal of Marriage and the Family, 43,* 675–692.

Hotaling, G. T., & Straus, M. A. (1980). Culture, social organization and irony in the study of family violence. In M. A. Straus & G. T. Hotaling (Eds.), *The social causes of husband-wife violence* (pp. 3–22). Minneapolis: University of Minnesota Press.

Hotaling, G. T., & Sugarman, D. B. (1986). An analysis of risk markers in husband to wife violence: The current state of knowledge. *Violence and Victims, 1,* 101–124.

Hudson, W., & McIntosh, S. (1981). The assessment of spouse abuse: Two quantifiable dimensions. *Journal of Marriage and the Family, 43*, 873–885.

Jaffe, P., Hastings, E., Reitzel, D., & Austin, G. (1993). The impact of police laying charges. In N. Z. Hilton (Ed.), *Legal responses to wife assault: Current trends and evaluation* (pp. 62–95). Newbury Park, CA: Sage.

Jang, D. (1994). Caught in a web: Immigrant women and domestic violence. *National Clearinghouse for Legal Services Review, Special Issue*, 397–405.

Johnson, H. (1996). *Dangerous domains: Violence against women in canada*. Toronto: Nelson.

Johnson, H. (1998). Rethinking survey research on violence against women. In R. E. Dobash & R. P. Dobash (Eds.), *Rethinking violence against women* (pp. 23–52). Thousand Oaks, CA: Sage.

Jones, A. (1981). *Women who kill*. New York: Holt, Rinehart & Winston.

Kalmuss, D. S., & Seltzer, J. A. (1986). Continuity of marital behavior in remarriage: The case of spouse abuse. *Journal of Marriage and the Family, 48*, 113–120.

Kantor, G., Jasinski, J., & Aldarondo, E. (1994). Sociocultural status and incidence of martial violence in hispanic families. *Violence and Victims, 9*, 207–222.

Kelly, E. E., & Warshafsky, L. (1987, July). *Partner abuse in gay male and lesbian couples*. Paper presented at the Third National Conference for Family Violence Researchers, Durham, NC.

Kelly, L. (1988). *Surviving sexual violence*. Cambridge: Polity.

Kelly, L., Burton, S., & Regan, L. (1994). Researching women's lives or studying women's oppression? Reflections on what constitutes feminist research. In M. Maynard & J. Purvis (Eds.), *Researching women's lives from a feminist perspective* (pp. 22–48). Britain: Taylor and Francis.

Kelly, L., & Radford, J. (1998). Sexual violence against women and girls: An approach to an international overview. In R. E. Dobash & R. P. Dobash (Eds.), *Rethinking violence against women* (pp. 53–76). Thousand Oaks, CA: Sage.

Koss, M. P. (1990). The women's mental health research agenda: Violence against women. *American Psychologist, 45*, 374–380.

Koss, M. P., Goodman, L. A., Browne, A., Fitzgerald, L., Keita, G. P., & Russo, N. F. (1994). *No safe haven: Violence against women at home, at work, and in the community*. Washington, DC: American Psychological Association.

Krenek, K. (1998, October). *Keynote address*. Annual Conference of PASSHE Women's Consortium and Mid-Atlantic Nation Women's Studies Association. Shippensburg University.

Leonard, K. E., Bromet, E. J., Parkinson, D. K., Day, N. L., & Ryan, C. M. (1985). Patterns of alcohol use and physically aggressive behavior in men. *Journal of Studies on Alcohol, 46*, 279–282.

Lerner, M. J. (1980). *The belief in a just world: A fundamental delusion*. New York: Plenum.

Letellier, P. (1994). Gay and bisexual male domestic violence victimization: Challenges to feminist theory and responses to violence. *Violence and Victims, 9*, 95–106.

Levinson, D. (1989). *Family violence in a cross-cultural perspective*. Newbury Park, CA: Sage.

Lindquist, C. U., Telch, C. F., & Taylor, J. (1985). Evaluation of a conjugal violence treatment program: A pilot study. *Behavioral Counseling and Community Intervention, 3*, 76–90.

Lipchik, E., Sirles, E. A., & Kubicki, A. D. (1997). Multifaceted approaches in spouse abuse treatment. In R. Geffner, S. B. Sorenson, & P. K. Lundberg-Love (Eds.), *Violence and sexual abuse at home: Current issues in spousal battering and child maltreatment* (pp. 131–148). New York: Haworth Press.

MacEwen, K. E., & Barling, J. (1988). Multiple stressors, violence in the family of origin, and marital aggression: A longitudinal investigation. *Journal of Family Violence, 3*, 73–87.

Maiuro, R. D, Cahn, T. S., & Vitaliano, P. P. (1986). Assertiveness deficits and hostility in domestically violent men. *Violence and Victims, 1*, 279–289.

Maiuro, R. D, Cahn, T. S., Vitaliano, P. P., Wagner, B. C., & Zegree, J. B. (1988). Anger, hostility, and depression in domestically violent versus generally assaultive men and nonviolent control subjects. *Journal of Consulting and Clinical Psychology, 56*, 17–23.

Makepeace, J. M. (1983). Life events, stress, and courtship violence. *Family Relations, 32*, 101–109.

Makepeace, J. M. (1986). Gender differences in courtship violence victimization. *Family Relations, 35*, 383–388.

Margolin, G., & Burman, B. (1993). Wife abuse versus marital violence: Different terminologies, explanations, and solutions. *Clinical Psychology Review, 13*, 59–73.

Martin, D. (1981). *Battered wives*. San Francisco: Volcano Press.

Martin, M. E. (1997). Double your trouble: Dual arrest in family violence. *Journal of Family Violence, 12*, 139–157.

McHugh, M. C. (1987, June). *Woman blaming*. Paper presented at the annual meeting of the National Women's Studies Association, Baltimore.

McHugh, M. C. (1990, August). *Gender issues in psychotherapy: Victim blame/woman blame*. Invited address presented at the annual meeting of the American Psychological Association, Boston.

McHugh, M. C. (1993). Battered women and their assailants: A methodological critique. In M. Hansen & M. Harway (Eds.), *Battering and family therapy: A feminist perspective.* Newbury Park, CA: Sage.

McNeely, R. L., & Mann, C. R. (1990). Domestic violence is a human issue. *Journal of Interpersonal Violence, 5, 1,* 129–132.

McWilliams, M. (1998). Violence against women in societies under stress. In R. E. Dobash & R. P. Dobash (Eds.), *Rethinking violence against women* (pp. 111–140). Thousand Oaks, CA: Sage.

Mignon, S. I., & Holmes, W. M. (1995). Police response to mandatory arrest laws. *Crime and Delinquency, 41,* 430–442.

Murphy, C. M., & O'Leary, K. D. (1989). Psychological aggression predicts physical aggression in early marriage. *Journal of Consulting and Clinical Psychology, 57,* 579–582.

Myers, B. A. (1989). *Lesbian battering: An analysis of power, inequality and conflict in lesbian relationships.* Unpublished doctoral dissertation, Indiana University of Pennsylvania, Department of Psychology.

Neff, J., Holamon, B., & Schluter, T. D. (1995). Spousal violence among Anglos, Blacks and Mexican Americans: The role of demographic variables, psychosocial predictors, and alcohol consumption. *Journal of Family Violence, 10,* 1–21.

Neidig, P. H. (1986). The development and evaluation of a spouse abuse treatment program in a military setting. *Evaluation and Program Planning, 9,* 275–280.

Neidig, P. H., Freidman, D. H., & Collins, B. S. (1985). Domestic conflict containment: A spouse abuse treatment program. *Social Casework,* April 1985, 195–204.

Neidig, P. H., Freidman, D. H., & Collins, B. S. (1986). Attitudinal characteristics of males who have engaged in spouse abuse. *Journal of Family Violence, 1,* 223–232.

O'Carroll, P., & Mercy, J. (1986). Patterns and recent trends in black homicide. In D. Hawkins (Ed.), *Homicide among Black Americans.* Lanham, MD: University Press of America.

O'Leary, K. D., & Curley, A. D. (1986). Assertion and family violence: Correlates of spouse abuse. *Journal of Marital and Family Therapy, 12,* 281–289.

Pagelow, M. (1981). *Woman-battering.* Beverly Hills, CA: Sage.

Pagelow, M. D. (1982). *Social learning theory and sex roles: Violence begins in the home.* Paper presented at the annual meeting of the Society for the Study of Social Problems, San Francisco.

Pagelow, M. D. (1984). *Family violence.* New York: Praeger.

Pagelow, M. D. (1985). The battered husband syndrome: Social problem or much ado about little? In I. N. Johnson (Ed.), *Marital violence.* London: Routledge and Kegan.

Pagelow, M. D. (1997). Battered women: A historical research review and some common myths. In R. Geffner, S. B. Sorenson, & P. K. Lundberg-Love (Eds.), *Violence and sexual abuse at home: Current issues in spousal battering and child maltreatment* (pp. 97–116). New York: Haworth Press.

Pate, A. M., & Hamilton, E. E. (1992). Formal and informal deterrents to domestic violence: The Dade County Spouse Assault Experiment. *American Sociological Review, 57,* 691–697. Abstract from Silver Platter File: PsycLIT Item: 80–15826.

Pence, E. (1989). Batterer programs: Shifting from community collusion to community confrontation. In P. L. Caesar & L. K. Hamberger (Eds.), *Treating men who batter: Theory, practice, and programs* (pp. 24–50). New York: Springer.

Pressman, B. (1989). Treatment of wife abuse: The case for feminist therapy. In B. Pressman & G. Cameron (Eds.), *Intervening with assaulted women: Current theory, research, and practice* (pp. 21–45). Hillsdale, NJ: Lawrence Erlbaum.

Raymond, B., & Bruschi, I. G. (1989). Psychological abuse among college women in dating relationships. *Perceptual and Motor Skills, 69,* 1283–1297.

Renzetti, C. M. (1988). Violence in lesbian relationships: A preliminary analysis of causal factors. *Journal of Interpersonal Violence, 3,* 381–399.

Renzetti, C. M. (1992). *Violent betrayal: Partner abuse in lesbian relationships.* Newbury Park, CA: Sage.

Renzetti, C. M. (1993). Violence in lesbian relationships. In M. Hansen & M. Harway (Eds.), *Battering and family therapy: A feminist perspective.* Newbury Park, CA: Sage

Ridington, J. (1978). The transition process: A feminist environment as reconstructive milieu. *Victimology, 3,* 563–575.

Roberts, A. R. (1987). Psychosocial characteristics of batterers: A study of 234 men charged with domestic violence offenses. *Journal of Family Violence, 2,* 81–93.

Romero, M. (1985). A comparison between strategies used on prisoners of war and battered women. *Sex Roles, 13,* 537–547.

Rosenbaum, A., Geffner, R., & Benjamin, S. (1997). A biopychosocial model for understanding relationship aggression. In R. Geffner, S. B. Sorenson, & P. K. Lundberg-Love (Eds.), *Violence and sexual abuse at home: Current issues in spousal battering and child maltreatment* (pp. 57–80). New York: Haworth Press.

Rosenbaum, A., & O'Leary, K. D. (1981). Marital violence: Characteristics of abusive couples. *Journal of Consulting and Clinical Psychology, 49,* 63–71.

Rosewater, L. B. (1987). A critical analysis of the proposed self-defeating personality disorder. *Journal of Personality Disorders, 1,* 190–195.

Rouse, L. P. (1984). Models of self-esteem , and locus of control as factors contributing to spouse abuse. *Victimology International Journal, 9,* 130–141.

Russell, D. E. H. (1995). Politicizing sexual violence: A voice in the wilderness. In P. Chesler, E. D. Rothblum, & E. Cole (Eds.), *Feminist foremothers women's studies, psychology, and mental health.* Binghamton, NY: Haworth Press.

Russell, D. E. H. (1982). *Rape in marriage.* New York: Macmillan.

Russell, M. (1988). Wife assault theory, research, and treatment: A literature review. *Journal of Family Violence, 3,* 193–208.

Russo, N. F., Koss, M. P., & Goodman L. (1995). Male violence against women: A global health and development issue. In L. L. Adler & F. L. Denmark (Eds.), *Violence and the prevention of violence* (pp. 121–127). Westport, CT: Praeger Publishers.

Saunders, D. G. (1986). When battered women use violence: Husband abuse or self-defense? *Violence and Victims, 1,* 47–60.

Saunders, D. G. (1992). A typology of men who batter: Three types derived from cluster analysis. *American Journal of Orthopsychiatry, 62,* 264–275.

Saunders, D. G. (1996). Feminist-cognitive-behavioral and process psychodynamic treatments for men who batter: Interaction of abuser traits and treatment models. *Violence and Victims, 11,* 393–413.

Schechter, S. (1982). *Women and male violence: The visions and struggles of the battered women's movement.* Boston: South End Press.

Schulman, M. (1979). *A survey of spousal violence against women in Kentucky.* Study No. 792701 for the Kentucky Commission on Women. Washington, DC: U.S. Department of Justice-LEAR.

Sev'er, A. (Ed.). (1997). *A cross-cultural exploration of wife abuse: Problems and prospects.* Lewiston, NY: Edwin Mellen Press.

Shaw, E., Bouris, A., & Pye, S. (1996). The family safety model: A comprehensive strategy for working with domestic violence. *Australian and New Zealand Journal of Family Therapy, 17,* 126–136.

Sherman, L. W., & Berk, R. A. (1984). The specific deterrent effects of arrest for domestic assault. *American Sociological Review, 49,* 261–272.

Sherman, L. W., Smith, D. A., Schmidt, J. D., & Rogan, D. P. (1992). Crime, punishment, and stake in conformity: Legal and informal control of domestic violence. *American Sociological Review, 57,* 680–690. Abstract from Silver Platter File: PsycLIT Item: 80–15831.

Shields, N., & Hanneke, C. R. (1981). *Patterns of family and non-family violence: An approach to the study of violent husbands.* Paper presented at American Sociological Association Convention, Toronto, Ontario.

Shields, N. M., McCall, G. J., & Hanneke, C. R. (1988). Patterns of family and nonfamily violence: Violent husbands and violent men. *Violence and Victims, 3,* 83–97.

Smith, M. D. (1987). The incidence and prevalence of woman abuse in Toronto. *Violence and Victims, 2,* 173–187.

Smuts, B. (1992). Male aggression against women. *Human Nature, 3, 1,* 1–44.

Sonkin, D. J., & Durphy, M. (1985). *Learning to live without violence: A handbook for men* (2nd ed.). San Francisco: Volcano.

Sonkin, D. J., Martin, D., & Walker, L. E. (1985). *The male batterer: A treatment approach.* New York: Springer.

Stahly, G. B. (1996). Battered women: Why don't they just leave? In J. C. Chrisler, C. Golden, & P. D. Rozee (Eds.), *Lectures on the psychology of women* (pp. 289–308). New York: McGraw-Hill.

Steinman, M. (1988). Evaluating a system-wide response to domestic abuse: Some initial findings. *Journal of Contemporary Criminal Justice, 4,* 172–186.

Steinmetz, S. (1977–1978). The battered husband syndrome. *Victimology, 2(3–4),* 499–509.

Stets, J. E. (1991). Psychological aggression in dating relationships: The role of interpersonal control. *Journal of Family Violence, 6 (1),* 97–114.

Straus, M. A. (1973). A general systems theory approach to a theory of violence between family members. *Social Science Information, 12,* 105–125.

Straus, M. A. (1979). Measuring intrafamily conflict and violence: The Conflict Tactics Scales. *Journal of Marriage and the Family, 41,* 75–88.

Straus, M., & Gelles, R. (1986). Societal change and change in family violence from 1975–1985 as revealed by two national surveys. *Journal of Marriage and the Family, 48*, 465–479.

Straus, M. A., Gelles, R. S., & Steinmetz, J. K. (1980). *Behind closed doors: Violence in the American family.* Garden City, NJ: Anchor/Doubleday.

Straus, M., Hamby, S., Boney-McCoy, S., & Sugarman, D. (1996). The Revised Conflict Tactics Scales (CTS): Development and preliminary psychometric data. *Journal of Family Issues, 17(3)*, 283–316.

Sugarman, D. B., & Hotaling, G. T. (1989). Violent men in intimate relationships: An analysis of risk markers. *Journal of Applied Social Psychology, 19*, 1034–1048.

Sullivan, C. M., Basta, J., Tan, C., & Davidson II, W. S. (1992). After the crisis: A needs assessment of women leaving a domestic violence shelter. *Violence and Victims, 7*, 3, 267–275.

Telch, C. F., & Lindquist, C. U. (1984). Violent vs. nonviolent couples: A comparison of patterns. *Psychotherapy, 21*, 242–248.

Tifft, L. L. (1993). *Battering of women: The failure of intervention and the case for prevention.* Boulder, CO: Westview Press.

Tolman, R. M. (1989). The development of a measure of psychological maltreatment of women by their male partners. *Violence and Victims, 4 (3)*, 159–177.

Tolman, R. M. (1992). Psychological abuse of women. In R. T. Ammerman & M. Hersen (Eds.), *Assessment of family violence: A clinical and legal sourcebook* (pp. 291–310). New York: John Wiley & Sons.

Tolman, R. M., & Bennett, L. W. (1990). A review of quantitative research on men who batter. *Journal of Interpersonal Violence, 5*, 87–118.

Tolman, R. M., & Weisz, A. (1995). Coordinated community intervention for domestic violence: The effects of arrest and prosecution on recidivism of woman abuse perpetrators. *Crime and Delinquency, 41*, 481–495.

Van Hasselt, V. B., Morrison, R. L., & Bellack, A. S. (1985). Alcohol use in wife abusers and their spouses. *Addictive Behaviors, 10*, 127–135.

Vivian, D., & Langhinrichsen-Rohling, J. (1994). Are bi-directionally violent couples mutually victimized: A gender-sensitive comparison. *Violence and Victims, 9*, 107–124.

von Erden, J., & Goodwin, B. J. (1992, March). *The unidentified battered woman: The importance of the intake interview.* Paper presented to the Association for Women in Psychology, Long Beach.

Walker, L. E. (1977). Battered women and learned helplessness. *Victimology, 2*, 252–354.

Walker, L. E. (1979). *The battered woman.* New York: Harper & Row.

Walker, L. E. A. (1983). The battered woman syndrome study. In D. Finkelhor, R. J. Gelles, G. T. Hotaling, & M. A. Straus (Eds.), *The dark side of families: Current family violence research* (pp. 31–47). Beverly Hills, CA: Sage.

Walker, L. (1984). *The battered woman syndrome.* New York: Springer.

Walker, L. E. A. (1995). Foreword. In L. L. Adler & F. L. Denmark (Eds.), *Violence and the prevention of violence* (pp. ix–xiii). Westport, CT: Praeger Publishers.

Walker, L. E. A., & Browne, A. (1985). Gender and victimization by intimates. *Journal of Personality, 53*, 179–195.

Weidman, A. (1986, April). Family therapy with violent couples. *Social Casework: The Journal of Contemporary Casework*, 211–218.

White, S. O., & Straus, M. A. (1981). The implications of family violence for rehabilitation strategies. In S. E. Martin, L. E. Sechrest, & R. Redner (Eds.), *New directions in the rehabilitation of criminal offenders.* Washington, DC: National Academy of Sciences.

Yllo, K., & Bograd, M. (Eds.). (1988). *Feminist perspectives on wife abuse.* Newbury Park, CA: Sage.

# III

# Relationships and Sexuality

---

This section addresses women's sexuality and relationships, as well as their experiences with motherhood and reproduction. By now you have noticed the interconnectedness between the larger social context and women's personal experiences. The topics in this section must also, of course, be understood in their social context.

Kristine Baber tellingly entitles her chapter "Women's Sexualities" and suggests that there is much diversity among women in their experiences of sexuality. Baber also points out some problems with our traditional conceptualizations of sexuality and challenges us to think about what we mean by the words and constructions that we apply to the categories we use to understand sexual experience. How do you define sexual orientation, and how did you arrive at this understanding? Do you believe that sexual orientation is stable across the life span? Have shifting sexual scripts led to changes in the experience of sexuality among young women? What variables are related to sexual satisfaction for women? Baber provides an impressive integration and analysis of the research to frame the above questions for you.

Intimate relationships and their role in women's lives is the focus of Rhonda Jeter's chapter. Jeter explores the relationship among love, romance, and intimacy: What is your understanding of these different aspects of relating? Have your views changed over time or as a result of your experiences? The chapter author also discusses marriage and long-term relationships, how they are influenced by cultural standards, and the variables that impact relationship quality. What do you consider the keys to relationship satisfaction? Jeter summarizes the research on relationship satisfaction, divorce, adjustment to divorce, and lesbian relationships.

Joan Chrisler and Ingrid Johnston-Robledo address an array of topics in Chapter 10: menstruation, menopause, pregnancy, birth, contraception, and motherhood. They discuss the trends in research on menstruation over the past 100 years and note the recent shift in focus as more feminists have brought their perspective to the topic. Here you can see a clear example of what the authors of Part I alluded to as the influence of feminist reconceptualizations. The authors also discuss abortion, a topic hotly debated issue in the contemporary United States. What can we learn from the research here on decision making about and coping with abortion? Can this research inform the social debate? Chrisler and Johnston-Robledo provide much valuable information about pregnancy and motherhood, and present a cogent discussion of the reproductive strategies currently available to women and their partners. This chapter brings together a wealth of research on motherhood and reproduction.

# 8

# Women's Sexualities

## Kristine M. Baber

## INTRODUCTION

Positive sexual experiences contribute to women's personal and relationship satisfaction throughout life (Brecher, 1984; Spector & Fremeth, 1996). Until recently, however, women's sexuality either has been seen as a problem or ignored (Ussher, 1993). Therefore, we lack a comprehensive understanding of how women develop a sense of themselves as sexual beings. We also know little about the meaning and importance to women of their sexual identities and experiences. Particularly lacking is information about women's sexuality after the reproductive years of 15 to 44 (di Mauro, 1995). What we do know about women's sexuality is fragmented, problem focused, often biomedical in nature, and based primarily on the experiences of white women. Summarizing the results of a comprehensive assessment of sexuality research in the United States, di Mauro (1997) might have been talking about women's sexuality specifically when she noted that:

> What we know about childhood sexuality is what the literature on child abuse tells us. What we know about adolescent sexuality is what the literature on teenage pregnancy and HIV/AIDS tells us. What we know about the sexuality of the college-age population is HIV/AIDS and coercive sexuality, such as date rape. After that, adult sexuality is barely represented in the literature. (p. 4)

Feminist researchers criticize much of the existing research for overlooking important factors that affect women's sexuality and for perpetuating faulty assumptions about women's experiences by accepting stereotypes derived from research by and about men (Baber & Allen, 1992; Chalker, 1994; Rothblum, 1994; Schneider & Gould, 1987; Wyatt & Riederle, 1994; Ussher, 1993). By integrating feminist theorizing about sexuality into an interdisciplinary framework, it is possible to help women understand the social forces that constrain their sexuality; provide accurate, useful information to women; and help women have satisfying sexual relationships. To date, the accomplishment of these goals has proven elusive and sometimes the means to accomplishing them hotly contested, making open and direct discussion of

Kristine M. Baber ● Department of Family Studies, University of New Hampshire, Durham, New Hampshire 03824

*Issues in the Psychology of Women,* edited by Biaggio and Hersen. Kluwer Academic/Plenum Publishers, New York, 2000.

women's sexuality perhaps "the final frontier feminism has yet to cross" (Berman in Valdes-Rodriquez, 1998, p. E3).

This chapter contributes to this project by providing information about physical, relational, and psychological aspects of women's erotic experiences. It begins with a theoretical perspective to assist in integrating often fragmented information, presents research on the variety of women's sexual experiences across the life span, considers the risks associated with sexuality for women, discusses pleasure and satisfaction, and concludes with suggestions for revising social constructions of women's sexuality. Data from large-scale studies such as the National Health and Social Life Survey [NHSLS] (Laumann, Gagnon, Michael, & Michaels, 1994; Michael, Gagnon, Laumann, & Kolata, 1994) are used to present the broad contours of women's sexual experiences. Qualitative research such as Thompson's (1995) work with adolescent females provides finer detail and is more woman focused in conceptualization and interpretation. A postmodern feminist perspective offers a useful approach to organizing this information, challenging prevailing knowledge, and deconstructing taken-for-granted assumptions about women and sexuality.

## A POSTMODERN FEMINIST PERSPECTIVE

A combination of postmodern and feminist approaches provides a powerful perspective for investigating current knowledge about women's sexuality. From this perspective, sexuality is assumed to be complex and fluid, with sexual beliefs, attitudes, and behaviors constructed through a sociocultural process influenced by political, economic, and historical forces (Tiefer, 1995). The feminist viewpoint puts women's experiences and thinking at the center of attention and sees women's sexuality as having been distorted, repressed, exploited, and mystified by gender inequities in power and opportunity (Schneider & Gould, 1987). A valid understanding of women's sexuality must take into consideration these power relationships and acknowledge that their legacy continues to be played out in theology, education, therapy, and in the everyday sexual relationships of women of all ages.

Postmodern feminism deconstructs not only ideologies and practices that maintain and legitimate male domination, but also feminist theories that ignore differences related to categories such as race, class, age, or sexual orientation that structure women's experiences (Best & Kellner, 1991; Flax, 1990; Fraser & Nicholson, 1990). By "deconstructing" concepts usually taken for granted, it is possible to critically analyze and decompose prevailing ideas that may be seen as essential and unchangeable but that have actually been created and maintained by existing social relations. Deconstructive approaches attempt to destabilize accepted theories, acknowledge the experiential and behavioral range of social constructions, and manipulate social constructions to bring about change (Tiefer, 1995).

### Women's Sexualities

One of the fundamental assumptions needing revision is the idea that there is a unitary way in which women experience their sexuality—a "women's sexuality." Unfortunately, much of the existing research on women's sexual experiences focuses on white, middle-class, heterosexual women. For example, relatively few studies include lesbian or bisexual women in their samples; if they are included, they may be excluded from analysis because of small numbers of participants in those categories. Information that is available, however, suggests that factors such as age, experience, race, class, sexual orientation, and relationship status provide for rich diversity in women's sexual lives. In acknowledgement of the plurality of women's sexual interests, desires, and experiences, this chapter addresses "women's sexualities" (Baber & Allen, 1992; Daniluk, 1998) and encourages students, researchers, practitioners, and women themselves to abandon simplistic or unitary conceptions of women's sexual feelings and activities.

Even while acknowledging the importance of taking into consideration the influence of categories of analysis such as race, class, or sexual orientation, a postmodern feminist approach demands that these categories themselves be challenged. For example, although researchers today are more frequently considering race or ethnicity in sexuality research, it is important to question how useful these concepts really are as correlates of sexual behavior. Armstrong (1995) argues that "race is a simplistic and ill-defined measure of a much more complex set of socially-defined behaviors, beliefs, and customs" (p.9). Racial categories are imprecise and often limited to white, black, or other. The assumption that all members of such categories share a similar heritage, the same experiences, and congruent beliefs may promote faulty assumptions and stereotypes (Armstrong, 1995). The interpretation of meager data from different "racial" groups raises a related concern. Samuels (1995) cautions that a meaningful investigation of sexuality in the lives of African-Americans, for example, requires not only more information from a broad spectrum of individuals, but also a methodology and interpretation that is Afrocentric and founded on the philosophical beliefs of those being investigated.

Another example of the problems with categorization involves prevailing constructions of sexual orientation. A methodological issue in research on sexual orientation concerns how to differentiate lesbians from heterosexual women (Dancey, 1994). Laura Brown (1995), in an article on lesbian identitities, presents a working definition of lesbian identity as:

> primarily a self-ascribed definition held by a woman over time and across situations as having primary sexual, affectional, and relational ties to other women. This identity may or may not be congruent with overt behavior at any point during the life span, and the variables making up this definition may come and go from the foreground of a woman's definition as life circumstances change. (p. 4)

Brown then goes on to point out that a lesbian identity might be ascribed to a woman by others if she behaves in ways that have been culturally defined as lesbian even if she does not identify as such. Or a woman may feel attracted to another woman, but identify as heterosexual. Two women may live together and share an emotionally close relationship, but not identify as lesbians. Brown asks, "Who among these women are the 'real' lesbian" (p. 5)?

Whenever possible, this chapter includes differences in women's experiences reported in the research literature with the caveat that women may be categorized in ways that are invalid or reductionistic. Fortunately, a postmodern perspective can accommodate the tension that results from presenting research findings showing differences reported among women in the literature while simultaneously acknowledging the problems of categories such as race or sexual orientation—themselves socially constructed. It is important to be aware of constructions of sexuality among women of different ages, ethnic groups, and/or sexual orientations because differences, socially constructed though they might be, may have important implications for education, health care, or therapy. Clinical and educational models based on Euro-American norms and assumptions, for example, may not be effective in working with or assisting those of other racial/ethnic groups (Samuels, 1995). Understanding the sociocultural process by which varying constructions of sexuality and the related sexual scripts are developed and manifested provides an important conceptual tool for both attending to and critiquing differences.

## The Construction of Sexual Scripts

A constructivist perspective rejects the idea that there is some authentic female sexuality waiting to be discovered and attempts to identify factors that enhance or constrain the sexual possibilities for women. A key assumption is that there is no basic, fundamental sexuality that is transhistorical or transcultural (Kitzinger, 1995). Although biological factors are not totally ignored by one taking this theoretical position, sociocultural influences are seen as more critical in determining what is perceived as sexual and how individuals construct, interpret, and express their sexual thoughts and desires (Laumann & Gagnon, 1995). The concept of sexual scripts provides a useful way of understanding how this process functions. Sexual scripts refer to the "repertoire of acts and statuses that are recognized by a social group, together with the rules, expectations, and sanctions governing these acts and sanctions" (Laws & Schwartz, 1977, p. 2).

Scripting theory differentiates among cultural scenarios (instructions embedded in cultural narratives), intrapsychic scripts ( the ideas individuals use to choose and reflect upon their activity), and intrapersonal scripts (the structured pattern of interaction between and among actors) (Laumann & Gagnon, 1995). Such a scripting model builds on the assumption that individuals acquire through a lifelong process a culturally influenced sexual framework that guides sexual beliefs, desire, and behavior. The scripting approach proposes that "a reflexive individual participates in concrete social interaction with others, guided in part by a meaningful system of individually interpreted cultural instructions" (Laumann & Gagnon, p. 190). Individuals approach activity that has been culturally defined as sexual with what appears to be "natural" inclinations regarding appropriate behaviors, desirable partners, acceptable timing and location of activity, and proper motivation for participation in the activity. Because gender and sexuality are linked, males and females tend to develop different and complementary scripts (Gagnon, 1990). The traditional male script encourages men to act assertively, to initiate and lead in sexual activity, and to be knowledgeable regarding sexuality. The female script supports a role characterized by passivity, compliance, and responsiveness to the male's sexual prowess.

Although scripting theory itself is politically neutral, it easily accommodates a postmodern feminist adaptation that sees women's sexualities shaped through interaction with cultural scenarios that reflect gender inequalities, heterosexism, and racism. The cultural backdrop for women's sexualities traditionally has set male sexuality as the normative baseline for all human sexuality and viewed heterosexuality as the only normal expression of sexual intimacy (Schneider & Gould, 1987). As a result, for women, the appropriate partner has been a male with whom she has a committed relationship. The appropriate activity is one that brings the male satisfaction when he desires it. Sexual problems result when the female has some difficulty accommodating the appropriate activity (which is usually penetrative in nature).

Such a conceptualization of women's sexual scripts is simplistic and narrowly drawn. We know that women resist cultural scenarios, transgress boundaries, and participate in a wide variety of sexual activities with both male and female partners. As gender inequities in other aspects of society are addressed and a wider variety of alternative scripts become available, women are becoming more active in defining and exploring their own sexuality (Blumstein & Schwartz, 1990; Schneider & Gould, 1987). Sexual agency, or the capacity to choose and control one's own sexual life (Laws, 1980), to deconstruct and reconstruct one's sexual script, becomes more of a possibility for women. Because the meanings of their sexual experiences are posited to be so central to women's sense of self as a sexual being, "the negotiation of more affirming and empowering sexual meanings is central to developing and maintaining a sense of sexual agency throughout life" (Daniluk, 1998, p.11). Revisions in women's (and men's) sexual scripts are dependent on the way cultural scenarios are depicted in social discourse about sexuality.

## Social Discourse/Sexual Discourse

Sexual scripts are constructed in interaction with the system of statements, terms, categories, and beliefs that cohere around common meanings and values about sexually related information (Gavey, 1993; Scott, 1994). An understanding about how women are supposed to act, think, and feel about sexuality is socioculturally constructed and conveyed through parents, friends, partners, teachers, the media, religion, and public policies. In the process of constructing an understanding of the world and developing a sense of self as a sexual being, each woman locates herself within an available discourse that influences her thoughts and actions. Although most women tend to be positioned within the dominant discourse, they may relocate themselves as the result of contradictions and ambiguities in their experiences (Gavey, 1993), exposure to alternative discourses, and reflection.

Michelle Fine (1988) identified four prevailing discourses of female sexuality that influence the way young women develop a sense of themselves as sexual beings. These include sexuality as violence, sexuality as victimization, sexuality as individual morality, and a discourse of desire.

The discourse representing women's sexuality as victimization appears to be the most dominant and pervades media, sexuality education, sexual assault prevention programs, and many feminist approaches to thinking about women's sexuality. In this discourse, women are the potential victims of men and are at risk for unwanted pregnancies, sexually transmitted diseases, and exploitation if they do not avoid sexual activity until they are safely located in a heterosexual marriage. Fine points out the irony that protection from male predation is to be achieved by coupling with another male. Discourses of sexuality as violence and sexuality as individual morality also focus on the dangers of sexual involvement for women and the importance of restraint and self-control until marriage.

A fourth discourse, the discourse of desire, is described by Fine (1988) as merely a whisper, barely existing in social institutions, historical constructions of women's sexuality, or modes of thought. This repression and distortion of a discourse of desire leaves women without the capacity to acknowledge, understand, and respond to their feelings (Tolman, 1991). Women become disconnected from their sexual feelings or face the dilemma of acknowledging feelings that are dangerous, unnamed, and therefore unspeakable.

Common forms of discursive practice provide socially meaningful ways for women to organize their thinking and experiences and develop their own sexual repertoire (Kitzinger, 1995). Popular media such as magazines, advertisements, and romance novels depict and shape women's cultural scripts regarding sexuality by encouraging girls and young women to locate themselves within an available discourse which then influences their thoughts and actions. Carpenter (1998) analyzed depictions of young women's sexuality featured in *Seventeen* magazine between 1974 and 1994 and found that, although editors increasingly recognized new scripts for young women, they continued to depict dominant cultural scripts as preferable to alternatives. Carpenter argued that the expansion of sexual scripts for young women might enhance the development of sexual agency; however, *Seventeen*'s focus on heterosexual romance, lack of attention to sociostructural issues such as gender equality, and targeting of middle-class, white teens might discourage the deconstruction of dominant scripts and thereby discourage sexual agency.

Fictional depictions of sexuality that target adolescent females also reinforce dominant sexual scripts (Christian-Smith, 1998). These novels present romance as the only legitimate context for sexuality. A young woman's sexuality appears dormant until awakened by a male; the proper channel for sexual expression is heterosexual romance, but the female is expected to show low levels of sexual desire and to be the enforcer of sexual limits. Christian-Smith notes that, " As these readers turn pages of their romance novels, their consent to traditional views on sexuality is negotiated" (p. 109).

Media and other forms of social discourse affect not only young women, of course. The dominant discourse on women and aging stresses the importance of being slim and fit and ties the possibility of maintaining an active sexual life to a youthful body (Dinnerstein & Weitz, 1998). The alternative depiction is of the asexual, menopausal woman (Gannon, 1994). For women and men of all ages, the dominant discourse also prescribes the centrality of the act of penetration, the focus on orgasm for both partners as the goal of all sexual engagements, and the imperative of heterosexuality (Nicolson, 1993).

These prescriptions are implicit in sexual language. Deconstructing the vocabulary of sexuality is important because of language's power to structure the way we conceptualize our everyday lives. Sexual language exhibits a male, heterosexist bias and is devoid of a nonpejorative vocabulary that expresses women's experiences, desires, and feelings (Baber & Allen, 1992; Rothblum, 1994; Schneider & Gould, 1987). "Having sex" is almost always conflated with penile–vaginal intercourse or coitus. "Foreplay" and "afterplay" suggest they are secondary to the central activity. During penile–vaginal intercourse, what happens is "penetration" rather than "enclosure" (Schneider & Gould, 1987) and heterosexual "sex" is likely to conclude as soon as the male has had an orgasm. If a woman does not have an orgasm she may be labeled as frigid, anorgasmic, or inhibited. Sexual activity is referred to as premarital, marital, or extramarital, excluding and denying the sexuality of those who do not choose to marry or who are prohibited by law from doing so. Terminology referring to "extramarital" sexual relations—adultery, cheating infidelity, and unfaithful spouse—reflect negative sanctions (Edwards & Booth, 1994).

In this chapter, an attempt is made to use language that is women centered without obscuring the information from studies that used traditional terminology. Rather than using the term "sex," particular activities such as oral–genital activity are referred to specifically. The term "Lesbian" is used if that concept appeared in the original research, but other times the phrase "women with female partners" or "women who have sex with women" is used in discussing sexual orientation.

## SEXUAL ORIENTATION

A critical aspect of women's sexual scripts identifies appropriate sexual partners. The dominant cultural script dictates that women be attracted to, fall in love with, and interact sexually with men. Yet research indicates that, across time and across cultures, some women prefer female partners and some women are attracted to and fall in love with both men and women.

In the NHSLS (Laumann et al., 1994; Michael et al., 1994), estimates of sexual orientation depended upon the way the question was worded. Approximately 98 percent of women had sexual activity exclusively with males in the previous five years, 1.4 percent with females only, and .8 percent had both female and male partners; fewer than 2 percent had a female partner in the past year. When asked about identity, 1.4 percent of the women said they thought of themselves as lesbian or bisexual. Five and a half percent of the women thought the idea of having sex with a woman was appealing, but only about 4 percent reported ever having done so. Most of these women had their first experience with a same-sex partner at age 18 or older and were more likely to have had sex with both men and women than with only same-sex partners. Women with a college education were eight times more likely to identify as lesbian than women with a high school degree alone. Overall, 8.6 percent of the women in this study defined themselves as homosexual based on behavior, desire, or self-identity. This was only slightly less than the 10.1 percent of men who so defined themselves.

The interrelationships among desire, behavior, and self-identification in these data are intriguing. Among the 8.6 percent of women who were defined as homosexual in any way, 59 percent desired other women, but had not acted on that desire (Michael et al., 1994). Thirteen percent both desired other women as partners and had acted on that desire, but did not identify as lesbian. In his research on women and men over age 50, Brecher (1984) found that although more men than women reported experiences with same-sex partners, more women than men reported having been attracted to other women. Findings such as these support the idea of orientation as socially constructed. Identity is the result of personal interpretation of constructs available in sexual discourse (Rust, 1993). Rust proposes that coming out is the process of locating oneself within a social context rather than discovering one's essential identity. In addition, one's location can change as the result of new relationships with individuals, groups, or sociopolitical institutions. People whose experiences are highly varied may have difficulty fitting themselves into existing categories. A woman in Dancey's (1994) study demonstrates this difficulty:

> I'm not sure how I define lesbian or heterosexual—they can mean several things, and the meanings shift according to the context . . . I am really unsure what I am . . . I believe we all have the capacity to fall in love and to relate sexually to either sex, but social conditioning usually turns us one way . . . For myself, I think I have the ability to relate sexually to either sex. (p. 35)

Although young women may experience same-sex attraction during adolescence, those identifying as lesbian generally do not define themselves as such until their early 20s; bisexual women may not so identify until later in their 20s (Rust, 1993). However, there is evidence that some young women may be constructing socially variant sexual identites for themselves earlier than this. The young lesbians that Thompson (1995) interviewed are examples. They saw their attraction to other females as "an identity, a source of pleasure and love, fantasy and hope" (p. 179). They integrated their relationships into their everyday lives and "insisted on their right to be lesbians and stay in the families, friendships and schools that nurtured them" (p. 201). It is not clear, however, why or how these young women are able to successfully challenge the social expectation of heterosexuality and construct sexual scripts for themselves that accommodate their desire and relationships.

The effect of ethnicity on women's sexual orientation has received little systematic attention, but Rust's (1996) cross-cultural research indicates the value of such work because many lesbians and bisexual Latinas, Asian-American, and African-American women experience their coming out as "a process of further marginalization from the mainstream" (p. 69). Rust notes that lesbian or bisexual women of these ethnicities may feel particular disapproval because identifying themselves in this way violates cultural norms regarding (1) privatization of sexuality, (2) women's commitment to roles as wives and mothers, (3) women's sexual naivete, and (4) respect for one's family and culture. She found that Jewish participants were most likely to report their ethnicity having a positive effect on recognition and acceptance of their sexual orientation.

Our understanding of sexual orientation is minimal, and heterosexuality, in particular, is untheorized because it is seen as normal and natural (Kitzinger & Wilkinson, 1993). However, it seems clear that there is not a single cause or simple developmental path that determines orientation. In addition, there is increasing evidence that sexual orientation may be more fluid than generally believed—that sexual self-labeling may change several times during one's life (Dancey, 1994; Rust, 1993; Sanders, Reinisch, & McWhirter, 1990). It is not clear, however, whether it is women's sexual identity that changes over time, or whether the perception of change is due to the inadequacy of the models used to explore and understand sexual attraction and partner choice.

Historically, the options for women's sexual identities have been primarily dichotomous—lesbian or heterosexual. Research that seriously considered sexual orientation as a category of analysis generally compared heterosexual women and lesbians (Blumstein & Schwartz, 1983; Hurlbert & Apt, 1993). Bisexuality, both in research and in popular discourse, was either missing entirely as a construct or was seen as a steppingstone on the way to a lesbian identity (Rust, 1993). Sexual orientation is being reconceptualized and some authors predict a paradigm shift that will radically restructure concepts, practices, and discourses about sex, gender, and sexual orientation (Firestein, 1996; Fox, 1995, 1996). This shift from a binary and dualistic model that emphasizes stability to one in which sexuality and sexual orientation are seen as multidimensional, fluid, and continuous in nature may narrow, and eventually close, the gap between homosexuality and heterosexuality (Fox, 1996). Revisions in the way sexuality and sexual orientation are conceptualized change the social discourse and provide new possibilities for women in constructing and interpreting their sexual scripts.

Dancey (1994) proposes a way of thinking about women's sexual orientation that addresses heterosexuality, lesbianism, and bisexuality and considers both sexual and nonsexual factors, the balance of which may change over time. Starting with an assumption of bisexual potential as the norm, Dancey posits that a heterosexual orientation will be the default because of conditioning, social reinforcement, and possibly biological factors. Relative strength of attraction to women and men, the perceived consequences of heterosexuality and lesbianism, and social contact with lesbians are all variables that may play into the equation, resulting in differential attraction to men and women. Such a theory takes into consideration the compulsory nature of heterosexuality (Rich, 1980) and would accommodate the fluidity observed in research on women's sexual orientation.

Perhaps even further deconstruction of sexual orientation is necessary. It may be that part of the problem in understanding sexual orientation is that we are asking the wrong question. Stearns (1995) suggests that the whole notion of defining sexual identity around sexual attraction and gender is problematic. She contends that "sexual attraction provides a limited mapping of social relationships and thus serves to highlight sexuality as central while downplaying other aspects of sociality " (p. 9). She argues that our preferences in partners can be affected by many characteristics other than gender. Although gender has been reified as the fundamental variable, other unexamined categories such as age, physical appearance, attitudes, and personality may be more important in understanding attraction. She notes, for example, that heterosexual women are not attracted to all men equally, nor are lesbians attracted to all females. Dancey's (1994) data would support such a position. She reported that women were more likely to choose their same-sex partners for nonsexual reasons such as intimacy, closeness, and friendship than for any explicit sexual reasons.

Whatever the reasons for women's choices of sexual partners, those decisions influence the experiences women have throughout their sexual lives. Although we have only begun to chart the dimensions of women's sexualities, it is clear that the sex of one's partners is intimately associated with a woman's sexual activities and the context within which those activities occur throughout her life.

## WOMEN'S SEXUALITIES ACROSS THE LIFE SPAN

This section provides information about women's sexuality from adolescence through older adulthood. Although the foundation of women's sexualities obviously is developed throughout childhood, pragmatic and ethical constraints of doing sexuality research with children limits the information available. The focus here is on research that provides a broad perspective on women's sexualities, that challenges taken-for-granted assumptions, and that elaborates our understanding of the diversity of women's experiences from adolescence through later adulthood.

### Adolescent Women and Sexuality

Sexuality plays a significant role in young women's sense of self. Becoming involved in sexual activity is an important marker of the transition to adulthood and the restructuring of interpersonal relationships (Upchurch, Levy-Storms, Sucoff, & Aneshensel, 1998). For both female and male adolescents, puberty is a time when sexual scripts are elaborated as most young people participate in a series of sequenced behaviors that begin with kissing and petting and proceed to intercourse in middle adolescence (Miller, Christopherson, & King, 1993). A young woman's sexual debut, however, is usually not something that is celebrated and seen as a positive event. It is more likely to be seen as a turning point marking increased exposure to the risks of unintended pregnancy and HIV and other sexually transmitted infections (Abma, Driscoll, & Moore, 1998). Much of our knowledge about adolescent sexuality comes from research about behaviors that are deemed risky and most of these studies are quantitative in nature. There are, however, a few recent exceptions to this research approach; these studies acknowledge that adolescent sexuality is complex and nuanced and includes desire and pleasure as well as danger.

The average age at first intercourse for young women in the United States in now about 16.5 years. There is some evidence that a relationship exists between ethnicity and age at first intercourse, with white and black females reporting an earlier sexual debut than Hispanic females (Upchurch et al., 1998). However, gender and ethnic differences seem to be converging. In 1995, 53 percent of high school females reported ever having had sexual intercourse, a rate almost identical to that of teen males (Warren et al., 1998). A higher percentage of black young women (67 percent) reported having had intercourse than did Hispanic (53 percent), or white (49 percent). However, the age at first intercourse no longer is significantly different for black, white, or Hispanic females. Young black women were significantly more likely to report having had more sexual partners than white or Hispanic high school females, but they also were more likely to report that their partners used a condom at last intercourse.

Family structure influences rates of first intercourse for adolescent females; teens living with a single parent or in a step family have higher rates of first intercourse than those living in two-parent, biological families (Upchurch et al., 1998). One explanation for this is that family structure is related to the experience of family disruption which may influence age at first intercourse. An alternative explanation for the higher rates of first intercourse and the higher number of sexual partners for black female adolescents may be derived from Samuels (1995) more Afrocentric perspective. He suggests that many blacks do not have control over traditional categories of resources, but they do have control over their sexuality, which can become a source of power leading to a more positive sense of self and a bond to the larger community.

Research with adolescents that considers sexual experiences from their perspectives provides a more elaborated picture. Thompson (1990) found among the young women with whom she spoke a group she referred to as "pleasure narrators" who saw their early sexual experiences as a "voyage of discovery" and related their first experience in detail. According to Thompson, these young women took sexual initiative, satisfied their own sexual curiosity, instigated sexual petting and coition, and took their sexual subjectivity for granted. These pleasure narrators related that their mothers were open with them about their own sexuality and therefore they approached their own sexual debut prepared by the knowledge of pleasure their bodies held in store. For them, sex was not a problem or something they were coerced into, but something they looked forward to with a sense of knowing their own mind.

Thompson's (1995) more recent analysis of data from 400 adolescent females suggests contemporary young women are constructing themselves as sexual beings in ways that suggest agentic variations in their sexual scripts. Among the females with whom she spoke, Thompson identified, "popular girls" who met boys as equals and "could say yes and get sex or say no and make it stick" (p. 76). There were "fast track achieving girls" who viewed intercourse as a growth experience that rounded out their preparation for womanhood, college, and their life beyond. Those identified as "equality narrators" derived ideas about how to construct themselves as sexual beings through their beliefs in equality with males and their own abilities to negotiate and strategize their sexual lives. According to Thompson, they positioned themselves as active subjects of their own sexuality who never gave a lover the ability to affirm or destroy them. Young lesbian women presented agentic narratives of coming out, making lesbianism visible, and taking great pleasure in their sexuality.

The narratives of the young women in Thompson's (1990, 1995) work reveal the rich diversity in their sexual lives that is often obscured when we consider only whether a young woman is or is not sexually active. Similarly, we find extensive diversity in the sexual lives of adult women.

## Women's Sexual Behavior

Women's sexual scripts also mediate the ways in which they express their intimate and erotic interests and desires. Behavioral data provide information about women's repertoire of sexual experiences and estimates of current sexual activity (Andersen & Cyranowski, 1995). However, they provide little insight into the meaning of these activities, the desire and pleasure involved, or the motivation for participating in them. The findings of both large-scale national studies and more focused research with smaller samples indicate women participate in a wide range of sexual experiences throughout their lives. Sexual touching and kissing, vaginal intercourse, oral–genital stimulation, anal intercourse, and self-pleasuring through masturbation are among the experiences in women's sexual repertoires.

Consistent with the dominant discourse that prescribes heterosexual penetrative sexual activities, more attention has been paid in research to vaginal intercourse than any other type of sexual experience for women. Its pervasiveness is incontrovertible. The NHSLS data (Laumann et al., 1994) indicated it was the most appealing type of sexual practice among women; almost 80 percent of female participants rated it very appealing and another 18 percent indicated it was somewhat appealing. Ninety-five percent of the participants reported having vaginal intercourse the last time they had "sex." Generally the frequency of vaginal intercourse decreases for women as they age, but this may be related to the quality of the relationship rather than purely to age (Hawton, Gath, & Day, 1994).

The NHSLS (Laumann et al., 1994) found significant differences among women in regard to their involvement in oral–genital sexual activity. Overall, white women were more likely to both receive (79 percent) and perform (75 percent) oral stimulation than were Hispanic American (60 percent and 64 percent) or African American (49 percent and 34 percent) women. Oral sex was more likely to be included in the repertoire of better-educated women and women under 50 years of age. The rates for women who identified as bisexual or lesbian or who did not so identify but had same-sex partners approached 90 percent to 95 percent.

Twenty percent of women in the NHSLS reported having participated in anal sexual activity sometime during their lives, but only 9 percent had done so during the last year (Laumann et al., 1994). Women who were white and those more educated had a higher likelihood of including anal intercourse among their sexual practices. One study that looked at the reported satisfaction level of different sexual activities (Hurlbert, Apt, & Rabehl, 1993) found it to be the least satisfying type of sexual practice for the women involved.

Masturbation is an activity that receives relatively little attention in the research literature. Although a frequent occurrence, it is socially stigmatized and among the most sensitive of sexual topics (Laumann et al., 1994). Contrary to the common belief that masturbation is an activity chosen by those who are without a sexual partner, the NHSLS data indicate that masturbation is actually a component of a sexually active lifestyle. It is an activity that stimulates, and is stimulated by, other sexual behavior and therefore is reported more frequently by women living with a sexual partner. White, more highly educated, and liberal women are more likely to report masturbating. These national data confirmed that men are more likely to masturbate than women and that they do so more frequently. Only 42 percent of women, compared to 63 percent of men, reported masturbating in the last year, with 27 percent of men and 8 percent of women saying they masturbated at least once a week. Guilt about masturbating appeared to have a different effect on women than it did on men. Although half of all those who masturbated reported feeling guilty, women who felt guilty appeared to masturbate less often. For men, there was little difference in masturbation frequency among those who reported feeling guilty and those who reported no guilt.

It is interesting that an activity with no associated risks should be missing from so many women's sexual scripts. It is worth noting that women who have sex with women are more likely to masturbate, to integrate masturbation into partner-related sexual activity, and to experience orgasm through self-masturbation than are women who have sex with men (Coleman, Hoon, & Hoon, 1983; Hurlbert & Apt, 1993; Loulan, 1988).

Masturbation can have important benefits for women throughout their lives. In addition to helping young women learn about their bodies and how they can increase the likelihood of orgasms, masturbation to orgasm may reduce menstrual cramping quickly and effectively. As women age, masturbation has the additional advantage of keeping the vagina healthy by maintaining the lubrication process (Barbach, 1993). Mutual masturbation with a partner provides an alternative to other riskier penetrative activities and self pleasuring is a safe, enjoyable option for women at any point in their lives. Later in life, women are much less likely than are men to have a sexual partner; if women are comfortable with masturbation, they can continue to enjoy sexual stimulation and orgasm whether they have a partner or not.

## Frequency of Sexual Activity

The frequency of sexual activity in women's lives has received considerable attention. In the NHSLS, the average frequency of any type of sexual activity with a partner for women was six times per month (Laumann et al., 1994). The highest proportion of women in this study said they had sexual activity a few times a month (36 percent) or two to three times per week (30 percent). Only 7 percent reported having sex four or more times a week. Those who were married or cohabiting had sex more frequently than women not living with a partner.

Research comparing women who identify as heterosexual and those identifying as lesbian generally finds lesbians having sexual activity less frequently (Blumstein & Schwartz, 1983; Hurlbert & Apt, 1993). This often is attributed to problems of initiation resulting from lesbians, like heterosexual women, having sexual scripts that discourage them from being the initiators in sexual activity (Blumstein & Schwartz, 1983). Alternatively, it might be the case that genital sexual activity may not be as important as emotional aspects of intimacy (Hurlbert & Apt, 1993; Loulan, 1988). It is important to note, however, that other research found lesbians having sex more frequently, being more sexually responsive, and more sexually satisfied than heterosexual women (Coleman et al., 1983). In this study, the lesbians were significantly older, better educated, and had more partners than the heterosexual women. Only 53 percent of the lesbians rated themselves as exclusively lesbian, suggesting that a sizable percentage of them may have been having sexual activity with men, which emphasizes the problem of categories that might not validly reflect women's identities and lived experiences.

The operational definition used to determine "frequency of sexual activity" is important. What is included or excluded as "sex" (Frye, 1990)? In a society where sex is conflated with vaginal intercourse or, at the most, other penetrative practices, comparison of sexual frequency among women having sex with women and women having sex with men is probably risky.

Frequency of sexual activity tends to decrease over time for both lesbians and heterosexual women (Blumstein & Schwartz, 1983; Hawton et al., 1994; Laumann et al., 1994; Loulan, 1988), but it is often difficult to tease apart the effects of women's aging, partner variables, and relationship variables. Perhaps the most important variable for women as they age is the availability of a partner. Many studies fail to control for relationship status, making it impossible to know whether variation in sexual activity is related to women's own interests and desires or to partner availability (Levy, 1994).

## Women's Sexualities at Midlife and Beyond

Although historically ignored by researchers, the sexual experiences of aging women are now receiving attention as increasing numbers of Baby Boom women reach middle age and menopause. However, the fact that the first major study on sexuality in the United States since Kinsey's work did not even consider menopause as a variable in investigating women's experiences suggests the lack of concern about these issues. The word *menopause* does not appear in the index of the 718-page book (Laumann et al., 1994) reporting on results of the NHSLS study. This lack of information about aging and sexuality is significant because women today can reasonably expect to live well into their 80s or even longer, and satisfying intimate relationships, including sexual relationships, can enhance their well-being and improve their perceived quality of life (Edwards & Booth, 1994; Gibson, 1992; Spector & Fremeth, 1996). Without accurate information, women are unable to anticipate possible changes in sexual functioning over time and health care providers may be limited in their ability to provide appropriate and effective assistance.

To further complicate the issue, much of the writing about women's midlife sexuality tends to be problem-oriented and stresses declining interest and function. The idea that aging women may experience positive changes in their sexuality is rarely considered. A significant portion of the literature is based on a medical model that attributes negative changes in sexual functioning to decreasing hormonal levels and resultant physiological changes (Freedman & Nolan, 1995; McCoy & Davidson, 1985; Rosen, Taylor, Leiblum, & Bachmann, 1993; Sherwin, Gelfand, & Brender, 1985). The discourse focuses on vaginas that become dry and atrophy, orgasms that become muted and infrequent, and libido that wanes and disappears. This same message is disseminated through the popular press. For example, an article in *Time*

(Wallis, 1995) quoted the author of a popular handbook on estrogen. "Without it (estrogen), you may soon have no sex life at all . . . The natural waning of estrogen in the middle years often brings physical changes that can ruin a woman's pleasure in sex . . . The libido may also dry up, if only because sex becomes painful (p. 50)."

The major issues addressed by the bulk of the scholarly research on midlife sexuality are still those identified by Morokoff (1988) over a decade ago: (a) whether menopause causes a decline in women's sexual interest, activity, and responsiveness; (b) if observed changes are hormonally related; and (c) whether replacing hormones affects women's interest, activity, and responsiveness. The results of this work are equivocal, and when taken together, often raise more questions than they answer.

Many menopausal women do experience decreased desire, lack of lubrication, reduced frequency of activity, and fewer orgasms (Baber, 1998; Barbach, 1993; Cole, 1988; Leiblum, 1990; Mansfield, Koch, & Voda; in press; Mansfield, Voda, & Koch, 1995; Morokoff, 1988; Sterk-Elifson, 1994). Decreased estrogen levels are associated with vaginal changes that can result in painful intercourse, changes in sensitivity to touch; orgasms that may be less frequent, less intense, or painful; and other problems such as hot flashes or sleep deprivation that might affect sexual interest (Barbach, 1993; Freedman & Nolan, 1995). Reduced levels of testosterone may result in decreased sexual desire and more difficulty in achieving orgasm (Barbach, 1993; Kaplan & Owett, 1993; Naftolin, 1994). However, not all women encounter these changes and some report improved sexual experiences; there appears to be no clear and predictable effect associated with menopause itself (Gannon, 1994; Hawton, Gath, & Day, 1994; Mansfield et al., 1995). Decreased lubrication is one of the most consistent changes reported by midlife women and it may result in less sexual interest, activity, and responsiveness if lack of lubrication results in pain during sexual activity (Hagstad, 1988; Morokoff, 1988; Mansfield et al., 1995, in press). However, some (Gannon, 1994) believe that even changes in lubrication may be associated with relationship problems that reduce sexual arousal, which in turn would reduce lubrication.

## Hormone Replacement Therapy

Hormone replacement therapy (HRT) is often recommended to alleviate sexual problems women experience at menopause (Leiblum, 1990; Sherwin et al., 1985; Wallis, 1995) even though the efficacy of HRT for this purpose is not well documented. A recent meta-analysis (Myers, 1995) indicated that hormones do seem important to some aspects of sexuality, but that the amount of variance accounted for by hormonal factors is quite small. Discrepant results in studies comparing users and nonusers of HRT may be related to the aspects of sexuality considered in the analysis. For example, in one study (Mansfield, Koch, & Voda, 1998), changes in sexual response were not significantly different between women using and not using hormone replacement. In another study (Baber, 1998), no significant differences were found in arousal levels experienced, need for longer period of stimulation to achieve orgasm, frequency of orgasms, decreased levels of sexual interest, or pain or bleeding during intercourse between users and nonusers. However, women using hormone replacement did report more intense orgasms and increased interest in sexual activity than nonusers.

Some of the more persuasive data on the efficacy of hormone replacement come from experimental research. Bellerose and Binik (1993) compared five groups of midlife women to determine the effect of estrogen and androgen replacement. Three of the groups consisted of women whose ovaries had been removed during hysterectomies. Another group had had hysterectomies but retained at least one ovary, and the fifth group was a nonsurgical control. Women without ovaries received either (1) no hormone replacement, (2) estrogen only, or

(3) estrogen and testosterone. Women without ovaries who received no estrogen replacement reported more problems with lubrication and painful intercourse. Women with no ovaries and either no hormone replacement at all, or only estrogen replacement, reported lower levels of sexual desire and arousal than women in the other groups. There were no differences among the five groups regarding frequency of orgasm, erotic touching, oral sex, intercourse, and overall sexual satisfaction. Sherwin (1998) claims compelling evidence of enhanced desire and arousal among women who received combined estrogen–androgen; however, frequency of sexual activity and orgasm were not affected. Hormones undoubtedly contribute to the sexual changes women report at midlife, but their effects may be fairly circumscribed and interact with other psychosocial variables in women's lives.

## Psychosocial Variables

Research (mainly by women) guided by a more contextual perspective that acknowledges biological changes, but also considers the roles of sociological and psychological factors, has contributed useful information about women's sexualities at midlife and beyond (Baber, 1998; Gannon, 1994; Mansfield et al., 1995, 1998, in press). This research takes a more woman-centered approach (McCormick, 1996) that does not limit itself to the study of problems, but also explores positive midlife changes. Such a perspective attempts to understand women's experiences and how they are influenced by factors such as partner variables, relationships, and societal expectations.

Partner and relationship variables appear central to women's midlife sexual experiences with sexual satisfaction more linked to marital intimacy and the quality of the relationship (Edwards & Booth, 1994). Among the important variables are whether a woman has a partner and the sex of the partner. Hawton and colleagues (1994) found that women's sexual behavior was largely unrelated to gynecological symptoms accompanying menopause, but that marital adjustment was the major predictor of frequency of intercourse, orgasm, and enjoyment of sexual activity. Strong positive associations were found between marital adjustment and (1) satisfaction with sexual activity with the partner, (2) perceptions of pleasure, and (3) enjoyment. Mansfield et al. (1995) found a significant difference between married and single women in regard to decline in sexual interest and enjoyment. Possible reasons they offer for this finding are boredom or dissatisfaction with a long-term partner, the partners' decreased interest or activity level, or psychological differences between married and single women. Edwards and Booth's (1994) research suggests that wives, particularly those in midlife, are also more dissatisfied with sex in marriage than husbands.

Another relationship variable to be considered is the sex of the partner. There is little research on the differential effects of menopause on sexuality and intimate relationships for women of different sexual orientations, even though related research suggests important differences might exist (Cole & Rothblum, 1990; Leiblum, 1990; Loulan, 1988). Kimmel and Sang (1995) reported in a review of research on midlife lesbians that a majority of these women reported being sexually active and enjoying sex more than at earlier times in their lives. Lesbians in this sample tended to focus more on the quality of their relationships, including loving, touching and sharing, and less on sexual functioning and orgasms. Because lesbians are not focused on penile–vaginal intercourse and there is no dependence on male sexual performance, the physiological changes associated with menopause may have less sexual or psychological significance for them (Cole & Rothblum, 1990; Kimmel & Sang, 1995).

Another important variable for women as they age is the availability of a partner. If a partner is not available for dyadic activity, a woman may not be sexually active or masturbation may become the central activity of her sexual life. There is a general decline in partnered sex as people age, but a marked difference exists between women and men. "Starting at age 30, the number of women without a sexual partner in the last year starts to climb, until eventually more women are not having partnered sex than are having it" (Michael et al., 1994, p. 122). According to NHSLS data, about one fifth of women aged 50 to 54, 41 percent of those 55 to 59, and 70 percent of women in their 70s reported having no partnered sex in the last year. Michael et al. (1994) attribute this lack of partnered sex to "logistics in the marketplace, the higher mortality rate for men, and the value women place on affection and continuity in sexual relations" (p. 122) rather than on women's lack of desire. Clearly, women's sexual scripts prescribing male sexual partners (preferably older and more experienced) with whom to have an intimate, if not committed, relationship interact with male sexual scripts prescribing female sexual partners who are young and meet society's norms for attractiveness. The result is a higher likelihood that women find themselves without a sexual partner later in their adult life. What we do not know is how much this matters to women.

African-American women experience an additional challenge if they desire a male sexual partner because of the perceived unavailability of suitable black men (Sterk-Elifson, 1994). The lower ratio of adult males to females among African-Americans is an issue for younger women as well, but increasingly becomes a problem as women age. In addition, the low sex ratio increases competition among women and makes it harder for women to be assertive with male partners for fear men will leave. Sterk-Elifson found that older black women were more likely "to redefine being real women as independent of a relationship with a man" (p. 122).

Even among women who are married, it can be expected that there will be variability in dyadic sexual activity and self-pleasuring. One study using national data on frequency of intercourse found that, in heterosexual couples, after age 50 the relevant question was not how frequently they are having intercourse, but whether they were having intercourse at all (Call, Sprecher, & Schwartz, 1995). Decline in sexual intercourse was gradual until age 50, when sharp reductions were reported. Age itself, beyond decreases associated with illness and poor health, was the strongest predictor of decline, but the second most important factor was sexual satisfaction.

Sexual satisfaction is multiply determined and we know little about the role played by partner variables such as interest in sexual activity, health, hygiene, and attractiveness. Similarly discrepancies between partners' sexual scripts, interest, and enthusiasm are rarely considered. Larger societal issues almost never enter the analysis.

## Positive Changes at Midlife

It is important to note that many women report no changes in their sexual responsiveness during midlife and a sizable proportion report positive changes. In one recent study (Mansfield et al., 1998), 60 percent of the married, midlife women reported no changes in the last year. In another study (Mansfield et al., 1995), 26 percent of the women reported more enjoyment with a partner in the last year, 19 percent found having orgasms easier, and 15 percent reported more sexual desire. A study comparing women of different menopausal statuses found 35 percent of menopausal women experienced higher levels of arousal during sexual activity and 13 percent had more frequent orgasms than in the past (Baber, 1998). A third of the women in Bellerose and Binik's (1993) control group reported positive changes in sexuality over the last five years, indicating they were feeling more comfortable and confident, enjoying themselves more, and feeling closer to their partners. Women in the control group indicated more positive than negative change for desire (29 vs. 25 percent), orgasm (32 vs. 18 percent), and overall physical (39 vs. 7 percent) and emotional (43 vs. 4 percent) changes in lovemaking.

Research on sexual attitudes and behaviors of lesbians at midlife indicates the majority reported their sex lives were as good, if not better, than earlier in their lives (Kimmel & Sang, 1995). Better communication, less pressure about orgasms, and greater importance of touching, loving, and sharing characterized sexual activity. In their study of lesbians at midlife, Cole and Rothblum (1990) found that relationships and not sexual activity were emphasized and that most women's responses about their sexuality had a celebratory quality.

## Extrarelational Sexual Activity

There has been little research on women's extrarelational sexual behaviors. The available information focuses on rates of extrarelational activity for married women and generally ignores the phenomenon among unmarried women. More than 80 percent of married women in the NHSLS sample reported having no extramarital partners (Laumann et al., 1994). In a recent analysis of data from a national sample of 1288 women and 844 men (Wiederman, 1997), 12 percent of the women reported having an extramarital relationship at some point in their marriage, a rate about half that of the men studied. Only 1.7 percent of the women reported having a sexual partner other than their spouse during the last year compared to 4 percent of the men. These findings may reflect a cohort phenomenon because when only those under age 40 were considered, gender differences disappeared. Black women reported higher rates of extramarital sex than did white women.

Data from studies such as these provide fairly consistent estimates of the rates at which various behaviors occur. This is important information to have, but says nothing about the reasons for the behaviors or their meanings to the women involved. Researchers who have investigated "extramarital sexual involvement" (Masters, Johnson, & Kolodny, 1994) report that women tend to have affairs for different reasons than do men. Men indicate they primarily have sexual partners outside the relationship for sexual excitement and to find more frequent and better sex. Married women are less motivated by sexual variables than by a need for emotional satisfaction and a desire to be more appreciated. One woman explained, "I trade 15 minutes in bed for a whole week of feeling wanted. I don't think that's such a bad trade-off" (Masters et al., 1994, p. 494). Masters and colleagues note that in four decades of intensive sexual research they have found only a few men who had affairs to get revenge, but the revenge motive was common among women, with a quarter to a third indicating this as a reason for their having an affair. Frequently the purpose of the affair was to punish a husband who himself had had a sexual relationship with another, but sometimes it was to get back at their husbands for neglecting or physically abusing them.

Although extramarital or extrarelational sexual activity generally is destructive to a marriage or primary relationship because of the deceitfulness of the behavior, women report feeling a sense of empowerment through their affairs (Masters et al., 1994). These sources of empowerment stem from (1) having an active choice, (2) being treated with attentiveness and affection that makes them feel wanted, (3) endorsing their attractiveness and desirability, (4) giving them an alternate reality in their lives, and (5) discovering they are more sexually responsive than they had imagined.

Just as relationship issues motivate women to begin affairs, they often lead them to end these alliances as well. Guilt, usually about betraying their husbands, is apparently a serious problem for women having affairs and causes them to end the affairs in about a quarter of the cases (Masters et al., 1994). These researchers note that relatively few men express guilt about their affairs and end them because they are bored, have found a new partner, are worried about their wives finding out, or are having problems meeting the demands of the extra partner.

## PROBLEMS AND RISKS

Although the purpose here is not to emphasize the dangers and problems associated with sexuality for women, it is critical to acknowledge that they exist. Prevailing gender relationships and dominant constructions of sexuality in our society contribute to the negative aspects of women's sexual experiences. Problems that interfere with pleasure and satisfaction and risks related to pregnancy, sexually transmitted infections, and sexual coercion are realities in the lives of many women. Chapter 10 of this book addresses issues related to pregnancy and Chapter 6 considers sexual victimization. Sexually transmitted infections, sexual problems (often referred to as sexual dysfunction), and the wantedness of consensual sexual activity are discussed here.

### Sexually Transmitted Infections

According to the NHSL survey, nearly as many women reported having sexually transmitted diseases during the last year as reported having been pregnant (Laumann et al., 1994; Michael et al., 1994). Sexually transmitted diseases or infections cause discomfort and pain, require treatment, can cause infertility, and in the case of HIV, can be fatal. Women are more vulnerable to infection by a male partner than vice versa, so women who have sex with men are at an increased risk (Stine, 1996).

The HIV epidemic has introduced a new sexually related risk that women must think about as they make decisions about sexual activity with a partner. In 1985, 7 percent of adult and adolescent cases of AIDS were women; by 1994, the proportion had risen to 18 percent (Centers for Disease Control, 1995). Although 41 percent of women with AIDS in 1994 acquired HIV through injection drug use, almost the same proportion (38 percent) acquired it through heterosexual contact with at-risk male partners. The Centers for Disease Control identify heterosexual contact with an HIV-infected man as the most rapidly increasing risk category for women. Among adolescent females there has been a startling rise in infection and diagnosis—from 14 percent of diagnosed adolescent cases in 1987 to 44 percent in 1995 ("New HIV data," 1998; Office of National AIDS Policy, 1996). From 1995 to 1996, HIV diagnoses declined slightly among men but increased 3 percent among women ("New HIV data," 1998).

Women of color are at even greater risk for HIV infection. Black and Hispanic females make up 75 percent of all AIDS cases in the 20 to 59 year age group and it is estimated that black women are nearly 15 times more likely to contract AIDS than their white counterparts (Stine, 1996). As of 1996 there were 62 new AIDS cases per 1000 black women compared to just 3.5 per 1000 for white females (Mann & Tarantola, 1998).

### Sexual Problems

Research on women's sexual problems is limited, but the existing data provide striking evidence of sexual dissatisfaction and discontent for many women (Rosen, Taylor, Leiblum, & Bachmann, 1993; Ussher, 1993). In a recent survey of 329 healthy women, aged 18 to 73, who were clients of an outpatient gynecological clinic (Rosen et al., 1993), a substantial number of women reported significant dissatisfaction with their sexual relationships. Forty-one percent indicated that the frequency of their sexual activity was less than they desired. Anxiety or inhibition during sexual activity were reported by 38 percent of the women; 16 percent indicated a lack of sexual pleasure and 15 percent noted difficulty in achieving orgasm. Problems of lack of lubrication (14 percent) and pain during intercourse (11 percent) were more likely to occur among postmenopausal women. Data from the NHSLS (Laumann et al., 1994) indicated similar frequencies of these problems. Nearly 20 percent of the women had difficulty with lubrication and about 14 percent experienced pain during sexual activity. One out of three woman reported they were uninterested in sex and 20 percent said sex gave them no pleasure.

A more comprehensive analysis of the NHSLS data (Laumann, Paik, & Rosen, 1999) provided the first population-based assessment of sexual problems since Kinsey's work in the 1950s. Among this national sample, a higher proportion of women (43 percent) than men (31 percent) reported sexual problems. Married women and women who graduated from college were less likely to experience sexual problems. Black women had higher rates of low sexual desire and lack of pleasure than did white women, although white women were more likely to report experiencing pain. Hispanic women reported lower levels of sexual problems than the other two groups. The prevalence of sexual problems tended to decrease as women aged, except for lubrication problems. Women who were sexually abused as children or who experienced other forced sexual contact were more likely to experience arousal disorders. All types of sexual problems had strong positive correlations with low feelings of physical and emotional satisfaction and low feelings of happiness.

Caution is required in the interpretation of this information, however, because of conceptual and methodological problems with much of this research. The basic concept of women's sexual problems has been critiqued as sexist and heterosexist, partially because normative sexual activity is equated with penetration of the vagina by a penis and dysfunctionality defined by women's inability to accommodate or respond to that penetration (Boyle, 1993; Ussher, 1993). Boyle argues that an indirect way of making heterosexual intercourse central to sexual theory and therapy has been the focus on the "sexual response cycle."

Masters and Johnson's (1966) model of the sexual response cycle and later variations of this model (e.g., Kaplan, 1979; Loulan, 1988) provide the leading conceptual and clinical paradigm regarding sexual problems or "sexual dysfunction." Masters and Johnson posited four phases of response for women and men: excitement, plateau, orgasm, and resolution; Tiefer (1995) argued that Masters and Johnson's research was "designed to identify physiological functions of subjects who had experienced *particular* (emphasis in the original), preselected sexual responses" (p. 43). Claiming that the model guided the selection of the participants rather than the model reflecting the actual data, Tiefer rejects the idea that such a model of human sexual response should be applied as normative to the general population. She asserts that defining the essence of sexuality as a specific sequence of physiological changes is reductionistic and ignores women's particular responses, which tend to be much more variable and less genitally focused.

One of the major applications of Masters and Johnson's human sexual response cycle has been to identify sexual dysfunction as the lack of ability to move through the four stages of the model. Because the model did not effectively encompass the actual problems people experienced, particularly those related to desire, revisions of the model have been proposed. Kaplan (1979) proposed a three-stage model consisting of desire, excitement, and orgasm. Loulan (1988) used a five-stage model—willingness, desire, excitement, engorgement, and orgasm—but rejected the necessity of this being a linear procession. She claims that most women begin their sexual response from willingness, may skip some or all of the other stages or skip around among them, and that any stage may lead to pleasure or the "sense of being shut down." Her approach posits a stage model but implies that there might be great variability among women without their responses necessarily being labeled dysfunctional. The willingness phase of her model also acknowledges the power dynamic involved in sexual relationships.

The diagnostic nosology for sexual dysfunction continues to be based on Kaplan's (1979) triphasic model of the sexual response cycle, even though there has been little empirical support for the model and few studies of the reliability and validity of this diagnostic approach (Rosen & Leiblum, 1995). Female sexual problems are generally categorized as inhibited sexual desire, arousal and orgasmic disorders, and dyspareunia (painful intercourse) or vaginismus (involuntary spasms of the musculature of the outer third of the vagina). Underlying these categories is the assumption that the problem is situated within the woman, rather than with the partner, the relationship, or cultural constructions. Orgasmic "problems" provide an excellent example.

## Deconstructing Female Orgasmic Disorder

Female orgasmic disorder, which is defined as "persistent or recurrent delay in, or absence of, orgasm, following a normal sexual excitement phase" (American Psychiatric Association, 1994, p. 506), is generally regarded as the most prevalent sexual problem among women (Rosen & Leiblum, 1995). It also may be the most controversial. Although most women appear to have the potential to be multiorgasmic, a substantial number of women report lack of orgasm during intercourse. More than 50 percent of women in some studies report never having any orgasms through penile–vaginal intercourse, much less experiencing multiple orgasms (Hite, 1976). NHSLS (Laumann et al., 1994) data indicated that only 29 percent of women always experienced an orgasm during sex with their primary partner, considerably less than the 75 percent of men who said they always had an orgasm.

What is probably more important than frequency of orgasm is the discrepancy between the desired and actual frequency. A recent survey (Rosen et al., 1993) found that among a nonclinical sample, 58 percent of the women experienced orgasms less frequently than they desired. What is interesting is that those sexual activities that women participate in most frequently are those that are least likely to result in their having orgasms. In one study of young women in "nondistressed" marriages who kept diaries about their sexual experiences, although more than 98 percent of sexual activity involved vaginal intercourse, the women reported having orgasms only about 25 percent of the time (Hurlbert et al., 1993). Cunnilingus occurred in 32 percent of their sexual interactions and resulted in orgasms 81 percent of the time. Other low-frequency activities such as female self-pleasuring in partnered sex (occurring in 17 percent of interactions) and male masturbating female (found in 5 percent of interactions) resulted in orgasms 98 percent and 83 percent of the time.

## Reconstructing "Sexual Problems"

Feminist critiques argue that it is not that women have problems reaching orgasm, but rather that society has difficulty coming to terms with the *way* they achieve orgasms (Boyle, 1993). Physiological research indicates that maximum orgasmic response among women is experienced through self-stimulation, either mechanically or manually, and the next highest level is through partner manipulation regulated by the woman; the lowest intensity of response is achieved during vaginal intercourse (Masters & Johnson, 1966). With self-controlled, mechanical manipulation, such as that with a vibrator, it is estimated that an average female may have 20 to 50 consecutive orgasms, stopping only because of exhaustion (Sherfey, 1973). As many as 134 orgasms in an hour have been reported in laboratory research (Chalker, 1994), suggesting that woman's orgasmic potential may be limited only by her endurance and interest.

Most women may be potentially multiorgasmic if freed of the constraints of unskilled or uncaring partners, guilt, the focus on activities that provide inadequate stimulation, and the norm of ending sexual activity after one orgasm. In their review of treatment of sexual disorders in the 1990s, Rosen and Leiblum (1995) report that "masturbatory training alone is superior to conventional sex therapy procedures in achieving orgasm . . . and that the overall success rate for primary anorgasmia has been reported at 90 percent or better" (p. 882). They note that secondary anorgasmia is more frequently associated with emotional or relationship problems and treatment is less successful. They also question the value of treatments that seek to enhance coital orgasmic response in women. This suggests that the "problem" may not be with the women, but with the women's relationship or with the focus on vaginal intercourse as real sex—the standard against which all other activities are compared.

Focusing on difficulties that may well be socially constructed means that problems and issues of most concern to women are likely to be ignored (Tiefer, 1988). These include relational and contextual problems such as the timing of partner's interest, too little attention and stimulation before intercourse, and too little tenderness after intercourse. Tiefer (1988) refers to a 1979 study by Frank, Anderson, and Rubenstein that found that while 63 percent of a sample of 100 white, married women reported problems traditionally defined as dysfunction (e.g., difficulty getting excited, inability to have an orgasm), 77 percent of the women reported the emotional/relational type problems. This suggests that by attending only to sexual problems related to the response cycle, we may routinely underestimate problems women have in their sexual interactions, particularly those that are most salient to them.

Starting in the early 1980s, there was a shift to greater focus on organic and biomedical approachs to research and clinical practice in sex therapy—but primarily for problems experienced by men (Rosen & Leiblum, 1995). Recently, oral pharmacological treatments such as Viagra have received significant attention in the treatment of male erectile problems. Although it took the FDA only six months to approve the use of this drug for men, it is estimated that, because of a lack of basic sexual dysfunction research in women, the FDA will not be able to study the use of Viagra in women for three to four years (Valdes-Rodriquez, 1998). There is so little known about the possible usefulness of this drug for women that it is not clear whether such a delay is of any consequence to women.

Additional research is needed to provide a foundation for understanding the variety of women's sexual experiences before there can be an adequate response to what are described as women's sexual problems. Problems need to be conceptualized from the perspective of women themselves. It is likely that there are multiple causes of women's sexual dissatisfaction, including illness, relationship problems, psychological distress, effects of medications and other substances, lack of knowledge and experience, and narrow and limiting sexual scripts. Because the way in which sexual problems are conceptualized dictates the way in which they are treated, it is critical that we not posit a physical or psychological cause for a woman's sexual difficulty and then treat it out of the context of the rest of that woman's life (Ussher, 1993).

## Consent to Sexual Activity

Most attention to sexual coercion centers on rape and sexual assault. As important as this focus is, the issue of consent in women's sexual activity is much more complicated. Nicola Gavey (1993) investigated women's experiences of unwanted or coercive sexual activity in heterosexual relationships and found that women sometimes engaged in sex even if they didn't want to because they didn't feel they had the power to say no. Regardless of their own desire, women would participate in sex to avoid arguments, because they thought it was expected, because they wanted to give something to a needy male partner, or for pragmatic reasons such as just being free to go to sleep. Dominant discourses that stress male sexual needs and prescribe submission to male initiatives result in a subtle coercion for women to have sex whether they are interested or not. Because these injunctions are so woven into sexual scripts at an early age, even though women may not be involved in conscious, deliberate submission, there is a subtle force in operation that functions almost invisibly (Gavey, 1993). Women may feel a lack of control and power even in what appear to be "consensual" relationships or sexual interactions. The concept of consent is meaningless, of course, unless given freely without the feeling that saying no jeopardizes one's safety, standard of living, or relationship (Muehlenhard, 1996). We have little information about how frequently women merely acquiesce to sexual activity and how that affects their experiences and sense of self as a sexual being.

A recent study found that 9 percent of young women aged 15 to 24 said their first intercourse was nonvoluntary (Abma, Driscoll, & Moore, 1998). In addition, about a quarter of those who described their first intercourse as voluntary indicated that they had consented, but they had not wanted it to happen. A dichotomy of voluntary and nonvoluntary obscures the ambivalence many young women apparently experience even when they consent to intercourse. We have almost no information about the effects of unwanted intercourse on these young women's sexual development, relationships, or sense of self. To complicate our understanding further, Thompson (1990) found that some girls even may fail to recognize or name coercion when sex takes place with someone they do not care about.

In one study (O'Sullivan & Allgeier, 1998), both male and female college students reported relatively high rates of unwanted consensual sexual activity, but women were twice as likely as men to have done so during the previous two weeks (50 percent compared to 26 percent). For men, the undesired activity was most frequently "making out," while for women it was intercourse. The reasons women said they participated, even though they did not want to do so, was because they wanted to satisfy their partner's needs, they wanted to promote intimacy, they felt obligated because of previous sexual activity, they wanted to avoid tensions, or they felt it was the norm. Even though many women believed the unwanted activity promoted intimacy, half indicated negative consequences such as feeling uncomfortable or disappointed.

The fact that large numbers of women, particularly young women, participate in sexual interactions about which they feel ambivalent or negative deserves attention (Abma et al., 1998). Sexual scripts that privilege males' interests, needs, and pleasure encourage women to interact sexually with male partners even when they have little desire to do so. Deconstructing these expectations and constructing sexual scripts that emphasize the equal importance of women's desire, pleasure, and satisfaction can only enhance women's sexual lives.

## PLEASURE, DESIRE, AND SATISFACTION

Pleasure, desire, and satisfaction are commonly perceived to be fundamental aspects of sexual activity. Research on women's sexuality has paid little attention to these concepts or to interrelationships among them and other key variables. Until recently, the discourse of desire has been virtually absent (Fine, 1988), particularly in scholarly research. The exceptions to this are cautionary tales about what might happen if women pursue sexual pleasure too openly or outside a committed relationship with a male (Nicolson, 1993) and, more positively, recent research on adolescent sexuality (Thompson, 1990, 1995; Tolman, 1991).

Much of the research that does consider women's sexual satisfaction usually reports the proportion of women who are "satisfied" with their sexual relationships without delving into what that really means to women. Coleman et al. (1983) compared sexual experiences of 407 lesbians and 370 heterosexual women, aged 17 to 68, and found the majority, regardless of sexual orientation, reported having satisfying sexual lives. Sixty-nine percent of the lesbians and 53 percent of the heterosexual women were pleased or extremely happy with their sexual lives. When women who said they were usually pleased were included, the proportions increased to 85 percent and 78 percent respectively.

In the National Health and Social Life Survey (Michael et al., 1994), about 40 percent of women indicated they were extremely physically pleased and slightly fewer said they were extremely emotionally satisfied in their sexual relationships. Married or cohabiting women were likely to be more satisfied than women not living with a partner. Married people with additional sexual partners reported lower physical and emotional sexual satisfaction, but the authors acknowledged it was impossible to determine whether the decreased satisfaction or the infidelity came first.

In Loulan's (1988) study of 1566 lesbians, she found that 53 percent of the women were either fairly well or completely satisfied with their sex lives. She found no difference between women of different ages, between women who were disabled or able-bodied, or between those who had and who had not been sexually abused in childhood.

Although little research has been done to provide a more elaborated understanding of women's sexual satisfaction, there is indication that greater sexual satisfaction is associated with greater closeness, greater sexual assertiveness, higher positive responses to sexual cues, greater sexual excitability, higher frequency of sexual activity, orgasmic consistency, and greater sexual desire (Hurlbert et al., 1993). Hurlbert and colleagues asked women about what aspect of their partner-related sexual activities they found most sexually satisfying and which they would like their partners to pay more attention to in their relationship. Women focused on "foreplay" and "afterplay"; 58 percent found "foreplay" most satisfying and 65 percent wanted partners to pay more attention to it. More than a quarter of the women wanted afterplay attended to more by their partners, with 14 percent seeing that as most satisfying. Orgasms were seen as most sexually satisfying by only 16 percent of the women and only 4 percent wanted more attention to them. Other aspects of "sex" were found as most satisfying by 11 percent of the women and only 5 percent indicated they wanted their partners to pay more attention to them.

Pleasure, satisfaction, and psychological contentment are what people say they want most from their sexual experiences (Gibson, 1992). Women know what is pleasurable to them, but appear to participate frequently in activities which are not satisfying. We need a better understanding of this paradox so women can be empowered to make sexual choices that result in maximum pleasure for themselves and their partners.

## CONCLUSIONS

As we stand on the threshold of the twenty-first century, we know more about women's sexualities than ever before. Yet it is clear that there is still much to be learned. Although we know a fair amount about what women do in their intimate relationships, we lack knowledge about why they participate in these activities, how freely they enter into these sexual interactions, the meaning of the activities to them, and how much pleasure and satisfaction are derived from their sexualities. We also need a better understanding of how sexuality fits into the larger framework of women's lives and relationships. The ideal means for accomplishing this would be a comprehensive research project that used multiple methods to gather data about the sexual lives of women of all ages, sexual orientations, ethnicities, and relationship status. This might be most reasonably accomplished through a network of linked studies carried out by researchers who themselves have diverse backgrounds and experiences. Such an approach could provide a more useful foundation for theory revision, education, programming, health care provision, and public policy than does our current fragmented knowledge.

Implicit in any feminist perspective is the expectation that we will use knowledge to benefit women and develop interventions that are meaningful and useful them. Empowering women means not only providing information and encouraging them to perceive options, but also facilitating an understanding of the forces that shape the context of their lives (Chalker, 1994; Lather, 1991). Through this process women can develop an understanding of where "experience comes from, why it is contradictory or incoherent and why and how it can change" (Weedon, 1987, p.41). In regard to sexualities, this means that our practice not only should focus on helping women and their partners understand, communicate, and achieve sexual pleasure and satisfaction in their lives and interactions, but also should reveal what we know about the ways in which women's sexuality is exploited and distorted.

To understand women's sexualities, we must unpack the entire gender system and realize that sociocultural forces structure not only the sexual relationships that women have with men or with other women, but also the sexual relationships that different women have with men or other women (Gagnon & Parker, 1995). It is important to keep women at the center of attention as we attempt to understand and reconstruct female sexuality, but it is also critical that we concern ourselves with reconstructions of male sexuality. Most women have male sexual partners at some time in their lives. These partners may present attitudinal and behavioral barriers as women try to balance having a satisfying sexual life and making knowledgeable choices that will keep them safe. Just as Silverstein (1996) argued that redefining fathering is essential to the reconstruction of the masculine gender role and the achievement of equality for women, it seems clear that redefining male sexuality also is imperative if we are to achieve these goals.

Sexual reconstructions and social discourse are closely linked. Revising social constructs regarding women's sexualities and empowering women to deconstruct and reconstruct their own sexual scripts, if they so desire, requires that prevailing discourse also be revised or at least challenged. Professionals who work with and for women can participate in this process by informing themselves, reflecting on the assumptions that guide their practice, deconstructing "common knowledge" about women's sexualities, and using language that validly reflects women's experiences. Women should be seen as active agents in their sexual lives responding to their own desire rather than submitting because of social expectations or coercion by a partner. Sexual activity itself might be revisioned as pleasurable experiences that may or may not involve intercourse or even a partner (Gibson, 1992). Taking these steps moves women's sexuality outside the realm of pathology; gives women control over their sexual expression, pleasure, and bodies; and reclaims sexuality as a positive empowering force for women (Baber & Allen, 1992; Chalker, 1994; Rothblum, 1994; Schneider & Gould, 1987; Ussher, 1993).

# REFERENCES

Abma, J., Driscoll, A., & Moore, K. (1998). Young women's degree of control over first intercourse: An exploratory analysis. *Family Planning Perspectives, 30*, 12–18.

American Psychiatric Association. (1994). *Diagnostic and statistical manual of mental disorders* (4th ed.). Washington, DC: Author.

Andersen, B. L., & Cyranowski, J. M. (1995). Women's sexuality: Behaviors, responses, and individual differences. *Journal of Consulting and Clinical Psychology, 63*, 891–906.

Armstrong, K. A. (1995). The problems of using race to understand sexual behaviors. *SIECUS Report, 23*, 8–10.

Baber, K. M. (1998, April). *Women's midlife sexualities.* Paper presented at the Eastern Regional Conference of the Society for the Scientific Study of Sexuality, Boston, MA.

Baber, K. M., & Allen, K. R. (1992). *Women & families: Feminist reconstructions.* New York: Guilford Press.

Barbach, L. (1993). The pause: A closer look at menopause and female sexuality. *SIECUS Report, 21*, 1–6.

Bellerose, S. B., & Binik, Y. M. (1993). Body image and sexuality in ooporectomized women. *Archives of Sexual Behavior, 22,* 435–459.

Best, S., & Kellner, D. (1991). *Postmodern theory: Critical interrogations.* New York: Guilford Press.

Blumstein, P., & Schwartz, P. (1983). *American couples: Money, work, sex.* New York: William Morrow.

Blumstein, P., & Schwartz, P. (1990). Intimate relationships and the creation of sexuality. In D. P. McWhirter, S. A. Sanders, & J. M. Reinisch (Eds.), *Homosexuality/heterosexuality* (pp. 307–320). New York: Oxford University Press.

Boyle, M. (1993). Sexual dysfunction or heterosexual dysfunction? In S. Wilkinson & C. Kitzinger (Eds.), *Heterosexuality* (pp. 203–218). Newbury Park, CA: Sage.

Brecher, E. M. (1984). *Love, sex, and aging.* Boston: Little, Brown and Company.

Brown, L. (1995). Lesbian identities: Concepts and issues. In A. R. D'Augelli & C. J. Patterson (Eds.), *Lesbian, gay, and bisexual identities over the lifespan: Psychological perspectives* (pp. 3–23). New York: Oxford University Press.

Call, V., Sprecher, S., & Schwartz, P. (1995). The incidence and frequency of marital sex in a national sample. *Journal of Marriage and the Family, 57,* 639–652.

Carpenter, L. M. (1998). From girls into women: Scripts for sexuality and romance in *Seventeen* magazine. *The Journal of Sex Research, 35,* 158–168.

Centers for Disease Control and Prevention. (February 13, 1995). Facts about women and HIV/AIDS. *HIV/AIDS Prevention.* Rockville, MD: CDC National AIDS Clearinghouse.

Chalker, R. (1994). Updating the model of female sexuality. *SIECUS Report, 22,* 1–5.

Christian-Smith, L. K. (1998). Young women and their dream lovers: Sexuality in adolescent fiction. In R. Weitz (Ed.), *The politics of women's bodies: Sexuality, appearance, and behavior* (pp. 100–111). New York: Oxford University Press.

Cole, E. (1988). Sex at menopause: Each in her own way. In E. Cole & E. Rothblum (Eds.), *Women and sex therapy* (pp. 159–168). New York: Haworth.

Cole, E., & Rothblum, E. (1990). Commentary on "Sexuality and the midlife woman." *Psychology of Women Quarterly, 14,* 509–512.

Coleman, E., Hoon, P. W., & Hoon, E. F. (1983). Arousability and sexual satisfaction in lesbian and heterosexual women. *The Journal of Sex Research, 19,* 58–73.

Dancey, C. P. (1994). Sexual orientation in women. In P. Y. L. Choi & P. Nicolson (Eds.). *Female sexuality: Psychology, biology and social context* (pp. 27–52). New York: Harvester/Wheatsheaf.

Daniluk, J. C. (1998). *Women's sexuality across the life span: Challenging myths, creating meanings.* New York: Guilford Press.

di Mauro, D. (1995). *Sexuality research in the United States: An assessment of the social and behavioral sciences.* New York: Social Science Research Council.

di Mauro, D. (1997). Sexuality research in the United States. In J. Bancroft (Ed.), *Researching sexual behavior* (pp. 3–8). Bloomington, IN: Indiana University Press.

Dinnerstein, M., & Weitz, R. (1998). Jane Fonda, Barbara Bush, and other aging bodies: Femininity and the limits of resistance. In R. Weitz (Ed.), *The politics of women's bodies: Sexuality, appearance, and behavior* (pp. 189–203). New York: Oxford University Press.

Edwards, J. N., & Booth, A. (1994). Sexuality, marriage, and well-being: The middle years. In A. Rossi (Ed.), *Sexuality across the life course* (pp. 233–259). Chicago: University of Chicago Press.

Fine, M. (1988). Sexuality, schooling, and adolescent females: The missing discourse of desire. *Harvard Educational Review, 58,* 29–53.

Firestein, B.A. (1996). Bisexuality as paradigm shift: Transforming our disciplines. In B. A. Firestein (Ed.), *Bisexuality: The psychology and politics of an invisible minority* (pp. 263–283). Newbury Park, CA: Sage.

Flax, J. (1990). *Thinking fragments: Psychoanalysis, feminism, and postmodernism in the contemporary West.* Berkeley: University of California Press.

Fox, R. C. (1995). Bisexual identities. In A. R. D'Augelli & C. J. Patterson (Eds.), *Lesbian, gay, and bisexual identities over the lifespan: Psychological perspectives* (pp. 48–86). New York: Oxford University Press.

Fox, R. C. (1996). Bisexuality in perspective: A review of theory and research. In B. A. Firestein (Ed.), *Bisexuality: The psychology and politics of an invisible minority* (pp. 3–50). Newbury Park, CA: Sage.

Fraser, N., & Nicholson, L. J. (1990). Social criticism without philosophy: An encounter between feminism and postmodernism. In L. Nicholson (Ed.), *Feminism/postmodernism* (pp. 19–38). New York: Routledge.

Freedman, M. A., & Nolan, T. E. (1995). Genital atrophy: An inevitable consequence of estrogen deficiency. *The Female Patient, 20,* 10–15.

Frye, M. (1990). Lesbian "sex." In J. Allen (Ed.), *Lesbian philosophies and cultures* (pp. 305–315). Albany: State University of New York Press.

Gagnon, J. H. (1990). The implicit and explicit use of the scripting perspective in sex research. *Annual review of sex research, 1,* 1–43.

Gagnon, J. H., & Parker, R. G. (1995). Conceiving sexuality. In R. G. Parker & J. H. Gagnon (Eds.), *Conceiving sexuality: Approaches to sex research in a postmodern world* (pp. 3–16). New York: Routledge.

Gannon, L. (1994). Sexuality and menopause. In P. Y. L. Choi & P. Nicolson (Eds.), *Female sexuality: Psychology, biology and social context* (pp.100–124). New York: Harvester/Wheatsheaf.

Gavey, N. (1993). Technologies and effects of heterosexual coercion. In S. Wilkinson & C. Kitzinger (Eds.), *Heterosexuality* (pp. 93–119). Newbury Park, CA: Sage.

Gibson, H. B. (1992). *The emotional and sexual lives of older people.* New York: Chapman & Hall.

Hagstad, A. (1988). Gynecology and sexuality in middle-aged women. *Women and Health, 13,* 57–80.

Hawton, K., Gath, D., & Day, A. (1994). Sexual function in a community sample of middle-aged women with partners: Effects of age, marital, socioeconomic, psychiatric, gynecological, and menopausal factors. *Archives of Sexual Behavior, 23,* 375–395.

Hite, S. (1976). *The Hite report: A nationwide survey of women's sexuality.* New York: Dell.

Hurlbert, D. F., & Apt, C. (1993). Female sexuality: A comparative study between women in homosexual and heterosexual relationships. *Journal of Sex and Marital Therapy, 19,* 315–327.

Hurlbert, D. F., Apt, C., & Rabehl, S. M. (1993). Key variables to understanding female sexual satisfaction: An examination of women in nondistressed marriages. *Journal of Sex and Marital Therapy, 19,* 154–167.

Kaplan, H. S. (1979). *Disorders of sexual desire.* New York: Brunner/Mazel.

Kaplan, H. S., & Owett, T. (1993). The female androgen deficiency syndrome. *Journal of Sex and Marital Therapy, 19,* 3–24.

Kimmel, D. C., & Sang, B. E. (1995). Lesbians and gay men in midlife. In A. R. D'Augelli & C. J. Patterson (Eds.), *Lesbian, gay, and bisexual identities over the lifespan: Psychological perspectives* (pp. 190–214). New York: Oxford University Press.

Kitzinger, C. (1995). Social constructionism: Implications for lesbian and gay psychology. In A. R. D'Augelli and C. J. Patterson (Eds.), *Lesbian, gay, and bisexual identities over the lifespan: Psychological perspectives* (pp. 136–161). New York: Oxford University Press.

Kitzinger, C., & Wilkinson, S. (1993). Theorizing heterosexuality. In S. Wilkinson & C. Kitzinger (Eds.), *Heterosexuality* (pp. 93–119). Newbury Park, CA: Sage.

Lather, P. A. (1991). *Getting smart: Feminist research and pedagogy with/in the postmodern.* New York: Routledge.

Laumann, E. O., & Gagnon, J. H. (1995). A sociological perspective on sexual action. In R. G. Parker & J. H. Gagnon (Eds.), *Conceiving sexuality: Approaches to sex research in a postmodern world* (pp. 183–213). New York: Routledge.

Laumann, E. O., Gagnon, J. H., Michael, R. T., and Michaels, S. (1994). *The social organization of sexuality: Sexual practices in the United States.* Chicago: University of Chicago Press.

Laumann, E. O., Paik, A., & Rosen, R. C. (1999). Sexual dysfunction in the United States: Prevalence and predictors. *Journal of the American Medical Association, 281,* 537–544.

Laws, J. L. (1980). Female sexuality through the life span. In P. B. Baltes & O. G. Brim, Jr. (Eds.), *Life-span development and behavior* (Vol. 3, pp. 207–252). New York: Academic Press.

Laws, J. L., & Schwartz, P. (1977). *Sexual scripts: The social construction of female sexuality.* Hillsdale, NJ: Lawrence Erlbaum.

Leiblum, S. R. (1990). Sexuality and the midlife woman. *Psychology of Women Quarterly,14,* 495–508.

Levy, J. A. (1994). Sexuality in later life stages. In A. S. Rossi (Ed.), *Sexuality across the life course.* Chicago: The University of Chicago Press.

Loulan, J. (1988). Research on the sex practices of 1566 lesbians and the clinical applications. In E. Cole & E. D. Rothblum, (Eds.), *Women and sex therapy* (pp. 221–234). New York: Haworth.

Mann, J. M., & Tarantola, D. J. M. (1998). HIV 1998: The global picture. *Scientific American, 279,* 82–83.

Mansfield, P. K., Voda, A., & Koch, P. B. (1995). Predictors of sexual response changes in heterosexual midlife women. *Health Values, 19,* 10–20.

Mansfield, P. K., Koch, P. B., & Voda, A. M. (1998). Qualities midlife women desire in their sexual relationships and their changing sexual response. *Psychology of Women Quarterly, 22,* 285–303.

Mansfield, P. K., Koch, P. B., & Voda, A. M. (In press). Midlife women's attributions for their sexual response changes. *Health Care for Women International.*

Masters, W. H., & Johnson, V. E. (1966). *Human sexual response.* New York: Bantam.

Masters, W. H., Johnson, V. E., & Kolodny, R. C. (1994). *Heterosexualities.* New York: HarperCollins.

McCormick, N. B. (1996). Presidential address: Our feminist future: Women affirming sexuality research in the late twentieth century. *Journal of Sex Research, 33,* 99–102.

McCoy, N. L., & Davidson, J. M. (1985). A longitudinal study of the effects of menopause on sexuality. *Maturitas, 7*, 203–210.

Michael, R. T., Gagnon, J. H., Laumann, E. O., & Kolata, G. (1994). *Sex in America: A definitive survey*. Boston: Little, Brown and Company.

Miller, B. C., Christopherson, C. R., & King, P. K. (1993). Sexual behavior in adolescence. In T. P. Gullotta, G. R. Adams, & R. Montemayor (Eds.), *Adolescent sexuality* (pp. 57–76). Newbury Park, CA: Sage.

Morokoff, P. J. (1988). Sexuality in perimenopausal and postmenopausal women. *Psychology of Women Quarterly, 12*, 489–511.

Muehlenhard, C. L. (1996). The complexities of sexual consent. *SIECUS Report, 24*, 4–7.

Myers, L. S. (1995). Methodological review and meta-analysis of sexuality and menopause research. *Neuroscience and Biobehavioral Reviews, 19*, 331–241.

Naftolin, F. (1994). The use of androgens. In R. A. Lobo (Ed.), *Treatment of the postmenopausal woman: Basic and clinical aspects* (pp. 91–94). New York: Raven Press.

New HIV data show impact on women, minorities. (1998). *AIDS ALERT, 13*, 62–63.

Nicolson, P. (1993). Public values and private beliefs: Why do women refer themselves for sex therapy? In J. M. Ussher & C. D. Baker (Eds.), *Psychological perspectives on sexual problems: New directions in theory and practice* (pp. 56–76). London: Routledge.

O'Sullivan, L. F., & Allgeier, E. R. (1998). Feigning sexual desire: Consenting to unwanted sexual activity in heterosexual dating relationships. *Journal of Sex Research, 35*, 234–243.

Rich, A. (1980). Compulsory heterosexuality and lesbian existence. *Signs, 5*, 631–660.

Rosen, R. C., & Leiblum, S. R. (1995). Treatment of sexual disorders in the 1990s: An integrated approach. *Journal of Counseling and Clinical Psychology, 63*, 877–890.

Rosen, R. C., Taylor, J. F., Leiblum, S. R., & Bachmann, G. A. (1993). Prevalence of sexual dysfunction in women: Results of a survey study of 329 women in an outpatient gynecological clinic. *Journal of Sex and Marital Therapy, 19*, 171–188.

Rothblum, E. D. (1994). Transforming lesbian sexuality. *Psychology of Women Quarterly, 18*, 627–641.

Rust, P. C. (1993). "Coming out" in the age of social constructivism: Sexual identity formation among lesbian and bisexual women. *Gender & Society, 7*, 50–77.

Rust, P. C. (1996). Managing multiple identities: Diversity among bisexual women and men. In B. A. Firestein (Ed.), *Bisexuality: The psychology and politics of an invisible minority* (pp. 53–83). Newbury Park, CA: Sage.

Samuels, H. (1995). Sexology, sexosophy, and African-American sexuality: Implications for sex therapy and sexuality education. *SIECUS Report, 23*, 3–5.

Sanders, S. A., Reinisch, J. M., & NcWhirter, D. P. (1990). Homosexuality/ heterosexuality: An overview. In D. P. McWhirter, S. A. Sanders, & J. M. Reinisch (Eds.), *Homosexuality/heterosexuality* (pp. xix-xxvii). New York: Oxford University Press.

Schneider, B. E., & Gould, M. (1987). Female sexuality: Looking back into the future. In B. B. Hess & M. M. Ferree (Eds.), *Analyzing gender* (pp. 120–153). Newbury Park, CA:Sage.

Scott, J. W. (1990). Deconstructing equality-versus-difference: Or, the uses of poststructuralist theory for feminism. In M. Hirsch & E. F. Keller (Eds.), *Conflicts in feminism* (pp. 134–148). New York: Routledge.

Scott, J. W. (1994). Deconstructing equality-versus-difference: Or, the uses of poststructuralist theory for feminism. In S. Seidman (Ed.)., *The postmodern turn: New perspectives on social theory* (pp. 282–298). New York: Cambridge University Press.

Sherfey, M. J. (1973). *The nature and evolution of female sexuality*. New York: Random House.

Sherwin, B. (1998, April). The efficacy of combined estrogen–androgen preparations in postmenopausal women. Paper presented at Frontiers in Sexual Medicine, Burlington, Vermont.

Sherwin, B. B., Gelfand, M. M., & Brender, W. (1985). Androgen enhances sexual motivation in females: A prospective, crossover study of sex steroid administration in the surgical menopause. *Psychosomatic Medicine,47*, 339–351.

Silverstein, L. B. (1996). Fathering is a feminist issue. *Psychology of Women Quarterly, 20*, 3–37.

Spector, I. P., & Fremeth, S. M. (1996). Sexual behaviors and attitudes of geriatric residents in long-term care facilities. *Journal of Sex and Marital Therapy, 22*, 235–346.

Stearns, D. C. (1995). Gendered sexuality: The privileging of sex and gender in sexual orientation. *NWSA Journal, 7*, 8–25.

Sterk-Elifson, C. (1994). Sexuality among African-American women. In A. Rossi (Ed.), *Sexuality across the life course* (pp. 99–126). Chicago: University of Chicago Press.

Stine, G. J. (1996). *AIDS update 1996*. Upper Saddle River, NJ: Prentice Hall.

Thompson, S. (1990). Putting a big thing into a little hole: Teenage girls' accounts of sexual initiation. *The Journal of Sex Research, 27*, 341–60.

Thompson, S. (1995). *Going all the way: Teenage girls' tales of sex, romance, and pregnancy*, New York: Hill and Wang.

Tiefer, L. (1988). A feminist critique of the sexual dysfunction nomenclature. In E. Cole & E. D. Rothblum, (Eds.), *Women and sex therapy* (pp. 235–252). New York: Haworth Press.

Tiefer, L. (1995). *Sex is not a natural act and other essays*. Boulder, CO: Westview Press.

Tolman, D. L. (1991). Adolescent girls, women and sexuality: Discerning dilemmas of desire. In C. Gilligan, A. G. Rogers, & D. Tolman (Eds.), *Women, girls, and psychotherapy: Reframing resistance* (pp. 55–69). Binghamton, NY: Haworth Press.

Upchurch, D. M., Levy-Storms, Sucoff, C. A., & Aneshensel, C. S. (1998). Gender and ethnic differences in the timing of first sexual intercourse. *Family Planning Perspectives, 30*, 121–127.

Ussher, J. (1993). The construction of female sexual problems. In J. M. Ussher & C. D. Baker (Eds.), *Psychological perspectives on sexual problems: New directions in theory and practice* (pp. 9–40). London: Routledge.

Valdes-Rodriquez, A. (1998, December 7). Little heed to women's sexual problems. *Boston Globe*, pp. E1, E3.

Wallis, C. (1995, June 26). The estrogen dilemma. *Time*, pp. 46–53.

Warren, C. W., Santelli, J. S., Everett, S. A., Kann, L., Collins, J. L., Cassell, C., Morris, L., & Kolbe, L. J. (1998). Sexual behavior among U. S. high school students, 1990–1995. *Family Planning Perspectives, 30*, 170–172, 200.

Weedon, C. (1987). *Feminist practice and poststructural theory*. Oxford: Basil Blackwell.

Wiederman, M. W. (1997). Extramarital sex: Prevalence and correlates in a national survey. *The Journal of Sex Research, 34*, 167–174.

Wyatt, G. E., & Riederle, M. H. (1994). Reconceptualizing issues that affect women's sexual decision-making and sexual functioning. *Psychology of Women Quarterly, 18*, 611–625.

# 9

# Intimate Relationships

## Rhonda Felece Jeter

### INTRODUCTION

"Tale as old as time, song as old as rhyme"—love. Whether it is B*eauty and the Beast, Sleeping Beauty, Romeo and Juliet, All My Children, Sleepless in Seattle,* or the *Bridges of Madison County,* tales of love are ageless, timeless epics that encompass a precious part of the human experience. People, regardless of gender, race, social class, disability, cultural background, age, sexual orientation, or attractiveness, have an innate need for intimate connections with others. Thus, intimate relationships are a quintessential component of life.

It is difficult to encapsulate the many components of relational love. Each component is powerful in its own right. From novels to the news, stories of attraction and attraction gone awry, commitments made and commitments broken, marriage wonderful and fulfilling or marriage on the brink of divorce, relationships have one thing in common. They all possess an intensity that is characteristic of intimate relationships. It is this intensity that causes someone to skywrite their love across the clouds or to harass, embarrass, or even murder a love who has scorned them.

In an effort to explain relational love and its resulting behavior many ideas have been explored. Of late, some theorists are positing that there is a strong relationship between our early childhood attachment experiences and our adult attachment styles. This is a new idea that may help us understand our behavior in intimate adult relationships better. Also, in this age of computers, e-mail, and websites, one wonders how the love on-line phenomena will affect the attraction, connection, and partnering process.

This chapter examines the theoretical basis for connection and partnering in this society, and then discusses some of the major ideas about intimate relationships in connection with love and romance, marriage and long-term relationships, separation and divorce, and lesbian relationships.

### IDENTITY AND INTIMATE RELATIONSHIPS

Stage theorists such as Erikson, Havighurst, and Freud seek to explain human development across the life span by identifying the relevant issues and tasks that should be encoun-

Rhonda Felece Jeter ● Department of Education, Bowie State University, Bowie, Maryland 20715

*Issues in the Psychology of Women,* edited by Biaggio and Hersen. Kluwer Academic/Plenum Publishers, New York, 2000.

**Table 9.1.** Erikson's Psychosocial Stages of Development

| Age | Stage |
| --- | --- |
| Birth–1 Year | Trust vs. mistrust |
| 1–2 Years | Autonomy vs. shame and doubt |
| 3–5 Years | Initiative vs. guilt |
| 6–11 Years | Industry vs. inferiority |
| 12–Young adulthood | Identity vs. role confusion |
| Early adulthood | Intimacy vs. isolation |
| Middle adulthood | Generativity vs. stagnation |
| Late adulthood | Industry vs. despair |

tered and addressed at each age-appropriate stage. Erik Erikson's Psychosocial Model of Development views life as a set of crises that arise, the outcome of which impacts the personality across the entire life span (see Table 9.1). Successful completion of the developmental issues at one stage leads to a sense of competence and aids in the work of the next stage. If the developmental conflict is not resolved positively, the resulting negative outcome makes positive resolution at future stages more difficult (Erikson, 1963).

In Erikson's model, Early Adulthood is the stage during which issues of intimacy are prominent. At this stage, young adults seek a greater sense of personal identity and self-worth. This process is facilitated by forming intimate relationships. An *intimate relationship* can be defined as an ongoing emotional connection with another person in which each person is willing to " remove his or her mask" and take the risk of sharing inner thoughts and feelings with another.

Erikson's stage six, Intimacy versus Isolation, embodies a struggle or conflict that occurs for young adults—seeking an intimate relationship and risking the loss of self or a part of self versus maintaining independence. Most young people attempt to resolve this conflict by seeking a long-term relationship with a partner or by marrying. Failure to resolve the conflict of this stage successfully leads to emotional and sometimes physical isolation. To avoid this isolation, most people ultimately seek an intimate partnering relationship. About 95 percent of all people marry at least one time in their lives (U. S. Bureau of the Census, 1994).

One danger that can arise in this stage of life is the substitution of sexual for emotional intimacy. In these days of sexual freedom, people often elect to bond sexually with one another and forego the emotional bonding that can lead to true intimacy. The result of sexual contact without emotional connection is a deep sense of isolation. Relationship contact without intimacy can leave an emotional void.

Robert Havighurst (1979) also views development as a life span process. He suggests that there are developmental tasks that must be managed at each stage. The pressure to succeed in the tasks at every stage is both internal as well as external. In Havighurst's theory, there are eight developmental tasks that need to be addressed during young adulthood (see Table 9.2). Two of the tasks are related to intimate relationships: (1) dating and selection of a partner and (2) learning to live happily with that partner. Successful completion of these tasks leads to a happier existence because one gains self-approval as well as the approval of society.

**Table 9.2.** Havighurst's Developmental Tasks—Young Adulthood Stage

1. Courting and selecting a mate
2. Learning to live happily with partner
3. Starting a family and assuming parent role
4. Rearing children
5. Assuming home management responsibilities
6. Beginning career or occupation
7. Assuming appropriate civic responsibilities
8. Establishing a social network

Research supports the idea that there is a relationship between identity development and intimacy. However, it is still unclear which comes first. Does identity development precede intimacy or does intimacy precede development? Some research suggests that in females intimacy occurs prior to identity development (Josselson, 1987).

Erikson and Havighurst provide a clear explanation for the partnering and mating process that most people experience during young adulthood. It also may explain why young adults who focus on careers, to the exclusion of fostering intimate relationships, may feel isolated or unhappy in spite of financial and job success.

## LOVE AND ROMANCE

Typically, when someone mentions love and romance, people think of roses, romantic cards, a tingling sensation, boxes of chocolates, a special song, a kiss, or an intimate memory. These are some of the mysteries associated with the process of love and the idea of attraction. Attraction appears to be the bond that initially holds people of the same sex or the opposite sex together. It is this initial force that enables people to venture into the next stage, love. Love has been defined in many ways throughout history and in different cultures. This section explores these two processes, attraction and love, and their connection to the achievement of true intimacy.

### Attraction

#### *Physical Qualities*

What causes that initial attraction between two people? Common stereotypes characterize men as being interested in only a pretty face and an athletic body. Women, on the other hand, are characterized as primarily being interested in a man's occupation and his financial status. Indeed, a perusal of the personal ads in the newspapers or on-line reveals some of these stereotypes over and over again. Further, research supports these ideas. South (1991) studied 2000 adults and found that people's initial selection of potential mates was based on their perceptions of that mate's characteristics. Men placed a high value on physical attraction and youthfulness while women placed a high value on employment stability and money earned. Other research supports these findings as well (Feingold, 1990).

What physical characteristics do people tend to find attractive in others? Research suggests that both physique and facial appearance are elements in the perception of attractiveness. However, some research has concluded that a lack of an attractive physique is perceived in a far more negative way than a lack of facial comeliness (Alicke, Smith, & Klotz, 1986). While this is true for both sexes, it appears to be particularly true for men.

Some studies of attraction, which surveyed mostly white students, concluded that women are attracted to tall men with broad shoulders, small buttocks, and lean legs and waists who are not obese (Harris, Harris, & Bochner, 1982; Lynn & Shurgot, 1984). White men rated women with the following characteristics as being the most appealing: not overweight and medium-sized breasts (Franzoi & Herzog, 1987). Some recent studies concluded that women's perceptions of the ideal body size was much thinner than those selected by their male and female peers (Cohn & Adler, 1992). The general view that a thin body is desirable most likely is a contributing factor in the eating disorders problems that have become more prominent of late.

Does a person need to have outstanding good looks to be considered an acceptable partner? Apparently, this is not the case. Feingold (1990) states that people tend to marry other people who are in a similar range of attractiveness as themselves. There is some question as to whether people with similar levels of attractiveness choose each other or whether they initially strive for more attractive partners, then are rejected before seeking people in a more similar attractiveness range (Aron, 1988).

Lance (1998) found that in the 1990s both men and women were more concerned about finding a nonsmoking partner. With all the research on primary and secondary smoke, this finding may relate to an awareness of health problems attributable to smoking.

### Interpersonal Qualities

It appears that people tend to seek out mates who have positive energy and positive qualities. A British study of college students and dating agency clients found that people preferred others who were kind, considerate, honest, and had a good sense of humor (Goodwin, 1990). In a study on preferred personal qualities for dates in the American culture, college students rated the qualities of emotional stability, easygoing nature, friendliness, excitement, and a good sense of humor highly (Kendrick, Groth, Trost, & Sadalla, 1993). Other studies confirm that interpersonal qualities are a critical part of peoples' overall attraction to potential mates. People tend to be more attracted to people who are kind, generous, poised, interesting, confident, and humorous than those who are rude, insecure, clumsy, insensitive, unstable, or irresponsible (Buss & Barnes, 1986).

## Other Qualities That Influence Attraction

Many other factors need to be considered in a discussion on attraction. Unlike the variables listed in the preceding, these qualities tend to be more external and based on societal, cultural, or familial expectations.

### Propinquity

Propinquity or geographic proximity plays a major role in mate attraction and selection. It is easier to meet and maintain an ongoing interaction with someone who lives nearby and whom one can see with regularity. Research indicates that people are more likely to marry someone who lives nearby (South, 1991). Thus regardless of whether one has lived in an area for some time or has recently relocated, a potential mate or partner is probably right around the proverbial corner.

### Homogamy and Heterogamy

People often select mates who are similar to themselves in many ways, such as age, intelligence, educational level, race, religion, social class, ethnicity, and socioeconomic status (South, 1991; Surra, 1991). The tendency to choose people whose background resembles one's own is call *homogamy*. On the other hand, choosing a mate whose background is different from one's own is called *heterogamy*. Not only do we tend to meet people while participating in the activities that are socially, economically, and culturally congruent with our background, but these people also have an appreciation and understanding of the things we value. This increases the sense of connectedness and thereby the level of attraction.

When heterogamy does occur, it is usually one-sided and frequently the differences are in age or education. For example, older men sometimes marry younger women, or men of wealth and position marry women with fewer resources than themselves (South, 1991). A recent example of this phenomenon occurring in reverse was poignantly displayed in the 1998 movie *How Stella Got Her Groove Back*. In this movie, an older African-American woman with an established career falls in love and eventually marries a man 20 years her junior. The story tells of the difficulties that a couple encounters in a nonhomogamous relationship.

Lastly, when a person elects to be involved in a heterogamous relationship, he or she must manage the potential backlash from family, friends, and society, which can be painful and cause problems for the couple.

### Culture and Rules of Attraction

The concept of a marriage gradient is a good example of how the rules of attraction do not hold true in all cultures. The *marriage gradient* suggests that men tend to marry women who are younger, smaller, and lower in status than they. Conversely, women tend to marry men who are slightly older, larger, and have higher social status. This equation gives men more choice than women in terms of available partners (Bernard, 1982).

In the African-American community, black men and women are less likely to marry than their white counterparts. There is an acute shortage of African-American males who are in the marriageable age range and who are economically secure. There are 1.8 million fewer black men than women over the age of 14 (U. S. Bureau of the Census, 1995).

The marriage gradient creates great difficulties for college-educated African-American females. Considerably fewer black males attend college. This means that the pool of acceptable, available black men is small. So, unlike women of other races, African-American women tend to marry men with less education than they have (Taylor, Chatters, Tucker & Lewis, 1990; Tucker & Mitchell-Kernan, 1995).

It appears that African-American women still desire the marriage gradient. Compared to white women, African-American women place greater importance on having economic stability in place prior to marriage. They tend to resist marrying someone who has fewer resources (Bulcroft & Bulcroft, 1993). Thus, one third of college-educated black women remain unmarried past the age of 30. This is not true for white women of similar age and educational status.

## Love

What is love? Social scientists for years have studied it. Ordinary women and men have attempted to define it. Every day people all over the world state that they have fallen in love.

Have they truly fallen into this state? Why did they fall in love? Is this emotion they define as love temporary or permanent? Are there signs that indicate one is in love? The research in this area has yielded some interesting findings and theories that facilitate studying and defining the process of love.

## Definitions of Love

What is love? There is no easy answer to this question. Webster's dictionary lists about 20 different definitions of love. In addition, there are a variety of theoretical models that try to delineate the stages and components of love. One of the early researchers who explored this topic was Zick Rubin (1973). He conducted a study to determine if there was a difference between *like* and *love*. He asked students to fill out a "like" and a "love" scale in relation to a dating partner. Then he asked them to fill out the scales in relation to a same-sex friend. His results indicated that there was a clear difference between like and love. Only the dating partners scored high on the love scale; friends did not.

In Rubin's model of love, he cites three foundational elements upon which love is built. The first element is *caring*, which he defines as the understanding that another's needs are as important as one's own. *Attachment*, the second element, is defined as the need to be with another person and to gain the approval of that person. The third element, *intimacy*, includes relating in a personal and private way with that partner (Rubin, 1973).

Sternberg (1986) advances another theory, known as the triangular theory of love. His popular explanation of the types of love includes three major components: passion, commitment, and intimacy. These components are combined in different ways to create the eight different types of love. *Passion* is defined as a powerful, almost uncontrollable urge to be with another person. Passion is generally, but not always, sexual in nature. *Intimacy* is defined as a close, warm interaction between partners that creates a bond that includes trust, respect, and honest self-disclosing communication. *Commitment* entails the conscious decision to love and remain together despite difficulties or problems. Sternberg (1986) talks about commitment as being both short-term and long-term. The short-term commitment involves making a deliberate decision to love a particular person. The long-term commitment involves a dedication to the relationship over time and frequently includes plans to share living arrangements, children, marriage, or a partnering agreement (see Table 9.3).

## Is Love Important in Every Culture?

Love is a primary component in the selection of a life partner in the United States. In some other countries, however, love is a secondary concern. In some cultures, marriages are still arranged by parents and family. Even when parents no longer arrange the marriages, there tends to be more concern about parents' feelings in these countries than in countries where people are taught to follow their hearts (Trandis, 1994).

One cross-cultural study queried college students in several countries as to whether they would marry someone they did not love. Almost none of the students in the United States, Japan, or Brazil responded affirmatively. However, the majority of students in Pakistan and India indicated that they would marry a person they did not love (Levine, 1993).

Gender and culture have a significant effect on the factors that are considered essential in selecting a partner. In America, we value love and mutual attraction. In South Africa, men rated emotional stability and maturity as essential, while women indicated it was important that the person be dependable. In China, men indicated that good physical health was primary,

**Table 9.3.** Sternberg's Triangular Theory of Love

| Type of Love | Components | | |
| --- | --- | --- | --- |
| | Passion | Commitment | Intimacy |
| Non-love | | | |
| Infatuation | **** | | |
| Liking | | | **** |
| Romantic Love | **** | | **** |
| Companionate Love | | **** | **** |
| Fatuous Love | **** | **** | |
| Empty Love | | **** | |
| Consummate Love | **** | **** | **** |

Note. ****: Means that component is included in that type of love.

while women ranked emotional stability and maturity as essential (Buss, Abbott, Angleitner, & Asherian, 1990).

While there are great differences in what each culture values as primary in terms of attraction, there are some universals. For example, in most cultures men more than women focus on physical attractiveness. On the other hand, women more than men prefer someone whom is ambitious and hard working (Sprecher, Sullivan, & Hatfield, 1994).

## MARRIAGE AND LONG-TERM RELATIONSHIPS

Since the beginning of time, the practice of going through life with a partner, two-by-two, has always existed. The primary institution for committed partnering is marriage. Throughout the world festive rituals and ceremonies celebrate two people being joined in matrimony. Marriage is extremely culture bound. In some cultures, the marriage celebrations to marriage last for weeks. The expected apparel varies, and the significance of the colors of the wedding attire varies as well. Literally, the colors can range from white to red. In some countries people are allowed to have more than one spouse simultaneously.

In the United States, the idea of every young girl growing up to be a bride is pervasive. The traditional part of the ceremony includes a long white gown that denotes purity, the veil and the train, the bridesmaids in their carefully selected, expensive gowns (that the bride insists can be worn again), the groomsmen, and, of course, the groom. The reception that follows generally includes plentiful food and drink, a tiered wedding cake, the toast, the first dance, and the gifts bought by the well-wishers. Millions of little girls grow up dreaming of a day something like this. There is an entire industry consisting of wedding consultants, photographers, decoration shops, caterers, and wedding packages devoted to making the perfect wedding a reality.

Once the wedding is over and thousands of dollars have been spent, the journey of one's life has begun. How does one make the magic last? This is one of the most critical decisions of one's life, and people receive little or no training in what to do. When people think about the beginning of marriage, they think of the honeymoon and romance. In reality, the first year of marriage is one of the most challenging because a myriad of adjustments need to be made.

These realities are rarely discussed because many couples believe that love is enough to keep them together.

Perhaps by choice or by circumstance the above scenario does not reflect the future some people have selected or will select. Long-term relationships that do not involve marriage are an option. These relationships give the opportunity for emotional commitment, but without either the benefits or complications of a marriage. Many couples now choose this kind of secure arrangement.

This chapter examines such issues as attachment, marital quality, marital conflicts, and predictors of marital success. In addition, this chapter considers the benefits and issues related to other types of long-term relationships.

## Marriage Statistics

- By age 65 more than 95 percent of all adults in the United States have been married at least one time.
- In the United States 56 percent of the adult population are married and living with their spouses.
- Among people between ages 25 and 34 years old, 13.6 million or 34.7 percent have never been married.
- For African-Americans in the same age group, 53.4% have never been married.
- In 1993 there were more than 3.5 million unmarried couples living in the United States (U. S. Bureau of the Census, 1994, 1998).

## Marriage and Attachment Styles

Attachment has long been studied as a process relating to how infants bond with their caregivers in general and their female caregivers in particular. Such work by Bowlby and Ainsworth is well known in the psychology field. Lately, applying this work to an examination of the relationship between early attachment experiences and adult attachment styles has been gaining momentum. The underlying premise in these studies is that the mother's style of interacting with the infant determines the personality type and attachment style of the person later in life (Hazan & Shaver, 1987). Infants whose mothers responded regularly to their needs usually became confident and secure. Infants whose mothers responded slowly or inconsistently generally became anxious. Mothers who were unemotional and unresponsive generally had children who were aloof and detached.

Ainsworth, Blehar, Waters, and Wall (1978) created three categories to explain the attachment behavior described by Bowlby (1958): Secure, Anxious/Ambivalent, and Avoidant. Secure attachment denotes a warm bond between the infant and the caregiver. Anxious/Ambivalent attachment denotes a weak bond caused by inconsistent care given by the caregiver. Avoidant attachment denotes cold, distanced behavior from the caregiver, which causes the baby to become distant and cold.

Hazan and Shaver (1987) believe that early attachment experiences result in corresponding adult relational attachment styles. For example, they posited that people who had secure attachment experiences as infants would have romantic attachments that were warm and secure. Their first study supported this hypothesis. They found that adults could be grouped into the following categories:

*Secure adults:* People in this category found it easier to form close relationships with others, trusted others easily, and did not worry about being abandoned in intimate relationships.

These adults reported that their parents treated them and each other in a warm, caring manner (56 percent of the respondents were in this category).

*Anxious–ambivalent adults:* People in this category found that their partners did not connect as closely with them as they would like. They also feared that their partners would leave them. In addition, they reported strong feelings of sexual arousal and jealousy. These adults described their parents as less caring than secure adults did and felt that their parents were unhappy in the marriage (20 percent of the respondents were in this category).

*Avoidant adults:* People in this category felt uneasy getting close to others, and they had difficulty totally trusting their partners. They also tended to be jealous, had emotional highs and lows, and were afraid of intimacy. They found their parents to be less warm than secure adults did, and they experienced their mothers as unfeeling and rejecting (24 percent of the respondents were in this category).

The results of the study were interesting. Hazan and Shaver (1987) found that approximately the same percentage of adults fell into each attachment group as did infants. In addition, the childhood memories of relationships with parents supported the idea that there was an association between the infant's experiences and adult attachment.

Several studies support the findings of Hazan and Shaver (1987). Collins and Reed (1990) found that securely attached adults have stronger, more satisfying intimate relationships than people from avoidant and anxious–ambivalent attachment styles. Moreover, research has shown that the anxious–ambivalent style is indicative of not being in a relationship and/or of having shorter relationships. Also, the avoidant style is associated with shorter relationships (Shaver & Brennan, 1992).

Although more research needs to be done on adult attachment styles, there is some evidence that they may impact other aspects of a person's life. There may be some connection between attachment styles and job satisfaction, susceptibility to drinking problems, religious beliefs, and gender roles (Hazan & Shaver, 1994).

A longitudinal study and a cross-sectional study found that people who have strong attachments or commitments to romantic relationships: (1) think about their relationship in terms of "we-ness" and use more plural pronouns; (2) perceive greater connection between themselves and their significant other; and (3) perceive their relationship as central in their lives (Agnew, Van Lange, Rusbult, & Langston, 1998).

Attachment style may become an important consideration in understanding long-term relationships and marriage. Research in this area may produce new interventions for treating relationship and marital problems.

## Marital Adjustment

One of the common misconceptions about marriage in general is that it is mostly pleasure and very little work. In addition, many couples believe that the first year of marriage is a time of mostly romance and excitement. In reality, marriage is hard work mixed with fun, and the first year of marriage is one of the most difficult (Sabatelli, 1988) because a multitude of adjustments need to be made. Disagreements can arise over a myriad of topics, from the proper way to squeeze the toothpaste to which side of the family with whom to spend Christmas holidays. This section explores major areas of adjustment that many couples encounter.

### The Perfect Mate Syndrome

Often couples have high, unrealistic expectations of their new mates. As they interact day in and day out, they see more of the real spouse, and are often disappointed (Sabatelli, 1988).

This idealized, swept-up view of one's spouse frequently derives from the excitement of love, engagement, and marriage ceremony activities. The more that couples strive before marriage to see each other with their imperfections, the less they will be affected by "encountering their real spouse" after marriage.

## But I Thought You Would Be More Like . . .

The marriage begins, and each mate has expectations about what the interaction between the couple will be like. These expectations are impacted by society, culture, and family tradition. Society's view of gender roles has been and still is in transition. Today each individual has his or her own dynamic picture of what the gender role interaction should look like in his or her marriage relationship. Research shows that gaps between each partner's expectation of the gender role create dissatisfaction in the marriage (Wilkie, Ferree, & Ratcliff, 1998).

In the past, role definition was not a major problem. Men worked and brought home the earnings, and women cooked, cleaned, and were responsible for the emotional climate of the home. Today, however, we live with the pervasive impact of the women's movement and the feminist perspective. Women have many career possibilities, and many choose demanding careers that bring them personal satisfaction. Two-wage-earner families are the most prevalent type of household today. In 56 percent of married couples, both spouses work outside the home (U. S. Bureau of the Census, 1996).

Are couples who have flexible notions about gender roles happier than those with traditional views? This does not seem to be the case. Lye and Biblarz (1993) found that couples with nontraditional gender roles were less happy than those with the more traditional views. This may be because they are more open to selecting alternatives to marriage, and because they place a high value on personal gratification.

Women are particularly at risk in the gender role battle. Many of today's women want both a demanding career and marriage. The ideal mate is one who will treat them as an equal, share in the household chores, and help with child care. Even though women are assisting with the breadwinning, research shows that men's careers are still seen as taking priority. It is the wife who is expected to accommodate if a child is ill, or if the husband needs to relocate for a promotion or another position (Silberstein, 1992). Moreover, even when both spouses have careers, many men expect their wives to play the traditional spousal role in which women are primarily responsible for child care, housework, and domestic decisions.

Do working women receive more help with the housework from their mates? Research suggests husbands are helping out somewhat more when wives work, but not far more (Demo & Acock, 1993). Women still do most of the household chores regardless of employment status. Men do only about one third of the household chores (Greenstein, 1995), most of which still are the outdoor tasks. Women still do most of the dishes, laundry, and cooking (Blair & Johnson, 1992). The equation becomes more unbalanced when the couple has children. The household workload then increases even more for women, but men tend to assist very little in the everyday child care tasks.

Of course, this uneven division of labor is not true for all couples. About one third of the dual-career couples have a more equitable arrangement for doing household tasks. Wives who receive more help at home generally: (1) make a larger percentage of the family total income; (2) work longer hours; (3) have a husband with a less demanding job; or (4) either they or their husbands have nontraditional views about gender roles (Coltrane & Ishii-Kuntz, 1992).

The sharing of household labor is a critical point in many marriages. It is often a source of problems for a couple when either's expectations vary sharply from their day-to-day experience (McHale & Crouter, 1992). Wives see their husbands' help as an indication of their love, support, and care. In addition, a husband's household assistance is also related to marital satisfaction, personal contentment, and a decrease in depression (Perry-Jenkins & Folk, 1994; Pina & Bengston, 1993). Sharing of the household chores is in fact associated with marital satisfaction for both men and women (Heinicke, 1995).

Wilkie, Ferree, and Ratcliff (1998) studied 382 two-earner married couples to see how marital satisfaction is affected by the overall division of labor outside (paid) and inside (unpaid) the home. They found that men's and women's perceptions of fairness in the overall division of labor was gender based. When either partner felt that he or she was doing more than his or her fair share of the paid work or household tasks, that partner was less satisfied with the marriage. Women felt more satisfied when the household chores were shared more equitably. Conversely, men felt more marital satisfaction when there was more equity in earning of the overall family income.

Because of the extreme variations in gender role preferences in today's world, it is important that couples talk about their expectations. Addressing these issues before marriage will help make adjustment to marriage easier.

## Does Money Make a Difference?

There is no research that indicates that having money makes marriage work better. However, poverty can cause major problems in a marriage. Financial instability causes personal strain and general tension. A couple with marginal resources lives in constant fear of a financial emergency that will put their day-to-day existence at risk. This financial strain sometimes causes negative personal feelings between the spouses and can negatively affect communication between the partners (Klebanov, Brooks-Gunn, & Duncan, 1994).

Couples with higher income and more education report being more satisfied in their marriages (Wilke et al., 1998). However, couples with resources sometimes have problems negotiating differences in how the money should be spent. This can add financial stress to a couple's relationship regardless of their income and can ultimately affect marital satisfaction (Pittman & Lloyd, 1988). Thus, regardless of financial status, money can negatively impact a relationship.

## Is Talk Cheap?

Talk is not cheap. In fact, poor communication, miscommunication, and negative communication can be very costly in a relationship. Research shows that good communication is critical to a thriving relationship. Proficient communication skills and marital contentment were associated with nondistressed couples (Burleson & Denton, 1997). One of the main differences between satisfied and dissatisfied couples was the couples' comfort level in sharing important information, and their ability to successfully resolve conflicts (Kurdek, 1995).

Several studies examined the difference between the communication styles of couples in happy and unhappy relationships. Unhappy couples: (1) have trouble giving positive messages; (2) misunderstand each other more; (3) are less likely to know they have been misunderstood; and (4) use more frequent and more flagrant negative statements (Noller & Fitzpatrick, 1990; Sher & Baucom, 1993).

Buehlman, Gottman, and Katz (1992) conducted a major study that examined couples' communication styles. Through analysis of the couples' communications on several dimensions, they were able to predict which couples would divorce within three years. The predictions were correct 94 percent of the time.

Couples who are distressed tend to blame each other for their personal problems and see positive behavior as almost accidental (Karney, Bradbury, Fincham, & Sullivan, 1994). As is apparent, negative communications does cost, and it has cost many couples their relationship.

## Other Adjustment Tasks

In addition to those discussed in the preceding, there are other areas in which couples must make adjustments: sexual preferences and habits, personal habits, work, employment, achievement, social life, friends, recreation, morals, values, and ideology (Rice, 1998).

## Social Exchange Theory and Relationships

Social Exchange Theory is an economic theory that has been applied to understanding relationships. This theory implies that relationships are an equation that balances out rewards and costs:

Relationship Outcome (Profits) = Rewards − Costs

From the initiation of the relationship through marriage and divorce, this theory offers an explanation for why people connect, how they behave in the relationships, and ultimately why they elect to leave relationships. Some people are uncomfortable with the idea that relationships can be reduced to a bottom line like an accountant's ledger in a business, but it is one way to explain relationships.

When people consider a new relationship, they often consider their own resources versus those of the other person. Resources can be defined as love, status, services, information, goods, and money (Roloff & Campion, 1985). Thibaut and Kelly (1959) originally advanced the idea of comparison levels. This theory suggested that people evaluate their relationships or potential relationship in terms of : (1) the Comparison Level (CL)—what a person believes he or she deserves; and (2) the Comparison Level for alternative (CLalt.), the best available alternative to the current relationship.

When people feel that they have attracted someone who is "better than they deserve" they feel that they have profited. When people feel that they have "less than they deserve," they are technically in the red. If they believe, however, that they have limited alternatives, they will be happier with this choice than if they feel they have unlimited alternatives. Whether one sees oneself as the "up" or the "down" in the relationship (i.e., perceives the self or other as having greater resources) subsequently affects the balance of power in the relationship.

For example, if Mary (with her master's degree and good looks) believes that Ken (an average looking plumber) got a great deal when he married her, she might be looking for concessions from him when they argue. On the other hand, if Ken feels that he got a great deal (even if Mary does not necessarily feel that way about herself) he might go out of his way to give her special treatment.

Rusbult, Drigotas, and Verette (1994) updated and added to the Comparison Level concept. They called their theory the "Investment Model" by adding a Commitment Level. This term is defined as the investment that a partner has put into a relationship. These investments could be tangible, such as children or a house, or intangible, such as attachment or shared experiences. This additional concept helps to explain why people do not automatically leave a relationship whenever they see a more viable or attractive option.

Relationship negotiations and the balance of power are affected by the social exchanges between partners. This is the kind of information that can be helpful in understanding the dynamics that occur in both happy and unhappy couples.

## Marital Satisfaction

Does marriage make people happy? Are married people happier and more satisfied than other people? These are difficult questions to answer and depend on how and when marital happiness is measured. One cannot judge marital happiness only by how long the couple has been married. Some people remain married even though they are unhappy. In many cultures, happiness is not the point of marriage. People seek mutual respect, financial support, and a vehicle for societally approved sexual behavior and childbearing. In the United States, however, happiness has become an expectation.

Research suggests that married people are happier at every age than those who are unmarried. Coombs (1991) reviewed 120 relationship studies. The research indicated that married people are not only happier, but they also experience less stress than single people.

The amount of happiness seems to vary across the marriage. Couples report high levels of happiness early in marriage, which then declines somewhat during the childrearing phases. Satisfaction increases again later in life (Glen, 1995). The lowest point of satisfaction for a couple seems to occur around the 20-year mark (Vaillant & Vaillant, 1993), when couples with children are frequently dealing with teenagers, a time that can be particularly stressful for parents. This could also be a time when career demands are high as well.

An earlier study by Skolnick (1981) found several social factors related to marital happiness. For women, the age at first marriage was related to happiness. The older the woman at the time of her first marriage, the greater chance that she will remain happy in the relationship. Men's marital happiness seemed to be related to occupation and socioeconomic status (SES). Professional men and executives reported being happier in their marriages than men in other occupations. Women and men reported being happier if they were more educated, had higher socioeconomic status, and were childless. Somers (1993) also found that voluntarily childless couples were happier than those with children. This finding is surprising because happy couples with children are frequently promoted as the ideal in the media.

Interpersonal factors also impact marital satisfaction. Couples who are satisfied with the frequency and quality of their sexual interactions also reported more marital satisfaction (Skolnick, 1981). In addition, people who give feedback that confirms their partner's self-view have more satisfying relationships (Katz & Beach, 1997).

Happiness does seem to be correlated with educational and economic factors. More research needs to be done to find out how these findings vary across cultures and SES. Perhaps the indicators of happiness are different for couples from different ethnic, cultural, and social class groups.

## Cohabitation

Cohabitation refers to living with someone outside of marriage. In the not too distant past, living together, or "shacking-up" as it was sometimes called in slang, was seen as immoral and disgraceful. Today, it is seen far more positively. POSSLQ, which stands for Persons of the Opposite Sex Sharing Living Quarters, is the United States Census Bureau's term for this coupling arrangement. Even some cities such as Seattle and Berkeley and large businesses such as Levi Straus are making it possible for cohabiting coupling to receive medical and retirement benefits for their partners, much like those available to married couples (Duff & Truitt, 1991). Cohabitation is different from common-law marriage in that cohabitors do not present themselves in society as husband and wife (Nicole & Baldwin, 1995).

### How Common Is Cohabitation?

Today in the United States, Canada, and the Western world, cohabitation is more commonplace, and young people in particular see this as a suitable life choice (Hall & Zhao, 1995). In 1970, about 1.2 percent of the population was cohabiting, but by 1993 the number had risen to 6 percent (3.5 million couples) (U. S. Bureau of the Census, 1994). Of women between the ages of 14 and 44, about half have cohabited at sometime by age 35 (Bumpass & Sweet, 1989). In some European countries, such as Sweden, couples have a higher rate of cohabitation than in the United States (Popenoe, 1987).

## Why Is Cohabiting So Popular?

For college students, cohabiting may be based more on financial convenience than on intimate connection. Many students choose to cohabit even when sexual contact is not a part of the equation. The trend to marry later may also be a reason that cohabitation is on the rise. People enjoy the benefits of a relationship while they put their careers in place and sort out their willingness to make a more permanent commitment. Another factor in the rising popularity of cohabitation is that the majority of people now accept or overlook premarital sexuality. Furthermore, people who have been divorced, particularly those with children, frequently prefer cohabiting relationships. Perhaps having experienced one failed relationship makes cohabitation a more desirable option for them.

The women's movement has helped women feel less dependent on marriage as a necessary institution for survival. Financial freedom, viable careers, and a sense of empowerment have helped many women decide that a nonmarital option such as cohabiting is more desirable. Traditional patriarchal relationships tend to benefit men more than women (Fox & Halbrook, 1994). In addition, women may consider cohabitation because they experience the relational benefits and an increased sense of equality and partnership often absent in marriage (Fox & Halbrook, 1994).

Cohabiting is frequently easier than marriage because there are few if any legal ties, the partners frequently have separate finances, there are usually fewer joint possessions, and the emotional commitment tends to be less than for those who marry (Strong & DeVault, 1995).

## Does Cohabiting Make One More Ready for Marriage?

Many people see cohabitation as a trial marriage. Some couples use this living experience to ascertain their compatibility and the likelihood that they could have a successful marriage. In actuality, couples who cohabit do not usually see this arrangement as long-term or permanent. The majority of individuals in cohabitating relationships plan to marry each other or someone else eventually. Only about one third of cohabiting couples marry each other. For American white women, pregnancy may lead to marriage with the cohabiting partner. This is not true for African-American women (Manning, 1993).

While many couples think of cohabitation as a trial marriage, or as a step that will prepare them for marriage, research does not support this notion (Hall & Zhao, 1995). Married couples who have cohabited before marriage reported less satisfying marriages. Moreover, they viewed marriage more negatively, and were more prone to divorce. Individuals who cohabited and then married someone else reported that the past cohabiting relationship had a negative effect on their marriage. Moreover, the divorce rate for couples who cohabited is higher than that of the general public (Thomson & Colella, 1992). It appears therefore that cohabiting does not really make future marriage more successful.

Nicole and Baldwin (1995) suggest that cohabitation could be seen as a developmental stage that can be a transitional phase en route to marriage. This view of cohabitation would make it a functional stage in a relationship, rather than a controversial lifestyle choice.

Some individuals, however, see cohabitation as a permanent lifestyle option (Rindfuss & Van den Heuvel, 1990) and feel it is the best choice for their relationship. Many cohabiting couples also have children. According to Rindfuss and Van den Heuvel, there were 1.2 million cohabiting households with children in 1998.

### Are There People Who Are More Likely to Cohabit?

Cohabitation is definitively different from marriage. Cohabitors tend to be more heterogamous (selecting partners who are not similar to themselves). These couples are often less similar in age, race, or religion which are important variables for marital mate selection. However, cohabiting couples do tend to be similar in educational level (Schoen & Weinick, 1993).

People who cohabit tend to be younger than married couples, less religious, and less traditional about family values (DeMaris & MacDonald, 1993). Additional variables tend to be present in couples who cohabit in the United States. For example, people from large cities are more likely to cohabit; a higher percentage of blacks than whites cohabit; and women who cohabit tend to have higher levels of education than women who do not, while men tended to have lower levels of education and employment than male noncohabitors.

### Does Cohabiting Affect Mental and Emotional Well-being?

Horowitz and White (1998) examined the mental health of cohabitors in relation to that of married and single people. There were no differences in depression levels across the three groups. However, differences were found in the area of alcohol problems. Men who cohabit reported more alcohol problems than married or single men. Women who cohabit also reported more alcohol problems than married women. These findings further suggest that those who cohabit do not experience the level of satisfaction that married people do.

### Culture, Marriage, and Long-term Relationships

Most of the research on marital happiness cited earlier refers to patterns found in white middle-class American people. Are married couples in other cultures also happier than those who cohabit? Stack and Eshleman (1998) reviewed survey data on relationships from 17 countries. They found that in 16 countries, married couples did report being happier than cohabiting couples. Married people appeared to be happier because of financial stability and better health.

In Canada and Sweden, couples who cohabited prior to marriage were more likely to have marriages end than those who did not cohabit. These results parallel the findings about cohabitation and marriage in the United States (DeMaris & Rao, 1992).

Cohabiting is sometimes considered to be a living arrangement choice of the young. In reality, it is a lifestyle choice made by the young, middle-aged, and old alike. Cohabitation is here to stay and more and more people will choose it as a temporary or permanent lifestyle option.

## DIVORCE AND SEPARATION

Divorce and separation seem to be very common in today's world. Thirty years ago, getting a divorce or being a divorcee was enough to start a scandal in a small town. Women were often denigrated for not being able to keep the marriage intact. Some women were openly ostracized by their communities and by society at large for the dissolution of their relationships.

Today society has expanded its boundaries, now accepting that marriages may not last "till death do you part." Divorce, while not preferred, is an acceptable legal and moral way to dissolve the marital bond. With the reduction of the divorce stigma and an increase of women in the workforce, more women have choices about terminating a nonfunctional relationship. For some women, a divorce is enpowering; for others, it is the source of deep emotional and financial scars.

## Divorce Statistics

- About 50 percent of all marriages end in divorce.
- In 1998, 19.4 million adults were divorced.
- About 1,200,000 couples divorce each year.
- About half of all divorces occur during the first seven years of marriage.
- One third of all divorces occur during the first four years of marriage (U. S. Bureau of the Census, 1994, 1998).

Divorce is an unfortunate reality that affects many lives every day. Couples marry and hope for the best, yet many couples do not make it. What causes divorce? Do people fall out of love? How do people manage after divorce? Do women handle the aftermath of divorce better than their male counterparts? This section of the chapter attempts to answer these and other questions related to separation and divorce.

## Why Is Divorce So Prevalent?

There are many reasons why divorce is so prevalent in our society today. For one, the stigma that used to be attached to divorce has greatly diminished. People accept the reality of a marriage not working instead of viewing others as moral and personal failures. Another reason is the advent of no-fault divorce. In the past, unhappy partners had to prove that the other person had wronged them during the course of the marriage (e.g., mental cruelty, abandonment, abuse, adultery). Today, instead of assigning blame, a marriage can be ended because of irreconcilable differences (Nakonezny, Shull, & Rodgers, 1995). The women's movement has made it possible for many women to have financially sufficient careers. This in turn has freed many women to pursue divorce instead of staying in dysfunctional relationships which they literally could not afford to leave.

People are now less willing to stay in unsatisfying relationship even for the sake of the children. Kersten (1990) suggests that loss of intimacy and love are primary factors in marriage deterioration. People tend to commit to the individual rather than to the institution of marriage. Thus the phrase "as long as we both shall love" is now more characteristic of relationships than the traditional "as long as we both shall live." Studies that have examined why people leave have identified more reasons relating to personal dissatisfaction than did early studies on divorce (White, 1990). Commitment plays a tremendous role in whether people leave or stay in a marriage, regardless of the level of marital dissatisfaction (Stanley & Markman, 1992).

Ultimately, people leave marriages when the costs outweigh the rewards, the alternatives are viable, and the consequences of leaving are low. Whenever these components all surface together, a relationship is most likely at risk for divorce (Karney & Bradbury, 1997).

## Do People Fall Out of Love?

Kersten (1990) describes a process of marital disaffection. Marital disaffection is described as a gradual decline in affection and emotional attachment, with a simultaneous increase in negative or apathetic feeling toward a partner. According to Kersten (1990) marital disaffection is a three-stage process. The beginning phase is typified by angry, disillusioned feelings. Negative attributions are made about the partner's behavior. In the middle phase, feelings of anger and apathy intensify. There is also an expectation of negative behavior from the partner. Often the partner begins to contemplate the impact (e.g., personal, financial, religious) of leaving the relationship. In the final phase anger is very prevalent. While some partners are ambivalent, there are generally frequent, intense thoughts and potential plans for leaving the relationship.

Thus, it appears that loving feelings can diminish over time, especially if a person attributes his or her dissatisfied feelings to the partner. Marriage therapy can sometimes help couples recapture that "old loving feeling" and assist in the resolution of their problems.

## How Do People Manage after Divorce?

Divorce is traumatizing for all involved, but research shows that it seems to be the most difficult for a spouse who does not want to end the relationship (Huber & Spitze, 1983). Most people experience disarrangement, stress, anxiety, and loneliness (Myers, 1989). Often there is a domino effect. In addition to personal disorganization, there can also be disruption of relationships with children, relatives, and friends (particularly those shared by the couple).

Divorce can affect emotional and physical health as well (Umberson & Williams, 1993). Divorced people report more health problems, have a higher mortality rate, and tend to have more accidents than people who are married (Kitson & Holmes, 1992; White, 1990).

One of the major factors that influences how well people adjust to divorce is whether or not they have children. Divorcees without children can choose to leave the marriage behind and have limited or no contact with their former spouse. Contact for couples without children tends to be less frequent and less conflictive (Masheter, 1991). Couples with children, however, must have ongoing contact around complex issues such as childrearing, custody and visitation, and finances. This makes contact with an ex-spouse more frequent and often more difficult.

## Are There Gender Differences in Adjusting to Divorce?

Women and men do tend to experience the aftermath of divorce differently. Women, particularly those with children, tend to suffer financially after divorce. Some women have been home caring for children, and entering or returning to the job market means having to manage on low or entry level salaries. Even if a woman has a good job that is comparable to her ex-husband's, women tend to experience salary inequities. Women on average earn only about 62 percent of the income a man earns for the same job. So even if a female divorcee is working a comparable job, she will most likely bring home less than her divorced counterpart. The reality for many women is that their financial well-being declines afer a divorce. Men's financial circumstances, on the other hand, tend to improve after a break-up (Kitson & Holmes, 1992).

In relation to psychological well-being, however, women tend to fare better than men. Two years after the divorce, women report that they are less depressed, less anxious, use alcohol less, and have fewer health problems (Hetherington, 1993). Many feel a sense of pride at their newfound financial and emotional independence. In addition, most women report that they are happier at this point than they were the year before the divorce (Hetherington, 1993). Women are more likely to assume custodial care of children from the marriage. Fathers tend to reduce their contact with children after a divorce (Albitson, Maccoby, & Mnookin, 1990).

## Do People Try Marriage Again after Divorce?

About three fourths of people remarry after divorce (Bumpass, Sweet, & Martin, 1990). Men remarry more often than women; younger divorcees remarry more often than those who are older; and women without children remarry more often than those with children. People who remarry tend to experience cycles similar to those of first-time married couples. People start out happy, and that feeling wanes somewhat over time. One major difference between first and second marriages is that the latter have an even higher rate of divorce, about 25 percent higher (Karney & Bradbury, 1997). On the other hand, remarried couples report better communication, less reluctance to address conflicts, and more equity in sharing housework and child care than they experienced in the first marital relationship (Hetherington & Clingempeel, 1992).

With about half of the marriages in America ending in divorce, divorce will touch the lives of most people in some way. Premarital counseling and marital therapy may help some couples avoid marriage termination. If divorce becomes inevitable, it is most important that the individuals involved develop a plan on how to cope with this difficult transition.

## LESBIAN RELATIONSHIPS

"Hello, Anne. We're having a dinner party next weekend, and we would like you to come, and bring your significant other. I'll give you the directions later this week." When these kinds of invitations are extended, the assumption is generally made that one will bring a person of the opposite sex. If the term "significant other" recognizes differences in relationship status, people often mean variations of heterosexual status, not the possibility that your significant other could be of the same sex. This is the *heterosexual assumption* that is often made by the majority of society.

In addition, the majority of society views homosexual relationships as morally wrong, and there has been little understanding, support, or tolerance for gay and lesbian couples (Garnets & Kimmel, 1991). Thus, many gay and lesbian couples are not "out" to the public. Not only are gay and lesbian couples not able to legally marry, but in a few states some sexual acts practiced by gay couples are illegal. Gay and lesbian couples also are unable to receive many of the economic benefits that are available to married couples, such as filing joint tax returns or placing a partner on their health insurance (Rivera, 1991).

It follows, therefore, that much of the research on romantic love, couples, and long-term relationships focuses on heterosexuals and their issues. Little research is done on homosexual couples in general and lesbian couples in particular (Koepke & Hare, 1992). This section of the chapter examines whether lesbian couples' relationships are different from those of heterosexual couples, myths about lesbian relationships, and how societal attitudes affect lesbian and gay relationships.

### Myths about Lesbian and Gay Couples

One popular myth about lesbian and gay couples is that one partner takes on the masculine role, while the other takes on a more feminine role in the relationship. In actuality this is true for very few couples. Gay and lesbian couples tend to embrace more flexible gender roles that value equality rather than the traditional roles that are typical of heterosexual relationships (Marecek, Finn, & Cardell, 1988).

Another myth is that lesbian and gay relationships are extremely sexual in nature, and that casual, promiscuous sex is the norm. In actuality, this voracious sexual behavior is true only for a small segment of the gay male population. It is essentially not present in the lesbian community. In fact, in committed lesbian relationships sexual activity is reported to be very low (Nichols, 1990; Tripp, 1987).

A third misconception is that gay relationships are rarely long-term. In actuality, most gay men and almost all lesbians prefer steady, long-term commitment. Lesbian relationships are generally sexually exclusive. While lesbian and gay relationships are not as stable as marriage, they are as stable as heterosexual cohabitation. This is a better parallel because some of the social stigma and lack of family support that cohabitors experience is similar to that which lesbian and gay couples experience (Peplau, 1991).

## Does Dating Look Different for Lesbian Couples?

Research shows that overall there are few major differences between lesbian couples' relationships and those of heterosexuals. They both report similar levels of commitment, general satisfaction with their relationships, sexual satisfaction, qualities they want in a partner, and the issues that contribute to the dissolution of the relationship (Peplau, 1988, 1991). Although there are many aspects about coupling that are universal, there are some differences for lesbian couples.

Rose and Frieze (1993) studied the actual and expected behavior about dating, which they call *dating scripts,* of 135 white undergraduate students. They found that these dating scripts are influenced by culture and gender roles. For heterosexuals dating involves men planning and shaping the date, and women preparing themselves and reacting to the plans. Are dating scripts different when gender is not a factor? Research indicates a great deal of overlap in the dating scripts of lesbian and heterosexual women (Klinkenberg & Rose, 1994). The most striking differences seem to be that lesbian relationships tend to have more shared power, more concern about emotion and evaluating the relationship process, and more equilibrium between initiating and responding behaviors. Lesbians become anxious before a date just like heterosexual women, but the energy seems to be more focused on preparation of the house and food rather than on personal appearance. Lesbians select the same kinds of dating activities as heterosexuals, but the lesbian dating script tends to include more assessment of how the evening is going and how they feel about it (Klinkenberg & Rose, 1994).

## Do Lesbian Couples Vary from Their Heterosexual and Gay Counterparts?

In a nationwide study that Eldridge and Gilbert (1990) conducted on 275 dual-career lesbian couples, some important relationship patterns emerged. First, these couples were mostly not "out" to the people around them, in spite of the fact that they were in their relationships for an average of five years; most were cohabiting; and about 15 percent were raising children together. The study revealed that about 65 percent had not told their employers, 35 percent had not told co-workers, about 50 percent had not told their fathers, about 33 percent had not told their mothers, and about 75 percent had not told friends and neighbors. The burden of secrecy affects how satisfied lesbians are with their social relationships. They report being less satisfied with work relationships than heterosexual women (Peters & Cantrell, 1993). While secrecy is probably not the only factor, it most likely has a major impact on their interaction and connections on the job.

Eldridge and Gilbert (1990) also found that even though most couples are not out to the public, lesbian relationships are steady, long-lasting, and committed. In addition, these women had high self-esteem and overall life satisfaction. This is a direct contradiction to the stereotype that lesbian relationships are mostly sexual . While sexual intimacy is important in lesbian relationships, it is not the primary connection. Other research on the stability of gay and lesbian relationships indicate that while these relationships can be relatively stable, they tend to be shorter and more at risk of ending than heterosexual marriages (Peplau, 1991). This could be a result of fewer legal and financial impediments to the break-up of gay and lesbian relationships.

Several studies have examined the level of satisfaction that lesbian couples have in their relationships. Lesbian couples reported that they have high levels of attachment and intimacy with their partners. One study examined the psychological factors that the literature suggests are indicative of relationship satisfaction in heterosexual couples to determine if these factors were significant for lesbian couples as well. The psychological factors included in the study were: dyadic attachment, personal autonomy, power, emotional intimacy, social intimacy, sexual intimacy, intellectual intimacy, recreational intimacy, self-esteem, career commitment, life satisfaction, professional versus partner role conflict, professional versus self role conflict, and partner versus self role conflict. The results indicated that 13 of the 14 psychological factors were related to relationship satisfaction for lesbian couples. The only factor not related to relationship satisfaction was career commitment. When partners had very different career commitments, relationship satisfaction suffered (Eldridge & Gilbert, 1990; Hurlbert & Apt, 1993).

Lesbians in relationships value equality even more than gay couples do (Kurdek, 1995). Lesbians who are satisfied in their relationships report a feeling of equality. Lesbian couples tend to share household tasks. This is not true for heterosexual couples or gay male couples in which one partner does the majority of household chores.

Lesbian couples reported greater relationship satisfaction, more fondness for their partners, and greater trust and more joint decision-making than gay males. These differences are probably a result of the socialization that women receive that foster nurturance, expressiveness, and warmth toward other females (Kurdek, 1998).

In relation to conflict management, lesbian, gay, and heterosexual couples have few differences. No differences were found on conflicts about power, personal habits (e.g., smoking, drinking), and career and school obligations. Heterosexual couples tend to have more altercations over social issues such as politics and in-laws, and lesbian and gay couples to argue more over distrust and jealousy (Kurdek, 1994). The fact that lesbian and gay couples are members of a sexual minority that must battle society for equal rights may account for reduced conflict in this area. Because of the small size of the gay community in most areas, former lovers are often are a part of the same social network, which could account for the increased arguments about distrust and jealousy.

Some European countries are far ahead of the United States in recognizing lesbian and gay rights. Countries such as Norway and Denmark have formalized legal arrangements that resemble marriage for lesbian and gay couples. There was less resistance to the legal arrangement for lesbian and gay couples because of the widespread acceptance of heterosexual cohabitation, which continues to increase (Lutzen, 1998). Research suggests that these legal arrangements were made in part because society is more accepting of cohabitation in the heterosexual community, where it is on the rise. As marriage became devalued in that society, the drive for marriage-like recognition for lesbian and gay couples seemed less of a pressing issue. In actuality, few lesbian and gay couples used the legal vehicle that is available to solidify partnerships (Lutzen, 1998).

Unfortunately, there is little research on lesbian couples and their relationships. More interview and survey research will give us a more accurate picture of what the experience of lesbian couples is like in America.

# SUMMARY

This chapter has examined four major areas related to intimate relationships: love and romance; marriage and long-term relationships; divorce and separation; and lesbian relationships. The chapter opens with a discussion of the role that identity development plays in intimate relationships. Erikson's and Havighurst's theoretical perspectives, which are discussed in this section of the chapter, note that intimate relationships are prominent in early adulthood.

## Love and Romance

In this section of the chapter, physical, interpersonal, and demographic qualities that influence attraction were examined. Factors such as age, education, personality, and body type all impact attraction. In addition, the construct of love is discussed in the latter part of this section. Both Rubin's and Sternberg's theories, which acknowledge the multifaceted nature of love, are presented. Rubin sees love as being made up of three elements: caring, attachment, and intimacy. Sternberg, on the other hand, suggests that passion, intimacy, and commitment can be combined in different ways to configure eight distinct types of love. Regardless of the model used to explain love, it is a powerful experience that creates the joy and pain that people experience in their intimate relationships.

## Marriage and Long-term Relationships

This section highlights the fact that marriage is alive and well in the United States. About 95 percent of adults in the United States marry at least once by age of 65. Current research on marriage and other long-term relationships explores the connection between early attachment experiences and adult attachment styles. Another important topic discussed in this section is marital adjustment. Many couples have unrealistic expectations about what marriage will be like. Marital adjustment is further complicated by the evolution of gender roles in our society. Each individual brings his or her definitions and expectations about gender roles to the relationship. When either partner's expectations are not met, marital or relationship disharmony ensues.

In the latter part of this section, cohabitation is discussed. Although research supports the idea that married people in every culture tend to be happier than unmarried people, cohabitation is becoming a more commonplace life choice. Some research discussed in this section suggests that cohabitation may be a developmental stage en route to marriage. While cohabitation is popular, it does not make people more ready for marriage. The divorce rate for people who cohabit is higher than that for those who do not cohabit.

## Divorce and Separation

In this section, the reasons for and the impact of divorce were discussed. About 50 percent of all marriages end in divorce. Moreover, half of all divorces occur during the first seven years of marriage. Divorce is more prevalent today because of no-fault divorce, the impact of the women's movement, and decreased willingness to remain in the marriage for the sake of the children.

Men and women experience the aftermath of divorce differently. Women tend to fare better emotionally than men after divorce, and men tend to fare better financially than women after a divorce. In spite of the fact than many people suffer pain after a divorce, about 75 percent of divorced people choose to remarry at some point in their lives.

## Lesbian Relationships

In this last section of the chapter, lesbian relationships are discussed. Little research has been done specifically on lesbian couples. Consequently, there are many myths about lesbian and gay relationships. This section of the chapter begins by discussing some of the commonly held myths about lesbian and gay relationships. For example, some people assume that lesbian and gay relationships are rarely long-term. In actuality, many gay men and almost all lesbians prefer steady, long-term commitments. Moreover, lesbian relationships are generally sexually exclusive. Many lesbian couples are not "out" to the public. Secrecy does seem to place a burden on social and work relationships for lesbian couples. However, within their relationships, lesbians report high levels of attachment and intimacy.

In sum, this chapter examined several types of intimate relationships and their impact on women's lives. Statistics and research help us to make sense of the world around us and the experiences encountered in life. Few areas have the universality that love does. It impacts almost everyone, regardless of age, gender, race, culture, or sexual orientation. Exploring the complexities of love, romance, marriage, long-term relationships, separation, divorce, and lesbian relationships will help us better understand ourselves, other women, and the world around us.

## REFERENCES

Agnew, C. R., Van Lange, P. A., Rusbult, C. E., & Langston, C. A. (1998). Cognitive interdependence: Commitment and the mental representation of close relationships. *Journal of Personality and Social Psychology, 74,* 939–954.

Ainsworth, M. D., Blehar, M. C., Waters, E., & Wall, S. (1978). *Patterns of attachment: A psychological study of the strange situations.* Hillsdale, NJ: Erlbaum.

Albiston C. R., Maccoby, E. E., & Mnookin, R. R. (1990). Does joint custody really matter? *Stanford Law Review,* 167–179.

Alicke, M .D., Smith, R. H., & Klotz, J. L. (1986). Judgments of personal attractiveness: The role of faces and bodies. *Personality and Social Psychology Bulletin, 12,* 389.

Aron, A., (1988). The matching hypothesis reconsidered again: Comment on Kalick and Hamilton. *Journal of Personality and Social Psychology, 54,* 441–446.

Bernard, J. (1982). *The future of marriage.* New Haven, CT: Yale University Press.

Blair, S. L., & Johnson, M. P. (1992). Wives' perceptions of the fairness of the division of household labor: The intersection of housework and ideology. *Journal of Marriage and the Family, 54,* 570–581.

Bowlby, J. (1958). The nature of the child's tie to his mother. *International Journal of Psychoanalysis, 39,* 350–373.

Buehlman, K. T., Gottman, J., & Katz, L. F. (1992). How a couple views their past predicts their future: Predicting divorce from an oral history interview. *Journal of Family Psychology, 5,* 295–318.

Bulcroft, R. A., & Bulcroft K. A. (1993). Race differences in attitudinal and motivational factors in their decision to marry. *Journal of Marriage and the Family, 55,* 338–355.

Bumpass, L. L., & Sweet, J. A. (1989). National estimates of cohabitation: Cohort levels and union stability. *Demography. 25,* 615–625.

Bumpass, L. L., Sweet, J. A., & Martin, T. C. (1990). Changing patterns of remarriage, *Journal of Marriage and the Family, 52,* 747–756.

Burleson, B. R., & Denton, W. H. (1997). The relationship between communication skill and marital satisfaction: Some moderating effects. *Journal of Marriage and the Family, 59,* 884–902.

Buss, D. M., & Barnes, M. (1986). Preferences in human mate selection. *Journal of Personality and Social Psychology, 50,* 559–570.

Buss, D. M., Abbott, M., Angleitner, A., & Asherian, A. (1990). International preferences in selecting mates: A study of 37 cultures. *Journal of Cross-Cultural Psychology, 21,* 5–47.

Cohn, L. D., & Adler, N. E. (1992). Female and male perceptions of ideal body shapes: Distorted views among Caucasian college students. *Psychology of Women Quarterly, 16,* 69–79.

Collins, N. L., & Reed, S. J. (1990). Adult attachment, working models, and relationship quality in dating couples. *Journal of Personality and Social Psychology, 58,* 644–663.

Coltrane, S., & Ishii-Kuntz, M. (1992). Men's housework: A life course perspective. *Journal of Marriage and the Family, 54,* 43–57.

Demo, D. H., & Acock, A. C. (1993). Family diversity and the division of domestic labor: How much have things really changed? *Family Relations, 42,* 323–331.

DeMaris, A., & MacDonald, W. (1993). Premarital cohabitation and marital instability: A test of the unconventionality hypothesis. *Journal of Marriage and the Family, 55,* 399–407.

DeMaris, A., & Rao, K. V. (1992). Premarital cohabitation and subsequent marital stability in the United States: A reassessment. *Journal of Marriage and the Family, 54,* 178–190.

Duff, J., & Truitt, G. S. (1991). *The spousal equivalent handbook.* Houston, TX: Sunny Beach Publications.

Eldridge, N. S., & Gilbert, L. A. (1990). Correlates of relationship satisfaction in lesbian couples. *Psychology of Women Quarterly, 14,* 43–62.

Erikson, E. H. (1963). *Childhood and society.* New York: Norton.

Feingold, A. (1990). Gender differences in effects of physical attractiveness on romantic attraction: A comparison across five research paradigms. *Journal of Personality and Social Psychology, 59,* 981–993.

Fox, C., & Halbrook, B. (1994). Terminating relationships at midlife: A qualitative investigation of low-income women's experiences. *Journal of Mental Health Counseling, 16,* 143–154

Franzoi, S. L., & Herzog, M. E. (1987). Judging physical attractiveness: What body aspects do we use? *Personality and Social Psychology Bulletin, 13,* 19–33.

Garnets, L., & Kimmel, D. (1991). Lesbian and gay male dimensions in the psychological study human diversity. In J. D. Goodchilds (Ed.), *Psychological perspectives on human diversity in America* (pp. 143–189). Washington, DC: American Psychological Association.

Glen, N. D. (1995). Marital quality. In D. Levinson (Ed.)., *Encyclopedia of marriage and the family* (pp. 448–455). New York: Simon & Schuster Macmillan.

Goodwin, R. (1990). Sex differences among partner preferences: Are the sexes really very similar? *Sex Roles, 23,* 501–513.

Greenstein, T. H. (1995). Gender ideology, marital disruption, and the employment of married women. *Journal of Marriage and Family, 57,* 31–42.

Hall, D. R., & Zhao, J. A. (1995). Cohabitation and divorce in Canada: Testing the selectivity hypothesis: *Journal of Marriage and the Family, 57,* 421–427.

Harris, M. B., Harris, R. J., & Bochner, S. (1982). Fat, four-eyed, and female: Stereotypes of obesity, glasses, and gender. *Journal of Applied Social Psychology, 12,* 503–516.

Havighurst, R. J. (1979). *Developmental tasks and education* (4th ed.). New York: David McKay.

Hazan, C., & Shaver, P. (1987). Romantic love conceptualized as an attachment process. *Journal of Personality and Social Psychology, 52,* 511–524.

Hazan C., & Shaver, P. R. (1994). Deeper into attachment theory. *Psychological Inquiry, 5,* 68–79.

Heinicke, C. M. (1995). Determinants of the transition to parenting. In M. H. Bornstein (Ed.)., *Handbook of parenting* (Vol. 3, pp. 277–305). Mahwah, NJ: Erlbaum.

Hetherington, E. M. (1993). An overview of the virginal longitudinal study of divorce and remarriage: A focus on early adolescence. *Journal of Family Psychology, 7,* 39–50.

Hetherington, E. M., & Clingempeel, W. G. (1992). Coping with marital transitions: A family systems perspective. *Monograph of Society for Research in Child Development, 227* (whole No. 57, Nos. 2–3).

Horowitz, A. V., & White, H. R. (1998). The relationship of cohabitation and mental health: A study of a young adult cohort. *Journal of Marriage and the Family, 60,* 505–514.

Huber, J., & Spitze, G. (1983). *Sex stratification: Children, housework, and jobs.* New York: Academic Press.

Hurlbert, D. F., & Apt, C. (1993). Female sexuality: A comparative study between women in homosexual and heterosexual relationships. *Journal of Sex and Marital Therapy, 19,* 315–327.

Josselson, R. (1987). *Finding herself: Pathways to identity development in women.* San Francisco: Jossey-Bass.

Karney, B. R., & Bradbury, T. N. (1997). Neuroticism, marital interaction, and the trajectory of martial satisfaction. *Journal of Personality and Social Psychology, 72,* 1075–1092.

Karney, B. R., Bradbury, T. N., Fincham, F. D., & Sullivan, K. T. (1994). The role of negative affectivity in the association between attribution and marital satisfaction. *Journal of Personality and Social Psychology, 66,* 413–424.

Katz, J., & Beach, S. R. (1997). Self-verification and depressive symptoms in marriage and courtship: A multiple pathway model. *Journal of Marriage and the Family, 59,* 903–914.

Kendrick, D. T., Groth, G. E., Trost, M. R., & Sadalla, E. K. (1993). Integrating evolutionary and social exchange perspectives on relationships: Effects of gender, self-appraisal, and involvement level on mate selection criteria. *Journal of Personality and Social Psychology, 64,* 951–969.

Kersten, K. K. (1990). The process of marital disaffection: Intervention at various stages. *Family Relations, 39,* 257–265.

Kitson, G. C., & Holmes, W. M. (1992). *Portrait of divorce: Adjustment to marital breakdown.* New York: Guilford Press.

Klebanov, P. K., Brooks-Gunn, J., & Duncan, G. J. (1994). Does neighborhood and Family poverty affect mothers' parenting, mental health, and social support? *Journal of Marriage and the Family, 56,* 441–455.

Klinkenberg, D., & Rose, S. (1994). Dating scripts of gay men and lesbians. *Journal of Homosexuality, 26,* 23–35.

Koepke, L., & Hare, J. (1992). Relationship quality in a sample of lesbian couples with children and child-free lesbian couples. *Family Relations, 41,* 224–230.

Kurdek, L. A. (1994). Areas of conflict for gay, lesbian, and heterosexual couples argue about influences relationship satisfaction. *Journal of Marriage and the Family, 56,* 923–934.

Kurdek, L. A. (1995). Predicting change in marital satisfaction from husbands and wives' conflict resolution style. *Journal of Marriage and the Family, 57,* 153–164.

Kurdek. L. A. (1998). Relationship outcomes and their predictors: Longitudinal evidence from heterosexual married, gay cohabiting, and lesbian cohabiting couples. *Journal of Marriage and the Family, 60,* 553–569.

Lance, L. M. (1998). Gender differences in heterosexual dating: A content analysis of personal ads. *Journal of Men's Studies, 6,* 297–306.

Levine, R. V. (1993, February). Is love a luxury? *American Demographics, 2,* 37–39.

Lutzen, K. (1998). Gay and lesbian politics: Assimilation or subversion: A Danish perspective. *Journal of Homosexuality, 35,* 233–243.

Lye, D. N., & Biblarz, T. J. (1993). The effects of attitudes toward family life and gender roles on marital satisfaction. *Journal of Family Issues, 14,* 157–188.

Lynn, M., & Shurgot, B. A. (1984). Responses to lonely hearts advertisements: Effects of reported physical attractiveness, physique, and coloration. *Personality and Social Psychology Bulletin, 10,* 349–357.

Manning, W. D. (1993). Marriage and cohabitation following premarital conception. *Journal of Marriage and the Family, 55,* 839–850.

Marecek, J., Finn, S. E., & Cardell, M. (1988). Gender roles in the relationships of lesbians and gay men. In J. P. De-Cecco (Ed.)., *Gay relationships* (pp. 185–210). New York: Harrington Park Press.

Markman, H. J., & Standley, S. M. (1992). Assessing commitment in personal relationships. *Journal of Marriage and the Family, 54,* 595–608.

Masheter, C. (1991). Post divorce relationships between ex-spouses: The roles of attachment and interpersonal conflict. *Journal of Marriage and the Family, 53,* 103–110.

McHale, S. M., & Crouter, A. C. (1992). You can't always get what you want: Incongruence between sex-role attitudes and family work roles and its implications for marriage. *Journal of Marriage and the Family, 54,* 537–547.

Myers, M. F. (1989). *Men and divorce.* New York: Guilford Press.

Nakonezny, P. A., Shull, R. D., & Rodgers, J. L. (1995). The effects of no-fault divorce law on the divorce rate across 50 states and its relation to income, education, and religiosity. *Journal of Marriage and the Family, 57,* 477–488.

Nichols, M. (1990). Lesbian relationships: Implications for the study of sexuality and gender. In D. P. McWhirter, S. A. Sanders, & J. M. Reinisch (Eds.), *Homosexuality/heterosexuality: Concepts of sexual orientation* (pp. 350–364). New York: Oxford University Press.

Nicole, F. M., & Baldwin, C. (1995). Cohabitation as a developmental stage: Implications for mental health counseling. *Journal of Mental Health Counseling, 17,* 386–396.

Noller, P., & Fitzpatrick, M. A. (1990). Marital communication in the eighties. *Journal of Marriage and the Family, 52,* 832–843.

Peplau, L. A. (1988). Research on homosexual couples: An overview. In J. P. DeCecco (Ed.), *Gay relationships* (pp. 64–85). New York: Harrington Park Press.

Peplau, L. A. (1991). Lesbian and gay relationships. In J. C. Gonsiorek & J. D. Weinrick (Eds.), *Homosexuality: Research for public policy* (pp. 177–196). Newbury Park, CA: Sage Publications.

Perry-Jenkins, M., & Folk, K. (1994). Class, couples, and conflict: Effects of the division of labor on assessments of marriage in dual-earner marriages. *Journal of Marriage and the Family, 56,* 226–228.

Peters, D. K., & Cantrell, P. J. (1993). Gender roles and role conflict in feminist lesbian and heterosexual women. *Sex Roles, 28,* 379–392.

Pina, D. L., & Bengtson, V. L. (1993). The division of labor and the well-being of retirement-aged wives. *The Gerontologist, 35,* 308–317.

Pittman, J. F., & Lloyd, S. A. (1988). Quality of family life, social support, and stress. *Journal of Marriage and the Family, 50,* 53–67.

Popenoe, D. (1987). Beyond the nuclear family: A statistical portrait of the changing family in Sweden. *Journal of Marriage and the Family, 49,* 173–183.

Rice, F. P. (1998). *Human development*. Upper Saddle River, NJ: Prentice Hall.

Rindfuss, R. R., & Van den Heuvel, A. (1990). Cohabitation: A precursor to marriage or an alternative to being single? *Population and Development Review, 16,* 703–726.

Rivera, R. R. (1991). Sexual orientation and the law. In J. C. Gonsiorek & J. D. Weinrick (Eds.), *Homosexuality: Research for public policy*. Newbury Park, CA: Sage Publications.

Roloff, M. E., & Campion, D. E. (1985). Conversational profit seeking: Interaction as social exchange. In R. L. Street & J. N. Capplla (Eds.), *Sequence and pattern in communicative behavior* (pp. 161–189). Baltimore: Edward Arnold.

Rose, S., & Frieze, I. H. (1993). Young singles contemporary dating scripts. *Sex Role, 28,* 499–509.

Rubin, Z. (1973). *Liking and loving: An introduction to social psychology*. New York: Holt, Reinhart & Winston.

Rusbult, C. E., Drigotas, S. M., & Verette, J. (1994). The investment model: An interdependence analysis of commitment processes and relationship maintenance phenomena. In D. J. Candry & L. Stafford (Eds.), *Communication and relational maintenance* (pp. 115–140). San Diego, CA: Academic Press.

Sabatelli, R. M. (1988). Exploring relationship satisfaction: A social exchange perspective on the interdependence between theory, research, and practice. *Family Relations, 37,* 217–222.

Schoen, R., & Weinick, R. M. (1993). Partner choice in marriages and cohabitations. *Journal of Marriage and the Family, 55,* 404–414.

Shaver, P. R., & Brennan, K. A. (1992). Attachment styles and the "big five" personality traits: Their connections with each other and with romantic relationship outcomes. *Personality and Social Psychology Bulletin, 18,* 536–545.

Sher, T. G., & Baucom, D. H. (1993). Marital communication: Differences among maritally distressed, depressed, and nondistressed, nondepressed couples. *Journal of Family Psychology, 7,* 148–153.

Silberstein, L. R. (1992). *Dual-career marriage, a system in transition*. Hillsdale, NJ: Erlbaum.

Skolnick, A. (1981). Married lives: Longitudinal perspectives on marriage. In D. H. Eichorn, J. Clausen, N. Haan, M. P. Honzik, & P. H. Musssen (Eds.), *Present and past in middle life* (pp. 270–297). New York: Academic Press.

Somers, M. D. (1993). A comparison of voluntarily childfree adults and parents. *Journal of Marriage and the Family, 55,* 643–650.

South, S. J. (1991). Sociodemographic differentials in mate selection preferences. *Journal of Marriage and the Family, 53,* 928–940.

Sprecher, S., Sullivan, Q., & Hatfield, E. (1994). Mate selection preferences: Gender differences examined in a national sample. *Journal of Personality and Social Psychology, 66,* 1074–1080.

Stack, S., & Eshleman, J. R. (1998). Marital status and happiness: A 17-nation study. *Journal of Marriage and the Family, 60,* 527–536.

Stanley, S. M., & Markman, H. J. (1992). Assessing commitment in personal relationships. *Journal of Marriange and the Family, 54,* 595–608.

Sternberg, R. J. (1986). A triangular theory of love. *Psychological Review, 93,* 119–135.

Strong, B., & DeVault, C. (1995). *The marriage and the family experience* (6th ed). St. Paul, MN: West.

Surra, C. A. (1991). Mate selection and premarital relationships. In A. Booth (Ed.), *Comtemporary families* (pp. 54–57). Minneapolis, MN: National Council on Family Relations.

Taylor, R. J., Chatters, L. M., Tucker, M. B., & Lewis, E. (1990). Development in research on black families: A decade review. *Journal of Marriage and the Family, 52,* 993–1014.

Thibaut, J. W., & Kelly, H. H. (1959). *The social psychology of groups*. New York: John Wiley & Sons.

Thomson, E., & Colella, U. (1992). Cohabitation and marital stability: Quality or commitment? *Journal of Marriage and the Family, 54,* 259–267.

Trandis, H. C. (1994). *Culture and social behavior*. New York: McGraw-Hill.

Tripp, C. A. (1987). *The homosexual matrix*. New York: Meridian.

Tucker, M. B., & Mitchell-Kernan, C. (1995). *The decline in marriage among African Americans*. New York: Russell Sage Foundation.

Umberson, G., & Williams, C. L. (1993). Divorced fathers, parental role strain and psychological distress. *Journal of Family Issues, 14,* 378–400.

U. S. Bureau of the Census. (1994). Statistical abstract of the U. S., 1994 (114th ed.). Washington, DC: U. S. Government Printing Office.

U. S. Bureau of the Census. (1995). Statistical abstract of the U. S., 1995 (115th ed.). Washington, DC: U. S. Government Printing Office.

U.S. Bureau of the Census. (1996). Statistical abstract of the U. S., 1996 (116th ed.). Washington, DC: U. S. Government Printing Office.

U. S. Bureau of the Census. (1998). Statistical abstract of the U. S., 1998, (118th ed.). Washington, DC: U. S. Government Printing Office.

Vaillant, C. O., & Vaillant, G. E. (1993). Is the u-curve of marital satisfaction an illusion? A 40-year study of marriage. *Journal of Marriage and the Family, 55,* 230–239.

White, L. K. (1990). Determinants of divorce: A review of research in the eighties. *Journal of Marriage and the Family, 32,* 904–912.

Wilkie, J. R., Ferree, M. M., & Ratcliff, K. S. (1998). Gender and fairness: Marital satisfaction in two-earner couples. *Journal of Marriage & the Family, 60,* 577–595.

# 10

# Motherhood and Reproductive Issues

## Joan C. Chrisler and Ingrid Johnston-Robledo

## INTRODUCTION

The topics discussed in this chapter (menstruation, menopause, pregnancy, birth, contraception, and motherhood) are central to the psychology of women. They are, after all, experienced only by women, and most women, despite the diversity of their lives, will experience menstruation and menopause and consider whether (and when) to use contraception. The majority of women will become pregnant at some point in their lives, and most who do will become mothers. Thus, our menstrual, menopausal, and reproductive experiences have the potential to draw together women who otherwise might not have much in common, and women do, under congenial circumstances, enjoy sharing with each other stories about menarche and mothering or arguing about whose labor or hot flashes were the most difficult to endure.

Although menarche can be a source of pride, pregnancy exciting, and motherhood the fount of our greatest joys, reproduction can also become oppressive to women. Obstetrics and Gynecology, the only medical specialty exclusively focused on women, essentially defines women in terms of the traditional roles of wife and mother, and it redefines normal developmental events in women's lives into illnesses and medical emergencies (Gannon, 1998; Rosser, 1993). Medical imperialism (Gannon, 1998) and sociocultural pressures can combine to convince women that they have little control over their reproductive experiences or force them to be secretive about the decisions they have made. Therefore, counselors and psychotherapists who work with women should expect to hear a wide range of attitudes, concerns, and experiences with regard to the topics of this chapter.

## MENSTRUATION

Most Western women can expect to experience monthly menstrual cycles for three to four decades. The regular appearance of the menses is a sign of good health, is symbolic of a connection to other women, represents biological maturity, signifies our ability to bear children, but lets us know we are not pregnant (Chrisler, 1996). The menstrual cycle provides a clear distinction between women and men, and, as a result, "its correlates, concomitants, ac-

Joan C. Chrisler and Ingrid Johnston-Robledo ● Department of Psychology, Connecticut College, New London, Connecticut 06320

*Issues in the Psychology of Women,* edited by Biaggio and Hersen. Kluwer Academic/Plenum Publishers, New York, 2000.

companiments, ramifications, and implications have become intrinsically bound up with issues of gender equality" (Sommer, 1983, p. 53). Thus a consideration of attitudes toward, beliefs about, and the experience of menstruation is important to an understanding of the psychology of women.

## Attitudes Toward Menstruation

Most Americans believe that they have a good understanding of the process and concomitants of the menstrual cycle, although they prefer not to mention the topic in public (Tampax Report, 1981). Even psychotherapists (especially men) have reported experiencing discomfort when their clients want to discuss some aspect of menstruation (Rhinehart, 1989). Despite our apparent sophistication and our having left behind most of the taboos of the past (when menstrual blood was thought to be magical or poisonous and menstruating women needed to be controlled and their activities curtailed), many Americans continue to accept the taboo against sexual activity during menstruation (Golub, 1992), believe that women are particularly delicate or susceptible to stress or illness at certain phases of the cycle (Tampax Report, 1981), and think that premenstrual women are dangerous and unpredictable. In a survey of college students (Golub, 1981), men were twice as likely as women to believe that menstruation affects the personality, thinking ability, and general functioning of women—despite considerable scientific evidence to the contrary (see Sommer, 1983, for a review).

It is not surprising that people who express these beliefs would also have negative attitudes toward menstruation. These attitudes are formed early and are less influenced by personal experience than might be expected. Clarke and Ruble (1978) asked boys and pre- and postmenarcheal girls to rate severity of the symptoms that they believed women experience during menstruation. Boys and premenarcheal girls had well-defined beliefs and negative attitudes toward menstruation; they reported that it is accompanied by pain, emotionality, and a reduction in social and physical activities. The postmenarcheal girls did not let their own experiences guide their responses; they thought that most girls experienced more severe symptoms than they themselves did.

Researchers have found that men tend to view menstruation as more debilitating than women do; women tend to rate menstruation as merely a "bothersome" event (Brooks-Gunn & Ruble, 1980, 1986; Chrisler, 1988). Men are more likely than women to describe menstruation as embarrassing and to report that their sources of information about menstruation have been negative (Brooks-Gunn & Ruble, 1986). Older adults perceive menstruation as less debilitating and bothersome than do college students (Chrisler, 1988; Stubbs, 1989).

These negative attitudes and inaccurate beliefs are reinforced by popular culture. Jokes about menstruation and women's hormones are common, and several books of misogynist humor about the premenstrual syndrome have been widely read in the United States (Chrisler, 1990). A content analysis of articles published in North American magazines between 1980 and 1987 found a strong bias in favor of reporting on negative (and often exaggerated) menstrual cycle related changes (Chrisler & Levy, 1990). The articles presented a confusing array of symptoms (including some that do not appear anywhere in the medical or psychological literature) and contradictory treatment recommendations, supported stereotypes about women's erratic behavior, and suggested that premenstrual women may need psychiatric care. Articles analyzed included "Dr. Jekyll and Ms. Hyde" and "The Taming of the Shrew Inside of You." Many of the articles (as these titles suggest) emphasized a tendency toward violent, irrational, and out-of-control behavior during the premenstrual phase of the cycle, and the terms (e.g., "raging animals") they used to describe premenstrual women came directly from newspaper reports of the trials of two British women who were accused of murder in the early 1980s (Chrisler, 1998). These images remain current today and form the subject matter of many cartoons about premenstrual syndrome (PMS), despite the facts that women commit fewer than 5 percent of all violent crimes and that there is no credible scientific evidence that links aggression to menstrual cycle phase (D'Orban & Dalton, 1980; Harry & Baker, 1987).

Scientists as well as journalists have tended to focus their efforts on negative aspects of the menstrual cycle. During the past 100 years or so many dozens of studies have been designed by biomedical and psychosocial researchers to look for deficits in women's behavior and abilities that can be associated with menstrual cycle phases, and feminist researchers have had to use their energies to critique, deconstruct, and correct these misconceptions (see, e.g., Gannon, 1998; Parlee, 1973). There are a few studies (e.g., Chrisler, Johnston, Champagne, & Preston, 1994; S. Nichols, 1995) of positive aspects of the menstrual cycle, but they are overshadowed by the current efforts of the American Psychiatric Association to gain acceptance for one of its newest DSM categories: Premenstrual Dysphoric Disorder. (See Gloria Steinem's 1983 essay "If Men Could Menstruate" for an amusing and creative illustration of how women's experiences are easily made to seem defective, whereas men's experiences are sources of pride and considerable social interest.)

## Menarche

Menarche, the first menstruation, is a milestone in women's development and a psychologically significant event. Although it occurs relatively late in the pubertal process, as much as two years after breast buds develop (Tanner, 1978), it is menarche that provides the proof of puberty (Erchull, Chrisler, & Johnston-Robledo, 1999). Unlike the other gradual changes that accompany puberty, menarche is sudden and conspicuous (Golub, 1992), and it thus provides a rather dramatic demarcation between girlhood and womanhood. The importance of the menarcheal experience is illustrated by the fact that many women have vivid and detailed memories of it that are retained over time with surprising clarity.

Given the cultural images of menstruation discussed in the preceding section, it is no surprise that most girls approach menarche with ambivalence. In studies of North American girls, participants typically report mixed feelings about menarche, such as proud and embarrassed or happy and frightened (Chrisler & Zittel, 1998; Koff, Rierdan, & Jacobson, 1981; Woods, Dery, & Most, 1983; Zimmerman & Chrisler, 1996). African-American and Hispanic girls have reported less positive reactions to menarche than European American girls, and Hispanic girls also report the most negative beliefs about menstruation (Zimmerman & Chrisler, 1996). Many girls are unprepared for menarche and do not understand what is happening to them when they experience it (Logan, 1980); this is especially likely to occur in early maturing girls for whom menarche appears to be more traumatic than for those who are "on time" or late (Petersen, 1983; Scott, Arthur, Panzio, & Owen, 1989). In one study (Scott et al., 1989) of African-American girls, 27 percent of the participants said that they felt totally unprepared for menarche; this can be compared to the approximately 14 percent of European American girls in previous studies (Koff, Rierdan, & Jacobson, 1981; Whisnant & Zegans, 1975) who reported being unprepared.

Preparation is not everything, however, as Koff, Rierdan, and Sheingold (1982) found that even the 60 percent of their participants who rated themselves as prepared for menarche had negative feelings about the event when they experienced it. The films and pamphlets that girls are given to educate them about menstruation tend to use technical medical vocabularies to describe the physiological aspects of the menstrual cycle, but are otherwise vague and mysterious (Erchull et al., 1999; Havens & Swenson, 1989; Whisnant, Brett, & Zegans, 1975). Most of these materials are produced by companies that manufacture menstrual products, and they tend to present menstruation as a hygiene crisis that should be hidden from the rest of the world by following rules of careful management and concealment (and using the right products). This emphasis on secrecy reinforces the idea that menstruation is a negative and embarrassing event. The book *Period.* (Gardner-Loulan, Lopez, & Quackenbush, 1991) is a rare example of positive education about menstruation.

Adjustment to one's new menstrual status is entwined with adjustment to thinking of oneself as an adult. Girls are taught that menarche signals the beginning of their adult lives (Koff, Rierdan, & Sheingold, 1982). When they experience their menstrual periods for the first time, girls are told that they are now women, and they are usually taught about the menstrual cycle in relation to reproduction (Erchull et al., 1999). Adolescents look forward to adulthood, but the average age at menarche in the United States is 12.3 years (Tanner, 1991), which is very young to be an adult. Body image concerns often arise around the time of menarche, as girls cope with menstruation and other pubertal changes such as weight gain and changes in body shape. Koff, Rierdan, and Silverstone (1978) asked adolescent girls to draw pictures of a same-sex body on two occasions six months apart. The bodies drawn by postmenarcheal girls were significantly more sexually differentiated than those drawn by premenarcheal girls, and the contrast was particularly striking in the drawings of girls whose menarcheal status changed during the course of the study. These data show the importance of menarche to the way girls organize their body image and sexual identity.

In many societies menarche is celebrated as a rite of passage to adulthood. Celebrations range from parties with the girl's friends or with other women in the family or village to rituals of cleansing or separation (Delaney, Lupton, & Toth, 1987). Celebrations of menarche are rare in Western countries (Chrisler & Zittel, 1998; Thuren, 1994), and most girls think of menstruation as too embarrassing to discuss with anyone but their mothers and closest friends. Think about what a change it could make to adolescent girls' self-esteem and body image if their change in menarcheal status was openly acknowledged with pride. (See Chrisler & Zittel, 1998, Golub, 1992, and Taylor, 1988, for suggestions of ways to celebrate menarche.)

## Dysmenorrhea

Dysmenorrhea is the technical term used to describe the uterine cramps, headaches, backaches, and other unpleasant symptoms that may occur during menstruation. It typically starts no more than 2 to 12 hours prior to the onset of the menstrual flow and lasts about 24 to 36 hours (Golub, 1992). Dysmenorrhea occurs only during ovulatory cycles, and it is thought that the process of ovulation triggers the production of prostaglandins: that is, hormone-like substances, that cause the uterine contractions we call menstrual cramps (Dawood, 1981; Golub, 1992). The amount of prostaglandins produced differs from woman to woman and even from cycle to cycle in the same woman; therefore, women may experience dysmenorrhea only during some cycles. Dysmenorrhea generally begins in the early teens and is most severe in the late teens and early 20s; it then typically declines with age (Golub, 1992), although some women report its return prior to menopause. About 50 percent of women experience dysmenorrhea; about 5 percent to 10 percent of women experience symptoms severe enough to incapacitate them anywhere from one hour to three days (Golub, 1992).

Although the connection of prostaglandins to menstrual cramps was known in the mid-1960s (Pickles, Hall, Best, & Smith, 1965), prostaglandins were not generally accepted as the cause of cramps until around 1980. Prior to 1980, dysmenorrhea was commonly treated as a conversion disorder. Women who complained of severe symptoms were told that their problems were "all in their heads," advised to have a baby, or referred to a psychiatrist. Many physicians believed that only women who reject the feminine gender role would experience pain during menstruation. There is a large literature that documents the attempt by physicians and psychologists to prove that neuroticism causes dysmenorrhea. Many personality and attitude variables were examined, with contradictory or obscure results. What does it mean, for example, that anxious women with negative attitudes toward menstruation are more likely to experience dysmenorrhea? That anxiety and negative attitudes are the cause of dysmenorrhea? Or that the experience of dysmenorrhea leads to anxiety and negative attitudes toward the source of the pain?

Today women with dysmenorrhea are advised to take an anti-prostaglandin medication, such as aspirin or ibuprofen. If these medications do not work, women should see a gynecologist, who can prescribe a stronger medication and conduct an examination to determine that the dysmenorrhea is primary, as opposed to secondary to a more serious condition such as endometriosis or pelvic inflammatory disease. Other strategies that women find useful in coping with mild to moderate dysmenorrhea include muscle relaxation, pain control imagery, stretching exercises (e.g., yoga), warm baths, heating pads, rest, and orgasm. Systematic desensitization (Tasto & Chesney, 1974), autogenic training, and both temperature and electromyogramic biofeedback (Sedlacek & Heczey, 1977) have been used successfully in therapy to reduce menstrual pain.

## Premenstrual Syndrome

Premenstrual syndrome (commonly known as PMS) refers to the experience of psychological and physiological changes in the three to five days prior to the onset of menstruation. The most frequently reported symptom of PMS is fluid retention, particularly in the breasts and abdomen. Other commonly reported symptoms include headaches, backaches, constipation, food cravings, anxiety, tension, lethargy, sleep changes, irritability, depression, and acne (Debrovner, 1982). PMS was first described in the 1930s (Frank, 1931), but it did not become well known among physicians or the general public until around 1980—the time when the media were publicizing the British trials in which women accused of murder were described as PMS sufferers (Chrisler, 1996, 1998).

There is a large literature about PMS (also called PMT, premenstrual tension) in biomedical and psychosocial journals despite the fact that researchers and clinicians cannot agree on a definition for it. There is no known cause of PMS (although speculations have ranged from gonadal or adrenal hormones to sleep disturbances to inadequate nutrition to neuroticism to self-fulfilling prophecies); nor is there a cure. Estimates of the number of women who experience PMS vary from 2 percent to 100 percent, depending on how PMS is described and defined (Chrisler, 1996). Perhaps only 5 percent of women experience symptoms severe enough to require medical attention (Rose & Abplanalp, 1983), but most women experience premenstrual changes from time to time, and many women have diagnosed themselves as suffering from PMS.

Feminist scholars (Chrisler, 1996; Gannon, 1998; Laws, 1983; Rome, 1986; Zita, 1988) have argued that PMS has been socially constructed to provide ostensibly scientific evidence to support the status quo. It can be seen as a form of social control that helps to "keep women in their place" by insisting that women's physical "condition" requires medical management and makes them unsuited to step beyond their traditional roles. Even asymptomatic women suffer because of PMS when they are not considered for promotion by bosses who assume that all menstruating women are unstable; when their anger is dismissed by others who think it is the result of hormonal fluctuations and thus not "real"; when their self-efficacy is reduced because they believe they cannot control themselves; when they accept the notion that their problems are internal and individual rather than external and social.

Behavioral, nutritional, and pharmacological treatments that target individual symptoms can help women to cope with premenstrual changes. Vitamin B, aspirin, diuretics, exercise, relaxation techniques, extra sleep, and reduction of salt intake may be particularly useful. Counselors and psychotherapists should also encourage women to change their attributions about their premenstrual experiences. Instead of labeling their experience as "symptoms," call them "changes." Women can be encouraged to consider themselves "sensitive" rather than "ill" or otherwise "overreacting" (Koeske, 1983). If we lived in a society in which women wore loose clothing such as robes or saris, would we even notice water retention (Rome, 1986), much less consider it a symptom of a disorder? Why is an occasional urge to eat a candy bar or a salty snack seen as a sign of a medical condition (Chrisler, 1996)? Are there benefits to the experience of cyclic variations? Is not change preferable to stagnation? Finally, women should be educated about the fact that hormones do not make us angry or irritable, although they may intensify those reactions. There are always reasons for our anger, and it is those reasons, not our hormonal states, that should be discussed.

## CONTRACEPTION

The decision of whether or when to bear children is a crucial one that has long-term consequences for women's lives. Women's ability to make reproductive decisions depends on the availability of various, accessible, safe, effective, and inexpensive methods of contraception. Although no single method is best for all women, or completely safe and effective, a variety of alternatives allows women to make contraceptive choices that best match their bodies, relationships, and life circumstances.

Approximately 50 percent of pregnancies per year in the United States are unplanned (Henshaw, 1998), and about one million prospective mothers each year are teenagers. Unintended pregnancies are the result of nonuse of, ineffective use of, or failure of contraceptives. These statistics emphasize the need for (1) increased research and development of new, safe, and more effective contraceptives; (2) better education, counseling, and training for contraceptive users and potential users; (3) public policy initiatives to make contraceptives more accessible and less expensive, especially for teenagers and low income users; and (4) a shift away from cultural messages that either celebrate or condemn teenage mothers to a more realistic message about the effects of early motherhood on women's lives and goals.

Although 95 percent of American women favor contraception (Forrest & Henshaw, 1983), many do not use it because of the expense, lack of information about how to obtain it, religious constraints, anti-contraception messages from family or partner, or fear of possible or actually experienced side effects (Silverman, Torres, & Forrest, 1987). Adolescents may defer contraceptive use because of feelings of invulnerability ("That will never happen to me.") or beliefs in inaccurate notions about how and when pregnancy can occur (Gerrard & Luus, 1995). Perimenopausal women may discontinue contraceptive use after they begin to skip menstrual periods; however, they are at risk for conception at any time until one year without menstruation has occurred. Disabled women may not use contraceptives because their health care practitioners have never offered them.

Winter (1988) found that having a sexual self-concept is positively correlated with contraception use, that is, that women who admit to being sexually active and perceive themselves to be at risk for pregnancy are most likely to decide to use contraception. This may seem like an obvious point, but in a society that has traditionally divided good women and sexual women into different groups, many women are taught to be ashamed of their sexual needs and thus may deny them (Leonardo & Chrisler, 1992). Acquiring contraceptives means one is planning to have sex, and women who view sex as an event that happens to them, as when they are romantically "swept away," rather than as an event they can control are not likely to use contraceptives (Leonardo & Chrisler, 1992). Ceding control to a male partner who may or may not have a condom with him puts women at risk for sexually transmitted diseases as well as unintended pregnancy.

Once a decision to use contraceptives has been made, women must decide which of the variety available to choose. Factors in the decision include cost, safety, effectiveness, side effects, health contraindications, convenience, partner cooperation, future childbearing plans, and the woman's own behavior, abilities, and preferences. Barrier methods, such as spermicides and condoms, and fertility awareness methods require partner cooperation; women without cooperative partners may choose oral contraceptives, an intrauterine device (IUD), or sterilization. Oral contraceptive effectiveness relies on memory and requires a regular routine. The diaphragm and cervical cap require advance planning and comfort with one's body. See Hawkins, Matteson, and Tabeek (1995) for a complete overview of the benefits, drawbacks, and contraindications of currently available contraceptives.

Once contraceptive use has begun, it may be discontinued or continued intermittently or ineffectively because of poor training (e.g., incorrect insertion of cervical cap or diaphragm), failure to establish the habit of use (e.g., forgetting to take one's pill daily), partner's lack of cooperation (e.g., his refusal to wear a condom or wait for spermicide application), pain or discomfort (e.g., IUD-related uterine cramps or increased premenstrual water retention due to oral contraceptive use), or side effects (e.g., rubber or spermicide allergies, infection at site of Norplant insertion). Other variables that have been found to predict regular contraceptive use include health orientation, achievement orientation, educational goals (Costa, Jessor, Fortenberry, & Donovan, 1996), communication skills (Burger & Inderbitzen, 1985), favorable attitudes toward and previous experiences with contraception (Hawkins, Matteson, & Tabeek, 1995), self-esteem, self-efficacy, and nontraditional gender role ideology (Sable & Libbus, 1998).

Counselors and psychotherapists can play a role in the important public health goals of preventing unintended pregnancies and sexually transmitted disease (STD) transmission by discussing contraceptive use with their heterosexually active clients who are not attempting to conceive. Family planning and the assumption of control of one's own body can result in mental health benefits for women. Therapeutic interventions can be used to increase women's self-esteem and self-efficacy, help to overcome barriers to effective contraceptive use (e.g., teach negotiation skills, assist in the establishment of routines), encourage achievement orientation and goal setting, and "offset emotional, coercive, pronatal pressures" from clients' partners, peers, or parents (Moskowitz & Jennings, 1996, p. 789). Counselors and psychotherapists can provide support and assistance in acquiring information about contraceptives and making decisions about which to use. Active, directive counseling about contraception has been found to be particularly effective with adolescents (Moskowitz & Jennings, 1996).

## ABORTION

According to the United Nations (1991) at least 200,000 women die annually from illegal abortions, most of them in Africa, Asia, and Latin America. Abortion has been legal in the

United States only since 1973 when the Supreme Court ruled that reproductive choices are protected from government intrusion by the constitutional right to privacy. Despite its legal status, abortion is not universally available to American women. The federal government and many states have enacted laws to restrict or deny abortions to Native Americans who use federally funded health services on reservations, to military and Peace Corps personnel and their dependents, to poor women who cannot afford health services without financial assistance, and to minors without parental consent. Counselors and health care practitioners who work in federally funded medical settings risk losing those funds if they even mention the possibility of abortion to pregnant women. In some parts of the country it is difficult to find physicians or clinics offering abortion services because anti-choice protesters have harassed them out of business.

There are many reasons why a woman may consider seeking an abortion. Her pregnancy may be unintended because she lacked birth control information, because contraceptives were unavailable to her, or because her contraceptive failed. Sexual intercourse that led to the pregnancy may itself have been unwanted and due to rape, incest, domestic violence, or pressure from her partner. Perhaps she is homeless or addicted and exchanged sex for shelter, money, or drugs. Her pregnancy may have been planned, but then she found herself in a medical or financial situation that would make having her baby dangerous or unethical.

The decision to seek an abortion is never an easy one, but it is a decision that each woman must make for herself, without pressure from others. Counselors and psychotherapists should be aware of their own attitudes and values, and try to provide supportive, nonjudgmental assistance to women who are making reproductive decisions. Clients should be encouraged to consider all of their options and imagine the long- and short-range consequences of each. Raising a child (especially as a single parent) is expensive, often difficult, and results in constricted educational, occupational, and social opportunities. The psychological pain of giving up a child for adoption is often severe and long lasting (Lethbridge, 1995). Abortion is physically painful, and the later in gestation that it occurs, the more difficult it is (Wells, 1989). Giving birth is also painful, and it carries higher risks than abortion (Russo, 1996). Given that women have been socialized to put others' needs before their own, that they know others will condemn them for choosing to terminate their pregnancies, that they may fear walking past anti-abortion activists to enter the clinic, and that they may have difficulty raising the funds to pay for the procedure, making a decision to have an abortion will never be simple. If the pregnancy was wanted and the woman already feels an attachment to the fetus, the decision to have an abortion will be even more difficult.

How do women cope with abortion? When women freely choose legal abortions, they usually cope quite well. Negative emotional aftereffects are uncommon; the most frequently reported emotion is relief (Lemkau, 1988). Researchers have generally found that psychological distress scores drop immediately after abortions and remain low for several weeks afterward. (See Adler et al., 1990, for a review.) Women who expect to cope well with abortion generally do (Mueller & Major, 1989). The more social support women have from their families and friends, the better they cope. When their male partners' disagree with their decision to have an abortion, women appear to experience psychological distress only when they themselves are not certain they have made the right choice (Major, Cozzarelli, Testa, & Mueller, 1992). Predictors of poor coping include strong religious or cultural beliefs that abortion is wrong, low social support, a history of emotional problems, pressure from others to consent to an abortion, and the expectation that coping will be difficult (Adler et al., 1990).

Results of the research briefly described in the preceding suggest that counselors and therapists can best assist clients who choose abortion by ascertaining that their decision is their own and, if so, supporting it, encouraging them to find a supportive person to accompany them to the clinic for the procedure, teaching positive coping techniques, encouraging self-efficacy and the expectation that they will cope well, and intervening appropriately if any signs of psychological distress appear. Clinicians who expect to work frequently with women who are making reproductive decisions should familiarize themselves with the details of abortion procedures in order to answer questions about them. See Lethbridge (1995) for clear summaries of common procedures, a review of the literature on the emotional sequelae of abortion and of giving up infants for adoption, and suggestions about factors clients should consider in reaching their decisions.

# PREGNANCY

Pregnancy is a major life event that affects many important aspects of women's lives; it causes changes in body size and functioning, changes in roles and identity, and changes in relationships. Like other life events, pregnancy can be a stressful experience that necessitates adjustment and the implementation of coping strategies.

Although it is a normative experience, there is a paucity of psychological research on the normal course of events that occur during most pregnancies. Instead, pregnancy is commonly viewed as a nine-month-long illness (Myers & Grasmick, 1990), an emotional upheaval or crisis, or a time of bliss and emotional well-being. These views are extreme, and none is supported by empirical data. Pregnancy can perhaps be best described as a developmental transition.

Are there particular milestones that most women experience during this transition? Through his interviews with a diverse group of pregnant women, Lee (1995) identified a set of events that most participants considered to be the major or central events of their pregnancies. In a follow-up study, he asked a group of mothers to rate the emotional impact of each of the events. The four events with the most emotional impact (for both first and subsequent pregnancies) were seeing the baby for the first time, finding out about the pregnancy, getting the results of prenatal tests, and feeling fetal movements. Results of these studies have educational and clinical implications. Counselors, psychotherapists, and childbirth educators may be better able to help women adjust to pregnancy and prepare for parenthood by providing them with an opportunity to discuss the thoughts, feelings, and behaviors that accompany these milestones.

Knowledge of the normative events that women experience during pregnancy may also guide clinicians as they assist women in the identification and mastery of developmental tasks. The tasks of pregnancy have been described in different ways (Rubin, 1984; Seegmiller, 1993). Examples of these tasks include the provision of a safe environment for oneself and one's fetus, becoming attached to the fetus, preparation for the maternal role, and forming a new relationship with one's own mother. The salience of these tasks changes over the course of the pregnancy. During the first trimester, for example, pregnant women may be especially concerned with adopting a healthier lifestyle. Becoming attached to the fetus takes precedence during the second trimester when fetal movement is first detected. During the third trimester, a primary task is preparing for the new role of mother or for changes in family routines and interactions that an additional child will bring.

Women report a variety of physical and emotional experiences during pregnancy (Striegel-Moore, Goldman, Garvin, & Rodin, 1996). During the first trimester, women complain of moodiness, fatigue, nausea, and vomiting. Heartburn and fatigue are frequent problems during the second and third trimesters. Coping with these symptoms may require women to make changes in their work and family roles (O'Brien & Naber, 1992). Clinicians should validate these experiences as prevalent, normal, and uncomfortable and suggest strategies for adjusting to and managing them. Pregnant women have not been found to differ significantly from control groups on standardized measures of anxiety or depression (Striegel-Moore et al, 1996). These data refute the notion that pregnant women are either in a state of emotional turmoil or continual bliss.

Women's concerns or worries also vary across the course of pregnancy (Statham, Green, & Kafetsios, 1997). At 16 weeks women's most common worries were about miscarriage, money, giving birth, having a healthy baby, and coping with a new baby. The most common concern was about the baby's health. This concern was mentioned by some women throughout the course of pregnancy, but it was reported most frequently at 16 weeks (the time when many women have amniocentesis) and 35 weeks and least frequently at 22 weeks. The women who were the most worried about their babies' health were those who had high trait anxiety scores, had mixed reactions to their pregnancies, had previously given birth to unhealthy infants, or believed there was a high likelihood that their babies would have problems. Thus, concerns about infants' health are widespread, and some women may need social support and reassurance throughout their pregnancies. Results of prenatal testing may calm fear or heighten it, and counselors should be prepared to help women deal with either reaction.

High levels of stress and anxiety have important implications for fetal health, yet there is little research available about the duration and severity of different stressors that are associated with pregnancy. Psychosocial factors such as stressful situations, trait anxiety, and life changes have been associated with pregnancy and birth complications such as preeclampsia, preterm labor, and prolonged labor (Levin & DeFrank, 1988; Lobel, 1994; Paarlberg, Vingerhoets, Passchier, Dekker, & Van Geijn, 1995). Important health benefits could accrue to both mothers and babies if stress management techniques were routinely taught to pregnant women. The least that should be done is to identify women who are at high risk for stress and anxiety-related complications and refer them for specialized counseling, such as relaxation training, problem-solving skills, and support groups (Park, Moore, Turner, & Adler, 1997; Zayas & Busch-Rossnagel, 1992). Women who may be at elevated risk for stress during pregnancy include those with mental illnesses (Mowbray, Oyserman, Zemencuk, & Ross, 1995), low income women (Norbeck & Anderson, 1989), and Latina women (Zayas & Busch-Rossnagel, 1992). Weight gain during pregnancy may be particularly stressful for women who have a history of eating disorders (Siegel & Chrisler, 1998).

Counselors and psychotherapists can play an important role in helping women to adjust to and cope with the physical, psychological, and social changes they experience during pregnancy. They can also work with women and their partners as they prepare for childbirth. Sexual assault and abuse survivors may need to discuss painful memories or feelings of vulnerability that may interfere with coping during pregnancy and birthing. They can be helped to identify and practice strategies for managing their fears of giving birth, which may be exacerbated by their memories of sexual assault. Other issues that may influence women's progress and experiences during labor and delivery include conflicts in their romantic relationships and ambivalence about motherhood.

## BIRTH

Childbirth is a memorable, meaningful, and challenging event in women's lives. It can be both exhilarating and anxiety provoking, empowering and disappointing, a source of accomplishment or failure. Because there are many psychological aspects of birthing, psychologists could play an important role through both research and clinical practice in working to improve women's experiences. Knowledge of current research and theory about childbirth preparation, coping, and the meaning of childbirth experiences for women will assist counselors and psychotherapists in their efforts.

## Preparing for Birth

There are a variety of ways for pregnant women to prepare for childbirth. Most middle-class women attend a series of formal childbirth education classes with a "coach," who is usually the father of the baby. The primary objectives of childbirth education classes are to provide women with (1) factual information about pregnancy, labor, delivery, and the postpartum period; (2) social support; and (3) relaxation training. The classes are designed to help women make decisions about their health care, assume a central and active role in the process of childbirth, and cope with the concomitant pain and anxiety (F. H. Nichols & Humenick, 1988).

Owing to methodological flaws in the literature and the variability of women's experiences, it is difficult to make definitive statements about the effectiveness of childbirth education in realizing its goals (Beck & Siegel, 1980; Swanson-Hyland, 1995; Wideman & Singer, 1984). Attending childbirth education classes is generally associated with decreased pain perception (Lowe, 1989), decreased use of pain medication (Hetherington, 1990), increased perceived control (Hart & Foster, 1997), and increased confidence (Hillier & Slade, 1989). Childbirth preparation appears to have less impact on satisfaction with the birthing experience (M. R. Nichols, 1995; Waldenstrom, Borg, Olsson, Skold, & Wall, 1996).

Women also prepare for birth by reading and talking with friends and family about it. Johnston-Robledo (1998) found that low-income women are less likely than higher income women to attend formal classes and more likely to obtain information and guidance from their mothers. These alternative methods of preparation appear to be effective, as the birth outcomes of women who attend classes are often similar to those who do not (Johnston-Robledo, 1998; Lumley & Brown, 1993).

Researchers have emphasized the need to integrate more psychological aspects of pregnancy, labor, and birthing into the preparation process. These include acceptance of and adjustment to the pregnancy, preparing to become a parent or add another child to the family, developing self-confidence, and making major decisions about health care (Cook, 1997; Handfield & Bell, 1995; Lowe, 1996; Nolan & Hicks, 1997). Clinical and counseling psychologists can help to make these courses more comprehensive by offering to consult with local childbirth educators or by volunteering to give a lecture on psychological issues during the course. Peterson (1996) suggested that psychotherapists assist pregnant women and their partners with these and other issues through prenatal counseling services.

## Coping During Childbirth

Women cope with the pain and anxiety associated with birthing in many ways. One of the most effective ways is social support from their partners, friends, families, and health care providers. Social support during labor can be emotional (i.e., encouragement and comfort), informational (i.e., advice), tangible (e.g., massage), and advocacy (e.g., negotiating with medical staff) (Hodnett, 1996). Social support from partners has been found to be related to decreased pain perception (Dannenbring, Stevens, & House, 1997) and positive evaluation of one's performance during childbirth (Mackey, 1995). Social support from health care providers has been found to be related to increased perceived control, decreased pain medication

(Hodnett & Osborn, 1989), shorter labors, fewer forceps and cesarean sections, and higher levels of satisfaction (Zhang, Bernasko, Leybovich, Fahs, & Hatch, 1996). Health care providers are an especially important source of support for low-income women (Johnston-Robledo, 1997).

Other coping strategies that women use include breathing techniques, walking or remaining upright, gripping, backrubbing, medication, and visualization. Women who attend childbirth classes are given the opportunity to practice most of these techniques. More research is needed on the efficacy of these techniques and on development of women's self-efficacy.

## Childbirth Experiences

Women are often eager to discuss their childbirth experiences, regardless of whether they are positive or negative. Conversations with mothers about their experiences can help to identify the factors that contribute to the quality of the experiences and provide insights for psychological interventions. One of the most important predictors of a satisfying birthing experience is the ability to remain in control. This means control over one's own behaviors (Mackey, 1995), control over medical decisions regarding one's care (Green, Coupland, & Kitzinger, 1990), and physical and mental awareness during labor and delivery (Doering, Entwisle, & Quinlan, 1980). Other predictors of a positive experience include information about childbirth (Crowe & von Baeyer, 1989; Hallgren, Kihlgren, Norberg, & Forslin, 1995), social support, and satisfaction with maternity care. Women tend to be more satisfied with maternity care if they are able to assume an active role in decision-making (Brown & Lumley, 1998; Seguin, Therrien, Champagne, & Larouche, 1989).

DiMatteo, Kahn, and Berry (1993) conducted focus groups to provide postpartum women with an opportunity to discuss their childbirth experiences. The most important themes the researchers identified were pain and emotional reactions that differed from what the women had expected, financial concerns, loss of autonomy and control, and the value of support during labor and birth. In conversations with postpartum women Mackey (1995) found that they emphasized their performance during labor and birthing. The women compared their coping behaviors to the standards set by their childbirth educators, compared themselves to other women in labor, and related feedback about their performance that they had received from health care providers.

Results of these studies suggest the importance of encouraging pregnant women to discuss their goals, expectations, and plans for birthing. Counselors and psychotherapists can assist women in developing realistic expectations of the demands of childbirth and of their own performance. Postpartum women should be encouraged to discuss their childbirth experiences. This opportunity may help them to reconcile ambivalent feelings about the experience, themselves, their partners, or their infants. The quality of women's experiences with childbirth may influence adjustment during the transition to parenthood (Mercer, 1986) and may have a long-term impact on their self-esteem and self-confidence (Simkin, 1991). Clearly, there is a need for counselors and psychotherapists to become more involved in assisting women through the pivotal life event of childbirth.

## REPRODUCTIVE TECHNOLOGIES

A staggering number of new medical technologies have been developed in recent years, and several of the best known are associated with reproduction. In vitro fertilization, prenatal diagnostic testing, electronic fetal monitoring, and cesarean section are important to any consideration of women's reproductive experiences. The latter three were originally used only in high-risk situations, but are now applied much more widely. Cesarean sections, for example, were used in only 4.5 percent of births in the United States in 1965, but by 1991 they were used in 23.5 percent of U.S. births (Stanton & Danoff-Burg, 1995). The increasing use of technology has advanced the medicalization of pregnancy and birth, and it has changed women's experience of these processes.

Many women are ambivalent about reproductive technologies. On the one hand, they have been hailed as advancing the goals of women's liberation. With in vitro fertilization lesbians and heterosexual women without partners have been able to conceive and bear children. Prenatal testing has alerted parents to possible birth defects, which allows them time to adjust to the news before their children are born or to consider terminating the pregnancy. Cesarean sections and fetal monitoring during labor have saved the lives of many women and their babies. On the other hand, reproductive technologies have been described as instruments of patriarchal domination (Wajcman, 1991). Fertility treatments can be seen as enforcing the motherhood mandate and reducing women to egg donors and incubators. Prenatal testing has been used to abort fetuses that are the "wrong" sex or are otherwise deemed to be imperfect. Electronic fetal monitoring interferes with women's freedom of movement during labor, which may impair coping. Many women have felt robbed of the ability to control the birth process by medical personnel who have insisted on using fetal monitors or cesarean sections when the women preferred not to have them.

## Infertility

Infertility, which is defined as the inability to conceive after one year of regular attempts to do so, affects about 2.3 million American women. Another 2.6 million women in the United States are described as having impaired fecundity, which is defined as having difficulty or risking danger in carrying a fetus to term (Stanton & Danoff-Burg, 1995). Infertility rates do not seem to be increasing, although we hear more talk about it now than used to be common. This may be due to several factors, including that (1) fewer infants are available for adoption because abortion is legal and because it is now socially acceptable for unwed mothers to raise their own children, and (2) with the availability of reproductive technologies, infertility can be treated and is now considered to be a "disease."

Prior to 1980 most people thought of infertility as a psychosomatic disorder. Women who could not conceive were referred to psychiatrists because they were thought to be conflicted about their sexual identity or rejecting their traditional roles. Couples were told that anxiety was responsible for their failures to conceive; if they could "just relax and stop worrying," the woman would soon find herself pregnant. Although stress has been shown to impair ovulation and spermatogenesis in certain circumstances, now that 80 percent of infertility cases can be traced to organic causes, most medical and psychological professionals have ceased to give credence to the psychosomatic model (Stanton & Danoff-Burg, 1995). Infertile women, however, may still hear these blaming messages from lay sources or outdated advice books.

In their review of the psychological literature on infertility Dunkel-Schetter and Lobel (1991) found differences between clinical and empirical work. Clinicians whose work was based on people they had seen in therapy tended to describe infertility as producing serious and enduring distress that could interfere with normal activities. Results of empirical studies that compared infertile and fertile women tended to show that the two groups did not differ significantly from each other on measures of self-esteem, relationship satisfaction, and psychological functioning. It may be that only the most distressed women talk to therapists about their infertility and/or that people tend to volunteer for research projects when they are feeling upbeat (Stanton & Danoff-Burg, 1995). Furthermore, the women most likely to seek psychotherapy or infertility treatment come from the higher socioeconomic classes, and they may differ from other infertile women in many ways. What is clear is that counselors and therapists should not expect women to have any one reaction to infertility; women may feel distress, disappointment, ambivalence, or relief. They may adjust to the diagnosis easily or with difficulty. Social support and active coping have been found to predict psychological adjustment (Stanton & Danoff-Burg, 1995).

Studies (e.g., Abbey, Andrews, & Halman, 1991) of couples coping with infertility have revealed gender differences. Men rate having children as less important to them than do women. Women are more likely than men to initiate medical treatments, and they are more likely to bear the burdens of the treatments (i.e., submitting to repeated medical tests, experiencing painful procedures, and monitoring themselves for indications of pregnancy). Most women have been raised with the assumption that they would and should become mothers, and therefore the role of parent may be more important to their identity than it is to men's. As a result, women may feel implicit or explicit pressure to try infertility treatments, perhaps to prove to themselves and others how much they want a child (Unger & Crawford, 1996).

Infertility technologies, such as in vitro fertilization (IVF), are not universally available. They are very expensive and are not covered by many insurance plans. The procedures are time consuming, and result in some women taking leaves from their jobs in order to concentrate on trying to become pregnant. Success rates are low (15 percent to 20 percent), and many women try IVF several times. IVF is painful and risky. The fertility drugs and surgical procedures have unpleasant side effects and potentially dangerous complications (including multiple fetuses), and women rate IVF as very stressful (Adler, Keyes, & Robertson, 1991). Treatment that results in repeated failures is disappointing, can lead to depression, and may only result in delaying and prolonging adjustment to childless status (Adler et al., 1991; Unger & Crawford, 1996). Treatment that results in multiple births can strain families financially and emotionally.

Clinicians who work with infertile women should have a good understanding of the organic causes of the condition and of the potential treatments for it. See Garner (1995) for a thorough review of causes of infertility and Sandelowski (1995) and Adler et al. (1991) for clear explanations of IVF and related procedures.

## Prenatal Diagnostic Screening and Surveillance

Commonly used prenatal technologies include amniocentesis, chorionic villus sampling, α-fetoprotein testing, and ultrasonography. Amniocentesis is a test for chromosomal abnormalities, which is generally performed at around the 16th week of pregnancy. It involves removing a sample of amniotic fluid through a needle that is inserted into the uterus through the woman's abdomen. Chorionic villus sampling (CVS) is a method of evaluating the DNA of the fetus. It involves obtaining a sample of placental tissue through a catheter inserted into the cervix or via a needle inserted into the abdomen; this procedure can be done as early as the 9th week of pregnancy. α-Fetoprotein testing is a test for elevated antigen levels that indicate neural tube defects (e.g., spina bifida) in the fetus. A sample of the woman's blood can be drawn and examined around the 16th week of pregnancy. If abnormal levels are found, amniocentesis is usually recommended. Ultrasonography is the use of inaudible high-frequency sound waves to produce an image of the fetus by recording echoes as they strike tissues of different densities. It can be used as early as the 4th week of pregnancy, and can be repeated at intervals to follow the development of the fetus throughout the pregnancy. Ultrasonography is the most commonly used of the prenatal technologies; in fact, many obstetricians believe that each pregnant woman should have at least one ultrasonic examination (Merck Research Laboratories, 1992).

Some feminist scholars and women's health activists have expressed concerns that these technological advances have interfered with the normal biological and experiential rhythms of pregnancy and replaced them with technological milestones (Beeson, 1984; Rapp, 1988; Rothman, 1986). For example, the ultrasound picture, which is often printed and given to the couple to take home, may replace quickening (the first felt fetal movement) as the indication that the pregnancy is "real" and as the motivation to form an attachment to the fetus. Thus, ultrasound changes the "realization" of one's baby from a private event in the second trimester to a public medical/technological event in the first trimester. Rothman (1986) has suggested that technology erodes the very idea of the trimesters; pregnancy may now be experienced as having only two phases: before and after prenatal testing. She has found that some women are reluctant to accept or "invest" in their pregnancies until the technologies have assured them that it is "safe" to do so, and this can inhibit psychological adjustment.

Two other issues are important to consider. First, prenatal technologies alter the balance of medical attention between the woman and her fetus. It used to be clear who the obstetrician's patient was. Prenatal care once consisted entirely of monitoring the woman's health, educating her about nutrition and other matters that would promote good health for her and her future child, and preparing her for the birth experience. Fetal surveillance through ultrasound has brought the previously hidden fetus into view, and diagnostic technologies have added another "patient" who may need medical care. This creates a dual allegiance for the physician, may promote a notion of the woman as a vessel rather than as person or patient, and, in cases where the medical needs of the woman and fetus conflict or where the woman and physician differ on what steps should be taken, can result in the woman being compelled to accept medical interventions against her will. In the majority of cases in which physicians and hospitals sought court ordered treatment interventions, the women were ethnic minorities (Kolder, Gallagher, & Parsons, 1987).

Second, the technologies provide information that once learned cannot be forgotten. Women who have been told the sex of the fetus, for example, may later regret that they did not get to experience that as a surprise at birth. Similarly, information about genetic abnormalities is often not definitive and may lead to difficult decisions that parents may prefer not to make. Philosophical questions such as what constitutes a disability need to be addressed. Questions about how severe the disability will be and whether the parents can cope with the care required cannot be answered by prenatal tests. For example, the knowledge that one's offspring has Down's syndrome does not provide information about whether the mental retardation and physical defects will be mild and allow a good quality of life or severe and result in a poor quality of life.

Counselors and psychotherapists may thus be called upon to assist women in making more than one set of decisions: (1) whether to have the tests and (2) whether to have an abortion if the tests result in a diagnosis. Amniocentesis and CVS are painful, and they are not without risk. Miscarriages can and do result from these procedures. A considerable amount of stress and anxiety are caused by the procedures, especially in couples who have family histories of genetic disorders. Women who know that they would never choose to have an abortion may worry that the test results would spoil their enjoyment of pregnancy and anticipation of birth, and, in fact, people with pro-choice attitudes have also been found to have positive attitudes toward prenatal genetic screening (Furr & Seger, 1998). However, it is difficult to resist technologies that have become part of routine practice, and health care professionals may imply that submitting to the procedures is part of being a good and responsible mother (Sandelowski, 1995). α-Fetoprotein testing results in a high number of false-positives, and additional tests may be required (Sandelowski, 1995). Amniocentesis results are not available until the second trimester, which means a later abortion than is usual. Second trimester abortions are more physically painful and emotionally difficult (Adler et al., 1990).

Clinicians who work with pregnant women should help them to weigh the costs and benefits of prenatal diagnostic screening. The test results can provide comfort and reassurance or increase risks and worries. They may increase the woman's control by allowing her to make reproductive decisions, or they may reduce her control as the physicians shift their sense of who their patient is. The tests also create new standards for good mothers and perfect babies, and the personal, social, and political consequences of these standards need to be understood. (See Asch, 1988, for a disability activist's perspective.) Counselors and therapists can be valuable in assisting parents in adjusting to the idea that their children will have genetic disorders, and they can teach stress and pain management techniques (e.g., distraction, imagery, deep breathing) for use in coping during the test procedures.

## Birth-Related Technologies

The electronic fetal monitor permits continual fetal surveillance during labor via ultrasound and electrocardiography. It allows medical personnel to monitor fetal heart rate and the frequency, intensity, and duration of uterine contractions. Results of studies of the effectiveness of fetal monitoring equipment do not provide solid support for its routine use, even in high-risk pregnancies; although it provides more information than would otherwise be available, the interpretation of the information is complicated and subject to error (Sandelowski, 1995).

Why would not any woman in labor want as much information as possible to guide the process? As stated earlier, technological devices alter the experience of birth. The woman's movement and the positions she can assume are restricted because she is attached to the machinery and because her movements interfere with the information being recorded. The machine may interfere with tactile contact (e.g., massage, hugging) from her partner or birth coach. Mere presence of the machine draws attention to it and away from the laboring woman. Information about contractions is gained from the equipment rather than from questioning, palpating, or observing the woman herself. Starkman (1976) questioned women about their responses to the electronic fetal monitor. Women variously reported perceiving the machine as an extension of themselves or their obstetricians, as a protector of themselves and their babies, or as a "mechanical monster" responsible for additional discomfort during labor.

Finally, it is important to realize that the electronic fetal monitor is likely to lead to further technological intervention. The machine itself is a reminder of technology's potential, it provides information about intrauterine events that would not otherwise be available, and it is associated with obstetrical risks. Therefore, some have suggested that the very presence of fetal monitoring equipment increases the probability that a cesarean section or other invasive technique will be performed (Sandelowski, 1995).

Cesarean section is the most common type of major surgery in the United States, and it accounts for almost 25 percent of all births (National Center for Health Statistics, 1990). Cesareans were first performed in the 1800s, and cannot be considered a "new" reproductive technology. However, the increase in the frequency of cesarean sections can be traced, at least in part, to the other technologies we have discussed, as they have changed the definition of "fetal distress" (Hurst & Summey, 1984). Most medical texts recommend cesareans in cases of fetal distress, prolonged labor, unusually large fetuses or women with unusually small pelvises, or when the woman has a condition such as herpes that could be transmitted to the infant during birth (Marieskind, 1982).

Rates of cesarean sections vary from hospital to hospital and from one geographical region to another. The procedure tends to be performed more frequently in women of higher socioeconomic classes, who have private medical insurance, and who have had cesarean sections in previous births (Gould, Davey, & Stafford, 1989; Hurst & Summey, 1984; Stafford, 1990). Cesarean rates are correlated with number of malpractice claims against the hospital and with how likely the physician thinks the patient would be to sue if something went wrong (Localio et al., 1993). Cesareans are also performed for older mothers, when the fetus is in the breech position, and to time the birth for the physician's convenience (Hurst & Summey, 1984). The maternal mortality rate for cesareans is about four times higher than for vaginal births, and at least one third of women contract infections following a cesarean section (Ruzek, 1991).

Women who have unplanned cesareans report being less satisfied with their birth experience than those who expected to have a cesarean or those who gave birth vaginally (Marut & Mercer, 1979; Padawer, Fagan, Janoff-Bulman, Strickland, & Chorowski, 1988). The emergency nature of the surgery is frightening and disruptive; it results in a loss of control for the laboring woman and violates her expectations for the experience. Cesarean births are associated with more postpartum anxiety and depression (Edwards, Porter, & Stein, 1994). Women who are recovering from abdominal surgery are fatigued and in pain, and they find it difficult to care for themselves and their infants (Davies, 1982). Surgical aftereffects usually result in a delay between the birth and the woman's opportunity to bond with her baby. She may find lifting, holding, and feeding the baby difficult for some time (Davies, 1982). Recovery from a cesarean section can take as long as three to six months, which is longer than most maternity leaves (Tulman, 1988). The stress of coping with postsurgical pain and other recovery matters may interfere with a woman's adjustment to motherhood and complicate her resumption of other roles. After a meta-analysis of 43 studies of psychosocial outcomes of cesareans, DiMatteo and her colleagues (1996) reported that women who had had cesarean sections were less satisfied with the childbirth experience, delayed longer before first interacting with their infants, were less likely to breastfeed, reacted less positively to their infants, and interacted less with their infants once they went home than did other new mothers.

## MOTHERHOOD

When women become mothers for the first time, they are faced with many challenges. These may include recovering from childbirth, meeting the demands of an infant, negotiating new issues with a partner, making decisions about paid employment, and facing the realities of motherhood, which often vary from expectations. These tasks are difficult, yet women are rarely given the support and encouragement they need to accomplish them. As a result, new mothers may experience depression, anxiety, frustration, and isolation. Counselors and psychotherapists can facilitate this transition by encouraging women to discuss their expectations, needs, and concerns and by providing them with the information, coping strategies, skills, and resources they need to meet the challenges of motherhood.

### Postpartum Adjustment

The postpartum period (i.e., the six weeks following the birth of an infant) is a difficult time for new mothers, yet psychologists have paid very little attention to women's experiences during this time. In their focus groups with new mothers, DiMatteo, Kahn, and Berry (1993) found two predominant themes: unexpected pain and emotions. The women reported being disturbed and surprised by the physical pain that arose from incision sites (episiotomy or cesarean) and hemorrhoids. The women also reported feeling detached from their babies, critical of their birthing experiences, and unprepared for apparently uncontrollable emotions, especially sadness. Other physical sources of discomfort during the immediate postpartum period include breast engorgement, nipple soreness, uterine cramps, constipation, and pain in the vagina, perineum, and rectum. New mothers must also cope with vaginal bleeding and discharge, which can last up to 45 days, and the difficulty and delay in resuming normal activities (e.g., sitting, lifting, driving, sexual intercourse).

Women have expressed many concerns during the postpartum period. Researchers have found the following to be among the most frequent: infants' feeding, health, and behavior; fatigue; sore breasts; body image issues (Smith, 1989). New mothers also worry about their competence as mothers, changes in their intimate relationships, and career or job-related matters (Mercer, 1986). See Walker (1995) for a review of the literature on weight gain after childbirth. As during pregnancy, body image and weight concerns may be especially complicated for women who have struggled with eating disorders.

Postpartum women have information needs that parallel their concerns. Moran, Holt, and Martin (1997) interviewed women seven weeks after their babies were born and found that their participants wanted more information about self-care (e.g., exercise, nutrition, fatigue, resuming normal activities) and baby care (e.g., consoling infants, recognizing illnesses, getting the babies on a schedule). First-time mothers, young mothers, and those with less than a high school education and less social support had the highest needs for information.

New mothers are not routinely provided with the education and support necessary for a smooth postpartum adjustment. Women who give birth vaginally typically spend less than 48 hours after childbirth in the hospital, and therefore have limited opportunities to acquire information and support from health care practitioners. Childbirth education classes focus on pregnancy, labor, and birthing; attendance at these classes is unrelated to postpartum adjustment (M. R. Nichols, 1995), need for additional postpartum information (Moran et al., 1997), and decision-making about postpartum issues (Handfield & Bell, 1995). Cook (1997) has argued for an expansion of the childbirth education curriculum; however, expectant parents may not be ready to assimilate the information. Formal postpartum follow-up programs may be a more effective way to provide women with the support and information they need (Moran et al., 1997). Counselors and psychotherapists can work to improve women's postpartum experiences by discussing concerns and expectations for the postpartum period toward the end of pregnancy, leading support groups for new mothers, and recognizing and addressing problems in postpartum adjustment as they arise.

## The Transition to Motherhood

The process of becoming a mother is complicated by popular beliefs about mothers. The motherhood mandate (Russo, 1976), the expectation that all women desire to be mothers, leads to the assumption that adult womanhood is synonymous with motherhood. Women themselves have often associated motherhood with "official" adulthood (Johnston-Robledo & Torres, 2000; Mercer, 1986). New mothers are also influenced by a set of popular beliefs known as the motherhood mystique (Hoffnung, 1989), namely that motherhood is natural, easy, and always enjoyable. These beliefs may hinder communication about the difficulties of being a mother, and they probably contribute to the unrealistic expectations many pregnant women have about parenting.

Genevie and Margolies (1987) found pregnant women's fantasies about motherhood to be extremely idealistic. Their participants believed that motherhood would be easy for them and that they would be more patient than other mothers with their children. The women who held these romantic notions later reported more negative feelings about motherhood than the more realistic women. Mercer (1986) found that most postpartum women she interviewed were either unsure about what motherhood would be like or expected motherhood to be fun, exciting, or easy. Few women in her study had realistic expectations about parenting that included both its positive and negative aspects. Pregnant women who are married or in committed heterosexual relationships may also have high expectations for an egalitarian division of labor (Ruble, Fleming, Hackel, & Stangor, 1988), which are likely to be violated; researchers often find that parenthood leads to a more traditional division of labor (Perkins & DeMeis, 1996; Sanchez & Thomson, 1997).

Based on surveys of new mothers at six weeks postpartum, McVeigh (1997) identified five major categories of concerns. These were the difficulty of infant care (e.g., boring, isolating), fatigue, lack of time, lack of preparation, and need for support from partners. She concluded that there is a conspiracy of silence about the difficulties of motherhood, and she suggested that women need structured community-based opportunities to share knowledge and experiences with other women. Mercer (1986) asked new mothers at one month postpartum if they had any advice for other new mothers. Several had no advice; the others said women needed to know that mothering is difficult and time consuming, that mothers need to learn to be flexible and patient, and that it helps to talk to others about the experience.

Counselors and psychotherapists can facilitate the transition to parenthood for expectant parents by enhancing their communication skills, preparing them for what to expect (especially in regard to infant behavior), helping them to anticipate and plan for changes in lifestyle and roles, and suggesting coping strategies. Mercer (1986) found that the most common coping strategies used by new mothers at one month postpartum were talking with others, asking questions or reading, and taking time to be alone or to go out without their babies. Psychologists can help prepare women for new motherhood by discussing with them the difficulties inherent in the normal adjustment process and minimizing guilt, depression, and anxiety when women's expectations about new motherhood are violated. For first-person accounts of mothering experiences under a diverse set of circumstances, see Coll, Surrey, and Weingarten (1998).

## Postpartum Depression

Although some level of anxiety and depression accompanies any stressful life event, some new mothers may experience a longer and more serious depression that requires clinical attention. Approximately 10 percent of women experience a diagnosable postpartum depression, which is characterized by sadness, crying, self-blame, loss of control, irritability, difficulty sleeping, anxiety, and tension (Cox, 1986). Risk factors for postpartum depression include a family history of depression (O'Hara, Schlechte, Lewis, & Varner, 1991), depression during pregnancy (Graff, Dyck, & Shallow, 1991), or a preexisting psychological disorder (Mowbray, Oyserman, Zemencuk, & Ross, 1995).

Empirical research does not support a direct connection between hormones and postpartum depression (Llewellyn, Stowe, & Nemeroff, 1997; Nicholson, 1998). Researchers (Cutrona & Troutman, 1986; Gotlib, Whiffen, Wallace, & Mount, 1991; Terry, Mayocchi, & Hynes, 1996; Whiffen, 1992) have examined the role of various stressors and found that a dissatisfying marriage, ineffective coping strategies, and fussy infants can complicate the transition to parenthood and contribute to postpartum depression. Social support may alleviate these stressors and help to prevent postpartum depression (Collins, Dunkel-Schetter, Lobel, & Scrimshaw, 1993; Terry et al., 1996). Whether postpartum depression is distinct from other forms of depression is currently being debated (Nicholson, 1998; Whiffen, 1992), yet "postpartum onset" is a subtype of clinical depression according to the *DSM-IV* (American Psychiatric Association, 1994). Some feminist psychologists (Lee, 1997; Mauthner, 1993; Nicholson, 1998) view postpartum depression as a normal reaction to the major social and personal adjustments that women are required to make without the necessary social and structural support. It is interesting to note that women are less likely to experience postpartum depression in cultures that recognize and support the efforts of new mothers (Stern & Kruckman, 1983; Zelkowitz, 1996).

Counselors and psychotherapists can help women to cope with postpartum depression by validating their experiences and emotional reactions and acknowledging that depressive reactions often follow major life events. Psychological researchers should continue to examine the psychosocial factors that may contribute to postpartum depression, such as role changes, disappointment with the childbirth experience, and lack of social support. Clinical psychologists should design interventions to prevent or treat postpartum depression that focus on these variables. Finally, feminists and women's health activists should advocate for new mothers by working for changes in social structures and public policy that may provide women with the resources they need to adjust optimally to motherhood.

## MENOPAUSE

Menopause refers to the cessation of reproductive capacity, and it is defined as 12 months without a menstrual period. It occurs as a result of age-related changes that lead to the gradual diminishing of the production of ovarian hormones. The average age of American women at menopause is 51 years, but it can occur naturally at any age between 40 and 60 (Golub, 1992). The process that leads to menopause (known as perimenopause) takes about seven years to complete. Therefore, a woman who will reach menopause at age 50 will probably notice the first changes in her menstrual cycle at around age 43. Early changes are likely to include menstrual cycle irregularity, including shorter or longer cycles and heavier or lighter bleeding, and, for some, the return of menstrual cramps.

Perhaps because it is associated with aging, menopause is often viewed in Western societies as a negative event. However, surveys (e.g., Maoz, Dowty, Antonovsky, & Wijsenbeek, 1970; Neugarten, Wood, Kraines, & Loomis, 1968) of midlife women have typically found that participants have mixed feelings. The downside of menopause, women say, is loss of fertility, physiological changes that accompany it, feeling less feminine, having a clear sign of aging, and a belief that it has come too soon. The upside is the end of dealing with menstrual periods, the end of contraceptive concerns, and a general sense of liberation. Older women typically have more positive attitudes toward menopause than younger women, and they are more likely than younger women to agree that postmenopausal women feel freer, calmer, and more confident than ever. Many women find that the worst part of the perimenopause is not knowing what to expect.

One reason why women do not know what to expect is that until recently menopause was not spoken about very much; women tended to keep their experiences private. However, knowing about others' experiences doesn't help much in predicting one's own. Peri-menopausal physiological changes and women's emotional reactions to them are highly variable. The most common menopause-related symptom is the hot flash (or flush), which, surveys show, is experienced by between 43 percent and 93 percent of women (Woods, 1982). Other frequent symptoms include sweating, headaches, vertigo, fatigue, weight gain, aches and pains, insomnia, irritability, tingling sensations, and anxiety. Stress is known to trigger hot flashes, as do caffeine, alcohol, hot weather, and spicy foods (Voda, 1982). The notion that depression is linked to menopause (involutional melancholia) is not empirically supportable; data from large surveys (e.g., McKinley, McKinley, & Brambilla, 1987) indicate that women are no more likely to be depressed at midlife than they are at other developmental stages.

Despite the increasing medicalization of menopause, it is not a deficiency disease that requires hormonal replacement. It is best thought of as a developmental phase to which one must adjust or a normal transitional condition with which one must cope. Women may have difficulty adjusting to the idea of menopause if they have negative attitudes toward aging, if they accept the idea that menopause is a disorder, or if they regret that they will not have further opportunities to become pregnant. These are all issues with which talking to a good counselor or psychotherapist can help. Menopause may also be a more difficult adjustment when it is artificial (i.e., surgically induced) than when it occurs naturally.

Coping with physical symptoms is an important task during the menopausal transition. Good health habits such as exercise, proper diet, and stress management are often helpful. Vitamins E and C and increasing dietary sources of estrogen may help to control hot flashes, and many cognitive-behavioral techniques also assist coping. Women might try dressing in layers, carrying a fan, standing in front of an air conditioner or open refrigerator, sipping cool drinks, and using imagery (e.g., walking through a snowstorm, swimming in a mountain stream) (Golub, 1992; Greenwood, 1996; Voda, 1997).

Physicians are increasingly urging midlife women to begin hormone replacement therapy (HRT), not only for perimenopausal symptoms, but also for prevention of age-related illness, such as coronary heart disease and osteoporosis. HRT is controversial, and women may have difficulty deciding what to do. In addition to considering her own health behavior, health status, and risk factors (including family history), every woman should seek a variety of opinions about HRT and learn something about hormones and their actions. A good source of information for both clinicians and clients is Ann Voda's (1997) book *Menopause, Me and You.*

## SUMMARY

There is much more that could be said about each of the topics in this chapter. Entire books can be (and have been) written about each of them. We provide what we think is the minimum that psychologists ought to know and to emphasize the psychological importance of these experiences.

Each of the topics has clinical implications. Counselors and psychotherapists should be open to discussing these experiences with their clients, and they should be alert to opportunities to assist them with adjustment, coping, and decision-making. Furthermore, counselors and therapists should consider engaging actively in community outreach to childbirth educators and to hospitals, churches, and community centers that might like to offer support groups to women with infertility, postpartum depression, difficult infants, severe hot flashes, or other special concerns.

Each of the topics invites the attention of psychological researchers. There are many questions yet to be answered, and in those areas that have been well studied researchers have tended to rely on homogeneous convenience samples. As we wrote we thought of many provocative issues we could not address. For example, what is the transition to motherhood like for women who adopt children? Are pregnant lesbians comfortable attending community childbirth education classes? How do lesbians make decisions about whether and how to conceive? How do low-income women who can not afford reproductive technologies adjust to infertility? Are there ethnic or cultural differences in the experiences of premenstrual and menopausal symptoms? Perhaps some of our readers will one day find the answers.

# REFERENCES

Abbey, A., Andrews, F. M., & Halman, L. J. (1991). Gender's role in responses to infertility. *Psychology of Women Quarterly, 15*, 295–316.

Adler, N. E., David, H. P., Major, B. N., Roth, S. H., Russo, N. F., & Wyatt, G. E. (1990). Psychological responses after abortion. *Science, 248*, 41–44.

Adler, N. E., Keyes, S., & Robertson, P. (1991). Psychological issues in new reproductive technologies: Pregnancy inducing technology and diagnostic screening. In J. Rodin & A. Collins (Eds.), *Women and new reproductive technologies: Medical, psychosocial, legal, and ethical dilemmas* (pp. 111–133). Hillsdale, NJ: Lawrence Erlbaum.

American Psychiatric Association (1994). *Diagnostic and statistical manual of mental disorders* (4th ed.). Washington, DC: Author.

Asch, A. (1988). Reproductive technology and disability. In N. Taub & S. Cohen (Eds.), *Reproductive laws for the 1990s: A briefing handbook* (pp. 59–101). Newark, NJ: Rutgers University Press.

Beck, N. C., & Siegel, L. J. (1980). Preparation for childbirth and contemporary research on pain, anxiety, and stress reduction: A review and critique. *Psychosomatic Medicine, 42*, 429–447.

Beeson, D. (1984). Technological rhythms in pregnancy: The case of prenatal diagnosis by amniocentesis. In T. Duster & K. Garrett (Eds.), *Cultural perspectives on biological knowledge* (pp. 145–181). Norwood, NJ: Ablex.

Brooks-Gunn, J., & Ruble, D. N. (1980). The Menstrual Attitude Questionnaire. *Psychosomatic Medicine, 42*, 503–512.

Brooks-Gunn, J., & Ruble, D. N. (1986). Men's and women's attitudes and beliefs about the menstrual cycle. *Sex Roles, 14*, 287–299.

Brown, S., & Lumley, J. (1998). Changing childbirth: Lessons from an Australian survey of 1336 women. *British Journal of Obstetrics and Gynecology, 105*, 143–155.

Burger, J., & Inderbitzen, H. (1985). Predicting contraceptive behavior among college students: The role of communication, knowledge, sexual activity, and self-esteem. *Archives of Sexual Behavior, 14*, 343–350.

Chrisler, J. C. (1988). Age, sex-role orientation, and attitudes toward menstruation. *Psychological Reports, 63*, 827–834.

Chrisler, J. C. (1990, Fall). Menstrual humor: Funny or not? *Association for Women in Psychology Newsletter*, p. 9.

Chrisler, J. C. (1996). PMS as a culture-bound syndrome. In J. C. Chrisler, C. Golden, & P. D. Rozee (Eds.), *Lectures on the psychology of women* (pp. 106–121). New York: McGraw-Hill.

Chrisler, J. C. (1998, March). *Hormone hostages: The cultural legacy of PMS as a legal defense*. Invited address at the meeting of the Association for Women in Psychology, Baltimore, MD.

Chrisler, J. C., Johnston, I. K., Champagne, N. M., & Preston, K. E. (1994). Menstrual joy: The construct and its consequences. *Psychology of Women Quarterly, 18*, 375–387.

Chrisler, J. C., & Levy, K. B. (1990). The media construct a menstrual monster: A content analysis of PMS articles in the popular press. *Women & Health, 16*(2), 89–104.

Chrisler, J. C., & Zittel, C. B. (1998). Menarche stories: Reminiscences of college students from Lithuania, Malaysia, Sudan, and the United States. *Health Care for Women International, 19*, 303–312.

Clarke, A. E., & Ruble, D. N. (1978). Young adolescents' beliefs concerning menstruation. *Child Development, 49*, 231–234.

Coll, C. G., Surrey, J. L., & Weingarten, K. (1998). *Mothering against the odds: Diverse voices of contemporary mothers.* New York: Guilford Press.

Collins, N. L., Dunkel-Schetter, C., Lobel, M., & Scrimshaw, S. C. M. (1993). Social support in pregnancy: Psychosocial correlates of birth outcomes and postpartum depression. *Journal of Personality and Social Psychology, 65*, 1243–1258.

Cook, S. S. (1997). Configuring childbirth education to survive in managed care. *Advanced Practice Nursing Quarterly, 2*, 22–26.

Costa, F. M., Jessor, R., Fortenberry, J. D., & Donovan, J. E. (1996). Psychosocial conventionality, health orientation, and contraceptive use in adolescence. *Journal of Adolescent Health, 18*, 404–416.

Cox, J. L. (1986). *Postnatal depression*. New York: Churchill Livingstone.

Crowe, K., & von Baeyer, C. (1989). Predictors of a positive childbirth experience. *Birth, 16*, 59–63.

Cutrona, C. E., & Troutman, B. R. (1986). Social support, infant temperament, and parenting self-efficacy: A mediational model of postpartum depression. *Child Development, 57*, 1507–1518.

Dannenbring, D., Stevens, M. J., & House, A. E. (1997). Predictors of childbirth pain and maternal satisfaction. *Journal of Behavioral Medicine, 20*, 127–141.

Davies, K. (1982). A conflict of roles. *Nursing Mirror, 155*, iii–iv.

Dawood, M. Y. (1981). Hormones, prostaglandins, and dysmenorrhea. In M. Y. Dawood (Ed.), *Dysmenorrhea* (pp. 21–52). Baltimore: Williams & Wilkins.

Debrovner, C. (1982). *Premenstrual tension: An interdisciplinary approach*. New York: Human Sciences.

Delaney, J., Lupton, M. J., & Toth, E. (1987). *The curse: A cultural history of menstruation* (2nd ed.). Urbana, IL: University of Illinois Press.

DiMatteo, M. R., Kahn, K. L., & Berry, S. H. (1993). Narratives of birth and the postpartum: Analysis of the focus group responses of new mothers. *Birth, 20*, 204–211.

DiMatteo, M. R., Morton, S. C., Lepper, H. S., Damush, T. M., Carney, M. F., Pearson, M., & Kahn, K. L. (1996). Cesarean childbirth and psychosocial outcomes: A meta-analysis. *Health Psychology, 15*, 303–314.

Doering, S. G., Entwisle, D. R., & Quinlan, D. (1980). Modeling the quality of women's birth experience. *Journal of Health and Social Behavior, 21*, 12–21.

D'Orban, P. T., & Dalton, J. (1980). Violent crime and the menstrual cycle. *Psychological Medicine, 10*, 353–359.

Dunkel-Schetter, C., & Lobel, M. (1991). Psychological reactions to infertility. In S. L. Stanton & C. Dunkel-Schetter (Eds.), *Infertility: Perspectives from stress and coping research* (pp. 29–57). New York: Plenum.

Edwards, D. R. L., Porter, S. M., & Stein, G. S. (1994). A pilot study of postnatal depression following cesarean section using two retrospective self-rating instruments. *Journal of Psychosomatic Research, 38*, 111–117.

Erchull, M. J., Chrisler, J. C., & Johnston-Robledo, I. K. (1999, June). *Fact or fiction? A content analysis of educational materials about menstruation*. Paper presented at the meeting of the Society for Menstrual Cycle Research, Tuscon, AZ.

Forrest, J. D., & Henshaw, S. K. (1983). What U.S. women think and do about contraception. *Family Planning Perspectives, 15*, 157–166.

Frank, R. T. (1931). The hormonal causes of premenstrual tension. *Archives of Neurology and Psychiatry, 26*, 1053–1057.

Furr, L. A., & Seger, R. E. (1998). Psychosocial predictors of interest in prenatal genetic screening. *Psychological Reports, 82*, 235–244.

Gannon, L. (1998). The impact of medical and sexual politics on women's health. *Feminism & Psychology, 8*, 285–302.

Gardner-Loulan, J., Lopez, B., & Quackenbush, M. (1991). *Period*. San Francisco: Volcano Press.

Garner, C. (1995). Infertility. In C. I. Fogel & N. F. Woods (Eds.), *Women's health care: A comprehensive handbook* (pp. 611–628). Thousand Oaks, CA: Sage.

Genevie, L., & Margolies, E. (1987). *The motherhood report: How women feel about being mothers*. New York: Macmillan.

Gerrard, M., & Luus, C. A. E. (1995). Judgments of vulnerability to pregnancy: The role of risk factors and individual differences. *Personality and Social Psychology Bulletin, 21*, 160–171.

Golub, S. (1981). Sex differences in attitudes and beliefs about menstruation. In P. Komnenich, M. McSweeney, J. A. Noack, & N. Elder (Eds.), *The menstrual cycle: Research and implications for women's health* (pp. 129–134). New York: Springer.

Golub, S. (1992). *Periods: From menarche to menopause*. Newbury Park, CA: Sage.

Gotlib, I. H., Whiffen, V. E., Wallace, P. M., & Mount, J. H. (1991). Prospective investigation of postpartum depression: Factors involved in onset and recovery. *Journal of Abnormal Psychology, 100*, 122–132.

Gould, J. B., Davey, B., & Stafford, R. S. (1989). Socioeconomic differences in rates of cesarean section. *New England Journal of Medicine, 321*, 122–132.

Graff, L. A., Dyck, D. G., & Schallow, J. R. (1991). Predicting postpartum depressive symptoms: A structural modeling analysis. *Perceptual and Motor Skills, 73*, 1137–1138.

Green, J. M., Coupland, V. A., & Kitzinger, J. V. (1990). Expectations, experiences, and psychological outcomes of childbirth: A prospective study of 825 women. *Birth, 17*, 15–24.

Greenwood, S. (1996). *Menopause naturally* (4th ed.) Volcano, CA: Volcano Press.

Hallgren, A., Kihlgren, M., Norberg, A., & Forslin, L. (1995). Women's perceptions of childbirth and childbirth education before and after education and birth. *Midwifery, 11*, 130–137.

Handfield, B., & Bell, R. (1995). Do childbirth classes influence decision making about labor and postpartum issues? *Birth, 22*, 153–160.

Harry, B., & Balcer, C. (1987). Menstruation and crime: A critical review of the literature from the clinical criminology perspective. *Behavioral Sciences and the Law, 5*, 307–321.

Hart, M. A., & Foster, S. N. (1997). Couples' attitudes toward childbirth participation: Relationship to evaluation of labor and delivery. *Journal of Perinatal and Neonatal Nursing, 11*, 10–20.

Havens, B., & Swenson, I. (1989). A content analysis of educational media about menstruation. *Adolescence, 24*, 901–907.

Hawkins, J., Matteson, P. s., & Tabeek, E. S. (1995). Fertility control. In C. I. Fogel & N. F. Woods (Eds.), *Women's health care: A comprehensive handbook* (pp. 281–322). Thousand Oaks, CA: Sage.

Henshaw, S. K. (1998). Unintended pregnancy in the U.S. *Family Planning Perspectives, 30*, 24–29.

Hetherington, S. E. (1990). A controlled study of the effect of prepared childbirth classes on obstetric outcomes. *Birth, 17*, 86–91.

Hillier, C. A., & Slade, P. (1989). The impact of antenatal classes on knowledge, anxiety, and confidence in primiparous women. *Journal of Reproductive and Infant Psychology, 7*, 3–13.

Hodnett, E. D. (1996). Nursing support of the laboring woman. *Journal of Obstetrics, Gynecology, and Neonatal Nursing, 25*, 257–264.

Hodnett, E. D., & Osborn, R. W. (1989). Effects of continuous intrapartum professional support on childbirth outcomes. *Research in Nursing and Health, 12*, 289–297.

Hoffnung, M. (1989). Motherhood: Contemporary conflict for women. In J. Freeman (Ed.), *Women: A feminist perspective* (4th ed.)(pp. 157–175). Mountain View, CA: Mayfield.

Hurst, M., & Summey, P. S. (1984). Childbirth and social class: The case of cesarean delivery. *Social Science & Medicine, 18*, 621–631.

Johnston-Robledo, I. (1997, March). *A study of the effects of childbirth preparation and social support on childbirth experiences of primiparous low income women.* Paper presented at the meeting of the Association for Women in Psychology, Pittsburgh, PA.

Johnston-Robledo, I. (1998). Beyond Lamaze: Socioeconomic status and women's experiences with childbirth preparation. *Journal of Gender, Culture, and Health, 3*, 159–169.

Johnston-Robledo, I., & Torres, K. (2000, March). *"My greatest accomplishment and contribution": Women reflect on their experiences with motherhood.* Paper presented at the meeting of the Association for Women in Psychology, Salt Lake City, UT.

Koeske, R. D. (1983). Lifting the curse of menstruation: Toward a feminist perspective on the menstrual cycle. *Women & Health, 8*(2/3), 1–16.

Koff, E., Rierdan, J., & Jacobson, S. (1981). The personal and interpersonal significance of menarche. *Journal of the American Academy of Child Psychiatry, 20*, 148–158.

Koff, E., Rierdan, J., & Sheingold, K. (1982). Memories of menarche: Age, preparation, and prior knowledge as determinants of initial menstrual experience. *Journal of Youth and Adolescence, 11*, 1–9.

Koff, E., Rierdan, J., & Silverstone, E. (1978). Changes in representation of body image as a function of menarcheal status. *Developmental Psychology, 14*, 635–642.

Kolder, V. E. B., Gallagher, J., & Parsons, M. T. (1987). Court-ordered obstetrical interventions. *New England Journal of Medicine, 316*, 1192–1196.

Laws, S. (1983). The sexual politics of premenstrual tension. *Women's Studies International Forum, 6*, 19–31.

Lee, C. (1997). Social context, depression, and the transition to motherhood. *British Journal of Health Psychology, 2*, 93–108.

Lee, R. E. (1995). Women look at their experience of pregnancy. *Infant Mental Health Journal, 16*, 192–205.

Lemkau, J. P. (1988). Emotional sequelae of abortion: Implications for clinical practice. *Psychology of Women Quarterly, 12*, 461–472.

Leonardo, C., & Chrisler, J. C. (1992). Women and sexually transmitted diseases. *Women & Health, 18*(4), 1–15.

Lethbridge, D. J. (1995). Unwanted pregnancy. In C. I. Fogel & N. F. Woods (Eds.), *Women's health care: A comprehensive handbook* (pp. 455–473). Thousand Oaks, CA; Sage.

Levin, J. S., & DeFrank, R. S. (1988). Maternal stress and pregnancy outcomes: A review of the psychosocial literature. *Journal of Psychosomatic Obstetrics and Gynecology, 9*, 3–16.

Llewellyn, A. M., Stowe, Z. N., & Nemeroff, C. B. (1997). Depression during pregnancy and the puerperium. *Journal of Clinical Psychiatry, 58*, 26–32.

Lobel, M. (1994). Conceptualizations, measurement, and effects of prenatal maternal stress on birth outcomes. *Journal of Behavioral Medicine, 17*, 225–272.

Localio, A. R., Lawthers, A. G., Bengtson, J. M., Hebert, L. E., Weaver, S. L., Brennan, T. A., & Landis, J. R. (1993). Relationship between malpractice claims and cesarean delivery. *Journal of the American Medical Association, 269*, 366–373.

Logan, D. D. (1980). The menarche experience in twenty-three foreign countries. *Adolescence, 15*, 247–256.

Lowe, N. K. (1989). Explaining the pain of active labor: The importance of maternal confidence. *Research in Nursing and Health, 12*, 237–245.

Lowe, N. K. (1996). The pain and discomfort of labor and birth. *Journal of Obstetrics, Gynecology, and Neonatal Nursing, 25*, 82–92.

Lumley, J., & Brown, S. (1993). Attenders and nonattenders at childbirth education classes in Australia: How do they and their births differ? *Birth, 20*, 123–130.

Mackey, M. C. (1995). Women's evaluation of their childbirth performance. *Maternal-Child Nursing Journal, 23*, 57–72.

Major, B., Cozzarelli, C., Testa, M., & Mueller, P. (1992). Male partners' appraisals of undesired pregnancy and abortion: Implications for women's adjustment to abortion. *Journal of Applied Social Psychology, 22*, 599–614.

Maoz, B., Dowty, N., Antonovsky, A., & Wijsenbeek, H. (1970). Female attitudes toward menopause. *Social Psychiatry, 5*, 35–40.

Marieskind, H. I. (1982). Cesarean section. *Women & Health, 7*, 179–198.

Marut, J. S., & Mercer, R. T. (1979). Comparison of primiparas' perceptions of vaginal and cesarean births. *Nursing Research, 28*, 260–266.

Mauthner, N. (1993). Toward a feminist understanding of 'postnatal depression.' *Feminism & Psychology, 3*, 350–355.

McKinley, J. B., McKinley, S. J., & Brambilla, D. (1987). The relative contribution of endocrine changes and social circumstances to depression in mid-aged women. *Journal of Health and Social Behavior, 28*, 345–363.

McVeigh, C. (1997). Motherhood experiences from the perspective of first-time mothers. *Clinical Nursing Research, 6*, 335–348.

Mercer, R. T. (1986). *First-time motherhood experiences from teens to forties.* New York: Springer.

Merck Research Laboratories (1992). *The Merck manual of diagnosis and therapy* (16th ed.). Rahway, NJ: Merck & Co.

Moran, C. F., Holt, V. L., & Martin, D. P. (1997). What do women want to know after childbirth? *Birth, 24*, 27–34.

Moskowitz, E., & Jennings, B. (1996). Directive counseling on long-acting contraception. *American Journal of Public Health, 86*, 787–790.

Mowbray, C. T., Oyserman, D., Zemencuk, J. K., & Ross, S. R. (1995). Motherhood for women with serious illnesses: Pregnancy, childbirth, and the postpartum period. *American Journal of Orthopsychiatry, 65*, 21–38.

Mueller, P., & Major, B. (1989). Self-blame, self-efficacy, and adjustment after abortion. *Journal of Personality and Social Psychology, 57*, 1059–1068.

Myers, S. T., & Grasmick, H. G. (1990). The social rights and responsibilities of pregnant women: An application of Parson's sick role model. *Journal of Applied Behavioral Science, 26*, 157–172.

National Center for Health Statistics (1990). *Vital statistics of the United States, 1988: Vol. 1. Natality.* (DHHS-PHS Publication No. 90–1100). Washington, DC: U. S. Government Printing Office.

Neugarten, B. L., Wood, V., Kraines, R. J., & Loomis, B. (1968). Women's attitudes toward menopause. In B. L. Neugarten (Ed.), *Middle age and aging* (pp. 195–200). Chicago: University of Chicago Press.

Nichols, M. R. (1995). Adjustment to new parenthood: Attenders versus nonattenders at prenatal education classes. *Birth, 22*, 21–26.

Nichols, S. (1995). Positive premenstrual experiences: Do they exist? *Feminism & Psychology, 5*, 162–169.

Nichols, F. H., & Humenick, S. S. (1988). *Childbirth education: Practice, research, and theory.* Philadelphia: W. B. Saunders.

Nicholson, P. (1998). *Post-natal depression: Psychiatry, science, and the transition to motherhood.* London: Routledge.

Nolan, M. L., & Hicks, C. (1997). Aims, processes, and problems of antenatal education as identified by three groups of childbirth teachers. *Midwifery, 13*, 179–188.

Norbeck, J. S., & Anderson, N. J. (1989). Life stress, social support, and anxiety in mid- and late-pregnancy among low income women. *Research in Nursing & Health, 12*, 281–287.

O'Brien, B., & Naber, S. (1992). Nausea and vomiting during pregnancy: Effects on the quality of women's lives. *Birth, 19*, 138–143.

O'Hara, M. W., Schlechte, J. A., Lewis, D. A., & Varner, M. W. (1991). Controlled prospective study of postpartum mood disorders: Psychological, environmental, and hormonal variables. *Journal of Abnormal Psychology, 100*, 63–73.

Paarlberg, K. M., Vingerhoets, A. J., Passchier, J., Dekker, G. A., & Van Geijn, H. P. (1995). Psychosocial factors and pregnancy outcome: A review with emphasis on methodological issues. *Journal of Psychosomatic Research, 39,* 563–595.

Padawer, J. A., Fagan, C., Janoff-Bulman, R., Strickland, B. R., & Chorowski, M. (1988). Women's psychological adjustment following emergency cesarean versus vaginal delivery. *Psychology of Women Quarterly, 12,* 25–34.

Park, C. L., Moore, P. J., Turner, R. A., & Adler, N. E. (1997). The role of constructive thinking and optimism in psychological and behavioral adjustment during pregnancy. *Journal of Personality and Social Psychology, 73,* 584–592.

Parlee, M. B. (1973). The premenstrual syndrome. *Psychological Bulletin, 80,* 454–465.

Perkins, H. W., & DeMeis, D. K. (1996). Gender and family effects on the "second shift" domestic activity of college-educated young adults. *Gender & Society, 10,* 78–93.

Petersen, A. E. (1983). Menarche: Meaning of measures and measuring meanings. In S. Golub (Ed.), *Menarche: The transition from girl to woman* (pp. 63–76). Lexington, MA: Heath.

Peterson, G. (1996). Childbirth-the ordinary miracle: Effects of devaluation of childbirth on women's self-esteem and family relationships. *Pre- and Perinatal Psychology Journal, 11,* 101–109.

Pickles, V. R., Hall, W. J., Best, F. A., & Smith, G. N. (1965). Prostaglandins in endometrium and menstrual fluid from normal and dysmenorrhoeic subjects. *Journal of Obstetrics and Gynecology, 72,* 185–192.

Rapp, R. (1988). Chromosomes and communication: The discourse of genetic counseling. *Medical Anthropology Quarterly, 2,* 143–157.

Rhinehart. E. D. (1989, June). *Psychotherapists' responses to the topic of menstruation in psychotherapy.* Paper presented at the meeting of the Society for Menstrual Cycle Research, Salt Lake City, UT.

Rome, E. (1986). Premenstrual syndrome through a feminist lens. In V. L. Olesen & N. F. Woods (Eds.), *Culture, society, and menstruation* (pp. 145–151). Washington, DC: Hemisphere.

Rose, R. M., & Abplanalp. J. M. (1983). The premenstrual syndrome. *Hospital Practice, 18*(6), 129–141.

Rosser, S. V. (1993). Ignored, overlooked, or subsumed: Research on lesbian health and health care. *NWSA Journal, 5,* 183–203.

Rothman, B. K. (1986). *The tentative pregnancy: Prenatal diagnosis and the future of motherhood.* New York: Viking Press.

Rubin, R. (1984). *Maternal identity and maternal experience.* New York: Springer.

Ruble, D. N., Fleming, A. S., Hackel, L. S., & Stangor, C. (1988). Changes in the marital relationship during the transition to first time motherhood: Effects of violated expectations concerning division of household labor. *Journal of Personality and Social Psychology, 55,* 78–87.

Russo, N. F. (1976). The motherhood mandate. *Journal of Social Issues, 32,* 143–153.

Russo, N. F. (1996). Understanding emotional responses after abortion. In J. C. Chrisler, C. Golden, & P. D. Rozee (Eds.), *Lectures on the psychology of women* (pp. 260–273). New York: McGraw-Hill.

Ruzek, S. (1991). Women's reproductive rights: The impact of technology. In J. Rodin & A. Collins (Eds.), *Women and new reproductive technologies: Medical, psychosocial, legal, and ethical dilemmas* (pp. 65–87). Hillsdale, NJ: Lawrence Erlbaum.

Sable, M. R., & Libbus, M. K. (1998). Gender and contraception: A proposed conceptual model for research and practice. *Journal of Gender, Culture, and Health, 3,* 67–83.

Sanchez, L., & Thomson, E. (1997). Becoming mothers and fathers: Parenthood, gender, and the division of labor. *Gender & Society, 11,* 747–772.

Sandelowski, M. (1995). Out of Eden: Philosophical perspectives on reproductive technology. In C. I. Fogel & N. F. Woods (Eds.), *Women's health care: A comprehensive handbook* (pp. 701–721). Thousand Oaks, CA: Sage.

Scott, C. S., Arthur, D., Panzio, M. I., & Owen, R. (1989). Menarche: The Black American experience. *Journal of Adolescent Health Care, 10,* 363–368.

Sedlacek, K., & Heczey. M. (1977). A specific treatment for dysmenorrhea. *Proceedings of the Biofeedback Society of America, 8,* 26.

Seegmiller, B. (1993). Pregnancy. In F. L. Denmark & M. A. Paludi (Eds.), *Psychology of women: A handbook of issues and theories* (pp. 437–474). Westport, CT: Greenwood Press.

Seguin, L., Therrien, R., Champagne, F., & Larouche, D. (1989). The components of women's satisfaction with maternity care. *Birth, 16,* 109–113.

Siegel, H. N., & Chrisler, J. C. (1998, August). *Pregnancy weight gain attitudes of disordered eaters and new mothers.* Poster presented at the meeting of the American Psychological Association, San Francisco, CA.

Silverman, J., Torres, A., & Forrest, J. (1987). Barriers to contraceptive services. *Family Planning Perspectives, 19,* 94–102.

Simkin, P. (1991). Just another day in a woman's life? Women's long term perceptions of their first birth experience. Part I. *Birth, 18,* 203–210.

Smith, M. P. (1989). Postnatal concerns of mothers: An update. *Midwifery, 5*, 182–188.

Sommer, B. (1983). How does menstruation affect women's cognitive competence and psychophysiological response? *Women & Health, 8*(2/3), 53–90.

Stafford, R. S. (1990). Cesarean section use and source of payment: An analysis of California hospital discharge abstracts. *American Journal of Public Health, 80*, 313–315.

Stanton, A. L., & Danoff-Burg, S. (1995). Selected issues in women's reproductive health: Psychological perspectives. In A. L. Stanton & S. J. Gallant (Eds.), *The psychology of women's health: Progress and challenges in research and application* (pp. 261–305). Washington: APA Books.

Starkman, M. N. (1976). Psychological responses to the use of the fetal monitor during labor. *Psychosomatic Medicine, 38*, 269–277.

Statham, H., Green, J. M., & Kafetsios, K. (1997). Who worries that something might be wrong with the baby? A prospective study of 1072 pregnant women. *Birth, 24*, 223–233.

Steinem, G. (1983). *Outrageous acts and everyday rebellions*. New York: Putnam.

Stern, G., & Kruckman, L. (1983). Multi-disciplinary perspectives on post-partum depression: An anthropological critique. *Social Science & Medicine, 17*, 1027–1041.

Striegel-Moore, R. H., Goldman, S. L., Garvin, V., & Rodin, J. (1996). A prospective study of somatic and emotional symptoms of pregnancy. *Psychology of Women Quarterly, 20*, 393–408.

Stubbs, M. L. (1989). *Attitudes toward menstruation across the life span*. Paper presented at the meeting of the Society for Menstrual Cycle Research, Salt Lake City, UT.

Swanson-Hyland, E. F. (1995). Childbirth preparation. In M. W. O'Hara, R. C. Reiter, S. R. Johnson, A. Milburn, & J. Engeldinger (Eds.), *Psychological aspects of women's reproductive health* (pp. 179–183). New York: Springer.

*Tampax Report, The.* (1981). New York: Ruder, Finn, & Rotman.

Tanner, J. M. (1978). *Foetus into man: Physical growth from conception to maturity*. Cambridge, MA: Harvard University Press.

Tanner, J. M. (1991). Secular trends in age of menarche. In R. Lerner, A. Peterson, & J. Brooks-Gunn (Eds.), *Encyclopedia of adolescence* (pp. 637–641). New York: Garland.

Tasto, D. L., & Chesney, M. A. (1974). Muscle relaxation for primary dysmenorrhea. *Behavioral Therapy, 5*, 668–672.

Taylor, D. (1988). *Red flower: Rethinking menstruation*. Freedom, CA: The Crossing Press.

Terry, D. L., Mayocchi, L., & Hynes, G. J. (1996). Depressive symptomatology in new mothers: A stress and coping perspective. *Journal of Abnormal Psychology, 105*, 220–231.

Thuren, B. M. (1994). Opening doors and getting rid of shame: Experiences of first menstruation in Valencia, Spain. *Women's Studies International Forum, 17*, 217–228.

Tulman, L. J. (1988). Return of functional ability after childbirth. *Nursing Research, 37*, 77–81.

Unger, R., & Crawford, M. (1996). *Women and gender: A feminist psychology*. New York: McGraw-Hill.

United Nations (1991). *The world's women 1970–1990: Trends and statistics*. New York: United Nations.

Voda, A. M. (1982). Menopausal hot flash. In A. M. Voda, M. Dinnerstein, & S. R. O'Donnell (Eds.), *Changing perspectives on menopause* (pp. 136–159). Austin: University of Texas Press.

Voda, A. M. (1997). *Menopause, me and you*. New York: Harrington Park Press.

Wajcman, J. (1991). *Feminism confronts technology*. University Park: Pennsylvania State University Press.

Waldenstrom, U., Borg, I., Olsson, B., Skold, M., & Wall, S. (1996). The childbirth experience: A study of 295 new mothers. *Birth, 23*, 144–153.

Walker, L. O. (1995). Weight gain after childbirth: A women's health concern? *Annals of Behavioral Medicine, 17*, 132–141.

Wells, N. (1989). Management of pain during abortion. *Journal of Advanced Nursing, 14*, 56–62.

Whiffen, V. E. (1992). Is postpartum depression a distinct diagnosis? *Child Psychology Review, 12*, 485–508.

Whisnant, L., Brett, E., & Zegans, L. (1975). Implicit messages concerning menstruation in commercial educational materials prepared for adolescent girls. *American Journal of Psychiatry, 132*, 815–820.

Whisnant, L., & Zegans, L. (1975). A study of attitudes toward menarche in White middle-class American adolescent girls. *American Journal of Psychiatry, 132*, 809–814.

Wideman, M. V., & Singer, J. E. (1984). The role of psychological mechanisms in preparation for childbirth. *American Psychologist, 39*, 1357–1371.

Winter, L. (1988). The role of sexual self-concept in the use of contraceptives. *Family Planning Perspectives, 20*, 123–127.

Woods, N. F. (1982). Menopausal distress: A model for epidemiologic investigation. In A. M. Voda, M. Dinnerstein, & S. R. O'Donnell (Eds.), *Changing perspectives on menopause* (pp. 220–238). Austin: University of Texas Press.

Woods, N. F., Dery, G. K., & Most, A. (1983). Recollections of menarche, current menstrual attitudes, and perimenstrual symptoms. *Psychosomatic Medicine, 44*, 285–293.

Zayas, L. H., & Busch-Rossnagel, N. A. (1992). Pregnant Hispanic women: A mental health study. *Families in Society, 73*, 515–521.

Zelkowitz, P. (1996). Childbearing and women's mental health. *Transcultural Psychiatric Research Review, 33*, 391–412.

Zhang, J., Bernasko, J. W., Leybovich, E., Fahs, M., & Hatch, M. C. (1996). Continuous labor support from labor attendant for primiparous women: A meta-analysis. *Obstetrics & Gynecology, 88*, 739–744.

Zimmerman, N. S., & Chrisler, J. C. (1996, August). *Menstrual attitudes and beliefs in adolescent girls.* Poster presented at the meeting of the American Psychological Association, Toronto, Canada.

Zita, J. N. (1988). The premenstrual syndrome: "Dis-easing" the female cycle. *Hypatia, 3*(1), 77–99.

# IV

# Psychological and Health Issues

This section presents material on physical and mental health issues for women, as well as feminist psychotherapy approaches. As the authors of Chapters 2 and 3 explained, women's development and psychology have often been viewed as a variation on the male theme. The chapters in this section explain how the feminist perspective has been used to critique this approach and forge a perspective that considers women in their own right, rather than as derivatives of the male model.

Linda Porzelius, an authority in the field of health psychology, explains that recent years have seen a dramatic increase in attention to women's health issues. Her excellent overview of these issues demonstrates the influence of gender-role attitudes and cultural factors on women's health. The contemporary woman has much better access to health care specifically designed to meet her needs than did women of earlier eras. If this trend continues, what changes do you believe you will see over your life span?

The chapter by Laurie Roades on mental health issues for women raises many interesting questions. One set of questions relates to the finding of different prevalence rates for several disorders as a function of gender. What is the explanation for this difference in rates? Are these "real" differences, artifacts of clinician bias, or reflections of differences in life experience and gender-role strain for men and women? How do ethnicity, social class, sexual orientation, and marital status affect mental health? And what are the practical ramifications in terms of treatment: Should men's and women's mental health problems be treated differently?

Ballou's and West's chapter on feminist therapy traces the development of feminist therapy from its early elucidation of several key principles to its critique of traditional approaches to diagnosis, assessment, and treatment, and finally to its emergence as a variety of diverse perspectives espoused by contemporary feminist therapists. If you were interested in seeking therapy, what would you expect from a traditional versus feminist therapist? For what types of persons and problems do you think feminist therapy might be especially helpful?

# 11

# Physical Health Issues for Women

## Linda Krug Porzelius

---

## INTRODUCTION

The past 30 years has seen a dramatic move away from a biomedical model of understanding health toward a "holistic" biopsychosocial model. Whereas in the early 1900s most disease was related to microorganisms, today the major diseases are influenced greatly by lifestyle, as well as by environmental, social, and physiological factors. Behavior contributes greatly to major diseases today, including heart disease, stroke, lung cancer, and breast cancer. As a result, the role of the psychologist in health and health care has grown tremendously. The field of health psychology emphasizes understanding health within the context of the person, including individual psychological factors, social and cultural factors, and the health care system with which they interact. Health psychology applications include methods to change lifestyle behaviors, relieve pain, reduce stress, improve coping with disease, and increase compliance with medical advice.

Historically, health care and health research have defined men as the "norm," with most health research including women minimally, at best (Lee, 1998). The field of health psychology has tended to follow this practice, focusing on diseases most important to men, and often excluding women as research participants. Although health research primarily used white men as research subjects, findings were often generalized to all people (Johnson & Fee, 1997; Lee, 1998). Women's health was greatly ignored. What research was done tended to focus on reproductive health, ignoring other diseases in women.

Recent history has witnessed a dramatic increase in attention to women's health that promises real progress (for a discussion of policy changes in women's health care, see Blumenthal & Wood, 1997). In 1986, The National Institutes of Health (NIH) began requiring that women be included in clinical trials. When this requirement proved insufficient, NIH established the Office of Research on Women's Health, which advocates with health care, scientific, and governmental organizations, including Congress. The Society for the Advancement of Women's Health Research was established in 1990 to increase the quality of health care for women by identifying needed areas of knowledge, increasing funding for women's health research, and ensuring the inclusion of women in health research. Rodin and Ickovics, in their

---

Linda Krug Porzelius ● School of Professional Psychology, Pacific University, Forest Grove, Oregon 97116

*Issues in the Psychology of Women,* edited by Biaggio and Hersen. Kluwer Academic/Plenum Publishers, New York, 2000.

*American Psychologist* article (1990), called for greater focus on women's health and outlined a research agenda for women's health psychology. Women's health psychology research is needed given our inadequate understanding of health concerns unique to women, a lack of research on disorders primarily affecting women, and health psychology's failure to include women in research in general. In 1995, The American Psychological Association developed the Research Agenda for Psychological and Behavioral Factors in Women's Health, which promotes multidisciplinary research on women's health.

Increased attention to women's health issues has already expanded our understanding of health concerns unique to women. However, the same research heightened concerns about the inadequacy of women's health care, accentuating the profound need for women's health care research. A complete understanding of the complex issues in women's health will need to extend beyond the study of gender differences from a psychological framework, as feminist scholars have noted (Lee, 1998). Feminist theory provides a useful theoretical approach for understanding women's health by examining the social, cultural, and political context of women's health. Women's health must be considered in the context of the poverty, violence, and sex roles that limit women's power. Feminist approaches also call for the inclusion of women from diverse racial, ethnic, age, and cultural groups. Feminism has a strong tradition of focusing on women's health, beginning with women gaining control of their bodies through access to contraception. A focus on women's health in feminism reflects the value of empowerment, in which each woman is responsible for her own health, and women are empowered by gaining information about their bodies and participating in their own health care.

This chapter briefly summarizes research on key topics in women's health, combining feminist and health psychology research perspectives on how gender is related to health care and health outcomes, how individual and societal factors impact women's health behaviors, and how psychological factors impact chronic illness in women.

## WOMEN, SES, AND HEALTH OUTCOMES

In the United States, women live, on average, seven years longer than men, with a similar gender gap in mortality across many cultures [for a review of epidemiological data on women, socioeconomic status (SES), and health, see Adler & Coriell, 1997]. The leading causes of death for women in the United States today are heart disease, stroke, lung cancer, and breast cancer. Although women live longer than do men, women suffer from greater morbidity, that is, have more disease and disability impacting the quality of life. Thus, for example, although more men than women die from cardiovascular disease, more women actually have the disease.

The causes of gender differences in morbidity and mortality are poorly understood, but likely include biological causes as well as social and psychological factors related to gender roles. Feminist formulations attribute women's poorer health to social factors in which women have less education, lower income, and less political power than men (Lee, 1998). Gender differences in stress related to gender roles and poverty, and gender differences in coping and social support are well documented and are known to be related to health (O'Leary & Helgeson, 1997). Gender roles also impact access to and quality of health care, symptom reporting and health seeking, and interactions with health care professionals, which are discussed in the following sections.

SES also impacts mortality and morbidity, with the poorest people having the worst health and the wealthiest the best health (Adler & Coriell, 1997; Williams & Rucker, 1996). Race is also strongly related to poorer health outcomes, largely through its relation to SES. Chronic diseases are more prevalent among low SES groups, particularly osteoarthritis, hypertension, and cervical cancer (Adler, Boyce, Chesney, Cohen, & Folkman, 1994; Carroll, Bennett, & Smith, 1997). However, in the upper SES levels, women appear to have fewer health benefits than do men (Adler & Corriell, 1997). Although the relationship of SES to health outcomes is clear, the ways in which SES impacts health are not well understood. Complex relationships among gender, SES, race, and illness illustrate the need for examining gender and racial differences in health psychology research.

## WOMEN IN THE HEALTH CARE SYSTEM

### Inequities in Health Care

Social and political forces create inequalities in access to and quality of health care across gender, race, and SES, in large part through their impact on health insurance (for a summary of data on women's health insurance, see Litt, 1997). Lack of adequate insurance has direct consequences for adequacy of health care for women. Women who do not have insurance tend to delay using reproductive services, to have no regular health provider, and to use the emergency room for regular care. Approximately 10 million people in the United States have no health insurance, and disproportionate numbers of the poor, minorities, and women are without such insurance. Part-time workers and the unemployed often go without insurance if they cannot afford to pay for it on their own, and do not qualify for Medicaid. Women are frequently not insured because they more often work part-time, in temporary positions, or for small businesses. However, length of time on a job, number of hours working, and size of company cannot fully explain the discrepancy in health insurance coverage between men and women (Litt, 1997). Women are less likely to have employer insurance, but more likely to have public insurance, which provides minimal coverage for health services. Women constitute the majority of those on Medicaid (Medicaid Professional/Technical Information, Table 10, 1998). Women also comprise more of those on Medicare than do men.

### Using Health Services

Despite a lack of insurance, women are more likely to use health care services than are men. Throughout the life span, women report more symptoms, see their doctors more often, and are more likely to be hospitalized than are men (Aday & Awe, 1997). Explanations for this gender difference in using health services abound, but adequate research is lacking. Prenatal and childbirth care account for only part of the gender difference in health care use. Women's poorer health status, perhaps resulting from social factors such as stress and poverty, also contributes to greater use of health services. In addition, women are more willing than men to seek help when ill (Verbrugge, 1985). Some propose that gender role socialization may prevent men from seeking help, while encouraging women to seek help (Verbrugge, 1985). Alternatively, women may engage in more help-seeking behavior because they are socialized to be sensitive to internal signals, thus reporting a greater number of symptoms, even when they are no more ill than men (Pennebaker, 1982). SES is also related to help-seeking, with higher SES groups experiencing fewer symptoms, but being more likely to seek health care (USDHHS, 1995). Lower SES groups wait longer to seek help, but are more likely to be hospitalized.

Use of health care is clearly complex, with many factors influencing when individuals seek health care. Recent research attempts to predict individuals' use of health care through models, which combine cognitive, social, and emotional factors (Aday & Awe, 1997). Cognitive predictors of help-seeking include the perceive threat of the illness or symptoms, perceived susceptibility, and beliefs about the effectiveness of medical treatment. Fear of painful medical procedures is an important emotional predictor of help-seeking. Social factors also impact help-seeking, with women more socialized to seek help in our society.

## Communicating with Health Care Practitioners

Communication between health care practitioner (HCP) and patient is extremely important to most patients, and is a potent predictor of patient compliance with medical advice (Di-Matteo & Lepper, 1998). Thus, a great deal of research has studied communication with HCPs, most focusing on physicians during office visits. Physician behaviors that interfere with communication include frequent interrupting, directive questioning, and overly technical language. In addition, HCPs are subject to the American culture's gender stereotypes and biases (for review, see Roter & Hall, 1997). Research indicates that male physicians report liking male patients more than female patients, even when controlling for age, education, income, and occupation. Physician biases against patients who have psychological problems, are sicker, or are chronically ill, are consistently found, all of which tend to be more common among female patients.

Feminist scholars highlight the importance of power as part of the traditional physician role. The traditional medical model contributes to a large power differential between patient and physician, particularly for female patients (Cline & McKenzie, 1998). Research on physician–patient communication finds some evidence of sexist patterns in health care, with particularly poor communication between male physicians and female patients. For example, research has found that physicians recommend greater activity restrictions for women than for men, even when symptoms and symptom complaints are equal (Safran, Rogers, Tarlov, McHorney, & Ware, 1997). Other research has found a tendency to attribute physical complaints to psychological causes more for women than for men. Consistent with this, physicians prescribe antidepressants and anxiolytics more often for women than for men. In a recent national study, it was found that prescription of psychotropic drugs is 55% greater in office visits by women than those by men, and was greater even with comparable symptoms (Simoni-Wastile, 1998). A willingness to ask for help, combined with more observable affect in women, may lead physicians to overattribute symptoms to psychological causes. Goudsmit (1994) termed this the "psychologisation" of women's health, in which physicians believe women exaggerate their complaints, and that psychological symptoms play a large role in women's symptoms.

In general, physician biases against female patients are not consistently found in the research literature, particularly when the research involves taped interactions of office visits. Research indicates that with female patients physicians spend more time interacting and less time interrupting, use more empathy, and give more information than with male patients (for a review of research, see Roter & Hall, 1997). Female patients tend to ask more questions, express more tension, and ask for more help than male patients ask. Male patients assert themselves more with suggestions and opinions, and are more likely to disagree with the physician. Perhaps as a result of these communication style differences, physicians are less aware of satisfaction levels of female than of male patients, as found in one large study (Hall & Roter, 1995). Beck (1997) calls for understanding the complexity of physician–patient communication as an interactional dynamic in which female patients co-construct the nature of the interaction. In Beck's view, women must take the initiative to assert themselves in order to forge a collaborative relationship with their physicians.

In contrast to the extensive literature on gender in physician communication, little research has addressed the issue of racial, ethnic, or other biases. There is evidence of bias among physicians, similar to the biases among others in American society, related to ethnicity, race, gender orientation, SES, and weight (Hall & Roter, 1997). In addition, many lesbian women report that their physicians are not aware of their health needs, and that physicians respond negatively to them if they disclose their sexual orientation (VanScoy, 1997).

A large quantity of research focuses on the question "Do male and female physicians differ in their interactions with patients"? In fact, physician gender appears to be more important than patient gender in determining communication patterns during visits (Roter & Hall, 1997). Research indicates that female physicians spend more time with patients than do male physicians, particularly with female patients, although findings may be explained by the more complex patient problems seen by female physicians (for a review see Bertakis, 1998). Female physicians tend to spend more time on preventive services, such as screening for chronic disease, and more time on understanding the patient's current life circumstances rather than obtaining a health history. As a result, research consistently finds greater patient satisfaction among patients of female physicians. In the past, almost 90 percent of physicians were male, but number of female physicians has increased dramatically in recent years. As more women enter the field of medicine, the nature of physician-patient communication will likely continue to change.

## LIFESTYLE FACTORS AND WOMEN'S HEALTH

Increasingly, American culture views lifestyle as a critical component in achieving and maintaining good health. The feminist movement played a large role in the cultural shift toward healthy lifestyle by emphasizing the individual's responsibility for health, and by shifting power away from the doctor to the individual. The movement toward health promotion and disease prevention calls for good health behaviors, including eating a balanced diet, exercising regularly, using seat belts, and decreasing stress. Health promotion also involves avoiding unhealthy behaviors, such as alcohol abuse or cigarette smoking. Health-related behaviors are clearly important in combating chronic disease and can save money by preventing disease.

At the level of the individual, health psychology research has greatly contributed to an understanding of demographic and other individual predictors of health behavior. Health behaviors are related to gender, age, ethnicity, and SES (Gochman, 1997). In general, women are more likely to avoid unhealthy behaviors than are men. Older adults are less likely to engage in unhealthy behaviors, but also less likely to exercise than younger adults. Children and adolescents may engage in more risky behaviors, such as substance use, because of unrealistic perceptions about their vulnerability. Among those of lower SES, high levels of stress and fewer resources lead to such unhealthy behaviors as smoking or alcohol abuse. Individuals who do not have regular health care are less likely to use routine preventive screening practices, such as Pap smears. Relatively little is known about health behaviors among different ethnic minority groups.

Research on health behaviors has studied many individual psychological factors as they relate to health behaviors (for reviews, see Carmody, 1997; O'Leary & Helgeson, 1997). Stress is a potent contributor to health status, both by its physiological impact on the immune system and the sympathetic nervous system, and through its impact on health behaviors. Gender differences in stress levels are found in some studies and not in others, depending upon what types of stressors are assessed. In our society, women clearly experience greater stress related to poverty, rape and domestic violence, sexism, lower pay or lower status work, and competing roles. In addition, women may be more vulnerable to relationship conflicts than men. Stress effects can be buffered in individuals who have greater social support, better coping skills, more perceived control, and more optimistic personality styles, but a clear understanding of gender differences in these areas is lacking (O'Leary & Helgeson, 1997). Women are more likely than men to express feelings and seek social support in coping with stressors (Thoits, 1991). However, social support may or may not be helpful to women, depending upon the quality of the relationships. Emotional factors impact the performance of health behaviors, often by disrupting successful self-management—planning and problem-solving to achieve one's goals. Cognitive factors influencing health behaviors include one's personal goals, one's perception of symptoms or vulnerability to disease, one's belief that a particular health behavior can prevent illness, and one's belief in being able to perform the behavior. Perceived control is important in predicting health behaviors, and would seem to be related to the traditional male role (O'Leary & Helgeson, 1997). However, gender differences in perceived control over health behaviors are not well understood. Further research is needed to fully understand the role of gender as it relates to demographic, social, and individual factors in health behavior.

## Physical Activity

Regular exercise offers a myriad of health benefits, including increased cardiovascular fitness and endurance, reduced risk for heart attack, improved muscle tone and strength, improved joint flexibility, control of hypertension, improved cholesterol level, improved glucose tolerance, and decreased alcohol and cigarette consumption (for a review of research, see Bouchard, Shephard, & Stephens, 1994). Exercise delays mortality due to cardiovascular disease and cancer. Psychologically, exercise can improve mood, decrease anxiety and stress, and decrease depression. Although much of this research on the health benefits of exercise has excluded women, available research indicates that women derive equal health benefits from exercise (Brownson, Eyler, King, Brown, Shyu, & Sallis, 2000).

Despite the remarkable benefits, most people do not engage in regular physical activity. Some never begin an exercise program; others fail to maintain regular exercise. Women exercise less than men from childhood, through middle age and older adulthood (USDHHS, 1996). However, this may be an artifact of how exercise is assessed, as women are more likely to engage in moderate, rather than intensive, exercise. Many survey studies ignore moderate physical activity or occupational activity, which can be more difficult to assess (Brownson et al., 2000). Women over 40 and less educated women have lower levels of physical activity (Ransdell & Wells, 1998). African-American and other minority women are less active than white women even when SES is controlled (King & Kiernan, 1997). Inactivity among ethnic minority women is of great concern, given the higher prevalence of chronic diseases and higher rates of obesity in this group. Recent data from a large survey found that 40 percent of African-American, and 45 percent of Hispanic American women reported no physical activity in the last month (Crespo, Keteyian, Heath, & Sempos, 1996).

Discouraging statistics on exercise prevalence, led the Public Health Service to list physical activity as the number one goal in Healthy People 2000, recommending moderate exercise for 30 minutes, 5 times per week (USDHHS, 1991). Moderate activities, such as brisk walking, are more easily maintained and are less likely to cause injury than intensive exercise (King et al., 1992 in King & Kiernan, 1997). However, relatively little is known about how to effectively increase activity among sedentary women. Research is needed to identify the important barriers to physical activity and the most useful strategies to increase physical activity among women. Intervention strategies must be tailored to meet the needs of diverse groups of women, including African-American, Hispanic, and other minority women, young girls, working women, and elderly women (Eyler et al., 1997).

Although gender roles in our society are changing, the traditional female role still acts as a barrier to physical activity among women, particularly older women. Historically, women were discouraged from exercise and sports to prevent damage to reproductive organs or delayed menarche (Brownson et al., 2000). Sports activities were geared almost exclusively to men until 1972, when Title IX, requiring athletic opportunities for girls and women in schools. However, girls' participation in formal sports during youth is still less than boys' participation even today (DiLorenzo, Stucky-Ropp, VanderWal, & Gotham, 1998), with gender differences in attitudes toward sports appearing at a very young age (Eccles & Harold, 1991). Unfortunately, women who were not physically active in youth are less likely to be physically active as adults (Sallis, Hovell, & Hofstetter, 1992). Perhaps related is a study in which older women identified perceived ability to exercise as an important barrier to beginning and maintaining an exercise program (Clark, 1999). Negative attitudes toward physical activity in youth could lead to lack of positive experiences with exercise and sports, and to a lack of perceived ability in later life.

Another barrier to physical activity is time. Women cite lack of time as the most important barrier to exercise (Johnson, Corrigan, Dubbert, & Gramling, 1990), with family demands a major competitor for time resources (Verhoef & Love, 1994). Access to childcare is closely tied to the problem of time limitations for women and should be addressed in interventions. In minority subgroups where family and community are central, taking time for oneself may be especially difficult (Kriska & Rexroad, 1998). Focusing on physical activity, rather than a formal program of exercise allows women to incorporate activity into their everyday responsibilities without adding an additional responsibility into overly full lives.

Kriska & Rexroad (1998) outline strategies for increasing physical activity among women, particularly minority women. Interventions must assess the social support needs for each group of women, including support from friends, family, church, and community. Women must have access to safe, affordable places to exercise. In addition, interventions must address time limitations for women struggling with child care, work, and household responsibilities. Community-based interventions offer a promising means to successfully address these issues, by sensitively dealing with strengths and barriers for a particular subculture. Broadscale efforts to promote physical activity through environmental and policy interventions also offer promise (Sallis, Bauman, & Pratt, 1998).

## Smoking

One of the most important unhealthy behaviors is smoking. Smoking is the greatest single cause of preventable death in the United States, accounting for 125,000 deaths from cancer annually, and 170,000 deaths from cardiovascular disease (USDHHS, 1991). Smoking increases the risk of chronic bronchitis, emphysema, peptic ulcers, respiratory disorders, and injuries due to fires and accidents (USDHHS). In addition, smoking in women is associated with osteoporosis, early menopause, decreased fertility, pregnancy complications, lower estrogen levels, and increased risk for cervical cancer. The dangers of smoking also effect non-smokers who have regular contact with smokers, including children, co-workers, and spouses. Children whose mothers smoke are at much higher risk of sudden infant death syndrome and asthma (USDHHS). For women, the risks of smoking are synergistic with other health risks, greatly amplifying morbidity and mortality rates when added to high cholesterol, stress, and overweight.

The Surgeon General's 1964 report on the dangers of smoking had a dramatic impact on smoking levels, reducing male smoking by 39 percent (Husten, 1998). However, women's smoking decreased only 11 percent from 1965 to 1993. Currently, 23 percent of women and 28 percent of men smoke in the United States (Husten, 1998). Smoking rates are highest among American Indian and Alaska Native women, and lowest among Asian and Hispanic women (Husten). Rates for black and white women are similar (Husten, 1998). Smoking rates are considerably higher in poorer and less educated groups (Grunberg, Brown, & Klein, 1997).

In the 1990s, almost all people who take up smoking do so as teenagers, rather than as adults. The number of teens taking up smoking remains high and appears to be increasing (Elders, Perry, Eriksen, & Giovino, 1994). The number of adolescent girls who begin smoking is currently higher than the number of boys who begin smoking (Killen, 1998). Smoking rates are highest among Native American boys and girls and lowest among Asian American and African-American boys and girls (Killen, 1998). Community prevention efforts, such as tobacco tax, mass media campaigns, and school-based prevention programs, have some documented impact on initiation rates (Kaplan, Orleans, Perkins, & Pierce, 1995). However, research on why girls start smoking is urgently needed in order to develop more effective prevention programs.

Reasons for starting to smoke include social influences and individual factors such as personality or beliefs about the benefits of smoking. Social influences seem to be the most important contributor to an adolescent's decision to begin smoking, with both peer and parent smoking among the strongest predictors (Friestad & Klepp, 1997). Individual factors that predict adolescent smoking include low levels of social support, rebelliousness and risk-taking, and the desire to appear mature and independent (DeBon & Klesges, 1995). Relatively little is known about how girls' reasons for smoking differ from those of boys. However, one study indicated that girls who begin smoking might be more outgoing than boys and might start smoking earlier than boys, suggesting different patterns of initiation (Friestad & Klepp, 1997). Other studies indicate that weight control is a major reason given by girls for why they take up smoking, particularly white girls (DeBon & Klesges, 1995). Cigarette advertising targeting girls, presenting an image of smokers as thin and glamorous, has increased tremendously, resulting in increased smoking rates among girls (Mermelstein & Borrelli, 1995).

Clinical smoking cessation programs have received considerable research attention during the past 20 years, adding considerably to an understanding of effective cessation techniques (for a review see Lichtenstein & Glasgow, 1992). Smoking cessation treatment programs are generally offered in small groups and have been widely disseminated through clinics, hospitals, and the American Lung Association. The most effective interventions involve multicomponent techniques, consisting of behavioral and cognitive self-management skills to help people manage triggers and resist cravings (DeBon & Klesges, 1995). Components include self-monitoring of smoking patterns to obtain information about triggers, stimulus control techniques, problem-solving strategies, and contingency contracting. Relapse prevention techniques provide strategies for coping high-risk situations for resuming smoking, such as drinking alcohol or experiencing interpersonal stress. Newer treatments include an assessment of the individual's stage of readiness for smoking cessation, with targeted interventions geared to the individual's stage (Mermelstein, 1997). Most treatments are directed at individuals who are in the action stage of readiness for change, although there is some indication that women may more often be in the precontemplation stage, where motivation is low (Mermelstein, 1997).

Multimodal smoking cessation programs are highly successful at getting people to quit smoking, but relapse rates are high (Ockene, Emmons, Mermelstein, Perkins, Bonollo, Voorhees, & Hollis, 2000). Effectiveness is greater with light smokers than with heavy smokers, and is enhanced with the use of nicotine replacement. Research has not consistently identified any gender differences in successful quitting, although relapses for women are more often related to stress, depression, or weight gain (Mermelstein & Borrelli, 1995). Women who have difficulty regulating negative affect may use smoking as a way to cope with stressors. Smoking a passive method for coping with stress and research has found that women use more passive, rather than active, coping strategies as compared to men, perhaps based upon perceptions that stressful events in their lives are uncontrollable (Solomon & Flynn, 1993). Smoking cessation programs that address problems with stress, depression, and coping skills may be more helpful to women and need further investigation.

Graham (1994), a feminist researcher, identifies mood regulation as a central reason for smoking in women. According to Graham, smoking provides a way to cope with a stressful life created by social inequality, particularly for low SES women. Graham relates smoking to women's lifestyle, particularly traditional mothers of young children, who are primarily responsible for child care and household duties. Their lives are entirely taken up in responding to their children's and husband's needs and schedules. Smoking offers a brief time out from serving others, that can be easily fit into this demanding schedule. Smoking relieves the boredom and isolation that can go with caring for children and running a household on a low income. Smoking also helps in regulating mood, as women struggle to cope with stress and anger in dealing with children. According to Graham, smoking cessation programs that focus on lifestyle change inappropriately attempt to change what the individual does, rather than the circumstances in which the individual lives. Quantitative research is needed to fully explore why economically and socially disadvantaged groups continue to smoke. Social, political, and economic factors may need to be addressed in order to reduce smoking among women.

Another important factor in relapse for women is concern about weight gain after quitting, which is not unfounded (Solomon & Flynn, 1993). Smoking may keep body weight down by decreasing taste sensitivity, affecting energy utilization through insulin levels, or providing a way to cope with stress. Women may experience greater metabolic effects of smoking than men and therefore greater weight reductions from smoking (USDHHS, 1990). Ironically, pressures on girls and women in our society to be thin lead many to believe that smoking is better (and healthier!) than gaining weight. Many have called for research on smoking cessation programs that specifically address concerns about weight gain. Initial evaluations of treatment programs that address weight concerns show mixed results (Mermelstein & Borelli, 1995).

Although smoking cessation programs are far less than perfect in their long-term effects, the cumulative effects of smoking programs are more promising. Repeated attempts at quitting seem to increase an individual's chance of staying quit, perhaps through repeatedly learning and practicing skills (Grunberg, Brown, & Klein, 1997). This is consistent with Prochaska's view of smoking cessation as a process, with identifiable stages (Lichtenstein & Glasgow, 1992).

One important limitation of clinical programs is that they do not reach many people. Thus, many efforts are geared toward quick and efficient dissemination of information on smoking cessation through physician office visits, mailing programs, and less intensive self-help programs (for a review, see Lichtenstein & Glasgow, 1992). Worksite smoking cessation programs can have a modest impact on smoking. Community efforts at intervention are becoming more widely used, based upon research demonstrating successful smoking cessation rates in these communities compared to control communities (Lichtenstein & Glasgow, 1992). Health care providers can also have a significant impact on smoking cessation through brief office visits, particularly when physicians are trained in patient-centered counseling techniques. Healthy People 2000 set a goal of increasing physician counseling for smoking cessation (USDHHS, 1991). Unfortunately, a significant change in physicians' treatment of smoking has been difficult to achieve as yet. A recent national study found that physicians addressed smoking in only 23 percent of office visits by patients who were smokers (Thorndike, Rigotti, Stafford, Singer, 1998).

## EATING AND WEIGHT

### Body Dissatisfaction and Eating Disorders

Feminist scholars identify body image and eating disorder problems as central issues for women in our society (Gilbert & Thompson, 1996; Fallon, Katzman, & Wooley, 1994). Girls and women are frequently judged according to their physical attractiveness, primarily determined by body weight. Our culture's current ideal for a woman's body is extremely thin, and thinness is promoted as a way to happiness and success for women. Overweight people are stigmatized as lazy, unattractive, and undisciplined, contributing to the pervasive fears of fat found in American culture (Rothblum, 1994). The women's fashion industry and the cosmetic industry make millions of dollars each year by instilling appearance anxiety and body dissatisfaction.

Feminists equate pressures on women to be thin with similar efforts to control women's bodies throughout history, such as Chinese foot-binding or wearing of corsets (for a review, see Gilbert & Thompson, 1996). According to some feminist perspectives, society's pressures on women to be thin arise from fears of women's power, and represent an attempt to silence the voices of the women's movement. Today's advertising portrays the ideal woman as weak and emaciated, thereby sending a message that women should be powerless. Women are forbidden to take up either space, by being large. Women should not take up resources, by eating food. The outcome is that girls and women are obsessed with weight and dieting, which promotes divisive competition between women, and drains energy from women's lives.

Body dissatisfaction and fear of fat are rampant, and dieting is pandemic, with about half of adolescent girls (Grigg, Bowman, & Redman, 1996), and 30 percent of adult women dieting at any given time (Neumark-Sztainer, Jeffery, & French, 1997). Half or more of women in the U.S. report significant dissatisfaction with their appearance (Cash, 1998). Eating disorder symptoms occur on a continuum, with body dissatisfaction and dieting occurring in almost all women, and more extreme eating disturbances effecting fewer women. However, strikingly high numbers of young women have subclinical eating disorders involving strong fears of getting fat, intense body dissatisfaction, and obsessional, restrictive dieting.

Rates of eating disorders are highest among western, industrialized cultures, and appear to be increasing. Approximately 1 percent to 3 percent of girls and women in the United States develop severe symptoms of anorexia nervosa or bulimia nervosa (Hoek, 1993). Anorexia involves obsessional fears of fat, and weight loss to 80 percent or less of normal body weight. Bulimia nervosa typically involves dieting, frequent binge eating, and purging through self-induced vomiting. In addition, approximately 2 percent of individuals with an eating disorder have symptoms that do not quite fit diagnostic criteria (Kendler et al., 1991). The gender difference in rates of eating disorders is striking, with approximately 95 percent of eating disorders diagnosed in girls or women. Anorexia has a mortality rate of 5 percent to 15 percent, higher than any other psychological disorder, and both anorexia and bulimia have potentially serious health, interpersonal, work, and academic consequences (Sullivan, 1995). Dieting has been identified as an important risk factor in the development of eating disorders, although not all dieters develop eating problems. Eating disorders are extremely complex, with multifaceted etiologies, including biological, psychological, and social factors.

Feminist professionals in the areas of treatment or prevention of eating disorders call for changes at a societal level that target destructive advertising and prejudice against the obese (Gilbert & Thompson, 1996). Feminist therapy for eating disorders helps women challenge society's definition of physical attractiveness. Girls and women are encouraged to develop a healthy self-esteem that is not dependent on body size or appearance, and to accept their current body size, eliminating efforts to lose weight (Fallon, Katzman, & Wooley, 1994).

## Obesity

Rates of obesity in our country have risen dramatically in the last 20 years. Currently, 25% of women, and 20% of men in the United States are classified as obese, which is approximately 20% over normal weight (Flegal, Carroll, Kuczmarski, & Johnson, 1998). Obesity rates are even higher among African-American and Mexican-American women. Higher rates of obesity are also found among older women, and those of lower SES.

Obesity is associated with numerous health risks, including non-insulin-dependent diabetes, coronary heart disease, hypertension, and cancer. Recent research indicates that distribution of body fat may be more important than amount of body fat in determining health consequences. Lower body or pear-shaped obesity, common among women, is associated with fewer health consequences than is abdominal obesity (Wing & Klem, 1997). Other studies indicate that weight cycling may have more adverse health consequences than obesity, although a review of studies on weight cycling did not support these findings (Brownell & Rodin, 1994). In addition to physical consequences of obesity, obese individuals, particularly women, suffer from prejudice and discrimination from employers, health care professionals, and many others (Rothblum, 1994).

The causes of obesity are complex and differ between individuals (for a review, see Wing & Klem, 1997). Genetic factors are clearly important, impacting metabolic rate and fat distribution. Despite a plethora of research, obesity does not seem to be associated with psychological disorders or personality variables. An exception is the subgroup of obese individuals who have problems with binge eating, which is associated with higher levels of psychopathology. Considerable research has also failed to clearly establish differences in caloric intake between obese and normal weight individuals, although high fat diet likely contributes to obesity in some individuals. Obese individuals are less physically active than lean individuals, which appears to play a role in causing and maintaining the obesity. Women are most likely to gain weight with smoking cessation, with pregnancy, and during menopause (Williamson, Kahn, Remington, & Anda, 1990).

Health care's response to the problem of obesity has traditionally been to recommend weight loss through a wide array of methods, including self-directed diets, prescribed dietary regimens, commercial weight loss programs, exercise programs, university- and hospital-based programs, pharmacotherapy, and even surgery. The most extensively researched weight loss programs are university- and hospital-based behavioral modification programs, utilizing primarily female participants (for a summary, see Grilo, 1996). These multicomponent programs include self-management techniques, cognitive restructuring, nutrition education, and exercise interventions. Programs typically last 12 to 24 weeks, and result in an average weight loss of about 20 pounds. Weight loss maintenance is poor, with one third of the weight regained one year posttreatment, and all of the weight regained after five years. Men and women tend to fare equally well in these programs (Wing & Klem, 1997). Weight loss maintenance research is badly needed, as is research on African-American women, who have been under-studied. African-American women tend to lose less weight than white women (Wing & Klem, 1997). However, discouraging results from behavioral weight loss treatment programs may reflect the fact that people who participate in these programs have already failed at many other types of weight loss programs, thus representing a biased sample of obese persons (Brownell & Rodin, 1994). According to a large-scale survey, only about 6 percent of people who try to lose weight join a hospital-based program (Consumers Union, 1993).

In contrast to clinic-based programs, very little research has evaluated the effectiveness of commercial and self-initiated attempt at weight loss. It is estimated that Americans spend more than three billion dollars a year on commercial programs for weight loss (Consumers Union, 1993). *Consumer Reports* conducted a large-scale survey people who participated in self-help and commercial programs. Approximately one fourth of the participants reported losing weight successfully and keeping it off. Most participants lost weight in the short term, but had regained part or all of the weight two years after the program ended. There were no major differences between programs. Self-initiated weight loss attempts tended to use sensible strategies that resulted in modest weight losses of about 10 pounds and generally good long-term maintenance of losses. Interestingly, in the *Consumer Reports* study and other studies, rates of dieting exceed rates of overweight. In fact, among normal weight individuals, approximately 50 percent of women, and 20 percent of men diet regularly (French & Jeffery, 1994).

The "anti-dieting" movement, strongly supported by many feminist professionals who treat eating disorders, developed in part as a reaction to American culture's obsession with thinness, and in part because of discouraging results from weight loss research (Garner & Wooley, 1991). Anti-dieting professionals argue that weight loss efforts are rarely effective in the long term, that dieting is harmful because it contributes to weight cycling and eating disorders, and that obesity is associated with health problems, but does not necessarily cause the problems. Therapists working with individuals who have an eating disorder generally focus on acceptance of body size. Some advocate body acceptance and abstension from dieting, even for severely overweight individuals who have associated health consequences (Chrisler, 1989). Other health professionals argue that the anti-dieting mentality is overstated, and that weight loss is a reasonable goal for individuals who are obese and have health problems (Brownell & Rodin, 1994; French & Jeffery, 1994). Arguments for and against weight loss for the obese are complex. Research to date does not clearly support an extreme pro-dieting or anti-dieting stance. Further research is needed to understand when and for whom dieting benefits outweigh negative consequences.

At present, health care professionals who treat obesity most often advocate weight loss through moderate changes in eating and physical activity. Wing and Klem (1997) outline a conservative approach to recommending weight loss, depending upon degree of overweight, genetic factors, the health consequences of the overweight for that person, and the individual's other health risks. More effective weight loss methods are needed in order to help obese individuals suffering from serious health problems. Some promising research indicates that modest weight losses of 15 to 20 pounds can significantly lower blood pressure and improve cholesterol, and may be more reasonable than achievement of normal body weight (Jeffery, Wing, & Mayer, 1998). However, such programs may need to provide body acceptance components if participants are to agree to small weight losses.

# CHRONIC HEALTH PROBLEMS

The role of psychologists in treating people with chronic health problems has broadened tremendously with the growth of health psychology (Belar & Deardorff, 1995). Rather than simply treating psychopathology in individuals who have chronic illness, psychologists may intervene with behavioral, affective, cognitive, or psychophysiological aspects of illness, with etiolgical and maintaining factors in illness, or with compliance issues. Health psychologists may work as individual, group or family therapists, consultants, patient or staff educators, researchers, or administrators in health care settings. Health psychologists may help with changing lifestyle health behaviors that can impact prognosis for surviving most major illnesses, such as heart disease, cancer, and diabetes. Health psychologists may also help individuals to cope with the impact of physical illness on emotional, social, and occupational functioning.

## Cardiovascular Disease

Cardiovascular disease (CVD) is the number one cause of mortality for both men and women, and contributes greatly to disability and reduced quality of life. Until recently, CVD has generally been thought of as a man's disease. CVD kills more women than men, yet the vast majority of medical and psychological research on CVD has often only used men as subjects (King & Paul, 1996). As a result, there is little understanding of the psychological aspects of CVD for women.

Coronary heart disease (CHD), a major type of CVD, develops from deposits of fat and calcium on the artery walls in the heart. Deposits that build up can block the arterial openings, reducing blood flow (for an overview, see Evanoski, 1997). Narrowing of the artery walls can cause angina pectoris (chest pain) and heart attack. Rates of CHD are greater for men than for women at all ages, although rates of CHD for women increase greatly after menopause (Shumaker & Smith, 1995). Genetic factors are known to be important contributors to CHD, but genetics are greatly influenced by lifestyle, particularly exercise, diet, and smoking behaviors (Evanoski, 1997). In fact, lifestyle changes in the United States, such as reduced fat intake, smoking cessation, and increased physical activity have contributed to a decline in death rates from CHD in the 1960s and 1970s. Unfortunately, the decline in CHD has slowed considerably in the 1990s.

CHD is not detectable in early stages, but can be predicted by risk factors, including family history, age, hypertension, diabetes, high cholesterol, smoking, overweight, and sedentary lifestyle (Evanoski, 1997). Although most risk factors present comparable risks for men and women, smoking and high cholesterol pose a greater risk for women. Smoking doubles a woman's risk of heart disease, and smoking while using oral contraceptives exacerbates the effects of smoking. Low SES is a strong risk factor for CHD for both women and men. The prevalence of lifestyle risk factors is generally higher among poorer and less educated women.

Chronic levels of psychological strain can increase the likelihood of CHD (for a review of gender, stress, and CHD, see Shumaker & Smith, 1995). Chronic strain impacts the endocrine and central nervous systems, which raises blood pressure, contributing to CHD. Increased risk for CHD is seen in people who are low SES with few resources; people who have a hostile, cynical approach to life; and people who exhibit type A behavior, including impatience, hostility, and irritability. In addition, social isolation is more often reported in low SES persons and is a risk factor for CHD, although more so in men than women.

Prior to menopause, women are protected from heart disease by the hormone estrogen, which prevents buildup of fats and calcium on the artery walls and keeps blood vessels pliable (for reviews see Evanoski, 1997; Stampfer, Colditz, & Willett, 1990). Estrogen also tends to increase levels of high-density lipoprotein (HDL) cholesterol (good cholesterol), and to decrease levels of low-density lipoprotein (LDL) cholesterol (bad cholesterol). Following menopause, women are at much higher risk for high cholesterol, hypertension, and heart disease. Cholesterol levels tend to rise sharply after age 40 and to continue increasing as a woman ages. For women over 45 in the United States, 50 percent of white women, and 79 percent of African-American women have hypertension.

Hormone replacement therapy (HRT) after menopause to reduce risk of heart disease is the subject of much debate in feminist and medical research communities. HRT represents an important feminist issue in that menopause has been viewed in a sexist manner, as a pathological state, a "hormone-deficiency problem" (Hunt, 1994), rather than as a normal process in a woman's life. Hunt describes this sexist notion of menopause. "The notion of 'replacement' emphasizes that, in passing through the menopause, a woman has reached a stage of need, of loss, of deficiency . . . it is not only her hormones that need to be restored but her gender, her womanhood, the essence of her femininity" (Hunt, 1994, p. 159). In the medical field, HRT has been administered widely, with claims of 50 percent reduction in risk of CHD, based on uncontrolled, epidemiological studies (Derry, Gallant, & Woods, 1997). These studies have come under criticism more recently, as there are no prospective, controlled clinical trials of HRT, and there are risks associated with HRT, including gallbladder disease, migraine headaches, and cancer (Schenk-Gustafsson & Al-Khalili, 1998). However, research has demonstrated that estrogen can improve several physiological indicators of CVD (Schenck-Gustafsson & Al-Khalili, 1998). A cautious view espoused by many is that each woman needs to evaluate the relative benefits for prevention of CHD against possible side effects in making a decision about HRT. Data from the Women's Health Initiative will provide prospective evaluations of CVD in women using HRT (Matthews et al., 1997).

Among individuals who develop CHD, prognosis is worse for women than for men (for reviews, see Cave, 1998; Czajkowski, 1998). Women are more likely to die from a heart attack than are men. Women who survive a heart attack tend to recover more slowly than men do. Women who undergo coronary artery bypass surgery are more likely to die than are men. Those who survive surgery show less improvement of symptoms. These poorer outcomes of CHD for women are partially explained by the fact that women develop CHD about 10 years later than do men. Women may also fare less well than men because of biases in detection and treatment of CHD in women. Studies have found that women are referred less frequently for expensive procedures, such as angiography, than are men, even after controlling for age and disease severity (Berry, 1995). Although the reasons for this are not fully understood, one study found that even when men and women's symptoms were similar, physicians were more likely to refer men for diagnostic tests. Other studies indicate that women may delay reporting symptoms longer. Perhaps because CHD has been viewed as a "man's disease," women themselves often greatly underestimate the likelihood of their developing CHD. Research is needed to understand the attitudes of women and their physicians that may contribute to delayed treatment.

Women also show poorer psychosocial functioning after a heart attack or heart surgery compared to men, reporting more depression and anxiety, poorer sexual functioning, and greater sleep disturbance (see Czajkowski for a review). These findings appear to hold even when age and other illnesses are equal. Some studies indicate that gender differences in psychosocial functioning exist prior to heart attacks or surgery, with women reporting more social isolation, lower incomes, and poorer emotional functioning. Importantly, poor psychosocial recovery heightens the risk of future CHD and death. Cardiac rehabilitation programs have been shown to help with physical and psychological recovery from heart attack in both men and women. However, women are much less likely to attend cardiac rehabilitation programs and are more likely to drop out (Konstam & Houser, 1994). Initial research indicates that women have different patterns of barriers and motivators for participation in rehabilitation programs (Lieberman, Meana, & Stewart, 1998).

## HUMAN IMMUNODEFICIENCY VIRUS/ ACQUIRED IMMUNE DEFICIENCY SYNDROME

Although acquired immune deficiency syndrome (AIDS) has traditionally been considered a "gay man's disease", approximately 20 percent of individuals with AIDS are women, and the number of women diagnosed with AIDS is increasing at alarming rates (for a review, see Kalichman, 1998). AIDS is now the fourth leading cause of death for women between the ages of 25 and 44, and the leading cause of death for young African-American women, and young women in many major cities in the United States. Most women with AIDS are African-American (59 percent), followed by Caucasian (21 percent) and Hispanic (19 percent) (Kalichman, 1998). In Africa, some regions report human immunodeficiency virus (HIV) infection rates as high as 25 percent of the population (Caldwell & Caldwell, 1996). Despite these statistics, research on AIDS in women has been slow to develop. What research there is on women with HIV or AIDS has tended to focus on pregnant women with HIV, with the primary concern being transmission to the fetus (Sherr, 1995).

The majority of women with HIV were exposed through injection drug use or through unprotected intercourse with an intravenous drug user (for a review see Gavey & McPhillips, 1997). Women are at greater risk of infection from sex with an infected man than are men from sex with an infected woman. Little data are available on woman to woman sex, but rates of HIV infection are low among lesbian women. However, lesbian women who have sex with men, or who are intravenous drug users are at much higher risk of infection (Kennedy, Scarlett, Duerr, & Chu, 1995). In prison populations, rates of HIV infection are alarming, particularly among women. Incarcerated women have 130 times higher rates of HIV infection than women in the general population (Kalichman, 1998).

AIDS is a result of exposure to HIV, which causes the immune system to lose its effectiveness. When the body is unprotected by the immune system, opportunistic diseases attack the body's organs, causing death (Kalichman, 1998). The progression of HIV to AIDS occurs over a decade or more, with enormous differences between individuals (see DeHovitz, 1995 for a review). Faster progression of the virus is associated with older age, smoking, contraction through intravenous drug use, and poor health care. African Americans also appear to have shorter survival times (Kalichman, 1998). Use of antiretroviral drugs, such as AZT, slow the rate of progression. Some studies find a faster rate of progression for women than for men, and it appears that sociocultural factors best explain the difference (Melnick et al., 1994). Sociocultural factors, such as poverty and poor access to health care, result in delayed and inferior treatment, and shorter survival times (Ickovics & Rodin, 1992). Studies have found that women are diagnosed later in the course of the illness, receive fewer medical services, are less likely to receive antiretroviral medications, and are less likely to be hospitalized (Kalichman, 1998). Once hospitalized, women die sooner than men, even when healthier at the time of hospitalization.

The first diseases to appear in people with HIV differ somewhat for women and men, with women most likely to develop vaginal candidiasis, pelvic inflammatory disease, and cervical dysplasia (DeHovitz, 1995). Later stage diseases associated with AIDS include neurological disease, pneumonia, pulmonary tuberculosis, and cervical cancer. Kaposi's sarcoma, commonly associated with AIDS in men, is rarely found in women (DeHovitz, 1995). The incidence of cervical cancer in AIDS has increased dramatically, in part because of the increased incidence of HIV/AIDS in women (Kalichman, 1998).

HIV infection usually results in a lifelong decline in health, with numerous psychological and social consequences, although much of what we know is based upon research using men as participants. Initial diagnosis of HIV can be extremely traumatic, resulting in shock, followed by anger, depression, anxiety, and obsessive concerns about health (Huggins, Elman, Baker, Forrester, & Lyter, 1991). People diagnosed with HIV face not only health concerns, but also stigmatization and potential rejection from friends and family, loss of employment, fears of infecting others, and fears of developing AIDS symptoms. The first sign of AIDS symptoms often causes intense emotional trauma related to fears of physical decline, financial problems, pain, and death (Mulder & Antoni, 1992).

Little is known about women's psychological adjustment to HIV/AIDS as most research on psychological adjustment to AIDS has been conducted on men. Sherr (1995) emphasizes the need to understand HIV and AIDS in women in a sociopolitical context in which women, particularly poor women, have little power. Women with HIV infection, who are often a part of marginalized groups in our society, face stigmatization from minority status and drug use, as well as stigmatization for their disorder (Jaccard, Wilson, & Radecki, 1995). Women who live in urban centers must cope with stress from crowded conditions, poor access to health care, and poverty (Sherr, 1995). Women exposed to HIV through injection-drug use had psychological and social problems prior to becoming infected that impair their ability to cope with the severe stressors associated with HIV/AIDS. Women who are heads of households must concern themselves with care for their children when health declines. The infected pregnant woman must cope with threats to her own life and that of her unborn baby.

Psychological interventions and support groups are available for persons with AIDS, particularly in urban areas, and can be quite helpful. Unfortunately, many support groups focus primarily on the needs of men with HIV and can be quite uncomfortable for women (Kalichman, 1998). Therapy for women with HIV must provide information about the disease, and help with lifestyle changes, decisions about disclosure, problems in relationships, thoughts of suicide, coping with illness and the health care system, and self-esteem problems (Kalichman, 1998). Therapists must also be prepared to assess and treat substance abuse problems. Research on treatment programs for individuals with HIV/AIDS supports cognitive behavioral interventions that include stress reduction, cognitive restructuring, and coping skills training (for a review see Sikkema & Kelly, 1996). Interpersonal therapy shows initial promise in improving emotional adjustment to HIV (Markowitz, Koesis, Fishman, Spielman, Jacobsberg, Frances, Klerman, & Perry, 1998). Although there is little research on psychodynamic treatments of individuals with HIV, Cadwell (1997) provides an important discussion of transference and countertransference issues in therapy with AIDS-infected clients. In general, pharmacological treatments may be underutilized, as emotional problems are often viewed as normal reactions to HIV infection. As the disease increases in prevalence, health care providers will be badly needed. Healthy Project 2000 objectives call for increased HIV testing, and increased numbers of primary care and mental health care providers who provide counseling on prevention of HIV (USDHHS, 1991).

HIV prevention must obviously be a priority, given the lack of a cure for the disease. Although many prevention programs have been developed, there is a lack of research on which prevention programs are effective, and a lack of research on prevention among women (Sikkema, 1998). The most crucial intervention targets for women are information about how to clean needles and information about the use of condoms for preventing infection. However, political forces often inhibit the dissemination of such information. By far the most common approach to prevention has been HIV counseling and testing, which are known to have limited effects on sexual risk behavior of women (Ickovics et al., 1994). Sikkema (1998) reviewed the only two controlled evaluations of prevention programs designed for women, and concluded that the most helpful interventions included skills training, such as sexual assertiveness and negotiation, problem solving, risk behavior self-management, condom use, and coping skills. Programs that address social support needs and emphasize empowerment are also helpful for women.

## SUMMARY AND CONCLUSIONS

Women's health has historically been greatly neglected, but has received much attention in the last decade as a result of national policy changes. Although our understanding of women's health is growing, much work remains, as can be seen in reviewing research on women's health behaviors, and research on major diseases as they impact women. Thus, the crucial important of women's health care research is seen in differential patterns of disease, as well as differential patterns of risk factors, treatments, and outcomes across gender, race, age, and SES. The complex patterns of disease, formed from interactions of physiological, environmental, social, and behavioral factors, cannot be fully understood without an appreciation of a cultural and political context of poverty, violence, and sex roles that limit women's power.

## REFERENCES

Aday, L. A., & Awe, W. C. (1997). Health services utilization models. In D. S. Gochman (Ed.), *Handbook of health behavior research l: Personal and social determinants* (pp. 153–172). New York: Plenum.

Adler, N. E., Boyce, T., Chesney, M. A., Cohen, S., & Folkman, S. (1994). Socioeconomic status and health: The challenge of the gradient. *American Psychologist, 49*, 15–24.

Adler, N. E., & Coriell, M. (1997). Socioeconomic status and women's health. In S. J. Gallant & G. P. Keita (Eds.), *Health care for women: Psychological, social and behavioral influences* (pp. 11–23). Washington, DC: American Psychological Association.

Beck, C. S. with Ragan, S. L. & Dupre, A. (1997). Partnership for health: An introduction. *Partnership for health: Building new relationships between women and health caregivers* (pp. 1–24). Mahwah, NJ: Lawrence Erlbaum.

Belar, C. D., & Deardorff, W. W. (1995). *Clinical health psychology in medical settings: A practitioner's guidebook.* Washington, DC: American Psychological Association.

Berry, T. A. (1995). Gender bias in the diagnosis and treatment of coronary artery disease. *Heart and Lung, 24*, 427–435.

Bertakis, K. D. (1998). Physician gender and physician-patient interaction. In E. A. Blechman, & K. D. Brownell (Eds.), *Behavioral medicine and women: A comprehensive handbbook* (pp. 140–141). New York: Guilford Press.

Blumenthal, S. J., & Wood, S. F. (1997). Women's health care: Federal initiatives, policies, and directions. In S. J. Gallant, G. P. Keta, & R. Royak-Schaler (Eds.), *Health care for women. Psychological, social and behavioral influences* (pp. 3–10). Washington, DC: American Psychological Association.

Bouchard, C., Shephard, R., & Stephens, T. (1994). Consensus statement. In C. Bouchard, R. Shephard, & T. Stephens (Eds.), *Physical activity, fitness, and health: International proceedings and consensus statement* (pp. 9–76). Champaign, IL: Human Kinetics Books.

Brownell, K. D., & Rodin, J. (1994). The dieting maelstrom: Is it possible and advisable to lose weight? *American Psychologist, 49*, 781–791.

Brownson, R. C., Eyler, A. A., King, A. C., Brown, D. R., Shyu, Y. L., & Sallis, J. F. (2000). Patterns and correlates of physical activity among US women 40 years and older. *American Journal of Public Health, 90*, 264–270.

Cadwell, S. A. (1997). Transference and countertransference. In I. D. Yalom (Ed.), *Treating the psychological consequences of HIV* (pp.1–32). San Francisco, CA: Jossey-Bass.

Caldwell, J. C., & Caldwell, P. (1996). The African AIDS epidemic. *Scientific American, 274*, 62–63.

Carmody, T. (1997). Health-related behaviours: common factors. In A. Baum, S. Newman, J. Weinman, R. West, & C. McManus (Eds.), *Cambridge handbook of psychology, health and medicine* (pp. 117–120). Cambridge, England: Cambridge University Press.

Carroll, D., Bennett, P., & Smith, G. D. (1997). Socioeconomic status and health. In A. Baum, S. Newman, J. Weinman, R. West, & C. McManus (Eds.), *Cambridge handbook of psychology, health and medicine* (pp. 171–173). Cambridge, England: Cambridge University Press.

Cash, T. F. (1998). Negative body image. In E. A. Blechman & K. D. Brownell (Eds.), *Behavioral medicine and women. A comprehensive handbook* (pp. 386–391). New York: Guilford Press.

Cave, W. (1998). Women and heart disease: Same disease, different issues. *Canadian Journal of Cardiovascular Nursing, 9,* 29–33.

Chrisler, J. C. (1989). Should feminist therapists do weight loss counseling? In L. S. Brown & E. D. Rothblum (Eds.), *Overcoming fear of fat* (pp. 31–38). Binghamton, NY: Harrington Park Press.

Clark, D. O. (1999). Identifying psychological, physiological, and environmental barriers and facilitators to exercise among older low income adults. *Journal of Clinical Geropsychology, 51,* 51–62.

Cline, R. J., & McKenzie, N. J. (1998). The many cultures of health care: Difference, dominance, and distance in physician-patient communication. In L. D. Jackson & B. K. Duffy (Eds.), *Health communication research: A guide to developments and directions* (pp. 57–74). Westport, CT: Greenwood Press.

Consumers Union. (1993, June). Losing weight. What works. What doesn't. *Consumer Reports,* pp. 347–352.

Crespo, C. J., Keteyian, S. J., Heath, G. W., & Sempos, C. T. (1996). Leisure time physical activity among U.S. adults: Results from the third National Health and Nutrition Examination Survey. *Archives of Internal Medicine, 156,* 93–98.

Czaijowski, S. (1998). Psychological aspects of women's recovery from heart disease. In K. Orth-Gomer & M. Chesney (Eds.), *Women, stress, and heart disease* (pp. 151–164). Mahwah, NJ: Lawrence Erlbaum.

DeBon, M. & Klesges, R. C. (1995). Smoking and smoking cessation: Current conceptualizations and directions for future research. In A. J. Goreczny (Ed.), *Handbook of health and rehabilitation psychology* (pp. 135–156). New York: Plenum.

DeHovitz, J. A. (1995). Natural history of HIV infection in women. In H. Minkoff, J. A. DeHovitz, & A. Duerr (Eds.), *HIV infection in women* (pp. 57–72). New York: Raven Press.

Derry, P. S., Gallant, S. J., & Woods, N. F. (1997). Premenstrual syndrome and menopause. In S. J. Gallant, G. P. Keita, & R. Royak-Schaler (Eds.), *Health care for women: Psychological, social, and behavioral influences* (pp. 203–220). Washington, DC: American Psychological Association.

DiLorenzo, T. M., Stucky-Ropp, R. C., VanderWal, J. S., & Gotham, H. J. (1998). Determinants of exercise among children. II. A longitudinal analysis. *Preventive Medicine, 27,* 470–477.

DiMatteo, M. R., & Lepper, H. S. (1998). Promoting adherence to courses of treatment: Mutual collaboration in the physician–patient relationship. In L. D. Jackson, & B. K. Duffy (Eds.), *Health communication research: A guide to developments and directions* (pp. 75–86). Westport, CT: Greenwood Press.

Eccles, J. S., & Harold, R. D. (1991). Gender differences in sport involvement: Applying the Eccles' expectancy-value model. *Journal of Applied Sport Psychology, 3,* 7–35.

Edmunds, M. (1995). Policy and research: Balancing rigor with relevance. *Women's health: Research on gender, behavior and policy, 1,* 97–119.

Elders, M. J., Perry, C. L., Eriksen, M. P., & Giovino, G. A. (1994). The report of the surgeon general: Preventing tobacco use among young people. *American Journal of Public Health, 84,* 543–547.

Evanoski, C. (1997). Myocardial Infarction: The number one killer of women. *Critical Care Nursing Clinics of North America, 9,* 489–496.

Eyler, A. A., Brownson, R. C., King, A. C., Donatelle, R. J., & Heath, G. (1997). Physical activity and women in the United States: An overview of health benefits, prevalence, and intervention opportunities. *Women & Health, 26,* 27–49.

Fallon, P., Katzman, M. A., & Wooley, S. C. (Eds.). (1994). *Feminist perspectives on eating disorders.* New York: Guilford Press.

Flegal, K. M., Carroll, M. D., Kuczmarski, R. J., & Johnson, C. L. (1998). Overweight and obesity in the United States: Prevalence and trends, 1960–1994. *International Journal of Obesity and Related Metabolic Disorders, 22,* 39–47.

French, S. A., & Jeffery, R. W. (1994). Consequences of dieting to lose weight: Effects on physical and mental health. *Health Psychology, 13,* 195–212.

Friestad, C., & Klepp, K. (1997). Social influences on the development of boys' and girls' smoking behavior. *Journal of Gender, Culture, and Health, 2,* 287–304.

Garner, D. M., & Wooley, S. C. (1991). Confronting the failure of behavioral and dietary treatments for obesity. *Clinical Psychology Review, 11,* 729–780.

Gavey, N., & McPhillips, K. (1997). Women and the heterosexual tramsmission of HIV: Risks and prevention strategies. *Women & Health, 25*, 41–63.

Gilbert, S., & Thompson, J. K. (1996). Feminist explanations of the development of eating disorders: Common themes, research findings, and methodological issues. *Clinical psychology: Science and practice, 3*, 183–202.

Gochman, D. S. (1997). Demography, development, and diversity of health behavior: An integration. In D. S. Gochman (Ed.) *Handbook of health behavior research III: Demography, development, and diversity* (pp. 325–350). New York: Plenum.

Goudsmit, E. M. (1994). All in her mind! Stereotypic views and the psychologisation of women's health. In S. Wilkinson, et al., (Eds.), *Women and health: Feminist perspectives* (pp. 7–12). London, England: Taylor & Francis.

Graham, H. (1994). Surviving by smoking. In S. Wilkinson, C. Kitzinger, et al., (Eds.), *Women and health: Feminist perspectives* (pp. 102–123). London, England: Taylor & Francis.

Grigg, M., Bowman, J., & Redman, S. (1996). Disordered eating and unhealthy weight reduction practices among adolescent females. *Preventive Medicine, 25*, 748–756.

Grilo, C. M. (1996). Treatment of obesity: An integrative model. In J. K. Thompson (Ed.), *Body image, eating disorders, and obesity: An integrative guide for assessment and treatment* (pp. 389–424). Washington, DC: American Psychological Association.

Grunberg, N., Brown, K., & Klein, C. (1997). Tobacco smoking. In A. Baum, S. Newman, J. Weinman, R. West, & C. McManus (Eds.), *Cambridge handbook of psychology, health and medicine* (pp. 606–610). Cambridge, England: Cambridge University Press.

Hall, J. A., & Roter, D. L.. (1995). Patient gender and communication with physicians: Results of a community-based study. *Women's Health, 1*, 77–95.

Hoek, H. W. (1993). Review of the epidemiological studies of eating disorders. *International Review of Psychiatry, 5*, 61–74.

Huggins, J., Elman, N., Baker, C., Forrester, R., & Lyter, D. (1991). Affective and behavioral response of gay and bisexual men to HIV antibody testing. *Social Work, 36*, 61–66.

Hunt, K. (1994). A "Cure for All Ills"? Constructions of the menopause and the chequered fortunes of hormone replacement therapy. In S. Wilkinson, et al. (Eds.), *Women and health: Feminist perspectives* (pp. 141–165). London, England: Taylor & Francis.

Husten, C. G. (1998). Cigarette smoking. In E. A. Blechman & K. D. Brownell (Eds.), *Behavioral medicine and women: A comprehensive handbook* (pp. 425–432). New York: Guilford Press.

Ickovics, J. R., Morrill, A. C., Beren, S. E., Walsh, U., & Rodin, J. (1994). Limited effects of HIV counseling and testing for women. *Journal of the American Medical Association, 272*, 443–448.

Ickovics, J. R., & Rodin, J. (1992). Women and AIDS in the United States: Epidemiology, natural history, and mediating mechanisms. *Health Psychology, 11*, 1–16.

Jaccard, J. J., Wilson, T. E., & Radecki, C. M., (1995). Psychological issues in the treatment of HIV-infected women. In H. Minkoff, J. A. DeHovitz, & A. Duerr (Eds.), *HIV infection in women* (pp. 57–72). New York: Raven Press.

Jeffery, R. W., Wing, R. R., & Mayer, R. R. (1998). Are smaller weight losses or more achievable weight loss goals better in the long term for obese patients? *Journal of Consulting and Clinical Psychology, 66*, 641–645.

Johnson, C. A., Corrigan, S. A., Dubbert, P. M., & Gramling, S. E. (1990). Perceived barriers to exercise and weight control practices in community women. *Women & Health, 16*, 177–191.

Johnson, T. L., & Fee, E. F. (1997). Women's health research: An introduction. In B. G. Jacobson & F. P. Haseltine (Eds.), *Women's health research: A medical and policy primer* (pp. 3–26). Washington, DC: Health Press International.

Kalichman, S. C. (1998). *Understanding AIDS: Advances in research and treatment* (2nd ed.). Washington, DC: American Psychological Association.

Kaplan, R. M., Orleans, C. T., Perkins, K. A., & Pierce, J. P. (1995). Marshalling the evidence for greater regulation and control of tobacco products: A call for action. *Annals of Behavioral Medicine, 17*, 3–14.

Kendler, K. S., MacLean, C., Neale, M., Kessler, R., Heath, A., & Eaves, L. (1991). The genetic epidemiology of bulimia nervosa. *American Journal of Psychiatry, 148*, 1627–1637.

Kennedy, M., Scarlett, M. I., Duerr, A., & Chu, S. (1995). Assessing HIV risk among women who have sex with women: Scientific and communication issues. *Journal of the Medical Women's Association, 50*, 103–107.

Killen, J. D. (1998). Smoking prevention. In E. A. Blechman & K. D. Brownell (Eds.), *Behavioral medicine and women: A comprehensive handbook* (pp. 228–232). New York: Guilford Press.

King, A. C., Blair, S. N., Bild, D. E., Dishman, R. K., Dubbert, P. M., Marcus, B. H., Oldridge, N. B., Paffenbarger, R. S., Jr., Powell, K. E., & Yeager, K. K. (1992). Determinants of physical health activity and intervention in adults. *Medicine and science in sports and exercise, 24*, S221-S236.

King, A. C., & Kiernan, M. (1997). Physical activity and women's health: Issues and future directions. In S. J. Gallant, G. P. Keita, & R. Royak-Schaler (Eds.), *Health care for women: Psychological, social, and behavioral influences* (pp. 133–146).

King, K. & Paul, P. (1996). A historical review of the depiction of women in cardiovascular literature. *Western Journal of Nursing Research, 18.*

Konstam, V., & Houser, R. (1994). Rehabilitation of women post myocardial infarction—a new look at old assumptions. *Journal of Applied Rehabilitation Counseling, 25*, 46–51.

Kriska, A. M., & Rexroad, A. R. (1998) The role of physical activity in minority populations. *Women's Health Issues, 8*, 98–103.

Lee, C. (1998). The social context of women's health. *Women's health. Psychological and social perspectives* (pp. 1–13). London: Sage.

Lichtenstein, E., & Glasgow, R. E. (1992). Smoking cessation: What have we learned over the past decade? *Journal of Consulting and Clinical Psychology, 60*, 518–527.

Lieberman, L., Meana, M., & Stewart, D. (1998). Cardiac rehabilitation: Gender differences in factors influencing participation. *Journal of Women's Health, 7*, 717–723.

Litt, I. F. (1997). *Taking our pulse: The health of America's women.* Stanford, CA: Stanford University Press.

Markowitz, J. C., Koesis, J. H., Fishman, B., Spielman, L. A., Jacobsberg, L. B., Frances, A. J., Klerman, G. L., & Perry, S. W. (1998). Treatment of depressive symptoms in human immunodeficiency virus-positive patients. *Archives of General Psychiatry, 55*, 452–457.

Matthews, K. A., Shumaker, S. A., Bowne, D. J., Langer, R. D., Hunt, J. R., Kaplan, R. M., Klesges, R. C., & Ritenbaugh, C. (1997). Women's Health Initiative: Why now? What is it? What's new? *American Psychologist, 52*, 101–116.

Medical Professional/Technical Information, Table 10 (1998, Feb. 6). (Online). HCFA. <http://www.hcfa.gov/medicaid/2082-10.htm> (2000, March 28).

Melnick, S. L., Sherer, R., Louis, T. A., Hillman, D., Rodriguez, E. M., Lackman, C., Capps, L., Brown, L. S., Carlyn, M., Korvick, J. A., & Deyton, L. (1994). Survival and disease progression according to gender of patients with HIV infection. *Journal of the American Medical Association, 272*, 1915–1921.

Mermelstein, R. J. (1997). Individual interventions: Stages of change and other health behavior models—The example of smoking cessation. In S. J. Gallant, G. P. Keita, & R. Royak-Schaler (Eds.), *Health care for women: Psychological, social, and behavioral influences* (pp. 387–404). Washington, DC: American Psychological Association.

Mermelstein, R., & Borrelli, B. (1995). Women and smoking. In A. L. Stanton & S. J. Gallant (Eds.), *The psychology of women's health* (pp. 309–348). Washington, DC: American Psychological Association.

Mulder, C., & Antoni, M. (1992). Psychosocial correlates of immune status and disease progression in HIV-1 infected homosexual men: Review of preliminary findings and commentary. *Psychology and Health, 6*, 175–192.

Neumark-Sztainer, D., Jeffrey, R. W., & French, S. A. (1997). Self-reported dieting: How should we ask? What does it mean? Associations between dieting and reported energy intake. *International Journal of Eating Disorders, 22*, 437–449.

Ockene, J. K., Emmons, K. M., Mermelstein, R. J., Perkins, K. A., Bonollo, D. S., Voorhees, C. C., & Hollis, J. F. (2000). Relapse and maintenance issues for smoking cessation. *Health Psychology, 19*, 17–31.

O'Leary, A., & Helgeson, V. S. (1997). Psychosocial factors and women's health: Integrating mind, heart, and body. In S. J. Gallant, G. P. Keita, & R. Royak-Schaler (Eds.), *Health care for women: Psychological, social, and behavioral influences* (pp. 25–40). Washington, DC: American Psychological Association.

Pennebaker, J. W. (1982). *The psychology of physical symptoms.* New York: Springer-Verlag.

Ransdell, L. B. & Wells, C. L. (1998). Physical activity in urban white, African-American, and Mexican-American women. *Medicine and Science in Sports and Exercise, 30*, 1608–1615.

Roter, D. L. & Hall, J. A. (1997). Gender differences in patient–physician communication. In S. J. Gallant, G. P. Keta, & R. Royak-Schaler (Eds.), *Health care for women: Psychological, social, and behavioral influences* (pp. 57–72). Washington, DC: American Psychological Association.

Rothblum, E. D. (1994). "I'll die for the revolution but don't ask me not to diet": Feminism and the continuing stigmatization of obesity. In P. Fallon, M. A. Katzman, & S. C. Wooley (Eds.), *Feminist perspectives on eating disorders* (pp. 17–52). New York: Guilford Press.

Safran, D. G., Rogers, W. H., Tarlov, A. R., McHorney, C. A., & Ware, J. E., Jr. (1997). Gender differences in medical treatment: The case of physician-prescribed restrictions. *Social Science and Medicine, 45*, 711–722.

Sallis, J. F., Bauman, A., & Pratt, M. (1998). Environmental and policy interventions to promote physical activity. *American Journal of Preventive Medicine, 15*, 379–397.

Sallis, J. F., Hovell, M. F., & Hofstetter, C. R. (1992). Predictors of adoption and maintenance of vigorous physical activity in men and women. *Preventive Medicine, 21*, 237–57.

Schenk-Gustafsson, K., & Al-Khalili, F. (1998). Reproductive hormone effects on the cardiovascular system in women. In K. Orth-Gomer & M. Chesney (Eds.), *Women, stress, and heart disease* (185–204). Mahwah, NJ: Lawrence Erlbaum.

Sherr, L. (1995). Psychosocial aspects of providing care for women with HIV infection. In H. Minkoff, J. A. De-Hovitz, & A. Duerr (Eds.), *HIV infection in women* (pp. 57–72). New York: Raven Press.

Shumaker, S. A. & Smith, T. R. (1995). Women and coronary heart disease: A Psychological perspective. In A. L. Stanton, & S. J. Gallant (Eds.), *The psychology of women's health: Progress and challenges in research and application* (pp. 25–50). Washington, DC: American Psychological Association.

Sikkema, K. J. (1998). HIV prevention. In E. A. Blechman & K. D. Brownell (Eds.), *Behavioral medicine and women: A comprehensive handbook* (pp. 198–202). New York: Guilford Press.

Sikkema, K. J., & Kelly, J. A. (1996). Behavioral medicine interventions can improve the quality-of-life and health of persons with HIV disease. *Annals of Behavioral Medicine, 18*, 40–48.

Simoni-Wastila, L. (1998). Gender and psychotropic drug use. *Medical Care, 36*, 88–94.

Solomon, L. J., & Flynn, B. S. (1993). Women who smoke. In C. T. Orleans & J. T. Slade (Eds.), *Nicotine addiction: Principles and management.* (pp. 339–349). New York: Oxford Press.

Stampfer, M. J., Colditz, G. A., & Willett, W. C. (1990). Menopause and heart disease: A review. In M. Flint & F. Kronenberg (Eds.), *Multidisciplinary perspectives on menopause: Annals of the New York academy of sciences* (pp. 193–203). New York: New York Academy of Sciences.

Sullivan, P. F. (1995). Mortality in anorexia nervosa. *American Journal of Psychiatry, 152*, 1073–1074.

Thoits, P. A. (1991). Gender differences in coping with emotional distress. In J. Eckenrode (Ed.), *The social context of coping. The Plenum series on stress and coping* (pp. 107–138). New York: Plenum.

Thorndike, A. N., Rigotti, N. A., Stafford, R. S., & Singer, D. E. (1998). National patterns in the treatment of smokers by physicians. *Journal of the American Medical Association, 279*, 604–608.

United States Department of Health and Human Services. (1990). *The health benefits of smoking cessation: A report to the Surgeon General* (PHS Publication No. 90–8416). Washington, DC: United States Department of Health and Human Services.

United States Department of Health and Human Services. (1991). *Healthy people 2000: National health promotion and disease prevention objectives* (PHS Publication No. 91–50213). Washington, DC: United States Department of Health and Human Services.

United States Department of Health and Human Services. (1995). *Health United States: 1994* (PHS Publication No. 95–1232). Washington, DC: United States Department of Health and Human Services.

United States Department of Health and Human Services. (1996). Physical activity and health: A report of the surgeon general. Atlanta, GA: Centers for Disease Control and Prevention, National Center for Chronic Disease Prevention and Health Promotion.

VanScoy, H. C. (1997). Health behavior in lesbians. In D. S. Gochman (Ed.), *Handbook of health behavior research III: Demography, development, and diversity* (pp. 141–159). New York: Plenum.

Verbrugge, L. M. (1985). Gender and health: An update on hypotheses and evidence. *Journal of Health and Social Behavior, 26*, 156–182.

Verhoef, M. J. & Love, E. J. (1994). Women and exercise participation: The mixed blessing of motherhood. *Health Care for Women International, 15*, 297–306.

Williams, D. R., & Rucker, T. (1996). Socioeconomic status and the health of racial minority populations. In P. M. Kato & T. Mann, (Eds.), *Handbook of diversity issues in health psychology* (pp. 407–423). New York: Plenum.

Williamson, D. F., Kahn, H. S., Remington, P. L., & Anda, R. F. (1990). The 10-year incidence of overweight and major weight gain in U.S. adults. *Archives of Internal Medicine, 150*, 665–672.

Wing, R. R., & Klem, M. L. (1997). Obesity. In S. J. Gallant, G. P. Keita, & R. Royak-Schaler (Eds.), *Health care for women: Psychological, social, and behavioral influences* (pp. 115–132). Washington, DC: American Psychological Association.

# 12

# Mental Health Issues for Women

## Laurie A. Roades

## INTRODUCTION

Recent epidemiological studies suggest that anywhere from almost one third (Robins et al., 1984) to almost one half of Americans will experience psychological distress sufficient to warrant diagnosis of a formal mental disorder at some time during their lives (Kessler et al., 1994). Although women and men share much in common in the area of mental health, women's and men's experiences differ sufficiently to yield significant distinctions in this area (Kessler et al., 1994). This chapter examines mental health issues specifically for women. First, conceptualizations of mental health and disorder, especially as they are impacted by gender, are discussed. Second, prevalence rates for specific disorders are examined, followed by possible explanations for gender-related differences. Finally, an expanded framework for understanding women's mental health is presented. Stress related to poverty and gender role strain, as well as violence against women, will be explored.

Historically, most research in psychiatry and psychology has focused on the experiences of men, even when women were seen as the primary clients. This chapter utilizes a feminist framework in which all women's experiences are central to conceptualizations of mental health and distress, the diagnostic tools and nomenclatures used, and the therapeutic interventions developed. In addition, most available research on women's mental health has been limited in scope, focusing on white, middle-class women (Reid & Comas-Diaz, 1990). Although women share a number of common experiences based on gender, women's experiences reflect great diversity related to ethnicity, sexual orientation, age, social class, and physical ability. Numerous researchers (Brown, 1997; Reid & Comas-Diaz, 1990; Russo, 1995) have called for attention to such diversity to better understand mental health issues for all women and to provide the most appropriate services when needed. Effort is taken to examine this diversity among women as each topic is discussed.

Laurie A. Roades • Department of Behavioral Sciences, California State Polytechnic University, Pomona, California 91768

*Issues in the Psychology of Women,* edited by Biaggio and Hersen. Kluwer Academic/Plenum Publishers, New York, 2000.

## CONCEPTUALIZATIONS OF MENTAL HEALTH
## AND PSYCHOLOGICAL DISORDERS

Conceptualizations of "mental health" and "mental disorder" have varied dramatically across time and cultures (Showalter, 1985). Historically, expectations for how healthy women should act have been quite different from what was expected for healthy men. Women's roles were quite restrictive and women's (primarily white women's) mental and physical health were seen as quite fragile. Women who challenged the status quo were seen as irrational and violently mad (Showalter, 1985). It should come as no surprise then that women have frequently been viewed as having more psychological disorders than men.

Showalter (1985), in her book, *The Female Malady,* provides a detailed discussion of how women have been viewed historically and how these views have been related to perceptions and treatment of women's mental illness. During the middle 1800s, the Victorian era, women's reproductive organs were deemed to make them vulnerable and mentally unstable. Showalter quotes one author, George Man Burrows, as writing that "The functions of the brain are so intimately connected with the uterine system, that the interruption of any one process which the latter has to perform in the human economy may implicate the former." (p. 56). Showalter suggests that "Given so shaky a constitution, it seemed a wonder that any woman could hope for a lifetime of sanity, and psychiatric experts often expressed their surprise that female insanity was not even more frequent" (p. 56). As a result, women were viewed as needing care and protection, and thus were sheltered and denied opportunities for work or activities outside the home. Refusal by women to accept these limitations was met with quick rebuke and punishment.

Steen, in her 1991 review of historical perspectives on women and mental illness, described how this view continued into the 1900s.

> Henry Maudsley and T. S. Clouston saw women as natural helpmates of men with all the placid, altruistic, and nurturant qualities needed to fit women to breed and rear children. Thus, mental illness began when women defied their "nature" and attempted to compete with men instead of serving them, or sought alternatives or even additions to their maternal functions. Once such deviant, mentally disordered behavior appeared, it could be passed on to the next female generation, endangering future mothers. This became one of the primary causes for the predominance of women among asylum patients (Clouston, 1911). (p. 363)

More recently, Phyllis Chesler (1972) in her controversial book *Women and Madness,* has discussed in detail how the medical and psychiatric establishment have been biased and discriminatory against women. Chesler described how women's social roles have been related to "madness" in women. She also examined how clinicians held different views of mental health for women versus men, and how many women increasingly came to have "careers" as psychiatric patients.

"Mental health," and consequently "mental disorder," remain difficult concepts to define. Today, psychological disorders are generally diagnosed according to criteria outlined in the fourth edition of the Diagnostic and Statistical Manual (DSM-IV) (American Psychiatric Association, 1994). This manual lists the specific symptoms required to diagnose each mental disorder, as well as information regarding prevalence, the course of the disorder over time, and limited information related to gender and age. Clinicians check for presence and number of specific diagnostic criteria before judging a specific disorder to be present and diagnosable. One of the stated goals for development and use of the DSM-IV was that it have an "extensive empirical foundation" in order to best serve as a guide to clinicians and to help facilitate reliable communication between clinicians (American Psychiatric Association, 1994, p. xv).

Numerous mental health professionals and researchers, however, have offered significant criticisms of the DSM-IV and this mode of diagnosing mental illness. Of particular concern is the notion that mental health and mental disorder can be separated into two discrete categories. Mental health and difficulties are much more likely to fall on a continuum, with many individuals having more or less of some behaviors and characteristics rather than simply having or not having them (Maxmen & Ward, 1995). In addition, formal DSM-IV diagnosis seems to locate the origin and cause of many disorders within the individual her- or himself without taking into account important environmental and social factors that may influence psychological distress (Marecek & Hare-Mustin, 1991).

Feminist researchers and clinicians have argued that both previous and current conceptualizations of mental health have been far too narrow and have been closely aligned with traditional gender stereotypes (Chesler, 1972; Kaplan, 1983). This has led to different ideas about what mental health means for women and men. In a now classic study by Broverman, Broverman, Clarkson, Rosenkrantz, and Vogel (1970), mental health professionals were asked to describe a "healthy man," a "healthy woman," and a "healthy adult." Although women and men were described similarly on a number of traits, significant differences in how clinicians perceived healthy women and men were noted. Descriptions of the healthy man included higher ratings of traits such as "independent," "aggressive," "logical," and "direct." Healthy women were more often described as "submissive," likely to have their "feelings easily hurt," and "excitable in minor crises." Obviously, "healthy" meant different things for women and men, even in the eyes of trained clinicians. However, most noteworthy was the description of the healthy adult. Clinicians described a "healthy" adult as being more similar to a man than to a woman. This presents a double bind for women. Whereas men can be seen as healthy both in their gender and as adults, women can be healthy in only one way at a time. Women who are healthy as "women" may be less likely to be seen as healthy adults in our society. In contrast, a woman we would identify as having the traits of a healthy adult in our society runs the risk of being seen as not healthy for her gender, perhaps not subscribing adequately to her gender role, being "unfeminine."

The study of Broverman and colleagues (1970) has been criticized on methodological grounds (Widiger & Settle, 1987). However, its main point remains valid. There does not appear to be one objective standard for mental health. Rather, what is mentally healthy differs based on one's gender. In addition, what is seen as mentally healthy more often reflects men's behavior rather than women's behavior.

McHugh (2000) summarizes how a feminist perspective of psychological disorders differs from more traditional approaches and reminds us of the importance of taking a feminist perspective when we ask how gender may be related to disorders more prevalent in women than men.

> Feminists urge us to consider the sociopolitical context in which women experience mental disorders. A feminist perspective includes an analysis of how cultural gender roles and sexual inequality create stress for women or affect the ways in which women react to stress. A feminist approach considers the possibility that women's problems in general, and an individual woman's problem in particular, may be rooted in gender roles or gender inequalities. (p. 345)

However, this is not always easy to do. Clinicians are trained to focus on individuals and their specific symptoms, and treatment interventions are usually geared toward individual clients (McHugh, 2000). It is a challenge not to look at what might be "wrong" within the individual, but to look beyond any particular woman simultaneously at the sociocultural and political contexts in which women live (Marecek & Hare-Mustin, 1991).

## PREVALENCE OF PSYCHOLOGICAL DISORDERS BY GENDER

It is difficult to know exactly how many people experience psychological difficulties that are serious enough to warrant formal DSM-IV diagnosis. Epidemiological studies are large community-based investigations which endeavor to provide information as to prevalence and incidence rates for various disorders. These studies may take place within a relatively limited geographical area (e.g., a particular city or region) or may include a national sample.

Two national epidemiological studies, the Epidemiological Catchment Area study (ECA) and the National Comorbidity Survey (NCS, conducted between 1990 and 1992), provide estimates of the prevalence rates for various psychological disorders in community samples. The ECA study examined incidence and prevalence rates for many DSM-III-R diagnoses in five U.S. cities, targeting both individuals in the community and in institutions (Robins et al., 1984). The NCS was a study mandated by Congress to examine "the comorbidity of substance use disorders and nonsubstance psychiatric disorders in the United States" (Kessler et al., 1994, p. 8). This national study was designed to include a representative probability sample of noninstitutionalized adolescents and adults (15 to 54 years old). Although there are limitations to any large-scale study, results from these projects provide us with some of the most current and comprehensive prevalence estimates for many psychological disorders. Combined with clinical studies of individuals seeking mental health services, this research helps us to understand both the types and frequencies of disorders experienced by women and men.

Previous researchers have disagreed about whether women and men differ in their overall rates of psychological difficulties, with some authors suggesting that women have higher rates of mental disorders than men and others suggesting that there is no difference in overall rates between women and men (Kessler et al., 1994; Robins et al., 1984). This question is difficult because the answer depends on which psychological disorders one chooses to include as well as how one calculates level of disorder. What is clear, however, is that women and men often receive different diagnoses (Fabrega, Mezzich, Ulrich, & Benjamin, 1990; Kessler et al., 1994; Robins et al., 1984).

Kessler and colleagues (1994) provide a detailed discussion of the lifetime prevalence rates for DSM-III-R diagnoses found in the recent NCS study. Data suggest that a large percentage of the U.S. population experience significant psychological difficulties, with 48 percent of the population estimated to meet criteria for at least one mental disorder at some time during their lives. No differences between women and men were noted in overall prevalence rates (47.3 percent vs. 48.7 percent, respectively) for a DSM-III-R diagnosis. Results from the ECA study suggested a lower overall lifetime prevalence rate for both women and men, but were consistent in noting no overall differences between women and men (Robins et al., 1984). This conclusion of no differences has been criticized, however, because not all relevant disorders were included in either study and there is some disagreement as to whether or not substance abuse/dependence should be included in rates of mental disorder (Russo & Green, 1993).

Gender differences in prevalence rates have consistently been found for the three diagnostic categories most frequently diagnosed: substance abuse and dependence disorders, anxiety disorders, and affective (mood) disorders (Kessler et al., 1994; Robins et al., 1984). Women are significantly more likely than men to be diagnosed with many of the anxiety and affective disorders. Men, in contrast, are more likely to be diagnosed with substance abuse/de-

pendence disorders. However, although there may be no gender difference in overall prevalence rates, women in the NCS study reported higher levels of comorbidity than men. That is,
women were more likely than men to have a lifetime history of three or more disorders
(Kessler et al., 1994).

Studies examining axis II personality disorders have also found a pattern of gender differences in diagnosis. Women are likely to be diagnosed with borderline and histrionic personality disorders (American Psychiatric Association, 1994). Men are more frequently diagnosed
with antisocial personality disorder (American Psychiatric Association, 1994; Kessler et al.,
1994). However, although rates once again differ by disorder, this does not necessarily suggest
a difference in overall rates of axis II disorders for women and men (Widiger, Corbitt, & Funtowicz, 1994).

Results of these studies suggest that in many ways women and men are similar in overall level of psychological difficulty, although they often exhibit different patterns of psychological symptoms. In addition, some women seem to be at additional risk by virtue of having
more disorders across their lifetimes. Disorders that are frequently diagnosed in women
and/or that present significant challenges to women's mental health are discussed below.
These include: depression, anxiety disorders, substance abuse/dependence disorders, and
personality disorders.

## DEPRESSION

### Diagnosis of Depression

Affective disorders, commonly known as mood disorders, include both primarily depressive disorders (e.g., major depressive disorder, dysthmic disorder) as well as bipolar disorders
which consist of both depressive and manic or hypomanic symptoms (e.g., bipolar I and II disorders, cyclothymia). Prevalence rates, course, treatment and gender differ greatly across these
two classes of mood disorders (American Psychiatric Association, 1994; Kessler et al., 1994;
Myers et al., 1984).

Major depressive disorder is a clinical syndrome in which individuals exhibit depressed
mood accompanied by difficulties in functioning. Symptoms include emotional difficulties
(e.g., depressed mood), cognitive changes (e.g., decreased concentration, loss of interest in
previously pleasurable activities, feelings of worthlessness), behavioral changes (e.g., difficulties eating or sleeping, fatigue and physical slowing), and possible suicidal ideation or behavior (American Psychiatric Association, 1994). Many people describe feeling "down" or "depressed" at times, but anywhere from 7 percent to 17 percent of the population will experience
difficulties serious enough to warrant a formal diagnosis of major depressive episode at some
time during their lives (Kessler et al., 1994; Robins et al., 1984). Approximately 6 percent of
the population will experience another form of depression, called "dysthymia," a longer-term,
lower-level depression in which a person experiences depressed mood over a period of years
(American Psychiatric Association, 1994; Kessler et al., 1994). Many additional individuals
will experience "subclinical" depressive symptoms that are not diagnosable, but are important
to note and treat nonetheless. Bipolar disorders, which include symptoms of elevated mood,
are far less common; lifetime prevalence rates are between .5 percent and 1.6 percent (American Psychiatric Association, 1994; Kessler et al., 1994). However, the course of the disorder is
quite stressful and its lower frequency should not be taken to suggest that this disorder is not
serious. Given these overall high prevalence rates for mood disorders, depressive difficulties
are obviously a serious concern for many people and their families.

### Gender Differences in Depression

Gender is significantly related to diagnosis of depression. Women are generally reported to be twice as likely as men to be diagnosed with a unipolar depressive disorder, both in community and clinical samples (American Psychiatric Association, 1994; Fabrega et al., 1990; Kessler et al., 1994; Weissman, 1987). This gender difference appears consistent across demographic groups (McGrath, Keita, Strickland, & Russo, 1990; Russo, Amaro, & Winter, 1987; Turner & Avison, 1989). These gender differences are not seen, however, in bipolar I disorder which includes both manic and depressive symptoms (Kessler et al., 1994). Kessler and colleagues (1996) analyzed rates of major depressive disorder further in terms of whether or not the disorder occurred alone ("pure") or was comorbid with another axis I disorder (primary or secondary depression). Results showed that for both women and men depression tends to be a secondary disorder, following another disorder. However, women are more likely than men to report "pure" depression (30.1 percent vs. 18.6 percent), with no additional disorder, and somewhat less likely to exhibit secondary depression (57.7 percent vs. 69.3 percent). This suggests that depression is a primary disorder for women more often than for men. The importance of examining the issue of depression for women is evidenced by the formation by Dr. Bonnie Strickland, president of the American Psychological Association in 1987, of a national Task Force on Women and Depression to examine the risk factors and treatment issues of women experiencing depression (McGrath et al., 1990).

Although gender differences exist across demographic groups, all women are not identical with regard to mood. Age, marital status, motherhood, ethnicity, and sexual orientation may all interact with gender to influence the experience of depression. For example, we know that rates of depression for females increase significantly during adolescence (see Nolen-Hoeksema, 1990). Women who are unhappily married and do not get along with their spouses report significantly higher rates of depression than women who are happily married, single, are separated or divorced (Weissman, 1987) and than men in similarly unhappy marriages (Barnett, Raudenbush, Brennan, Pleck, & Marshall, 1995).

Accurate diagnosis of depression is important, because both under- and overdiagnosis of depression can be serious errors with severe consequences (American Psychiatric Association, 1994; Russo, 1995). Some researchers have suggested, however, that clinicians may be more likely to overdiagnose depression in women and to see women as depressed even when they are not (Russo, 1995). Research by Loring and Powell (1988) revealed a tendency for clinicians to misdiagnose depression in white women who clearly were not depressed. They provided 290 psychiatrists with two case histories each describing client symptoms consistent with an axis I diagnosis of schizophrenia and an axis II diagnosis of dependent personality disorder. They varied the cases only by gender (female or male) and ethnicity (African-American or white); a fifth case contained no information regarding gender or ethnicity (neutral). Male clinicians (African-American and white) diagnosed women, regardless of ethnicity, as depressed more often than any other disorder, a bias not seen in female clinicians. However, this tendency was more pronounced for white women than for African-American women. Results of this study highlight the importance of possible clinician bias in diagnosing depression in women. They also underscore the need to examine client gender and race simultaneously, rather than independently, given that women of diverse ethnic backgrounds may be viewed differently. Research by Jenkins-Hall and Sacco (1991) suggests that African-American women who are depressed are likely to be evaluated more negatively by therapists than depressed white women.

A particularly pressing concern regarding overdiagnosis of depression for women is the fact that many depressed clients are treated with antidepressant medication, and there is concern that antidepressants may be overprescribed for women (McGrath et al., 1990). Hohmann (1989) examined data from the 1985 National Ambulatory Medical Care Survey to determine whether or not psychotropic drug prescribing by primary care physicians differed for males and females visiting physicians offices. She concluded that the rate of antidepressant prescriptions for women exceeded what would logically be expected. Women in the study ". . . were 82% more likely than men to receive an antidepressant" (p. 486).

This overprescription of antidepressant medication for women is not particularly surprising given the results of a recent study examining the drug advertisements that appeared in two medical journals, *American Family Physician* and *American Journal of Psychiatry* (Hansen & Osborne, 1995). Hansen and Osborne (1995) suggested that given that women are diagnosed with depression approximately twice as often as men, one might expect to see a 2:1 ratio of women to men in antidepressant ads. Unfortunately, the actual ads presented quite a different picture. In the journal for psychiatrists the ads depicted females five times more often than they did males. The greatest disparity was seen, however, in the journal for family physicians where the ratio was 10:0. These researchers suggest that this pattern is particularly problematic given that previous research has shown primary care physicians frequently diagnose mental disorders, with only limited mental health training.

It is important, however, not to dismiss use of antidepressant medication, or any other medication, completely. Antidepressant medications have been shown to help a number of clients seeking professional treatment, generally in combination with psychotherapy (McGrath et al., 1990). Marsh (1995), in her discussion of feminist psychopharmacology, highlights the need to keep appropriate psychopharmacologic interventions available for treating women who will benefit from them.

## Explanations for Women's Higher Rates of Depression

Several explanations have been advanced for understanding the gender differences in rates of depressive disorders. One popular explanation for women's relatively high rates of depression is that women's physiology is directly linked to their depressive difficulties. In their examination of risk factors for depression in women, McGrath and colleagues (1990) examined a wide range of research on the relationship between "reproduction-related events" (e.g., menstruation, pregnancy, childbirth, menopause) and depression. They concluded that it is important to consider a woman's reproductive life history in evaluating and understanding depression, but that these events alone cannot account for the overall difference in depression rates between women and men. This conclusion is supported by Nolen-Hoeksema's (1990) extensive review examining biological explanations for gender differences in depression. She states:

> The biological explanations of sex difference in depression have not been well supported. There is no evidence that women have a greater genetic predisposition to depression than men, and the hormonal explanations have received mixed and indirect support at best. . . . Social and environmental factors cannot be ignored as we try to explain the variations across groups in sex differences in depression. (pp. 75–76)

A second proposed explanation for women's higher rates of depression focuses on personality characteristics and styles responding to and dealing with life stressors. Examination of the relationship between personality characteristics and the differing rates of depression for women and men, however, has not supported the idea that this is an adequate explanation. Nolen-Hoeksema (1990) examined research in the areas of assertiveness, influenceability, risk-taking, dependency, and reactivity to the evaluations of others and concluded that differences in these areas were not always strong nor straightforward, nor could they account for the levels of depression experienced by women. Research has supported the idea, however, that women may respond differently to feelings of depression than men. Nolen-Hoeksema and her colleagues in a number of studies (Nolen-Hoeksema, 1990) have found that women often have a more ruminative response to dealing with depression in contrast to men's more distracting response style. Many women tend to spend time thinking about why they feel depressed, whereas men are more likely to do something to take their mind off feelings of depression. This ruminative style may lead women to experience both higher levels and longer periods of depressed mood.

Finally, a third explanation for why women might reasonably be expected to experience high levels of depression has to do with women's and men's different life experiences. Poverty (Belle, 1990), gender role strain (Aneshensel et al., 1981; Turner & Avison, 1989), and violence directed against women (Kilpatrick et al., 1992) have all been related to increased levels of depression in women.

An alternative view on these differing base rates in depression for women and men, however, is that they do not reflect accurately women's and men's depressive difficulties. Rather, these rates may reflect a rather biased representation of women's mental health, as suggested by the Loring and Powell (1988) research that was just described. It seems likely, however, that there is a middle ground between these two seemingly opposite positions. Most research supports the conclusion that women do experience depression more often than men (McGrath et al., 1990) as a result of a combination of biological factors, gender role expectations, discrimination and misogynistic violence directed toward them. These factors should not be ignored and women's depression should be understood within this context. However, it also seems appropriate that clinicians should guard against overdiagnosing depression in women when other diagnoses may be more appropriate, which possibly leads to artificially inflated gender differences in depression.

## ANXIETY DISORDERS

### Diagnosis of Anxiety Disorders

Anxiety disorders represent a class of disorders that include a wide range of symptoms associated with fearfulness and apprehension. Specific symptoms may range from fearfulness of single objects or situations (as seen in specific phobia) to unexpected, intense feelings of panic accompanied by symptoms such as heart palpitations, fear of losing control, or dying (e.g., panic disorder) to a fear of being in places from where it may be difficult to escape which often makes it difficult to leave one's home (agoraphobia). In contrast, some people feel anxious much of the time and in most situations (generalized anxiety disorder). Posttraumatic stress disorder (PTSD), in contrast, involves symptoms which follow a specific, terrifying trauma. (PTSD is discussed later in this chapter.) Combined, these anxiety disorders make up one of the most frequently diagnosed class of disorders, second only to substance use disorders (Kessler et al., 1994), although prevalence rates vary considerably across disorders.

### Gender Differences in Anxiety Disorders

Women and men differ significantly in their rates of many of these anxiety disorders, with women generally exhibiting higher levels of most anxiety disorders (Kessler et al., 1994; Regier, Narrow, & Rae, 1990). For example, data from the NCS study suggest that women are approximately twice as likely as men to exhibit agoraphobia (9 percent vs. 4.1 percent) (Magee, Eaton, Wittchen, McGonagle, & Kessler, 1996), generalized anxiety disorders (6.6 percent vs. 3.6 percent) (Wittchen, Zhao, Kessler, & Eaton, 1994), and simple phobias (15.7 percent vs. 6.7 percent) (Magee et al., 1996), and their rate of social phobia is almost 40 percent higher (15.5 percent vs. 11.1 percent) (Magee et al., 1996). Individuals, who identified their employment status as "homemaker," presumably mostly females, had higher rates of agoraphobia and simple phobia. The role of "homemaker" was also consistent with higher rates of generalized anxiety disorder, an effect that was even stronger than the effect for gender, suggesting the influence of gender roles yet again (Wittchen et al., 1994).

Wittchen and colleagues (1994) examined prevalence rates for generalized anxiety disorder. Rates for generalized anxiety disorder did not differ among women of different ethnic groups (African-American, Latina, and white), but did vary across the life span. Women under 24 years of age were least likely to experience generalized anxiety (2.5 percent), with rates increasing between 25 and 44 years (~7.1 percent) and again after age 45 (10.3 percent). No information was available for women over age 54, leaving open the question about levels of generalized anxiety found in older women. In addition, no information was provided about sexual orientation or physical ability.

Finally, anxiety disorders are seldom the only diagnosis a person receives; there is a high level of comorbidity with other disorders. More than 90 percent of individuals with lifetime generalized anxiety disorder (Wittchen et al., 1994) and more than 80 percent of those with agoraphobia or a phobia (Magee et al., 1996) indicated they had experienced one or more additional DSM-III-R disorders sometime during their lives. In addition to other anxiety disorders, the most common diagnosis was major depression. This finding is particularly important because depressive disorders are also more commonly diagnosed in women, suggesting that many women struggle with both anxiety and depression at some time during their lives.

## Agoraphobia

Agoraphobia is an area that is receiving the attention of feminist researchers and clinicians trying to understand both women's difficulties in this area, as well as mental health professionals' conceptualizations of and explanations for women's anxiety (Gelfond, 1991; McHugh, 2000). Agoraphobia often occurs concurrently with panic disorder, and women are diagnosed with this dual disorder three times as often as men, in contrast to the double rate for panic disorder without agoraphobia (American Psychiatric Association, 1994). Given that agoraphobia is so much more prevalent in women than in men, McHugh (2000) asks why we have not examined this connection.

> Given these numbers, isn't it likely that the experience of agoraphobia has something to do with being a woman in our culture? Shouldn't the theories about the causes of agoraphobia and the intervention strategies employed to treat agoraphobes incorporate some form of gender analysis or sensitivity? Yet authors of articles and books on agoraphobia rarely attempt to explain why most agoraphobes are women. (pp. 344–345)

Gelfond (1991) suggests that what we learn about the fears of women with agoraphobia may tell us much about fears of many women in our society. Rather than seeing women with agoraphobia as being pathological and qualitatively different from women without these specific symptoms, it is possible that women with agoraphobia have much in common with the many women who voice concerns about their place in the public sphere. Gender role socialization, which encourages girls from a young age to remain close to home and frequently discourages venturing out confidently into the world, is an important consideration in understanding agoraphobia, but one that has seldom been examined by researchers (Gelfond, 1991). McHugh (2000) adds to this the relationship between agoraphobia and marital status and marital conflict, as well as violence against women, to help us understand better women's increased tendency to remain close to home. Although all women clearly do not meet the diagnostic criteria for agoraphobia, there is some question as to whether or not there is a clear demarcation between women with and without these symptoms. Rather, it seems more likely that there is a continuum for these symptoms, with many of them found among a wide range of women (Gelfond, 1991). As a result, it seems unlikely that agoraphobia should be seen solely as a pathological disorder residing within a specific woman. Rather, a more comprehensive, feminist explanation would require us to consider this disorder in the context of women's (versus men's) experiences in our society (McHugh, 2000). Interventions aimed only at treating individual women, one by one, will do little to alleviate rates of agoraphobia among women overall; social changes directed at preventing agoraphobia are needed (Gelfond, 1991).

## SUBSTANCE ABUSE AND DEPENDENCE

### Diagnosis of Substance Abuse and Dependence

Substance abuse and dependence disorders include a wide range of symptoms resulting from problematic use of chemical substances. Substances often included in these disorders are alcohol, cocaine, amphetamines, hallucinogens, and sedatives. Individuals can be diagnosed with substance abuse if their use of one or more of these substances leads to significant impairment within a one-year period. This may involve difficulties in important roles (e.g., work, family), legal problems resulting from substance misuse, or use of the substance in dangerous situations (e.g., driving while under the influence) (American Psychiatric Association, 1994). Substance dependence may develop after a substance has been abused for some time and includes the additional symptoms of physiological tolerance (e.g., need for more of the substance to produce similar effect) or withdrawal (symptoms resulting from not using the substance) (American Psychiatric Association, 1994).

### Gender Differences in Substance Abuse and Dependence

Women are diagnosed with significantly lower rates of all substance abuse and substance dependence disorders than men, although specific rates vary by class of drug (Kessler et al., 1994; Robins et al., 1984). For example, results from the recent NCS study (Kessler et al., 1994) indicated that women's lifetime prevalence rates for alcohol abuse or dependence are between 41 percent to 51 percent those of men. Their rates for drug abuse or dependence are approximately 64 percent to 65 percent those of men. Overall, estimates of women's lifetime prevalence rates for any substance (alcohol or drug) abuse or dependence disorder have been as high as 17.9 percent (Kessler et al., 1994).

Because women are so much less likely than men to experience difficulties with substance abuse and dependence, these disorders may be ignored when discussing women's mental health (Schmidt, Klee, & Ames, 1990). However, although women's rates of substance abuse and dependence are lower than those of men, these disorders are still more frequent for women than dysthymia and many anxiety disorders. It is important not to underestimate either frequency of these disorders among women or the impact of these disorders on the mental health of women who experience these difficulties (Wilsnack, Wilsnack, & Hiller-Sturmhofel,

1994). Estimates suggest that anywhere from 4 to 18 percent of women will experience serious problems with alcohol or drug abuse/dependence at some time during their lives (Kessler et al., 1994; Vogeltanz & Wilsnack, 1997). This is not an insignificant number of women in the United States. In addition, many women who do not have diagnosable alcohol disorders engage in "problem drinking" (see Vogeltanz & Wilsnack, 1997).

Patterns of alcohol use vary among women of different ethnic groups, ages and sexual orientations (Caetano, 1994; Hughes & Wilsnack, 1997; Wilsnack, Vogeltanz, Diers, & Wilsnack, 1995). African-American and Latina women are more likely than white women to report either abstaining from alcohol completely or drinking only "infrequently" (Caetano, 1994). Acculturation to the United States is often related to lower abstention rates and increased alcohol use for Latina immigrants (Caetano, 1994). As women age, alcohol use tends to decrease, and overall rates of alcohol abuse and dependence are relatively low in the elderly female population (Wilsnack et al., 1995). However, there are still many older women who exhibit problems with alcohol, and this is particularly dangerous given that many older women may take over-the-counter or prescription medications while drinking (Wilsnack et al., 1995). A recent review of research examining alcohol use among lesbians (Hughes & Wilsnack, 1997) suggests that they are less likely than heterosexual women to abstain from drinking and somewhat more likely to report higher levels of problem drinking.

Although women experience many difficulties similar to their male counterparts, they also experience a somewhat different pattern of substance-related problems (see Vogeltanz & Wilsnack, 1997). Women who are dependent on alcohol often have co-occurring anxiety (Kessler et al., 1997) or mood disorders (Grant & Harford, 1995; Kessler et al., 1997). Compared to men, women are more likely to report that alcohol dependence followed these other psychological difficulties (Kessler et al., 1997). In their review of physical consequences of alcohol abuse in women, Vogeltanz & Wilsnack (1997) report that women who drink excessively experience higher rates of a number of illnesses (e.g., liver disease, hepatitis), as well as higher mortality rates than men.

Recently, Wilsnack and colleagues (Hughes & Wilsnack, 1997; Wilsnack et al., 1994; Vogeltanz & Wilsnack, 1997) have examined specific risk factors for problem drinking among women. In addition to the depressive and anxiety disorders described, at least three additional risk factors are important in understanding women's drinking. First, women are often influenced by the drinking behavior of their partners, more than men are influenced by their partners. Second, many women with alcohol problems have histories of childhood sexual abuse and/or adult victimization. Third, women with sexual dysfunctions often show an increased risk for alcohol-related problems.

# PERSONALITY DISORDERS

## Gender Differences in Diagnosis of Personality Disorders

Personality disorders involve problems resulting from a person's characteristic ways of behaving, thinking, and interacting with others. Such a pattern of behavior is longstanding and either causes the individual personal distress or interferes significantly with important areas of functioning (e.g., social or occupational) (American Psychiatric Association, 1994). Ten specific personality disorders are identified in the DSM-IV, and there are significant gender differences in prevalence rates for many of them (American Psychiatric Association, 1994), although men and women do not seem to differ in their overall rates of personality disorder (Widiger et al., 1994).

Given these disparate diagnoses for women and men, it is important to examine possible explanations for this discrepancy. Personality disorders are generally organized into three clusters each with a different theme. Themes include: (1) oddness or eccentricity; (2) appearing overly emotional, dramatic, and/or erratic; and (3) fearfulness or anxiousness. The clearest gender differences are for the disorders in which a person appears emotional or dramatic. Although women and men are both represented within this cluster, women are significantly overrepresented in two of these disorders (e.g., histrionic and borderline personality disorders) and men in another (antisocial personality disorder) (American Psychiatric Association, 1994).

Histrionic personality disorder is a diagnosis used to describe a person who is overly emotional and excessively seeks attention from others. Additional characteristics include provocative or seductive interactions with others, drawing attention to oneself through physical appearance, and dramatic and exaggerated speech and emotional expression (American Psychiatric Association, 1994). Borderline personality disorder is characterized by longstanding instability both in a person's relationships with other people as well as with one's own self-image, emotions, and behaviors. Specific characteristics also include: potentially dangerous impulsivity, self-mutilation or suicidal gestures, feelings of emptiness and concerns about abandonment, and difficulties controlling anger (American Psychiatric Association, 1994). Antisocial personality disorder involves behaviors that violate the rights of others. This may include lying or failure to obey laws, as well as impulsivity, irresponsibility, and aggression toward others for which the person exhibits no remorse (American Psychiatric Association, 1994).

There is significant controversy within the mental health field about what gender differences in these personality disorders mean. Widiger and colleagues (1994) suggest that there are similar levels of difficulty for women and men, but that problems are merely exhibited in different ways. Given that women have often been socialized to be expressive with their emotions and to be somewhat dramatic and dependent in interactions with others, one might reasonably expect exaggerations of these traits, personality disorders, to be more commonly seen in women (e.g., histrionic personality disorder). Men, in contrast, are encouraged to be more detached interpersonally, to be independent, and to be more aggressive. Exaggerations of these traits and behaviors would lead to different personality disorders (e.g., antisocial personality disorder). It is reasonable to expect that if certain personality characteristics and behaviors are going to be exaggerated it is likely to be done by the group (or gender) most likely to exhibit them in the first place. Generally accepted behaviors for women and men would *not* be diagnosed, and thus women would be no more vulnerable to a personality diagnosis than men. These differing prevalence rates for specific disorders would then reflect accurately women's and men's very real difficulties (Widiger et al., 1994).

Numerous feminist researchers and clinicians, however, have suggested that the personality disorder classifications are riddled with bias, particularly bias against women (Kaplan, 1983; Walker, 1994). These criticisms generally focus on two areas. First, behaviors identified as stereotypically "feminine" are more likely than those identified as stereotypically "masculine" to be viewed negatively and labeled as disordered. Women who merely conform to traditional feminine stereotypical behaviors (e.g., openly expressing emotion, using physical attractiveness to garner attention), behaviors that are socialized, expected, and rewarded in our society, are still at risk for being labeled less mentally healthy and viewed as potentially personality disordered as in histrionic personality disorder (Kaplan, 1983). The exception to this would be women judged to exhibit "unfeminine" behaviors. Women who do not conform to expected behaviors (e.g., are angry or unpredictable in their behaviors) are subject to a different personality disorder diagnosis—borderline personality disorder. Thus, women have a very narrow range of acceptable personality characteristics and behaviors. In addition, Walker (1994) notes that "It is important to recognize that the criteria in those disorders more frequently assigned to males are more behaviorally based, whereas those for women include more distortions of affect and cognition" (p. 25). This leaves disorders most often diagnosed in women open to more subjective clinician bias given that it is easier to measure and evaluate behaviors as opposed to thoughts and feelings.

Second, research on clinician bias in diagnosing of axis II personality disorders reveals that clinicians do indeed diagnose women and men differently with regard to personality disorders, even when they exhibit identical symptoms (Ford & Widiger, 1989; Hamilton, Rothbart, & Dawes, 1986). Ford and Widiger (1989) examined potential clinician bias in the diagnosis of histrionic and antisocial personality disorders. Clinicians were asked to rate one of the following case histories: histrionic, antisocial, or balanced (symptoms of both, but insufficient to warrant diagnosis). Case histories were varied by gender to include a woman, a man, and a neutral case (no gender information provided), but all other information within each diagnostic case was identical. Results showed that the clinicians' personality disorder diagnoses were more related to the gender of the client that to the specific symptoms exhibited, clear evidence of gender bias. Seventy-sex percent of the women in the histrionic condition were correctly identified with histrionic personality disorder, compared with only 44 percent of the men in this condition. Men were more likely to be diagnosed accurately in the antisocial condition (42 percent), but women were seldom diagnosed with antisocial personality disorder (15 percent). In fact, when women were described as exhibiting antisocial behavior they were more likely to be evaluated as histrionic than antisocial. Thus even if the diagnostic criteria and disorders themselves are shown not to be inherently biased against women, clinicians use these diagnostic categories in biased ways that treat women and men differently.

## AN EXPANDED FRAMEWORK FOR EXAMINING WOMEN'S MENTAL HEALTH

Traditional explanations for gender differences in psychological disorders have focused primarily on biological, behavioral, cognitive, and emotional factors within individual women or within women as a group. Biologically, we have asked what about women's bodies (e.g., genes, hormones, reproductive functioning) makes them different from men. Behaviorally, we have asked what skills or abilities are women lacking. Cognitively, we question what a particular woman is thinking and how this might impact her feelings and activities. Finally, we wonder whether women's personality make-up might simply be more emotional than men's, perhaps making them more vulnerable and less able to cope when they encounter distressing events.

However, although each of these approaches may offer something meaningful, each misses an important piece of the puzzle in helping us to understand women's mental health and why many women exhibit different types of psychological difficulties than men. McHugh (2000), in her examination of agoraphobia, argues eloquently for a new perspective, a feminist perspective, on understanding both women's specific psychological differences in rates of disorders, as well as their life experiences in general.

> Feminists have argued for a thorough examination of the sociological, historical, cultural, economic, political, and psychological factors that affect and limit women's experiences. Women's experiences and problems are seen as occurring in a sociocultural context, as affected by gender socialization and as limited by gender roles. (p. 356)

Examined below are two sociocultural factors related to women's mental health. Specific factors discussed include stress and gender role strain and violence against women.

## Stress and Gender Role Strain

Stress has frequently been implicated as a factor in a number of psychological disorders (Mirowski & Ross, 1989). Women and men are both exposed to numerous stressors in daily life; neither gender has a monopoly on this experience. However, it is important to ask whether women might experience some stressors more frequently than men in ways that differentially impact the mental health picture for women. The impact of two specific stressors, poverty and gender role strain, are important for understanding women's mental health. (The impact of violence against women can be discussed as an important stressor, but is discussed separately.)

### Poverty

Poverty is one of the most consistently documented sources of physical and psychological distress (Belle, 1990; Kessler et al., 1994; Mirowsky & Ross, 1989). Individuals in the lowest income category are the most likely to exhibit a psychological disorder; show the highest rates of anxiety, mood, and substance abuse/dependence disorders; and are significantly more likely to exhibit multiple psychological disorders than those with higher incomes (Kessler et al., 1994).

Women are significantly more likely than men to live below the poverty level, a fact that has come to be described as the "feminization of poverty." Women, particularly Latinas (Amaro & Russo, 1987) and other women of color, are often confined to low-paying jobs with little hope for promotion or easing of financial strain. High levels of depression and anxiety are often seen in single mothers with children, likely the result of the financial struggle associated with this role (Weissman, Leaf, & Bruce, 1987). McGrath and colleagues (1990), in the final report of the American Psychological Association's National Task Force on Women and Depression, identified poverty as a "pathway to depression," having a particularly powerful impact on women's mental health (p. xii).

### Gender Role Strain

Research in the area of gender role strain has traditionally examined how the number and quality of roles women occupy is related to women's mental health. This research has generally focused on three specific roles for women: spouse, employed worker, and mother. Two theoretical perspectives on the impact of these roles have been proposed. One theory suggests that women who hold fewer roles should exhibit better mental health because there is less risk of role overload or role conflict. The other approach proposes that increased roles should prove beneficial because gratification can come from many sources and difficulties in any one area can be offset by other roles.

It is interesting to note that the question of how various roles impact mental health primarily arises when one is discussing women's rather than men's lives. It is assumed that men can successfully work, have intimate relationships, and be parents to a number of children simultaneously. For women, however, there is the often asked question, "Can she have it all?" This question seems rather biased and reflects our differing expectations for women's and men's lives. However, women's experiences in these roles differ somewhat from men's and it is important to examine the impact this different experience may have on women's mental health.

Research examining the relationship between various roles and mental health presents a complex picture, suggesting it is difficult to address the impact of any of these roles for women (or men) in a single sentence. Baruch and Barnett (1987) suggested that the clearest statement in this regard is that

> What most affects well-being is not the number of roles but rather the specific roles occupied and their quality. . . . The psychological consequences of occupying multiple roles, furthermore, depends not only on the number of roles a woman plays but also on how much she enjoys each role. (p. 64)

Thus, both the number and quality of roles must be examined.

Employment is generally related to improved mental health for women and men (Coleman, Antonucci, & Adelmann, 1987; Gove & Zeiss, 1987). Women who are employed have been found to report higher levels of happiness (Gove & Zeiss, 1987), as well as better physical health, higher self-esteem, and lower levels of anxiety (Coleman et al., 1987) compared to women who are not employed. One exception to this pattern seems to be that women with children at home who are employed, but would rather not be employed, report being less happy (Gove & Zeiss, 1987). This is consistent with Thoits' (1987) suggestion that it is the "congruence" between our roles and expectations of roles that is important. Most research, however, has been conducted with primarily white samples. Research on employment among Latina women has suggested that they often work in lower paying, lower status jobs (Amaro & Russo, 1987) which may evidence a different relationship to mental health.

Marital status also seems to promote a sense of well-being for many women, although its protective status is larger for men than for women. Gove and Zeiss (1987) report that in their study of more than 2000 adult women and men, married women, regardless of employment status and parenting status, reported higher levels of happiness than any group of unmarried women. They note, however, that the quality of the marriage was more important for women than for men in the study. Results of a study by Barnett and colleagues (1995) support this idea. In their study of dual-earner couples they found that women showed a greater psychological reaction to changes in marital quality than did men. Women's psychological distress (anxiety and depression) increased more when their relationship worsened and mental health improved more significantly when there were improvements in their marital relationships.

Finally, the role of parenting, specifically motherhood, has been examined for its relationship to mental health. Research in this area presents some of the most complex findings. This may be because the experience of motherhood differs depending on marital status, quality of the relationship for married women, and employment status. Although a number of studies (Coleman et al., 1987; Gove & Zeiss, 1987) report relatively high levels of health, self-esteem, and happiness among married, employed mothers, this often seems related more to employment status than to motherhood per se. Weissman and colleagues (1987) examined possible differences in psychological functioning between African-American and white married and single mothers of one or more children under the age of 18. In general, these mothers reported similar levels of psychological functioning regardless of marital status. Two differences, however, were noted. Single mothers had higher levels of dysthymia than married mothers and lower self-perceptions of mental health (26 percent vs. 9 percent rated their mental health as "fair" or "poor"). Thus, employment, marital status, and parenthood combine to present different pictures of mental health for women.

Research by Hughes and Galinsky (1994) supports the notion that although both work and family roles may be beneficial for women in many ways, these roles differ for women and men. They studied three groups of married, primarily white, women and men employed full time in office jobs. The three groups included: full-time employed women with full-time employed husbands, full-time employed men with full-time employed wives, and full-time employed men with spouses who were not employed. Overall, participants reported generally low levels of psychological symptoms. However, women reported more symptoms overall and reported more specific stressors both at work and at home. Full-time employed women were more likely than either group of men to report less job enrichment and less time spent at work, as well as higher levels of housework inequity and child care inequity at home. In addition, women reported higher levels of work–family interference making their jobs difficult than did men. Thus, it is not simply the number or types of roles women play, but their experiences within these roles that impact mental health. In addition, when family and work conditions were controlled, gender differences in psychological distress decreased, suggesting that these conditions mediate the relationship between gender and psychological distress across various roles.

One possible explanation for this is the impact of young children for women's lives. Gender differences between women and men appear most prominent when children are in the home (Aneshensel et al., 1981). Child care continues to be the primary responsibility of women, regardless of employment status, and increased responsibility for child care has been related to increased depression and somatic complaints (Steil & Turetsky, 1987). Marks and MacDermid (1996) found that women who described less role balance in their lives reported higher levels of depression and lower self-esteem than women who described less role overload and more role ease.

A second explanation for this role strain may have to do with women's and men's different experiences of undesirable life events (Kessler & McLeod, 1984). Kessler and McLeod (1984) examined women's and men's exposure and vulnerability to a number of different types of undesirable life events. They found that women and men reported the same type of impact when they experienced loss of income in the workforce or marital disruption (separation or divorce). Women were no more vulnerable when they experienced any of these stressful life experiences. However, women were more impacted both in the number of negative life events they were exposed to in their social networks compared to men and were more vulnerable to these stressors. The authors suggest this shows that "women are exposed more than men to acute life stresses which are centrally associated with their nurturant roles, and that this role-related difference is one important source of the mental health advantage of men" (p. 629).

## Impact of Violence on Women's Mental Health

Although both women and men are victimized, women are significantly more likely to experience many forms of violence in their lives. Rape, incest, and domestic violence all occur more frequently for women than men, regardless of ethnicity (Root, 1996). Often, perpetrators are family members or acquaintances (Koss, Woodruff, & Koss, 1991b), and women are significantly more likely than men to be shot or killed by a spouse or intimate partner (Kellermann & Mercy, 1992). These forms of violence are linked to a number of physical (Golding, 1996; Kimmerling & Calhoun, 1994; Koss, Koss, & Woodruff, 1991a), sexual (Golding, 1996), and psychological (Kilpatrick et al., 1985, 1992; Kimmerling & Calhoun, 1994; Koss et al., 1991a) consequences for women. Although violence against women is covered in depth elsewhere in this text, its impact on women's mental health will be discussed in this chapter.

Violence against women is related to a number of difficulties in psychological functioning and emotional well-being. Posttraumatic stress disorder (PTSD), depression, anxiety and substance abuse are all difficulties commonly reported by women experiencing rape, incest, or partner violence (Kilpatrick et al., 1992). PTSD is a disorder that involves exposure to a traumatic stressor in which the person feels fearful for her/his safety and helpless to do anything about the experience. Common symptoms include: reexperiencing the event (e.g., flashbacks, nightmares); avoidance of reminders of the event and emotional numbing; and increased physiological arousal (e.g., heightened startle response, difficulties sleeping) (American Psychiatric Association, 1994).

Estimates of PTSD among women vary, but research suggests that women are more likely than men to experience PTSD (Kessler, Sonnega, Bromet, Hughes, & Nelson, 1995). Results of two recent studies confirm that PTSD, depression, anxiety, and substance abuse among women are often related to sexual assault. Kilpatrick et al. (1992) reported findings from The National Women's Study, which surveyed more than 4000 adult women nationally in the United States. PTSD was evidenced by almost one third of the women who had been raped, and 30 percent of the rape victims had experienced one or more major depressive episodes. One-third of these women also reported seriously considering suicide, and 13 percent had actually attempted suicide. Finally, women who had been raped reported both higher usage of drugs and alcohol and more problems related to alcohol and drugs than women who had not been victimized. Kessler and colleagues (1995) found that in the NCS study almost 46 percent of women who identified rape and 26.5 percent of women who identified sexual molestation as their most traumatic experiences developed PTSD. In addition, women with PTSD were often diagnosed with depression, anxiety, and/or substance abuse disorders. Although it is difficult to determine the chronological order of these difficulties, estimates based on the age for the PTSD event suggest that PTSD generally preceded depression and substance abuse, and often preceded anxiety disorders for women. There were no differences related to ethnicity once other demographic variables were controlled.

Even when women do not meet full diagnostic criteria for a formal diagnosis of PTSD, their lives are still significantly affected by trauma. Stein, Walker, Hazen, and Forde (1997) conducted a community survey in Canada to examine current (past month) PTSD and partial-PTSD (person met a significant number of PTSD criteria, but not all needed for DSM-IV diagnosis). They found that individuals diagnosed with full PTSD had higher levels of impairment in work/school functioning, but that there was no difference between full and partial PTSD in levels of functioning at home and socially or in help-seeking behaviors; both exhibited significantly lower levels of functioning and sought more assistance than persons without PTSD.

Partner violence, like rape, is experienced by large numbers of women throughout the world and is also related to a number of psychological difficulties (Fischbach & Herbert, 1997). Fischbach and Herbert (1997) conducted a review of the domestic violence literature examining women's experiences in a number of countries. They identified a strong relationship between partner violence and much of the psychological distress women experience. Studies of women who experience violence in their intimate relationships have found high levels of PTSD, depression, anxiety, and a wide range of physical complaints (e.g., headaches, stomach problems) reported (Astin, Lawrence, & Foy, 1993; Follingstad, Brennan, Hause, Polek, & Rutledge, 1991).

Although research on partner violence among ethnic minority couples is frequently overlooked and is thus limited (West, 1998b), researchers have begun to examine both the rates of violence and the experiences of women who are Asian/Asian American (Ho, 1990), African American (see West, 1998b), Latina (Kantor, Jasinski, & Aldarondo, 1994), and Native American (Chester, Robin, Koss, Lopez, & Goldman, 1994). In addition, researchers have begun to examine violence in lesbian relationships (Lockhart, White, Causby, & Isaac, 1994). Two detailed reviews of this literature on violence in same-sex relationships have been conducted by Renzetti (1997) and West (1998a). Research on partner violence within these various groups suggests that women of color and lesbians often experience unique challenges associated with being members of nondominant groups in our society (e.g., prejudice and discrimination, socioeconomic stresses, acculturation for some women). However, many of the prominent mental health consequences related to partner violence remain the same for women regardless of these differences.

Much of the violence directed toward women involves sexual abuse of women during childhood (Finkelhor, Hotaling, Lewis, & Smith, 1990). Wyatt (1985) has found high rates of childhood sexual abuse among African-American and white women living in the community. The majority of the time this involved bodily contact which was usually committed by either a member of the girl's family or someone she knew (Wyatt, 1985), and in many instances the girl told no one about the abuse (Wyatt, 1990). Sexual assault during childhood is associated with a wide range of emotional and behavioral difficulties. Laws and Golding (1996) reported that childhood sexual assault, particularly if there were repeated assaults, the perpetrator was a parent, or the child was coerced by threats of "love withdrawal," was linked to a number of symptoms associated with anorexia nervosa. Depression and PTSD are common symptoms for victims of incest (Roesler & McKenzie, 1994), a finding that has consistently been supported by research on childhood sexual abuse using clinical samples (e.g., Bryer, Nelson, Miller, & Krol, 1987; McLeer, Deblinger, Atkins, Foa, & Ralphe, 1988).

Unfortunately, most clinicians have not been trained to consider the impact of physical and sexual assault when diagnosing and treating clients (Briere & Zaidi, 1989; Carmen, 1995; Kilpatrick et al., 1992). Clinicians often rate their graduate and internship training in this area as "poor" or "very poor" (Pope & Feldman-Summers, 1992), and as a result, most clinicians do not ask about sexual abuse histories (Briere & Zaidi, 1989). Women are often reluctant, however, to offer this sensitive information spontaneously. A two-part study by Briere and Zaidi (1989) found that female patients seen in an emergency room almost never volunteered information about childhood molestation. However, when clinicians were instructed to directly ask about childhood sexual abuse, many women reported this history. Mental health clinicians must discuss these issues with women, for omission can lead to an underestimate of the prevalence of abuse, an inability to evaluate the relationship between the sexual abuse and the client's present difficulties, and potentially ineffective treatment for women with abuse histories.

Yet, although violence can be detrimental to women's physical and psychological well-being, being victimized does not necessarily doom a woman to a life of misery or emotional problems. Women do recover and go on to live fulfilling and satisfying lives. This is not to underestimate the impact of victimization, but to emphasize that women victimized at the hands of others are not necessarily "victims" forever. Many women improve and recover over time, either with or without professional help. Follingstad et al. (1991) reported that emotional and physical health do improve for many women after they leave a violent relationship. Astin and colleagues (1993) studied factors related to resiliency among battered women and found that social support was negatively correlated with the intensity of PTSD symptoms. Research examining the effectiveness of therapeutic interventions for PTSD resulting from rape suggests treatment can be helpful. Resick and Schnicke (1992) reported that women who had been raped showed decreases in psychological symptoms following 12 group sessions of cognitive-processing therapy, and improvement was maintained when assessed six months after the end of treatment.

## SUMMARY

Conclusions about women's mental health are not simple nor easy to summarize in a sentence or two, contrary to what popular literature or the media might suggest. Rather, women's experiences vary greatly, and there is no single picture for all women. Discussions of women's mental health must include examination of the social context in which all women live, as well as the unique circumstances of each particular woman. Women's mental health is greatly affected by a number of factors, some of which are related to gender, but that are also influenced by ethnicity, sexual orientation, social class, marital/relationship status, physical ability, and a host of other factors. Research examining mental health and mental distress among these various groups is just beginning, and feminist psychologists are at the forefront in emphasizing the importance of this work (Reid & Comas-Diaz, 1990; Russo, 1995). Women's experiences will not be identical; the diversity of women's lives cannot be underestimated.

However, it is important to understand that women do face some special challenges to their mental health which are directly related to their gender. The impact of gender role stereotypes, stress and gender role strain, physical and sexual assault, and possible clinical bias in diagnosis and treatment are all likely to impact women's mental health and their treatment within the mental health system. It is important to recognize that many women will seek individual solutions to their difficulties as they strive to take responsibility for their own mental health and their own lives. However, it is also important that we as a society work to remove barriers and roadblocks to women's mental health that impact individual women, but have their origins within our larger society. Decreasing restrictive gender stereotypes, increasing economic opportunity, and decreasing violence directed against women are all goals that require attention at a societal level and that should only serve to improve mental health for women.

ACKNOWLEDGMENTS  I would like to thank Dr. Carolyn West and Ms. Carol Rosholm for comments and assistance as this chapter was being prepared. I am also grateful to Ms. Linda Adams and Ms. Elizabeth Turdevich who served as research assistants and helped gather information for this chapter.

## REFERENCES

Amaro, H., & Russo, N. F. (1987). Hispanic women and mental health: An overview of contemporary issues in research and practice. *Psychology of Women Quarterly, 11,* 393–407.

American Psychiatric Association. (1994). *Diagnostic and statistical manual of mental disorders* (4th ed.). Washington, DC: Author.

Aneshensel, C. S., Frerichs, R. R., & Clark, V. A. (1981). Family roles and sex differences in depression. *Journal of Health and Social Behavior, 22,* 379–393.

Astin, M. C., Lawrence, K. J., & Foy, D. W. (1993). Posttraumatic stress disorder among battered women: Risk and resiliency factors. *Violence and Victims, 8,* 17–28.

Barnett, R. C., Raudenbush, S. W., Brennan, R. T., Pleck, J. H., & Marshall, N. L. (1995). Change in job and marital experiences and change in psychological distress: A longitudinal study of dual-earner couples. *Journal of Personality and Social Psychology, 69,* 839–850.

Baruch, G. K., & Barnett, R. C. (1987). Role quality and psychological well-being. In F. J. Crosby (Ed.), *Spouse, parent, worker: On gender and multiple roles* (pp. 63–73). New Haven, CT: Yale University Press.

Belle, D. (1990). Poverty and women's mental health. *American Psychologist, 45,* 385–389.

Briere, J., & Zaidi, L. Y. (1989). Sexual abuse histories and sequelae in female psychiatric emergency room patients. *American Journal of Psychiatry, 146,* 1602–1606.

Broverman, I. K., Broverman, D. M., Clarkson, F. E., Rosenkrantz, P. S., & Vogel, S. R. (1970). Sex-role stereotypes and clinical judgments of mental health. *Journal of Consulting and Clinical Psychology, 34,* 1–7.

Brown, L. S. (1997). New voices, new visions: Toward a lesbian/gay paradigm for psychology. In M. M. Gergen & S. N. Davis (Eds.), *Toward a new psychology of gender* (pp. 295–308). New York: Routledge.

Bryer, J. B., Nelson, B. A., Miller, J. B., & Krol, P. A. (1987). Childhood sexual and physical abuse as factors in adult psychiatric illness. *American Journal of Psychiatry, 144,* 1426–1430.

Caetano, R. (1994). Drinking and alcohol-related problems among minority women. *Alcohol Health and Research World, 18,* 233–241.

Carmen, E. H. (1995). Inner-city community mental health: The interplay of abuse and race in chronic mentally ill women. In C. V. Willie, P. P. Rieker, B. M. Kramer, & B. S. Brown (Eds.), *Mental health, racism, and sexism* (pp. 217–236). Pittsburgh, PA: University of Pittsburgh Press.

Chesler, P. (1972). *Women and madness.* Garden City, NY: Doubleday.

Chester, B., Robin, R. W., Koss, M. P., Lopez, J., & Goldman, D. (1994). Grandmother dishonored: Violence against women by male partners in American Indian communities. *Violence and Victims, 9,* 249–258.

Coleman, L. M., Antonucci, T. C, & Adelmann, P. K. (1987). Role involvement, gender, and well-being. In F. J. Crosby (Ed.), *Spouse, parent, worker: On gender and multiple roles* (pp. 138–153). New Haven, CT: Yale University Press.

Fabrega, J., Jr., Mezzich, J., Ulrich, R., & Benjamin, L. (1990). Females and males in an intake psychiatric setting. *Psychiatry, 53,* 1–16.

Finkelhor, D., Hotaling, G., Lewis, I. A., & Smith, C. (1990). Sexual abuse in a national survey of adult men and women: Prevalence, characteristics, and risk factors. *Child Abuse and Neglect, 14,* 533–542.

Fischbach, R. L., & Herbert, B. (1997). Domestic violence and mental health: Correlates and conundrums within and across cultures. *Social Science and Medicine, 45,* 1161–1176.

Follingstad, D. R., Brennan, A. F., Hause, E. S., Polek, D. S., & Rutledge, L. L. (1991). Factors moderating physical and psychological symptoms of battered women. *Journal of Family Violence, 6,* 81–95.

Ford, M. R., & Widiger, T. A. (1989). Sex bias in the diagnosis of histrionic and antisocial personality disorders. *Journal of Consulting and Clinical Psychology, 57,* 301–305.

Gelfond, M. (1991). Reconceptualizing agoraphobia: A case study of epistemological bias in clinical research. *Feminism & Psychology, 1,* 247–262.

Golding, J. M. (1996). Sexual assault history and women's reproductive and sexual health. *Psychology of Women Quarterly, 20,* 101–121.

Gove, W. R., & Zeiss, C. (1987). Multiple roles and happiness. In F. J. Crosby (Ed.), *Spouse, parent, worker: On gender and multiple roles* (pp. 125–137). New Haven, CT: Yale University Press.

Grant, B. F., & Harford, T. C. (1995). Comorbidity between DSM-IV alcohol use disorder and the major depression: Results of a national survey. *Drug and Alcohol Dependence, 39,* 197–206.

Hamilton, S., Rothbart, M., & Dawes, R. M. (1986). Sex bias, diagnosis, and DSM-III. *Sex Roles, 15,* 269–274.

Hansen, F. J., & Osborne, D. (1995). Portrayal of women and elderly patients in psychotropic drug advertisements. *Women and Therapy, 16,* 129–141.

Ho, C. K. (1990). An analysis of domestic violence in Asian American communities: A multicultural approach to counseling. In L. S. Brown & M. P. P. Root (Eds.), *Diversity and complexity in feminist therapy* (pp. 129–150). New York: Harrington Park Press.

Hohmann, A. A. (1989). Gender bias in psychotropic drug prescribing in primary care. *Medical Care, 27,* 478–490.

Hughes, D. L., & Galinsky, E. (1994). Gender, job and family conditions and psychological symptoms. *Psychology of Women Quarterly, 18,* 251–270.

Hughes, T. L., & Wilsnack, S. C. (1997). Use of alcohol among lesbians: Research and clinical implications. *American Journal of Orthopsychiatry, 67,* 20–36.

Jenkins-Hall, K., & Sacco, W. P. (1991). Effect of client race and depression on evaluations by White therapists. *Journal of Social and Clinical Psychology, 10,* 322–333.

Kantor, G. K., Jasinski, J .L., & Aldarondo, E. (1994). Sociocultural status and incidence of marital violence in Hispanic families. *Violence and Victims, 9,* 207–222.

Kaplan, M. (1983). A woman's view of the DSM-III. *American Psychologist, 28,* 786–792.

Kellermann, A. L., & Mercy, J. A. (1992). Men, women, and murder: Gender-specific differences in rates of fatal violence and victimization. *The Journal of Trauma, 33,* 1–5.

Kessler, R. C., Crum, R. M., Warner, L. A., Nelson, C. B., Schulenberg, J., & Anthony, J. C. (1997). Lifetime co-occurence of DSM-III-R alcohol abuse and dependence with other psychiatric disorders in the national comorbidity survey. *Archives of General Psychiatry, 54,* 313–321.

Kessler, R. C., McGonagle, K. A., Zhao, S., Nelson, C. B., Hughes, M., Eshleman, S., Wittchen, J. U., & Kendler, K. S. (1994). Lifetime and 12-month prevalence of DSM-III-R psychiatric disorders in the United States. *Archives of General Psychiatry, 51,* 8–19.

Kessler, R. C., & McLeod, J. D. (1984). Sex differences in vulnerability to undesirable life events. *American Sociological Review, 49,* 620–631.

Kessler, R. C., Nelson, C. B., McGonagle, K. A., Liu, J., Swartz, M., & Blazer, D. G. (1996). Comorbidity of DSM-III-R major depressive disorder in the general population: Results from the U.S. National Comorbidity Survey. *British Journal of Psychiatry, 168,* 17–30.

Kessler, R. C., Sonnega, A., Bromet, E., Hughes, M., & Nelson, C. (1995). Posttraumatic stress disorder in the National Comorbidity Survey. *Archives of General Psychiatry, 52,* 1048–1060.

Kilpatrick, D. G., Edmunds, C. N., & Seymour, A. K. (1992). *Rape in America: A report to the nation.* Arlington, VA: National Victim Center.

Kilpatrick, D. G., Best, C. L., Veronen, L. J., Amick, A. E., Villeponteaux, L. A., & Ruff, G. A. (1985). Mental health correlates of criminal victimization: A random community survey. *Journal of Consulting and Clinical Psychology, 53,* 866–873.

Kimmerling, R., & Calhoun, K. S. (1994). Somatic symptoms, social support, and treatment seeking among sexual assault victims. *Journal of Consulting and Clinical Psychology, 62,* 333–340.

Koss, M. P., Koss, P. G., & Woodruff, J. (1991a). Deleterious effects of criminal victimization on women's health and medical utilization. *Archives of Internal Medicine, 151,* 342–347.

Koss, M. P., Woodruff, W. J ., & Koss, P. G. (1991b). Criminal victimization among primary care medical patients: Prevalence, incidence, and physician usage. *Behavioral Sciences and the Law, 9,* 85–96.

Laws, A., & Golding, J. M. (1996). Sexual assault history and eating disorder symptoms among White, Hispanic, and African-American women and men. *American Journal of Public Health, 86,* 579–582.

Lockhart, L. L., White, B. W., Causby, V., & Isaac, A. (1994). Letting out the secret: Violence in lesbian relationships. *Journal of Interpersonal Violence, 9,* 469–492.

Loring, M., & Powell, B. (1988). Gender, race and DSM-III: A study of the objectivity of psychiatric diagnostic behavior. *Journal of Health and Social Behavior, 29,* 1–22.

Magee, W. J., Eaton, W. W., Wittchen, H. U., McGonagle, K. A., & Kessler, R. C. (1996). Agoraphobia, simple phobia, and social phobia in the National Comorbidity Survey. *Archives of General Psychiatry, 53,* 159–168.

Marecek, J., & Hare-Mustin, R. T. (1991). A short history of the future: Feminism and clinical psychology. *Psychology of Women Quarterly, 15,* 521–536.

Marks, S. R., & MacDermid, S. M. (1996). Multiple roles and the self: A theory of role balance. *Journal of Marriage and the Family, 58,* 417–432.

Marsh, M. (1995). Feminist psychopharmacology: An aspect of feminist psychiatry. *Women and Therapy, 16,* 73–84.

Maxmen, J. S., & Ward, N. G. (1995). *Essential psychopathology and its treatment: Second edition, revised for DSM-IV.* New York: W. W. Norton & Company.

McGrath, E., Keita, G. P., Strickland, B. R., & Russo, N. F. (1990). *Women and depression: Risk factors and treatment issues.* Washington, DC: American Psychological Association.

McHugh, M. C. (2000). A feminist approach to agoraphobia: Challenging traditional views of women at home. In J. C. Chrisler, C. Golden, & P. D. Rozee (Eds.), *Lectures on the psychology of women* (2nd. ed.) (pp. 341–359). New York: McGraw-Hill.

McLeer, S. V., Deblinger, E., Atkins, M. S., Foa, E. B., & Ralphe, D. L. (1988). Post-traumatic stress disorder in sexually abused children. *Journal of the American Academy of Child and Adolescent Psychiatry, 27,* 650–654.

Mirowski, J., & Ross, C. E. (1989). *Social causes of psychological distress.* New York: Aldine de Gruyter.

Myers, J. K., Weissman, M. M., Tischler, G. L., Holzer III, C. E., Leaf, P. J., Orvaschel, H., Anthony, J. C., Boyd, J. H., Burke, J. D., Kramer, M., & Stoltzman, R. (1984). Six-month prevalence of psychiatric disorders in three communities. *Archives of General Psychiatry, 41,* 959–967.

Nolen-Hoeksema, S. (1990). *Sex differences in depression.* Stanford, CA: Stanford University Press.

Pope, K. S., & Feldman-Summers, S. (1992). National survey of psychologists' sexual and physical abuse history and their evaluation of training and competence in these areas. *Professional Psychology: Research and Practice, 23,* 353–361.

Regier, D. A., Narrow, W. E., & Rae, D. S. (1990). The epidemiology of anxiety disorders: The epidemiologic catchment area (ECA) experience. *Journal of Psychiatric Research, 24,* 3–14.

Reid, P. T., & Comas-Diaz, L. (1990). Gender and ethnicity: Perspectives on dual status. *Sex Roles, 22,* 397–408.

Renzetti, C. M. (1997). Violence and abuse among same-sex couples. In A. P. Cardarelli (Ed.), *Violence between intimate partners: Patterns, causes, and effects.* Boston: Allyn and Bacon.

Resick, P. A., & Schnicke, M. K. (1992). Cognitive processing therapy for sexual assault victims. *Journal of Consulting and Clinical Psychology, 60,* 748–756.

Robins, L. N., Helzer, J. E., Weissman, M. M., Orvaschel, H., Gruenberg, E., Burke, J. D., & Regier, D. A. (1984). Lifetime prevalence of specific psychiatric disorders in three sites. *Archives of General Psychiatry, 41,* 949–958.

Roesler, T. A., & McKenzie, N. (1994). Effects of childhood trauma on psychological functioning in adults sexually abused as children. *The Journal of Nervous and Mental Disease, 182,* 145–150.

Root, M. P. (1996). Women of color and traumatic stress in "domestic captivity": Gender and race as disempowering statuses. In A. J. Marsella, M. J. Friedman, E. T. Gerrity, & R. M. Scurfield (Eds.), *Ethnocultural aspects of post-*

*traumatic stress disorder: Issues, research, and clinical applications* (pp. 363–387). Washington, DC: American Psychological Association.

Russo, N. F. (1995). Women's mental health: Research agenda for the twenty-first century. In C. V. Willie, P. P. Rieker, B. M. Kramer, & B. S. Brown (Eds.), *Mental health, racism, and sexism* (pp. 373–396). Pittsburgh, PA: University of Pittsburgh Press.

Russo, N. F., Amaro, H., & Winter, M. (1987). The use of inpatient mental health services by Hispanic women. *Psychology of Women Quarterly, 11,* 427–441.

Russo, N. F., & Green, B. L. (1993). Women and mental health. In F. L. Denmark & M. A. Paludi (Eds.), *Psychology of women: A handbook of issues and theories* (pp. 379–436). Westport, CT: Greenwood Press.

Schmidt, C., Klee, L., & Ames, G. (1990). Review and analysis of literature on indicators of women's drinking problems. *British Journal of Addiction, 85,* 179–192.

Showalter, E. (1985). *The female malady.* New York: Pantheon Books.

Steen, M. (1991). Historical perspectives on women and mental illness and prevention of depression in women, using a feminist framework. *Issues in Mental Health Nursing, 12,* 359–374.

Steil, J. M., & Turetsky, B. A. (1987). Marital influence levels and symptomatology among wives. In F. J. Crosby (Ed.), *Spouse, parent, worker: On gender and multiple roles* (pp. 74–90). New Haven, CT: Yale University Press.

Stein, M. B., Walker, J. R., Hazen, A. L., & Forde, D. R. (1997). Full and partial posttraumatic stress disorder: Findings from a community survey. *American Journal of Psychiatry, 154,* 1114–1119.

Thoits, P. A. (1987). Negotiating roles. In F. J. Crosby (Ed.), *Spouse, parent, worker: On gender and multiple roles* (pp. 11–22). New Haven, CT: Yale University Press.

Turner, R. J., & Avison, W. R. (1989). Gender and depression: Assessing exposure and vulnerability to life events in a chronically strained population. *The Journal of Nervous and Mental Disease, 177,* 443–455.

Vogeltanz, N. D., & Wilsnack, S. C. (1997). Alcohol problems in women: Risk factors, consequences, and treatment strategies. In S. J. Gallant, G. P. Keita, & R. Royak-Schaler (Eds.), *Health care for women: Psychological, social and behavioral influences* (pp. 75–96). Washington, DC: American Psychological Association.

Walker, L. E. (1994). Are personality disorders gender biased? In S. A. Kirk, & S. D. Einbinder (Eds.), *Controversial issues in mental health* (pp. 21–39). Boston: Allyn and Bacon.

Weissman, M. M. (1987). Advances in psychiatric epidemiology: Rates and risks for major depression. *American Journal of Public Health, 77,* 445–451.

Weissman, M. M., Leaf, P. J., & Bruce, M. L. (1987). Single parent women: A community study. *Social Psychiatry, 22,* 29–36.

West, C. M. (1998a). Leaving a second closet: Outing partner violence in same-sex couples. In L. M. Williams & J. L. Jasinski (Eds.), *Partner violence: A comprehensive review of 20 years of research* (pp. 163–183). Thousand Oaks, CA: Sage.

West, C. M. (1998b). Lifting the "political gag order": Breaking the silence around partner violence in ethnic minority families. In L. M. Williams & J. L. Jasinski (Eds.), *Partner violence: A comprehensive review of 20 years of research* (pp. 184–209). Thousand Oaks, CA: Sage.

Widiger, T. A., & Settle, S. A. (1987). Broverman et al. Revisited: An artificial sex bias. *Journal of Personality and Social Psychology, 53,* 463–469.

Widiger, T. A., Corbitt, E. M., & Funtowicz, M. N. (1994). Are personality disorders gender biased? In S. A. Kirk & S. D. Einbinder (Eds.), *Controversial issues in mental health* (pp. 21–39). Boston: Allyn and Bacon.

Wilsnack, S. C., Wilsnack, R. W., & Hiller-Sturmhofel, S. (1994). How women drink: Epidemiology of women's drinking and problem drinking. *Alcohol Health and Research World, 18,* 173–181.

Wilsnack, S. C., Vogeltanz, N. D., Diers, L. E., & Wilsnack, R. W. (1995). Drinking and problem drinking in older women. In T. Beresford & E. Gomberg (Eds.), *Alcohol and aging* (pp. 263–292). New York: Oxford Press.

Wittchen, J. U., Zhao, S., Kessler, R. C., & Eaton, W. W. (1994). DSM-III-R generalized anxiety disorder in the National Comorbidity Survey. *Archives of General Psychiatry, 51,* 355–364.

Wyatt, G. E. (1985). The sexual abuse of Afro-American and White-American women in childhood. *Child Abuse and Neglect, 9,* 507–519.

Wyatt, G. E. (1990). The aftermath of child sexual abuse of African American and White American women: The victim's experience. *Journal of Family Violence, 5,* 61–81.

# 13

# Feminist Therapy Approaches

## Mary Ballou and Carolyn West

## INTRODUCTION

Carla is a mixed race adolescent who is referred for therapy following a suicide attempt. She is 14 years old and lives with her Irish immigrant mother and 11-year-old brother in the working class section of a predominantly white, middle-class community. Her Hispanic father left the family after a long history of marital discord. The mother had coped within a controlling and often abusive marital relationship by being quiet and passive, and had been repeatedly encouraged by Carla to stand up for herself. Since the separation, however, Carla has assumed an increasingly blaming attitude toward her mother.

It was shortly after her parents separated that Carla took an overdose of sleeping pills. She currently presents with eating and sleeping problems and repeatedly misses school because of complaints about headaches and stomach problems. She reports demeaning treatment at the time of hospitalization around her suicide attempt; medical professionals consistently tell her that her physical complaints have no physiological basis.

In attempting to gain support at Carla's middle school, her mother reports being told that only 2 percent of the school population is Hispanic and that statistics show that youngsters of Carla's ethnicity rarely complete high school. Carla's mother has no relatives in the United States and Carla is currently estranged from her father's family of origin. This mother does not know where to go for help. She does not know where she and her daughter fit or how to gain an understanding of how the American culture works. This chapter explicates the issues that a feminist therapist would consider as she works with Carla.

Feminist therapy is perhaps best understood as a philosophical orientation to therapy (Sturdivant, 1980) rather than a specific type or competing brand of therapy. Indeed some, for instance, Worell and Johnson (1997) and Landrine (1995), would hold that feminist therapy is the application of feminist psychology to clinical practice. While over time this characterization may have become accurate, the developmental beginnings of feminist therapy are rooted in a well-articulated stand against traditional mental health practices, including

Mary Ballou ● Northeastern University, Boston, Massachusetts 02478
Carolyn West ● Western New England College, Springfield, Massachusetts 01119

*Issues in the Psychology of Women,* edited by Biaggio and Hersen. Kluwer Academic/Plenum Publishers, New York, 2000.

the therapist–client interaction. The criticisms that underpin this stand evolved in the context of the contemporary women's movement and other struggles of liberation as detailed in Chapter 1.

The current chapter addresses feminist therapy and its principles and practice, and seeks to describe both what feminist therapy stands against in traditional therapy as well as what it stands for on its own terms. Perhaps because it is a philosophical orientation rather than a specific therapy, perhaps because practitioners come to it from a variety of life and training experiences, there is considerable diversity within feminist therapy. Its longstanding differences and variations continue today to provide vital discussions in such areas as the critical analysis of mainstream mental health, the development of rich theory, and the ongoing evolution of procedures and ethics within feminist therapy communities. Indeed, lively debates are just as common and engaging today as they were when the first text *Feminism as Therapy* was written in 1974 by Mander and Rush.

## FEMINIST THERAPY PRINCIPLES

Feminist therapy is remarkable in many regards. While the more traditional and widely used techniques emanate from somewhat imposing and distant theoretical frameworks, feminist therapy asserts its grounding in a model that can be thought of as circular and interactive rather than linear and static. Here, information flows naturally and bidirectionally from theorist and therapist to client, into the culture and back round again. Paraphrasing Marcia Westkott (1979), it is FOR women rather than ABOUT them and it is less a prescription or technique than it is a philosophy of therapy emerging out of the lived experiences of women within a social context. This philosophy, which is potentially mapped onto and informs a range of treatment modalities, is best articulated via a set of clear and consensual principles that have served as the building materials and unifying constructs of theory, practice, and ethics within feminist therapy.

Feminist therapy can be characterized by several key principles:

1. Feminist therapy is unwaveringly rooted in the search for and valuing of ALL women's experiences (Hill & Ballou, 1998). Essential to feminist therapy is the "valuing of the diverse and complex experiences of women from all racial, class, religious, age and sexual orientation groups" (Brown & Brodsky, 1992, p.51). "Considering behavior alone is insufficient to understanding women in patriarchy, nor is it adequate to link women's behavior only to the dominant, male-created ideology" (Westkott, 1979, p. 429). Rather than forcing women's experiences into the ideological frames constructed without attention to their voice and status by in so doing, devaluing and distorting both the experiences and the women themselves, feminist therapy inquires into, listens for, and attempts to understand the experiences of all women as "they have grown up and lived in social contexts that are opposed to their needs as human beings" (Westkott, 1979, p. 424).

2. Feminist therapy recognizes a primary need to consider behaviors and intrapsychic processes as they are embedded within a sociopolitical context. Feminist therapy rests on and respects the notion of "the personal is political," a way of viewing and analyzing experience WITHIN its sociopolitical context which evolved out of the consciousness raising groups of the second wave of the women's movement (Hill & Ballou, 1998). It has as its purpose the exploration of the "inherent contradictions in the prescribed social roles for women" (Espin, 1994, p. 271).

3. Feminist therapy seeks to redress the power imbalance that is typically maintained within the counseling relationship and that mirrors the power imbalance of the larger sociocultural context—a context in which the client has already experienced destructive misuses of power (Hill & Ballou, 1998). Holding issues of power at the forefront of all exchanges, feminist therapists seek to build an egalitarian therapeutic relationship that can empower the client and that models more collaborative ways of being in the world (Hill & Ballou, 1998). This sorting out and reconfiguring of power inequities includes all aspects and exchanges of the therapeutic relationship including such ordinary and at the same time power-laden issues as fees and payment schedules, the use of titles, therapist self-disclosure, touch, and therapist availability between sessions(Brown, 1994).

4. Feminist therapy attends not to issues of gender alone but also recognizes and names additional categories of oppression. At its core, feminist therapy honors and respects the inherent worth and dignity of all human beings while seeking to expose both subtle and overt manifestations of oppression directed toward gender, race, class, religion, age, ethnicity, sexual orientation, disability, and the identities that flow out of belongings anchored in multiple cultural contexts.

5. The goals of feminist therapy are not about achieving a better, a quieter, a more compliant fit within a system that oppresses, but are directed toward helping the individual to recognize the sociopolitical and economic forces, the societal structures and gendered expectations that contribute to pain and discomfort while simultaneously discovering personal resources and healthy resistances as means of empowerment. Feminist therapists deal not only with individuals, but also have an overarching commitment to social change (Morrow & Hawxhurst, 1998; Whalen, 1996).

6. Feminist therapy recognizes and respects a range of methods in its effort to seek out and validate knowledge. Multiple ways of knowing (epistemologies) replace singular, outdated and limiting constructions, and include a deliberate and concerted interdisciplinary effort (Ballou, 1990).

7. Feminist therapy adopts a questioning stance toward the status quo, consistently surveying dominant institutions, theories, practices, and research methods in an effort to expose ideas and practices that fail to include or account for, and are harmful to marginalized peoples. Feminist therapy does not reject science but it does note and mark its limits and continually attempts to locate the questions of research within a sociopolitical context. These principles serve as an organizing framework for a therapy model that both accepts and seeks diversity. They provide a conceptual framework as issues of feminist assessment, diagnosis, and therapy practice are discussed.

Early feminist therapists were like anthropologists, unearthing and exposing sexist problems, abuses to women, and power politics as these functioned in traditional mental health theory and practice. Brought to light and given voice were issues involving social control, the devaluing and pathologizing of women's roles and coping strategies, and the ignoring of contextual environments and structures. It is interesting to note that many of these early critiques seem to be reemerging within the context of the corporate mental health industry of today. Specifically, feminist therapists criticize mainstream views of women and the associated normative standards that are routinely applied throughout therapy—in assessment, in diagnosis, and in treatment planning. They also critique therapy practices and the very nature of the therapeutic relationship as it exists within traditional therapy.

## DIAGNOSIS AND ASSESSMENT

The problems with traditional theory as it has been historically critiqued by feminist therapists reemerge in a seemingly logical but nonetheless haunting and damaging way when diagnosis is considered. Once theory has set the standard for normal development, it is then but a short step to identifying variations from this standard as abnormal. Feminist critiques have long and loudly asserted that diagnosis is largely naming and norming and it is tied inextricably to the life experiences, values, achievements, and social expectations of the dominant group membership. Furthermore, feminist therapy asserts that diagnosis within psychology and psychiatry is controlled through a bio–psycho–medical model of illness, as Hannah Lerman (1996) discusses so ably and thoroughly in *Pigeonholing Women's Misery*.

Psychiatry, the mental health discipline responsible for the Diagnostic and Statistic Manual-Fourth Edition, or DSM-IV (American Psychiatric Association, 1994), nosology used in mental illness, is described critically by Greenspan (1993) as:

> the religion of contemporary society. . . . In psychologizing reality, psychiatry reduces a complex set of social, economic, emotional and spiritual dimensions to the terms of a single diagnosis. Ultimately what gets denied in all this is pathology of the social structure itself. . . . Diagnosis is ultimately a social act with social uses masquerading as a medical act with medical uses. (p.xxxi)

Greenspan's contemporary indictment is reminiscent of Phyllis Chesler's groundbreaking and revolutionary work *Women and Madness* (1972), in which she articulates the irony inherent in the disempowering control and abuse of women through an establishment purporting to recover and sustain mental health.

Since Chesler's definitive work, many have joined the chorus objecting to medical model diagnosis in general, and specifically to its effects relative to women and other marginalized groups. Critical analysis and subsequent activism have focused on exposing the routine pathologizing of any difference from that standard espoused as normative. Indeed, many feminist therapists have eschewed the traditional DSM medical model diagnostic system. The specific critiques have ranged from charges of sexism, racism, classism, xenophobia, and homophobia to charges of overt social control dressed appealingly as mental health support (Ballou, 1990; Kaschak, 1992; Szasz, 1961).

Feminist positions regarding diagnosis and assessment have evolved from critiquing the traditional model to providing a conceptualization of difference as it is situated in context—as it is influenced by external factors. Worell and Remer (1992) tackle these issues as they consider how women's symptoms can be understood through feminist perspectives. These authors explicate how behavior that has been socialized in accord with sex–gender role is too often renamed as pathology. The DSM-IV, for example, provides criteria for the diagnosis of Dependent Personality Disorder (American Psychiatric Association, 1994) at the same time that self-sacrifice, lack of independent initiative, deference, and subservience are embedded within the normative context of white female socialization. Worell and Remer also articulate the middle-class heterosexual role conflicts inherent in raising children AND carrying on a career or in being sexually attractive to males in dress and behavior while maintaining leadership positions in social and business spheres.

Consistent with feminist principles, it is also important to recognize and consider that particular customs and points of conflict differ sustantially in various ethnocultural and class experiences. Laura Brown (1995) points out that feminist therapists must use extreme caution in diagnostic formulations that have the potential to rename as pathology that which is troublesome to the dominant group, as when a woman's emotional expression is labeled "hysteria" or when vigilance and healthy distrust in people of color is renamed "paranoia." Brown speaks "in particular to the potentials for racism as well as sexism inherent in certain diagnostic categories" (Brown, 1995, p. 154). Worell and Remer also assert that many symptoms can, in fact, be coping strategies—the logical result of norms being defined through the life experience of one dominant group—and not pathology at all. That is, stereotypic female socialization may lead to pathology, as, for example, in powerlessness leading to poor self-esteem and depression. In the case of role conflict, certain behavioral choices that are contrary to dominant expectations can themselves be pathologized. For example, within the dominant culture it is considered socially unacceptable for women to demonstrate anger or to be unwilling to be subservient to others, or to be hostile or selfish or sexually aggressive. Sometimes, then, an individual woman's symptoms may signal damage and sometimes they may represent a reasonable response to an alien and threatening situation. Feminist therapy holds and considers both of these notions.

Echoing a basic feminist principle, Worell and Remer point out that in addition to the essential need to reframe symptoms, it is critical to assess not just behaviors but also the context of women's lives. These authors call for new diagnostic categories and, consistent with the feminist principle of sharing power within the therapeutic relationship, they suggest considering diagnosis as a collaborative activity between therapist and client.

Laura Brown, most recently in *Subversive Dialogues* (1994), adds an important multicultural and antiracist perspective to diagnosis so that earlier feminist analyses are extended beyond the dimension of gender. Any and all of the identities involved in race, class, ethnicity, sexual orientation, ability, status, or age may be salient and may interact in assessment. She also adds developmental perspectives, arguing convincingly that the stage of focus at the time of the insult or events will influence and shape the individual's particular vulnerabilities.

In a somewhat similar vein, Maria Root (1992) asserts that the diagnostic categories must be expanded to fit the complex natures of multiple lived experiences. Using the diagnostic category of posttraumatic stress disorder, she expands and contextualizes the notion of trauma and the dimension of its impact. Laura Brown, among others, reminds us that within the histories of women who are diagnosed as having a personality disorder, there is an extremely high rate of sexual and physical abuse (Brown & Ballou, 1992). The link between these traumatic events and the symptomatology that leads to the diagnosis of personality disorders is too often overlooked and the "problem" is located in the individual. Many other feminists have joined Brown and Root in expanding diagnostic categories, looking first critically and then differently at conventional diagnoses.

Clearly, assessment and testing are accepted roles for many psychologists. In fact, prior to World War II, testing was the main form of clinical practice, and developments in testing and assessment in clinical, vocational, and educational domains are largely the result of psychology. Testing, however, shares may of the same problems identified previously regarding the practice of naming and norming within narrow monocultural contexts. Several lines of feminist work have examined these issues and taken positions ranging from rejecting testing and assessment practices altogether to valuing the specificity they can render, to using specific testing to advocate for women in forensic situations.

Contemporary recommendations for feminist assessment are offered in a chapter by Santos de Barona and Dutton within *Shaping the Future of Feminist Psychology* (1997). To summarize their perspective, there are a number of problems inherent in the traditional assessment and diagnostic processes as they are viewed from a feminist perspective. These include views of human functioning and normative standards that are based on white, upper-middle class, male, American, and capitalistic world views. They also include a narrow biopsychological model, which ignores social, cultural, and structural realities and pathologizes their influences and interactions on individuals, families, and whole segments of the population. To view our client Carla merely as a depressed, malingering teen is to miss the interactive effects of issues connected with ethnicity and gender and structure and culture.

Feminist therapy, writes Laura Brown (1994), "is the practice of therapy informed by feminist political philosophy and analysis, grounded in multicultural feminist scholarship on the psychology of women and gender, which leads both therapist and client toward strategies and solutions advancing feminist resistance, transformation, and social change in daily personal life, and in relationships with the social, emotional, and political environment" (p.22). Feminist therapy embraces a much broader perspective than conventional models of therapy. In looking broadly and critically, feminist therapists use a bio–psycho–social–cultural–structural model of assessment and diagnosis—a model that provides not only a more complete understanding of personal functioning, but also informs and gives direction to the therapy itself.

## CRITIQUE OF TRADITIONAL THERAPY

Therapy as practiced in a conventional manner contains several inherent problems as critiqued through feminist principles. These problems reside in the very underpinnings of conventional practice involving hierarchical and dichotomous roles. Doing psychotherapy in conventional ways means setting up a hierarchical relationship that identifies the therapist as the expert and the client as the patient. Whether overtly, as in traditional psychodynamic treatment, or more subtly as in cognitive behavioral approaches, the therapist is the expert—an expert who controls the process and whose knowledge is used to change the person or some aspect of the person's thoughts, behaviors, or beliefs.

While the therapist is obliged to be competent and to act in the best interest of the client, the unmistakable assumption is that the well-trained, licensed professional will name the problem and prescribe the treatment. This treatment will, in turn, achieve outcome goals that are observable and measurable. The therapist not only formulates these goals in ways that are largely independent of client input, but all too often dutifully communicates them to the staff at the clinic, hospital, and managed care entity. Such is conventional psychotherapy as practiced in the 1990s in formal settings. It renders the ideas of therapeutic relationship, healing, and facilitation of growth and development as matters of biopsychological intervention initiated by medically oriented professionals in the pursuit of ameliorating disease and psychological dysfunction.

This sort of conventional therapy can indeed be helpful to some and perhaps many people. Certainly therapist–client interactions can be kind and guided by active listening skills, and symptoms can be decreased measurably. Yet, in this model clear distinctions exist between the knowledge of the therapist and the client's information, between measured outcomes and expert clinical judgement, on the one hand, and the client's perceptions and feelings, on the other. Clearly defined, too, are the appropriate interactions between therapist and client—the therapist is there to treat the client. It is easy to see that power and authority are basic to this medical model. Feminist therapy models, grounded in feminist principles, are guided by a quite different set of values, assumptions, and world views.

## TREATMENT ISSUES FOR WOMEN

Using a biopsychological model, the diagnostic protocol of conventional psychology typically identifies the problem, situates it within the woman, and proposes treatment based on this notion. The contextual elements, that is, factors within the relational, social, economic, racial–ethnic, cultural, and ecological structures associated with the individual, are not necessarily viewed as reletive to the clinical issues. It is true that in recent decades, conventional mental health has increased its attention to what are considered to be "women's issues," including sexual abuse, trauma, depression, eating disorders, somatic complaints, and even sharp decreases in adolescent self-esteem; further, there has been considerable conceptual and empirical work devoted to defining and elucidating these and other women's treatment issues. Both mainstream and feminist perspectives have contributed to this literature—indeed, several are discussed in other chapters in the present text.

Yet conventional clinical treatment has proceeded myopically as though these issues arise out of some inherent weakness in the individual rather than in collusion with the larger social, political, and economic structures. Familiar intrapsychic language and concepts regarding developmental vicissitudes, ego structures, organizational schema, irrational thoughts, family patterns, and neurobiology routinely become integral to the diagnostic and treatment protocol.

While few feminist therapists would argue that these factors are relevant in treatment and influence one's life, the feminist, multicultural, and liberation positions consider forces external to the individual as major influences in influencing the conditions in which such "women's issues" flourish. Not only is this so with regard to influential factors or phenomena of clinical notice, but, in a feminist tradition, these external conditions must also become part of the clinical treatment. Thus, feminist therapy often includes consciousness-raising and activism directed at social change.

Feminist clinical awareness has been influenced both by advances in mainstream and feminist psychology, and by critical interdisciplinary analyses of sociopolitical and economic factors. These interdisciplinary perceptions help to illuminate hegemonic influences and contribute to new understandings of old notions. For example, new content areas arise from an understanding of the intersect of multiple identities, the separation of notions regarding sex and gender, and the consideration of affect and spirituality. Radical feminist therapists consider ecological context and sociopolitical structures to be directly implicated in women's treatment issues. These would include, for example: the prevalence of and damage from violence—physical, emotional, and sexual; relational restrictions and disconnection, both developmental and contemporary; the myriad of discriminatory threats, interactions, practices, and structures; and the distorted media images aimed at control and profit. And women's treatment issues have, in turn, become symptomatic of social ills. Miriam Greenspan (1993, p. xxvii) for example, in her introduction to the second edition of *A New Approach to Women and Therapy*, writes of the problems women bring to therapy as "symptoms of female subservience in a man's world."

Feminist therapy provides a broader, more contextualized perspective of mental health treatment than the more typical focus on "clinical issues" that characterizes more traditional therapy models. An example may demonstrate this point:

> Beth, a working-class, white, single mother presents with fear, worry, and the experience of racing and jumpy energy, all symptoms of an anxiety disorder. An analysis of her experience reveals she is struggling to juggle at least three responsibilities—parenting a young family, maintaining a home, and working at a job in order to earn enough money to keep the family afloat—all within a cultural context that isolates her and devalues her status. Using a biopsychological model, traditional therapy might consider prescribing Ativan, a popular antianxiety medication that does, indeed, reduce such presenting symptoms and, for the most part, does so quickly and effectively. But authentic communication with a trusted friend or counselor, the security of a safe environment with re-

sources available to meet ongoing, real life responsibilities and demands, and perhaps some training in imagery or relaxation skills—these will also serve to quiet Beth's symptoms at the same time that they respectfully address the factors that influence her personal reaction. Feminist therapy would most probably explore all the options with Beth and support her treatment decision.

The important issues of timing and client readiness would indicate that, in these beginning stages, a feminist therapist would probably not engage Beth in a discussion of her situation and status relative to the larger context. As her symptoms decreased and as it was mutually determined to be appropriate, Beth and her therapist would be able to broaden their view to consider her personal and interpersonal resources, the embedded restrictions of her class/gender/economic status, and the possibilities of vocational counseling. This context as considered by a feminist therapist would include the influences of gendered politics and the impact of advanced capitalism on employment opportunities.

## THE BREADTH OF FEMINIST THERAPY

Many writers have described varying aspects of feminist therapy, each adding to the breadth of technique and process and, at the same time, reflecting a unique point of view. While a comprehensive discussion of the process and techniques within feminist therapy would be long and complex, and beyond the scope of this chapter, we offer a sample of the range of positions and strategies and encourage the reader to visit the many rich and enlightening original works cited here. Feminist therapy positions can be placed along a continuum ranging from a modification of such standard techniques as cognitive behavioral interventions, to a radical position that argues against any standard practice of individual therapy at all! The work of Kitzinger and Perkins (1993) represents the latter position in it's statement, for example, that therapy unavoidably individualizes and makes psychological a phenomenon that is essentially and irrefutably sociocultural sexism. These authors propose a return to political analysis and action, along with a recommitment to fostering loving and supportive women's communities. They also lobby for mental illness to be viewed in the same light as any other illness—that is, as an incidence wherein the coping abilities of the organism have been overwhelmed by environmental pathogens at a specific point of vulnerability.

The writings on feminist therapy by such authors as McLellan (1995), Burstone (1992), and Ballou and Gabalac (1985), while not so extreme as to eschew individual counseling, still occupy a radical position on the continuum of feminist therapy practice. The key factors for these authors involve an exposition of the sociopolitical causation of women's oppression coupled with a plan of action directed toward changing those structures and developing support for those who are damaged by them. From this perspective, therapeutic techniques include sex/gender role analysis, analyses of power structures, the development of women's communities and alternative forms of living/working/ economic arrangements, and social action projects that target harmful social structures and policies.

The position assumed by Worell and Remer (1992) seems to occupy a position near the midpoint of this feminist therapy continuum. Their work offers clear definitions of feminist therapy practice and descriptions of techniques unique to feminist therapy, as well as techniques adapted for its use. Hill and Ballou (1998) also offer some additional specifics on the practice of feminist therapy in their recent work. The efforts of Morrow and Hawxhurst (1998) to reemphasize political analysis in feminist therapy also exemplifies this midpoint position, as does Whalen's work (1996) within both professional and community-based groups addressing violence against women.

Those midpoint positions have offered clarification relative to both the process and technique of feminist therapy. Their focus is on promoting health in women and preventing damage to girls and women and other nondominant groups. A major emphasis is on understanding the influence of external factors—sexism, institutional oppression, hierarchical professional positions, and limited norms—on women's development and health. These assumptions also stress the effects of social conditions and social conditioning on women throughout the life span.

While authors such as Brown (1994); Kaschak (1992); Greenspan (1993); Greene (1994); Comas-Diaz and Greene (1994); Adleman and Enguidanos (1996); and Jordan, Kaplan, Miller, Stiver, and Surrey (1992) represent unique positions that cannot be described accurately in collective terms, their views can generally be characterized as "cultural speakers." Several are deeply committed to understanding and interpreting just how the patriarchal social norms control the nature of our experiences as women. Others wish to explore and develop the connections among women and those between women, spirit, and the earth. Many of the feminist therapy "cultural speakers" are thoughtfully engaged in looking at the intersection of culture and ethnicity and sexual orientation as they consider the best ways to do feminist therapy.

The aforementioned authors take the position that the larger culture is responsible for many, if not most, individual ills, and they speak to the importance of relationship as a primary mechanism for healing and growth. Given the isolation of many women within a culture that fails to support them, this notion includes—in many cases, begins with—the healing power of the therapeutic relationship itself. And many in this group of writers and theorists view the community as the place that can promote the positive development of women's culture by means of psychosocial interventions that address the complex needs of women. Thus, they recommend interventions and programs that extend beyond the boundaries of the individual office and the traditional therapist–client dyad and reach into the life settings of communities of women talking to and helping women.

## FEMINIST THERAPY PRACTICED

So just how does one do therapy that is feminist? Does it really differ from conventional psychotherapeutic practice? If so, in what ways? These are reasonable and important questions. Feminist therapy has evolved substantially over the 25 years since Mander and Rush wrote *Feminism as Therapy*. Guided by the basic feminist principles that introduced this chapter, it differs in both obvious and subtle ways from conventional therapy. It seems important to say, again, that unlike other therapeutic models, there is no single or predominant therapy school that dictates feminist therapy practice and so this presentation is organized around the feminist principles as they contribute to a range of feminist therapy techniques and considerations.

### Women's Experiences

"While feminist therapy is not about therapy with women, it is therapy practiced by feminist women whose insights are profoundly informed by living in diverse female realities" (Brown, 1994, p. 10). One of the central points of feminist therapy is that it is based in the valuing of ALL women's experiences (Ballou, 1995; Brown, 1994; Enns, 1997; Gilbert, 1980; Hill, 1990; Kaschak, 1992; Lerman, 1986, 1992; Worell & Remer, 1992).

This basic tenet holds a number of implications for the practice of feminist therapy. A client's description of her life, her feelings, and areas of concern are heard and believed as her truth. Unlike the custom in conventional therapies, they are not decontextualized and processed into intake histories and data that are later used to develop a diagnosis and treatment plan. Nor are misinterpretation, repression, or other "psychological mechanisms" presumed to distort her perceptions and descriptions. Yet, it seems important to say that while the valuing of women's experience is a central and complex aspect of feminist therapy, all perceptions are not necessarily assumed to be accurate or in full awareness. Thus, the careful process of reflecting, critical questioning, and learning are also essential features of doing feminist therapy.

One difference between feminist and conventional therapies is that in feminist therapy the descriptions of the client are not reinterpreted through some remote theory. Neither are expressions of fear, anxiety, pain, and depression represented in the traditional language of psychological distancing (e.g., "enmeshment," "irrational thought," "codependency"). Feminists consider that social images and messages as well as normative standards and theory emanate from the dominant ideology. Because such sources of information about women and how they ought to be are apt to be contaminated, women's direct experiences are centrally featured in feminist therapy.

Indeed, unless the agency, hospital, or cost management entity requires formal DSM diagnosis, the descriptions of concerns and problems are formulated by the client and counselor together without the distancing and sometimes prejorative labels of formal diagnosis. This collaborative process, perhaps possible only in such venues as a college counseling center, uses ordinary and accessible language and is negotiated in a way that respects both the expert knowledge of the therapist and the lived experiences of the woman. Even when interactions with an insurance company or similar gatekeeping agency is required, feminist therapists seek out creative ways to empower and respect their clients by involving them in such processes as diagnosis and negotiation about the number of sessions. Marcia Hill (1999), for example, describes her practice of talking to the insurance company case manager on a speaker phone while sitting with her client.

Unlike more standard formulations, a feminist therapy frame would consider the devaluation, danger, and difficulties of life alongside cultural and individual coping efforts. In the case of Carla, a feminist therapist would seek to understand Carla's experience of being devalued within her educational setting, of feeling misunderstood and dismissed by medical professionals and of feeling hopeless in the face of a culture that expects her to fail.

The valuing of women's experiences within the feminist therapy model also involves a recognition and honoring of the whole of women's lives and work. Here, in contrast to traditional models, women's lives replace men's as the basis for theory building and understanding. We gain valuable insights into the lived realities across the diversity of women through such descriptions as those provided by Beverly Greene (1994), who tells us about African-American women teaching their children how to cope with racism. Rather than capitulating to the helplessness engendered by the structures of racist oppression, Greene's mothers take a proactive stance. These women acknowledge and name racism and seek to resist its damage by preparing their children for its inevitability.

In a similar fashion, women-based theories such as the Stone Center's relational model (Jordan et al., 1992) and the work of Taylor, Gilligan, and Sullivan (1995) in adolescent girls' development are set squarely in this principle of valuing women's experience. Some of the interventions that have been developed around listening and finding voice demonstrate feminist therapy's clear commitment to valuing all of women's experiences. Feminist therapists evoke voice and experience through such means as bibliotherapy and journal and poetry writing (Rogers, 1993), as well as other expressive arts. All of these tools are used to encourage clients to find avenues of voice and self-expression by providing multiple opportunities to be heard and understood.

Two additional examples are now provided of this essential feature of feminist therapy—the process of listening carefully and of drawing insights from women's lived experiences in all their complexities. In its understanding of each of the following situations, feminist therapy would consider the woman's construction of meaning and her own awareness of possible alternatives.

The first example concerns the experiences of a Cambodian woman who endures physical abuse by her husband. When her experience is contextualized and situated culturally and sociopolitically, a story emerges of a family who has suffered great humiliation in refugee camps. The husband, who formerly maintained a professional status in Cambodia, is now working as a cook in an Asian restaurant. Understandably wary of authorities, given her experiences in Cambodia and in the refugee camps, the woman, in her silence, reflects her culture's constraints around shaming of the family and seeks to retain her family's respect in the Asian-American community.

Here, feminist therapy listens not only to what has happened to this woman, but also seeks to understand her experiences and the complex social, cultural, economic, and structural influences that combine and interweave to influence her decisions. Feminist therapy listens for these often difficult choices as described by the women themselves. A number of authors, including Cole, Espin, and Rothblum (1992), Ho (1990), and Root (1995), have expanded our understanding of the experience of Asian-American women.

A second example comes from the context of a mixed race, bicultural, adolescent female gang member. Gold (1998) reports these girls' experiences often include sex on demand, utilitarian sex devoid of the partners' emotional involvement, and sex used as an initiation rite with multiple gang members. Certainly a white, middle-class feminist may readily classify these experiences as sexual abuse. Yet, in listening to the girls' voices, Gold learns of the significant value placed on their relationships with the boy gang members. To the girls, these relationships involve being listened to in a way that has been glaringly absent from their experience. The coupling, here, of being listened to and of being sexually abused forms a very real contradiction for the feminist therapist. While these stories may be difficult to hear, what is critically important is that the girls' reality is understood in terms of what these relationships have meant to them.

Over the last decade, feminist therapy has made a commitment to understand women's experiences as multiple, diverse, and interactive. This is a basic principle of feminist therapy and occupies a central position within the therapeutic relationship. Feminist therapists are themselves engaged in raising their own consciousness about the multiple realities of various women's lives so as not to replicate and perpetuate the embedded normative notions of monocultural experiences (Barrett, 1998). So while feminist therapists thoughtfully analyze sociocultural contributions to their clients' distress they are, at the same time, committed to an ongoing analysis of their own understandings of diversity and multiple realities.

## External Factors and Sociocultural Influences

Women's experiences also provide us with compelling examples of sociostructural factors as they impact on individuals (Ballou, 1990, 1995; Ballou & Gabalac, 1985; Brown & Root, 1990; Brown & Ballou, 1992; Brown & Brodsky, 1992; Comas-Diaz & Greene, 1994; Kaschak, 1992; Rawlings & Carter, 1997; Worell & Remer, 1992). For instance, that many single mothers struggle with issues of child care and finances is a reality borne out of women's experience. Yet, it is a reality reflective of the values and patterns that are part of a much larger socioeconomic system. Highlighting this basic tenet of the personal as political, McGrath,

Keita, Strickland, and Russo (1990) concluded, in a major American Psychological Association (APA) task force report that gendered politics, are strongly associated with depression. Others have similarly analyzed the relationships between gendered politics and eating disorders and sexual conflicts.

Feminist therapy attempts to deconstruct, with the client, just how her experiences are tied to this sociocultural context and its structural factors. Just as the political context shapes the individual lives of women, so, too, do the specific aspects of individual experience reflect the political. For example, when women work for less pay than men and are also expected to do the unpaid work of child and man care within their families and workspace, their structural second-class position shapes not only the time/demand/resource realities but their self-evaluation as well. Gender stereotypes are not only unenlightened but oppressive and harmful to self-worth. Feminist therapy is directed toward exposing this reciprocal influence of the political and personal to help the client move beyond her overwhelming feelings of guilt and self-blame.

Carla's situation represents a bicultural example of ways in which a family's economic and social status can be radically affected by the loss of a family member due to separation and divorce. While Carla initially encouraged her mother to end the relationship with her father because of the ongoing spousal abuse, the current helplessness of both mother and daughter has resulted in Carla's feelings of guilt, ambivalence, and internalized anger. Aside from the personal and interpersonal complexities of their current situation, there are very clear social, economic, and cultural factors impacting this family.

This process of taking note of the intersection between personal issues (e.g., depression, anxiety, hopelessness) that often bring women into therapy, and their often less obvious sociopolitical context, involves recognizing the trauma, destructiveness, and devaluation that occur through such acts of power as rape, abuse, and domestic violence (Walker, 1999). Broadening our own and our clients' understanding of the damage incurred through such violations is an especially important endeavor. Among the many authors who have written extensively on this topic are Maria Root (1992), who provides sociocultural analyses of insidious trauma. While psychotherapy has traditionally been sought for the traumatic damage done to the individual by these crimes and human rights violations, feminist therapy has brought to the foreground the external causes of individual distress and their impact on the developmental patterns of girls and women.

Cole, Espin, and Rothblum (1992) provide an example of this in their reports of refugee women immigrating into the United States. These women are frequently assigned psychiatric diagnoses and given medication to minimize their "symptoms." Yet, as pointed out by such authors as Adleman and Enguidanos (1996), co-cultural community support, acknowledgement of the women's trauma, credible and understandable explanations of United States' rights and protections, and interventions for the women's physical and security needs both contextualize their problems and provide a socially responsive treatment.

Thus, lucid and thorough bio–psycho–social–cultural–structural analysis is a major aspect of the conduct of feminist therapy.

## Egalitarian Relationship

Another cornerstone of feminist therapy is its focus on the relationship between the client and therapist and the distribution of power within this relationship. In conventional therapy the therapist implicity holds the institutional, expert and referent-formal power. Feminist therapy, howver, demands that the power be shared between the client and the therapist. Therapeutic relationships that attempt to reduce the power asymmetries (Brown, 1994) and to coordinate the power to name and the right to bargain (Ballou & Gabalac, 1985) are quintessential aspects of the egalitarian relationship principle. In sharing power, feminist therapy engages in an ethic of respect (Hill, 1990) and strives to avoid replication of hierarchical structures which have sometimes wrought damage on the client.

While this tenet is implemented in a variety of ways in feminist therapy, there are some applications that are considered fundamental and consensual. For instance, decisions regarding the frequency and length of treatment, payment amounts and schedules, and treatment modalities are typically decided collaboratively through discussion. Depending on the readiness of the client, she will participate in naming her distress and establishing appropriate outcomes, goals, and areas of work. Consistent with the principle of an egalitarian relationship, some feminist therapists provide information to the client that addresses how to raise concerns about the therapy or the therapeutic relationship in the initial session (Hill & Ballou, 1998). Similarly, issues of progress, termination, respite, and the future availability of the therapist are discussed mutually.

Both the principles and ethics of feminist therapy call on feminist therapists to raise these matters on all levels of complexity and to enter into and consistently maintain an egalitarian relationship that questions and works out the responsibilities of each party.

> An example of the careful decision-making and often subtle issues involved in feminist therapy involves a feminist therapist and her client, Alice, both of whom live and work in a Western rural setting. The therapist is experienced in trauma work through a gender and power abuse perspective; Alice is 18 and the fourth generation to be born into and work on the family ranch. She has a high school education.
>
> Alice comes to therapy for treatment of symptoms related to the trauma of ongoing physical and emotional abuse perpetrated by her uncle, a man who owns one half of the ranch and who wields the power that accompanies this economic, gendered, and sociopolitical status. Alice's family is aware of her situation, but in the context of hierarchical notions gender roles and out of fear of losing the ranch, they minimize Alice's distress and chide her either to toughen up or leave. Alice has limited financial resources and few interpersonal supports outside of her abusive family.
>
> In this context of vulnerability, isolation, and distress, Alice seeks safety and security within the therapeutic relationship and requests frequent sessions and daily contact with the feminist therapist. While mental health resources are very limited in this rural setting, there is a community health center 50 miles away, a center that is known for its psychoanalytic approach and tendency to manage care through hospitalization.
>
> There is no easy answer, here. Conventional guidelines would sanction a referral for Alice to the community health center. Yet, therapeutically, this feminist therapist would note the incompatiblity of the psychobiological medical model with a feminist therapy interpretation of Alice's situation, and may choose instead to discuss with Alice the community treatment center and its perspective vis-a-vis her history and needs. The therapist would provide for Alice a supportive and healing relationship while engaging with her in taking a trauma history and in providing gender role and power analyses. She may work with Alice to expand her identities from that of "a bad person" to that of a daughter/woman/client who is caught in a damaging situation with little means of control or agency. The feminist therapist would attempt to assist Alice in making

connections between what has happened to her and the broader sociopolitical, economic, and gendered context of her situation.

And the therapist would be challenged to consider and negotiate with Alice regarding the request for and possibilities around frequent contact in terms of Alice's need and the therapist's attention to her own self-care. She would also discuss with Alice financial arrangements that would take into account both Alice's limited ability to pay and the therapist's regard for her own livelihood.

Feminist therapy offers no easy, programmed answers to the complexity of Alice's therapy, either in content or process. What is clear and imperative, however, is that feminist therapy is deeply, fully, and consistently reflective and involves a co-creation with the client around choices and meaning-making. In addition, its commitment to an egalitarian relationship insists that the feminist therapist and client collaboratively consider choices and consequences and arrive at mutual decisions.

Such mutual decision-making is infused into every level of the therapeutic process, including adaptation of standard techniques. For example, some feminist therapists use hypnosis, a practice that may seem antithetical to the mandate for an egalitarian relationship. Yet, from a feminist perspective, the therapist can practice the technique of hypnosis and simultaneously transfer power to the client by asking for explicit permission throughout each step of the process. Other feminist therapists who use hypnosis techniques do so by teaching SELF-hypnosis to their clients (Hill & Ballou, 1998).

The issue of therapist self-disclosure is also viewed differently by the feminist therapist than it is by more conventional therapists. A feminist therapist routinely articulates her own values and world views, for example, as well as her own needs regarding working conditions. Throughout her work, a feminist therapist also carefully considers to what extent self-disclosure regarding their common struggles as women will be of benefit to her client. With the well-being of her client always uppermost in her mind, she may choose to share age-related experiences or to model situations of coping or negotiation.

Indeed, the importance of an appropriate fit with a particular client's needs and unique, yet complex experience, as well as this process of joint negotiation, make the conduct of feminist therapy both tentative and flexible. This is not to be interpreted as anything goes, nor should it be assumed that the process is without standards and limits, for this is clearly not the case. In particular, feminist ethics, discussed in the next section, demand careful and responsible actions within and surrounding feminist therapy.

Perhaps this vigilantly thoughtful and reflective posture of feminist therapists emanates out of the history of feminist therapy, with its transformations of conventional psychology, and its newly developing theory and practices. By their very orientation, feminist therapists have learned to seek out and question the assumptions embedded within the standard workings of the social order and, thus, they also take great care to maintain a relationship with their client which is honest and forthright. It is important for a feminist therapist to share her expert knowledge about psychology, feminist analyses, and the counseling process with her client. She also defines herself in terms of her own questioning stance toward the standards and practices of conventional therapy as well as toward feminist practices that are inconsistent with her own.

The importance of the egalitarian relationship within feminist therapy has evolved beyond its initial efforts to address the power inequities inherent in the therapeutic relationship. In large part through the contributions of the developing Relational Theory model (Jordan et al., 1992), feminist therapy considers the therapist–client relationship to be a primary and valuable means of healing. Through the therapy relationship, feminist therapy can offer empathic connection, which is an essential step in ameliorating the disempowerment, shame, and negative, distorted self-evaluation too often resulting material, psychic, and/or cultural violations.

In addition, the therapeutic relationship itself becomes a means of treatment and healing. This mutually respectful and connected relationship, with its emphasis on health and caring and the clarification and negotiation of values and needs, provides an experience that the client can take out in the world to use in judging and negotiating relationships in her own life and community. And, recursively, it allows therapists to experience some of the further reaches of human connections which they can then infuse into their therapy practice as well as their efforts in community-building, within social action initiatives and in theory-building.

Feminist therapy encourages the building and maintaining of relationships within a dyadic model as well as through groups and communities. The process of connecting and healing in mutually growth enhancing relationships is a major development in feminist therapy. Feminist therapy in group settings is consistent with the notion of building community and also provides healing opportunities for women. Again, we can refer to Carla. She demonstrates feelings of disempowerment and disconnection—from her family, her culture, the institutional forces in her school and, ultimately, from herself. Feminist therapy would begin by providing Carla with a healing relationship that would eventually allow her to reconnect her with herself and with other caring individuals.

As we end the twentieth century, feminist therapy is moving beyond the well-established, traditional boundaries, both in perspective and in space. In addition to the care of individuals and groups in therapy practice, feminist practitioners are promoting health, and differentiated and multiple identities in the lives of girls, women, and other nondominant groups. Indeed, feminists are moving into the very spheres that have been the targets of earlier analyses. If sociopolitical oppression is the issue, then feminist therapy is finding ways to enter the social-political system, identify its oppression, and support healthy and liberating change.

The work of the Stone Center is now extending beyond its model of self-in-relation-to-another to a model of organizational change that speaks to (1) ways in which relational awareness can be made visible in the workplace and (2) how through an analysis of gender, power, and hierarchy, movement toward mutuality and "relational leadership" can be "cultivated as an organizational value" (Wellesley Research Report, 1998). This task is quite obviously monumental within a culture in which business is arranged in an entrenched, competitive hierarchy. Yet it is being addressed in the feminist tradition of women talking to women. A study group formed out of the Jean Baker Miller Training Institute (Wellesley College) is currently holding seminars to examine how to "bring relational awareness to the workplace, how to name and strengthen connections that create effective functioning in an organization and how to develop specific strategies to deal with the 'disappearing' of relational practice or the shaming that occurs around practices that are not valued by the dominant work culture" (Wellesley Research Report, 1998 p. 6).

A second project that speaks to relationship and community-building involves bringing together the mothers of adolescent girls in an effort to name the cultural, sociopolitical, economic, educational, and gender issues that silently, insidiously, and harmfully initiate these young women into the dark sisterhood of oppression (West, 1999). Tapping into "women's creative imagination," the place where "mainstream social science with its insistence on recording behavior" (Westkott, 1979, p. 429) has failed to go, this project and others like it are reminiscent of the consciousness-raising groups of the 70s. It uses a format in which consciousness can be acknowledged and safely given voice and in which what Debold, Wilson, and Malave (1993) call "revolutionary mothering can devise ways to "en-courage girls' resistance" (p. 246).

## Integrated Analysis of Oppression

The integrated analysis of oppression that is at the core of feminist therapy acknowledges the complexity of human experience. Pluralism, which refers to the valuing of differences among people, is critically important to the practice of feminist therapy as it opens up the range of acceptable life scripts. For example, having children or choosing to be childless, pursuing career, family, or some combination, working in the public or underground economy, living life alone, in community, or with one or more partners, are different, certainly, but not more or less right, healthy, or desirable. Instead of bringing the dominant group's rules and values into therapy as standard assessments of risks and benefits, a feminist therapist considers the individual merits of different choices. This obviously demands a therapist with experience and the capacity for self-reflection, and a client with appropriate developmental and life circumstance capabilities.

Feminist practice extends well beyond the analysis of gender to consider the multiple ways in which people have been categorized and evaluated through hierarchies disguised as normative standards. Some of the ways in which humans vary include size, age, race, ethnicity, disability, class, sexual orientation, religion, geographic region, type of work, economic status, cultural traditions, family structure, social organizations, kinds of intelligence, sensitivities, and relationships with power, people, and the earth. These multiple factors interact and overlap and influence individuals, their life conditions, others' evaluations of them, and the opportunities or lack thereof available to them.

Each of these classifications of human variation calls the feminist therapist to awareness and demands particular knowledge and literacy. Also, each aspect of individual identity comprises a complicated web of dimensions of influence, requiring models representing interactions of multiple influences and levels. Feminist therapists consider the multiple factors that are involved in personal, group, and institutional oppression. And as these realities are part of women's experiences, sociopolitical contexts, and power relationships, they are also coming to be addressed in the theory and practice of feminist therapy (Hill & Ballou, 1998): "In perhaps the last ten years, feminist therapy has evolved a more complex analysis of oppression and an awareness that gender cannot be separated from other ways in which a culture stratifies human difference, privileging some at the expense of others" (p. 3).

Hope Landrine (1995), in her introduction to readings of cultural diversity in feminist psychology, provides a compelling example of the intersect of multiple oppressions, external factors, and women's experiences. Landrine tells us that studies conducted in the late 80s and early 90s revealed the prevalence of AIDS to be significantly higher among young Latinas than among other ethnic groups. It was found that this difference could in part be accounted for by the higher incidence of anal intercourse (particularly with intravenous drug users) among young, unmarried, heterosexual Latina women whereas this behavior was relatively infrequent among other heterosexual populations. Without an integrated analysis of oppressive factors, it was easy to assume that these young women simply did not have information regarding the risks of unprotected anal intercourse.

What was missing from this line of reasoning, however, was an understanding of the sociopolitical, cultural, and structural context in which these young women lived their lives. A feminist analysis found that Latinas did *not* hold erroneous beliefs about the transmission of the AIDS virus through unprotected vaginal or anal intercourse. Indeed, they knew it was dangerous and especially dangerous with a partner who was also an intravenous drug user. Nor, Landrine points out, was this pattern representative of a "titillating" ethnic difference or an "exotic" or "primitive" sexual "deviance." Rather, these young women had found a way to satisfy the demands of their boyfriends for intercourse while remaining virgins, a status that was also demanded within their community. Therefore, to understand their behavior, a thoughtful and thorough analysis needed to consider the intersect of culture, gender, age, and class.

As mentioned previously, some feminist therapists approach their work through one of the more conventional models and infuse these models and techniques with the principles and ethics specific to feminist therapy. So, for example, the feminist application of cognitive behavioral techniques standpoint may address multiple oppressions by challenging cognitions based on learned responses to cultural and gender expectations. As used in feminist therapy, cognitive reframing would invite the client to join with the therapist in clarifying the cultural and structural influences of individual beliefs and distress, using such questions as "What do you get out of this?" "What does the other get out of this?" and "Are these equal?" (Hill & Ballou, 1998, p. 12).

Interestingly, while feminist therapy is in the process of expanding pluralistic, multicultural, and antiracist conceptual frameworks (Brown, 1994; Sue, Ivey & Pederson, 1996), multicultural psychology is moving toward feminist therapy's gender and sociopolitical analyses, its critiques of conventional theory and therapy, and its counseling processes, which include critical consciousness-raising, reflection, and social change.

## Social Change

With its foundation principle of social change, feminist therapy extends out of the office and into the world in a way that moves beyond analysis to action. At first glance, working to create social change seems a necessary but somewhat idealistic goal. Yet the initiation of social change (Worell & Remer, 1992) and the ultimate intention of creating social change (Hill & Ballou, 1998) is an unambiguous and consistent call within most of the feminist therapy literature and practice. Ballou (1990, 1995), Brown (1992, 1994), Enns (1997), Lerman and Porter (1990), Greenspan, (1993), Whalen (1996), Maracek and Kravetz (1998), and others all write of the need for broad social and institutional change. This engagement in social change may occur at a variety of levels.

Simply doing feminist therapy involves clients in gendered reflections on their distress, lives, and the larger sociocultural context. Creating change at any of a variety of levels—individual, relational, community, interpersonal, policy—is certainly a part of feminist therapy. The feminist therapist engages in social change in a variety of ways: by reframing pathology, by discovering coping strategies for oppressive devaluation, discrimination and damage, and by bringing her sex role and power analyses to bear in her work.

Additionally, it may be therapeutically important at particular points for particular clients to encourage them to engage in empowering social change activities. This may take the form of protesting welfare policies that serve to increase poverty and decrease safe child care, or of participation in "Take Back the Night" demonstrations to increase awareness regarding the violence women face in their communities. Social action may also take the form of negotiating healthful decisions and arrangements within relationships, families, and communities, or within the environments of work, school, or social service agencies. Therapist supported client social actions may address power and gender arrangements. They are activities that may be initiated within the context of the feminist therapy relationship and, at the same time, they are political actions which may strengthen the resistance of the client to the forces of the sociocultural context. Resistance, says Laura Brown (1994, p. 25), "means the refusal to merge with dominant cultural norms and to attend to one's own voice and integrity." Fostering and supporting healthy resistance is a primary goal of feminist therapy practiced.

However, to practice feminist therapy is also to be involved in social change within one's own community and sometimes within much broader spheres. The efforts of many feminist therapists to challenge and change mainstream mental health and to influence legal decisions and national policy are at once encouraging and enlightening. A current example of such work can be seen in the ideology and actions of ecofeminists who link personal pain and physical illness (increases in cancer, asthma, and environmental disease) to global damage perpetrated by patriarchal institutions, in particular, the greed of advanced global capitalism. In addition to their advocacy around expanding treatment issues to include the link between spirituality and healing, treatment issues for this group include active and collective resistance to global injustice.

Lenore Walker is an example of a feminist therapist who has been involved in change at multiple levels. She counsels women and has engaged in theory-building and research. She has moved into the legal arena to advocate for battered women and to educate judges. She has worked within professional associations to educate and change policy. And most recently, she has created alliances with other women's and professional groups internationally to name the violence against women and children as a human rights violation. While the extent of this involvement may be unusual, commitment to working toward social change in a variety of local community and professional efforts is an integral part of feminist therapy practiced.

# FEMINIST ETHICS

As feminist principles provide guidance for therapeutic practice, so too do feminist ethics offer grounding and coherence to this practice. Most professional groups have ethical standards that codify practice and guide the actions of its practitioners. However, since most of the conventional professions are in concert with the dominant culture's normative standards, this codification of good practice becomes merely a derivation of mainstream beliefs and politics. However, feminist therapy, through its questioning stance, reliance on women's experience, emphasis on egalitarian relationships, analysis of multiple oppressions, and sociocultural location of pathogens, sometimes stands outside of and is sometimes juxtaposed with standard practice. Therefore, as can be noted in some of the previous case examples, thorough and continuous attention to standards of behavior and guidelines for thinking are necessary, even essential, in feminist therapy. Sorting out what is and what is not in the best interest of the client is never an easy task. But when the best interest of the client raises questions regarding standard practice and is sometimes at odds with conventional thinking, even greater care must be taken.

For example, standard prohibitions against self-disclosure keep therapists from talking about their own experience with clients and maintain hierarchical, expert power roles. Stepping out of this tradition-steeped practice, feminist therapists must consistently and carefully evaluate self-disclosure as it relates to an individual client's growth, always being conscious of the purpose and motive for sharing. Another example might involve a client carrying a former diagnosis of borderline personality disorder with a life experience of sexual abuse. Does the therapist work especially hard on developing relationship, knowing that through feminist eyes the relationship will heal the woundedness, or does the therapist stay carefully and legalistically constrained because of the likelihood of anger and conflict? While feminist therapy ethical guidelines offer protections and safety for the client, they also offer guidance for the counselor in both practice and theory-building.

The Feminist Therapy Institute, a national group of advanced feminist therapists, developed Ethical Guidelines for Feminist Therapists in 1987 and revised and updated its code in 1999. They have also published two books that discuss ethics and cases considered through them. The first is *Feminist Ethics in Psychotherapy* (1990) edited by Lerman and Porter, and the second is *Ethical Decision Making in Therapy* (1995), edited by Rave and Larsen. The

Feminist Therapy Institute 1999 update of the Feminist Therapy Code of Ethics is reproduced below.

## FEMINIST THERAPY CODE OF ETHICS
## (REVISED, 1999)[1]

### Preamble

Feminist therapy evolved from feminist philosophy, psychological theory and practice, and political theory. In particular feminists recognize the impact of society in creating and maintaining the problems and issues brought into therapy. Briefly, feminists believe the personal is political. Basic tenets of feminism include a belief in the equal worth of all human beings, a recognition that each individual's personal experiences and situations are reflective of and an influence on society's institutionalized attitudes and values, and a commitment to political and social change that equalizes power among people. Feminists are committed to recognizing and reducing the pervasive influences and insidious effects of oppressive societal attitudes and society. Thus, a feminist analysis addresses the understanding of power and its interconnections among gender, race, culture, class, physical ability, sexual orientation, age, and antisemitism as well as all forms of oppression based on religion, ethnicity, and heritage. Feminist therapists also live in and are subject to those same influences and effects and consistently monitor their beliefs and behaviors as a result of these influences.

Feminist therapists adhere to and integrate feminist analyses in all spheres of their work as therapists, educators, consultants, administrators, writers, editors, and/or researchers. Feminist therapists are accountable for the management of the power differential within these roles and accept responsibility for that power. Because of the limitations of a purely intrapsychic model of human functioning, feminist therapists facilitate the understanding of the interactive effects of the client's internal and external worlds. Feminist therapists possess knowledge about the psychology of women and girls and utilize feminist scholarship to revise theories and practices, incorporating new knowledge as it is generated.

Feminist therapists are trained in a variety of disciplines, theoretical orientations, and degrees of structure. They come from different cultural, economic, ethnic, and racial backgrounds. They work in many types of settings with a diversity of clients and practice different modalities of therapy, training, and research. Feminist therapy theory integrates feminist principles into other theories of human development and change.

The ethical guidelines that follow are additive to, rather than a replacement for, the ethical principles of the profession in which a feminist therapist practices. Amid this diversity, feminist therapists are joined together by their feminist analyses and perspectives. Additionally, they work toward incorporating feminist principles into existing professional standards when appropriate.

Feminist therapists live with and practice in competing forces and complex controlling interests. When mental health care involves third-party payers, it is feminist therapists' responsibility to advocate for the best possible therapeutic process for the client, including short or long term therapy. Care and compassion for clients include protection of confidentiality and awareness of the impacts of economic and political considerations, including the increasing disparity between the quality of therapeutic care available for those with or without third-party payers.

---

[1] © Copyright 2000, Feminist Therapy Institute, Inc.

Feminist therapists assume a proactive stance toward the eradication of oppression in their lives and work toward empowering women and girls. They are respectful of individual differences, examining oppressive aspects of both their own and clients' value systems. Feminist therapists engage in social change activities, broadly defined, outside of and apart from their work in their professions. Such activities may vary in scope and content but are an essential aspect of a feminist perspective.

This code is a series of positive statements which provide guidelines for feminist therapy practice, training, and research. Feminist therapists who are members of other professional organizations adhere to the ethical codes of those organizations. Feminist therapists who are not members of such organizations are guided by the ethical standards of the organization closest to their mode of practice. These statements provide more specific guidelines within the context of and as an extension of most ethical codes. When ethical guidelines are in conflict, the feminist therapist is accountable for how she prioritizes her choices.

These ethical guidelines, then, are focused on the issues feminist therapists, educators, and researchers have found especially important in their professional settings. As with any code of therapy ethics, the well-being of clients is the guiding principle underlying this code. The feminist therapy issues which relate directly to the client's well-being include cultural diversities and oppressions, power differentials, overlapping relationships, therapist accountability, and social change. Even though the principles are stated separately, each interfaces with the others to form an interdependent whole. In addition, the code is a living document and thus is continually in the process of change.

The Feminist Therapy Institute's Code of Ethics is shaped by economic and cultural forces in North America and by the experiences of its members. Members encourage an ongoing international dialogue about feminist and ethical issues. It recognizes that ethical codes are aspirational and ethical behaviors are on a continuum rather than reflecting dichotomies. Additionally, ethical guidelines and legal requirements may differ. The Feminist Therapy Institute provides educational interventions for its members rather than disciplinary activity.

## Ethical Guidelines for Feminist Therapists

### I. Cultural Diversities and Oppressions

    A. A feminist therapist increases her accessibility to and for a wide range of clients from her own and other identified groups through flexible delivery of services. When appropriate, the feminist therapist assists clients in accessing other services and intervenes when a client's rights are violated.

    B. A feminist therapist is aware of the meaning and impact of her own ethnic and cultural background, gender, class, age, and sexual orientation, and actively attempts to become knowledgeable about alternatives from sources other than her clients. She is actively engaged in broadening her knowledge of ethnic and cultural experiences, non-dominant and dominant.

    C. Recognizing that the dominant culture determines the norm, the therapist's goal is to uncover and respect cultural and experiential differences, including those based on long term or recent immigration and/or refugee status.

    D. A feminist therapist evaluates her ongoing interactions with her clientele for any evidence of her biases or discriminatory attitudes and practices. She also monitors her other interactions, including service delivery, teaching, writing, and all professional activities. The feminist therapist accepts responsibility for taking action to confront and change any interfering, oppressing, or devaluing biases she has.

## II. Power Differentials

A. A feminist therapist acknowledges the inherent power differentials between client and therapist, and models effective use of personal, structural, or institutional power. In using the power differential to the benefit of the client, she does not take control or power which rightfully belongs to her client.

B. A feminist therapist discloses information to the client which facilitates the therapeutic process, including information communicated to others. The therapist is responsible for using self-disclosure only with purpose and discretion and in the interest of the client.

C. A feminist therapist negotiates and renegotiates formal and/or informal contacts with clients in an ongoing mutual process. As part of the decision-making process, she makes explicit the therapeutic issues involved.

D. A feminist therapist educates her clients regarding power relationships. She informs clients of their rights as consumers of therapy, including procedures for resolving differences and filing grievances. She clarifies power in its various forms as it exists within other areas of her life, including professional roles, social/governmental structures, and interpersonal relationships. She assists her clients in finding ways to protect themselves and, if requested, to seek redress.

## III. Overlapping Relationships

A. A feminist therapist recognizes the complexity and conflicting priorities inherent in multiple or overlapping relationships. The therapist accepts responsibility for monitoring such relationships to prevent potential abuse of or harm to the client.

B. A feminist therapist is actively involved in her community. As a result, she is aware of the need for confidentiality in all settings. Recognizing that her client's concerns and general well-being are primary, she self-monitors both public and private statements and comments. Situations may develop through community involvement where power dynamics shift, including a client having equal or more authority than the therapist. In all such situations a feminist therapist maintains accountability.

C. When accepting third-party payments, a feminist therapist is especially cognizant of and clearly communicates to her client the multiple obligations, roles, and responsibilities of the therapist. When working in institutional settings, she clarifies to all involved parties where her allegiances lie. She also monitors multiple and conflicting expectations between clients and caregivers, especially when working with children and elders.

D. A feminist therapist does not engage in sexual intimacies nor any overtly or covertly sexualized behaviors with a client or former client.

## IV. Therapist Accountability

A. A feminist therapist is accountable to herself, to colleagues, and especially to her clients.

B. A feminist therapist will contract to work with clients and issues within the realm of her competencies. If problems beyond her competencies surface, the feminist therapist utilizes consultation and available resources. She respects the integrity of the relationship by stating the limits of her training and providing the client with the possibilities of continuing with her or changing therapists.

C. A feminist therapist recognizes her personal and professional needs and utilizes ongoing self-evaluation, peer support, consultation, supervision, continuing education, and/or personal therapy. She evaluates, maintains, and seeks to improve her competencies, as well as her emotional, physical, mental, and spiritual well-being. When the feminist therapist has experienced a similar stressful or damaging event as her client, she seeks consultation.

D. A feminist therapist continually re-evaluates her training, theoretical background, and research to include developments in feminist knowledge. She integrates feminism into psychological theory, receives ongoing therapy training, and acknowledges the limits of her competencies.

E. A feminist therapist engages in self-care activities in an ongoing manner outside the work setting. She recognizes her own needs and vulnerabilities as well as the unique stresses inherent in this work. She demonstrates an ability to establish boundaries with the client that are healthy for both of them. She also is willing to self-nurture in appropriate and self-empowering ways.

## V. Social Change

A. A feminist therapist seeks multiple avenues for impacting change, including public education and advocacy within professional organizations, lobbying for legislative actions, and other appropriate activities.

B. A feminist therapist actively questions practices in her community that appear harmful to clients or therapists. She assists clients in intervening on their own behalf. As appropriate, the feminist therapist herself intervenes, especially when other practitioners appear to be engaging in harmful, unethical, or illegal behaviors.

C. When appropriate, a feminist therapist encourages a client's recognition of criminal behaviors and also facilitates the client's navigation of the criminal justice system.

D. A feminist therapist, teacher, or researcher is alert to the control of information dissemination and questions pressures to conform to and use dominant mainstream standards. As technological methods of communication change and increase, the feminist therapist recognizes the socioeconomic aspects of these developments and communicates according to clients' access to technology.

E. A feminist therapist, teacher, or researcher recognizes the political is personal in a world where social change is a constant.

The Feminist Therapy Institute, Inc.
Corporate Office: 50 South Steele, #850, Denver, CO 80209
Administrator: Polly Taylor
128 Moffat Street, San Francisco, CA 94131

The Code is immediately striking for its positively framed and accessible language. It is not a set of warnings, restrictions, and limitations. It does not so much confine as ethically empower and guide feminist therapists toward an ongoing, moment-by-moment awareness and enactment of the essential principles of feminist therapy. Laura Brown (1994) says that although ethical considerations and concerns arise consistently within all psychotherapeutic interactions, for feminist therapy "ethics has been an abiding, transcendent concern, one that ties together every issue and aspect of our practice" (p. 201).

It is important to note that the ethical guidelines for feminist therapists are not about providing a nicer, more positive frame for the ethical practice standards of other mental health organizations. Rather they respond positively and proactively to ethical dilemmas that arise

OUT of feminist therapy practice. They are not static cautions or strictures but rather dynamic formulations that are applied and reapplied in a thoughtful and vigilant manner. The overlap between ethical considerations and feminist principles can readily be noted in this document.

Feminist therapy ethics serve additional purposes beyond standards for practice and guides to action. They also educate and stimulate the further development of feminist therapy. For example, Laura Brown's (1990, 1994) expansion of multicultural and antiracist feminist therapy is in large measure supported by the interweave of feminist principles and ethics—in particular, the ethical guideline relative to cultural diversities and oppressions and the feminist principles related to the valuing of women's experience and the adoption of a questioning stance toward dominant institutions, theories, practice, and research.

As a final illustration, development of feminist supervision as "co-vision" (Porter & Vasquez, 1997) was guided by the ongoing development of theory and research within the psychology of women, and by feminist therapy ethics and principles related to social change, power differentials, therapist accountability, and self-care. Traditional supervision has concentrated on the trainee's clarity around her own feelings and issues and those of her clients, and around an understanding of treatment issues as they relate to conventional formulations. In a feminist tradition, however, Porter and Vasquez have expanded this frame to include the nature of the relationship between the supervisor and the trainee as well as of that between the trainee and the client. They have also offered a means of integrating newer feminist positions into standard practice by treating such issues as gender and culture and class like any other issue which the trainee may encounter within the clinical frame. This is not simply a matter of increasing sensitivity to issues of difference. Rather this model involves broadening the perspective of what makes a competent professional. Trainees, with the support and direction of their supervisors, need to read the literature and actively engage a curriculum that includes theory, research, and skill competency.

## CONCLUSIONS

Carla, Beth, and Alice; the unmarried Latina women; the girl gang members; the refugee women; and the African-American mothers each represent unique cases. Yet in each gender, class, and ethnicity, and values and cultural expectations result in a particular interaction of influences. These multiple identities and complex interactions also meet, and collide with, the often unspoken norms, standards, expectations, and dictates of the dominant culture. Each of these women could be labeled in standard diagnostic terms and treated by traditional mental health interventions. However, feminist therapy would seek to understand them in all of their complexity and would attempt to accept them as they are. Feminist therapy would engage these women in a relationship and would decide with them what actions would be in their best interests. Feminist therapy would further engage in social action efforts to diminish the harmful effects of the external forces that oppress them.

In this chapter we have tried to give the reader a sense of the wide range of perspectives within feminist therapy—perspectives that are grounded in feminist theory, principles, and ethics. In describing feminist therapy we have tried to note those domains in assessment, diagnosis and practice in which feminist therapy diverges from more traditional models at the same time that it attempts to address the complexity of human existence. At its foundation, feminist therapy represents a consciousness of multiple standpoints, multiple life experiences, multiple cultures, multiple inquiries, and multiple histories that continually challenge and engage those who do its work.

# REFERENCES

Adleman, J., & Enguidanos, G. (Eds.). (1996) *Racism in the lives of women: Testimony, theory, and guides to antiracist action.* New York: Haworth.

American Psychiatric Association. (1994). *Diagnostic and statistical manual of mental disorders* (4th ed., rev.). Washington, DC: Author.

Ballou, M. (1990). Approaching a feminist-principled paradigm in the construction of personality theory. In L. Brown & M. Root (Eds.),*Diversity and complexity in feminist therapy* (pp. 23–40). New York: Haworth.

Ballou, M. (1995). Women and spirit: Two nonfits in psychology. *Women and Therapy, 16,* 9–20.

Ballou, M., & Gabalac, N. (1985). *A feminist position on mental health.* Springfield, IL: Charles C Thomas.

Barrett, S. (1998). Contextual identity: A model for therapy and social change. *Women and Therapy, 18,* 3/4.

Brown, L. (1994). *Subversive dialogues: Theory in feminist therapy.* New York: Basic Books.

Brown, L. (1995). Cultural diversity in feminist therapy: Theory and Practice. In H. Landrine (Ed.), *Bringing cultural diversity to feminist therapy: Theory, research, and practice* (pp. 143–161). Washington, DC: American Psychological Association.

Brown, L., & Ballou, M. (Eds.). (1992). *Personality and Psychotherapy: feminist reappraisals.* New York: Guilford.

Brown, L. & Brodsky, A. (1992). The future of feminist therapy. *Psychotherapy: Theory, Research, Practice, Training, 29,* 51–57.

Brown, L., & Root, M. (Eds.). (1990). *Diversity and complexity in feminist therapy.* New York: Haworth.

Burstone, B. (1992). *Radical feminist therapy: Working in the context of violence.* Newbury Park, CA: Sage.

Chesler, P. (1972). *Women and madness.* Garden City, NY: Doubleday.

Cole, E., Espin, O., & Rothblum, E. (Eds.). (1992). *Refugee women and their mental health.* New York: Haworth.

Comas-Diaz, L., & Greene, B. (Eds.). (1994). *Mental health and women of color.* New York: Guilford.

Debold, E., Wilson, M., & Malave, I. (1993). *Mother–daughter revolution.* Reading, MA: Addison-Wesley.

Enns, C. (1997). *Feminist theories and feminist psychotherapies.* New York: Harrington Park Press.

Espin, O. (1994). Feminist approaches. In L. Comas-Diaz & B. Greene (Eds.), *Women of color: Integrating ethnic and gender identities in psychotherapy* (pp. 265–286). New York: Guilford.

Gilbert, L. (1980). Feminist therapy. In A. Brodsky & R. Hare-Musten (Eds.), *Women and psychotherapy* (pp. 245–265). New York: Guilford.

Gold, J. (1998). *Understanding girls and their involvement in gangs through their stories: A qualitative psychological study.* Unpublished doctoral dissertation. Boston, MA: Northeastern University.

Greene, B. (1994). African american women. In L. Comas-Diaz & B. Greene (Eds.), *Women of color: integrating ethnic and gender identities in psychotherapy* (pp. 10–29). New York: Guilford.

Greenspan, M. (1993). *A new approach to women and therapy.* New York: John Wiley & Sons.

Hill, M. (1990). On creating a theory of feminist therapy. In L.Brown & M. Root (Eds.), *Diversity and complexity in feminist therapy* (pp. 53–66). New York: Haworth.

Hill, M. (March, 1999). Address to Association of Women Psychologists. Providence, Rhode Island.

Hill, M., & Ballou, M. (1998). Making feminist therapy: A practice survey. *Women & Therapy, 21,* 1–16.

Ho, C. (1990). An analysis of domestic violence in Asian American communities: A multicultural approach to counseling. In L.Brown & M. Root (Eds.), *Diversity and complexity in feminist therapy* (pp. 129–150). New York: Haworth.

Jordan, J., Kaplan, A., Miller, J., Stiver, I., & Surrey, J. (1992). *Women's growth in connection: Writings from the Stone Center.* New York: Guilford.

Kaschak, E. (1992). *Engendered lives: A new psychology of women's experience.* New York: Basic Books.

Kitzinger, C., & Perkins, R. (1993). *Changing our minds: Lesbian feminism and psychology.* New York: New York University Press.

Landrine, H. (Ed.). (1995). *Bringing cultural diversity to feminist psychology.* Washington, DC: American Psychological Association.

Lerman, H. (1986). *A mote in Freud's eye: From psychoanalysis to the psychology of women.* New York: Springer.

Lerman, H. (1992). The limits of phenomenology: A feminist critique of the humanistic personality theories. In L. Brown & M. Ballou (Eds.), *Personality and psychopathology: Feminist reappraisals* (pp. 8–19). New York: Guilford.

Lerman, H. (1996). *Pigeonholing women's misery: A history and critical analysis of the psychodiagnosis of women in the twentieth century.* New York: Basic Books.

Lerman, H., & Porter, N. (Eds.). (1990). *Feminist ethics in psychotherapy.* New York: Springer.

Mander, A., & Rush, A. (1974). *Feminism as therapy.* New York: Random House.

Marecek, J., & Kravetz, D. (1998). Putting politics into practice: Feminist therapy as feminist praxis. *Women & Therapy, 21,* 17–36.

McGrath, E., Keita, G., Strickland, B., & Russo, N. (1990). *Women and depression: Risk factors and treatment issues.* Washington, DC: American Psychological Association.

McLellan, B. (1995). *Beyond Psychoppression: Feminist alternative therapy.* Melbourne, Australia: Scinifex Press Pry Ltd.

Morrow, S., & Hawxhurst, D. (1998). Feminist therapy: Integrating political analysis in counseling and psychotherapy. *Women & Therapy, 21,* 37–50.

Porter, N., & Vasquez, M. (1997). *Covision: Feminist supervision, process and collaboration.* Washington, DC: American Psychological Association.

Rave, E., & Larsen, C. (Eds.). (1995). *Ethical decision making in therapy: Feminist perspectives.* New York: Guilford.

Rawlings, E., & Carter, D. (1997). *Psychotherapy for women: Treatment toward equality.* Springfield, IL: Charles Thomas.

Rogers, A. (1993). Voice, play, and a practice of ordinary courage in girls' and women's lives. *Harvard Educational Review, 63,* 265–295.

Root, M. (1992). Restructuring the impact of trauma on personality. In L. Brown & M. Ballou (Eds.), *Personality and psychopathology: Feminist reappraisals* (pp.229–265) New York: Guilford.

Root, M. (1995). The psychology of Asian American women. In H. Landrine (Ed.), *Bringing cultural diversity to feminist psychology* (pp. 265–301). Washington, DC: American Psychological Association.

Santos de Barona, M., & Dutton, M. (1997). Feminist perspectives on assessment. In J. Worell & N. Johnson (Eds.), *Shaping the future of feminist psychology* (pp. 37–56). Washington, DC: American Psychological Association.

Sturdivant, S. (1980). *Therapy with women: A feminist philosophy of treatment.* New York: Springer.

Sue, D., Ivey, A., & Pederson, P. (1996). *A theory of multicultural counseling and psychotherapy.* Pacific Grove, CA: Brooks/Cole.

Szasz, T. (1961). *The myth of mental illness: Foundations of a theory of personal conduct.* New York: Dell.

Taylor, J., Gilligan, C., & Sullivan, A. (1995). *Between voice and silence: Women and girls, race and relationship.* Cambridge, MA: Harvard University Press.

Walker, M. (1999). Dual traumatization: A sociocultural perspective. In Y. Jenkins (Ed.), *Diversity in college settings* (pp. 52–65). New York: Routledge.

Wellesley Centers for Women. (1998). *Relational Approaches to workplace change.* Research Report. Wellesley, MA: Author.

West, C. (1999). *Strengthening the resistance: An exploration of how mothers can ally with and support their adolescent daughters.* Unpublished doctoral dissertation. Boston, MA: Northeastern University.

Westkott, M. (1979). Feminist criticism of the social sciences. *Harvard Educational Review, 49,* 422–430.

Whalen, M. (1996). *Counseling to end violence against women: A subversive model.* Thousand Oaks, CA: Sage.

Worell, J., & Johnson, N. (Eds.). (1997). *Shaping the future of feminist psychology.* Washington, DC: American Psychological Association.

Worell, J., & Remer, P. (1992). *Feminist perspectives in therapy: An empowerment model for women.* New York: Wiley.

# Index